About to Die

Arts & Ideas

The New York Times

SATURDAY, SEPTEMBER 15, 2

The Formula
For Portraying
Pain in Art

Frontispiece: The visual can only use "but a single moment of an action, and must therefore choose the most pregnant one, the one most suggestive of what has gone before and what is to follow."—Gotthold Lessing, *Laocoon*, 1776. Laocoon, Copyright © 2001 by The New York Times Co. Reprinted with permission.

BARBIE ZELIZER

ABOUT TO DIE

How News Images Move the Public

OXFORD
UNIVERSITY PRESS
2010

OXFORD
UNIVERSITY PRESS

Oxford University Press, Inc., publishes works that further
Oxford University's objective of excellence
in research, scholarship, and education.

Oxford   New York
Auckland   Cape Town   Dar es Salaam   Hong Kong   Karachi
Kuala Lumpur   Madrid   Melbourne   Mexico City   Nairobi
New Delhi   Shanghai   Taipei   Toronto

With offices in
Argentina   Austria   Brazil   Chile   Czech Republic   France   Greece
Guatemala   Hungary   Italy   Japan   Poland   Portugal   Singapore
South Korea   Switzerland   Thailand   Turkey   Ukraine   Vietnam

Published by Oxford University Press, Inc.
198 Madison Avenue, New York, New York 10016

www.oup.com

Oxford is a registered trademark of Oxford University Press

Library of Congress Cataloging-in-Publication Data
Zelizer Barbie.
   About to die : how news images move the public / Barbie Zelizer.
     p. cm.
   ISBN 978-0-19-975213-3 (cloth : alk. paper)—ISBN 978-0-19-975214-0 (pbk. : alk. paper)
1. Photojournalism—Social aspects—United States.
2. Death—Press coverage—United States.
3. Collective memory—United States.   I. Title
   TR820.Z45 2010
   070.4'9—dc22   2010012024

9 8 7 6 5 4 3 2 1

Printed in the United States of America
on acid-free paper

Contents

Acknowledgments

For one who spent nearly two decades living in Jerusalem, it is telling that the decade of my working on this project was bookended with events from the Middle East. It is not a coincidence that my interest in images of impending death was sparked by the coverage of the renewed Intifada and the killing of twelve-year-old Mohammad Aldura in 2000 and wrapped shortly after the death of Iranian student Neda Agha-Soltan in Tehran in 2009. Indeed, the centrality of depictions of events from the Middle East in driving this book from beginning to end reminds me of how rarely our choices of scholarly projects stray from the personal.

My gratitude for those around me over this decade is widespread and heartfelt. The project began at the behest of Barbara Biesecker and John Lucaites, who asked me to deliver a keynote for a conference they were hosting on visual rhetoric in 2001. Along the way, many individuals helped move it along: Roger Abrahams helped me conceptualize the project at its inception, while Larry Gross assisted me in seeing it to completion. Larry Gross, Michael Schudson, Linda Steiner, and Robin Wagner-Pacifici read drafts along the way, and Andrea Drugan, Peter Labella, and Jerome Singerman offered useful editorial advice. Shannon McLachlan, Brendan O'Neill, Lisa Force, and Jessica Ryan oversaw its production at Oxford University Press. The Joan Shorenstein Center on the Press, Politics, and Public Policy at Harvard University hosted me for a fellowship period that helped flesh out the project. And the Annenberg School for Communication was instrumental in ensuring it reach completion, remaining an ideal work environment for scholarly endeavors. There, Sharon Black and Min Zhong relentlessly searched for library titles to augment my own efforts; Eric Bowden, Elizabeth Cooper, Michael Olsen, and Tej Patel offered technical assistance, while Richard Cardona and Brendan Keegan enlisted lengthy hours respectively keeping my computer running and creating slides from amorphous documents. My dean, Michael Delli Carpini, was extremely generous with resources, funds for permissions, and research tips, and my assistant in the Annenberg Scholars Program on Culture and Communication, Emily Plowman, good-naturedly filled in with various tasks.

Multiple cohorts of students at Annenberg heard me talk year after year about this project, and I thank them for willingly assisting in the project's evolution: Dan Berger, Mary Bock, Matt Carlson, Julia Chang, Lauren Feldman, Rachel Gans, Caralyn Green, Brittany Griebling, Courtney Hamilton, Le Han, John Huxford, Bethany Klein, Angela Lee, Kyung Lee, Nehama Lewis, Jody Madeira, Oren Meyers, Nicole Maurantonio, Kimberly Meltzer, David Park, Ji Hoon Park, Joel Penney, Michael Serazio, Piotr Szpunar, Keren Tenenboim-Weinblatt, Lokman Tsui, Claire Wardle, and Louise Woodstock.

A host of people kept me going in other ways—Stuart Allan, Ruth Anolik, Barbara Biesecker, S. Elizabeth Bird, Gwen Borowsky, David Camp, Cecily and Warren Carel, James Carey, Nick Couldry, James Curran, Daniel Dayan, Peter Ehrenhaus, Isabel Gil, Larry Gross, Robert Hariman, Amy Jordan, John Lucaites, Alex Jones, Richard Juran, Amy Kaplan, Tamar Katriel, Ingrid Lehmann, Carolyn Marvin, DC Maxwell, Toby Miller, Ravi Narasimhan, Thomas Patterson, Kendall Phillips, Monroe Price, Kevin Robins, Marian Rogers, Eric Rothenbuhler, Pamela Sankar, Claudia Schmidt, Fred Shaurer, Marita Sturken, Howard Tumber, Sarah Banet Weiser, and Liliane Weissberg.

I was fortunate enough to try out many of the ideas presented here in multiple international venues. They include: Indiana University, University of Llublijana, University of Helsinki, Ryerson University, University of Colorado, Le Centre Pompidou, American University of Paris, Cambridge University, University of Maryland, New School University, Bilgi University, Sorbonne University, University of Tampere, Columbia University, Hamilton College, Universidad Catholica Portugesa, University of North Carolina, Oslo University, University of Stockholm, New York University, Texas A & M, Northwestern University, University of Pennsylvania, University of Buenos Aires, University of Washington, Central European University, University of California at Riverside, University of Southern California, Harvard University, University of Haifa, National Press Club, Middle Tennessee State University, The Human Rights Center and School of Journalism at University of California at Berkeley, University of Edinburgh, Nottingham University, Grand Valley State University, Wabash College, University of Minnesota, Museum of the City of New York, Institut d'histoire du temps present (CNRS), and L'ecole des

Hautes Etudes en Sciences Sociales. Pieces of this project were also presented at the yearly meetings of the International Communication Association, the National Communication Association, the American Sociological Association, the American Folklore Society and the Society for Cinema Studies.

In the end, scholarly projects inevitably rise or collapse by the most proximate circumstances. My three siblings—Judy Shifrin, Louise Haukka, and Ron Zelizer—kept me focused even when our mother's death made intellectual concerns feel trite and unimportant. My three children—Noa, Jonathan, and Gideon Glick—and as time moved on their significant others—shared a house with multiple images of people about to die, one sharing the nightmares produced by being in a guest room filled with so much death. For that I apologize. But they also spent ten years of their lives energetically tracking down pictures of impending death. For that, and for them, I am grateful.

Finally, it is fitting to end a book on images and impending death with two stories about one of the premier thinkers on photography, Susan Sontag. She and I met in April of 2003 and, over dinner, traded compliments for each other's work (the ones she tendered in my direction were far more appreciated, I am certain, than the ones I tossed her way). We spoke at length about this project and I looked forward to her response to it when completed, making tentative plans that she would write a forward to the book. She died, however, the following year and did not make it long enough to see what became of my ideas. But she reared her head, nonetheless. In 2007, I was offering a series of lectures at the Sorbonne and found myself strolling the corridors of Paris' Montparnasse Cemetery, reveling in the gravestones that rose from the ground. Turning a corner, I came upon Sontag's resting place. Not knowing she had been buried there, I was stunned but with some reflection realized she had emerged yet again just as the book began to enter its final phase. Sontag once wrote that "memory is, achingly, the only relationship we have with the dead." And so I dedicate this book to the memory of Susan Sontag, who, in lieu of the relationships she might have continued to nurture, taught generations of observers to probe deeply the images among us.

About to Die

Chapter 1

Journalism, Memory, and the Voice of the Visual

What are news images for? Still photos of a small John Kennedy Jr. saluting his father's coffin may have helped a grieving American public accept the death of its president in much the same way as a flag raising on Iwo Jima may have reduced the complicated reality of World War II to a symbolic gesture of victory. But neither example makes clear what equips an image to deliver the news and what makes some images work better than others, either on their initial display or in their recycling across time and space. Instead, multiple questions surface about these "flashbulb memories": Under which conditions does an image work most powerfully?[1] What kind of information does one need to understand an image and how much information is necessary? Who fosters an image's understanding? How does this impact public response to the news?

These questions motivate this book. As still photographs, videos, film, and digital images fill a growing and increasingly diverse print, broadcast, cable, and digital landscape, a fuller understanding of news images becomes critical. Because many images reflect unsettled public events—the difficult and often contested planned violence, torture, terrorism, natural disaster, war, famine, crime, epidemic, and political assassinations at the core of today's geopolitical environment—their consideration can help clarify how the public forms sentiments about the larger world. It can also elucidate under which conditions images promote broader political agendas and what happens to a healthy body politic when images reduce complex issues and circumstances to memorable but simplistic visual frames.

This book tracks the emergence, positioning, and use of one visual trope in U.S. news photographs—depictions of the moment at which individuals are about to die—as a prism for addressing news images more broadly. Reflecting a larger universe of news photos that similarly target the cusp of impending action—about to win, about to kiss, about to set sail, about to separate, about to fight—this trope exemplifies the strengths and weaknesses of news images as vehicles of information and memory. Drawing from pictures that have over time been deemed important enough to warrant sustained journalistic attention but stretch beyond familiar iconic depictions, this analysis of about-to-die images in nineteenth-, twentieth-, and twenty-first-century U.S. journalism, with some discussion of news images elsewhere, raises fundamental questions both about how these pictures depict the news, how they figure in collective memory, and how they connect with the public at multiple points in time. In so doing, it suggests a refinement of how news images have been thought to function and how the public has been thought to respond.

News Images, Information, and Memory

The eighteenth-century German dramatist Gotthold Lessing was among the first to address the singularity of visual representation, when, in his 1776 essay on the Laocoon, he distinguished painting from poetry: the visual can only use, he wrote, "but a single moment of an action, and must therefore choose the most pregnant one, the one most suggestive of what has gone before and what is to follow."[2] This ability to strategically freeze a moment in the sequencing of action has drawn the attention of various thinkers since photography's inception: Cartier Bresson coined it the "decisive moment," Victor Burgin the "pregnant moment," and Alfred Eisenstadt the "story-telling moment"—all in reference to an "instant arrested within a narrative flow" that coaxes the viewer to suspend disbelief, draw conclusions and invoke the "intended sentiment" of the depiction. Freezing a moment as a still photo turns a dynamic sequence into a "static scene...using space to replace or to represent time" and condenses action "into a single image, generally a moment of climax [representing] a process while avoiding the impression of simultaneity."[3]

As one kind of image, the photograph makes it particularly easy to suspend disbelief about what is shown. As Susan Moeller noted, "A photograph provokes a tension in us—not only about the precise moment that the image depicts, but also about all the moments that led up to that instant and about all the moments that will follow."[4] Its reduction of the world into miniature size, supposed flatness, predictable size and shape, traditional sidestepping of color, and fixation on a single moment in time all make it, in Oliver Wendell Holmes's term, a "mirror with the memory." Considered a primarily realistic mode of visual representation, photographs work through two forces, which scholars have termed denotation and connotation: denotation suggests that images reflect what "is there." Associated with "indexicality," "referentiality," and "verisimilitude," denotation—what William Henry Fox Talbot termed a "pencil of nature" and John Berger a "record of things seen"—shows things "as they are" and appears to capture life on its own terms. Connotation suggests that images provide more than what is physically caught by the camera, where, associated with symbolism, generalizability, and universality, the image draws from broad symbolic systems in lending meaning to what is depicted. Photographs have been thought to work by twinning denotation and connotation, matching the ability to depict the world "as it is" with the ability to couch what is depicted in a symbolic frame consonant with broader understandings of the world.[5]

Images have not been easily incorporated into much of the existing research on journalism. Adopting the sentiments of most journalists, complementary research strands on news production, content, and effects have tended to position news images in a supportive role to words, where the verbal record underpinning journalists' authority as arbiters of the real world takes precedence over its visual counterpart. Journalism, largely seen as a project of modernity, is presumed driven by words. Though images relate variously to them—bolstering, complementing, negating, and affirming what they stipulate—words remain journalism's authoritative cues because they are thought to enable information, evidence, reasoned testimony, and deliberation.[6] This means that for as long as journalists are thought to invoke reasoned and systematic reasoning, patterned procedures and standardized codes of behavior so as to encourage rational public response, accommodating a tool that works in other ways challenges longstanding notions of what journalism is for. It also leaves relatively unaddressed the related question of what news images are for.

The relationship between the words and images of news has not had a steady history either. Hanno Hardt, for instance, tracked some of the debates by which photographers came to be seen as appropriating journalistic authority, while Julianne Newton, Caroline Brothers, and Michael Schudson have been among those documenting the contradictory responses of journalists toward the visual tools of their trade.[7] Though the capacity to accommodate visual representation has always differed by news medium—Ericson, Baranek, and Chan provided a useful description of the ramifications of newspaper's reliance on the visual, radio on the audio, and television on a combination of the two, further complicated by the Internet—most news organizations use text-based editors rather than photographers to select pictures across all news media, with often ill effect: in the view of a former director of photography at the *New York Times*, "the editors didn't value what pictures did.[8] They were considered soft."[9] Even today, with the multimodal platforms of the digitally mediated environment displaying still pictures regularly across slide shows, video packages, and online galleries of images, words still retain authority. As one wire service bureau chief recently remarked, "Words can go deeper than pictures. What about ideas? Concepts? Explanations? Background?"[10] This disregard for the image has buttressed a default understanding of news as primarily rational information relay that uses words as its main vehicle and implicitly frames images as contaminating, blurring, or at the very least offsetting journalism's reliance on straight reason.

That is not to say that scholars have not considered news independent of information, evidence, facts, and reason. John Hartley, for instance, observed that "pictorial news creates the public sphere within the semiosphere... rendering visible the continuous (and necessary) dialogue between... a rational public sphere and the fantasy layers of the semiosphere." John Fiske, S. Elizabeth Bird, James Carey, Kevin Barnhurst, and John Nerone have used journalism's representational forms, the tabloids, popular and lifestyle journalism as opportunities for addressing news as exercises in pleasure, community building, meaning making and code breaking. Other scholars—John Taylor, Susan Moeller, Jean Seaton, Eleanor Singer and Phyllis Endreny, and Carolyn Kitch and Janice Hume—have looked at spectacle, emotions, and passion in the hard news coverage of difficult events.[11]

And yet framing journalism as primarily the relay of reasoned information persists as the default construct in journalism's study, providing a useful starting point for thinking about how news images might work differently, particularly in unsettled events where the public need for information is thought to be critical. This assumption is worth addressing, for as the circumstances for producing news are changing, the primary emphasis on reason may be less relevant than ever before. The wide diversification of journalistic forms across high and low, broadsheet and tabloid, serious and sensational exemplified by two centuries of illustrated magazines, tabloid news, broadcast news, and online news, calls for a reassessment of the lingering emphasis on hard information and its association with the mainstream news of record. Previous enclaves separating print from broadcast and online journalists have given way to a restructured convergent environment, where multiple platforms regularly display a single story, professional and amateur journalists are repeatedly brought into close and sustained contact, and many journalists pull together multimedia stories without explicit organizational cues, producing variant treatments of events on their own that involve video, still photos, sound, text, and graphics. New aspirations of digital collaboration incorporate viewers in news making, while contemporary pressures toward corporatization make multitasking and multiskilling the rule rather than the exception. The involvement of picture agencies like Getty, Magnum, or Newspixs, often at the expense of staff photographers, and the increasing importance of paparazzi, freelancers, citizen journalists, and archives, make the editorial task of finding one image for a story into a search among more possibilities than ever before.[12] All of this has made the work of news production substantially more varied and multidirectional today than it was in preceding years and more open to a less-strident reliance on reason.

Fault lines over the so-called appropriate display of news images also indicate that the emphasis on reason might be more uneven than assumed. Because most journalists still privilege a picture's denotation, relying on photographic realism to enhance their coverage of the real world, they tend to display pictures in greater numbers and prominence whenever they need to assert authority for their coverage. But connotation reveals itself as important, if not more, than denotation. The work of Stuart Hall has shown how pictures are frequently used in ways that depict not the core of a news story but its peripheral, symbolic, and associative sides—scenes removed from those described in the text but valuable because they play to broader mind-sets about how the world works, "material for interpretation...to be solved, like a riddle."[13] For example, in the still ongoing Iraq War, images of children proliferated according to the surrounding context: in the news media of those nations prosecuting the war, children were shown being nurtured by the military forces; in the media of those opposing the war, pictures of maimed and dead children appeared. Denotatively, it could be argued that both sets of images showed life "as it was," but each set made a certain kind of sense in a particular connotative context.

Moreover, further questions about reason are introduced as images move across time, where additional disconnects occur between information and understanding, on one side, and depiction, on the other. As markers of collective memory, "photos are most useful when they symbolize socially shared concepts or beliefs rather than present new or unfamiliar information." Moving beyond journalism to various carriers of collective memory, such as art installations, posters, and cartoons, news images offer arbitrary, composite, schematic, conventionalized, and simplified glimpses of the past in service of the present: one may not know or remember the name of the South Vietnamese villagers who stood huddled together as a U.S. military photographer snapped their last moments before being shot to death, nor the date or circumstances under which the photograph was taken, but the photo's resonance as an image of war atrocity charts its meaning without such detail. As David Perlmutter has shown, not even an image's impact can be guaranteed. For over time as people look at news images in different contexts, they may accept their preferred meaning by taking the fastest if not the fullest, most reliable, or most all-encompassing route. What remains is what makes sense: "The natural tendency of social memory is to suppress what is not meaningful or intuitively satisfying...and substitute what seems more appropriate or more in keeping with [a] particular conception of the world."[14]

All of this suggests that despite their marginalization by both journalists and academics, news images deserve more attention as vehicles of more than just straight reason. Acting as conduits of both news and memory, they draw public attention regardless of how fully they depict what viewers might know and understand. Over time, the tendency to disconnect what is understood from what is seen intensifies, suggesting that reasoned information relay is not the sum total of what images provide.

Qualifying Reason: Contingency, Imagination, and Emotion

Qualifying journalism's focus on reasoned information is supported on multiple levels when addressing news images. First, pictures function in ways that have little to do with a definitive set of certain and unambiguous cues for understanding the world: they are thought to be analogic—continuous and operating in more/less terms—rather than digital—discrete and operating in either/or terms. Generally offering an affective and often gestalt-driven view of the world, they tend to be indexical—directing attention to something; material—having a tangible form; iconic and syntactically indeterminate—representative of something but in a fuzzy, porous way. Most important, images are expected to offer only fragments of understanding, and thus direct their viewers elsewhere to understand what is shown—to the purposes, processes, and formulations at work beyond a camera's frame.[15] While words are valued for their evidentiary qualities, images offer instead implicative relays, suggestive slices of action that people need to complete by interpreting and imagining what unfolds beyond the camera's frame.

Second, the fact and actuality of photographic depiction has been so central to supporting the journalistic record that its opposite impulses—contingency and imagination—have been left unaddressed. Because photography dates to a time when its practitioners angled for its recognition as a tool of objective, scientific recording, contingency and the imagination were both associated with a set of "hand-me-down terms from the other arts...that did not fit very well and that hobbled assessment of the medium." Largely uninterested in terms that might complicate, modify, or qualify what was shown, some critics went so far as to identify contingency as one of photography's weaknesses and, accommodating the blunt force of the photograph's depiction of the here-and-now, pushed aside all that it entailed—possibility, qualification, play, supposal, conditionality, and implication.[16]

Nonetheless contingency and the imagination assert their presence in news images. Defined as the quality of being uncertain, conditional, or (im)possible, contingency softens the fact-driven force of the photograph by introducing chance, relativity, implication, and hypothesis into the act of viewing, forcing people to imagine and interpret a sequence of action beyond the picture's taking.[17] The imagination offers the possibility to interpret in a fanciful, illogical, baseless, or irrational fashion, with an uneven regard for what is actually shown. Both qualities can alter unseen sequences of action over time. A black-and-white photograph of a naked female corpse killed by the Nazis becomes an art installation years later, featuring a beautiful nude woman sleeping erotically under pastel strobe lights. A picture of a person dying of AIDS later transforms into a glossy advertisement for a popular clothing line. When dealing with events of an unsettled nature, contingency and the imagination may constitute a particularly useful stance for those needing to establish meaning. For the ambiguity of the codes through which images are set in place "allow[s] considerable play in the meaning of the work, [which] is not immanent."[18] In fact, contingency and the imagination suggest that closure around images is rarely achieved and that they may provide the necessary leakage through which visual meaning can change.

Third, the idea that news images might bypass the intellect to engage the emotions has been acknowledged as more of an irritation than strength when thinking about journalism. Drawing from John Stuart Mill's 1859 admonitions against the power of popular sentiment, Jurgen Habermas and Karl Popper are among those who have more recently argued that affect, the emotions, and passion undermine the development of the reasoned public that journalism is expected to bolster,[19] making a public emotional response to images undesirable. Rationalizing the public sphere, they maintain, enhances the public good, and journalism is implicated in its maintenance. It may be, however, that rationality has been overemphasized as a way of explaining public action, in large part because it supports journalism's own self-recognition as a project aligned with modernity. For as the British cultural critic Raymond Williams pointed out, collective existence cannot take on meaning without some recognition of the structures of feeling that drive it.[20]

Though these points of entry—contingency, the imagination, and the emotions—have not been the primary target of journalism scholarship, they have drawn attention elsewhere. For instance, Richard Rorty made the case for contingency as a useful parameter through which to conduct moral deliberation, Roger Silverstone argued that imagination "opens the door to understanding and in turn to the capacity to make judgments in and through the public world," and both George Marcus and Lauren Berlant suggested that the emotions enable rather than undermine rationality.[21] Multiple scholars have argued that late modernity encourages a rethinking of the centrality of reason. Though the emotions remain "the aspect of human experience least subject to control, least constructed or learned (hence most universal), least public, and therefore least amenable to socio-cultural analysis," a focus on the rational leaves "unarticulated its dependence on emotion-concepts [such as] how emotion enters into political theories, how pictures of emotional needs and pains legitimate political theories, how political regimes privilege, amplify, stunt or nurture actual political emotions."[22]

The importance of contingency, the imagination, and the emotions is also supported in developments beyond the academy, where a rise in identity politics, personal blogging, and nationalism suggest that many people engage in ways that cool reason cannot explain, remaining "little inclined to set aside the persuasive force of passion." Qualifying reason may thus be particularly important in shaping public response to events of an unsettled nature:

> So when do we think about politics? When our emotions tell us to.... In addition to managing our emotional reactions to things that are novel, threatening and familiar, affect influences when and how we *think* about such things.... Emotions enhance citizen rationality because they allow citizens to condition their political judgment to fit the circumstance.[23]

Or, as one scholar aptly summarized, "Our commitment to reason is an emotional one" that draws on "strong reserves of emotional capital [that] are necessary for matured and reasoning modes of conduct to prevail."[24]

The shooting of twenty-six-year-old Iranian philosophy student Neda Agha-Soltan, killed during election demonstrations in Tehran in June 2009, illustrates how images do more than provide reasoned information. The incident unfolded as quickly as its impact became known: a bystander's brief cell-phone video captured the shooting, its forty-second sequence depicting the young woman crumpling to the ground after being shot in the chest. As people rushed to assist her, she turned her panic-stricken face toward the camera and blood began to trickle from her mouth. Though she did not die on camera, her rapid demise was implied by the depicted sequence of action.[25]

The unnamed bystander's video was sent by e-mail to an Iranian asylum seeker in the Netherlands, who forwarded it to CNN, the BBC, YouTube, Facebook, and other news organizations and social networking sites. For a mediated environment hungry for pictures of the Iranian protests, the video's informational value was beyond doubt, and nearly every U.S. news organization ran some visual treatment of the story. Multiple news organizations offered links to the video, though journalists, worried about its verification, graphicness, low resolution, and shaky focus, struggled to explain what it showed: CNN at first blocked out the woman's face, then withheld her name and ran a pixilated version of the video on-air before eventually screening the full video; ABC withheld the video altogether and showed instead a few select still images on freeze frame, one of its news executives noting that "we don't show people on television at the moment of their death." Both CBS and NBC heavily edited the video's most graphic sequences. Social networking sites, however, exhibited no such hesitation, and they facilitated the full video's rapid transfer from site to site, many of which experienced thousands of hits in rapid succession and pushed the video to go viral, where it became a "trending topic" by nightfall on Twitter. As *Photo District News* later observed, "The clip proved too strong to be bogged down by fact-checking."[26]

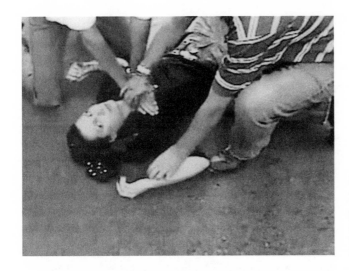

Figure 1.1:
Anonymous Cellphone
Video, YouTube/Public
Domain, "Iran–Neda
Girl killed in Tehran"
(Screenshot at 0:05),
June 20, 2009.

As coverage continued, the video soon gave way to still photos in much of its display. One still image, frame-grabbed from the video, froze a single powerful moment from the more extended sequence of action. Fuzzy and out-of-focus and taken before the blood started to flow, the picture targeted the woman prone on the ground, her wide eyes beseechingly searching out the camera (fig. 1.1).

The image was arresting, implicating the viewer in the woman's helplessness, vulnerability and anguish. One trade paper put it best, when it noted that a "viewer can't help but imagine being there."[27]

Though at first journalists conveyed their unease with the voyeurism of watching Agha-Soltan die—*Time* noted that the woman looked as if she were "begging to tell a story, but it is too late; she is dying as we watch"—the image was nonetheless widely displayed across the U.S. news media, appearing in still form in nearly every newspaper and newsmagazine, even above the fold on the front page of the often picture-free *Wall Street Journal,* on multiple TV news programs, and on online news sites. Many news organizations continued to link to the video alongside the still photo, but as an increasing number of people voiced discomfort with its display, the latter took over as the event's primary depiction, before long constituting its most prominent, shared visualization across all of its mediated forms.[28]

Helping to set the mnemonic template for remembering Neda Agha-Soltan—who within hours became a symbol of freedom of expression and human rights, martyred as the "Angel of Iran" in their defense—the photo, instrumental in capturing public attention, took on a role larger than that associated with a simple news picture of a topical and breaking news event. Over the following days and weeks, the image moved into other contexts as Agha-Soltan inspired poetry, stories, songs, documentary films, videos, posters, and other memorial activities.[29] At the same time, multiple news organizations hailed the picture as a symbol of the Iranian protests and positioned it within their lists of iconic photos of other unsettled events that they constructed on the spot. Compared with Robert Capa's picture of a Republican soldier during the Spanish Civil War, the shooting of a Vietcong officer in Vietnam, and a solitary man's assault on the tanks of Tiananmen Square, the image, though not necessarily a candidate for iconic status itself, reappeared in countless additional contexts, each time showing Agha-Soltan's languishing eyes piercing the image's third wall and connecting with the public on the other side. Calling her death "probably the most widely witnessed death in human history" and naming her "a battle cry for Iranian protesters, her face a symbol for the thousands of people who suffered under the government's heavy-handed crackdown," by the end of 2009 *Time* included the woman among its top ten heroes for the year, while the *Washington Post,* saying that she had "moved the world," suggested that she should have been given a posthumous Nobel Peace Prize instead of U.S. president Barack Obama.[30]

Each time the image appeared and reappeared, incessantly and in multiple contexts, its viewers, who already knew she was dead, engaged yet again with a picture of her facing death with animal-like fear. The frame-grabbed image not only appeared numerous times in the weeks after her death but months later too—when her grave was desecrated in November 2009, when discussions of women's rights highlighted Iran's repression of women, when her parents proclaimed the government responsible for her death in December 2009, and in yearly retrospectives of news photography. The image and its taking also ushered in widespread discussion among journalists of a change in journalistic practices: the Poynter Institute, a professional forum for journalists, called for a "next-step journalism" that could accommodate the kind of collaboration evident in covering the woman's shooting, while PBS Boston affiliate WGBH gathered journalists in a roundtable to address the squeamishness that had prompted the U.S. networks not to show the full video. Citing a slew of earlier similar images—the Zapruder film of the Kennedy assassination, images of dead U.S. soldiers in Mogadishu, the shooting of a Palestinian boy in Gaza, and a decapitation video of *Wall Street Journal* reporter Danny Pearl—one reporter noted that "the notion that the viewers of ABC, NBC and CBS cannot handle blood is ridiculous...you have to see what's going on in a war or conflict zone in order to understand." *Photo District News* pondered whether coverage of her death signaled a "turning point for conflict reporting," and the image punctuated debates at the *Columbia Journalism Review* about citizen journalism. Contemplating the confluence of new and old media in a somewhat more poetic fashion, one news magazine observed that Agha-Soltan "died on the Web, and she is being given a second, perhaps eternal, life on it."[31]

The image's display provoked similarly diverse responses from the public. Though many viewers felt the picture emblematized Iranian repression, the repeated display of her dying vexed viewers who lamented that "instead of being put to rest, her final, bloody image is being strewn across blogs and Twitter" and other settings in the mediated environment. "What does it say," wrote one blogger, "when we feel squeamish and protective about the deaths of some, but not others....People like Neda owe access to their deaths so Americans can access their own humanity." Complaints over the image were tied to a perceived disregard for women of color.³² Many viewers also expressed an irrational wish for her not to have died: as some social networking sites filled with messages lamenting how "the world cries seeing your last breath," others recontextualized the dying woman's last moments as taking on "new life, flickering across computer screens around the world." Irrational scenarios circulated imagining her still alive: "Stay, Neda, Don't go, Neda," lamented one poem, while the United for Neda video, put together by a group of Iranian singers and artists, sported lyrics calling on her to "be strong" and "keep your head held high." The *New York Times* noted how protestors filled the streets after her death chanting "Neda lives! Ahmadinejad is dead!' " OneWeb site— weareallneda.com—gave posters the chance to leave memorial messages to a woman who would never read them, and thousands of messages were logged within weeks.³³

The image's repeated and often illogical display patterns, evocative public response and importation into different discussions, which both debated professional standards and appropriateness and expressed wishful lamentations about imagined sequences of action, all show how images assert themselves beyond narrow invocations of reasoned information relay. Community building, recovering from trauma and grief, arousing empathy and indignation, concretizing complex events, creating new alliances, imagining alternative endings, debating parameters of coverage, expressing hope for a different order, creating context, rethinking professional practice, facilitating catharsis, enabling analysis and comparisons—all of these were brought to bear on a fuzzy image framegrabbed from a demonstration in Iran. Though each response built on an initial act of information relay, it was not the image's informational dimensions that sustained the picture's display. Rather, the image of Agha-Soltan continued to reappear for reasons having to do with nationalism, grieving, memory, identity, community, trauma, and compassion, all of which were more easily crafted through the event's visual representation than through its words.

It is thus possible, even probable, that news images, and particularly photographs, function through a qualification of reason—a combination of contingency, the imagination, and the emotions—that settles not at the image's original point of display but over time by different people putting it to multiple uses in new contexts. Images regularly travel across circumstances that are transformative, sometimes playful and hypothetical, and often internally contradictory. This means that an image's meaning relies not on individualistic whims but on fundamental collective impulses on hand to help people make sense of what they see. As Mark Johnson noted, "The capacity to share meaning and to reason is imaginative through and through, starting from our most mundane, unreflective bodily interactions and working up to our most impressive activities of hypothesis formation, problem solving and reasoning." Thus admitting contingency, the imagination, and the emotions more readily into discussions of journalism may help explain why news images are useful for viewers struggling to make sense of unsettled events of a difficult and complicated nature. Following John Dewey, who long ago noted that "imagination is the chief instrument of the good," it may be that to a greater degree than reasoned judgment these impulses help people engage with the news, and that is why images appeal to them.[34]

"As If": The Subjunctive Voice of the Visual

The power of contingency, the imagination, and the emotions has drawn the attention of some of photography's most renowned observers, even if it has not been at the top of their conversations. Walter Benjamin was fascinated by photography's illogical dimensions. Reporting a nineteenth-century encounter with photography where people said, "We didn't trust ourselves at first...we were abashed by the distinctiveness of these human images, and believed that the little tiny faces in the picture could see us," he argued for an object's "aura," an ineffable quality of the object that was simultaneously elusive yet compelled the public to make sense of the object. Roland Barthes insisted on the photograph's "third meaning," which compelled viewers after encountering both the image's literal/informational side and its symbolic dimensions; though the third meaning was both difficult to locate and describe, involving what he called the image's obtuseness, accent, or anaphoric side, Barthes used it to push discussions of the photograph toward the idea of "the punctum," which saw the onlooker's engagement with the image as key to understanding the image itself. While Susan Sontag maintained that images remained "inexhaustible invitations to deduction, speculation and fantasy," Terence Wright commented on the camera's play to the continuous present, where the viewer could

> take time to speculate on (or fantasize over) an event which could not be perceived in the same way in the normal course of events....It presents the opportunity to the viewer which goes beyond the bounds of everyday perception, offering the time and space to imagine, examine or analyze in a way that would not normally be possible.[35]

These ruminations suggest that something beyond denotation and connotation rests in photographs, a quality that enables their shaping and use in ways that have not been fully accounted for. When Dorothea Lange's acclaimed photo "Migrant Mother" is recycled into an advertisement for life insurance or a picture of a Palestinian raising hands bloodied from the Israeli soldier he just killed becomes a political cartoon, photographs seem to be crafting their power through more than just a combination of literal and figurative meaning. Because images of different events look similar even on their initial taking, recurrent visual impulses carry meaning across unusual contexts, and viewers make images meaningful in ways that might not be readily apparent, photographs facilitate making sense of the world in a way that is not necessarily rational, evidentiary, or reasoned.

The voice of the visual elucidates how this happens. The notion of voice is defined here as an image's orientation to the imagined, emotional, and contingent cues in its environment, which facilitate its relationship with a broad range of contexts, events, people, practices, and other images. Voice builds on an image's denotative and connotative sides so as to locate the image's use value beyond what it delineates and connotes at first glance.[36] While denotation grounds the image in reality, and connotation carries the meaning of an image across a set of possible associations, voice orients to the ways in which an image travels via these associations to other contexts, where it can be used by other people, seen through other images, and activated for other aims. Thus the image of Agha-Soltan not only denotes a dying woman and connotes state repression, but acts as a relay for community building, the expression of women's rights, recognition of amateur videography, and a new tweaking of the relationship between old and new media. Much as Clifford Geertz long ago distinguished between "culture of" and "culture for,"[37] voice refers to the ways in which an image's meaning is used *for* a wide variety of strategies and objectives, all of which increase over time and space.

This means that voice accounts for an image's larger environment—its transportation to other spatial and temporal contexts, its variable use value among viewers, its connection with other images, its reliance on the past. Loosely borrowed from linguistics, voice builds on associated linguistic terms—aspect, tense, voice, and mood—which complicate, qualify, and expand on what is shown. Defined grammatically as that which highlights the relationship between the subject and the word of action,[38] voice makes an image's completion dependent on features beyond its own parameters—other images in the same field of depiction, past similarity with events, a viewer's state of mind, attitude, temporal and sequential positioning. As Slavoj Zizek contended, "Voice does not simply persist at a different level with regard to what we see, it rather points to a gap in the field of the visible, toward the dimension of what eludes our gaze...ultimately, we hear things because we cannot see everything."[39]

Voice thus suggests rethinking how images work when they come into contact across time and space with other people, events, contexts, and images. Voice helps explain why a single image can be recycled to multiple contexts, where it plays to members of various publics, to cues from other events at other times and places, and to a public familiarity with other images. It facilitates the inclusion of contingency, the imagination and the emotions as necessary cues in visual representation rather than as adjuncts to reason, thereby introducing new dimensions to the terrain on which images are thought to work.

The voice of the visual is subjunctive in character. Taken too from linguistics, which defines subjunctivity as the mood or voice of a verb used to express condition, desire, opinion, hypothesis, or statements that are contrary to fact, the subjunctive grammatically couches what is depicted in an interpretive scheme of "what could be" rather than "what is." It situates action within the hypothetical, changing the statement "I shot that man" to "I might have shot that man." Usually signified in verbal language by auxiliaries like "might," "could," or "should," by the substitution of "would have" for "had," and by the use of "if" clauses, the subjunctive voice thus adds impulses of implication, contingency, conditionality, play, imagination, emotionality, desire, supposal, hypothesis, hope, liminality, and (im)possibility to the supposed certainty of visual representation. When added to the denotative and connotative impulses usually associated with photography, subjunctivity offers a way of transforming the relationship between the possible, probable, impossible, and certain by accommodating contingency, the imagination, and the emotions, and it becomes particularly useful in the unsettled times associated with war, terrorism, natural disaster, epidemic, torture, and planned violence. In this regard, it can readily appear and resurface across images in unexpected contexts.

As a mode of tackling experience, the subjunctive—often called the "as if"—has been addressed by scholars beyond news images. Originally surfacing as both a philosophical treatise and a psychological intervention at the turn of the twentieth century,[40] today the subjunctive reasoning used in law and philosophy; the thought experiments of physics, mathematics, and biology; and grammatically driven mood or voice characterizing the structure of multiple languages all foster an alternative engagement with reality. Anthropologist Victor Turner introduced the subjunctive into his discussion of ritual process and liminality:

I sometimes talk about the liminal phase being dominantly in the subjunctive mood of culture, the mood of maybe, might be, as if, hypothesis, fantasy, conjecture, desire....[It is] fructile chaos, a storehouse of possibilities, not a random assemblage but a striving after new forms and structures, a gestation process.

Roger D. Abrahams, Jerome Bruner, Charles E. Scott, Roger Silverstone, and Michael Schudson each elaborated on the notion in the different contexts of folklore, psychology, philosophy, cultural studies, and journalism; I addressed it in my discussion of journalism's live performances of media events. In her analysis of the standoff, Robin Wagner-Pacifici described the subjunctive as a "world in which strong emotions...uncertainty and ambiguity are foregrounded."[41] Moreover, the more recent emergence of the "as if" as the title of popular songs, movies, books, television shows, a Web comic, and a collective blog for authors concerned with intellectual freedom—almost every one of which surfaced after the events of 9/11—suggests that a drive for the subjunctive may increase in times of collective anxiety.[42]

The role that the subjunctive voice might play in visual representation is fruitful, for it helps explain how people might engage with images differently. Through its reliance on contradiction; on often illogical, unpredictable, and idiosyncratic connections; and on the changing use values of an image, the voice of the "as if" can be thought to provide contingent, imagined, or impossible conclusions to already-finished sequences of events, activate visual markers for subjunctive ends, and facilitate the depiction of disparate events through similar images. Equally important, it forces an event's meaning through the display of images that are themselves contingent. What all of this suggests is that the voice of subjunctivity—and its concomitant invocation of emotionality, contingency, and imagination—become particularly useful around events that are unsettled, ambiguous, difficult, contested, or in otherwise need of public consensus.

Voice thus offers a window onto a different kind of patterned response to the news, activated by news images. Although a move toward the emotions, contingency, and the imagination is not widely prevalent in default discussions of journalism, a closer look at news images may offer a different lens both on how journalism comports itself and on the different tools through which the body politic in its multiple formations can be maintained.

Images in Journalism: From the "As Is" to the "As If"

Today's mediated environment makes it difficult to be naïve about images. Four interrelated—and not mutually exclusive—interpretive communities have been particularly invested in articulating assumptions about the value of news images—journalists, news executives, politicians and officials, and viewers. Though not the only groups to voice their sentiments about what news images are for, their investment complicates the assumption that pictures document reality as it is.

On the face of things, journalists value images for their "eyewitness" authority and the act of "having been there" that a photograph implies. Though journalists tend to reduce images to supports to words, photographs help journalists credential their coverage by drawing on photographic verisimilitude and realism to show that one was present to witness an event. As one photographer who covered the battlefields of Vietnam and Lebanon said, journalism's need for pictures is undeniable: "Many people ask me 'why do you take these pictures?'...It's not a case of 'There but for the grace of God go I'; it's a case of 'I've been there.'" This would seem to suggest that the "as is" of visual relay helps journalists do a better job of being journalists, with journalists readily relying on images to substantiate their stories. One director of the French photo agency Vu noted that journalism makes "wholesale use of (photography) for the purposes of simple effectiveness....It's true because it's in the papers and it's even more true because it's in the photograph."[43]

But the resulting images of news are not necessarily the ones with the greatest truth value. As one photo editor maintained, "Since we've seen almost everything there is to see in this age, what photo editors are trying to do it make you feel something." During war, for instance, news organizations tend not to depict human civilian devastation on the "other" side, military casualties, battles gone badly, wounded or captured soldiers. Though journalists often maintain that they try to show a full and accurate depiction of the events they cover, regardless of the explicit parameters that may surface, a spokeswoman for the British *Independent* offered a more contained strategy about the war in Iraq when he said that "we are not keen on showing US or UK prisoners of war."[44] Instead one's own war tends to be depicted as clean, heroic, and just, with images limited to those that are consonant with prevailing sentiments about the war. When such sentiments involve securing and maintaining support for the war, images tend to reflect themes of patriotism, civic responsibility, and the good of the nation-state. They also tend not to be graphic. When they are transported into other fields of visual display—posters, film, postage stamps, T-shirts—it becomes clear that subjunctive notions of the world "as if" it were a better, more coherent, gentler, more equitable place than it may be on the ground regularly drive visual selection and presentation, and particularly around unsettled events.

Journalism's somewhat contained regard for images has had multiple ramifications. Although images have long been part of news, how images could or should be used to relay information about the real world was never fully addressed, and the challenges facing journalism as it accommodated visual representation, from its earliest introduction as lithographs, newspaper illustrations, early photographs, and drawings, were not clarified. Images were regarded as the fluff of news, material that was secondary and adjunct to the words at their side, and that sentiment continued even when the ascent of wire photos made it possible to access images as quickly as words. Nearly a hundred years after their onset, photographs were still derisively labeled the work of "newspaper illustrators" or "pictorial reporters," "a mechanical side-line to the serious business of fact-narration—a social inferior," while photographers were called "journalism's poor relation." Though trade forums debated photographers' membership in professional associations, resistance was high and photographers were denied membership on grounds that photography was "not journalism." This means that even the most basic standards for image use—where to put an image, how to title an image, how to caption an image, and how to position an image alongside words—were not developed at the time of their emergence.[45] Not surprisingly, today many journalists remain unclear about what to do with images and how to discern which image might be appropriate or relevant for a news story; they are also split on the value of graphic imagery. For instance, the *New York Times'* public editor lamented whether news images should be presented as art or news:

> I believe *Times* readers deserve more precise and consistent explanations of the images put before them. Making the wording and explanations uniform across all sections of the paper would help ensure that readers know whether they are looking at news or at art, no matter what part of the *Times* they are reading.[46]

This uncertainty intensifies when difficult targets of news depiction arise. Ambivalence probes more deeply than the question of whether viewers will flinch at seeing grotesque imagery, as some recent literature suggests. Because many journalists still see images not as constructions—the result of actions taken by individual photographers, their corresponding photo editors, and the larger institutional setting that engages both—but as mirrors of the events that they depict, the authority of images grows when the news increases in magnitude or importance. As one editor said of U.S. journalism, "It is a tradition...that when the event or history is raised to a level of great importance, we use pictures to reflect that importance." Coverage of unsettled events, then, turns to visuals when information is thought most needed, readily turning over column inches, airtime, and online spaces to accommodate an increased and more central pictorial presence in the news.[47] As often as not, these images push the "as if" side of events—the emotional, imagined, and contingent—as much as they reflect what transpires on the ground.

This is because the various kinds of journalistic practice that undergird journalism's truth claims to the real—the "as is"—also encourage journalists to gravitate toward the "as if." Practices of composition, uses of text, and conventions of presentation can all be developed in subjunctive ways. For instance, the "as if" has many helpers in news photography, where conventions insufficiently clarified as part of regular news relays—credits, captions, and the relation between text and image—blur a news image's denotative and connotative impulses and by extension bolster its subjunctive voice. Credits can be insufficient and pushed to the back of the news hole, captions are often overgeneralized and bear a questionable link to what they depict, and images tend to exist in an imprecise relationship with the words that they accompany. Such blurring is intensified when news organizations cover difficult events and images regularly appear that do not play to the key information points of a news story but are instead repetitive, aesthetic, memorable, dramatic, and familiar from other events.[48] In other words, in covering events where a greater public need for information relay has long been assumed, journalism often turns to images that offer familiarity, memorability, and ease of access but not necessarily reasoned information.

Additionally, journalists' mnemonic practices draw from the subjunctive voice, which helps viewers see and remember events across time through images that reduce complex and multidimensional phenomena into memorable scenes. Often they are memorable because they activate impulses about how the "world might be" rather than how "it is." When a depiction coaxes viewers to consider how it "might mean," "might look," or "might end," it involves many qualifications of reasoned information. A photograph of a kiss, tendered in a public square at the end of World War II, draws imaginary visions about who the people might have been, what kind of relationship they might have had, or where their engagement might have led. As the image travels to new contexts, it plays off of additional subjunctive impulses. This illustrates what Lessing said about the visual long ago: images break the sequencing of action in the middle. By freezing that sequencing midway at a particularly memorable representational moment, viewers are able to embellish numerous emotional, imaginary, and contingent schemes on the "about to" moment depicted in the photo. Moreover, when viewers complete the sequence of action, they often do so in ways that do not correspond with what happens on the ground.

The chief executives of news media organizations tend to value the "as if" dimensions of news images for a different reason, largely because they believe that imagined and contingent interpretations help compel public attention. Driven by what some photographers see as a strategic recognition of the image's power, recognition often rests alongside a conservatism about which images to use, by which executives often shy away from unusual or unfamiliar depictions. In one photographer's view, news executives "are afraid of pictures which they know are terribly powerful, for they are unable to show the real truth and are vulnerable to all kinds of manipulation. Their natural instinct is that of self-protection, the repetition of well-known types of pictures."[49]

This gravitation away from the world as it is and toward its subjunctive reflection tends to become particularly prevalent during large-scale crises, when news executives encourage images to literally come to the fore of the journalistic record. Following September 11, executive tweaking facilitated a "sea change" in the *New York Times'* then-current use of images, when its pages displayed more than double the number of images it had displayed in noncrisis times. During the beginning of the 2003 war in Iraq, broadcast and cable news organizations turned to photographic galleries and interactive visual displays, showing, in the words of then-news anchor Dan Rather, a "literal flood of live pictures from the battlefield"; the *New York Times* again doubled its daily display of photographs, while certain TV networks featured slide shows of photographs, profiling them against background music.[50] The pictures that appeared were repetitive, familiar, formulaic, and patterned, reflecting the "as if" of crisis and war as much as their "as is" dimensions.

This is not to say that graphic pictures of the "as is" do not appear. But often when they do, the responses that they generate provide an opportunity to gravitate back to the "as if." In 2004, for instance, photos of four dead U.S. contractors in Fallujah, Iraq surfaced, which showed their bodies defiled by an Iraqi mob. While the news stories were graphic and unrelenting in tracking what had happened, the equally graphic pictures were presented with marked ambivalence, as news executives and journalists pondered questions of decency, appropriateness, and the so-called "breakfast cereal test" fretted over the protection of children and public opinion either for or against the war and worried about possible charges of sensationalism, political bias, and lack of patriotism.[51] As one NBC news editor observed following the network's decision not to show one particularly gruesome image, "I think we can convey the horror of this despicable act while being sensitive to our viewers." Though death's depiction pushed news executives into debates over whether, where, and how they should display the images, their discussion moved toward a narrowing of possible imaging practices. Guidelines on photo display were published, reviewed, discussed, and revised, and ombudsmen's columns tracked whether the duty to publish changed if the bodies were military rather than civilian, Iraqi rather than American, visible as distinctive human beings rather than charred corpses, women and children rather than men. In the words of one newspaper, the incident "resulted in more mainstream media self-examination in one day than the entire attack on Iraq had in a year." Arguments—about our dead versus their dead about civilian versus military dead about showing the faces of the dead about class, race, and the dead about identifying the dead before their next of kin were notified—were caught in the tension between what John Taylor called "polite looking" and the "prolonged, uncontrolled staring" with impunity into another's misfortune, inviting revulsion, "identification and reflection, rejection and denial, and moments to be inquisitive about the dreadful fate of others." As the debates signaled conflicted measures of temperateness and a desire for graphic imagery among news executives, the former won out, reflecting, as the *New Republic*'s Adam Kushner said at the time, "something fundamentally amiss in . . . journalism—that an instinct to protect viewers is trumping an instinct to inform."[52] His words were prescient, for in the years since that graphic display from Fallujah, few other incidents in Iraq have received similarly explicit visual coverage.

Officials and politicians recognize the subjunctive value of news images in shaping public opinion and justifying policy, and they remain among the first tools of journalism to be discussed in unsettled times. The use of images for political purposes relies on the recognition that abstract concepts and complicated events can become visible and understandable through certain kinds of depiction. Connected here has been an assumption that seeing photos is enough to promote action or responsiveness of some kind. Particularly following the Holocaust, the sentiment prevailed that had there been pictures available of the atrocities as they unfolded, the Holocaust might never have happened. Though that notion was laid to rest in later wars whose related atrocities were depicted but still received no sustained official attention, the presumed connection between public action and photographs persists nonetheless.[53]

Thus, in the final stages of World War II, images of the victims of the concentration camps were used to help secure waning support for the war effort. In 1993, when images surfaced of a U.S. soldier being dragged through the streets of Mogadishu, the assumption was that officials changed policy due to the uproar it generated. Regardless of the assumption's accuracy, the images' impact was widely invoked as an impetus for withdrawing troops from Somalia. In the beginning of the war in Iraq, the Bush administration pushed the "as if" over the "as is," when it banned the display of coffins of the military dead on the basis that showing the coffins was insensitive to the dead soldiers' families. This remained the U.S. administration's stance, even though it went against public polls, which already by late 2003 sided with the caskets' public display. Although a shift toward more easily accommodating explicit images was expected to take place with the Obama administration, change was undercut by a turnaround in May 2009, when Obama refused to release photos showing the abuse of U.S. prisoners.[54] Again, the "as if" prevailed, when replaying to a pretended reality rested on a presumption that not displaying abuse would diminish attention to its unfolding.

Viewers use images to come to grips with the news, relying on their capacity to render the world more concrete, accessible, and readily understandable. But viewers can also be among the most vocal supporters of the image's play to the "as if." Though people tend to recall more about the news when visuals depict what is happening and exhibit certain empathetic bodily responses to what they see in images,[55] viewers have definite assumptions about what should and should not be shown, and many regularly try to constrain images by notions of decency, taste, appropriateness, and tone. Though this is not the case with all viewers and has not always been the case—Barbara Norfleet and Jay Ruby have separately documented the extensive practices of taking pictures of the dead, including one's own children and family members, which prevailed as recently as the middle of the twentieth century—most of the public supports journalism's moments of death as private and unseen.[56] And yet, that timidity about seeing death in the news is now regularly overturned by a mediated environment that foregrounds graphic images. Though the mediated environment is saturated with images of death and accommodates fictional, televised, cinematic and digital depictions of death which are dramatic, prolonged, and not ambiguous, very few photographs in the news actually depict death.[57] At a time when pictures of death and gruesome acts of violence proliferate elsewhere, it is curious that many viewers remain so uncomfortable by the same images when they are shown as part of news.

Moreover, the recent public trend against graphicness in the news has been steadily rising, at least in the United States. In 1993, U.S. survey respondents were evenly divided over whether or not pictures should be used to show violence, but by the following decade a preference for a more limited display of photos was widely articulated: in 2001, the *Boston Globe, Newsweek,* and *Time* were each deluged by readers who protested the display of photos of Osama Bin Laden—"We don't need to look at that evil face, big and bold on the cover of your magazine," wrote one angry woman to *Time.*[58] By March 2003, 57 percent of the U.S. population felt that the U.S. media should not show pictures of captured U.S. soldiers in Iraq, and one year later, when the images of the mutilation of four U.S. contractors in Fallujah, Iraq were published, a full 71 percent of the U.S. public said that the pictures had been too gruesome or explicit, and only 7 percent wanted even more explicit pictures.[59] In September 2009, the Associated Press took a picture of a mortally wounded Marine in Afghanistan, and though the Marine's father asked that the picture not be published, the AP distributed it nonetheless, justifying its decision "to make public an image that conveys the grimness of war and the sacrifice of young men and women fighting it." Letters to the editor and postings from readers deluged the newspapers that printed the picture, and U.S. defense secretary Robert Gates protested the decision in "the strongest terms, saying it was "appalling" and a "breach of public decency."[60]

Because this trend takes shape alongside journalists and news executives who are split on the value of explicit news images, debates among them over the degree of explicitness often become pronounced. When Sidney Schanberg—writing in a 2005 *News Photographer* commentary, titled "Not a Pretty Picture: Why Don't U.S. Papers Show Graphic War Photos?"—observed that a lack of graphic display of the Iraq war was undermining journalism's obligation to full reportage, his piece generated critical letters to the editor. A writer for *Broadcasting and Cable* urged the U.S. networks in 2007 to offer more graphic coverage of the Iraq war, and readers called him "an idiot" who was "heartless toward the families of those who have loved ones" in Iraq.[61] In June 2009, *New York Times* ethicist Randy Cohen argued that Obama's banning of photos of the abuse of detainees held abroad by the United States was wrong, likening the effect of their display to that achieved by seeing the video of the young

Iranian woman shot to death in Tehran. "There are many kinds of understand-ing," he wrote, "including the kind grasped from making a visceral emotional connection to an event." His column generated extensive disagreement among readers who argued that the Abu Ghraib photos were old news and did not merit display.[62]

Contemporary public discomfort with graphic display exists beyond the United States too, though the topic changes by context. The death of Princess Diana in 1997 saw the Italian news media publishing graphic images, while British journalism followed conventions of extreme restraint.[63] After the 2004 tsunami, Indian journalists protested the graphic display of their dead in the Western news media, arguing for the same restraint that the U.S. news media had shown its dead following the attacks of September 11.[64] And, as discussed earlier, Muslim and feminist Web sites were filled with laments about what was seen as a gratuitous display of Neda Agha-Soltan's streetside death in Tehran in 2009. As one writer for the *Toronto Star* phrased it:

> News organizations have been on the receiving end of grisly photos since the invention of the camera. But there's never any debate over whether we will show the blood-spattered body of a murder victim....We just don't do it....If the victims are not one of us, if they live far away or have no names or cultural commonalities, they're fair game. Hence, it's perfectly acceptable, if not mundane, to show piles of skulls in Rwanda or a skeletal and swollen-bellied African baby on the verge of death....Except last year, when the bombs were crashing down on Iraq and houses were flattened, their inhabitants incinerated, the very same networks and newspapers that proclaimed their high moral ground and concern for reader sensibilities refrained from running pictures of the civilian casualties.[65]

Graphicness thus is a moveable, serviceable, and debatable convention, depen-dent on those who invoke it and for which aim. As a standard of depiction whose moderation pushes the "as if" over the "as is," it often acts as a barrier when information is too proximate, either culturally or geographically.

Viewer involvement in pushing the "as if" over the "as is" is facilitated by today's porous mediated environment. As public lobbyists, religious and pedagogic leaders, members of militias and insurgencies, aggrieved or bereaved family members, celebrities and activists all articulate their sentiments about news images, the image moves into environments where multiple displays and meanings can be continuously recrafted. Not only does such involvement fur-ther complicate the image's status as a carrier of reasoned information, but the subjunctive voice alters, mutes, and sometimes suspends the questions nor-mally posed of journalism, drawing attention not to what people see but asking them to consider what it reminds them about or which possibilities it raises. All of this suggests that though there may be some general belief that seeing is believing, seeing is preferred only under certain circumstances. "As if" prevails over "as is."

No wonder, then, that journalism often embraces images that do not follow obvious lines of reasoned information relay, pushing the memorable shot over the topical one; the image that appears in every newspaper, newscast, and online news site on a given day; the picture that resembles a painting more than a less aesthetic but real street scene; the shot that recalls familiar images from earlier events, similar or disparate.[66] What is worthy of depiction, how, and why are thus decisions weighed on not only by journalists but by news executives, officials, politicians, and viewers, making the question of what news organizations do with images more porous than assumed. The patterning of these accommodations, made more pronounced in today's digital environment, suggests that news images often reflect more about subjunctive visions of the world than show what is transpiring on the ground.

The potential impact of all of this on a healthy body politic should by now be obvious. The ambivalence over photography's integration into news; the unevenness with which photos are used; the emotional, contingent, and imagined appeal that images wield in a supposedly rational mediated environment; the ongoing debates over what counts as an image; and the active involvement of nonjournalists in making calls about which images to show complicate the longstanding recognition of news images as carriers of reason and suggest instead that images play to different impulses altogether. If the power of news images derives in part from the "as if" of what they show, then images can be used to simplify, soften, and render contingent the untenable features of the geopolitical realities that they depict. Their invitation to respond as much to the imagined, conditional, and impossible as to the real and known may constitute a different kind of response to the unsettled events of the public sphere that deserves further attention. Though the "as if" may have both positive and negative consequences, it suggests that news images reside in a sea of potential leakages, which wedge in and around the words of news coverage, between the actual and aspired dimensions of journalism, and between journalism and the larger mediated environment.

Those leakages need to be more carefully charted. Susan Sontag was among the earliest and most prominent of cultural critics to change her mind on how images work: "As much as they create sympathy, I wrote, photographs shrivel sympathy. Is this true? I thought it was when I wrote it. I'm not so sure now."[67] It may be that images simultaneously do both, and it is in the intricate circumstances by which each picture is produced, distributed, contextualized, recycled, and viewed that its impact comes clear, if only for a fleeting moment and for a particular segment of the public.

About to Die

The about-to-die image invites a close consideration of the "as if" of journalistic relay. At its simplest level, the about-to-die image represents a range of ambiguous, difficult, and contested public events, which are shown by depicting individuals facing their impending death. Focusing on intense human anguish, it offers a simplified visualization of death-in-process in events as wide-ranging as natural disaster, crime, accidents, torture, assassination, war, illness, and acts of terrorism. Although not the only visual trope for depicting such events in journalism or the only way of visually treating death, its repeated appearance suggests a systematic pattern by which certain public events are reduced to heart-rending moments of intense personal fear and dread. Not surprisingly, over time such depictions often become the iconic images of the events that they show; more predictable is their repeated, patterned, and frequent use value among multiple sectors of the public.

By stopping action at a potentially powerful moment of meaningful representation, the frozen moment of impending death forces attention even though people know more than what it shows. Reminiscent of Aristotle's injunction to dramatists to place death offstage and drawing on Roland Barthes' interest in the special temporality created by the "will have been" of future anteriority,[68] the about-to-die image works by coaxing people to suspend disbelief, deferring knowledge of where the depiction leads long enough to respond to a scene that shows less information than is known. These images sanitize visualization in much the same way as euphemistic labeling sanitizes language: just as soldiers "waste" people rather than kill them or "collateral damage" obscures the devastation to people and buildings it wreaks, strategically visualizing people about-to-die hides the more problematic visualization of death itself.[69] Understanding is thus suspended so as to engage in the act of seeing. Showing and seeing the picture of Neda Agha-Soltan dying on a Tehran street facilitated multiple responses to the Iranian demonstration, not all of which furthered a clearer understanding of what had happened. At some point, the picture's recycled contexts became equally important, if not more so, to the original setting in which it was taken.

The about-to-die image thus provides an escape hatch for journalism, by which it counters its ambivalence about images and images of death by playing to a suggestive picture, sidesteps contradictory aspirations between the realized and desired dimensions of news, and stays abreast of the tensions between journalism and the larger mediated environment without alienating any of its residents. Centering not on the finality of death but on its possibility and, conversely, its impossibility, images of impending death allow journalism to remain open to the contingencies involved in the images that shape it. In so doing, the subjunctive voice becomes the impulse through which people can engage with the news, even if that engagement suspends the relationship between under-standing and depiction.

The choice to show and see impending death in the news draws from a set of broader impulses and attitudes about death's representation. Viewing death has long been associated with voyeuristic spectacles of suffering, where looking at those dead or about to die constitutes a public duty, often of an involuntary nature;[70] with aspirations about how life is supposed to be lived and ended, using what Michael Baxandall called a "period eye" to depict death's dramatic nature, graphicness, and publicness;[71] with multiple taboos about pri-vacy, dignity, and voyeurism;[72] and with an invitation to either empathize or dissociate.[73]

Viewing death has also been associated with mourning and grief, where gaz-ing on pictures of the dead can help mourners come to terms with their loss.[74] Photography, wrote Roland Barthes, keeps "time in a frame...making each installment hypothetically knowable" and seemingly "death defying"; belong-ing to the past but engaged in the present, it creates a temporal moment of "having been there." In that regard, his final work—*Camera Lucida,* where he called photographers "agents of death," was written as he grieved his dead mother and tracked the inherent connection he found between photography and his mourning of her. Susan Sontag famously observed that "all photo-graphs are *memento mori....* To take a photograph is to participate in another person's (or thing's) mortality, vulnerability, mutability."[75] Marianne Hirsch and Jay Ruby separately demonstrated how photographs provide a medium for mourning in everyday life.[76]

The about-to-die image in some ways addresses these impulses more effec-tively than depictions of people already dead. Offsetting the predictability and lack of surprise associated with death photos that Barthes attributed to the *studium,* the about-to-die image draws viewers through what he called the *punctum*—a piercing of the visual frame that forces a renewed engagement with a depiction that breaks with the expected. Coaxing people to complete understanding by filling in what they do not see, the encounter, like other instances of the sublime, "allows the observer to enjoy the threat it momen-tarily poses to his rationality."[77]

But the about-to-die image works beyond its compositional parameters. Presentationally, it draws attention through its generalizability, not specificity: the impending deaths from atrocities in Cambodia come to look like those in Iraq; assassinations in Guatemala resemble those in the United States. Giving journalists a way to show the unsettled events of the news while sidestep-ping the discomfort and ambivalence that throws people into disarray almost whenever they face death's depiction, these images draw viewer involvement rather than introduce distance, as images of death tend to do when they seal viewing with the impossibility of engagement. By lessening the discomfort caused by viewing and enhancing identification with what is seen, the about-to-die photo also works as a vehicle of memory, becoming the central and often iconic image that standsin for complex and contested public events. Not only is it often sustained over time but photos of people facing impending death are repeatedly used, recycled, and displayed in various contexts. They win awards, they reappear in retrospectives, and they often take on iconic status. No surprise, then, that they travel to contexts other than the news, appearing widely across educational, political, cultural, commercial, and religious venues.

What does it mean when the news encourages the emotions, imagination, and contingency as a way of responding to the world? The subjunctive voice provides a construct for understanding how and why certain images emerge as powerful and memorable depictions of events, even if they do so in ways contrary to both articulated journalistic conventions and assumptions of a rational public response to the news. This analysis of the about-to-die image challenges traditional understandings of the function of news images and their public response—moving the conversation from default notions of reasoned information toward an environment which privileges contingency, the emotions, and the imagination. It also brings the discussion of news images into the landscape of visual representation writ broadly—tracking how an occupational ideology meets up with a broader discussion about the nature of the image.

This book provides a close analysis of a select set of news pictures of impending death that have appeared in U.S. journalism since the mid-1860s, all chosen because they have appeared repeatedly, frequently, and over time and in so doing have generated sustained journalistic and public discussion. By combining the life histories of such images with a tracking of the journalistic and public responses they have enabled, a charting of their uses and recycling over time, and a thematic analysis of the ways in which their visual attributes have driven certain modes of public response, this analysis situates this strategically chosen subset of news images against the larger universe of news images that appear in the news.[78]

This book is comprised of seven additional chapters. Chapter 2 tracks the importation of the about-to-die image into journalism and the practices characterizing the trope. Chapters 3 through 5 address the different motifs that signal the trope's display. Chapter 6 charts the ways in which these motifs surface in unsettled events stretching across time and space. Chapter 7 tracks the about-to-die image in the so-called war on terror. Chapter 8 considers the impact of the trope of impending death on the intersection of U.S. journalism and its public. Taken together, these chapters consider the question of how the "as if" of news images helps to move the public in its response to unsettled events.

Through the trope of the about-to-die moment, this book considers how visual subjunctivity has shaped the treatment and response to a slew of unsettled public events over a century and a half of news images, and it targets the strengths and problems this raises. In so doing, it tracks how the "as if" of news relay shapes knowledge and understanding of the world. Given journalism's stature as a major institution of recording and memory, news images deserve attention on their own terms. This book demonstrates how powerful, complicated, nuanced, tenuous, internally contradictory, and often problematic those terms can be.

Chapter 2

Why Images of Impending Death Make Sense in the News

The events depicted by the "as if" vary in nature: a young boy herded from the Warsaw Ghetto under a Nazi machinegun, Lee Harvey Oswald being gunned down by Jack Ruby, a Palestinian child crouching in fear before being shot to death all replay the moment before death as a synecdochic stand-in for the diverse realities of natural disaster, war, torture, crime, illness, assassination, planned violence, accidents, and acts of terrorism. These events emerge as more similar via their depiction than reality suggests.

Reflecting broader painterly trends that have long been central in art—where Hellenistic representations of the Laocoon, the "dying Niobids" of classical art, the iconography of martyrdom, depictions of the crucifixion during the Middle Ages, and Renaissance representations of the deaths of both celebrated and anonymous figures all represented death in process rather than as a finished affair—the about-to-die image invites subjunctivity's reliance on the emotions, the imagination, and contingency in response to the news.[1] Both at the time of a photograph's initial display, where it replaces other images showing the more graphic evidence of death signaled by corpses, blood, gore, and body parts, and as the image is recycled over time, where the photo becomes the central and sometimes iconic image for remembering, the image undercuts a reliance on reasoned information.

The decision to show an about-to-die image reflects a corresponding decision not to show evidence of death. Significantly, the practicalities of showing about-to-die images go beyond the photographer because though images of dead people are often taken by photographers, they are not always shown. Rather, the responsibility for migrating away from death's graphic display is found primarily in the newsroom, where photo editors, graphics editors, subeditors, page editors, and layout editors together gravitate toward the about-to-die photo over photos of people who are already dead. Such judgments are often made without the photographer knowing which of his or her images have been selected for display. Seen as a less offensive, less graphic, and more ethical journalistic choice, images of impending death and their invocation of the "as if" are used by news organizations to cover the "as is."

The Importation of About-to-Die Images into Journalism

The importation of the about-to-die image into U.S. journalism in effect preceded mechanical modes of imaging, predating the use of the camera in news. It appeared first in the United Kingdom in the illustrated journals of the mid-1800s, when it was used primarily to craft moral messages about the social world. In the 1830s, *The Penny Magazine* reproduced facsimiles of the about-to-die moments of famous sculptures like *The Dying Gaul* and *Laocoon* as moral exemplars for a nineteenth-century, working-class public. In one view, they conveyed an "unwritten exhortation to the reader: Work hard, exercise restraint and value what you have—in short, be civilized."[2] Other impending death images, largely of suicides, showed girls and women leaping to their deaths in hand-drawn visual scenes of the early 1870s. Printed widely in the London-based *Illustrated Police News*, the images underscored a visual morality tale of sorts, which emphasized the attraction of visuals of morbidity, suggesting that "other folk's deaths or despair reminded those left behind that they were very much alive and well."[3]

About-to-die images started appearing in the United States in the latter half of the 1800s, though at first they did not circulate widely in the newspapers and illustrated magazines of the time. For instance, they surfaced as illustrations of the 1865 assassination of U.S. president Abraham Lincoln but were not centrally featured in the illustrated press, which tended to show different views of the event. Though engravers like Currier and Ives and other lithography firms showed the president about to be shot by his assassin, John Wilkes Booth, as he sat in a Washington, D.C., theater, the illustrated press gravitated toward the display of other scenes—of the assassin, the theater crowd, and the aftermath. Such choices continued: three weeks after Lincoln's death, the *National Police Gazette* featured a drawing of Booth escaping the scene of the crime, which was followed one week later by a front-page image on *Frank Leslie's Illustrated News* that showed Booth leaping from Lincoln's box seat onto the stage after shooting the president, who was nowhere to be seen. The front page of *Harper's Weekly* similarly depicted Booth, though two additional pictures—one an about-to-die image of the president—appeared inside.[4] Pictures of impending death also appeared in association with the lynching of African Americans in the south from the late nineteenth century onward. Though most lynching photographs showed their victims already dead and the images were circulated primarily in postcard form, some did include pictures of victims about to die, and they were circulated to such an extent that the U.S. Postmaster General banned the cards from the mail in 1908.[5] This early inclusion of both well-known and relatively unknown individuals at the same moment of impending death presaged what would become a broadly used trope for depicting unfolding death in the news. Indeed, once it became clearer that the about-to-die image could usefully depict breaking news—the most straightforward kind of news event and the most difficult to capture because it is still transpiring—images of impending death began to surface more readily across the illustrated newspapers and magazines of the United States.

From its earliest uses, the about-to-die image reinforced the commonly understood sentiment that death discriminated among none of its victims, leveling and equalizing those depicted, regardless of their stature, race, class, or ethnicity. From the late 1800s onward, news organizations recognized its usefulness in depicting breaking news events that involved the deaths of a wide range of people—such as assassinations, electrocutions, and jumping or falling from buildings—and turned with increasing readiness to it as cameras became faster and less cumbersome. Depicting famous people who were about to die from an assassin's hand, people made notorious, usually from crime, who faced an institutionally sanctioned death, and generally anonymous people made visible by their impending death, about-to-die images thus gained recognition as a trope that worked by neutralizing the specificity of the various people it depicted.

Two separate assassinations—of U.S. presidents James Garfield and William McKinley—were depicted by the "as if" in the late 1800s, but in both cases a strictly linear and realistic depiction of the act of the assassination was avoided. Both presidents died after the passage of time, but in the interim images of them facing death were put to a patterned use that would repeat in later years even when death was immediate. Though the trope's initial uses reflected the unfolding nature of what transpired on the ground—playing to the "as if" while the event took shape—its emergent strengths over time made it usable even when doing so undermined or contradicted what unfolded.

Garfield's shooting came less than four months after he had taken office on July 2, 1881. Making his way to a Williams College reunion in Washington, D.C., Garfield was shot by a disgruntled office-seeker, Charles Julius Guiteau. Garfield sank to his feet in front of a large crowd. Journalistic illustrations of his shooting drew from the practices of the time, with illustrated newspapers combining sketches from different temporal points into one image.

One resulting sketch in *Leslie's Illustrated Weekly*, which appeared two weeks later on July 16, depicted the president before he fell to the ground across two pages of the magazine. The shot targeted Garfield, looking surprised and leaning onto a nearby man for support, just after he had been hit by Guiteau's bullet (fig. 2.1). The artists—A. Berghaus and C. Upham—portrayed the president in front of a jumble of startled bystanders, all of whom looked in various directions; only Garfield looked straight at the artist and by extension the viewers. In the back of the frame, a number of people apprehended the assailant. The caption pronounced the sketch "an accurate rendering." In Kevin Barnhurst and John Nerone's view, the sketch offered a "temporal range that would have covered about a minute of actual time and could never have been captured by a camera. This drawing was based on the sketch artists' interviews with people on the scene; the journalists themselves had not been present but arrived two hours after the shooting."[6] Tellingly, missing from the drawing was what might have been expected following a shooting: there was no blood, no gore, no damaged flesh anywhere to be seen.

Garfield languished in hospital for weeks. The following September, largely due to unhygienic medical practices, infection set in and he died of complications. By then, the drawing of him about to die had predated his death by two months.

The assassination of William McKinley was drawn with similar parameters. Attending a reception at the Temple of Music in Buffalo, New York, McKinley was shot in the stomach on September 6, 1901, by a self-proclaimed disciple of Emma Goldman. No illustrators were present at the scene, because the one individual who had been contracted to take official pictures did not follow McKinley into the building and was not permitted inside until after

Figure 2.1:
A. Berghaus & C. Upham/Library of Congress/Public Domain; "The Attack on the President's Life," LC-USZ6Z-7622, *Frank Leslie's Illustrated Newspaper*, July 16, 1881, 332–333.

the president had been removed to the hospital. Although McKinley did not die until the following week, when gangrene set in from his bullet wound, drawings of the shooting were based on the verbal recounting given by one of McKinley's secret service agents to the Buffalo press. Though one scholar maintained that "none of [the accounts] were accurate according to eyewitness accounts," pictures appeared, as with the earlier assassination of Lincoln, of the assassin, of a bedridden McKinley being nursed by his wife, and the following month of the assassin facing his execution. About-to-die images surfaced unevenly at first: the *Philadelphia Inquirer* depicted one such drawing by Chas Bell on an internal page the day after the shooting, while the illustrated newspaper *Leslie's* "made no attempt to illustrate the shooting itself."[7] It did, however, publish a drawing by T. Dart Walker with some delay,[8] which, like that of Bell, targeted McKinley at the moment of his attack (fig. 2.2). In the drawing, McKinley stood mid-center, surrounded by advisors and looking bewildered, as a man, hair slightly amiss, stuck an object into the president's abdomen. Surrounding women, male counselors, and guards converged into the forefront of the image. As with the Garfield image, this picture too covered a longer span of time than could have been captured by the camera. Here too, the artist elected to eliminate the graphic nature of the assassination, showing no bloodshed, wounds, or human gore.

The delay in publishing the image—drawn at a time when it showed the president about to die or, potentially, about to recover—did not stifle its widespread use, and it surfaced over time in newspaper retrospectives, comparison pieces of presidential assassination attempts, and books on McKinley's assassination. This means that the "as if" of McKinley's death was primarily accommodated

Figure 2.2:
T. Dart Walker/Public Domain, "Assassination of President McKinley," Library of Congress, Prints and Photographs Division, LC-USZ62-5377, September 6, 1901.

after he had died. About to die became a stand-in for the assassination, even though the picture was drawn when the president was already dead.

Images of impending death were thus useful visuals for news organizations needing to depict a still unfolding news story. Their play with temporality and the event's sequencing facilitated journalists' visual treatment of the breaking news of death, although both Garfield and McKinley languished for a considerable time before perishing. Over time, those using the trope would be able to creatively vary the relationship between what happened in a death's sequencing, when it happened in connection with its relay as news, and which moment in that sequencing would be frozen for depiction.

From the beginning, then, the "as if" was patterned enough to suggest a death unseen, formulaic enough to encourage viewer identification with human anguish over an engagement with the larger structural circumstances surrounding death, and porous enough to accommodate wide-ranging engagement with the events it was used to depict, its play with temporality a useful entry point for those wanting to display the images for their own purposes. As news imaging technologies advanced and cumbersome engraving techniques were replaced with lighter cameras, the "as if" became an increasingly valuable mode of showing the breaking news of death.

This was central, for it suggested that journalists and news executives would have a vested interest in using the "as if" in the depiction of journalism's unsettled events. Two events, discussed here because they fronted journalism's involvement in such depictions, suggest how important and creatively far-reaching that investment would be.

The first instance recorded a moment whose outcome did not lead to death—the shooting of New York City mayor William J. Gaynor, on August 9, 1910. A disgruntled city employee boarded a docked ship in Hoboken, New Jersey, on which Gaynor was aboard waiting to sail for Europe. As Gaynor posed for a group of press photographers, the employee shot him in the neck.[9] Although the assassination attempt failed, the photo's taking was memorable, as *Evening World* photographer William Warnecke came late to the event and approached the crowd just as the would-be assassin drew his pistol. The resulting image, which appeared the next day in Warnecke's paper, showed a stunned Gaynor, stiffening with the impact of a gunshot wound to the back of the throat (fig. 2.3). In the photo, the mayor, portrayed in its center, leaned slightly onto a nearby aide while a second man rushed to help from behind. While the photographer might have been expected to reflect the bloodiness of the situation more so than had the illustrators of earlier images, in this photo no blood or gore tainted the shot though other images did show blood running down his face. Of those photos, the *Evening World* editor proclaimed, "Blood all over him, and an exclusive too!"[10]

The photo generated discomfort among officials in the mayor's office and instant acclaim among journalists. Consonant with more lenient attitudes toward

Figure 2.3:
William Warnecke/
New York World/
Public Domain,
Shooting of Mayor
William J. Gaynor,
August 10, 1910.

the display of graphic images at the time, viewers expressed little squeamishness about what the photo depicted or suggested. Appearing widely the next day, the picture crowned the front pages of numerous papers, including the *New York World* as a four column shot, *Washington Post*, and *Philadelphia Inquirer*, each of which cheered its taking "the instant after the shooting." Though additional images by other photographers appeared on the inside pages of other papers, showing Gaynor and his group of advisors from slightly alternative angles and at different points in the sequencing of action, most journalists and news executives lauded the preciseness of the scene that Warnecke had captured.[11]

As time moved on, Warnecke's photo generated additional professional kudos. The photo won the 1936 Press Photographers Award—twenty-six years after the fact—when it received first prize in the organization's first award for spot or breaking news. Years later, the photo was "still considered by editors one of the most dramatic [pictures] ever recorded." And though Gaynor died three years after the assassination, allegedly from a coughing fit caused by the bullet still lodged in the back of his throat, the image of him being shot continued to proliferate long after he was dead.[12]

A second image involved the *New York Daily News'* full-page cover photo of Ruth Snyder's impending electrocution in 1928, which the newspaper published three separate times over a two-day period. Snyder faced electrocution after being convicted of killing her husband in order to secure his insurance

Figure 2.4:
Tom Howard, "Dead!
Ruth Snyder," *New
York Daily News,*
DailyNews Frontpage,
Extra Edition, January
13, 1928.

policy and pursue an illicit affair with the man accused of helping her with the murder (fig. 2.4). The picture showed Snyder strapped in a chair as she was being electrocuted. Other than a somewhat fuzzy depiction of her blindfolded and sitting upright into a chair, nothing else was included in the frame except for a large bold headline, suggesting a different temporal moment: "DEAD," it proclaimed, though she was still alive in the image.[13]

Although Snyder was not the first person to be photographed during an electrocution—in August 1890, when William Kemmler became the first person executed by electricity and the first victim of a botched electrocution, a drawing of his impending death had appeared in the *New York Herald*[14]—the circumstances surrounding the picture of her made the event noteworthy. Taken illicitly by photographer Tom Howard with a miniature camera fastened to his ankle, the picture was later called "the most remarkable exclusive picture in the history of criminology." Issued first as part of an extra edition on January 13 and then again in a final edition the following day, the picture appeared with varying headlines and captions. On its first appearance it depicted Snyder atop the bold block-lettered caption "RUTH SNDYER'S DEATH PICTURED!"—titled in a way that foretold the outcome of impending death: "DEAD!" emblazoned a large point banner headline atop the photo's display. The next day it appeared as part of a final edition, its headline recounting that "Crowds Follow Ruth and Judd to Grave." The caption under the image underscored the moral import of her execution as it proclaimed, "WHEN RUTH PAID HER DEBT TO THE STATE!" and it hailed what the paper called "the most talked-of feat in the history of journalism." On the picture's third display, it appeared as only a quarter-page photo in an extra edition on January 14, under the headline "Gray's $30,000 Policy Paid Daughter." Again, the caption underscored the professional triumph of having scored "the greatest of picture beats." On both of the later occasions, a second more distant image of the execution also appeared. The photo of Snyder's death on the front page of the *New York Daily News* sold a million additional copies.[15]

While prison officials called the picture "a fake" and decried the propriety of a photographer taking the picture and a newspaper publishing it, later tightening the restrictions on journalistic access to such events, and viewers remained generally unbothered by the image, again in journalistic lore the feat was seen as unequaled. Called years later "one of the most powerful images in photojournalism," it circulated in multiple photojournalistic retrospectives over time and numerous papers later displayed it to illustrate exhibits on press photography.[16]

The picture also was used to signal shifting sentiments about the value of the death penalty, though in ways that illustrated both support and dissent for it. The *Daily News* claimed in 1975 that the "picture focused public attention on capital punishment and likely was a factor in its virtual abolition." By the 1990s, the *New York Times, USA Today,* and the *St. Petersburg Times* ran it to illustrate articles on changes in public opinion on the death penalty. In 1997, when the picture appeared as an advertisement for an exhibit in the Freedom Forum's Newseum, death-penalty opponents complained that it trivialized capital punishment.[17]

These two pictures suggest how the trope's porous—but patterned—nature and repeated—but suspended—temporal unfolding allowed for those who saw the image to engage with it. Though officials voiced discomfort and viewers tended to be silent about what they saw, journalists and news executives uniformly celebrated the images as landmarks in discussions of the burgeoning authority of news pictures. This would prove particularly important to the trope's continued display. Hailed by news executives for skillfully representing "events of great magnitude...photographed since the camera became fast enough," the pictures were taken at a time when cameras were easing the photographer's ability to capture an event as it happened and photographs were beginning to travel by wire. As imaging technologies became faster, lighter, and cheaper, photography seemed ever more poised to help realize a more equal relationship between journalism's images and words: in Vicki Goldberg's view, this was critical, for "disaster doesn't wait around for a photographer, who seldom has a chance to depict anything but the aftermath."[18] Both images thus reflected high points in journalistic practice that tellingly increased in salience among journalists retelling their unfolding over time, regardless initially of the dissonance that the images generated among politicians and officials or the muted response that it provoked among viewers.

The images thus hinted how central journalists and news executives could be in appraising pictures of impending death, regardless of what much of the public felt about their display. They also signaled that supporting a progressive discourse about photography could prove relevant in establishing a picture's professional acclaim. Later classified by the historian of the National Press Photographers Association as being among history's "great news photo stories,"[19] the photos' cogency understandably intensified over time, where their function as vehicles of memory, particularly among photographers eager to credential news images as valuable journalistic tools, was enhanced.

In offering the public an engagement with the breaking news of death by playing to the "as if," these images revealed a fundamental elasticity—of time, sequencing, salience, interpretation, and meaning—that would characterize the trope of impending death moving forward. Its porous and suggestive nature, reflected in the attention generated by these images, not only set in place what would become a wide-ranging set of imaging practices surrounding journalism's about-to-die moments but a clear use-value of the images for those hoping to establish the burgeoning credibility of photography in news. While both of these photos portrayed people dying who were already known to the public, for either renowned or notorious reasons, the trope's value would be further established once used to depict the breaking news of deaths associated with both anonymous and previously unknown individuals.

About to Die By Jumping/Falling

As pictures of famous and notorious people about to die sparked and sustained the attention of journalists and news executives, the trope began to be used to depict events involving anonymous and previously unknown people facing death. One recurrent image depicted such individuals jumping or falling from buildings—following fires, accidents, attempts at suicide or, more recently, terror attacks. Because response to the trope did not only depend on journalists and news executives but also on the separate interests of officials, politicians, and viewers, the usefulness that they found in the displays of impending death suggests how central they were to its resonance as a trope. Four such images, discussed here because they spanned half a decade of widespread public attention, exemplify how the trope shaped the news of impending death against different interests of the public, Here too the depiction of people formerly unknown to the public helped broaden the trope across the unsettled events of breaking news.

The first picture, taken in 1942, caught a woman in Buffalo, New York, on camera as she jumped from the eighth-story ledge of a hotel (fig. 2.5). Taken by the Buffalo's *Courier Express* staff photographer, I. Russell Sorgi, who noticed a speeding police convoy and followed it to the Genesee Hotel and Coffeeshop, the shot's capture reflected his resourcefulness and quick thinking. In his words, he waited until the woman was at a visible spot in midair and then captured her doll-like torso—whiteish and pale—falling in somewhat balletic right angles down the side of the brown hotel building. The act was incongruously juxtaposed with the rest of the frame, which was filled with the paraphernalia of middle America—unwitting bystanders, a coffee-shop sign, a barber shop pole, a poster celebrating the war effort.

Figure 2.5: I. Russell Sorgi, "Genesee Hotel Suicide," *Buffalo Courier Express*, May 7, 1942, Courtesy of the Buffalo State College Archives and the Buffalo & Erie County Historical Society.

The next day the photo appeared on the paper's front page under the caption "Camera Catches Death Leap in Mid Air." As with earlier images, the picture was widely applauded by journalists, who celebrated how a level-headed photographer could successfully document unfolding news. As Sorgi himself recounted in the paper:

> The chance that every news photographer dreams of—to be in the right spot at the right time—fell right into my lap...I snatched my camera from the car and took two quick shots as she seemed to hesitate....As quickly as possible, I shoved the exposed film into the case and reached for a fresh holder. I no sooner had pulled the slide out and got set for another shot than she waved to the crowd below and pushed herself into space. Screams and shouts burst from the horrified onlookers as her body plummeted toward the street. I took a firm grip on myself, waited until the woman passed the second or third story, and then shot.[20]

The photo was so celebrated by journalists that it was reprinted the following week as a full page photo in *Life*. Recycled in retrospectives on photography and hailed as a high point of photojournalism, it did not wither in journalism's memory; according to one reporter for the *Courier Express*, one copy hung on the newspaper's darkroom for over thirty years.

Equally relevant, although viewers had initially offered a muted response to its display at the time of the woman's death, the picture ignited public engagement over time, when it went on to serve as the impetus for psychological experiments in the mid-2000s.[21] As viewers—increasingly able to circulate the picture online by that time—used it to animate wide-ranging engagements with the "as if," the photo—by then sixty years after its taking—inspired poems, paintings, and short stories, most of which imagined the woman still alive. It also invited subjunctive considerations about suicide. As one blogger wrote in 2007, "She had two or three seconds to think as she fell. What would I think about if I were falling to my imminent death?"[22]

Other photos of jumping figures were received in a similarly variable fashion—professional celebration and a claiming by some sector of the public for some purpose. Four years later, in 1946, when a woman jumped from a burning hotel in Atlanta, Georgia, a twenty-five-year-old amateur photographer who had just bought himself a camera caught the fall in midair (fig. 2.6). The photo's downward movement was mesmerizing, as the woman, her clothes flying straight up and her white underpants starkly contrasting the hotel's dark wall, swept down the building feet first. The photographer, Arnold Hardy, then a graduate student at Georgia Tech, told the story of its taking as a breathless tale of professional triumph: "I looked up, raising my camera. A woman was plummeting downward. As she passed the third floor I fired, using my last flashbulb."[23]

Figure 2.6:
Arnold Hardy/AP,
"Winecoff Hotel
Death," December 7,
1946.

AP Picture Editor Ralph Johnson, whose organization distributed the photo under both the title "Winecoff Hotel Death" and "The Winecoff Fire," later described it as "a full front view of a burning hotel with a woman in midair, seconds from death."[24] The fire, which killed 119 people, was the most deadly hotel fire in U.S. history, increasing the picture's importance. Significantly, although it was not made public at the time, the woman did not die but survived the jump, her fall broken by a pipe and a railing. Nonetheless, the potentiality of her death enhanced the "as if" quality of its image and underscored its representativeness for the 119 deaths that did occur.

Again the photo was immediately hailed by journalists and news executives, who saw it as an exemplary action shot, awarding it the Pulitzer Prize in 1947 and ranking it among the top news photos of the time; Hardy was celebrated as the first amateur photographer to receive a Pulitzer.[25] As *Photo District News* later told it, Hardy "happened to be in the right place at the right time when he captured the iconic image of the country's most deadly hotel fire." But the photo had pragmatic effect too, where over time it was worked into discussions of necessary changes to existing fire codes. Because the fifteen-story hotel had had no fire escapes, fire stairs or fire doors, the fire—and its image—provided an impetus for retrofitting existing buildings and bringing them up to standard. As his son noted in his father's obituary in 2007, Hardy took pride that "after his photograph was published worldwide, fire codes were changed all over the country." Though Hardy decided against a career in photojournalism after taking the picture—in his son's view, "he stood on the sidewalk and watched people plummet to their deaths. He had almost a post-traumatic response to that"—the depiction nonetheless came to be seen as a picture with an important public afterlife.[26]

Thirty years later, a third shot again produced professional acclaim and galvanized public attention, when a fire escape gave way under a teenage girl and her two-year-old goddaughter after their Boston apartment building caught on fire (fig. 2.7). The picture, which appeared in the *Boston Herald American* on July 22, 1975, showed the two individuals, the toddler facing the camera in sheer terror, in full flight on their fall from a cracked fire escape, which hung precariously at right angles to the building on the left hand side of the picture.

The young girl's hair streamed straight up toward the building as she plummeted downward, a certain indicator of the speed of her fall.

The paper's photographer Stanley Forman, who heard the call from the fire department, followed one of the fire engines to the row house, where he saw the two girls standing on the fire escape. Thinking he was about to photograph a routine rescue, Forman readied his camera, but as the fireman stabilized his ladder, the fire escape gave way. Forman later said that he simply started shooting at that moment, capturing their plight on camera as they hung onto the fire escape and then tumbled to the ground five stories

Figure 2.7:
Stanley Forman/AP, "From Marlborough Street," *Boston Herald American*, July 22, 1975.

below. "I was shooting pictures as they were falling—then I turned away…I didn't want to see them hit the ground."[27] The *Boston Herald American* ran the photo of the two in mid-air, titled "From Marlborough Street," as a full-page image, five columns wide, on its front page. Additional pictures followed on page three of the newspaper. The Associated Press distributed them worldwide. Though the younger girl's fall was broken when she landed, the older girl died on impact.

As with earlier images of unknown people jumping to their deaths, the professional acclaim here was widespread, celebrating Forman's skill. But unlike earlier photos, public reaction was at first hostile. Reflecting a budding dissonance with journalism's graphic depictions, by which the public display of graphic pictures of death was beginning to pale,[28] viewers initially charged the photographer with sensationalism, arguing that he had invaded the woman's privacy. That dissonance only seemed to abide, when, as had been the case with the Winecoff Hotel fire, official response to the photos produced pragmatic effect: within hours of the photos' display a citywide inspection of all fire escapes was ordered, eventually upgrading existing fire-codes and softening public discord. In one view, "the impact of the shocking pictures carried the trend nationwide [and] Forman's memorable news photo contributed to the betterment of the public."[29] The following year, Forman received the Pulitzer Prize. The image was recycled onward—into retrospectives, books on photography, even the obituary for the firefighter who had tried to rescue the girls.[30]

Each of these images—Buffalo in 1942, Atlanta in 1946, and Boston in 1975—pictured the deaths by falling or jumping of previously unknown individuals. Establishing an association between the about-to-die image and aspired journalistic practice by playing to the "as if" of the breaking news of death, these images elicited a patterned response from the public that exhibited differences across journalists, news executives, politicians, officials, and viewers. Journalists and news executives hailed them as professional triumphs, where the awarding of prizes and breathless retellings of the photos' shooting underscored a progressive narrative about the growing value and recognition of news images. Officials and politicians protested the images' display but took pragmatic action in response—changing conventions for journalistic access, altering fire codes, updating building regulations, and setting new safety standards. Viewers' engagement with these images reflected the changing sentiments about graphic display of the time, but even as they moved from a lack of responsiveness to an articulated discomfort with graphic pictures, they remained amenable to the responses of others, to the image's changing display, and to the pragmatic effect that the images wielded. Significantly, the images' recycling in memory offered multiple opportunities for public engagement, with earlier celebratory impulses dominating their mnemonic trajectory. During the mid-2000s alone, the images—two of them taken some sixty years earlier—inspired poems, short stories, firefighters' tales, artwork, and psychological experiments, to say nothing of the more consistent professional journalistic lore.

Two more recent events depicting people jumping or falling to their deaths, however, suggest that contemporary about-to-die photos receive a different kind of patterned response from the public. The first involved the attacks of September 11, 2001, in which multiple individuals hurled themselves from skyscrapers to the ground to escape the fiery heat of the World Trade Center. The second involved a college student's suicide in March 2004, when a New York University (NYU) undergrad was caught on camera as she leapt from a midtown building, the fourth in a series of such suicides at the university.

The about-to-die depictions of the jumping or falling bodies of September 11 are significant because they signal how much more diverse were the responses of viewers, officials, and politicians as well as the journalists and news executives who in earlier times would have heralded their taking. During the rapidly evolving events of that Tuesday morning in 2001, among the hastily gathered documentation were ill-focused shots of people about to die by jumping from the World Trade Center. The shots, which appeared briefly and then just as quickly disappeared by giving way to shots of the World Trade Center instead, were taken as both professional and amateur photographers and video-camera personnel arrived on the scene, frantically taking pictures of whatever they could.

Images of people about to die appeared first on television. During the first few hours after the attacks, certain U.S. broadcast and cable news organizations—CNN, Fox News, and CBS—initially showed moving images of people jumping from the towers' upper floors to their presumed deaths on the pavement below. These pictures, which portrayed bodies like unreal stick figures tumbling jerkily into the gray sky from the side of the buildings, represented but did not depict actual death. No bodies were shown striking the pavement below, and little visual detail of those about to die was offered. The images were peculiar for the long view of action that they offered and for their failure to depict faces, identifiable human features, or detailing of clothing. At the same time, the distance between the photographers and camera-people, on the one hand, and the individuals on the towers' upper floors, on the other, made certain that the people remained anonymous and would not be recognized by relatives.[31] Spectators, instead, were expected to expand on the brutal fact of anonymous falling bodies with the presumption of their impending death on the pavement below. In a sense, then, these images, that aptly captured the horror of the attack as it unfolded, depended already at their original depiction on the public to fill in the narrative of a gruesome death beyond that actually depicted.

Significantly, however, the image in its moving version was pulled from the television screen almost immediately after its initial broadcast. Both ABC and MSNBC decided not to show it at all, with executives at both news organizations

wondering whether it was "necessary to show people plunging to their death."
NBC aired an image of one person jumping once and then pulled it, because,
in one executive's view, it was "disturbing." Although the image continued to
be shown on some foreign broadcast networks, such as the BBC and French
television, on the home front it was deemed inappropriate and taken off-air.[32]

The still images of people jumping and hanging out of the towers experienced a similarly peculiar shortlife in the print media, which underscored
the power of the "as if" in helping people deal with the World Trade Center
attacks. Two particular images appeared the day after the attack, when they
were positioned as black-and-white photos on the inner pages of certain daily
newspapers. An Associated Press photograph of a solitary person tumbling
headfirst out of the buildings, taken in two versions by Richard Drew, was
reprinted more widely than other images of people about to die. Taken from a
contact sheet of images in which the individual was pictured in various degrees

Figure 2.8:
Richard Drew/AP, Contact Sheet, September 11,
2001; Richard Drew/AP, Bodies Falling from Towers,
September 11, 2001.

of disarray as he fell from the building (fig. 2.8), Drew snapped frantically as
the jumper plummeted downward. Drew later recounted that "people on the
ground were gasping because people in the building were jumping." As he
heard people respond he began to take pictures. As *Esquire* later told it, Drew
was "standing between a cop and an emergency technician. Each time one of
them cried 'there goes another,' his camera found a falling body and followed it
down for a nine or twelve shot sequence. He shot ten or fifteen of them before
he heard the rumbling of the South Tower."[33]

One shot within the sequence caught a male figure jumping or falling in
parallel angles to the building at his side. As Drew later recounted, "that picture just jumped off the screen because of its verticality and symmetry. It just
had that look." The man's legs poised as if in a graceful dance position as he
dropped straight down the sides of the building, the image captured the event
in clear focus. The *Chicago Tribune*, the *Washington Post*, and the *Philadelphia*

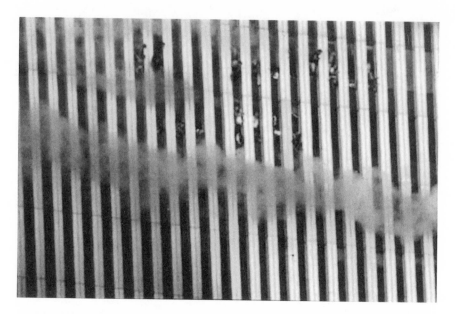

Figure 2.9: Jeff Chriestensen/Reuters, Trapped People Waving from Towers, RTXKQ20, September 11, 2001.

Inquirer all ran it on their inside pages; in the latter case, it appeared under the matter-of-fact title "A person falls from the World Trade Center's north tower"—alongside a much larger picture of a jetliner lining up to fly into one of the World Trade Center towers. A differently angled version of the same shot was displayed in the *New York Times* and also the *Washington Post*. *Time* labeled the picture "The Long Fall."[34]

A second image, taken by Reuter's Jeff Christiensen, also appeared in the first day or two after the attacks (fig. 2.9). The photograph showed people hanging out of the World Trade Center, waving frantically. Although Christiensen did not realize at first that his much larger shot of the building included in one corner scores of people caught between death by fire and death by jumping, the wire service blew up a small portion of the original frame into its own image once alerted to its contents. The picture appeared on inside pages in the *Washington Post,* the *Chicago Tribune, Newsweek* and the *Boston Globe.* Typically, it received a caption that generalized the depicted scene: *Newsweek* called it "After the Blast."[35]

The still images of people about to die at first raised the question of how the photograph could suddenly make the horrific display presentable when it had been banned from television. Why did the image of people jumping, considered too powerful and inappropriate when positioned as part of a video sequence, become appropriate for public display a mere twenty-four hours later, when transformed into a single, static shot? Those questions, however, were quelled by the fact that the static shots of people about to die disappeared as well.

This was in large part due to the discomfort raised by the graphic images—among journalists, news executives, officials, politicians, and viewers. So bothered was the *New York Times* by the image it ran that it printed an article detailing other journalistic decisions to run the same picture. While the *Times* justified its decision to publish because the photo appeared on an inside page and in black and white and *Newsday* justified it because it was a small image and the person unidentifiable, this was not enough for some viewers. The pictures' appearance immediately provoked complaints; one wrote to the *Denver Post*, "This is nauseating.... Do you have no feelings, no sense of respect for the families of the loved ones lost?" As *Esquire* put it later, "In a nation of voyeurs, the desire to face the most disturbing aspects of our most disturbing day was somehow ascribed to voyeurism, as though the jumpers' experience, instead of being central to the horror, was tangential to it, a sideshow best forgotten."[36] Thus images of people on the way to their deaths in the World Trade Center disappeared.

Significantly, this was not the case when the attacks received coverage beyond the U.S. news media. Television in Europe and the Middle East continued to play the footage of the people jumping from the towers through the week, and newspapers in Europe, South America, and elsewhere readily showed the falling or jumping bodies on their front pages the day after the attacks.[37]

By the weekend, the images of people about to die were virtually gone, appearing in very few of the newsmagazines, retrospectives, or other overviews of that first week's events.[38] By the time retrospective volumes went into print three months later, they reappeared hardly at all. One memorial volume comprised nearly one hundred photos but not one portrayed the tumbling bodies. An Associated Press retrospective, issued in September 2001, did not include its own photograph of a solitary jumper taken by its own photographer. As *Esquire* saw it two years later, "We—as Americans—are being asked to discriminate [on the jumpers'] behalf [and] have agreed not to look at them." Even in 2004, when the *New York Times* published a front-page think piece on why the jumping or falling bodies had disappeared from view, it included only an image of onlookers watching an unseen tragedy unfold beyond the camera's reach.[39]

This contradictory display of the "as if"—which appeared but without sustained force—is telling. On the one hand, its appearance could have been expected to be short-lived, given that news executives, journalists, politicians, officials, and viewers were reluctant to show and see human gore. On the other, the temporary reappearance of the about-to-die moment as a still shot offered a paused engagement with the subjunctive dimensions of the event, in a way not made possible by the image's moving footage. While most viewers within a day or two were able to fill in the tragic details of the larger narrative—the fact that beyond the camera's frame rested the harsh pavement on which the bodies landed—there was little in the images themselves that forced them to face that aspect of the event. Rather, the porous depictions allowed them to remain in a subjunctive space even longer than they had with the moving image. In that space, the people portrayed were not yet dead, and the depiction suggested the remote possibility that perhaps, as in one viewer's words, it was "all just a bad dream." As one ABC news correspondent said, "The most horrible thing was the sight of people hurling themselves from the building. I was telling myself maybe they weren't real people. They looked like little dolls."[40]

The tug of these two contradictory impulses facilitated the images' disappearance and brief return. However, the no-nonsense positioning of the bodies, some of them tumbling headfirst as they plummeted from the buildings, made it difficult to contain a subjunctive interpretation for long. What possibilities—other than a brutal death—could be entertained here? It was against this context that the portrayals of jumping bodies disappeared a second time. As the identity of the depicted individuals remained unclear, *Esquire* probed the anonymity of the jumping or falling figures. Lamenting that the "images of people jumping were the only images that became, by consensus, taboo— the only images from which Americans were proud to avert their eyes," its cover story asked, "Do you remember this photograph? In the United States, people have taken pains to banish it from the record of September 11, 2001. The story behind it, though, and the search for the man pictured in it, are our most intimate connection to the horror of that day."[41] The AP image, taken by Drew, appeared again in 2006 as the topic of a documentary, billed as "a journey to identify the falling man from one of 9/11's most startling images."[42]

But these attempts were short-lived. By and large, the U.S. news media eradicated the jumping or falling figures of 9/11 from its record of the event. In need of a visualization that could powerfully convey the tragic events as they unfolded, the 9/11 attacks came to be depicted instead through the collapse of the World Trade Center itself. In other words, images of the buildings in which people were about to perish took the place of depictions of people themselves about to die.

These erratic back-and-forth responses—among journalists, news executives, officials, politicians, and viewers—underscore a deeper and more frenetic variance in response to about-to-die images that had not been evident in earlier events. Moreover, an ambivalence among journalists and news executives about graphic images surfaced here that had not been displayed earlier. Though the sheer intensity of the attacks on the World Trade Center might have been partly responsible for this shift, it nonetheless suggests a complication of public response and a move away from the unambivalent heralding of such images by journalists and news executives.

That shift was further supported by a more intimate act of jumping to death three years later, in an event with little of the public import attached to 9/11. A rash of suicides—three in number—had taken place across a six-month period at NYU, during which faculty and students as well as the larger collegiate community pondered the mental state of U.S. college students. A fourth occurred on March 9, 2004.

The student, Diana Chien, an NYU sophomore, threw herself from a midtown high rise in the middle of a weekday, following a reported spat with her boyfriend. The *New York Post* featured a full front-page color photo of the woman midair in her suicide leap, caught by *Post* photographer Scott Schwartz (fig. 2.10). The picture captured the back of the woman as she jumped, depicting her head, shoulders and outstretched arms as she pushed away from the building and into the air. The rest of the image was taken up with the large structure from which she had jumped, its windows spanning across the back of the frame. The title emblazoned atop the images shouted "Death Plunge No. 4: NYU's Grief."[43]

The image reappeared in the paper the next day alongside a story quoting witnesses to the fall and again four days later on the front page once the student's identity was made public. Although a couple of publications followed suit, reprinting the front page of the *Post* with the photo, most abstained from doing so.[44] The image, however, remained on the Internet, where it was accessed repeatedly.

Unlike the earlier cases of suicide but parallel to the responses generated by the jumping or falling figures of 9/11, here journalists and news executives followed the lead of officials and viewers in criticizing the image. *Post* readers posted protests to the paper, calling the photo "irresponsible," "vulgar," "cruel," "gruesome," and "unconscionable"; one proclaimed it "a new low in journalistic baseness." In numerous places the decision to publish was compared unfavorably with the decision to pull back from publishing the jumping bodies of September 11 "because every other media outlet determined on 9/11 that images of those who jumped were beyond the boundaries of journalism."[45] A university spokesman critiqued the appalling lack of judgment and insensitivity to the young woman's family and a disregard for the feelings of NYU students. Mental health professionals warned that the picture could glorify suicide.[46]

At first journalists defended the photo, likening it to the trajectory of about-to-die images that had received acclaim in the past: "Not all news is good," said one. "But...it makes great visuals—ask Nick Ut or Robert Capa or 100 other lenspeople who have taken magnificent yet disturbing photos of death as it happens."[47] The *New York Post*'s chief copy editor defended the decision to publish, noting that while there had been dissension among the paper's editorial staff about whether to use the picture, it was precluded by the image's news value:

Figure 2.10: Scott Schwartz/NYP, "Suicide," *New York Post*, March 9, 2004, © NYP Holdings, Inc.

Is it a good news photo? Damn right! Photos like this used to be the stock-in-trade of tabloids. And they are far better than the posed, photo-op snapshots of newsmakers that too often pass for photojournalism these days. We had a damn good story—the fourth fatal plunge by an

NYU student since the beginning of the school year—and a damn good photo to go with it. Of course we were going to use it!

Critiquing the "piously outraged, self appointed moral compasses of good journalism" who would have prevented the display of numerous iconic photos had they been given the chance, including the Nick Ut photo of General Loan shooting a Vietcong suspect in 1968 and the Zapruder footage of JFK's assassination, he—and a handful of others—supported the paper's right to publish its picture of choice and decried calls for censorship.[48]

But by the following day, journalists' negative responses to the depiction dominated the conversation, as the picture was called "despicable," "sickening," "distasteful," and "not human."[49] Ombudsman and media critic Geneva Overholser protested its "naked grab at emotionalism on [the] front page," and editorials decried the "work of tasteless, shoddy journalism." Calling its publication "a new low," writer Katha Pollitt lamented that "it is so grotesque, so cruel, so voyeuristic and so irresponsible to cover suicide in this way. . . . It is chilling to think of the photographer waiting for just the right moment to click the button so he could make his however many dollars the *Post* paid him."[50] By the end of the week, nary a voice could be heard in support of the photo's publication.

The flux of responses associated with the NYU suicide is telling, for it suggests that the depiction invited and accommodated multiple responses, again underscoring a more frenetic and less settled nature of public engagement. Moreover, like the response accorded the jumping or falling figures of 9/11, it signals that an image's graphic content complicates its celebration by journalists and news executives. Not only has the public—including journalists—become more conflicted about the parameters in which it is willing to see and show images, but the ready articulation—among viewers, politicians, officials and other non-journalists—to a photo's display as soon as it is shown may be shifting the environment even further. In that light, in June 2005, the BBC decided it would begin using a time delay device to weed out upsetting images, saying that "the purpose is to avoid really distressing, upsetting images that our viewers might not want to see going straight out."[51]

Why has the public response to images become more diversified than in earlier times? And why does the nearly uniform professional acclaim earlier accorded such images now rest alongside a more critical reaction among journalists and news executives? Three reasons come to mind: First, shifts in the conventions for viewing death have moved public sentiments toward a more constrained expectation of viewing death and a less explicit range of its depiction. Though this figures differently among sectors of the public involved in an image's display, it nonetheless suggests that the earlier tendency toward showing and seeing death, and its various impending stages, is no longer a default assumption in journalism. Instead, the opposite has become the case, whereby the uncomfortable edges of graphic display can be enough to prevent an image from being shown and seen. Second, the early evaluations of the value of about-to-die images were swept up in the validation of the burgeoning technology of photography. As the cutting edge of visual documentation, still photos at that time offered a new modality for seeing news events, contrasted with the earlier verbal documentation by which viewers needed to create their own imagined visual form. In this regard, seeing images of impending death played to an evolving set of expectations about journalism's capacity to show more of the world than it had in precamera times. Third, today's digital environment suggests that the locus for evaluating images—and indeed, often for determining which images to show—no longer rests primarily with journalists but among all those who see and circulate them online. It thus may make sense that the public response to these images has become more varied and unsettled and that journalists' responses now more closely reflect those of the wider public.

All of this suggests that there may be a shift in public sentiment about what news images are for, facilitated by changes in the public appropriation of images of death, a diminishment of journalists' formerly exclusive and authoritative call on the images they show, and shifts toward a larger and more vocal public role in evaluating pictures. These later images hint too at a rise in the articulation of standards of decency, tastefulness, and propriety more than before, which increasingly sets the stage for determining which images appear. The about-to-die photo thus offers a prism through which to consider the shifting value of news images more generally.

Recognizing the About-to-Die Image

How generalizable is the about-to-die image? Journalism's images of impending death reflect many of the strengths and weaknesses evident more broadly in news depictions. A lack of clarity over titling, headlining, captioning and the broader link between text and image have come to characterize the latitude with which the "as if" is visualized and its pictures used. In playing to generalizability, each image builds on a set of formal attributes, which make the picture's form as central to the trope as its content.

The degree and fashion in which the undepicted end of the sequence—that is, death itself—is made known to the public vary widely. Because death is always beyond the camera's frame, the fact of death is central to an image's understanding and its placement within a broader sequencing. Conversely, if death is not made evident, viewers are illogically suspended without knowing the result of the sequencing to which the depiction leads. In other words, what the public sees is necessarily separated from what it understands. Cues must thus be offered to create the understanding that the photo fails to provide, and these cues often push form at the expense of content.

The about-to-die image depends on a variety of practices—compositional, textual, presentational, viewing, and mnemonic—by which its meaning can be established. As Gisele Freund noted more generally, "few people realize that the meaning of a photograph can be changed completely by the accompanying caption, by its juxtaposition with other photographs, or by the manner in which people and events are photographed."[52] Each of these practices is crucial to shaping the meaning of what people see.

Compositional Practices

The about-to-die shot tends to be conventional and repetitive in design. The aesthetic proffered here is one that has been already tried, has appeared in other images, and is known to have an established and familiar effect. Drawing from the balanced composition and form typical of journalistic images, the about-to-die image is assumed to record what happened in a direct and untampered fashion. In keeping with that impulse, it tends to draw from the longstanding middle-ground of photography, where intervention is presumed to be minimal. These images resemble action shots suspended at one moment in time, driven both by photographic verisimilitude and vernacular practice.

Though compositional choices differ slightly across the news media, these shots are uncluttered. Their visual center—the person or persons facing impending death—is generally salient or at least signified by other objects. Photojournalists are of two minds about taking these pictures. Some feel they are unavoidable. As the prize-winning war photographer Patrick Chauvel put it, "I don't take [pictures of] dead people, or very rarely. I'll take them killing the guy, but not when he's dead."[53] Others recoil from their taking. Horst Faas noted that "you shouldn't really ever take a picture of somebody dying...when somebody dies it's a private moment in a way and you shouldn't show it then and there...you don't stand there and wait till his eyes go over."[54]

When individuals are depicted, however, photographers almost invariably position them in the shot's middle and foreground, as its largest and simplest visual element. For instance, this picture, taken after Hurricane Katrina in 2005, pictured an anonymous young woman on the grounds of the Superdome in New Orleans (fig. 2.11). Taken by a photographer for the *Baton Rouge Advocate* and appearing in that paper on September 1, 2005, the unnamed woman took up the frame's foreground, her face—eyes closed, lips pursed—raised upward, while her head, limply cradled by a nearby police officer and onlookers, drew the only extra lighting in the photo. Serene, unmoving, and pristine, she looked as if she were comfortably sleeping, though those looking on showed signs of consternation. The caption told viewers she died shortly afterward. The photo appeared in multiple places. The *New York Times* told readers that "soon after this photo was taken, the woman passed away." *Newsweek* featured the same photo on a full page and titled it "Life on the Brink."[55] Portrayed usually in sharp focus and intricate detail, often the person facing death appears in exaggerated size or with brighter lighting than that given the rest of the frame, as seen in this photo. There is rarely a suggestion of artifice or hint that these individuals act on cue or perform for the camera; rather, the person or persons facing death appear to be wholly unselfconscious. When the individuals themselves are not depicted, the objects that signify them are shown in the same fashion.

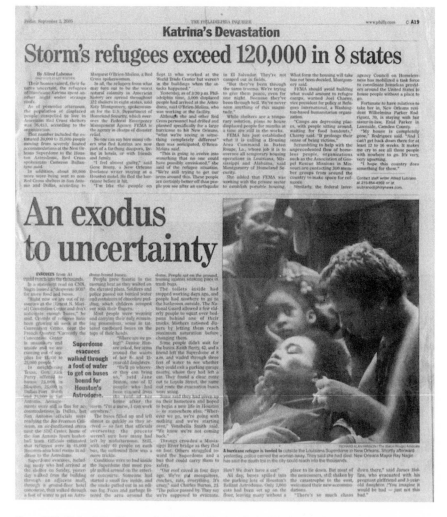

Figure 2.11: Richard Alan Hannon, Police Officer Tends to Dying Hurricane Refugee, *Baton Rouge Advocate*, September 1, 2005. Used with permission of *Philadelphia Inquirer* Copyright © 2008. All rights reserved.

Thus the picture of Neda Agha-Soltan bleeding out on a Tehran street (fig. 1.1) featured her front and center. Though taken by an amateur bystander's cell-phone, the image frame-grabbed across the news media echoed the compositional focus of this photo combined with the more distant framing of the women jumping from buildings during the 1940s (figs. 2.5, 2.6). Each starkly contrasted the women with their backgrounds—in focus, color, lighting, size, and position—pulling viewers toward their most emotive features.

Once a trope's visual parameters are established, its photos can display a substantial degree of latitude toward what is shown. This latitude relates to what Kress and van Leeuwen have called the differences between the "given" and the "new" in images: the "new" refers to the message or issue associated with the image, drawing attention because it is problematic or contestable; the "given" is the part of the depiction that is commonsensical and self-evident, presented as something the viewer already knows. While the actual person facing death is the "new" aspect of the image, the remainder of the image is "given" and therefore already somewhat understandable. Latitude ranges across these parameters: individuals of varying genders, ages, races, classes, and ethnicities who face death are depicted from various vantage points—close-up, medium-close, medium, medium-long or long shot, tight or loose framing, frontal or side view, alone or in a group.[56] Often they are presented as representative of broadly defined groups (commoners, villagers, refugees) and are buttressed within the frame by elements that support, point to, or otherwise mark their centrality as the target of depiction.

For instance, this image from Vietnam, taken by AP photographer Horst Faas in January 1964, focused on an encounter between a suspected Vietcong collaborator and a South Vietnamese soldier (fig. 2.12). Neither person was identified beyond his affiliation with one of the warring sides. Faas later said that the shot, which showed the two as the victim apparently faced his death, was useful because the "event was not a singular event, not even occasional. It was a routine event. . . . The knife was a threat—and I think he used it."[57]

Depicting the "as if" departs from photojournalistic convention because it does not provide the clean shot typical of photojournalistic display but rather an incomplete and suggestive shot of implication. But implication depends on providing the right cues—settings that are easily identified as threatening, dangerous, or unstable; a victim's cowering gestures that unambiguously convey fear and dread; or, as the Faas picture from Vietnam shows, a perpetrator's overbearing and menacing bodily posture signified in the guards, militia, or military police who often perpetrate violence. Sometimes this involves stock depictions that the public readily associates with war, poverty, disasters, accidents, sickness, and violence—a close focus on the physical encounter between assassins and their intended victims (figs. 2.1, 2.2, 2.3), for instance—or scenes that juxtapose individual danger with dangerous natural settings, imprisonment, or institutional control—the limbs of Ruth Snyder (fig. 2.4) tacked tightly to the instruments of her electrocution.

Figure 2.12:
Horst Faas/AP, "Crime
and Punishment,"
Vietnam, January 1964.

Blended here are multiple aspects of the impending deaths of those individuals who know they are about to die and those who do not, those who are about to die by choice and those by accident, those about to die naturally and those about to be killed. Contrast these two pictures—one of a child about to die in the Ethiopian famine of 1984, which later won the Pulitzer for its *Boston Globe* photographer, Stan Grossfeld, and one taken by photojournalist Don McCullin, which showed a 1964 freedom fighter about to be shot by a Congolese soldier (fig. 2.13). In each image, the frontal gaze of the person about to die, magnified by large, doleful eyes and unselfconscious posturing, takes over the space connecting the photo with its viewers. The individual confronts those who watch without flinching, underscoring their voyeurism and generating a suggestion of complicity. There is little about these individuals which can differentiate their impending deaths from each other. Rather, it is the gestures of those around them—the futile embrace of the child's mother versus the gun menacingly stuck into the freedom fighter's neck—that cues the public to the difference between death by neglect or accident and death by design.

Figure 2.13: Stan Grossfeld, "An African Madonna, Holding Her Starving Child Only Hours before the Child Perished in a Refugee Camp," *Boston Globe*, 1984; Don McCullin, "Lumumbist Freedom Fighters about to Be Killed by Congolese Soldiers," Contact Press Images, 1964.

These images exude a sense of dread and foreboding. As shown in the images of jumping or falling figures (figs. 2.5, 2.6, 2.7, 2.8), the depicted individuals cut across categories of gender, age, race, class and ethnicity. But they are uniform in their actions—cues of desperation and often subjugation, eyes wide open, pursed or gaping mouths, acts of screaming, crying, crouching, kneeling, clutching or begging for mercy, and collective embraces. The photos are situated within the final moment in which it is still possible to hope, where the inevitability of death might yet be avoided.

This compositional focus means that it is up to the public to provide the end—the inevitability of death—to the picture by appending contingent and imagined sequences of action to what is shown. The emotional overload that drives these images makes it possible for them to do so. The images tend to communicate simplistic messages about the impending end of life, with little elaboration of the geopolitical realities that lie beyond the frame. One does not need extensive knowledge to appreciate the fear and dread being depicted. For this reason, the depictions leave unvisualized instrumental identifying features of what is being depicted. Often the settings are not identifiable: Do viewers know from the picture that it depicts Atlanta's Winecoff Hotel? Similarly, unless the people are known beforehand, they often remain anonymous in depiction. The broader reasons for impending death also tend not be evident. But the lack of such detail does not diminish the image's power, for the capacity to codify a photograph as involving the impending death of an unsettled event lies in the picture's generalizability.

And yet in the about-to-die image, composition is but a part of the actual interpretive frame. By definition it does not show death. Yet it is death, and its realization beyond the frame of the camera, that makes the picture meaningful.

Textual Practices

Underlying the relationship between images and texts is the degree to which verbal detail—in titles, headlines, captions, and other modes of accompanying text—tracks what transpires in the image. The texts of the "as if" are critical, for it is through texts that the fact of an undepicted death is made clear. These photos rely on texts to import value and meaning to the conventions set in place through composition, to anchor meanings suggested by the image, and to impart understanding.

The relationship between words and images can take on numerous forms: words and images can support each other by recounting in text what is shown in pictures; words can narrow what an image shows by directing viewers toward parts of the depiction deemed relevant to the story; words can broaden what a picture shows by generalizing it through a broader message; words can diminish or refute what the image shows by directing attention to aspects of the story that are not depicted. Which aspects of the about-to-die image are underscored in adjoining texts is critical.

But not all texts are equal. The words surrounding about-to-die images can be found across a range of textual practices, which vary in prominence, length, detailing, proximity, and type size. Headlines or titles tend to be bold, brief summary phrases that adjoin an image and proclaim in large type what is thought to be its most significant or newsworthy aspect; these can be "screamer headlines" that shout "DEAD!" or "HORRIFIC DEATH"—as with the Ruth Snyder execution photo (fig. 2.4). Captions tend to provide one or two sentences that summarize an aspect of what is being depicted; usually displayed underneath a news image, they can provide varying levels of explanatory or contextualizing information—as with the wide-ranging captions adjoined to the jumping or falling figures of 9/11 (fig. 2.8, 2.9). Credits tend to be noted in the corner of an image's display and denote the photographer who took the shot, the photographic agency that employs the photographer, or the archive that owns the image: the award-winning image of Gaynor's attempted assassination (fig. 2.3) mentioned the photographer's name in none of the photo's original displays. Extended texts can be found in adjoining news stories or alongside adjoining photographs, and they refer to any explanatory information that describes what is shown in the image. In each case, the information provides either "supporting information" or "extending information" to that established by the image: supporting information "refers to information and detail already contained within the photograph by drawing attention to certain features...it acts as a guide which tells the viewer how to view the image." Extending information "adds facts or information derived from a different source to the photograph...[it may be] beyond the scope of the photographic system of representation and may serve to broaden the restrictions of the single image."[58] When combined with all of its adjoining texts, the about-to-die image takes on elaborated meanings.

Who writes the texts appended to about-to-die images remains one of the quandaries of news practice. For instance, while photographers almost always provide their own explanatory information about what is depicted in their photos—using batch captioning to identify people, places, sequences of action, the proper spelling of names—that information does not always find its way into the image's caption. There is no guarantee that a photographer's information will be used, as photojournalist Susan Meiselas admitted, "The images are out of my control...once the material goes...difficulties can develop, [like] examples of images used to accompany text that misrepresented the feelings I had at the time I photographed. Some were just mistakes and some were intentional."[59]

Instead, decisions about texts are taken in discussions with the graphics editor, photo editor, page editor, subeditor, and at times the reporter responsible for the news story. Because photographers, who tend not to play active roles at the home office of a news organization and who in fact may be physically far away, tend not to be part of these discussions, the final captions are generally written instead by editors. Deferring to their judgment, however, is often problematic, for as one photographer termed it, "many have no basic knowledge of visual display, and so make decisions on a relatively uninformed basis."[60] Thus the texts adjoining about-to-die images offer varying levels of explanatory material, much of it provided without the knowledge of the photographers who took the pictures. Moreover, these decisions change as deadlines change, narrowing the individuals involved in decision making when decisions are taken under stress and high stakes.

The most central fact to be determined by the adjoining texts of about-to-die images is the death of those depicted. In many cases, death is clearly admitted in one of the accompanying texts—the title or headline, caption, or adjoining news story. References to death might also be offered in accompanying news stories, in the captions to sequenced photos, and possibly in the adjoining text to recurrent photos.

But the degree of detail surrounding the fact of death varies. The particulars of death, cause of death, manner of death, impact of death, wider circumstances surrounding death, and even the fact of death can all be included or not. This uneven verbal detail takes on particular importance because the image depends on its text to move the story beyond the visible scene of impending death. Sometimes death is suggested when it does not occur: the texts adjoining the display of the picture of the woman jumping from Atlanta's burning Winecoff Hotel (fig. 2.6) all suggested that she died. That presumption prevailed for forty years, until in 1993 she was identified as a badly-wounded survivor.[61] Just as often, the opposite occurs: rather than designating a person as having "died," captions and adjoining texts can offer language which euphemistically blurs the fact, noting instead that his or her "fate remains unknown." Euphemisms are wide ranging: suicides can be described as a person having "fallen," executions as a person being "dragged away," assassinations as a person being "shot," and fatal beatings as a person being "roughed up." Because the fate of the depicted persons is not shown, words can thereby complete the scene in imaginary, contingent, or sometimes erroneous ways.

Presentational Practices

Not only do the settings in which a photograph appears help establish its importance and worth, but the range of presentational options is critical in shaping the understanding of what it shows. Options vary: the same photo can run with different captions, headlines, or stories and in different news organizations or sections of a news site. It can also run at multiple points in time.

Images are selected for presentation from the photographer's proofs—either contact sheets or digital image files. The photographer generally does not make the final decision about which image to display but transmits the image to editors, who make the selection "with or without the photographer's permission or agreement." In theory, "the picture editor acts as mediator between the photographer's vision and the aims and objectives of the publication,"[62] but there is no guarantee that the will of the photographer, who is often geographically distant from decision making, will be honored. In fact, the picture editor, graphic editor, or photo editor—any of whom might run the electronic picture desk in contemporary news organizations—has been seen as such a problematic juncture that one trade columnist recently remarked that "if there is a crisis in world photojournalism today, it is a crisis of editing and publishing, not of photography."[63]

The about-to-die image is presented in ways that support more common presentational practices. Because these images are associated with generally newsworthy events, they tend to be prominently displayed. Though they range in size and shape, their presentational aspects tend to convey to viewers that the image is of note. Generally square or oblong, the about-to-die image is often larger and more compelling than its surrounding photos and might be appended to the lead story on the page or lineup. Boxes or bold frames might encircle it, and it might bear its own headline, title, or lengthy caption. Sometimes it appears in tandem with other photos.

Generally found above the fold on newspapers' front pages, it leads sections and graces the covers of newsmagazines and tabloids: the Ruth Snyder execution image (fig. 2.4) shouted at readers from its front page display. It highlights television's featured stills: the streetside death of a young Iranian protester (fig. 1.1) appeared as a still photo on televisions around the world. It appears in the easily accessed and visible links on the Internet: the picture of the suicide of an NYU student (fig. 2.10) traveled extensively across online sites. If multiple platforms for a news story exist, the about-to-die image typically appears repeatedly across all of them. When the about-to-die image is shunted to less-visible presentational options, like a newspaper's internal pages, that choice suggests that the image's visibility is problematic.

Moreover, presentational practices of cropping and juxtaposing multiple images are used extensively. Cropping, for instance, helps the public focus on the image by highlighting its emotional dimensions. As Harold Evans noted more generally, there is a distinction between "cropping which accepts the main subject as presented in the print, and cropping which creates a new focus of interest. The first is concerned mainly with excluding extraneous detail; the second is the recognition that a portion within the picture is really its main story."[64] In cropping about-to-die pictures, news organizations can either feature a focused concentration on the person about to die—facilitating a more undiluted emotional encounter with the victim—or target the larger context—persons facing death alongside people taunting them, an approaching tidal wave, an officer pointing a gun in their direction.

Similarly, juxtaposing more than one image, described by onetime *Life* editor Wilson Hicks as generating a "third effect" among viewers,[65] facilitates the creation of a spatial and temporal continuity around the depicted scene and reestablishes pieces of the sequencing of action that have been frozen by the single still photograph. Only sometimes, however, does such juxtaposition provide images of the person actually dead; rather, news organizations tend instead to visually elaborate the events leading up to death, still concluding the photographic sequence before death occurs.

But the "as if" is also presented in ways that differ from more common presentational formats. About-to-die images tend to appear more than once, undercutting the journalistic mandate to show primarily images that are new and topical. Repetitive display can occur in different forms of the same image, as in cropped and uncropped versions of one image positioned side by side; at different points in time, as on a weekday and again a news site's weekend review; in different places, as in a newspaper's front page and inside page; in association with different news stories, as in the initial story and a follow-up story occurring later in time; and across different media, as in a featured still on television and part of an online photo gallery. This means that one about-to-die photo can appear more than once in a given news site in different places, on more than one day in the same news site, across journalism's multiple platforms at one or various points in time, and over time in association with more than one news story: the image of a dying Neda Agha-Soltan (fig. 1.1), for instance, appeared multiple times on the same day and on different days, as well as in multiple social networking sites and news sites. Given the topicality and novelty that motivate much of journalism, the about-to-die image instead works by an opposite impulse, through frequent, familiar, and repeated displays over time.

Viewing Practices

Viewing images of impending death helps establish their longevity in news and memory. But not everyone sees these images in the same way. Griselda Pollock observed that "what is at stake in representation is not so much a matter of what is shown as it is of who is authorized to look at whom with what effects."[66] Relevant here is how the public navigates the gap between experience and representation. The longstanding distinction between linear and nonlinear composition offers one way to do so, for about-to-die images require a viewer's involvement that goes beyond that usually associated with a news photo's linear composition, arousing the imagination and contingency. While these images perform a narrative role—positioned within a known or imagined sequence that takes the depicted individuals to their deaths—and they follow the clear and strictly coded sequence associated with linear composition, they also rely on a viewer's interpretation and response to gain the stature with which they are typically associated. Viewing is thereby not only relevant but critical.

The about-to-die photo engages the public emotionally. Its reliance on affect draws from the positioning of an overly emotive (fearing, trembling, dreading) body in some kind of threatening situation, forcing a viewer's powerful emotional response as a means of generating meaning, and possibly action. Viewers tend not to pass these photos without attending to the dread they embody and articulating responses to it. So do journalists: as photographer Ron Haviv said of an image he made of a young Muslim about to be killed by Serbian paramilitaries in Bosnia, "He looked me straight in the eyes, pleading for help....It's a memory that will stay with me forever."[67] The "as if" is thus built on emotional display and on the emotional responses it generates. This affective bonding is central to the image's power.

What kind of emotional responses do about-to-die images raise? On the one hand, the photos can facilitate the articulation of a certain degree of moral indignation, responsibility, empathy, and compassion, forced by the fact that viewers need to decide where they stand in regard to what they see. On the other hand, the images can produce more deleterious responses—shame, voyeurism, spectacle, complicity, and indifference. The gravitation toward imagination complicates both sets of emotions, for one of the most patterned responses to these photos is the articulation of the possibility that death does not occur. Lamentations about reversing time, stopping guns, and shutting off bombs are all common responses. As one TV critic proclaimed after the repeated viewings of the Challenger explosion, "Maybe on the 10th or 20th replay, you think as you watch, it won't happen. Maybe this time the shuttle will continue its upward climb and not disappear in a cloudy ball of fire."[68] Equally important, although the drive for emotional engagement is instrumental to these images, which emotions they drive is not predictable. The same photo can generate opposite emotional cues of compassion and disgust, pity and vengeance.

It is for these reasons that viewing these photos is both active and intervening, though it does not necessarily lead to collective public action. Typically, these photos are not seen and then forgotten. Rather, they are almost invariably marked by degrees of public attention and discursive response, stimulating multiple topics of conversation both within and beyond the journalistic setting. Within journalism, they serve as starting points for discussions about the appropriate role of news photography, where news executives, editors, journalists, and ombudsmen can weigh in on the complications of journalistic practice that these images raise—of ethics, values, morality, and privacy and the tensions created by simultaneous compassionate viewing, spectacle, and voyeurism. About-to-die images also often comprise the high ground of journalistic practice, where they win journalistic and photographic prizes.

Beyond journalism, about-to-die images are discussed not only as powerful representations of a certain moment in time, but they become facilitators of conversations about the unsettled events of the public sphere. They surface in readers' letters, blogs, and postings on the Internet, talk shows and other public forums. Politicians, public officials, human rights workers, bereaved parents, and lobbyists all actively invoke them in their discussions. In this sense, about-to-die images are dissimilar to other kinds of news images, which tend to fall beneath the public's radar once displayed. They are dissimilar too because an about-to-die image's display is generally flanked by knowledge of death before the photo is seen.

Mnemonic Practices

One of the key attributes of images of impending death is their recycling over time. The about-to-die image appears in additional presentational venues to that of news, for it does not end as a journalistic display but is rerouted into the work of memory, where news retrospectives, anniversary issues on journalism, anniversary albums about specific events, and other instances of recycling the original journalistic record replay the image time and again. The about-to-die image is also readily transported from the news into other modes of visual representation.

Consider this photo, taken of a young AIDS activist about to succumb to the disease, which appeared in *Life* in November 1990. It showed thirty-two-year old Ohioan David Kirby, surrounded by his father, sister, and niece as he languished before death (fig. 2.14). The photo, which was taken by Ohio University student Therese Frare and showed Kirby in the throes of death's embrace while family members wept over his approaching death, portrayed the dying man in a serene position, leaning against a pillow as his beard and long

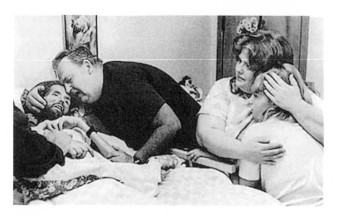

Figure 2.14:
Therese Frare,
"David Kirby's Final
Moments," *Life*,
November 1990, 8–9.

hair conjured a Christlike visage. His face was lifted ever so slightly toward the ceiling, highlighted with what looked like streaks of light, as his family members crumpled in grief and anguish around him. *Life*'s caption relayed the scene in full:

> THE END. After a three year struggle against AIDS and its social stigma, David Kirby could fight no longer. As his father, sister and niece stood by in anguish, the 32-year-old founder and leader of the Stafford, Ohio AIDS foundation felt his life slipping away. David whispered "I'm ready," took a labored breath, then succumbed.

Perhaps because the photo differed from other AIDS pictures at the time, which tended to exploit the disease-ridden bodies of its inflicted individuals, the photo won multiple awards, among them the Budapest Award and second place in the World Press Photo Award in 1991. Within a few years it became part of *Life*'s collection of images and was recycled as part of its retrospective literature.[69]

But the photo was to have another life outside of journalism. In 1991, thinking it would raise AIDS awareness, Kirby's family gave permission to the Italian clothing company Benetton to use it for advertising. Later called "the most shocking photo used in an ad," the photo appeared widely as part of its advertising campaign linking commercialism with social and humanitarian concerns in the early 1990s. Trying to brand its clothing with humanitarian activism, Benetton colorized the picture and displayed it widely under the title "Final Moments." The photo raised both admiration and dissonance in its advertising frame. Seen as markedly innovative by advertising executives and informally dubbed the "Benetton Pieta" by those made uncomfortable by its display, it circulated the still-dying Kirby over and over, never making clear that he had died. Throughout the campaign, AIDS activists lamented why the picture never included a hotline phone number for AIDS information. Today, its use regularly punctuates scholarly texts on advertising.[70] Such recycling, however, is typical of about-to-die images, in that even when a death is clearly articulated in the original display of its photo, that is no guarantee that the person depicted dying will be portrayed as dead once the image moves on.

Thus, about-to-die images are recycled energetically into almost every available venue of visual representation, complicating more recent sentiments that their graphic nature of suggestion of death renders them inappropriate for public display. The "as if" image of impending death has been transformed into the raw material of postage stamps, where a Palestinian boy about to be killed in the Gaza Strip became the face of a stamp in over half a dozen countries in the early 2000s; political posters, where Vietnamese civilians about to die embodied antiwar protest placards during the 1970s;

advertising, where the Tiananmen Square standoff of 1989 sparked a Chik-Fil-A advertisement in the late 1990s; toys, where a doll and its accompanying noose surfaced on the Internet after the hanging of Saddam Hussein in the late 2000s; and educational treatises, where a boy being herded out of the Warsaw Ghetto in 1945 appeared on informational pamphlets in the 1980s about the Holocaust.

Even the jumping or falling figures of 9/11 (figs. 2.8, 2.9), which disappeared from the journalistic record in 2001, later found their way into art installations, fiction, and theater years after the event. Reemerging as the focus of primarily nonjournalistic attempts to remember, the figures reappeared as sentiments about 9/11 were rewoven into reappraisals of the so-called "war on terror," and the more predominant image of the World Trade Center towers came to be seen as unworkable, too strong, perhaps even too manipulative in its depiction of the event. Against this circumstance, the jumping or falling bodies of 9/11 reemerged as a challenge to journalism's widespread adoption of the towers' image.

The picture transformed into art already in 2002, when Eric Fischl's "Tumbling Woman," a life-size bronze sculpture of a woman plunging from the trade center tower, was put briefly on display at Rockefeller Center and then removed after public protest.[71] It emerged again in 2005, when a performance artist used the fall to stage a reenactment from a Chicago skyscraper, suspending himself in a harness from the building and repeating the falling man's fall from the photograph of 9/11 (fig. 2.15). As seen on CNN's Web page, the image was strikingly similar to the event it imitated and the earlier photograph taken of it, which by then had more or less disappeared. In 2007, the figure occupied the titular role of Don DeLillo's book, *The Falling Man*.[72]

Thus about-to-die images often take on an afterlife through mnemonic practices that create a curious separation of the images of impending death from the events themselves. It is significant that this afterlife is not necessarily associated with the image's iconic status. Nonetheless, its retrospective display means that individuals are shown facing death long after they are already dead.

All of this suggests that the about-to-die image depends precisely on what has not been emphasized in discussions of news images more generally: the subjunctive voice of the visual—the "as if"—carries a picture beyond its denotative and connotative impulses to engage with other contexts, people, events, and pictures, and thereby take on meaning. The variant but patterned informational detail carried by these images may make the "as if" a litmus test for how news images function more broadly. Because they are more pronounced about what lurks under the radar in the more general workings of news images, they may be ahead of the curve in addressing the emotional, imagined, and contingent nuances that images bring to the forefront of journalism's relay of reasoned information.

Figure 2.15: AP Photo/Chicago Tribune, "Artist Kerry Skarbakka Leaps Off Museum Roof to Recall 9/1 Horror," June 17, 2005. Used with permission of The Associated Press © 2005. All rights reserved. Used with permission of CNN.

The Informational Load of an About-to-Die Image

Compositional, textual, presentational, viewing, and mnemonic practices all show that the U.S. news media display impending death by making a series of choices about how to do so. The question of how much information is needed to make sense of a photograph is flanked by other questions that probe which deaths the camera most readily intrudes on and under which circumstances that intrusion makes sense. How "about" an about-to-die image needs to be depends on a host of temporal, spatial, cognitive, cultural, and contextual loads that are constructed, implied, and suggested. Together, they render the image of impending death as dependent on form as on content. While the "as if" is regularly used to depict unsettled news events, different kinds of images gravitate toward different kinds of choices.

Work on responses to different informational strategies has established a continuum by which people decide what makes sense. Attempting to draw a theory of speaker meaning, Paul Grice argued for different kinds of implicature, by which the audience brings its own assumptions to its engagements with messages and not all of them work in expected ways.[73] Similarly, Sol Worth and Larry Gross stipulated a distinction between different modes of sense making: attribution references the interpretation of natural events, while inference refers to the interpretation of symbolic events.[74] A close analysis of images of impending death, however, suggests that neither scheme accommodates the full range of nuances that emerge here.

Three separate levels of information are evident in news images of impending death, which generate different informational loads around the photograph, organized across three motifs. These include images of presumed death, images of possible death, and images of certain death. These three motifs of the trope of impending death exist on a continuum of implicature, by which the least amount of detail—in images of presumed death—requires a greater degree of interpretive work by the public to complete what is not shown. Conversely, the greatest amount of detail—in images of certain death—calls for less interpretation on the public's part. In between, the work of inference facilitates the engagement with images of possible death. This is not to say that the images work so neatly across the board, for as this book will show, such a continuum is but a starting point for a varied range of practices related to images of impending death. Each relies on differing levels of contingency, the emotions, and the imagination in helping to craft the messages that they bring.

Images of Presumed Death

The about-to-die image of presumed death offers the least explicit level of informational detail and thereby relies to the greatest degree on the emotions, contingency, and the imagination on the part of the public. The victims of images of presumed death are never shown and rarely identified. Imagined and usually hypothesized to be members of identified groups—refugees, villagers, passengers—they are the unseen and often anonymous victims of indeterminate numbers who have died from usually large-scale tragedies or disasters but whose deaths are neither confirmed nor seen. In this sense, the impending nature of their death depends on an image which freezes the devastation at a moment prior to their death's visualization or confirmation.

While the tragedies depicted here involve an extensive loss of life, such as that caused by wide-ranging physical or structural devastation, humans dying or dead are not seen. Largely inanimate physical landscapes provide the form that encourages the public to presume death in these images.

This front-page picture of the *Philadelphia Inquirer*, taken in the spring of 2003, is a case in point (fig. 2.16). Though the image showed the city of Baghdad, lit on fire in the first throes of attack during the start of the recent war in Iraq, it obscured the fact that thousands were in the process of dying from that same frontal assault. No people appeared in the image. The structural devastation stood in for the imagined dying and dead who remained unseen.

In instances of presumed death, people need to fill in the details that the news media do not show. Buried under the mounds of earth caused by landslides, lost in the waters of typhoons or shipwrecks, disintegrated by the force of a terrorist's bomb, the victims of presumed death rely on the public to imagine their demise. Although death tends to occur rapidly, its confirmation often comes with a delay, allowing for presumption to stand in for evidence of its occurrence within the evolving news timetable. Death is assumed to be causal and is anticipated within a finite and proximate period of time. Images of presumed death call on the public to engage in substitution, to let the rubble from the earthquake or the shards of the airplane wreckage become an implied relay about the loss of human life.

In this regard, the moment of "about to die" is itself a visible prelude to an invisible unfolding of events. Although people may know they are being shown a smashed building, the depiction becomes significant in light of what it implies, not in terms of what it shows. Images of presumed death, then, require acts of presumption on the public's part, where people fill in details about the nature, scope, scale, and impact of human devastation that remain beyond the camera's eye.

Images of Possible Death

The about-to-die image of possible death offers more explicit informational detail than that given presumed death. Usually separated in time from the actual event causing death, these images mark deaths that tend to occur to large numbers of generally unnamed people at many points in time. What this means is that the usual markers for circumstances causing death are not available for depiction within the normal parameters of news making: they stretch across time and involve more people than can easily be captured by the tools of news relay, particularly images.

Figure 2.16: Ramzi Haidar/AFP/Getty Images, "Baghdad on Fire," March 21, 2003. Laura Raugh/ AP, "Iraqi Soldiers Surrender to US Marines," March 21, 2003. Used with permission of the *Philadelphia Inquirer*.

Images of possible death thus involve the public in a different kind of substitution work, where people are asked to assume a linkage between what is shown and what is not shown, even if they are not given cues for how to connect them. The public infers not only that people are about to die, even if they do not, but that the action anticipated beyond the camera's frame causes death, even if it does not.

Endangered human bodies are the form that encourages people to infer a possible death. This AP picture, for instance, taken during a two-day attempt to overthrow the government in the coastal town of Puerto Cabello, Venezuela in June 1962, showed a priest holding a wounded soldier as bullets whizzed by (fig. 2.17). Although people were told that the priest was administering last rites to a number of wounded soldiers and that more than two hundred people died, they were not told what happened to the unnamed wounded individual who was depicted. The picture won the Pulitzer Prize the following year. Said one overview simply years later, the priest "gave the sacrament to the soldier, then moved on to others who had fallen."[75]

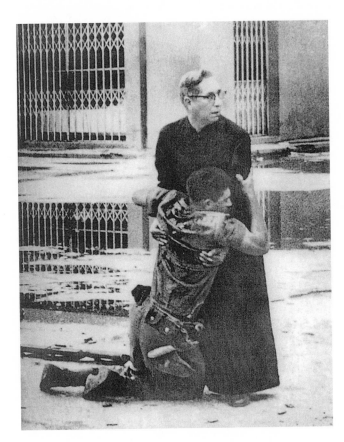

Figure 2.17:
Hector Rondon/
AP, "Aid from the
Padre," Puerto Cabella,
Venezuela, June 4,
1962.

Similarly, images of sports disasters often show anonymous people on the cusp of a possible death. Pictures of Brussels's Heysel Stadium in 1985 showed soccer fans being crushed against a wall during a riot, which moments later collapsed and killed thirty-nine persons. Four years later, similar pictures depicted British crowds crushed against a chain-link fence at a soccer game in Hillsborough Stadium. The pictures of both disasters did not make clear who of the depicted died, though the latter disaster's images, which showed the fans' faces as they were bring crushed to death, prompted more than three hundred complaints to the British press council and were then used to catalyze change in the United Kingdom's soccer clubs, control of fan behavior, and improvement of stadiums.[76]

Depicting hypothetical rather than presumed or certain death, these images draw on a synecdochic or symbolic connection between what is depicted and what actually transpires in an event's unfolding, building on the possibility that the person depicted eventually dies. Although the persons depicted may or may not die, that is incidental to the fact that they stand in for those who do. Because death lingers as a potentiality only, it is up to the public to make the contingent death certain by inferring death from what is depicted.

In this regard, the targets of depiction reinforce what is already known rather than offer new information, and they tend to do so at a delay from the event itself. Necessarily recognized by the public as symbols, these images emblematize a fate that may or may not befall the depicted individuals but which they are used to represent nonetheless. Calling on the public to infer numerous aspects of a sequence of action that it does not see, images of possible death work best when people assume a death that is not depicted and agree to assume the death of those depicted, regardless of whether or not this actually occurs. Additionally, the public needs to generalize impending death to those not depicted, engaging in an act of imagination that extends beyond what is visualized. These circumstances make images of possible death useful beyond journalism, where humanitarian organizations, governmental tribunals, and truth commissions are among those that build on an image's original appearance as a news relay for other aims.

Images of Certain Death

The about-to-die image of certain death offers the most extensive load of informational detail. Unlike the others, this image tends to establish the death of the person or persons being depicted. Because death is never established by about-to-die images themselves—which depend on a sequence of visuals beyond the about-to-die image that shows death itself—the relevance of verbal detail is key here. Words here provide the form by which people accept or refute the certainty of death in these images.

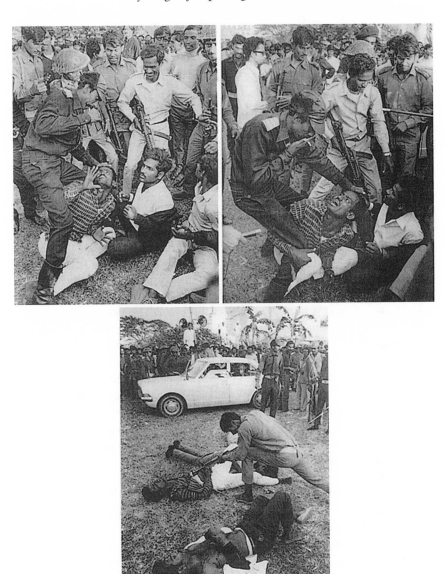

Figure 2.18: Horst Faas and Michel Laurent/AP, "Death in Dacca," Bangladesh, December 18, 1971.

This sequence of pictures depicted a 1971 victory rally in a Dacca racetrack on the eve of Bangladesh's move to freedom. The fighters for Bangladesh's liberation, under the name "Mukti Bahini" (Liberation Army), sought revenge against those who they felt had sided with Pakistan during the fight for independence. After torturing them for hours, they bayoneted and executed four men who were suspected of collaboration with Pakistani militiamen. Though photographers were invited to the racetrack for a "photo opportunity," many chose not to take pictures of the scene for fear it would incite violence.[77] Those who stayed recorded a sequence of action that led to the depicted men's death (fig. 2.18). Among the photographers who remained were Associated Press photographers Horst Faas and Michel Laurent. Doing so, in their words, pulled them in two directions. They asked for the torture to stop but when it did not, they stayed and documented the men's bayoneting, though the act of taking the images proved arduous: Faas later recalled that his "hands were trembling so much I couldn't change the film.... The crowd cheered and took no notice of us. I hoped the men would die quickly, but it took almost an hour."[78]

After the AP distributed the pictures, their depiction of the bayoneting aroused anger in the region. India, citing "national interests," refused permission for them to be transmitted through Calcutta.[79] The result, said one observer, was that "the story was played in the worldwide media for a much longer period than it might have been. The written story was published first, and the pictures that were transmitted [through London] were printed a day later."[80] The pictures won a 1972 Pulitzer for their AP photographers. Though they were published at a delay from the story, viewers were repeatedly told that the men had died.[81]

Unlike other kinds of about-to-die images, these images establish death's inevitability by providing patterned, explicit, and elaborated verbal leads, and in this they require people to accept or reject what they see as valid and consonant with the interpretation they are being verbally given. Images of certain death show individuals perched on the precipice of death and use texts—headlines, captions, the titles of adjoining news stories—to establish a death not typically seen: consider the image of Ruth Snyder's execution (fig. 2.4), which was banner headlined "DEAD!" though she was still alive. The contingency of the image needs to be necessarily undone by the public, which relies on the various leads and conventions to turn the image into one of certainty, even though certainty is not depicted.

The information that accompanies these about-to-die images appears both together with the image's display and afterward. The continued recycling of these images is central, for here the picture of a person facing death tends to be presented even in situations where alternative visual documentation shows that the same person is dead. Such verbal detail can offer varying degrees of identity to the depicted victim: it can leave the victim anonymous, offer a name made relevant by the impending death, signal notoriety, or suggest immortality. In each case, people tend to know that the depicted person or persons are dead even before they see the images of them facing death.

Images of certain death rank among those generating the most fanfare among journalists, news executives, officials, politicians, and viewers. Prompting discussion across much of the public, they not only serve as launch pads for larger conversations about the appropriate role of photography in journalism but facilitate extensive debates over the meaning of unsettled events in the public sphere. Because images of certain death can foster multiple kinds of responses, not all of them related to the reasoned relay of information, this underscoring of the "as if" as an impulse for shaping public response deserves pause.

Imagining Unseen Death

Within these parameters, the "as if" plays on a longstanding lack of clarity between what is depicted in an image and what can be understood from its depiction. Powerful, contingent, and emotive, the about-to-die images of journalism push form as much as content when engaging the public. They invite the emotions, contingency, and the imagination, and they use these impulses to play to multiple public sentiments about what the breaking news of death means. When events are unsettled, standards and conventions for their depiction ambiguous, relations between words and images unclear and often contradictory, and multiple interpretive communities actively staking claims to meaning, the chance that such images will be sideliners to the events they depict is slim. This is worth considering, because the "as if" can shift public sentiments in wide-ranging and creative ways about the events it depicts.

The capacity to presume, infer, and accept or reject meaning from images is built into the image-making enterprise. But in the cases under discussion here, the capacious ability to craft meaning regardless of an image's clear relevance to what is being depicted deserves further attention. Journalists, news executives, officials, politicians, and viewers can and do go in many directions in their engagement with images of impending death, impacting the larger question of what news images are for. What ultimately counts as evidence of impending death? Who decides? And what does this reveal about the broader function of news images?

Chapter 3

Presumed Death

One way of showing the "as if" without graphic detail is by encouraging the public to presume a death not shown. Images of presumed death signal impending death through inanimate landscapes—fallen buildings, devastated physical settings, and crushed structures—but no people about to die. Instead, the public needs to presume the death of undepicted persons so as to make sense of what they see. A picture of a sinking *Titanic,* for example, pushes people to engage with the event by imagining its unseen passengers about to drown.

Images of presumed death draw broadly from notions of spectacle, where death, endangered human beings, and bodies of the dead are erased so as to more fully emphasize extravagant, memorable, and striking visual scenes in their stead. Theories put forward by scholars as wide-ranging as Jean Baudrillard, Guy de Bord, and Douglas Kellner[1] posit that spectacles displace necessary dimensions of social experience and collective life, undermining critical reflection, meaningful engagement, and deliberative democracy. Images of presumed death, then, and the substitution of physical and structural devastation for people about to die, offer a spectacular engagement with the unsettled and difficult events of the news that obscures the human loss at their core.

Following a broader tendency among journalists to use inanimate objects so as to sidestep the difficulties of graphic portrayal,[2] images of presumed death tend to emerge in news coverage about large-scale tragedies where a large and often indeterminate number of people perish quickly. The individuals facing death in these tragedies cannot be easily or readily depicted, for the loss of human life tends to be extensive. Devastation can be natural, manmade, unanticipated, predictable, accidental, or intentional, caused by tornadoes, earthquakes, mudslides, volcanic eruptions, landslides, hurricanes, tidal waves, floods, fires, train wrecks, shipwrecks, airplane crashes, war, and terror attacks. Though death tends to occur rapidly, its confirmation generally comes with a delay, allowing for presumption to stand as evidence of its occurrence within the evolving timetable of journalism. Often, then, the people presumed about to die in these images may in fact already be dead, but using the camera to freeze a moment before their death can be confirmed suspends the image's temporality and facilitates its "as if" status.

Systematic about what gets emphasized and hidden in the events being depicted, the form of these images is familiar. Devastation is generally beyond doubt, its parameters disproportionate to the photo and often spilling beyond the camera's frame. Mounds of dirt run off the sides of an image of a mudslide; the clouds of atomic disaster billow across the horizon framed by the camera's lens. Devastation is portrayed as an enormous tragedy with seemingly limitless dimensions. While the people who face death or are dying as the picture is taken remain beyond the camera's frame, unseen and anonymous, they are attested to by the details of the unfolding news event. When these images do depict individuals, they are not people about to die but those trying to rescue them—police officers, EMT personnel, villagers looking for survivors; less often, these images depict survivors fleeing the disaster area. Framing the devastation by their positioning alongside it, they stand in for the undepicted victims, insert an additional level of witnessing, and mark the collective efforts to reassert control over an event unfolding seemingly without discrimination or reason. Accompanying captions tend to underscore these individuals' supporting roles.[3]

Images of presumed death thereby provide multiple levels of distancing from the depiction of death itself, forcing the public to fill in a number of gaps created by their informational load. As with other images of impending death, they suggest an undepicted death. But unlike other images, these images coax people to imagine undepicted individuals dying or dead from situations in progress. The viewer's act of presumption thus completes the process of interpretation, giving the image meaning by completing a narrative that reaches closure in death, even if death and the people who die are not seen. Doing so cannot only mitigate any ambivalence about displaying and seeing graphicness but can also enhance a certain kind of public attentiveness and involvement in an event with high existential stakes.

What Does Presumed Death Look Like

Images of presumed death extend across the full trajectory of news depictions and date to the earliest uses of images in daily news, when they were prevalent in illustrating the large-scale disasters that accompanied the heights of modernization, industrialization, and urbanization. From the late 1850s, the capacity to use images—drawings, woodcuts, engravings, and eventually photographs—to address the unanticipated accidents, mishaps, and problems of the industrial age as well as the ever-present human tragedies caused by natural disasters helped legitimate journalism's role in documenting the timely and immediate events of public life. For instance, an 1880 cover of the *Illustrated London News* depicted a man balancing on the edge of the Tay Bridge to peer into the rough waters into which an unseen train had plunged on a stormy New Year's Eve in 1879, taking all seventy-five passengers with it.[4] By the turn of the second millennium, similar images were produced as video footage, with still frames grabbed from sequencing often provided by on-site citizen journalists: consider how the Internet filled in December 2008 with still images, grabbed from video, of onlookers watching the Indian security forces surround the terrorist-occupied buildings in Mumbai, no hostages or victims in sight.

Across this stretch of technological development, the types of events relying on presumption have had certain common parameters, as evidenced by two seemingly disparate events separated by nearly eighty years—the Great Chicago Fire and the bombings of Hiroshima and Nagasaki (fig. 3.1). One involved natural disaster, the other intentional destruction; considered here in tandem, they highlight how about-to-die images—from the earliest days of newspaper illustration to a highpoint in the development of war photography during World War II—have used presumption to blend death by nature, accident, and design.

The Great Chicago Fire of 1871, in which thousands of individuals perished in flames that ravaged four square miles of the city, was said to have been the "first instant media event" in the United States. One of the first major disasters to receive immediate and widespread coverage in the news, it struck down a city that many took to be the emblem of America's age of urbanization.[5]

By 1871, fires in cities had been depicted in journalism for over ten years, but those portrayals had focused on the tragedy's aftermath. By contrast, the Great Chicago Fire, which blasted the city in early October, was an event drawn in progress. Coming during a year so dry that newspapers dubbed it the "Black Year," it was seen as one of the significant disasters of the nineteenth century. The fire occurred in the middle of a hundred-year period in which "America became urban," with no other U.S. city growing as fast or as much as Chicago. While some hailed the city's tenacity and determination, many saw its industrialization as a "regrettable decline," its physical disarray after the fire reflecting

Figure 3.1:
John R. Chapin,
"Chicago in Flames–
The Rush for Lives
over Randolph Street
Bridge," *Harper's
Weekly*, October 28,
1871; George R. Caron,
"Atomic Bombing of
Hiroshima," Time &
Life Pictures/Getty
Images, August 6,
1945.

an internal social disorder associated with the many immigrant groups in which social and economic problems simmered under the surface.[6] As Carl Smith later observed, "How Americans discerned the disorderly [in this] most well-known urban fire in this country's history [took shape] in relation to the development of an understanding of the meaning of modernity." The fire thus comprised a "kind of historical node," reflecting both the perils of urbanization and the victory of the nineteenth-century urban setting—"a unique moment in time, when, it seemed, an old order was instantly gone and a new one appeared in a flash of flame."[7] As one resident wrote the Saturday after the disaster, "An age has closed and a new epoch, obscured in doubt and uncertainty, is about to begin."[8]

What this new age would look like depended in part on how the story of the great fire would be told. Working from mostly makeshift quarters, the local press struggled to provide coverage while keeping in mind the contradictory public sentiments about the blazing urban setting, but, as the *Philadelphia Inquirer* noted, it was "almost impossible to get any reliable particulars" because only one telegraph—in the suburbs—was working.[9] Flames put the *Chicago Tribune* out of commission before daylight, and other papers contended with difficult logistics in getting the news out: the *Chicago Evening Journal* turned out an edition that day, while the *Chicago Evening Post* reprinted its full-page account on the following day due to "universal demand for extra copies"; over the following weeks, a dozen or so instant histories saw print.[10]

Spawning eyewitness accounts, illustrations, essays on the fire's lessons, and as time went on, updates on the city's condition, much of the coverage was fragmented, incomplete and contradictory. Correspondents repeatedly voiced the limitation of words in telling the story: *Chicago Tribune* editor Horace White said the disaster was "simply indescribable in its terrible grandeur," *Harper's Weekly* observed that "no pen can describe the horrors of the night," and one city editor was said to have told his reporters to "all sit here and write whatever comes into your heads."[11] The result was that "the accounts disagree[d] almost unanimously as to details."[12] The verbal record produced what was later called a "willful, wishful separation of terrifying fact and materialist aspiration." Such a prevalent disconnect characterized the link between what had happened and its record that one magazine, published in 1880, went so far as to declare that nobody died from the fire.[13] As John J. Pauly later noted, "Because Chicago was the most rapidly expanding city of the industrial age, the fire there offered a perfect occasion for reflections on the state of American society."[14] The fire cast shadows over collective aspirations associated with urban growth, industrialization, and social mobility while giving vent to those who saw value in their development, forcing a bipolar collective reevalution of where people stood on the issue of the city's future. Connected here was a sense of oneness that many felt with Chicago. As *Scribner's Magazine* told it, "Never in the history of the world was a local calamity more remarkably national in its character and consequences than the burning of Chicago," while another journal noted that the "great destruction of property furnishes an...illustration of the manner in which we are all united together."[15]

Journalists thus played a dual role: they were responsible for the account of what happened, and they "were part of a widespread desire to put the disaster to rest."[16] This meant that squelching the disaster's hard facts was one way of skirting the tensions raised by contradictory sentiments about the urban setting. Against this problematic verbal documentation, the illustrated weeklies offered the fire's first visual depictions. Already in the early hours of the fire, artists rapidly set out to sketch what was left of the city: "The artists of the illustrated papers are seated at every coign of vantage, sketching for dear life against the closing of the mail," reported one journalist.[17]

But images could only do so much in depicting a vast burning landscape whose reportage was so uneven. One woman lamented the incomplete documentation pictures could provide: "I know your paper will contain valuable illustrations of our fire," she wrote *Harper's Weekly,* "but half the sad events will never be made public."[18] Both journalists and readers were concerned with the scenes of death that were cluttering the burning landscape, and though the newspapers reported that "hundreds of charred bodies are lying in the streets and floating in the river,"[19] illustrators followed the press's lead in providing less than complete documentation: no dying or dead made it into the fire's depictions.

Instead, the sketches of the Chicago fire depicted barreled-out buildings, fragments of structures, and groups of newly homeless survivors. While journalists lamented a disaster that was "too vast, too swift, too full of smoke, too full of danger for anybody to see it all,"[20] the ruins, rebuilding, and survivors safely beyond it dominated the bulk of the drawings. Popular illustrator Alfred R. Waud, for instance, drew numerous pictures of the devastation without showing victims, while *Harper's Weekly* showed burnt or burning buildings and shaken—but safe—survivors. Although death was rampant, the illustrations showed no dying individuals or corpses.[21]

It was here that the moment of presumed death, embodied by a city ablaze, found its way into numerous illustrations of the disaster, offering a way to suggest death but not show it. The powerful moment of live flames overwhelming a still-intact city took over the disaster's depictions. They appeared repeatedly in *Harper's Weekly,* the *Illustrated London News,* and various lithographs of the fire.[22]

Harper's led the way in the fire's visualization, though at a delay typical of the illustrated weeklies. Its October 21 issue was able only to show what it called "a bird's eye view of Chicago as it was before the fire."[23] The following week, however, it offered a multivista depiction of the city ablaze. In a series of illustrations that spread across seven pages, it offered multiple versions of the fiery horizon. Drawings portrayed both the blazing landscape and specific buildings on fire—the Crosby Opera House, the Chamber of Commerce, the central grain elevators; three additional pictures showed, in the magazine's words, "the general character of the buildings which have been swept away by the fire."[24]

One version of a mass exodus across the Randolph Street Bridge was sketched by artist John R. Chapin, who drew a broad city scene for the magazine's readers, much of it overwhelmed in the drawing by black billows of smoke and swirling flames. As Chapin later wrote, "No language which I can command will serve to convey any idea of the grandeur, the awful sublimity, of the scene." Though swarms of people were depicted running from the fire, they were shown safely positioned on the unlit side of the river. In the background across the bridge, the sketch targeted a blazing urban horizon which filled the top of the drawing's frame. No detail depicted the individuals fatally trapped, dying, or dead inside its burning buildings and structures. In a lengthy laudatory commentary, *Harper's* commended its illustrators—Chapin and the others—for a job well done. In its view, they had offered "a more graphic idea than can be expressed in words of the privations and sufferings endured."[25]

Harper's displayed the image alongside a two-page narrative by Chapin of what he saw. In it, Chapin provided a detailed tale about the unimaginability of its scenes—the pressing masses of people across the bridge, the frantic activity to and fro, the sheer panic. Calling himself a second Nero as he attempted to sketch the scene, he noted that "nothing but the importance of preserving a record of the scene induced me to force my nervous system into a state sufficiently calm to jot down the scenes passing before me." In turn, the magazine noted that Chapin's double-page illustration "will enable our readers to form some conception of the somber desolation that hung over the city."[26]

An example of presumed death, Chapin's image sparked interest among other illustrators, many of whom copied it. The drawing drew its strength from the fact that it provided enough detail to capture the horror but not so much to turn the public off: as an editorial in *Every Saturday* remarked, "It is a fact that sorrow and calamity ultimately deaden the faculty of apprehension, and there is a blessed limit beyond which not even the tenderest heart can go in sympathy."[27] Frozen at a point in time in which the fire still raged, some of its unseen victims still lived and the ensuing calamity had yet to fully unfold, the drawing portrayed a moment in which Chicago could have either gone under or emerged triumphant in its rebuilding. Viewed thus, it accommodated evolving and contradictory public responses to the fire and what they suggested about modernization, urbanization, and industrialization. While the verbal record simply got many details of the fire wrong, the visuals charted a safer course by not depicting the same details. Those who were traumatized by the sheer horror of the fire, those who remained nostalgic for a preurban time and imagined a city cleansed of its impure traits, or those who were ready to take on the challenge of turning loss into gain and rebuilding from anew could ponder the significance of the fire and engage with the image, regardless of the understanding it did or did not offer.

Equally important, the image made it possible to linger in the impossible contingency that damage might be minimized, disaster halted in its tracks. A writer for the *World* noted that "there is little to be said of such a calamity which the imagination of every reader cannot build for himself."[28] Even though the drawing and others like it came at a delay, it did not clearly depict the fire's impact; instead it disconnected both the fire from the deaths it caused and the disaster's official and journalistic representation from its effect. Journalists and officials encouraged viewers to imagine what they did not see. An editorial in the *Christian Union* noted, "What shall make possible in a crisis to be the actual, the natural current of their lives."[29] The Chicago Relief and Aid Society counseled a play to the imagination, which remained "the only faculty of the human mind equal to any comprehension of the appalling night when Chicago was in flames."[30]

As the image moved into memory, its positive association with modernization and urbanization prevailed. The moment of presumed death—blazing buildings with no visible people in them already dead or about to die—carried into later years, reproduced in lithographs and commemorative efforts. The following year an engraving, titled "Chicago on Fire," went on sale, showing, according to its advertisement, "the entire city by night and one half of it in flames—shipping, buildings, etc." By 1878 buildings ablaze with no people in sight were being copied widely by artists in the Currier and Ives stable and appeared as a frontispiece for the Griswold Opera House's reenactment of the event.[31] As time went on, the burning, unpeopled buildings were cemented into a memory of the disaster that upheld the blazing city as a hallmark in urban resilience. They became the leitmotif underlying a range of commemorations, made more poignant as the value of modernity and urbanization pushed aside its perceived perils—fireworks simulating the fire alongside reenactments of firefighters extinguishing a simulated burning building in the 1970s or a 1996 Fire Diorama re-creating the night that Chicago burned, including the "roar of spreading flames and the explosion of burning buildings." Called "one of the most dramatic recreations of a disaster scene ever depicted," an unpeopled city ablaze was embraced as a marker of Chicago's durability and renewal, becoming the disaster's most lasting depiction.[32]

Significantly, though the fire was among the first natural disasters for which photography was available as a tool of visual documentation, it was the Chapin *drawing*—not a photograph—of the burning city that persevered. This was because Chapin had addressed multiple aspects of the fire by collapsing them into one frame—its immediacy, its high stakes, the ensuing public danger, and no visible human loss. By remaining open, suggestive, and implicative, this image of presumed death worked at the time and in the following years because it accommodated a public working through a range of existential uncertainties exacerbated by the fire. Playing to the fire's "as if" dimensions rather than providing a relay of primarily reasoned information about it, the image thus serviced a public needing to figure out where it stood in relation to what it saw.

Not surprisingly, the city ablaze marked the initial organized efforts at urban fire prevention. The Chapin drawing appeared widely when Fire Prevention Day was proclaimed by U.S. President Woodrow Wilson on the fire's fortieth anniversary. Nearly 150 years later, it still adorns informational materials marking fire prevention week and historical chronicles of the city's various immigrant groups.[33] Through these efforts, the city under siege from the elements, but without people dying or dead, became most actively associated with the triumph of urbanization and industrialization, and the city's successful response to natural disaster, rather than its inverse.

Nearly eighty years later, another image of presumed death entertained the same patterned response to disaster, though the meaning of the image gravitated over time in an opposite direction. It also encouraged the involvement of the emotions, contingency, and the imagination because they completed a fundamental lack of clarity in the depiction. The dropping of the atomic bombs on Hiroshima and Nagasaki offered perhaps one of the most curious—and then unimaginable—images of presumed death to circulate in journalism. The bombings occurred on August 6 and 9, 1945, killing more than 100,000 people. How news organizations scrambled to cover an event without precedent, alongside an official containment of news of what had happened, depended largely on the images of presumed death through which it circulated.

Coming at a time when wartime photography was reaching its zenith and explicit images documented the multiple fronts of World War II with zeal, making it "not only the most photographed war in history but the best photographed,"[34] the gravitation to an image of presumed death and its lack of explicit detail constitutes a telling choice in a time of extensive visual documentation. The dropping of the bomb occurred with little clear prior public discussion. Though *New York Times* science reporter William L. Laurence had published accounts of atomic power in 1937,[35] news organizations were prohibited from printing anything related to the actual wartime experiments involving atomic energy. The largely hypothetical discussion of the value and peril of atomic warfare that ensued thus addressed imagined aspects of an imagined bomb—its potential impact, the level of destruction it might cause, and what it might look like—but it was not yet addressed with any degree of public certainty.

This meant that the bombings occurred at a moment in which the U.S. public did not know what to make of them, making it difficult to distinguish them from firebombings, the Blitz, and other mass attacks. Journalists, when briefed by U.S. president Harry Truman's press secretary, at first could not convince their news desks of the bombings' importance, and as the news unfolded people remained unclear about how to appraise what they were being told.[36] The *New York Times* offered two perspectives the day after the bombing: "Atomic energy may well lead to a bright new world in which man shares a common brotherhood or we shall become—beneath the bombs and rockets—a world of troglodytes."[37] Though the likelihood was high that images could help viewers make sense of the event, no image appeared initially in the U.S. news media.

No photographs of the bomb, the cloud or the destruction were released on the day of the announcement, making the news "oddly abstract."[38] Said to "stagger the imagination," the bombings' initial coverage came in large part from *New York Times* reporter William L. Laurence, who had been loaned to the Manhattan Project as its historian and was able to produce ten pages of the *Times'* thirty-eight-page edition on that day.[39] The bombings were thus first described in what the *New York Times* called "word pictures" from one of the earlier test explosions in New Mexico:

> The lighting effects beggar description. The whole country was lighted by a searing light with the intensity many times that of the midday sun. It was golden purple, violet grey and blue. It lighted every peak, crevice and ridge of the nearby mountain range with a clarity and a beauty that cannot be described but must be seen to be imagined. It was that beauty which the great poets dream about, but describe most poorly and inadequately.[40]

Such word pictures, coming in place of the first photographs, divorced the explosion from its destruction, the event from its context, the aesthetic appeal from its pragmatic effect. The delay in publishing the images, attributed by the U.S. War Department to technical difficulties and due in part to the complications in securing ground images with fighting continuing, left the "visual effects of the equivalent of twenty thousand tons of TNT...to the imagination."[41]

The first images of the bombings were released on August 11 and appeared in print the next day, five days after Truman's initial announcement. Caught between "the alternative futures of nuclear devastation and nuclear utopia,"[42] the aerial mushroomlike photos were striking examples of presumed death, because the connection between what people saw and the loss of human life it caused was unclear. Taken by George R. Caron from the aircraft, the bird's-eye view he captured pitted white and black billowing smoke against a grey, indiscriminate background. Depicted primarily as mushroomlike clouds that hovered serenely above unseen devastation, the billowing smoke blocked vision of all else on the horizon. Nothing beyond the mushroomlike clouds was visible, and the clouds were therefore not visibly connected with destruction. Taken before the smoke cleared and so depicting no ground, by extension the images also showed no sign of life—or death. Missing from the images were the scale, scope, magnitude, and context of the disaster, only that of the clouds. Seeming familiar and uncomplicated, in fact the images were undecipherable. Because the public had no idea of what the effect of a bombing would look like, the lack of a referent complicated the presumption of death.

The images were displayed unevenly by the U.S. news media. The *Los Angeles Times* showed Hiroshima on its front page on August 12 under the title "First Photo of Atomic Bombing of Japan" alongside an aerial view of ground devastation on an inside page. But it was unique in doing so: the *New York Times* ran three photos of mushroom clouds on an inside page; other newspapers followed suit.[43] One simply worded caption, offered first by the Associated Press, was adopted by most papers, and it positioned the clouds as distinct and separate from the damage they caused. Proclaiming that "fire and smoke reach toward the sky as atomic bombs are dropped on Japanese cities," the caption both contextualized the bombs as wartime action, described them with the recognizable descriptors of "fire" and "smoke," failed to delineate the damage— either human or structural—that they caused, and drew attention to the upward movement of fire and smoke over the downward force of the blast. The caption offered no information beyond what was immediately visible in the image, even if it was not readily understandable. This made an image of presumed death well suited for the event, for it built on the subjunctive voice—and its possibilities of the imagination, contingency, and the emotions—in much the same way as did the verbal descriptions. When *Life* magazine made the bombings a central frontispiece on August 20, the disjunction between what viewers saw and what they read was further cemented. Using a pictorial essay that included seven full-page illustrations, *Life* displayed the bombings in two full-page mushroomlike images. The accompanying captions quoted an eyewitness as saying that after the "lightninglike flash," he saw "dead and wounded all around...bloated.... burned with a huge blister."[44] The images, however, showed none of this. As Susan Moeller later observed, the images remained

> uncomfortably otherworldly. The atomic cloud pictures included no hints of the ground-level destruction they had wreaked, yet the enormity of their existence portended ill. A child could do the calculations. If a puff of smoke rising a story high from the ground could kill and maim a squad or platoon of soldiers, a mushroom cloud almost four miles high was apocalyptic. The photographs were awful.[45]

All of this underscored that in order to understand, viewers needed to piece together information that was not necessarily compatible, presuming death while not understanding what was being shown. Nor would the public be given more visible evidence of the bombs' effect for quite some time: the first photos of the devastated cities did not appear in the U.S. press for nearly a month.[46]

And yet the reliance on inanimate depictions of death, by which the clouds stood in for the human loss caused by the bombs, was precisely in keeping with the official U.S. line about keeping the news of human devastation from the papers. As the *London Daily Express*'s Wilfred Burchett later observed, "I was forced to recognize the existence of an official policy to suppress accurate reportage of the terrible after-effects of nuclear war."[47]

Against this context, an ambiguous image made it easier to accommodate a public still unclear about what had happened. Though at first readers' letters simultaneously praised the fact that "modern science had found a way to end all wars" and decried the bombings as "sheer terrorism" and "a stain upon our national life,"[48] over time public reaction shifted in collectively more uniform ways. Each time the images reappeared in newspapers, newsmagazines, and journals, advertising copy, documentary films, and cartoons, they were used to support a shifting message. In the beginning, the value of nuclear warfare persevered: even the timing of the images' release, coinciding with the day Japan pronounced its surrender, lent the depictions the status of victory shots, "photographs of nuclear weapons being used to wage war."[49] Through the 1960s they came to signify, primarily in children's textbooks, scientific accomplishment, a strong America, and a stern threat to the Soviet Union about containing communism.[50] But as time moved on, the images came more and more to reflect conversations about the dangers of nuclear warfare: during the 1970s and 1980s, they were seen as markers of U.S. imperialism, symbols of the end of the world, and an embodiment of U.S. atrocity against Japanese civilians.[51] By the 1990s, when debates over remembering World War II pitted the Enola Gay against Hiroshima as the appropriate token of remembrance, the images of the bombs dropping were seen almost solely through their negative impact. As Robert J. Lifton had presciently noted, "The danger comes from our own hand, from man and his technology. The source is not God or nature but ourselves."[52] By the time the images were engrained in the retrospective literature on photography,[53] they were seen as having documented a problematic turn in the evolution of warfare.

Like the images of the Great Chicago Fire, then, the images of Hiroshima and Nagasaki stood for more than a particular disaster. Taken at a moment in which people were unclear about where they stood on nuclear warfare, the images served as porous carriers for its discussion over time, giving "form to the hopes and fears in which different groups in society regard[ed] nuclear weapons" in much the same way that images of the fire gave shape to evolving and contradictory positions on modernization, industrialization, and urbanization.[54] Offering an antiseptic visual that implied death but did not depict it, the images made it possible for the news media to depict what it could of the disaster, at a point when the military was either not providing more detailed images or did not have them in hand. The images' ambiguity made it easier for the public to engage regardless of what it understood about the bombings, its presumption of death instrumental to entertaining the existential uncertainties and shifting public sentiments that ensued in response to the event.

In both the Great Chicago Fire and Hiroshima, images of presumed death were relevant because they facilitated a play to the "as if" of visual depiction, which could accommodate evolving public interpretations about an unsettled event. That these depictions disconnected the event from its impact is telling, for the reliance here on images of presumed death—stretching from the earliest uses of images in news to a critical apex in wartime photography eighty years later—underscores the motif's emergence in difficult times, when the impact of disasters, wars, and other complicated events may be challenging to address. Although news images across this same time span did show evidence of death in other events, the decision in these two cases to migrate away from corpses, blood, gore, and body parts and show instead burning buildings and mushroomlike clouds created a backdrop through which journalists, news executives, officials, politicians, and viewers could wrestle with the events through contingency, the imagination and the emotions.

At the same time, however, in playing to presumed death and its suggestive and ambiguous inanimate representations, the main difference between the events was minimized: no element of the images explained why death had occurred. Instead, death's differential causes—natural disaster and fire versus warfare and intentional barbarism, death by nature, accident, or design— were depicted as indistinct from each other. This play to form over content meant that those presuming death needed to imagine an undepicted causality beyond what they saw. As the depictions of other events will show, however, public response to images does not necessarily reflect what transpires on the ground, raising the question of how much is lost in making death by nature, accident, or design more similar to each other as depictions than the events might warrant.

Presumed Death: Natural/Accidental/Intentional

What kinds of causality underlie images of presumed death? Because death occurs across a range of events warranting news coverage, images of presumed death depict events resulting from faulty human judgments or technological mishaps—shipwrecks or plane crashes; natural occurrences—earthquakes or hurricanes; predictable disasters—floods or fires; and intentional destruction— terrorist attacks or war. Agreements on the causes underlying the breaking news of death do not necessarily develop: consider how observers continue to lament that Hurricane Katrina's devastation of New Orleans in 2005 was caused by a lack of responsive action to rising water levels in the city. Nonetheless, the events depicted by images of presumed death display characteristics that situate them across various categories of unsettled events. Deemed by Robert Hariman and John Lucaites as events embodying "modernity's gamble"—by which the simultaneous tensions of progress and risk, or control and catastrophe play out—they surface in news as naturally occurring events, as accidental sequences of action that result from faulty human judgments or technological mishaps, and as intentional action that is inflicted to impose harm.[55]

Three kinds of news events across the last century invoked each of these frames by repairing to then-common modes of journalistic relay—the 1906 San Francisco earthquake, which depended on the print media for its shaping; the aerial explosions of the *Hindenburg* dirigible in 1937, the *Challenger* space shuttle in 1986, and the *Columbia* space shuttle in 2003, all of which were shaped as photo opportunities for journalists with live audiences in attendance and were relayed through on-site broadcasting, enhanced in the latter case by the Internet; and the attacks of September 11, 2001, considered here not through its emphasis on jumping or falling bodies, as discussed in chapter 2, but through the central motif of the towers of the World Trade Center, shaped across the multiple platforms of the digitally mediated environment. In each case, despite changes in technology and the kinds of information it made available, death was rendered open, suggestive, and implied through a device, building, or landscape. In none of these events were people about to die seen in a sustained fashion, making it possible to stall causality as people wrestled to come to grips with what had happened.

Natural Death: Presumed Death in San Francisco

As suggested by the Great Chicago Fire, images of presumed death—rather than those of possible or certain death—surface frequently in the depiction of natural disaster, where they play to the obvious point that the floods, tidal waves, and other seemingly spontaneous tragedies unfold without human intervention. As journalism's stories of human sacrifice in the face of natural disaster tend to recount unanticipated and uncontrollable events that overshadow and often outpace human attempts to survive, those viewing the disaster can do little other than join in collective grief over the consequent deaths. And, indeed, this may be the reason that "historic events caused by natural phenomena have a way of escaping the past,"[56] becoming easy fodder for the work of collective memory.

The images of natural disaster are most powerful in their suggestion of the range, scale, and scope of destruction that asserts itself in a seemingly fierce and uncompromising manner, against which the fragility of human life generally loses out. One such disaster was the 1906 San Francisco earthquake. Earning placement among the worst natural disasters in popular memory, the earthquake measured between 7.8 and 8.3 on modern earthquake scales, becoming "the benchmark against which all other tremors [would be] measured."[57] Said to have killed between one thousand and five thousand people, though neither estimate was ever fully confirmed, the temblor hit the city at 5.12 A.M. on the morning of April 18. Within the first minute, it opened the pavement six feet wide and at places twenty feet deep, crumbling civilization along a path that scarred nearly three hundred miles of landscape. Following the earthquake, fires ravaged the city, burning for three days and eradicating nearly a quarter of the built environment.

The earthquake came amidst widespread national ambivalence about San Francisco. For half a century, Americans had been split on the value of the westward expansion, and San Francisco, a city created in response to the Gold Rush, provoked antipathy among those who saw its residents as adventurers seeking instant wealth. As the city's inhabitants embraced what some saw as rugged individualism, others decried what they saw as materialism, greed, and marked degrees of self-gratification. One minister wrote, "In the city there is still greed, lust and intemperance. Good there is, too, but the good has always to fight for its existence." After the quake, one paper cautioned that "in this hour of our pain, we know that nothing comes to us by chance," while the *New York Observer and Chronicle,* chiding San Franciscans for their "insecure moral and religious foundations," warned that "the craze for wealth, the greed of power and the pride of dominion in the appalling disaster...may well be accepted as a sign of divine displeasure." Many readers agreed: "Earthquake and fire may demolish a great city," wrote one, "but they cannot wipe out the sin and selfishness of the human heart."[58]

A widespread sentiment that the city's residents had not done enough to prepare for a big quake stoked the criticism. While San Francisco had been a tiny hamlet of less than a thousand residents when the Gold Rush began in 1848, by 1900 it numbered more than 340,000 inhabitants. The city's infrastructure was consequently built rapidly and often without the necessary supports, guidance, or caution. Mud was used in place of concrete, and people lived in wooden shanties and in pieces of abandoned ships transformed into more permanent structures. Though the disaster followed seven major fires, little had been done to ensure public safety should a larger calamity occur, and words of caution that the city's infrastructure might be in danger were proffered at least through the final quarter of the nineteenth century. The *San Francisco Call* issued an editorial after an earthquake in 1868 that "the lives lost yesterday are not chargeable to the earthquake but to the vanity, greed and meanness of those who erected the buildings."[59]

But most city residents remained oblivious to the forewarnings. "We have here a different civilization," said one observer.[60] With the city relying on poorly constructed, fire-prone buildings with no clear escape route and a water system that remained vulnerable to shifts in the earth's surface, the quake hit hard, and in some views the region got what it deserved: U.S. president Teddy Roosevelt labeled San Franciscans "infernal fools," and readers' letters were as pointed, remembering that before the disaster "San Francisco had been a wicked city.... Immorality was flaunted."[61]

Coverage thus took shape against a larger ambivalence about how "natural" the 1906 earthquake really was. Though the earthquake itself could not have been prevented, critics maintained that much of its consequent destruction—the fires, the widespread devastation, the crumbling buildings—was brought on by its residents not having attended to the signs of imminent disaster before it occurred. The Associated Press led the way in telling the story, largely because buildings housing two of the city's local newspapers—the *San Francisco Call* and *San Francisco Examiner*—had been destroyed. The *San Francisco Daily News* was the only paper fully able to publish, offering two abbreviated extra editions and printing one of them on a pink sheet of paper with the headline "HUNDREDS DEAD!"; a combined paper—the *Call-Chronicle-Examiner*—was distributed free the next day. A press committee was set up to organize the distribution of news, and an emergency panel—with one representative from each of the city's papers and the Associated Press—was formed.[62]

The stories journalists told of the disaster were dire. Hundreds of eyewitness accounts circulated in single articles, whole issues and multiple editions of the daily press and magazines like *Collier's, Harper's Weekly, McClure's* and *Everybody's Magazine.* Coverage detailed how individuals watched buildings around them crumble, fled in panic over unstable surfaces, listened to the screaming, moaning and pleading of the trapped, and helped rescue survivors trying to crawl from the wreckage. Eyewitnesses recounted the frantic search for survivors, the discrimination of the living from the dead, and the stacking and removal of the crushed and burned corpses. Survivors recounted "trenches one hundred feet long and a mean's length wide," whose dead were laid to rest "side by side in their burial sheets." The accounts were graphic, explicit, and detailed, and headlines shouted the news of mounting fatalities.[63]

Some felt the regional press, which initially printed hundreds of stories, did a yeoman's job. Writing two years later, one professor lauded the newspaper enterprise which "shone preeminent during the critical days."[64] As prevalent, however, was a critique of that same journalism. Reporter James Hopper admitted that "in spite of what we had already seen, our power of realization was behind time as it was to be through the three days' progressive disaster." What newspapers reported was a "rushed and hurried job...[with] substantive factual errors," accompanied by hearsay, rumor, innuendo, and blocked information.[65] Following the lead of local officials who deliberately tried to gloss over the quake's impact, at first claiming no one died and minimizing the damage and ensuing danger, some local journalists refused to call the event an "earthquake," preferring instead to label it a "fire." Numerous residents protested the accusation that San Franciscans should have been better prepared.[66] As one city archivist later maintained, city officials were concerned about the financial impact of the quake, and so decided "let's not talk earthquake. Let's talk fire. Because cities could recover from fire, and many of them did."[67] Embedded within what was later dubbed a "culture of suppression," the "simplest way for a newspaper to deal with an earthquake was to refuse to acknowledge its occurrence." Thus, "the closer the magazines were to the epicenter, the more they participated in the campaign of cultural disinformation . . . the further away they were, the more they gave credence and space [to more accurate information]. In both cases the information they printed was incomplete."[68] All of this made images of presumed death a convenient way to signal, however reluctantly, the widespread loss of life. The least graphic and thereby potentially least reprehensible available visual alternative, these images left open the possibility that the widespread deaths were more limited than was being confirmed and sidestepped further criticisms that San Franciscans were at fault. As one resident rather charitably saw it, "I am glad I lived to see things that happened in the first ten days after the catastrophe. Those days were the best and most inspiring in my life."[69]

In some ways, the gravitation to images of presumed death was curious, because regardless of how one appraised the coverage, its images far outpaced its words. "Only the massive photographic record," said one observer, "came close to documenting the catastrophe in an accurate manner."[70] And indeed, photographs of the earthquake helped prove the mettle of budding cameramen. As the trade journal *Camera Craft* told it at the time,

> The probabilities are that never since cameras were first invented has there been such a large number in use at any one place as there has been in San Francisco since the eighteenth of last April. Everyone who either possessed, could buy or borrow one, and was then fortunate enough to secure supplies for it, made more or less good use of his knowledge of photography.[71]

To that effect, thousands of photographs recorded the city's broken landscape during the first two days of the quake. The images were "sobering—a city of rubble engulfed in smoke and flame."[72] Photo after photo recorded buildings cracking and slipped at right angles to the structures on either side, angular gashes where chimneys used to be, streets that buckled like ocean waves. Though the professional images of photographers like Arnold Genthe or Louis J. Stellman were noteworthy, many pictures taken by amateurs showed stark black-and-white unpeopled scenes of widespread devastation. Tracking the suddenly crumpled landscape, the images conveyed the horrific scale of the tragedy, as photo after photo recorded similar broken scenes in different sections of the city. Though limited by uneven terrain, dangling wires, unavailable security passes for access, and over time the pall of smoke and intense heat, photographers tracked the region relentlessly, knowing that "the photos that were in most demand were those that spouted smoke and fire" and "anything showing ruins went."[73] The first panoramic images showing the devastation from the air were also taken within days of the disaster.

But what the images did not show was the loss of human life: few images showed the badly wounded, the dying, or the corpses mounting rapidly inside the caved-in structures, crushed or buried in the ruins. Even when news stories verbally pointed to wounded and dying individuals, accounts of bodies being pulled from the wreckage and tales of frantic rescue attempts, no human victims or survivors were found in the pictures. In part this was because the about to die and the dead remained one of the disaster's unknowns. As Jack London wrote at the time, "An enumeration of the dead will never be made. All vestiges of them were destroyed by the flames. The number of the victims of the earthquake will never be known." The *Los Angeles Times* lamented the large number of unnamed victims "cremated in the fiery furnace without corporeal vestige being left to record the tragedy."[74] But the hesitation was also due to a broader ambivalence surrounding both confirmation of the dead and their photographic documentation.

The images thus reflected an imbalance between what people experienced and what people saw. Widely distributed instead were inanimate images of crumpled buildings and unseen victims.[75] One such image depicted the once four-story Valencia Street Hotel in the Mission District. The image depicted a tumbled structure on a seemingly intact street with upright buildings on either side (fig. 3.2). The boarding house was the most damaged building on the street, perched grotesquely askew and squashed in height, with what appeared to be its smashed upper stories pouring off the sidewalk and into the street. The front of the shot was filled with scores of people who lined the street, gaping open-mouthed at its misshapen structure. Bystanders reported "seeing numerous people trapped beneath the heavy timbers" and remarked on how the building cracked: "As we ran we heard the hotel creak and roar and crash. I turned to look at it: It was then daylight and the dust of the falling buildings had not time to rise. The hotel lurched forward as if the foundation were dragged backward from under it, and it crumbled down over Valencia Street."[76]

Various versions of the same scene circulated. A photo of the hotel appeared on April 21 on the front page of the *Los Angeles Times,* in a picture taken by the newspaper's own correspondent.[77] Though the image showed no people other than onlookers, the captions and accompanying texts told of two hundred individuals who were trapped on the hotel's lower floors, many of whom would soon drown when the two water mains on the street broke. As rescue

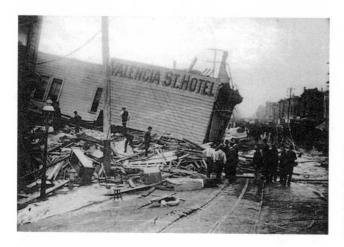

Figure 3.2:
Unknown
photographer,
"San Francisco
Earthquake—Valencia
Street Hotel," April
21, 1906. Courtesy of
San Francisco History
Center, San Francisco
Public Library.

efforts continued for two full days and nights, the image appeared repeatedly, depicting stories about unseen corpses about to be transported into a waiting coroner's wagon and shown again as a roofless battered structure sitting atop a deserted street once rescue attempts were abandoned.[78] Yet despite the flux of activity that took place at the site, in each case all people saw in the images was an inanimate building, angled peculiarly to the street. There were no victims, no wounded, no corpses. Called years later "a horrifying hotel collapse...of which there is ample photographic evidence," by the end only a dozen people were pulled from the hotel's wreckage, with the hotel housing the single largest number of fatalities from the earthquake.[79] But about-to-die images showed no evidence of those fatalities or of the dying; instead people needed to presume the deaths of those they could not see.

Presuming the death of unseen persons through a crumbling structure was an act that occurred repeatedly across the earthquake coverage. The burned shell of the Southern Pacific Company Hospital (where eight people eventually died), the crumbling façade of the multiple storied Palace Hotel, and the rubble of the Wilcox House, where most of the inhabitants perished, were all shown as charred, inanimate structures in which people were still dying at the time the pictures were taken.[80] Once the Navy evacuated people from the area and news of the quake spread, the images of inanimate buildings housing people about to die or already dead circulated more widely. Thirteen such images, almost all taken within the first two days of the quake, illustrated the *New York Times*' front page story, even as its headline pronounced "Hundreds of Bodies Found in the Ruins of Buildings."[81] Images of presumed death decorated the covers and inside pages of the illustrated papers and magazines, including Leslie's, *Sunset,* and *Overland Monthly.*[82] They continued to appear in the retrospective literature, in books on photography, and volumes of Californian history over the decades that followed, lingering long after the quake was over.[83]

Many observers felt that the images were the strongest part of the quake's journalistic record. Not only did they appear in the illustrated papers, but thousands of two and three-dimensional photographs found their way into the card collections of private individuals. Widely recorded by amateurs, who frenetically used their cameras to record what they saw,[84] in none of these efforts was there mention of the failure to visually record the disaster's human victims.

Why were people not bothered by the fact that they saw no wounded, no dying, and no dead, even while the headlines and accompanying texts tracked a mounting body count? First, the ambiguity of the images ensured public engagement: Who would refuse to look at a picture of a grossly crumpled building? But equally important and like other images of presumed death, the pictures signified more than just the aftermath of an earthquake. In playing to a public struggling with evolving sentiments raised by the earthquake, their ambiguity made sense. San Francisco's devastation generated questions about the expansion westward, a rugged and adventurous national character, an alternative American Dream. While observers at first saw the city's response to the quake as one of San Francisco's finest hours—"Together, soldiers and civilians battled the fires. Rich and poor struggled to survive side by side. The city's courageous efforts to rebuild…[took] on an epic tone," wrote one observer—over time the devastation came to be seen broadly as a combination of poor planning, human error, and insufficient imagination.[85] Philip Fradkin later wrote that San Francisco was "the city that nearly destroyed itself" because "San Franciscans, not the inanimate forces of nature, were primarily responsible for the extensive chaos, damage, injuries, and death in the great earthquake and firestorms of 1906." Citing the "unparalleled period of racial, political and social strife" that followed the quake, he observed that "the human fabric that tenuously held the city of San Francisco together was rent. The forces of nature shaped the city's subsequent culture and its history. Violence in the landscape begat violence in the human history that followed."[86]

Thus death in the 1906 earthquake remained suggestive and unseen by design. Not only illustrations of a natural disaster, these ambiguous images of presumed death accommodated evolving public sentiments about the value of the western expansion and the alternative American Dream that San Francisco had embodied. Though San Franciscans saw the tragedy as natural, much of America saw it as a sequence of events that could have been prevented, a result of local residents' unwillingness to prepare for the disaster before it had occurred. As one scholar years later phrased it, "The old American dream was a dream of the Puritans…of men and women content to accumulate their modest fortunes a little at a time, year by year by year. The new dream was the dream of instant wealth, won in a twinkling of audacity and good luck."[87]

What remained unclear at the time of the earthquake was whether the new model of prosperity would endure. Images of presumed death were thus a manageable way of facilitating public exposure to the quake while accommodating the discomfort and the ambivalence it raised, even if they made for a less-than-complete visualization of the disaster itself.

No surprise, then, that the images of the quake surfaced in debates that had little to do with the earthquake per se. As the expansion westward and its relevance to the American Dream prevailed as a project of value over time, the images of crumpled buildings repeatedly appeared, becoming part of the iconography of the United States,[88] as much for what they offered about natural disaster as for what they had to say about the West and the durability of the American Dream.

Accidental Death: Presumed Death in Midair

Images of presumed death have long figured in news stories about the botched uses of technology, where technological mishaps or faulty human judgments involving technology cause human death. Though this includes the faulty devices of everyday life—images of the burned shell of a Rhode Island nightclub were used to depict the story of a 2003 fire caused by faulty equipment, for example—much coverage has been primarily associated with the technological devices of human transportation. Errant technology in ships, trains, planes, and space shuttles have all caused the loss of human life, and death in such images needs to be presumed because its individuals tend not to be easily visible. Instead, they are hidden by the transporting mechanism that defaults—the ship, plane, or train—and then stands in for those who perish while aboard.

Perhaps because these images combine the reliance on technology with a fundamental uncertainty about it—combining a man-made device or instrument with the accidental sequences of action that bring it down—the events depicted here often generate lengthy discussion of culpability, missed opportunities, and ill planning. The devices that fail in a sense are never fully redeemed in discussions about them. Thus one newspaper typically lamented after the *Titanic* sank off the Newfoundland coast on August 14, 1912, killing thousands, "It is nothing less than criminal that a steamer crossing the Atlantic runs the risk of disaster by taking the shortest route, where icebergs are to be expected, just to save time at the risk of life."[89]

These images of presumed death reflect developments in two parallel technologies—transportation and communication. In the early days of news illustration and photography, the breaking news of death by transport was signaled by images of the transporting vehicle still intact. Coverage of the sinking of the steamer *Lusitania,* for instance, hit by a German submarine off the coast of Ireland on May 6, 1915, and killing some one thousand people in fifteen minutes, was illustrated by pictures of the still-standing steamship.[90] Nearly half a century later, as wire services increasingly made the distribution of pictures as fast as words, mishaps were initially illustrated by intact ships and then replaced the next day with images of the listing vehicles: when two ships—the *Andrea Doria* and the *Stockholm*—collided off the coast of Nantucket Island on July 26, 1956, newspapers first showed images of both ships before the accident and replaced them with images of the Andrea Doria going underwater the next day.[91] As the technologies of communication moved on to broadcasting and then the digitally mediated environment, this pattern has taken on additional nuances reflecting those developments.

Images of three separate midair explosions forced the U.S. public to presume death in circumstances caused by accidental technological failure—the explosion of the *Hindenburg* dirigible in 1937, and the explosions of the *Challenger* and *Columbia* space shuttles in 1986 and 2003. Spanning nearly three quarters of a century, each event—shaped as photo opportunities for journalists with onlookers in attendance—involved deaths caused by aerial technology, given shape by immediate on-site coverage that varied as communication technologies developed. And yet, despite the evolution of increasingly varied forms of broadcast relay—radio with the *Hindenburg,* television added with the *Challenger* and the Internet added with the *Columbia*—coverage in all three cases settled on still photos, which became central to the accident's understanding and recollection over time (fig. 3.3). In each case, the events' central pictures depicted the still-unfolding disaster in the midst of killing unvisualized persons in midair.

Accidental Death: Hindenburg

The explosion in 1937 of the *Hindenburg,* a state-of-the-art German aircraft, in front of a live crowd burst apart not only a dirigible but also a resonant technological success story of the time. The latest in a long line of so-called "flying hotels," the dirigible was hailed as "the supreme achievement of modern air ship construction."[92] Its physical explosion and the rupture of the expectations associated with its successful voyage raised questions about technology and progress and their dependence on mechanistic devices that were not fail safe.

The *Hindenburg* had been seen as a technological curiosity from its inception. Although attempts to fly by balloon went back at least to the late eighteenth century, the *Hindenburg* was larger and faster than anything yet devised. Expected to speed up transatlantic travel in lighter-than-air airships, the 245 meter dirigible had crossed the Atlantic Ocean in about three days and was making its first transatlantic crossing of the 1937 season. For that reason, its arrival at Lakehurst, New Jersey, on May 6, 1937 was awaited by hordes of journalists and bystanders, including twenty-two photographers.

The Washington Post

Hindenburg Explodes With 97 Aboard; D. C. Man Escapes, 33 Die at Lakehurst

F.L. Belin, Jr. Leaps From Blazing Ship

Others Near Death Given Last Rites

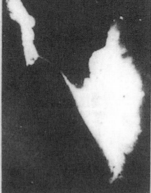

Today's Index

Figure 3.3: Scott Shere, Hindenburg Explosion, © 1937, *The Washington Post*, May 6, 1937, Reprinted with permission; NASA/Public Domain, "Challenger Accident after Launch," S86-38989, January 28, 1986; Jason Hutchinson/AP, "Columbia Breakup," February 1, 2003, AP/Courtesy of NASA. Used with permission of *Newsweek*.

The landing never happened. As the airship approached its mooring in light rain nearly eleven hours late, a small explosion and fire occurred at 7.21 P.M., followed by a second explosion. The dirigible burst into flames, and in less than a minute it fell three hundred feet to the ground. Some passengers jumped to the ground, many dying in the fall. Others were burned inside the airship, pinned by other passengers or shifting furniture. Still others were rescued from the ship after it struck the ground. Happening so fast that one observer said the catastrophe was "a blur rather than a series of remembered incidents," the explosion sent debris flying in every direction and froze witnesses in shock, transforming instantly, in the *Philadelphia Inquirer's* view, into a scene at "the end of the world." The injured were taken to the airfield's infirmary, the dead to an impromptu morgue set up in a nearby press room.[93]

Coverage of the explosion, in which thirty-five passengers died, surpassed most standards for news coverage at the time. The event belonged first to radio, where emotional on-the-scene accounts could be audibly relayed. Radio broadcaster Herbert Morrison, on the scene for WLS-Chicago, was preparing a relay for later broadcast, and in the midst of his description of the airship's mooring, the *Hindenburg* caught fire. "It's burst into flames," he said, his voice breaking. "Get out of the way, please, oh my, this is terrible…Oh, the humanity and all the passengers.…This is one of the worst things I've ever witnessed." In the background listeners could hear shocked bystanders screaming and the sounds of the explosion, producing a report so realistic that in Robert J. Brown's view, "to this day writers often mistake it for a live broadcast."[94] It was not: because Morrison did not have facilities for broadcasting live, the report was taped and a fifteen-minute excerpt broadcast in the middle of the night after his return to Chicago. The full forty-minute report was broadcast to national audiences over the four major networks the next morning, itself a suspension of their ban on recorded reports.[95] Called "radio news at its finest, news events reported as they happened,"[96] one writer for the *Chicago Tribune* called the account "the most dramatic broadcast of all time," another "one of the best pieces of word-eye broadcasting."[97]

What radio could not provide, however, were pictures. It was up to the print media to offer complementary coverage that could equal the potency of radio's emotional sound relays. Adding their own verbal accounts of the explosion, the print media turned much of their attention to the disaster's images. Both newsreel and still photographers were on site to immediately record the dirigible from multiple angles.[98] The largest proximate newspaper to the event, the *Philadelphia Inquirer,* began working on a special edition minutes after the explosion and set a record for the most papers printed on any single weekday in the paper's history. Images were a large part of its coverage, and a day later the paper's editorial staff lauded the fact that it had been able to provide "more fine action pictures than any other paper in the nation." Using the available photos, nearly every U.S. daily, including the *New York Times, Washington Post,* and *Los Angeles Times,* and within the week *Life* magazine, gave the event front-page coverage. The *New York World Telegram* printed twenty-one pictures of the airship, with nearly a dozen appearing in the *New York Daily Mirror* and *New York Post*. Photographic sequences—ranging from half a dozen to over twenty pictures—provided shots of the blazing dirigible accompanied by sober images of wreckage and debris.[99]

Though survivors jumped from the airship and were rescued once it hit the ground and a few corpses appeared in the foreground of broader shots of the hull of the burning airship, no people appeared in the pictures that dominated the media. The focus narrowed onto the inanimate about-to-die moment—the moment at which the dirigible set ablaze—and newspapers played to its visualization in patterned ways: the *Philadelphia Inquirer,* for instance, published twelve separate pictures, four of which showed the airship before or as it was exploding. They were arranged not by sequence but around the shot of impact, which showed, in the headline's words, "the exact moment that the Zeppelin blew up" front and center on the newspaper's first page. The following day, the *Inquirer* published additional photos of the moment of impact. The *Los Angeles Times* showed eight photos on the day of the explosion, half of which showed the still-airworthy dirigible exploding in flames, and three additional sketches of the same moment appeared over the following days.[100] Viewers were expected to presume deaths they could not see, despite the fact that they saw no evidence of humans aboard the airship or attempting to flee its fiery embrace.

One particular photograph was widely picked up by news organizations. Taken by Sam Shere for the International News Service and distributed by the Associated Press Photo Service, the image showed a huge balloon dangling in the air as part of it went up in flames. The image implied an unusual temporal sequencing about the event—a four quadrant timeline dividing left from right and top from bottom: the dirigible hung in the middle; on the right enormous spirals of flame erupted skyward, while on the left the front half of the dirigible hung in midair suspension, as if undisturbed by the fire raging across its backside. The contrast between the light background below the aircraft and the dark background atop it created a surreal before and after moment. Called by Robert Hariman and John Lucaites "a beautifully balanced representation of an unpredicted, uncontrolled explosion," the image was praised for its beauty and successful redrawing of horror though a "picturesque element of impressive fireworks." No surprise, then, that the image played across the U.S. news media, appearing in multiple newspapers and news magazines, even in newspapers, like the *Philadelphia Inquirer,* which had their own staff photographers on site.[101]

Alongside the journalistic triumph of recording the event in sight and sound, however, the event marked a significant downturn for aerial technology. The fears associated with air travel, despite its promise of mobility and progress, were at the heart of responses to the tragedy, and numerous observers challenged the "accidental" nature of the explosion, arguing that a rushed reliance on the airships had for some time been a tragedy in waiting. Speculation about the cause of the explosion filled the newspapers the next day, and it ranged across the scope of possibility: mechanical failure, an explosion of hydrogen gas, sabotage, lightning, an in-sky shooting, or some combination of the above were all raised as complications of the simple notion that the explosion had accidentally occurred. Three separate investigations were conducted—by the Navy, the Commerce Department, and the FBI—but turned up no clear reading of what happened, and the reason for the airship's demise remained unknown for some time. The following year, the *Hindenburg*'s German owner—the Zeppelin company—announced the roll out of a successor to the airship that ran on helium instead of hydrogen. But the first line of an article reporting its impending arrival aptly summed up a rapidly growing American disenchantment with airships: "Dinosaur of the air," it queried, "or future luxury liner of the heavens?" Years later, archival records of the Zeppelin company were found suggesting that the flammable coating of the dirigible's outer skin had probably sparked the fire.[102]

News coverage reflected the fact that the public did not know what to make of the disaster. Reminding its readers that air travel remained "too useful" and "too promising," the *Los Angeles Times* predicted that "this disaster will not end lighter-than-air navigation." But others were not as hopeful: the *New York Times* reminded its readers that the disaster "had [been] feared for some time." And, indeed the *Times'* words proved prescient: with travelers newly alerted to the dangers of flying in highly combustible vehicles, it was not long before paid passenger flights on dirigibles were discontinued. The explosion thus stalled progress in air travel. One editorial cartoon framed public sentiment at the time by showing the dirigible—titled "Man's Ingenuity"—being set on fire while an individual man—titled "The Will to Conquer"—struggled to set himself free of the flames. "Too much, too fast" was how many summed up what had happened, or as one popular online site later succinctly observed, "The *Hindenburg* marked the beginning and the end of transatlantic airships."[103]

A second technology—communication—took on a different shape in memory of the event, however. Journalists' widespread audio and visual capture of the moment of impending death appeared front and center in the retrospective literature on journalism, where the story became equally about the tale and its telling; observers maintained that the coverage "marked a new era....Never before had a disaster been so thoroughly documented." Held responsible for changing public expectations of news, the event initiated a "reign of instant news that addressed both the eye and the ear."[104] Both the radio recording and Shere's photo moved onward in time, drawing from these impulses: easily accessed today on the Internet, for example, one or the other repeatedly appears in satirical Web sites, children's textbooks, and comedic TV programming. The History Channel even aired an advertisement in 2004 that combined the explosion's photographic and radio relay: a man and dog appeared against a background that dissolved into a picture of the *Hindenburg* exploding, as Morrison's voice again issued his famous cry, "Oh, the humanity."[105]

Images of the *Hindenburg* explosion thus accommodated evolving sentiments about human loss, seen against two technologies—sight and sound journalism and air travel. Accepting the facts of the explosion and the deaths it had caused required the public to adjust expectations of the airship's technological prowess. At the same time, the explosion facilitated a celebration of radio and photojournalism: "The *Hindenburg* lived on, but only in photographs—forever burning, forever in the throes of death."[106] Central here was journalism's success in meeting the challenges of breaking news. As one observer later recalled:

> The catastrophe of the *Hindenburg* marked the end of passenger Zeppelins. But even as Herb Morrison's chilling eyewitness report chronicled the end of one era, it signaled the beginning of another—an age in which electronic media would routinely report shocking events in the moment they occur[107]

Two technologies were pitted against each other, both central to the infrastructure of daily life, but the demise of one pushed the other to acclaim.

It was fitting, then, that the most ambiguous and porous of about-to-die images, requiring the greatest degree of the imagination, contingency, and the emotions to make sense of what had happened, would have prevailed here. The fact that people saw no bodies or corpses—in other words, no impact—made it easier to accommodate the tensions that arose from simultaneously being disturbed by its content—the horrific loss of life in an accident that might have been prevented—and celebrating its form—the immediacy and on-site nature of its capture by journalism.

Accidental Death: Challenger

Uncertainty about the technologies of transportation alongside a celebration of journalistic relay again became evident in the *Challenger* space shuttle explosion decades later. An accident that took place in the midst of a journalistic photo opportunity, the capture of the explosion on live television showed the moment at which the shuttle broke apart in real time. Again, no evidence of dying or death was shown, and the inanimate images of presumed death that journalists produced remained at best suggestive.

The shuttle exploded a minute after liftoff forty-six thousand feet above a public crowd at Cape Canaveral on January 28, 1986. All seven astronauts on board were killed immediately. No victims were seen; nor were the masses on the ground visibly depicted in the main images that ensued. What was witnessed—and recycled repeatedly—were the shuttle's exploding fragments, disintegrating into aesthetic plumes of white smoke as the rocket boosters veered away from the vessel.

Recognition of what had happened was not immediate. In the *Washington Post*'s view, both for those on the ground and those watching on television, "the horror dawned slowly. For one very long moment after the explosion, few realized they had witnessed a disaster."[108] Reporters on the scene assumed that the astronauts had aborted the shuttle and were on their way back to earth, and they ran to the landing strip for emergency landings. As the *Boston Globe* later noted, "there was, in the aftermath of the explosion, a momentary respite from horror when the sight of a parachute raised hope that miraculously, perhaps, they had survived.[109]

They had, of course, not survived. Called the "worst accident in the history of space exploration,"[110] the disaster's coverage played to an already assembled audience waiting to see the launch. Millions of school children watched the shuttle explode in real time from their school's television sets. "Stunning a world made witness to the event by television," the arranged exposure—set to accommodate the first civilian teacher flying into space—had the opposite effect.[111]

Television took the lead in coverage. Although the only live coverage occurred on CNN and NBC's *Today* program, the networks shifted to uninterrupted coverage within minutes, where they "played, replayed and re-replayed videotaped footage, sometimes in slow-motion, sometimes frame by agonizing frame, of this truly terrible occurrence."[112] At the heart of the coverage, the shuttle exploded across the horizon, again and again. This image of presumed death charted the appearance and dissipation of spectacular spirals of smoke, which first billowed across the television screen like spiraled cotton candy and then melted into the horizon. The shuttle—and the astronauts inside—seemed to simply disappear. Even if the visual sequence's implications were not immediately understandable, it was the only depiction available, and though it showed no people or bodies, no ground or impact, it remained simultaneously otherworldly and all-authoritative. As *Time*'s Lance Morrow noted, "The moment was irrevocable. Over and over, the bright extinction played on the television screen, almost ghoulishly repeated until it had sunk into the collective memory. And there it will abide, abetted by the weird metaphysic of videotape."[113]

Coverage was relentless. As with the *Hindenburg* fifty years earlier, journalism turned all its resources to the story, offering eyewitness accounts, analytical pieces on the space program, sidebars, and repeated broadcasts of the shuttle breaking apart. Dropping commercials and alternative programming, television sustained marathon coverage, which was structured not chronologically or sequentially but by repeatedly targeting the moment of presumed death as the event's central visualization. Exposure to the coverage was high, with surveys reporting that 95 percent of the public saw some part of the broadcast that day.[114] And yet, people did not believe what they were seeing. As NBC news anchor Tom Brokaw said on the air, "We were all suspended for a time between a state of belief and disbelief." Bewildered TV viewers noted that "this can't be real. We can't be watching this."[115]

By the following day, the videotaped footage gave way to frame-grabbed images. The images that proliferated most widely were part of an Associated Press multishot depiction of the plumes of smoke veering erratically across the camera's frame. One or more of the images appeared on the front pages of nearly every U.S. newspaper. The *New York Times* printed one image on an inside page as part of a seven-shot sequence titled "The Last Moments." The *Washington Post* ran one image twice: once on its front page and once inside as part of a six-shot sequence, four of which showed the process of the shuttle's disintegration. An additional eight-shot sequence, provided by NASA, showed close-up shots of the flames engulfing the fuel tank. Significantly, the shots appeared repeatedly across the same issue of various newspapers as well as on subsequent days: for instance, both the *New York Times* and *Los Angeles Times* showed eight images of the shuttle's disintegration, two of them twice.[116]

Much of the draw to repetitive display reflected an irrational hope that what was depicted would change. "Oh, my God, this is real," said one observer. "It's not a space movie."[117] The *Washington Post* lamented that "cruel visions, over and over, bring the nightmare home,"[118] but the reality of what had happened was slow in coming. When the Air and Space Museum in Washington, D.C., decided to reair the explosion footage on television sets in the museum's lobby, reporter Richard Cohen charted the museum-goers' persistent disbelief: "The monitor showed the tape of the catastrophic blastoff. A kid in a Superman cap looked into it, uncomprehending. A woman slowly brought her hand up to her face as if to ward off the coming blast and, at the moment, a man's mouth just dropped open."[119] Noting a widespread desire to deny what had happened and see the shuttle instead "continue its upward climb and not disappear," *Washington Post* TV critic Tom Shales commented that "we may not be able to believe that something truly terrible has happened anymore unless we see it six or seven times on television."[120]

Alongside collective disbelief in what the images showed were wavering sentiments about the technology it depicted. As with the *Hindenburg,* it was not immediately clear what had caused the explosion. As numerous theories circulated—faulty decision making, failures in communication, misunderstandings, mechanical failure—the suggestion that NASA had been "too keen to meet a tight launching schedule and rushed ahead despite warnings"[121] resulted in the *Miami Herald* pronouncing "an end of the age of innocence in space" and multiple reports that the *Challenger* had "damaged [the space program's] future."[122] As *U.S. News and World Report* later remarked,

> The disaster was freighted with more than just human tragedy.... We had been watching a mighty symbol of American technology climbing toward the heavens on a pillar of flame. The shuttle was so safe, so reliable, we were told, that NASA could send a teacher along to give televised science lessons from space. Suddenly, all that was left on our TV screens was an awful tangle of rocket-smoke trails. It seemed a terrible confirmation that

all our technology was going awry. America in the middle 1980s was losing its cars and microchips to superior foreign competitors. The one area where we thought we were unchallenged, human space flight, was disintegrating, too.[123]

Tied into U.S. nationalism, patriotism, global competition, the Cold War and embodying remnants of the New Frontier, questions arose about whether the space program had rushed its own demise. Though the accidental nature of the event was front and center to its discussion, many wondered whether the program's enthusiasts had brought the disaster on themselves by doing too much, too fast, like the *Hindenburg*. In particular, as news spread of a meeting the night before the launch in which NASA officials were urged to delay due to cold weather, advice which they ignored, the question of negligence reared its head.[124]

At the same time, again like the *Hindenburg,* journalism's live coverage of the event was a triumph. Hailing the coverage for relaying—and then retelling—a "defining moment for the nation,"[125] journalists—tellingly, not on-the-spot reporters but media and television critics whose role was to evaluate the coverage—praised the immediacy, vividness, and thoroughness of the accident's reportage. Notable was a linking of the coverage to that of other events in U.S. history—the *Hindenburg* disaster; the assassinations of John F. Kennedy, Robert Kennedy, and Martin Luther King; the attack on Pearl Harbor—not similar events but events with similar kinds of coverage, each of which had been depicted by pictures of people about to die. The *Washington Post* summed up the parallel across events best:

> "Oh, the humanity!" Those words, spoken by a weeping radio announcer as he witnessed the explosion and fire that claimed the dirigible *Hindenburg* nearly 50 years ago, must have come to the minds of some people yesterday as they watched the terrible short flight of the space shuttle *Challenger*. For a few moments that announcer in New Jersey in 1937 was doing his best as a journalist, describing a disaster that was to prove a turning point in the history of aviation. But suddenly he was overcome by the sight of fellow human beings dying. The radio and television journalists who brought the first word of yesterday's loss were similarly affected. For a few moments they were, like the rest of us, shaken and horrified by what they had seen, by what was the last thing they or any of the rest of us expected to see: the deaths of seven people we thought were beginning a routine voyage into space.

Other news organizations invoked the parallel in other ways. The *San Francisco Chronicle* ran a reaction to the explosion from *Hindenburg* radio announcer

Herbert Morrison, while some newspapers showed the *Hindenburg*'s picture alongside the *Challenger* image. The *Boston Globe* recalled multiple events that all featured "images that flickered on television [and] cannot be forgotten.[126]

No surprise, then, that this image of presumed death traveled onward in time. A version of the photo inhabited nearly every collection of photojournalism's high moments. In 1996 it inspired a memorial that took the "twisted Y of the contrails formed by the solid rocket boosters as they diverged, a graphic depiction of vast power gone berserk" as its architectural impulse. Today it continues to illustrate the Web pages of multiple news sites and social networking sites detailing what happened in 1986.[127]

Like that of the *Hindenburg*, the *Challenger* image worked because it invited and sustained evolving and contradictory responses to what it depicted without overpowering the public with graphic detail. It facilitated initial grief over the shuttle's loss, which gave way to praise for the explosion's live coverage and questions about the continued viability of the space program. Like the *Hindenburg*, the *Challenger* explosion facilitated an engagement with two technologies—one legitimating media triumph, the other cementing a downward turn for space travel. Ushering in a new period of doubt about the viability of space exploration and hailing the capacity of the news media to record what had happened, similarities in form were celebrated at the expense of differences in distressing content. As space travel drew uncertainty and concern, journalism drew celebration; the laudatory capacity to see was coupled with the disbelief and disappointment that seeing engendered.

Accidental Death: Columbia

Seventeen years later, coverage of the explosion of the *Columbia* space shuttle followed the parameters set in place by both the *Hindenburg* and *Challenger* disasters. The *Columbia* shuttle broke up on reentry into the earth's atmosphere on February 1, 2003, and its explosion killed all seven astronauts on board immediately. As the shuttle slowed on reentry, minutes shy of reaching its destination at the Kennedy Space Center in Florida, a last verbal relay— "Roger, uh"—was followed by silence and then static. As NASA officials scrambled to figure out what had happened, debris had already begun to fall across East Texas and Louisiana.

The *Columbia*'s reentry had been scheduled as a photo opportunity for journalists, but it did not excite the public in the way that both the *Hindenburg* and *Challenger* had. While the *Challenger* explosion had set skeptics in motion about the space program's viability, by 2003 space travel had multiple doubters. The reentry was thus less charged, involved fewer bystanders, and drew less journalistic attention than had been the case earlier. MSNBC was the only cable channel providing live coverage, and CNN had asked ABC's Dallas affiliate—WFAA-TV—to shoot footage of the shuttle as it passed over Texas. That request turned, in CNN's words, a "beauty shot" into a "telling piece of tape that captured the moment of disintegration."[128]

Largely thanks to the Internet, word spread quickly that the shuttle was in trouble. News organizations turned to marathon coverage, as professional and amateur photographers and cameramen across two states trained their cameras on the sky. TV viewers were immediately shown footage of a white streak flashing across a clear blue sky and then breaking into pieces. Though the verbal story continued to be updated throughout the day, that visual sequence did not change, showing the shuttle's last moments "over and over again, too many times to count—but such is the tradition of national tragedies on live television. It's as if the images have to be seen repeatedly to be believed."[129] From the beginning, the story was crafted through its subjunctive voice, and this helped because by mid-afternoon the broadcast media had run out of new angles. In a bid to trump their competitors, they reverted instead to "the catchy graphics packages, the dreaded parade of marginal 'experts' and endless hours of pointless speculation from talking heads."[130] One Knight Ridder reporter later admitted that two stories needed coverage—" 'How did it happen?' and 'how could it happen?' The latter, he said, was 'the better story.' "[131] Thus speculative and imaginary trajectories of action surfaced across the media: *Slate* magazine revisited a two-month long online thread that had tracked the shuttle's preexplosion progress, which read "almost like a dark novel, full of foreboding clues to the pending disaster."[132]

Newspapers and newsmagazines, many of which now sported online sites, sprinted into the story almost immediately. Multiple newspapers put out extra editions in the middle of the day; *Florida Today,* which served the local community around the space center, put out two extras—one at 1.30 P.M. and one at 5.30 P.M. Other newspapers produced special pages, special sections, and lists of stories online before the newspapers themselves were published.[133]

Following a "blueprint" set in place after the coverage of the 9/11 attacks of 2001, the Internet shaped the *Columbia*'s reporting in powerful ways. It offered multiple additional sources of information, valuable in particular once broadcast news began repeating itself. It also opened the unfolding story to journalists and nonjournalists alike. Google News had more than six hundred *Columbia*-related stories within hours of the explosion. NASA had launched a new Web portal the night before the accident, which received a record 49 million hits within the first twenty-four hours after the disaster, while an Internet site specializing in saturation reporting on space travel—space.com—saw its visitors increase tenfold during the day. MSNBC ran a direct link with NASA-TV, and newspapers like the *Washington Post* set up discussion groups for readers. At sites like cyberjournalist.net, assignmenteditor.com, poynter.org, slate. com, lostremote.com, and others aggregated explosion-related coverage—offering pointers on where to find debris, collections of videos and photos, and biographical material on the astronauts and the shuttle—bloggers tackled the disaster energetically, updating links and providing sidebars to the main story: BoingBoing's Doctorow, for instance, posted a photo of a Dallas road sign that implored the public to "CALL POLICE TO REPORT SPACE SHUTTLE DEBRIS," e-bay sported a short-lived auction for "shuttle debris," and bloggers offered an animated map of the shuttle's debris trail.[134]

Convergence meant that the coverage at points took on unpredictable shape. The regional New England Cable News (NECN) showed pictures of the debris before the networks, because one of its news executives knew where to find them online. An Associated Press prewrite about the shuttle's reentry had the *Columbia* streaking into a landing rather than exploding, largely because the editors at washingtonpost.com neglected to take it off the Web site once the story veered off-course. As the sheer volume of information increased, stories moved into long lists of related items and disappeared by the next day, though the sites remained cluttered with pop-up ads. Automated news sorting went off when the algorithms of Google News missed keeping the *Columbia* explosion on its primary news screen. Nonetheless, as one reporter later remarked, "Convergence wasn't some lofty ideal on February 1....The *Columbia* story was a watershed" of information for all those who cared to look online.[135]

As the story moved aggressively across the mediated environment, it moved increasingly beyond the grasp of professional journalists. As one *Boston Globe* columnist later remarked, "Much of the reporting was done not by journalists but by ordinary citizens—witnesses, video camera owners, and law enforcement officials."[136] Though the initial broadcast images were taken by WFAA-TV in Dallas, amateur photographers and camerapersons bolstered the professional images with their own. Still photos taken by two Texan amateur photographers—Scott Lieberman and Jason Hutchinson—were distributed by the Associated Press within hours. Their digital images, strikingly similar to each other, showed the vapor trails shooting across the sky at jagged angles across the horizon, and one or the other topped the covers, front pages, broadcasts, and online sites of nearly every U.S. newspaper, newsmagazine, newscast, and online news site. Said one AP executive of the Lieberman image, "I have never seen a single image get such universal front page play. It is the digital image that played around the world." The photos showed seven or eight white smoke trails streaking across the sky, although the vapor trails were not particularly definitive. Simultaneously described as "unforgettable" and "oddly empty," both images told viewers "next to nothing until we fill [it] up with words."[137]

And yet, news organizations displayed both images repeatedly—alone and together, in sequenced and singular forms. A special edition of *U.S. News and World Report* featured ten pages of images in its fifty-page issue, and *Time,* showing Lieberman's image on its cover, increased its national print run by

51 percent. The *New York Times* featured a lone shot of the *Columbia* on its front page and twice more on inside pages—part of a three-shot sequence of radar images of the explosion and as part of a four-shot sequence of the vapor trails. The corresponding online news sites featured an even larger number of still photos. The *Orlando Sentinel,* closely following the story because of the city's proximity to the Kennedy Space Center, had an eight-page extra on the streets within four hours of the explosion and a twenty-eight-page special section, featuring multiple pictures, before the end of the day, later winning one of the Society of Professional Journalists' Sigma Delta Chi awards for best deadline reporting.[138] Alongside the images of trailing smoke were numerous pictures of fallen debris—pieces of the shuttle, an astronaut's helmet, equipment—but no pictures of human remains, corpses, blood, gore or body parts.

This was telling, because unlike the follow-up to the *Challenger* explosion, body parts of the astronauts surfaced almost immediately. The next day reports recounted how pieces of human torsos had hit the ground in Texas and Louisiana, but none were shown by news organizations. Though scattered pictures suggested body parts among debris,[139] no evidence of human death or suffering was immediately visible in the *Columbia* story. The closest that news organizations came were pictures of NASA workers, members of the FBI, or workers for the Department of Public Safety praying over undepicted human remains.[140] Presuming death, then, remained among journalists the preferred strategy for depicting what had happened, even when more graphic alternative visual documentation might have been secured independently by viewers searching online. Though presumption itself was at times hard to come by—one BBC News report mistakenly incorporated file footage of a shuttle landing safely into its tracking of the *Columbia* disaster—images with an incomplete informational load remained the accident's central visual motif, requiring viewers to engage in extensive interpretive activity to make sense of what they depicted.[141]

Interpretive activity was called for in other ways too, for the shuttle exploded in a field of skepticism. At stake was NASA's image and congressional and public support for the space program. In the years since the *Challenger* accident, journalists had stopped tracking the space program closely, with a distant hook-up press conference scheduled with the *Columbia* astronauts three days before it exploded eliciting the participation of only two journalists. By 2003 many people had stopped caring about outer space and saw the explosion as an unnecessary loss of human life and a waste of public funds and energy. Theories about what had happened—bad decision making, terrorism (facilitated by the confluence of an Israeli astronaut on board and the shuttle's breakdown over Palestine, Texas), tile damage and broken foam insulation, a failure to develop contingency plans once early evidence of tile damage surfaced—were hard to dissociate from bewilderment over how it could have happened again. What the *San Francisco Chronicle* called "cynical, even nasty" readers' letters popped up immediately. The critiques they raised about the space program's viability led editors to openly ponder the fact that people cared less about the *Columbia* than they had about earlier shuttles, leaving the sentiments of one astronaut— that "no human endeavor has inspired our nation and captivated our imagination like space flight...quintessentially American [for] the love of speed and mobility, the hunger to explore new frontiers"—with few takers.[142]

Those who valued continued space travel responded to the criticisms by contextualizing the disaster through an almost apocryphal lens: astronauts wrote columns celebrating the space program's achievements, and some viewers hailed the dead astronauts as "falling from the sky," calling them "God-like" and representing "the best of what we are." NASA took pains to respond to queries promptly and openly, though it was attacked once it denied what became the reigning explanation for the explosion—debris on the shuttle's foam tiles.[143]

Nonetheless, criticism prevailed, best summed up by the *Los Angeles Times* as a "great perversity, willfulness and destructiveness accompanied by an almost undetectable, homeopathic admixture of pure hope and love, an overwhelming stupidity and a perfect faith." *Time* reporter Gregg Easterbrook called for a shutdown of the shuttle program, and the *New York Times* remarked that the explosion "jolted [Americans] out of a sustained period of success and safety in exploring the world outside our planet." The *Philadelphia Inquirer* contextualized the accident against a string of disasters that had dampened American morale. "It's possible that our current grief over the deaths of the *Columbia* astronauts would have been stronger had we not endured the September 11 assaults," wrote the paper's Dick Polman. Suggesting a certain fatigue with the need to respond to repeated disaster, he continued:

> More than ever we understand with visceral clarity that bad things can happen....We will grieve for the astronauts, assign blame—and try to move on. It's in our national character to believe that we are masters of our own fate. And even though our faith has been badly shaken by September 11, we will no doubt strive again, in the spirit of Horatio Alger.[144]

The *Challenger* figured centrally in these parallels, with reporters crafting their stories through the "lessons learned" from the earlier disaster. The *Washington Post, Philadelphia Inquirer,* and *Time* were among those news organizations that posted images of the exploding *Challenger* in their *Columbia* coverage. The *Hindenburg* surfaced as well: recalling the 1937 aerial explosion, the *Los Angeles Times* noted that "if you caught a whiff of déjà vu, join the crowd." Perhaps it was no surprise, then, that the image became associated with a breakdown of the space shuttle program. Just five days after the explosion, the number of reporters attending NASA press conferences dropped by two thirds, and within the year, U.S. president George W. Bush suspended the space shuttle program. In the multiple instances of the images' recycling onward in time, the association between the *Columbia*'s aerial disintegration and the demise of space exploration became routine.[145]

At the same time as the images played a role in articulating the discomfort with space travel, they were again used to prove journalism's mettle. Journalism's capacity to capture the disaster on live television and, thanks to the Internet, to distribute its still and moving images widely and rapidly showed yet again that images of presumed death could powerfully depict the breaking news of death. This is itself curious, for the differences in the *Columbia*'s circumstances from those surrounding the *Hindenburg* or *Challenger* disasters—the centrality of the Internet, the involvement of multiple nonjournalists providing and seeking documentation, and the availability of pictures depicting more graphic aspects of the disaster that were not used—might have suggested a tamped-down version of journalism's celebration of its own breaking news of death. But like the images of earlier aerial explosions, the images of the *Columbia*'s disintegration remain its central depiction, hailed in journalists' professional lore and recycled across time, marked as a high moment of the picture-taking of journalism. Displayed across multiple newspapers, news magazines, newscasts, books, Web sites, and other memory work, images of the *Columbia* breaking apart yet again underscore the "as if" not only of the event but of journalism's role in it.[146]

Thus the *Columbia*'s coverage closely followed the template already set in place with both the *Hindenburg* and the *Challenger*. Across multiple communication technologies, the depiction of aerial death remained the same. A focus on the repeated visual display of a technological fiasco midair, a reliance on the public's presumption of death, the absence of people dying or dead, a triumph of the news media, and questions raised about the safety of air travel provided a familiar context in which to display the image. Left unaddressed was the degree to which form could push aside offending content, made all the more evident across a different mediated environment that made this coverage less of a journalistic triumph than was claimed.

In all three cases of accidental death—the *Hindenburg*, the *Challenger* and the *Columbia*—visual coverage migrated from a wide-ranging repository of various kinds of images to a picture of presumed death that required the public to complete the unseen deaths of invisible persons. Focusing on the faulty machine of transport that brought people to their deaths as the stand-in image for understanding what had happened, these disasters worked well with images of presumed death because death was not expected in the context of the larger narrative about progress and technical advancement. While the loss of human life was regrettable, the technological setback was equally mourned, and contradictory responses to its accidental nature—Was it truly an accident? Could it have been prevented?—made death's visualization a further exacerbation of what was already broadly troubling about the disaster itself. The "as if" thus offered a fitting choice of depiction, encouraging the public to engage in extensive interpretive work—through the imagination, the emotions, contingency—so as to complete what was not seen as people struggled to give the event meaning. Pushing form over content, these images of presumed death thus accommodated the entertainment of unsettled sentiments regarding the prevalent technologies of the time, and what they suggested about those who used and viewed them.

Intentional Death: Presumed Death on 9/11

The decision to depict intentional disaster by images that call on the public to presume death is revealing of the larger opportunistic strategies through which news images can be shaped, because their absence of causality facilitates a diminished recognition of the intentional nature of certain disasters. For instance, images of the 1991 war in the Persian Gulf resembled spectacle in the most fundamental sense of the term: facilitating viewers' presumptions of undepicted and inanimate death, computer-driven sensors showed an antiseptic war that resembled a computer game more than a battlefield, and as sensors tracked the pathways of the smart bombs on their way to wreaking destruction, viewers were given little sense of the devastation and human loss they caused.[147]

Perhaps nowhere was the reliance on viewers to presume death as aptly represented as in the depictions of the September 11, 2001, attacks on the World Trade Center and the Pentagon.[148] As three separate planes hit their targets, some 3,000 persons perished in less than ninety minutes. Because the World Trade Center attack occurred in the midst of the nation's media capital, camera crews and news photographers "all had ample time to capture the most horrific moments."[149]

The widespread visualization of these moments—captured in real time across multiple platforms of the digitally mediated environment—matched the vivid horror of spectacle with a clear inability to read its cues. Fundamental questions about the intentional nature of what had happened—Who had done this? Why? To what end?—received no address in the initial rush to cover the event. But the familiar form of that coverage encouraged contingency, the imagination, and the emotions as a means of engaging with what people saw, regardless of whether or not they understood it.

The attacks began at 8.48 A.M. An American Airlines flight from Boston crashed into the North Tower of the World Trade Center. Seventeen minutes later, a United Airlines flight, also from Boston, barreled into the South Tower. After smoking and lighting on fire in multiple places, both towers collapsed—one after another—before 10.30 A.M. In between, terrified people on the ground escaped the disaster's wake. Though planes also crashed in close sequence into both the Pentagon and a wooded area in Shanksville, Pennsylvania, most coverage centered on the New York City attacks.

The attacks' brutality, nearness, scope, and scale—and the disbelief they provoked over their unfolding as intentional acts of terror—pushed the news media into immediate response. As one newspaper columnist put it: "I needed facts in the confusion following the attacks, but even more I needed stories, narratives that ordered experience and instructed me on how to behave in the face of tragedy...I needed to know what others thought and felt."[150] Within minutes, broadcast coverage went wall to wall, as the four major TV networks, agreeing to share video and satellite footage, suspended commercials and regularly scheduled programming. The information came in so fast that CNN started running several lines of text from multiple threads simultaneously across the bottom of its screen. Radio stations broadcast live television news feeds.[151] Newspapers printed special late editions—the *Chicago Tribune* two in one day—and newsmagazines published special midweek vignettes. Biweekly newspapers turned into weeklies. The event's coverage in each case underscored its sheer intensity: broadcasts were continuous and live, editions came earlier and grew in size, headlines were bigger and bolder, pictures were more prevalent. Precedents were broken: for the first time in its nineteen-year history *USA Today* dropped its traditional front-page ears, entertainment cable and satellite stations showed news clips, National Public Radio broadcast live for more than a day, the *Atlanta Constitution* ran a front page with only one story, and newspapers ran multiple pictures prominently.[152]

Relatively new to the journalistic environment, the Internet emerged as one shaper of 9/11's coverage. Though trade overviews later called the coverage "a convergence story," those managing the Internet were somewhat unprepared for what ensued. WNBC's Internet partner—feedroom.com—provided live footage of the area, which, significantly focused on the towers following the attack of the first plane and thus captured the second as it happened. But upsets to the Internet's infrastructure—key here was the severing of long distance telephone lines with the World Trade Center's collapse—compromised multiple online relays at precisely the moment they were most needed. Information seeking was so unprecedented—in Stuart Allan's view, "news sites, which the day before had been counting their 'hits' in the hundreds of thousands per hour, suddenly experienced millions"—that news sites, the Web sites of the affected airlines and businesses in the disaster area shut down, cnn.com, abc.com, cbs.com, and msnbc.com, among them. At the same time, however, hundreds of nonnews sites, such as slashdot.com and scripting.com, stepped in to facilitate information sharing, and they encouraged onlookers to post their own eyewitness reports, still photos and videos. Though one trade report later noted that the Internet mostly followed the lead of television, which remained the primary source of information during the attacks' early hours, these interactive platforms offered an important opportunity to engage with the disaster; once news sites resumed functioning, they too created sections for viewers to post their images and stories. Thus, though at first uneven, the Internet established its instrumentality for sharing information and community in the wake of the attacks, to be used as a blueprint for covering later unsettled events, as discussed earlier in the case of the *Columbia* shuttle explosion.[153]

Across the mediated environment, pictures—moving and still—were everywhere. As television relentlessly replayed eclipsed footage of the attacks—"it looks like a movie," said NBC's Katie Couric—and online news sites filled with the photos and videos of onlookers, the print media published extra editions bursting with photography. Pictures came in many shapes and sizes, covering full pages, half pages, and quarter pages and stretching across pullouts three-pages wide with simple broad captions and little extraneous text. For instance, the *New York Times* featured more than fifty photos in its front section the day after the attacks, a tendency echoed elsewhere, compared with the twenty or so normally displayed. Even one month later, the use of photos remained proportionately high, when a full fifty-two photos graced the paper's front section and accompanying reportage. Similarly, in its first full issue after the attacks, *Newsweek* featured ten separate double and triple page photographic spreads only four days after it had put out its own independent midweek photographic supplement. Certain newspapers initiated new features to accommodate the marked interest in the event's visual representation, such as the *New York Times'* "Portraits of Grief," a memorial tribute to the dead with photographs and short vignettes about each person, and "A Nation Challenged," a special section devoted to the stories and photographs of 9/11. Pictures on theInternet, displayed as galleries of onlookers' images, revealed new practices among viewers: as one online editor said, "People really wanted to look at images in their own time, contemplating and absorbing the tragedy in ways that the rush of television could not accommodate." In one picture editor's words, 9/11 "caused a sea change" in the then-current display and use of pictures.[154]

But more pictures did not necessarily mean more or more varied information. Though stories described the loss of life in 9/11 in detail, only two graphic photos—one of a severed hand in the *New York Daily News* the day after the attacks and a photo of a dead chaplain being carried out of the towers—were published.[155] Depictions of body parts, blood, and gore were generally nowhere to be found. Pictures instead targeted the site of the attacks—both during and after their unfolding, survivors, and people witnessing the destruction. The same images tended to be shown over and over. One magazine published eighteen separate images of people running from the World Trade Center in the same issue. Footage and still photos of the planes striking the towers were shown repeatedly across broadcasts, print, and online media. Even the Internet—which made it possible for the public to share its own pictures—grouped them in thematic galleries organized around the towers, the destruction, and the survivors. As the names of the victims became known, their pictures—taken in calmer times—proliferated too across the Web as memorial tributes to the dead.[156]

The play to a narrowed visual aesthetic is telling, for in much the same way that the images of 9/11 offered repeated depictions of familiar scenes, so too did the disaster's verbal accounts begin to repeat themselves. Stunned by the intentional nature of the attacks and the associated fact that neither the U.S. political establishment nor the news media had seen them coming, journalists, news executives, officials, politicians, and viewers all struggled to make sense of what had happened. Disbelief prevailed that such attacks could happen in the United States: as the *New York Time's* Caryn James succinctly observed, "After the terror attacks, stunned and baffled 'Why do they hate us?' articles flooded the news media, addressing a public that had been blinkered to what other parts of the world were thinking." Questions about American imperialism, culture, exceptionalism, and foreign policy in the Middle East, among others, all reared their heads. But even as the coverage stretched across weeks and months, the full context for understanding the intentional nature of the attacks did not play centrally across the U.S. news media. Instead, multiple news organizations offered largely patriotic and ethnocentric explanations of the rationale and reasoning behind the attacks. As one observer said, the U.S. news media are "reflecting a mood of patriotism rather than informing viewers of the complex, sometimes harsh realities they need to know." That narrowness seemed especially prevalent on television, where in the *New York Times'* view, "television's cautious approach has turned into knee-jerk pandering to the public." Attending to the larger questions underlying the attacks seemed to many journalists an exercise in futility, as CNN president Walter Isaacson implied when he claimed that "in this environment...if you get on the wrong side of public opinion, you are going to get into trouble." Because viewers were "in no mood to listen to views they dismiss as either loopy or treasonous," journalists tended not to address the broad stakes of global risk that rested at the heart of the disaster. In Silvio Waisbord's view, this pushed them toward safe cultural and political narratives of patriotism and heroism instead, as a way of minimizing the unsettledness that the attacks induced.[157] The narrowed visual aesthetic thus mirrored the narrowed verbal interpretation that the news media provided.

But this did not hinder journalists' ability to celebrate themselves. As the event unfolded, they lost no time in evaluating how they had responded, and most focused on their immediacy of their initial coverage of the attacks rather than the inadequacy of their interpretations later on. Already by October, the American Press Institute published a seventy-five-odd-page booklet for crisis reporting "because the kind of advice we offer...will be of value if we ever have to do this again." Public forums ran symposia outlining journalism's role following acts of terror, and trade journals—like *Editor and Publisher* and the *American Journalism Review*—ran overviews of coverage they called "stunning" and "comprehensive." The *Columbia Journalism Review* pushed aside its own anniversary issue to accommodate the story. Because the immediacy of live coverage was key to these positive appraisals, television received high marks: one CBS news executive trumpeted "the networks for knitting the country together," ABC's Peter Jennings likened TV coverage to a campfire, when "people pulled the wagons around, and sat down and discussed what was going on and tried to understand it," and the *New York Times* praised television as a "lifeline to what was happening." Not surprisingly, the coverage of 9/11 topped the journalism awards ceremonies in 2002: the Peabody awards went to ABC and NPR; the Pulitzer awards delivered a round of tributes to the coverage of September 11, with the *New York Times* winning a record six prizes—one for "A Nation Challenged," one for the *Times'* Web site, and two for photography—and coverage of the attacks received eight of the fourteen awards given for journalism that year.[158]

The celebration of the disaster's live coverage makes it all the more notable that it gravitated to one visual motif—the towers under attack. Images of the burning World Trade Center buildings, filled with individuals who were not visualized but poised in an imaginary or presumed space on the brink of death—not only prevailed at the time but in memory too. Its suggestiveness—depicting presumed death in buildings on way to collapse rather than people about to die—accommodated those struggling with the attacks' intentional nature without overwhelming them with human gore. Though pictures of people jumping or falling to their deaths, discussed at length in chapter 2, were taken and appeared in the first bursts of coverage, they abruptly disappeared—within hours from television, days from the print media—and reappeared in almost none of the retrospective literature. Instead, drawing from an established motif of crumpled buildings and structural devastation, images of the towers in which people were about to perish took the place of depictions of people themselves about to die.

Images of the towers—functioning as what the *American Journalism Review* later called "a kind of wallpaper"—segmented the larger story of the attacks into neat before and after portions. Portraying multiple points in the process of their destruction—the planes approaching the towers, the planes striking the towers, the towers smoking, the towers alighting on fire, the towers collapsing and crumbling to the ground—they played over and over on television, in the print media, and online. For instance, they appeared on the front pages of most newspapers—85 percent of one collection of papers from that day—and multiple times on inside pages, with some front pages showing a visual sequence of the building crumbling; they graced the covers of multiple journals, including *Newsweek, Time, Business Week,* and *TV Guide;* and they appeared widely

Figure 3.4:
Peter C. Brandt/Getty Images, World Trade Center Towers before Collapsing, September 11, 2001.

online, taken by both journalists and onlookers and used to illustrate the links to the story's rapidly multiplying threads. Taken together, the towers surfaced as the predominant visual marker of the events of 9/11.[159]

One particular mid-sequence shot dominated the visual landscape—a picture of the towers ablaze (fig. 3.4). Freezing the moment at which the towers burned before crumbling prolonged the "as if" aspects of the event's depiction. Showing the fury of rapidly billowing flames as they engulfed the upper quadrant of the towers' sleek structure, viewers could look at the image and improbably hope that things would turn out otherwise, that the buildings would not fall and the people not die. As one viewer said, "I kept looking and looking and wishing that the story would take a different turn." Or, as a *New York Times* columnist commented on a moment in which the tape of the just-struck buildings played backward momentarily from their fiery embrace, "We saw history reverse itself; the building appeared whole, as if in a wishful dream."[160]

Afterward, news executives admitted that the towers offered a more admissible image than the corresponding shots of human gore that were not shown. MSNBC's president said that his staff pushed aside numerous pictures showing blood and body parts to find the more antiseptic images. "We chose not to show a lot," he said. "How more horrifying and graphic can you get than a 110-story building, blowing up and disintegrating before your eyes?"[161] In other words, the about-to-die moment of presumed death took precedence as a motif of the attacks' visual representation from the beginning.

In each case of the towers' display, people needed to suspend what they knew—that the towers did in fact come down, killing all those still trapped inside. And yet playing to the "as if" seemed to provide a degree of comfort. Continually met with incredulity—in MSNBC anchor Brian Williams' words, "It just never ceases to amaze people to watch that piece of videotape" and *Business Week* advised its readers to "close your eyes and try to make the images go away"—journalists gave the images a context borrowed from other events, including the assassination of John Kennedy, the 1972 Munich Olympics hostage crisis, the *Challenger* explosion, the Persian Gulf War, the death of Princess Diana, and the Columbine high school shootings.[162] That inventory of other images of presumed death again rested on the familiarity of the visual trope of impending death, with form pushing a parallel across events with significantly different content.

At the same time as the images of the burning towers were used to illustrate different news stories, they took on additional functions. For instance, an image of the towers on fire was used as a logo by multiple news organizations covering the attacks; the *Philadelphia Inquirer* turned it into a front-page logo already the day after the attacks and then transformed it into a smaller emblem for inside pages during the later days of coverage. United Way featured the burning towers in its advertisements, while the burning towers surfaced one month later as pictures witnessed by onlookers, once photographic exhibits were set up to show still photos from the event. Multiple pictures showed people gazing on the towers or looking at pictures of the towers, offering an additional level of witnessing the disaster.[163]

Images of the burning towers persisted over time, displayed at year's end where, in the *New York Times'* view, "they freeze-frame a calamity so great that the mind struggles, even months later, to comprehend the data being sent by the eyes."[164] Adorning the covers of retrospective memorial volumes, special issues, and Web sites, the towers emblematized the attacks: for instance, the cover of *Newsweek*'s double year-end issue surveyed the year with the single word "September" topping a picture of the burning towers, while the image illustrated the *New York Times* section on "The Year in Pictures." The towers ablaze appeared on both volume covers and the inside pages of numerous books: a Reuters commemorative volume designated 10 percent of its 130 photos to them; in another book—*New York: September 11, 2001*—a full fifth of the total images portrayed the burning or smoking towers. Additionally, the images were affixed to numerous popular cultural artifacts, including calendars, buttons, T-shirts and posters.[165] Though the towers ablaze continue to appear, though less frequently, as in 2008 to mark a *New York Times* article on the attacks' anniversary, they appeared repeatedly across the various "decades in review" retrospectives by multiple news organizations.[166]

Thus the towers invoked a workable combination of the imagination, contingency, and the emotions as responses to an event overflowing with the brute force of reality's depiction and a public inability to understand why it had occurred. As one viewer, trying to take his own photograph of the towers before they collapsed, wrote in the *New York Times:* "It had been a nice shot. And certainly it had been easier to shape the horror into an aesthetic distance and deny the human reality. There was safety in that distance."[167] The formulaic and familiar aspects of the towers' visual representation and their sidestepping of human gore facilitated public exposure to the attacks. By freezing the story at its most porous and suggestive moment and asking people to do no more than presume death, the images prolonged public engagement long enough for them to come to grips with what was being depicted. Even if that did not reflect an understanding of the event's causality and offered no real answer to the lingering questions about America's changed place in the global imaginary, engagement was nonetheless important in its own right.

When Presumption Fuels the "As If"

What does it mean to understand unsettled events through the motif of presumption? Journalism's substitution of physical and structural devastation for unseen people about to die makes sense when considering the role of the subjunctive in the popular imagination. As shown in events as wide-ranging as fire, earthquakes, nuclear bombing, midair explosions, and terror attacks, these depictions draw multiple responses from viewers: they make it possible to engage with an event's visualization without being repulsed by graphic imagery of the dying. They prolong the subjunctive possibility of muting the finality of death and softening its severity with the improbable but strategically useful sentiment that time might thwart death's intention. They offer a continuous reactive loop, by which the public can act out the horror of the moment by imagining, rather than seeing, the countless, nameless, faceless victims who meet their deaths. And they allow viewers to feel as if they are responsibly acting as witnesses to horror, even though they do not attend to its structural conditions, its causality, its purposive nature or its impact.

In all cases, the tragedy comes to be visualized through its "as if" rather than its "as is" dimensions. Offering people a space of contingency, the imagination, and the emotions for as long as they need it, these images postpone the logical acceptance of the about-to-die image's next step in the sequence—death itself. This space facilitates the airing of evolving, contradictory responses to issues broader than the disaster itself, suggesting that the photo's lack of definition facilitates its interpretation in ways that might be wholly variant with each other. That openness, however, itself has strategic value if for no other reason than it facilitates public engagement.

Equally important, the "as if" pushes form over content, where the shape of the trope obscures the distinguishing features of the events being depicted. Whether a disaster is natural, accidental, or intentional is indiscernible, as causality is absent in these images. It is not incidental that the various events portrayed through images of presumed death—the Great Chicago Fire, Hiroshima, the 1906 earthquake, the *Hindenburg* disaster, the *Challenger* and *Columbia* explosions, and 9/11—are invariably compared with each other for their effect, the inhumanity of their mode of death and their journalistic treatment, which is itself repeatedly celebrated.[168] But how similar are they other than their shared reliance on the public's act of presumption in making sense of the images? And what gets lost by virtue of the comparison?

Significantly, the about-to-die representation of presumed death does not disappear as it moves into memory and into what could be a gradual acceptance of the horror of its underlying events. Despite its strategic representativeness for certain kinds of public events, it lingers as a marker of complex events in history, persisting in manifold forms, turning in journalism into prize-winning photos, celebrated images, and even iconic representations that become, in one newspaper's words "defining statements of the events from which they have arisen."[169] Such is the power of the informational load attached to the act of presuming death. For as pictures that remain in memory by offering little definition or detail about the physical events that they depict, these images further a suggestion of impending death at the expense of clearly delineating the circumstances causing death. Blurred are the natural unfolding of the event, the intervention of human agency, and the degree of purposive action. Such images, then, are easily invoked in a wide range of often incompatible and contradictory conversations and debates, where they highlight the anguish of human loss. Their reliance on affect and emotion—and their concomitant corollaries of contingency and the imagination—thereby become powerful impulses for judging action in the public sphere, in a way not always admitted into discussions of the relay of reasoned information. Facilitating exposure and engagement more than understanding, they suggest an alternative mode of response to public events.

All of this means that a subjunctive response to the horrors that images of presumed death embody persists too, lingering as vehicles of the "as if."

To paraphrase Vincent Leo's observations about the photographs of Hiroshima, images of presumed death suggest much but define little. Or as one observer said of the *Columbia* disaster, "The picture of *Columbia* breaking into pieces doesn't do what news shots are supposed to do. It isn't self-explanatory. It doesn't tell the story. It's more an emblem, or a symbol. It's practically abstract."[170] As this chapter has shown, those attributes, at odds with how journalism likes to see itself operate as a project of modernity and a vehicle of reasoned information relay, have nonetheless becomes the trope's strength rather than its failing. The fact that it continues to surface across diverse technologies of news delivery, each providing different kinds of information, suggests that it wields a fundamental salience for the public.

In being "practically abstract," then, images of presumed death carry the meaning of events in a way that allows the public to find a more acceptable understanding of the loss caused by disaster and the reestablishment of equilibrium required in a postdisaster period. Journalism's call to presume death tends to come at the expense of some expected or aspired development—a city thriving, a shuttle landing, a world free of terrorism—and in this regard presumption is a response to sequences of action that go against the grain of anticipation: assumptions of a harmonious blend of nature and civilization are upset when nature rears its head; assumptions of technological mastery are upset when accidents happen; and assumptions of physical safety are undermined when malicious action turns it upside down. In all three cases, death is the unanticipated consequence, yet its visualization—too early, too graphic, and too much—threatens to sidestep the engagement needed in a postdisaster period and so does not appear.

Presuming death, then, is a strategic coping mechanism, an act of interpretation that uses the imagination, the emotions, and contingency so as to coax journalists, news executives, officials, politicians, and viewers beyond their comfort zones enough to show and see suggestive images of death in times of disaster. Though the motif is used by news organizations seeking not to show graphic images, it also plays to those looking for more visual contingency and ambivalence than might be provided by more explicit pictures showing dying or dead individuals. Presuming death may thus provide the act of interpretation that works most effectively in certain types of existential crisis, for it may be as proximate as those who view it can get to the depiction of human loss.

In the best of cases, presuming death draws people into larger debates than what is depicted in the image. In the worst of cases, its images leave open the first draft of history that journalism aims to provide. Either way, images of presumed death make possible a different kind of engagement with the news—both for those who make it and those who receive it. It may be that the coverage of certain kinds of crises functions best by offering no more.

Chapter 4

Possible Death

Images of possible death show more detail of death than do pictures of presumed death, requiring the public to invoke less of contingency, the imagination, and the emotions in engaging with what it sees. Focusing on the human body, these images target people about to die. This greater informational load, however, does not undo their "as if" status, for they remain suggestive, providing no texts confirming that the people depicted do indeed die.

Unlike images of presumed death, which use inanimate objects and landscapes to depict exact moments of catastrophe or devastation, images of possible death depict events whose scope, scale, and magnitude cannot be easily captured at the time of actual death—famine, illness, planned violence, torture, mass extermination, epidemic—all circumstances in which death occurs to multiple individuals over a prolonged period of time. In suggesting the hypothetical death of those depicted, these images build on a synecdochic connection between what they show and what actually transpires: a picture of a person ailing from an advanced case of the swine flu raises the possibility that she dies, but her death is never articulated or confirmed.

Instead, the "as if" in these images draws from the work of inference. People need to complete what the image does not show and offset death's contingency by inferring death from what is depicted. Individuals are shown in ways that suggest that they are about to die—even if they do not in fact die—and the action anticipated beyond the camera's frame is assumed to cause the individual's death—even if it does not actually cause death. Consciously or not, the public must transform the image's denotative aspects—what it actually depicts and what its caption often says it depicts—into a symbolic proxy for what is not shown or said. Images of possible death ask people to infer numerous aspects of an event that they do not see: inferring the death of a villager shown suffering from forced starvation means both assuming a death that is not depicted and assuming the death of the depicted individual, regardless of whether or not it actually occurs. Additionally, viewers need generalize and broaden the impending death to people who are not depicted, extending its significance beyond the picture. Like other images of impeding death, then, the image's "as is" dimensions need to be shunted aside in order to accommodate its subjunctive ones, the "as if" of what is shown. Impending death can be remotely possible, vaguely possible, distinctly possible, or even probable, but it is never certain, and information conveying certainty is not made available by the news organization.

Journalists signal death's possibility by showing endangered or weakened human bodies. Multiple visual cues act as its facilitators: these pictures might show bodily behaviors that suggest fear (widened eyes, clenched lips, a slouching, slinking, or cowered posture, raised eyebrows, furrowed brows and other facial expressions of dread;) sickliness (gauntness and emaciation, pale demeanors, balding heads, shriveled faces, figures lying in fetal positions;) threat (raised fists, guns, overbearing posture, rifle butts, and looks of menace;) and support (embraces of caregivers, uniforms of doctors or relief workers, religious symbols, and hospital beds). Verbal cues necessarily suggest that death is imminent, even if they stop short of pronouncing the deaths of those in the picture.

For instance, this Pulitzer Prize–winning photo of war-torn Rwanda, taken by AP photographer Jean-Marc Boujou in 1994, offered a close-up of a man as he lay prostrate on the ground, his hand cradling his bony and emaciated face in a gesture that suggested a total depletion of energy (fig. 4.1).

The caption outlined the photo's synecdochic connection to the larger issue of civilian well-being in the region:

A man lies starving at a makeshift health clinic in Ruhango, 30 miles southwest of Kigali, Rwanda, Monday, June 6, 1994. Thousands of civilians caught in fighting between government troops and the Rwanda Patriotic Front (RPF) rebels have taken refuge in Ruhango, but have no access to sufficient medical care. Doctors say that 20–50 people die every day in Ruhango from disease and hunger. (AP Photo/Jean-Marc Boujou)

AP titled the photo "Rwandan Refugee Starving," though Boujou himself had no role in captioning the photograph.[1] The title was itself misleading, for the photo was about more than it revealed, suggesting not only the effects of

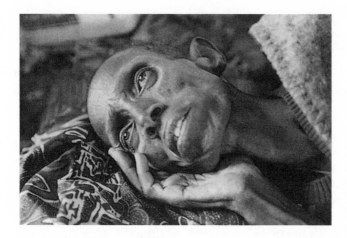

Figure 4.1:
Jean-Marc Boujou/AP,
"Rwandan Refugee,"
June 6, 1994.

starvation but also death from civil war. But the caption too was telling for what it did not offer—no name, no identity, and no suggestion of whether the man depicted was one of those who were dying daily in the region. Typical of the summarizing titles or captions associated with images of possible death, which recount the impending death of large numbers of individuals though not necessarily those shown, it suggested that the person still living in the picture was believed to be dying—and by the time the photo appeared was probably already dead. These pictures are generally presented with broad attributes that push aside first-order informational detail; the people they depict are symbolic surrogates, remaining anonymous, inarticulate, largely unidentified, usually unnamed, and often without any characteristic other than their positioning as representatives of certain groups. Typical captions recount "a starving Ethiopian refugee" or "a mother of five lies dying of Ebola."[2]

The formulaic nature of these cues makes images of possible death useful tools for nonjournalists—humanitarian workers, prosecutorial teams, members of truth commissions, politicians, NGOs, celebrities—who build on the original journalistic relay for use in channels outside of journalism. While the lack of a definitive time frame is problematic for journalism, as it complicates the ability to make death newsworthy within the timetables and temporal registers of periodic news delivery, it makes images of possible death particularly workable as a mode of visualizing continuing news, where the story still unfolds. It also makes the images amenable to memory work, with photographers themselves often sanctioning the borrowing of their pictures: in 1997, for instance, Don McCullin agreed for his pictures of abuse in Cyprus, Biafra, the Congo, and elsewhere to be distributed by Amnesty International, years after they had originally appeared in the news media. As journalism has expanded across evolving platforms of technological relay and exchanges of information have become easier between journalism and the rest of the information environment, the capacity to recycle these images in various ways has grown.

What Does Possible Death Look Like?

Since the earliest days of journalism, images of possible death have ranged across the multiple unsettled events that were difficult to visualize at the time of their unfolding. They surfaced among some of journalism's earliest pictures of widespread illness, when drawings of the Black Death, appearing in the beginnings of the illustrated press, depicted individuals across Europe gravely ill, dying, and dead from the bubonic plague; these images typically portrayed large courtyards cluttered with individuals in various stages of physical decay.[3] Not long afterward, pictures of the wounded during the U.S. Civil War helped those distant from its battlefields visualize the reality of war (fig. 4.2).

This front cover of *Frank Leslie's Illustrated Newspaper* showed eight wood engravings of emaciated former Union prisoners at Andersonville in 1864. Shown so as to prove the willful malevolence of the Confederate high command, the images of the unnamed soldiers with rotting limbs, vacant faces, and thin, disjointed bodies made their death possible, if not probable. As Vicki Goldberg observed, "They are not yet dead, for their eyes still look at us—sad, resigned, passive—but their bodies waver on the way to the grave." When the images appeared in *Harper's Weekly,* the illustrated journal pronounced them "photographs from death in life…No evidence is like these pictures." The nonjournalistic use of images of possible death dates to one of the earliest known human rights campaigns, a crusade by British evangelicals at the turn of the twentieth century to stop the atrocities then rampant in the Congo Free State.[4]

In offering sufficient information to stimulate the imagination and the emotions about what is shown but not so much as to close off variant—and contingent—interpretations of what it means, these images, which stretch across the journalistic and nonjournalistic visual relays of epidemic, war, and human rights violations, provide the inferential latitude that encourages engagement and accommodates evolving responses to what is seen. That latitude makes the images valuable to news organizations needing to depict circumstances that cause large numbers of unconfirmed deaths over a prolonged period of time and helps explain why they often surface in unsettled events that are still unfolding. Not only are such circumstances difficult to depict—how does one show the start of famine?—but their temporal sequencing, spread, scope, and scale remain undepictable by any single picture. Rather, they take on clarity over time, as the number of deaths in an unsettled event accumulate and become public.

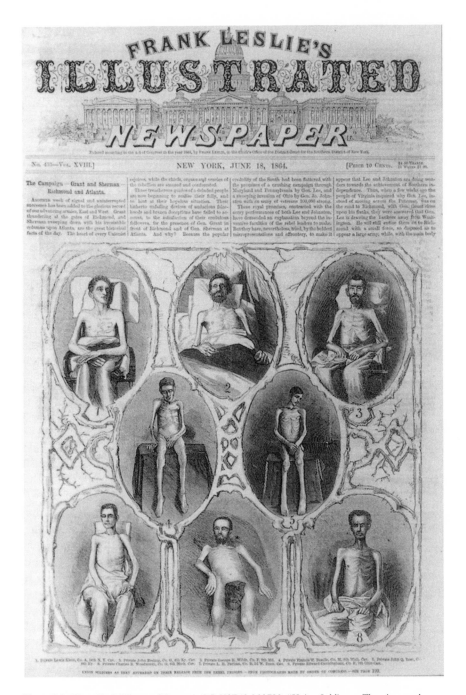

Figure 4.2: Uncredited/Library of Congress, LC-USZ62-130792, "Union Soldiers as They Appeared on Their Release from the Rebel Prisons," *Frank Leslie's Illustrated Newspaper*, June 18, 1864.

Unlike the breaking news of images of presumed death, images of possible death are thus often retrospective displays, coming at a time when viewers already know that death is more widespread than any single image can show. Functioning less to drive new information—about famine, mass extermination, or epidemics—than to reinforce information already in hand, these depictions draw power from the fact that what is understood from the photo is always larger than what is depicted. Acting as what Robert Hariman and John Lucaites called the "individuated aggregate,"[5] they tend to be among the most formulaic about-to-die photos: they often rely on close-ups, frontal stares, and intimately framed visages bearing high expressive appeal, and on aesthetic juxtapositions of anonymous and unnamed individuals standing in for the groups who can most easily carry the symbolic message they embody—children, babies, the elderly, and prison guards, relief workers, soldiers, members of militias. Equally important, images of possible death regularly activate nonjournalists involved in humanitarian efforts, public relations, prosecutorial tribunals, and governmental action to ensure that they get seen.

Though death remains at best possible here, these images nonetheless position people about to die in ways that cue viewers to death by nature, accident, or design. While images of presumed death collapse differences by focusing on inanimate structures and mechanistic devices that look the same in each, the focus here on the human body facilitates a distinction that is tempered by what Elaine Scarry called a fundamental referential instability associated with the hurt or endangered body.[6] Central aspects of the picture's compositional framing—Does the person about to die look fearful or sickly? Do other objects or figures constrain or console the person facing death?—help signal the difference.

Two images taken during the 1980s, discussed here because they signal natural death through bodily frailty and intentional death through bodily harm, reveal how patterned death's possibility can be. Though both underscore the body's centrality, one image uses the body to suggest a physical shutdown already in process while the other positions the body as the receptacle for harmful actions from others. Unlike images of presumed death, where bodies are absent, images of possible death can only work if bodies are made visible enough for viewers to ascertain some incipient danger to their well-being. And yet the actual danger of death is inferred, not delineated, which suggests that multiple vagaries of interpretation can ensue.

Bodily frailty and bodily harm do not work entirely in the same fashion: cues of bodily frailty suggest that the depicted individuals are afflicted with some kind of physical malaise that naturally or accidentally leads to death. Cues of bodily harm suggest that the depicted individuals face undepicted circumstances which cause death intentionally—mass extermination, extreme incarceration, torture, violence, physical mishandling. Though the conditions of bodily frailty may themselves result from strategic military or political action, it is the effect of physical malaise that is seen as hastening an individual's demise. In both cases, the individuals are depicted in ways that seem to suggest death as the primary if not the only eventuality, and the body—either in decay or under threat—is the relay for driving home its possibility.

Both pictures—one of a child languishing from famine in Uganda, the other of a confrontation between students and soldiers in China—signal widespread deaths befalling large numbers of people across time in locations far from the settings regularly covered by the U.S. news media, a circumstance that made the images good candidates for suggesting the scale and scope of impending death's temporal unfolding. Both pictures relied as much on nonjournalistic venues for their display as on the news media (fig. 4.3).

The first image from Uganda rested within then-consonant parameters for showing and seeing famine—nongraphic, suggestive, anonymous, generalizable. Taken in 1980 at a refugee camp in the rural Karamoja district of northeastern Uganda, the picture targeted a region known for its dry and dusty climate, frequent droughts, and primitive lifestyle, an area regarded by many as "backward and troublesome."[7] Populated largely by nomads whose wandering had been curtailed for security reasons under the government of Idi Amin, the region had endured a series of broader misfortunes alongside frequent bouts of drought. The ascent of raiding between rival groups, cattle-stealing, thefts, and killing by armed bandits, and general political instability undermined the region and helped turn the drought into a full-fledged famine.

Against these circumstances, the famine that developed in 1980 was brutal: it killed nearly a quarter of the Karamojong population and over half its infants in less than a year, making it one of the worst famines in history.[8] Even today, its reverberations are still felt as longstanding ethnic violence further undermines the potential for stability in the distressed and barren region.[9]

This image, taken in April of that year, was aesthetically jarring in its choice of compositional features. The image juxtaposed two hands, unattached to faces, individuals or identities, yet clearly drawn from different populations— one black, frail, tiny, childlike, and painfully malnourished, the other white, adult, and robust. Missing from the image were names, faces, full torsos, and settings. Though the public never learned whose black hand they saw and therefore never learned whether the child lived or died, they did learn that the white hand belonged to a missionary. Driving home the redemptive power of the consolation being depicted and drawing viewers into the possibility of engagement, the image worked regardless of what it did not reveal: what people did not know did not matter, for the hand stood in for the hands of millions who had already perished. What was important was that the shriveled fragility and skeletal appendage of a Ugandan child, made smaller by the proximity of the missionary's healthy hand, raised the specter of possible death and sparked responsiveness among those who saw it. As Marcel Marceau

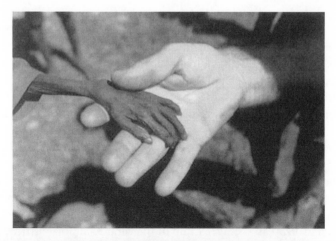

Figure 4.3: Mike Wells/Aspect Picture Library, "'Hands' Uganda." April 1980; Stuart Franklin for Magnum Photos, "Tiananmen Square–Revolution," Beijing, China, June 4, 1989.

commented on seeing the picture, "That terrible symbol, that dried-up hand of a black child, a small faded hand like a leaf in the palm of a strong, living white hand, the compassion of well-meaning but impotent energy in the face of death."[10]

The image was not immediately well received. The photographer's news organization held up its display for five months, and it was not widely published by the news media, presumably because it was taken before attention generated by TV footage in 1982 fueled public attention to the African famine. But when it was entered into news image competitions, reportedly by the same news organization that had sat on the image without publishing it, it won its photographer, Michael Wells, the World Press Photo award of the year.

After it won the award, the image began an active second life in campaigns against hunger and famine. Rumored to have moved the United Nations and other agencies to intervene with provisions to the Horn of Africa, its appeal was notable, topping numerous lists of the most powerful photographs and reappearing in retrospectives on photography.[11] Its relevance was further enhanced in the late 2000s, when famine in Karamojo reared its head again. Then recycled aggressively across the Internet, it was used to illustrate blogs on famine in Africa, discussions of iconic photographs, and attempts to intensify peacemaking efforts in Uganda. The Web site www.friendsforpeaceinafrica.org, for example, used the photo in 2009 to warn people about a resurgence of famine in the region, through a depiction taken nearly thirty years earlier.[12]

Flush with the force of contingency and implication over evidentiary fact, the photo suggested but did not depict human death. Bodily frailty in this case acted as a suggestive cue of death by nature. Its formal attributes and its play to the imagination, the emotions, and contingency dominated the content of the shot, which though stopping short of a fuller depiction of the child nonetheless remained distressing.

The second image depicted one of a series of confrontations between students and the military in China during the spring and summer of 1989. One such demonstration took place that June, in Beijing's massive Tiananmen Square. As thousands of students protested human rights violations, the government called in troops to quell the protests. What began peacefully ended in the wounding, incarceration, and death of thousands. Though numerous images of people being beaten, constrained, or lying dead were published, one set of images, captured on video and separately by three still photographers, seemed to encapsulate the event best.

The images offered a simple, contained juxtaposition of man and military machine. A single unnamed young man, plainly dressed in black pants and a white shirt and holding a shopping bag, stood down a long and overbearing convoy of tanks. The slight figure's fate was unclear, for the next shot of the sequence—Do the tanks stay halted or move forward? Does the man run away or get killed?—remained undepicted. Significantly, not even the video of the event offers a clear visual depiction of whether the man about to die in fact met his death. All of the footage and still photos were taken from afar, as photographers—ABC and BBC crews and still photographers from the Associated Press, Magnum, and UPI—stood on the balconies and in the windows of the nearby Beijing Hotel as they took their pictures. The video showed a sequence that remained as ambiguous as the scene captured by still images: the soldiers on the tanks fired warning shots and then began a blocking exercise with the protester, who climbed halfway up the nose of the first tank and then descended; friends were seen coaxing him to leave, and after a few minutes he yielded his position and the tanks continued onward. Though that sequence still left open what happened to the man in the event's aftermath, particularly whether or not he was taken into custody and killed, the still image that persevered provided even less information.

One of the event's photographers proclaimed his dissatisfaction with the photo's ambivalence, noting that it required a "bit of a reach [that was] too dependent on what people are prepared to read into it...you can go off into disparate vagaries."[13] But by freezing the action at the moment in which the man's fate—survival or death—remained unknown, its force aligned precisely with that typical of about-to-die images, for it coaxed public engagement without overwhelming graphic content. Additionally, by not being clear, it enabled people to entertain numerous interpretations of what it depicted. Even if the sequence of action it implied was not definitive, the bodily harm signaled in the image was. Its juxtaposition of the vulnerable figure of the man, shown with his back to the camera, and the ominous and threatening positioning of the line of tanks—three or four in number, depending on the image—left no ambiguity about the threat being communicated. Though one observer later remarked, "It is not clear what [the man's] name is or what happened to him after he took his stand," reports from that day's incident in Tiananmen Square recounted that thousands were killed, a toll added to even larger numbers who had died on earlier days.[14] As with other images of impending death, then, a familiar form for suggesting impending death prevailed over the uncomfortable content of death itself.

That same day and in the days that followed, the images of Tiananmen Square generated a literal media blitz, plastered across the news media and pushing aside other more graphic images showing death and detainment. Because the photographers had been located at the same place—the Beijing Hotel—the images they produced were highly similar. Both the footage and stills were shown across the U.S. networks on the evening of June 5, appearing on CNN and ABC's *Nightline* with deliberate lapses in voiceover. Still photos, displayed copiously, appeared more than once in the same journal or newspaper and were reprinted the next day in the *New York Times, Los Angeles Times,* and *Chicago Tribune*.[15] Numerous newspapers ran sidebars about the images, querying who the man was and what had happened to him.[16] Though some reporters were discomfited by the subjunctive aspirations about freedom that the photos raised—for instance, when reporting on *Nightline,* Ted Koppel cautioned that much of its reportage "may have more of a basis in wishful thinking of angry demonstrators than in any reality"[17]—the display of the "as if" was still widespread. Over the next six months alone, the image of the solitary man challenging the cordon of tanks appeared four separate times in *Time,* twice in *Newsweek,* and twice in *Life.*[18]

Though the event unfolded seemingly as the breaking news of the protestor's possible death, an inability to follow what happened next, clarify the man's identity, or uncover news of his fate not only that day but over the weeks that followed made the images part of a continuing story, where meaning prevailed in multiple ways. Information about who the man was or what had happened to him was never made clear. Was he a student or a worker? Did he carry groceries or books? Did he shout political slogans at the tanks or say nothing? Multiple claims ensued but were not resolved.[19] The protestor's anonymity and the absence of clear information as to whether he in fact died were central to establishing the photo's force over time. For many, the photos became "a permanent and universal symbol" about the triumph of the human spirit and human courage, and in that vein they were recycled to book covers, Web sites, posters, T-shirts, cartoons, coffee cups, and other artifacts of popular culture.[20] In 1998, *Time* proclaimed the man "the unknown rebel" when it included him on its list of the twenty most influential "leaders and revolutionaries" of the twentieth century, with his image "instantly decipherable in any tongue, to any age." That decipherability, though, had multiple shapes. David Perlmutter saw the photos' cogency as drawn strategically by the elite news media and politicians: "Tiananmen was framed through Western eyes."[21] In Robert Hariman and John Lucaites's view, the image of the man and tanks was most effectively codified as a simultaneous performance of democratic virtue and liberal autonomy, though the relationship between the two tilted in uneven directions over time.[22] Certain Chinese officials set forth a countermyth, presenting the image "as proof of the enormous restraint that the military showed under stress."[23] Even today the image continues to appear as what the *Philadelphia Inquirer* recently called "an image of defiance, an image of possibility," where it reigns as a porous symbol of contradictory possibility in most retrospectives of good journalistic photography.[24] Its capacity to entertain multiple agendas—taken in conjunction with a widespread exposure to the image, familiarity with the event, and relevance of the image to circumstances broader than the picture itself—bolstered the power that the image wielded.

Both of these photos drew attention when there was some degree of prior public awareness about the causal circumstance for death, their retrospective positioning following, rather than preceding, public knowledge of the circumstances in which people died. Useful for depicting events involving widespread and often unconfirmed death, which by definition afflict more people than those depicted in the image and occur over a prolonged period of time, they were driven by an assumption that numerous people died in both the Ugandan famine and the Chinese demonstrations, regardless of whether or not death involved those in the picture.

But what of the deaths suggested? These two photos—situated at opposite ends of a continuum stretching from cues of bodily frailty to cues of bodily harm—seem to suggest a clear distinction between death by nature and design. One photo suggested a person faced death through a disembodied hand, unconsoled by another's futile attempt at solace. The other showed from afar a person facing death, his back faced to the camera as the instruments of his potential death overpowered the image. Yet neither event was as clear as the unambiguous cues of a fragile malnourished child or a foreboding military tank might suggest.

Interpretations of the famine in Uganda as a naturally occurring tragedy underplayed the specific political and socioeconomic landscapes in which it was able to flourish. The strategic curtailing of the nomadic movements of the population of Karamoja and undermining of its autonomy, the ascent of cattle raiding and tribal assaults, influx of guns, broader restrictions on hunting and grazing activities, the breakdown of civil order and resulting political and social unrest offer multiple signs that this famine had been as intentionally wrought as it was naturally occurring.[25] Some claimed that years of British colonial rule in the area had transformed the former "grass savanna" of the region into burned-out bush.[26] Regardless of whether intentional action was wreaked from within or beyond Ugandan administration of the region, this suggests that the same bodily cues that seem to distinguish between death by nature and design do not necessarily hold up when considering the circumstances more closely.

Similarly, interpretations of the Tiananmen Square image as a symbol of human rights and courage overplayed the gesture at the expense of the lingering human rights violations that ensued. Questions about whether Tiananmen was even one event, about earlier—and more violent—protests that went unreported, about the centrality of student participation in the protests, about the media's role in stimulating the event, even about a woman who also tried to stop the tanks but was run down earlier all went unanswered. As David Perlmutter argued, "The blocking agent was victorious, but *only in the icon,* for minutes later, as the man was hustled away, the tanks passed, and, of course, the government crackdown proceeded."[27] No surprise, then, that the image raised opposite interpretations in China, where it was seen widely as evidence of the humanitarian gestures of a military that could have inflicted bodily harm but chose not to.

Nonetheless, both of these pictures show that images of possible death are particularly potent as they move from journalism into other venues of public display. As John Taylor noted in his discussion of Amnesty International's humanitarian and political program, pictures with less than maximum intensity—suggestive rather than graphic—are good candidates for recycling: advocates of humanitarian organizations "choose images that sit within mainstream photojournalism [and use] photographs which may have already appeared in the press or whose horror is exceeded by media images."[28] Politicians, government officials, human rights workers, prosecutorial teams, celebrities, and filmmakers are among those engaged in piggybacking on the image's initial status as a news relay.

Because these images tend to come at a later point in the development of public awareness about the circumstances being depicted, their ability to invoke engagement is clear. While the motif of possible death depends on the public completing the undepicted aspects of the image by imagining what it does not see, the differential cues of bodily harm and bodily frailty can be interpreted in different ways as the images gravitate toward possibility. Moreover, such a tendency intensifies over time.

Possible Death from Bodily Harm

The cues of bodily harm typical of images of possible death surface frequently in the depiction of events involving the violation of human rights. Because these are generally implemented and sustained by institutional settings—governments, militias, the military—the ability to secure visuals remains one of journalism's major challenges. Images of possible death are useful in this regard for they can be easily transported after the fact into broadly scoped stories about such violations, where they take advantage of journalism's long-standing laxity about matching image to word.

Images of possible deaths involving bodily harm have stretched across the range of journalism's imaging technologies. They surfaced in the early pictures of the U.S. Civil War, when Union prisoners were released from Andersonville. More recently, for instance, an image of an Iraqi woman holding her dying child in a Baghdad Hospital in 1998 was used to illustrate a story on UN arms inspection. Although no names or identities were appended to the image, the caption linked the depiction with the larger, though tenuously connected, issue. Similarly, Ugandan elections in 2001 were accompanied by wide-ranging violence, in which voters opposing President Yoweri Museveni were allegedly beaten and killed by soldiers; photos circulated depicting situations of harassment but provided no comment on whether the persons depicted actually died.[29] Today these images of possible death regularly appear across the digitally mediated environment.

That said, the gravitation toward about-to-die images in situations marked by scores of people who have already died by intentional action is a choice worthy of contemplation. For it raises the question of whether and how the engagement of these images promotes understanding when it is offered in such a delayed, broadly scoped, and porous fashion. To what uses are such images put? And what does it mean when circumstances of wide-ranging bodily harm are depicted after the fact by the "as if" rather than the "as is"?

Possible Death in the Holocaust

Images of stacks of dead individuals killed by the Nazis during World War II remain one of the most memorable visualizations of the Holocaust, and their proliferation following the liberation of the concentration camps constituted a watershed moment in journalism's depictions of death.[30] At their side, however, a separate set of images, many of which surfaced after the fact, attested to the impending death of individuals being herded to their deaths by the Nazis. As information about the nature of Nazi terror was pieced together over time, the images that depicted Nazi activity as it was unfolding played a key role in facilitating the development of a clearer retrospective understanding of what had happened. Often taken by individuals who were responsible for killing their victims, these images documented in horrific detail a steady stream of mass evictions, evacuations, deportations, and killings in the 1940s that were structured around the impending death of the depicted. The pictures were themselves reprehensible for the mundane and cold-hearted attitude evinced toward death. Images included individuals in various stages of disarray and humiliation, and at times in degrees of physical undress, being paraded from the ghettoes, through the concentration camps, across the nearby forests and fields, and into large pits in the ground. Victims were often made to undress, humiliated, and degraded before being killed. Some images showed scores of women, children and elderly men being gunned down, their naked bodies pushed into readied mass graves. Who took the pictures and whether or not the victims knew of a photographer's presence was left unclear. As a reporter for *The Guardian* later observed, "Was it an official photographer for the files of the Reich or an unofficial photograph, a memento for the album of a Nazi sympathizer?" Included in albums produced at the time by Nazi guards recording their various actions, the photos became "a way of celebrating a much greater ideal: the unity and purity of the nation-state itself."[31]

Though many of these images did not appear as part of journalism's record of the Holocaust per se, they nonetheless drew a marked degree of public attention when they did appear. In that most, if not all, were distributed with considerable delay after the fact, the presentation of impending death brought with it a confused temporality. But that was precisely these images' power, in that in order for journalists, news executives, officials, politicians, and viewers to be willing to generalize the fate of impending death beyond the individuals being depicted, they needed to be already aware of the devastation that had occurred. Images of possible death in the Holocaust thus by definition appeared after there was extensive knowledge of what had happened. The role of the public in response, then, was to infer death by generalizing more broadly from what was suggested to people who remained undepicted, in most cases because they were already dead.

Many pictures of this type depicted responses to the atrocities perpetrated by the Nazis. Attempts at armed resistance under the Nazi occupation, for instance, which were concentrated in the eastern European ghettoes from 1942 onward, produced a number of uprisings that took place once the underground leaders sensed that there was no other way out. They "knew they were bound to lose. There was no longer a choice between life and death."[32] The Nazis responded in most cases with severe collective punishment, usually deportation and death. Often, they took pictures of their victims before they killed them.

One such uprising broke out in the Warsaw Ghetto on April 19, 1943. Ghetto residents battled the Nazis for nearly a month, making it the largest underground resistance in Nazi territory. Its images reflected a brief but intense Nazi intervention: seven thousand residents were shot, seven thousand taken to the concentration camp of Treblinka and fifteen thousand to Lublin.[33] One image, taken sometime after April 19 but before May 16 when the uprising was quashed, was circulated not at the time but only years later, when it was found in the files and personal collection of one of the Nazi guards. Who took it, when exactly it was taken and to which purpose remain unknown (fig. 4.4).

The image depicted a group of people leaning against a brick wall, their backs to the camera, suggesting mass detainment though no instruments of coercion were visible. What the public saw was a simple picture—nearly three dozen individuals facing the wall, their arms stretched skyward, wedged in between the wall and piles of rubbish on the ground. They had no faces, no names and no identities. But that did not matter, for the image of possible death worked as a symbolic proxy, becoming understandable only through a broader context that explained the uprising as having provided a moment of dignity for the oppressed. Later described as a depiction of "nothing less than a revolution in Jewish history" by which the Jews "resisted the Nazis with armed force,"[34]

Figure 4.4:
Unknown
photographer,
Warsaw, Poland April
19, 1943–May 16,
1943, USHMM,
courtesy of National
Archives and Records
Administration,
College Park.

the image underscored the value of an honorable death and those about to die stood in for the many undepicted persons who had been killed. The picture's broad symbolic force facilitated its appearance after the fact of millions dead had already permeated public consciousness. It also fueled its recycling in retrospective literature on the Holocaust, where it was seen to emblematize the Jewish underground resistance.[35]

One of the most poignant images portraying the actions in the Warsaw Ghetto portrayed a young boy being herded from the ghetto under a Nazi machinegun (fig. 4.5). Depicting part of the deportation of thousands of Jews in May 1943 after the attempted uprising, the image caught the deportees before they were reportedly taken to Treblinka, where they were believed to have perished. The image documented one moment in that process, during which a group of women, men, and small children was shepherded from the ghetto under the watchful eye of Nazi guards. Front and center to the image was a small boy, his arms raised in terror above his head. The photo displayed frenetic energy, with people confusedly looking in all directions and signaling to others in the group; only the soldiers remained steadied and calm, their guns turned on the group. The boy stood somewhat apart from the others. Half the size of the rest, his body was made all the more vulnerable by his clothing— dark-colored knee socks, short pants, an oversized beret and knee-length pea jacket. Positioned a few steps away from the rest of the group, the boy seemed particularly frail and alone as he looked frontally at the photographer, his eyes widened in fear.

Later captioned "Forced from the bunkers," the photograph was taken by an unnamed personal photographer of SS General Jurgen Stroop, who masterminded the ghetto's evacuation. Stroop collected the photo together with

Figure 4.5: Unknown photographer, Warsaw, Poland, April–May 1943, USHMM, courtesy of Instytut Pamieci Narodowej.

fifty-five others and made a seventy-six-page scrapbook, titled "The Jewish Quarter of Warsaw Is No More!" which he donated to Heinrich Himmler.[36] After the war, the scrapbook was found by the Allied forces, and it was used as a central piece of evidence in the Nuremburg Trials of 1945 and 1946, where it was employed to convict and sentence to death Corporal Josef Bloesche, the German soldier holding the gun on the boy. Remarked on at length during the trials by Robert H. Jackson, chief of counsel for the United States, it had already appeared in numerous publications on the trials by the end of 1946.[37] As Charles Alexander, the tribunal's director of photography, noted in his 1946 book of photos, the photo captured a memorable moment in the sequencing of actions that were central to Nazi terror: "This small Jewish boy knows he is about to be shot and holds up his hands in agonized fear."[38] The image, poignantly accessible, remained largely unknown in any venue other than the books detailing the tribunal, and it received no major coverage at the time from the news media.

Ten years later, however, once a number of contemporaneous events drew attention to the photograph, the boy's impending death became one of the most widely distributed images of the Holocaust. In 1956, the image appeared in Alain Resnais's Holocaust film, *Night and Fog*, and in 1960 it graced both the first book of Holocaust-related photographs—Gerhard Schoenberner's *Der gelbe Stern* (*The Yellow Star*)—in Germany and the first German exhibition to display photographs of Nazi crimes against European Jewry in poster form.[39] A second public tribunal connected to the Holocaust—the internationally televised trial of Adolf Eichmann in 1961, following his capture by Israeli intelligence agents from Buenos Aires one year earlier—gave it the widest exposure. When Israeli attorney general Gideon Hausner showed the image during his opening remarks at the trial,[40] the photo captured the news media's attention.

Within the year, news organizations reproduced the image in a wide variety of related news stories. Some had to do with creating public consensus around the upcoming trial, planned while Israel was still defending its kidnapping of Eichmann to Argentine authorities; in this regard, the news coverage had a propagandistic demeanor, as numerous news organizations agreed to give Israeli premier David Ben-Gurion a platform to espouse the legitimacy of Israel's actions. For instance, the image was used to illustrate a *New York Times Magazine* interview with Ben-Gurion in 1960 on the upcoming Eichmann trial. Appearing as a half-page image above Ben-Gurion's prose, it was titled "In the Fury of the Nazi Terror." Though the picture depicted the Warsaw Ghetto, no mention was made of the ghetto in the body of the article, reinforcing the symbolic status of the image in regards to broader actions related to the Holocaust.[41] *Life* magazine published a two-part series on Eichmann, which again showed the image alongside excerpts from his memoirs. In 1962 the

Saturday Evening Post ran a three-part series on Eichmann's trial, displaying the image. And it appeared in 1969 alongside an article about the execution of the soldier who had trained his gun on the boy in the picture.[42] Though sporadic, the image's display was sufficiently central to cement it as the iconic representation of the Warsaw Ghetto in the public eye.

And so it continued. From the 1960s onward, the photo inhabited nearly every photographic book on the Holocaust and adorned covers of memoirs from the Warsaw Ghetto, was displayed in museums like Yad Vashem in Jerusalem and the Anne Frank House in Amsterdam, and represented the Holocaust in a wide range of educational materials.[43] In 1976 a BBC television series, *The Glittering Prizes*, featured a subplot around the photo, and it was made the topic of Holocaust paintings, films, and poems, one of which erroneously commented on the yellow star atop the boy's jacket but, on discovering no star in the original image, produced an altered version of the photo that included one.[44] The boy, coined "the Warsaw Ghetto Boy," was seen as a substitute for numerous other children who perished, and survivors gave him constructed identities which addressed their own loss.[45] The invocation of the "as if" dimensions of the photo prevailed. As late as the 1990s, *Progressive* editor Erwin Kroll commented thus:

> It is the photograph that has come to symbolize the Holocaust: a small Jewish boy, frightened eyes downcast, hands raised above his shoulders, surrounded by Nazi troops. This is the final roundup of Jews scheduled for execution during the Warsaw Ghetto uprising of 1943. More Jews, hands raised, can be seen in the background. We know as we stare at the photo that soon they will all be dead. The photo appears in archives and exhibitions, in magazine and newspaper articles about the Holocaust, in television documentaries and history books. By now I must have seen it hundreds of times, and each time my reaction is what it was when I first saw it almost half a century ago: It could have been me.[46]

The image was both particular and universal, representing both "the suffering of those who lived in the Warsaw Ghetto" and everything connected to "the Holocaust in one photograph."[47] Because the boy remained anonymous and his actual death was never confirmed, his depiction functioned as a stand-in for the death of others. For instance, the *Washington Post* ran an article titled "Warsaw Ghetto Boy: Symbol of the Holocaust," where it noted that the photograph "wrenches the heart because it appears that the boy, like millions of Jews and others, is to die at the hands of the Nazis." The *Jerusalem Post* ran three separate articles on the image through the decades, detailing the image's symbolic power. The photo also inhabited numerous collections of photojournalism's memorable images.[48]

That status changed as people attempted to identify the boy. Numerous individuals—Arthur Domb Siemiontek, Israel Rondel, and Levi Zeilinwarger, among them—made claims that the image depicted them. Each time an additional person surfaced, newspaper headlines celebrated his emergence: the Danish *Ekstrabladet* declared "He's Alive" and the French *L'Humanite* proclaimed "His Name Was Arthur Schmiontak" in July of 1978. The most persistent claim came in 1982 from Zvi Nussbaum of Rockland, New York, who said he had been sent to Bergen Belsen from the ghetto and was liberated there in 1945. Claiming to be the boy in the picture, the New York physician gave the *New York Times* reason to run the image, where the paper noted, "It is one of the indelible images of history: a Jewish boy, arms in the air and terror in his eyes, standing on a Warsaw street under the watchful gaze of a Nazi soldier. Though others, largely women and children, stand in horror nearby, the boy seems utterly abandoned, his fate seemingly sealed."[49]

The response that met Nussbaum's assertion that he was the image's little boy underscored how powerful were the subjunctive impulses surrounding the image. Many preferred the image's "as if" dimensions to its "as is" connection to reality. In the *Times'* words, "Concerned that the symbolic power of the picture would be diminished were the boy shown to have survived, [many] refuse to consider [Nussbaum's claim] at all." Historians remained "cautious and extremely skeptical" because they "considered the photograph a sort of sacred document."[50] Said one, "This great photograph of the most dramatic event of the Holocaust requires a greater level of responsibility from historians than almost any other. It is too holy to let people do with it what they want."[51]

Claims aside, the photo's ambiguity and its suggestion of bodily harm came to be seen as an emblem of universal suffering demarcating the divide between good and evil. It was labeled by the Israeli museum Yad Vashem "a symbol of German brutality," and the Anti-Defamation League used it in its promotional materials against racism.[52] With time, the image came to stand in for evil and suffering rather than the Holocaust per se. In 1993, it buttressed a comparison of genocides, when a *New York Times* article on the war in Bosnia, titled "Does the World Still Recognize a Holocaust?" reprinted the picture alongside a more contemporary image from the Balkans. Nearly a decade later, the *New York Times* again used the image in an obituary for anti-Nazi activist Jan Karski, where the photo was titled "What He Saw," implying (erroneously) that Karski had seen the boy being evacuated from the Warsaw Ghetto. A reader's letter lamented the choice of image, noting that "the picture you selected of the small boy was a moving but much reproduced image and could not convey the unique authority of Karski's own visage."[53] At the same time, the image also drew the attention of the Holocaust deniers, who maintained that the boy's identity and survival supported their claims that the Holocaust never happened.[54]

The picture's reputation as the symbolic marker of the Warsaw Ghetto uprising, Nazi brutality, or even brutality more broadly meant that it was an easy target for both supportive and oppositional discourses. At the core of both was the suggestion of bodily harm that the image conveyed. One prevalent response had to do with Israel and its treatment of the Palestinians. Because the child's implied victimhood was so central to the original image, its reversal made it a valuable conveyor for a message about Israeli brutality in various venues of visual representation. In 1982, when hundreds of Palestinians were slaughtered by Lebanese Phalangist militiamen after relocation to the Sabra and Shatilla refugee camps by the Israel Defense Forces, cries of Israeli brutality were widespread, and Portuguese artist Antonio Moreira Antunes expressed his outrage in a political cartoon based on the 1943 photograph in the Portuguese newspaper *Expresso.* In the cartoon, the boy with raised hands and the other deportees wore PLO scarves while the helmets of the soldiers bore the Jewish Star of David. Although it won the Grand Prize at the Twentieth International Salon of the Cartoon in Montreal the following year, the cartoon's display provoked demonstrations.[55] In 2003, artist Alan Schechner addressed the renewed Intifada, in which Palestinians and Israelis clashed violently across the region, by creating an installation that combined the Holocaust with the politics of contemporary Israel. He depicted both the Warsaw Ghetto boy and a Palestinian boy being arrested by Israeli border police clutching photographs of each other, saying he hoped to offset the either/or question that seemed to permeate discussions of Israeli brutality by focusing on the perpetrators.[56] In 2000, when twelve-year-old Mohammad Al-Dura was shot by Israeli troops in the Gaza Strip and an image of him facing death became a symbol of the Intifada, linkages between the two photos—juxtaposing the Jew as victim with the Jew as perpetrator—encouraged the cartoonist Latuff to portray the Warsaw Ghetto boy with a sign around his neck proclaiming him to be Palestinian; similarly, a Greek editorial cartoon in the newspaper *Eleutherotypia* recycled both the original image alongside a tweaked version which combined an Israeli firing on a Palestinian boy with raised arms.[57] By 2006 the parallels between the two photos had moved into a faux journalistic environment, where the picture was the centerpiece of an urban legend drawn from the People's Cube, which created a fake *New York Times*' front page, dated May 10, 1943, replete with the image positioned under a banner headline proclaiming "Warsaw Ghetto Uprising an Over-Reaction." The piece was crafted as a response to calls against Israeli militarism in the Intifada.[58]

The image was also over time put to unpredictable uses—as the centerpiece for an online recruitment campaign for the militaristic Jewish Defense League, a British musical based on the events of the Warsaw Ghetto, and a genealogical search site for lost relatives in Poland.[59] The boy's raised arms were the discussion of numerous scholarly projects, which saw them as both a variant of the sacrifice of Isaac and the crucifixion of Christ.[60]

Each display of the photo introduced variants on the meanings attached to it. Through it all, the suggestion of bodily harm, the child's anonymity, and the image's ambiguity were central to maintaining the image's power as a depiction of possible death. As David Roskies observed, "Whose child is he? It doesn't matter, because they will all eventually perish. Yet the child alone is surely all of us."[61] One artist reflected the prevailing sentiments well when he noted that "I know that such a boy did perish, one among an entire million of Jewish children, and even if this specific boy in the photo should happen to be still alive (he would now be seventy), that fact would be irrelevant."[62]

The Warsaw Ghetto Boy was thereby useful because the openness of the image's retrospective display kept the Holocaust front and center for a public still struggling decades later with it. The assumption of bodily harm central to the photo was fueled by keeping the boy unnamed and the death possible, but not certain.

Possible Death from the Khmer Rouge

The pictures of individuals facing death at the hands of the Khmer Rouge in Cambodia during the 1970s constitute one of the more troubling contemporary documentary records of people about to die, but it was not one that journalists covered at the time of the story's unfolding. The account of what transpired under the Khmer Rouge was pieced together bit by bit over the years of the Pol Pot regime, but its visual record in effect only came together years after the regime had been dismantled. Against that delay, it was the images—numerous, formulaic, and repetitive in the horror they forced viewers to imagine—that eventually coaxed the public to attention on a story whose broad plotline it had come to know already through words. As with other images of possible death, then, these pictures augmented public awareness after journalists, news executives, officials, politicians and viewers had already been primed for its visualization.

The atrocities committed by the Khmer Rouge in Cambodia were systematic, expansive, and bureaucratic in detail. Herded from cities and into torture centers and prisons, about 1.7 million people—a quarter of Cambodia's population—died during the four years of the Khmer Rouge's rule, helmed by Pol Pot. The photographic record of these individuals' last moments before death provided depiction of the final moments of lives lived under a brief but intense reign of terror.

The Khmer Rouge government came to power following the war in Cambodia under the radar of most of the U.S. news media, which managed to uncover very little about the so-called Communist-led Cambodian insurgents. As Sydney Schanberg reported in the *New York Times* as late as March of 1975, "The 'enemy' is red, cruel and, after five years, little known." When

Pol Pot took over the government that year, forcing the evacuation of Phnom Penh and other large cities, news organizations verbally reported a massive bloodbath with thousands of victims and a death toll expected to rise to tens of thousands of individuals, but they provided no pictures. In the *Wall Street Journal's* view, observers were focused on the atrocities—"the question becomes: How many will they kill?"—but the news media were unable to interpret what was happening. The Khmer Rouge kept the country sealed from outside eyes, barring the foreign news media and generating uncertain, often speculative reporting and no visual documentation. As William Safire wryly commented, "What kind of bloodbath is it, after all, that goes on unrecorded by videotape?"[63]

In 1978, a CBS News documentary gave a certain visual form to the atrocities, but it offered so little visual information that the *New York Times* remarked that "the Cambodia story does not lend itself to easy 'visuals.'" The documentary, said the *Times,* provided pictures that were "largely unremarkable. Deserted city streets are contrasted to crowded rice and salt fields, and a few factories."[64] One year later a second documentary on PBS generated a similar impression. "Cambodia is proving a difficult subject for television to cover," wrote the *Times.* "On the one hand, there is too little, as American crews have limited access to the country. On the other, there is too much, as the few films that are available provide scenes of devastating horror."[65] Though verbal estimates of the dead already stretched to more than a million victims, the only evidence the news media could gather were the unsubstantiated and subjective eyewitness reports of those who had been tortured and escaped. This meant that the story of the Cambodian atrocities remained in need of visualization. Much like the liberation of the concentration camps of World War II, the story needed to be seen to be believed, even if its visualization were to come at a delay.[66]

That situation changed in 1979, when the Pol Pot government was overthrown by the Vietnamese. It was then that the story of the Khmer Rouge atrocities began to take on visual and material form. Within the year the archive of the main prison south of Phnom Penh, Tuol Sleng, or S-21 Prison, was discovered, and UN workers and human rights activists who traveled to the region made available thousands of personal snapshots of victims that the Khmer Rouge meticulously ordered by number and filed neatly into storage.[67] The photographic files provided a detailed record of close to fifteen thousand men, women and children in their last moments before they had been killed. Bits and pieces of their story, largely told through its visual documentation, began to come together.

The prison's photographic unit, controlled by the security police, had been responsible for taking photos of each man, woman, and child who had entered the prison. Framed as either full-length or head and shoulder frontal shots, the images of Cambodians about to die, later called "portraits of the condemned," documented mass and systematic execution in various locations across Cambodia from 1975 onward. More than fourteen thousand images were made by Cambodian photographers at the prison of Tuol Sleng alone, and countless others were made elsewhere.[68]

The pictures were arresting, both for their strict patterning and their undiluted engagement with the photographer and by extension the viewer (fig. 4.6). Each image portrayed a single individual, positioned squarely in the middle of the frame. Male and female, young and old—all nameless, anonymous, and voiceless—they stared frontally into the lens of the camera. Their hands tied behind their backs, standing stiffly and in identical poses against a bare wall, some pursed their lips and widened their eyes, while others looked stoic, expressionless, and vacant; some bore the marks of beatings on their faces. Dressed in simple black or white clothing, each individual bore a number pinned to his or her shirt.

Taken by Khmer Rouge officials—or their designates—the process for visual recording was simple: "As each prisoner was brought in, a blindfold was ripped from his face. 'Where am I?' some of the prisoners asked. The young photographer was not permitted to talk to them. 'Look straight into the camera,' he replied." Immediately after having their picture taken, the depicted individuals were either taken for hard labor or killed on the spot.[69]

When the pictures were found, they were not immediately displayed by the news media. Though a handful of print news organizations gave the images coverage, they did so sporadically and relegated them to inside pages.[70] Instead, the pictures surfaced in other venues first. A small museum space was set up at Tuol Sleng, displaying some of the images. United Nations officers who had seen the pictures when the archive was discovered organized small photographic exhibits, which began to tour in late 1983. Called "Cambodian Witness," the exhibits showed the pictures alongside other images of mounds of human skulls and mass burial pits at Cheung Ek, Tuol Sleng in Phnom Penh, and elsewhere, suggesting the systematic brutality of Pol Pot's regime."[71] By 1988, when the museum spaces inside Cambodia began to include human remains, the news media showered attention on a glass tower filled with skulls and bones, some still bearing patches of clothing.[72] Missing, however, from each of these efforts was the scope and magnitude of the Khmer Rouge atrocities. The visuals, while an improvement over the absence of visual documentation in earlier years, did not sufficiently convey to a broad viewing public what had transpired and in which fashion. They were thus insufficient vehicles for enabling the public to infer what had happened.

In 1996, those circumstances changed. Only then—a full twenty years after the Pol Pot atrocities—were the photos of Tuol Sleng widely, centrally, repeatedly, and systematically circulated. Though doing so did not lend a certainty to the impending death of those depicted, it made the scale, scope, and magnitude

Figure 4.6: Unknown photographer, Tuol Sleng, Cambodia, 1975, appended to "Flawed Khmer Rouge Trial," April 16, 2003. Copyright © 2003 by *The New York Times* Co. Reprinted with permission.

of the atrocities clearer. Citing "a huge, meticulously kept archive of what came to be known as Cambodia's 'bureaucracy of death,'" *New York Times* reporter Seth Mydans published a series of news stories on the atrocities, mostly on the newspaper's front page. With each story a gallery of pictures of people about to die appeared.[73]

The first images of individuals about to die appeared in the *Times* on the paper's front page on June 7, 1996. Under the title, "Cambodian Killers' Careful Records Used against Them," Mydans outlined the process by which the Khmer Rouge had meticulously "recorded the names and personal histories of thousands of prisoners who were led blindfolded...to be tortured and killed."[74]

Illustrated by four images of people about to die, the story was immediately picked up by other news organizations, which remarked widely on the visuals. Journalists were unnerved by the frontal display of the faces they depicted. In one reporter's view, "the faces linger in the visitor's memory, rows and rows of mug shots taken on entry to the prison, men, women and even small children....Their faces show they know what is to come."[75] Another noted that the Cambodian pictures were "mute. We can never be sure what their expressions mean. Is it defiance or doom on the faces of the Cambodians? Does a frown indicate anger or confusion or concentration? The implicit message behind showing these photos...is precisely that the faces are so unremarkable, so indistinguishable from the rest of us. [They] could be anyone."[76] The assumption in each case, twenty years hence, was that the individuals depicted facing death were now dead. Of "16,000 people who entered Tuol Sleng, the Khmer Rouge's secret police prison, between 1975 and 1979, perhaps seven of them emerged alive."[77] Not knowing which seven survived, of course, only enhanced the "as if" dimension of what the photos showed. As one art critic remarked on looking at the images, "we see the dead walking."[78]

The *Times'* display of the images was incessant: the shots of Cambodians about to die appeared in the paper at least once every three or four weeks for nearly half a year, always in different sections. Bearing titles like "Faces from Beyond the Grave," "Poignant Faces of the Soon-To-Be-Dead," and "Hypnotized By Mug Shots That Stare Back," the articles drew directly on the photographs to rekindle public interest in a story long faded from front page news.[79] Stories on Tuol Sleng populated the features sections, lifestyle sections, film and book review sections as well as the sections devoted to hard news. The result was a variegated conversation about the set of photos, late to arrive but powerful nonetheless. Through it all, the images continued to reappear, haunting those who saw them.

Within weeks of their initial display, the images literally tumbled across the front pages and broadcast spaces of other news organizations, books, films, and retrospectives.[80] By the mid-1990s, they moved into other display venues. New exhibits of photos, more extensive than the small displays of the early 1980s, toured in the late 1990s, where they were shown in venues like New York City's Museum of Modern Art and Boston University's Photographic Resource Center.[81] Large images appeared on the walls of the Tuol Sleng prison in Phnom Penh, which had been turned from a simple memory site into a full-fledged genocide museum. Though "the idea of showing these pictures in art museums at all" was criticized on moral grounds, because "their subjects were murdered after the pictures were taken or [because] many Cambodians are still trying to discover the fate of their loved ones," the exhibits were nonetheless well-attended.[82] An online program was set up at Yale University with U.S. congressional funding to make the photographs available online so as to facilitate victim identification. Titled the Cambodian Genocide Program—available online at www.yale.edu/cgp—it scanned more than five thousand images of unidentified individuals for Internet display and the program's Web site invited Cambodians around the world to put names to the photos.[83] From the late 1990s onward, the photos became the topic of books, gallery exhibits, and museum retrospectives, illustrating book reviews on the Cambodian genocide, surveys of art exhibits, articles about the meaning of torture, updates on the prosecution of the Khmer Rouge leaders, discussions about the nature of photographic images, and the reporting of Pol Pot's death.[84] Two films focused on the actions at Tuol Sleng prison, and both featured the photographs.[85] Given that these efforts at recycling the photos took place twenty years or more after Pol Pot's atrocities, their repeated and variegated display was evidence of the images' retrospective power.

The images of Cambodians facing their death from Pol Pot were given another focused public display on two other occasions—first in the mid-2000s when the Tuol Sleng prison, which became nominally a genocide museum in 1999, drew attention as Cambodia became a favored site for "genocide tourism" or "dark tourism."[86] Stories of tourism to the region were illustrated with pictures of tourists looking at pictures of the condemned that lined the walls of the museum: noting that the images helped remind tourists how benign the current government was when compared with the Pol Pot regime, the *Boston Globe* told its readers that "at Tuol Sleng, one walks across bloodstained tile to the metal bedframes where suspects were found shackled and bloodied. To the extent that the museum's curators offer any interpretation, it's meant to shock."[87] As before, the reportage centered on the faces of the condemned: one reporter noted that "to look at these people is to see the living dead. Their stares are captivating....The eyes are vacant, empty, lifeless," while another remarked that "it is nearly impossible for visitors to escape the feeling of being watched by the faces on the walls."[88] It was not long before the lines of Cambodian mug shots filled travel Web sites for offbeat travel destinations and Phnom Penh travel guides.[89] Not everyone was captivated by the display, however, and one commentary in *Asia Times* remarked that the site constituted an "overkill of atrocity tourism."[90]

A second event that occasioned additional visual coverage was when the tribunals for the Khmer Rouge leaders began in earnest in late 2007, after exceedingly protracted delay. Although Pol Pot himself died in 1998—or by some reports was murdered before being turned over to prosecutors—his lieutenants went on trial for crimes against humanity nine years later.[91] Although the thirty-two-year delay meant that "accountability has been long in coming in Cambodia,"[92] by the time the proceedings began it was clear that the images from Tuol Sleng would play a central role in the prosecutorial efforts. Photographers from the prison were called to testify in late 2007 and were photographed in the halls of pictures that lined the museum; one photographer talked of his plans to exhibit and sell his images.[93]

What does all of this suggest? The display of the atrocities of Tuol Sleng Prison worked effectively as images of possible death, drawing attention at a delay that facilitated their employment for strategic reasons other than news relay. Needing the exposure to the public and the inference of widespread death to make the pictures meaningful, these images, later called "incontrovertible evidence of genocide," were central to helping identify the victims and spearheading the prosecutorial efforts against the Pol Pot regime.[94] The bodily harm implicit in these photos—so frontal, dispassionate, cold, and bureaucratic that it left the depicted little dignity in their last moments alive—turned its suggestion of intentional death into a visual emblem of Khmer Rouge complicity in war crimes.

Possible Death from Bodily Frailty

Journalism's ability to target circumstances that cause the human body to shut down naturally—illness, malnutrition, accidents, epidemics, starvation—has long drawn from recognizable cues of bodily frailty. Portraying the fragility of human lives has come in tandem with an assumption that death is caused by "naturally occurring" rather than purposive circumstances. That distinction, of course, is not always tenable, as seen in the numerous cases of government-orchestrated mass famine.

The target of these images is invariably the same—people. Anthropomorphizing the events they depict, individuals or groups lie prostrate and helpless on the grounds of hospitals, hospices, refugee camps, and other caregiving centers. The camera generally focuses on their faces and upper torsos. As they languish from reduced bodily function, death advances impersonally, set in either desolate and wasted outdoor landscapes or antiseptic and frigid hospital settings. Little denotative detail is provided about the causal circumstance behind the malfunctioning body, and the images and their captions focus instead on bodily frailty as an event in and of itself. The captions to these photos recur formulaically across images from different circumstances—"Starvation Brings Final Days Closer" or "Awaiting Death from Malaria"—playing off of journalism's own looseness in matching image to word.

Differences in the depiction of impending death from famine or illness, though, can be inferred from visible cues of the institutional processes at work in assisting the individual or not: when dying from famine, individuals tend to be portrayed alone and outdoors, seen against barren landscapes; when dying from illness, individuals tend to be depicted with others—family members, hospice workers, or medical practitioners—and in some kind of caregiving facility. Though viewers are never told that these particular individuals die, their possible death is always described in the adjoining captions and always linked with others who have died: for instance, a photo of a Rwandan refugee "dying within a makeshift clinic for the sick and weak who are unable to continue walking" was linked to further description by Red Cross workers "who say at least 50 refugees are now dying of disease and malnutrition each day."[95] Whether depicting a woman dying from Ebola in Zaire or a child dying of meningitis in Iraq,[96] captions necessarily reference the larger body of people dying from illness, for it is the larger body that makes the image newsworthy. In most cases the individuals depicted are given no names or identities, though when the illness involves proximate individuals, there is a greater chance that additional informational detail will be provided. Images of terminal cancer patients, for instance, typically portrayed in the stages of dying rather than after death, are often accompanied by extensive information about the individuals involved. The *Detroit News* ran one such feature, which addressed the cost of dying and was illustrated by two pictures of in-house patients at a hospice center who were identified by name.[97] But most depictions of illness remain anonymous, generalizable, and categorical.

News images of possible death have depended on cues of bodily frailty since the earliest drawings of the Black Death, which portrayed the dying sprawled alongside corpses on the streets of European cities. The two largest epidemics of the late eighteenth and early nineteenth centuries were depicted by large-scale settings in which people were shown dying: pictures of cholera showed street scenes with healthy people strolling alongside the dying, while the influenza outbreak of 1918 was depicted by emergency hospitals in which scores of individuals in long lines of hospital cots were being treated. Ireland's Potato Famine was similarly shown through pictures of people starving and dying a possible death.[98]

As with other images of possible death, these pictures tend to appear in alignment with the efforts of individuals outside journalism. Days or months dedicated to raising awareness about a particular disease or fund-raising campaigns for certain illnesses are reasons to run pictures of impending death. Similarly, celebrity visits to drought-stricken regions generate a flourish of media coverage. The response to these cues for media attention has been mixed, and observers have lamented the insufficient governmental attention at their side. As the *Wall Street Journal* ironically noted in 1985, "Can rock stars stem Ethiopian hunger?"[99]

Like other images of possible death, these images showcase people in circumstances in which they malinger, suggesting but not confirming that they die. In like fashion, viewers are expected to infer death even when it is not depicted and even if it does not occur to those in the picture. But unlike pictures of an intentional possible death, which rely on cues of bodily harm, these photos depend primarily on the body's frailty to drive home the message that death is near. A depleted body is thus central to the public's act of engagement.

Possible Death from Disease

The coverage of disease across time has taken on different characteristics, depending on the nature, proximity, intensity, and novelty of the illness it depicts. Typically using vivid language and dramatic photos, it reflects the fear and emotion an outbreak of disease provokes and the degree of trust in medicine to set things right. At the heart of much of this coverage has been a visual focus on the physical decay of degenerating bodies. As Sander Gilman noted more than twenty years ago, disease provokes a "fear of collapse, the sense of dissolution which contaminates the western fear of all disease."[100] Cues of bodily frailty are powerful cues for relaying such a message.

That said, images of disease do not tend to generate as much coverage as do other kinds of images of impending death. Often involving less dramatic sequences of action leading to death and less obviously connected to the large social and political issues that drive news coverage, illness becomes newsworthy when it involves known persons or takes on characteristics that connect the social fabric to the deaths it causes. Deaths with dramatic characteristics and unusual symptoms, deaths of multiple people and deaths connected to various policy issues are among the traits that enhance the chances that disease will secure coverage as news. Diseases that have "an emergency tilt" also merit attention, leaving to the background the greyer circumstances surrounding measles, most cases of flu, tuberculosis, and the various diarrheic diseases. In Susan Moeller's view, six types of images tend to depict epidemic disease—scientific charts and diagrams, depictions of the epidemic's source (rats, monkeys, insects), images of people protecting themselves from disease (gloves, masks, space suits), victims, funerals and clean-up efforts. Though as a rule illnesses with gruesome symptoms tend to be covered because of the terror they provoke, coverage takes shape in different ways: for instance, the Ebola epidemic drew from the multiple fictional cinematic and TV representations released at the time of its outbreak in 1995, while Mad Cow Disease was depicted the following decade most effectively in cartoons because the disease's development was not photogenic. Similarly, the coverage of diseases causing graphic injury tends to show pictures of individual victims, while that of less disfiguring but highly contagious illnesses depicts many individuals. In the U.S.

news media, Euro-Americans are more likely to be depicted as individuals and people from the global South as groups, though this changes when depicting children who are almost always shown individually.[101]

All of this makes pictures central to the public engagement with disease. As one guest on CNN commented during an outbreak of deaths from strep-A in 1994, "The doctors say, 'Don't worry,' but the pictures say 'Oh, yes, you should.'" What the pictures show, however, and how they in turn reflect what is understood about the disease can take on multiple shapes. As Roland Bleicker and Amy Kay observed, symbolic representations "can easily turn into an archetype....Suffering, then, becomes idealized and stigmatized at the same time."[102] The "as is" gives way to the "as if."

These qualities make images of possible death from disease useful for non-journalistic aims. When tuberculosis resurfaced in South Africa in late 2006 after a new strain of the disease proved resistant to existing anti-TB drugs and killed thousands in the less-developed regions of Africa, India, and Asia in under two years, James Nachtwey, a contract photographer for *Time,* tracked its spread. In October 2008, he showed his images as part of an eight-page photographic spread in *Time* and a larger online video photo-essay. Said the titles to the *Time* slideshow:

> This is happening now. One person dies every 20 seconds. An ancient disease is taking on a deadly new form. TB is preventable and curable. But it is mutating due to inadequate treatment. There is no reliable cure. Patients often die within weeks of diagnosis. We can stop this now. Spread the story, stop the disease. We are the treatment.

Still photos from the video essay appeared that same week in newspapers like the *Boston Globe* and *USA Today,* Web sites like wired.com and slate.com, and elsewhere across the digitally mediated environment; each time the photos appeared, the photo essay itself was uploaded to online news sites.[103]

It was not long before Nachtwey's pictures moved from their journalistic venues to the forums of NGOs needing such images for their own promotional literature. Though multiple photographers engage in such a practice—where organizations like the World Health Organization, the United Nations, Medecins Sans Frontieres, and Christian Aid all provide access to the areas of suffering in return for depictions of what transpires there—the intimacy and close focus of Nachtwey's images generated particular appeal. Given a TED (Technology, Entertainment and Design) Award of $100,000 to act on "one wish to change the world," he knew that XDRTB did not draw public attention because it remained a "disease of the poor," and—noting that "I'm a witness and I want my testimony to be honest and uncensored. I also want it to be powerful and eloquent and to do as much justice as possible to the experience of the people I'm photographing"—he put it to the development of new uses of digital news photography in spreading information about the story. With his initiative sponsored by the medical technology company of BD (Becton, Dickinson and Company) and the nonprofit medical advocacy organization RESULTS USA, he formed xdrtb.org—a Web site dedicated to spreading information about Extreme Drug-Resistant Tuberculosis (XDR-TB). Launching this Web site's public health media campaign in October 2008, he circulated his images widely online. Helped by Mammalfish in developing the Web site's software technology, YouTube in disseminating the images, and RESULTS USA in promotion, Nachtwey's pictures were also projected in public spaces, with viewing events on all seven continents. As the Web site's viewers were urged to share pictures, sign letters of support, plan events, and raise money, these photos of possible death caused by tuberculosis functioned simultaneously as markers of the journalist record and as advocacy in nonjournalistic forums.[104]

One of the most longstanding portrayals of disease has centered on the depiction of AIDS. Seen as a "long wave" event, whose progression has spanned decades, the circumstances for depicting AIDS differed from those of other epidemics, which were over in a matter of weeks. From its early recognition in the early 1980s, when it was seen mostly as a "gay disease" and thought imported to the United States from Africa, it broadened across gender and sexuality—from gay men to straight men, women and children; across spatial boundaries—from the largely urban environments of the advanced nations in the West to the impoverished countries of the global South; and across temporal spans—from a relatively short progression to death to one that either progresses across decades or becomes a chronic but manageable illness. And yet, it is estimated that more than 21 million individuals have died from the disease since its first known diagnoses in 1981. Paradoxically, however, though the disease has continued to spread, its coverage has declined since the late 1980s.[105] This has made the coverage that does exist representative of a disease that is more diverse and widespread than ever before.

During much of the disease's development, coverage was driven by attention-grabbing events, and it took some time before news organizations settled into ongoing coverage of the disease.[106] Structured as what Douglas Crimp and Jenny Kitzinger separately called a morality tale and what Paula Treichler saw as an "epidemic of signification," the coverage of AIDS dropped precipitously around the point at which it was reframed from constituting a death threat to a chronic disease.[107] This raised other problems, for as Laurie Garrett noted, the chronic form of AIDS impacted multiple aspects of the infrastructure in which it resided. Its continued prevalence is now partly responsible for

the reshaping of the demographic distribution of societies, massive orphaning, labor shortages in agricultural and other select trades, strong challenges to military forces, an abiding shift in spiritual and religious views, fundamental economic transformations, and [changed] concepts of civil society and the role of the state.[108]

Its persistence have increased dependency ratios, depleted work forces, changed family relations, and lowered life expectancies. Coupled with the international spread of AIDS, these circumstances have prompted some to call it a global threat—where, like the Ebola virus, Mad Cow Disease, or H1N1, it reflects a fundamental "disquiet about globalization and the end of the supremacy of nation-states." Paralleled by its importation into concerns about securitization, the disease has come to be seen by many as endangering global security and stability.[109]

Pictures of people about to die have been part of the disease's visualization from its earliest coverage. The gravitation toward pictures of possible death is notable, though, because for much of the disease's progression, bodily frailty is contained and invisible, suggesting no recognizable symptoms. As one photographer said, "you can photograph a sea of refugees leaving Afghanistan or Albania or a city razed to the ground—but you cannot photograph 25 million Africans living with HIV. It's invisible." At the same time, as the disease progresses—often toward ugly skin lesions and a wasting syndrome—it becomes uncomfortably evident, as photojournalist Don McCullin noted, "The disease is visually unkind to the eye. It infringes upon the comforts of magazines themselves because it's difficult to run advertising up against certain stories, and AIDS is one of the most unattractive, powerful and important visual stories on earth." This makes images of possible death—where "emaciation, jutting bones, sunken eyes and a listless expression of despair" need to be shown early on—all the more central as AIDS's visualization in the news.[110] Suggesting the possibility of death may be as much as is comfortable for the journalists, news executives, politicians, officials, and viewers who look on its depictions.

Though pictures of possible death have not been the only mode of representing people about to die from AIDS in the news, the depictions have offered a formulaic, though narrowed, representation of what a person with AIDS looks like. In Jenny Kitzinger's view, in the disease's early days "photojournalists deliberately sought out people with AIDS who looked particularly ill, rejecting healthier 'specimens' who volunteered to be photographed or filmed because they did not 'look the part.'" Bodily degeneration was key, and many news organizations showed before and after pictures that underscored the downward transformation. Most persons depicted dying from AIDS were shown often alone and sometimes with families, but rarely with their male partners or friends. Such visuals underscored the consequence of "deviant" lifestyles, imparting a clearly moralistic message to viewers, which was reinforced by captions and voiceovers. For instance, one early CBS TV special on AIDS, broadcast in 1986, reminded viewers of "hopelessness. Whenever a person with AIDS is allowed to utter words of optimism, a voiceover adds a caveat, such as 'Six weeks after she said this, she was dead.' "[111] Roland Bleiker and Amy Kay argued that early depictions of AIDS drew strongly from colonial stereotypes, which positioned death from AIDS as a phenomenon that was "not part of daily life...something less real and more remote," an "attempt to capture the universal nature of death, stripped free of context and culture."[112]

Some early depictions drew from associations with Africa, where generalizable pictures of usually anonymous African men and women in stages of decay from the disease lent it the aura of an illness "removed from the everyday realities of the western world...passive victims, void of agency, history, belonging or social attachment."[113] One such picture was taken in 1986 by Edward Hooper, showing a Ugandan mother and baby, both in the last stages of AIDS-related illness. Titled "Florence and Ssengabi," it pictured the mother and infant in the entranceway to their unseen home in Gwanda, Uganda (fig. 4.7). Underscoring passivity in the face of AIDS, the picture was emblematic of the early visualization of the disease, whose sufferers remained universal, lacking in agency, and clearly marked by decline. They also remained the other in nature.

The image offered a close almost dispassionate portrayal of the two ravaged bodies—emaciated frames, bony extremities, listless facial expressions that signaled a tired resignation, and used-up energy. Though holding the almost unrecognizable shape of her failing infant, the mother displayed maternal gestures that amounted to little more than the mechanistic provision of physical support for the child, tendered much like one would break the impact of a falling glass, without affect, warmth, or nurturing impulse. The picture shouted despair, failure to thrive, lack of a way out.

In a manner similar to that reflecting the display of other images of impending death, the picture portrayed little of the initial moral discomfort Hooper had experienced in taking the photo or the context in which the photo had been taken. Hooper and the French photojournalist he accompanied on the shoot ended up spending five days—twice as long as intended—in the area once they realized the gravity of what they were witnessing. Hooper later said the event "came to represent a pivotal moment in my life." He recalled photographing "the mother and child from every angle, with every lens," but later added that this trip to southern Uganda and "the photographing of Florence went on to affect fundamentally my personal response to the pandemic." Devoting the twenty-four years since that episode to researching and writing about AIDS, in 1999 he produced a well-received tome of more than a thousand pages that provided fresh evidence supporting the hypothesis that the AIDS pandemic was iatrogenic. In his words, "I believe that had Florence known the role that this photograph would eventually play, she might well have felt that at least something good had come out of a tragic situation."[114]

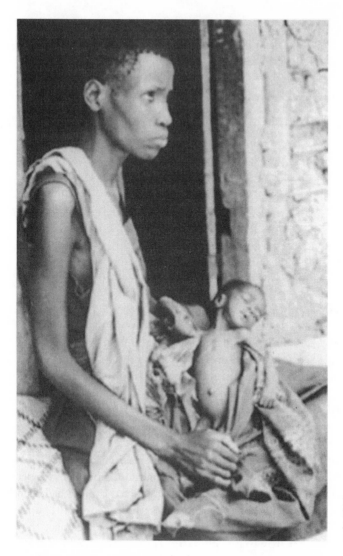

Figure 4.7: Edward Hooper, "Florence and Ssengabi," Uganda, 1986.

Little of that context was reflected by the photo's display. It was soon picked up by *Newsweek*, where Hooper's image encapsulated what Americans were willing to show and see about AIDS in its early manifestations and was generically titled "Two Victims: Ugandan Barmaid and Son." Two years later, the *Washington Post's* affiliated journal *Health* published a photo from the same series—with Florence's head now turned toward the photographer—on the cover of its weekly to illustrate a broad story about exaggerated fears of AIDS, rendering its use even more universal, though its caption now mentioned her full name. That article and the picture appeared yet again that same year in

Africa Report, the following year in *The Guardian* and in the Nairobi-based *Weekly Review,* where Florence and her child became "African AIDS Victims." Though Florence died within four weeks of the picture and her baby Ssengabi a few months later, the photograph was instrumental in giving a human face, however decontextualized, to the disease long after the moment of its taking.[115] And yet that face belonged elsewhere.

From its earliest depictions, then, AIDS was anthropomorphized through often distant, disfigured, and debilitated people. As Paula Treichler argued, the understanding of AIDS that such pictures proffered drew on "a series of filtering devices, a layering of representational elements, narrative voices and replicating images" that positioned the disease as coming from elsewhere.[116] Usually seen through close-ups, the images left those with AIDS little privacy or dignity, what Douglas Crimp called "phobic images" without context that generated fear.[117] But these images—which appeared beyond journalism too—generated multiple responses. As early as 1988, when Nicholas Nixon exhibited pictures of people with AIDS across time at MOMA, photographic critics hailed the images as intimate and authentic—Robert Atkins celebrated how "one feels both vulnerable and privileged to share the life and (impending) death of a few individuals"[118]—while ACT-UP members protested outside the museum: "No More Pictures Without Context," read their fliers. "Stop Looking at Us; Start Listening to Us."[119]

By the early 1990s, journalism's images of people with AIDS began to reflect some of these impulses. As AIDS gradually turned from a death sentence to a chronic and manageable disease, depictions of people living with AIDS began to offset pictures of people dying. Though still somewhat stigmatized, a combination of

> activism which turned HIV/AIDS into a cause at the heart of gay liberation, celebrity calls for a normalization of social attitudes, and recognizable "faces of AIDS" in the media and popular culture meant that, in North America at least, identification with the domestic victims has trumped the blaming of stereotypes.

Pushed by the successful intervention of antiretroviral drugs, an active commercial interest in the gay market, and pharmaceutical companies anxious to use pictures which could represent the shift, pictures of possible death gave way to pictures of healthy Americans with HIV, such as Arthur Ashe and Magic Johnson.[120]

This development, however, required a different, more somber target for the disease's centering and consequent coverage because the images still needed to signify illness. It is here that Africa became even more central to the depictions that ensued. As AIDS became more manageable in the United States, its spread across Africa hit unprecedented heights. This aggressive spread facilitated a reshowing of images reminiscent of the early days of the disease's visualization, but now they showed primarily dying Africans. David Campbell called these images

> a relocation of the phobic images from the domestic space of northern societies to the foreign realm of the global south.... Replayed colonial stereotypes of the 'dark continent' through an iconography of anonymous victimization ... has meant that images of death abroad have helped secure life at home.

Homogenizing a continent of 900 million people in fifty-seven countries and thousands of cultural groups, Africans came to be routinely seen in the U.S. news coverage of AIDS as a single diseased population. Coupled with crude notions of African sexuality, colonialism, and racial difference, these images allowed for the importation of impulses that had circulated during the disease's first years—when AIDS was originally seen as an importation from Africa—but now with a newly global relevance.[121]

That the locus for addressing AIDS in the U.S. news media has shifted to Africa has been supported by numerous studies. In a survey of AIDS coverage between 1981 and 2002, one study found that a decline in coverage, begun in 1987, revealed a shift from overwhelmingly U.S.–focused coverage with American datelines (86 percent and 94 percent respectively) to less focus on the United States and fewer American datelines (60 percent and 80 percent respectively); most of the other news coverage addressed Africa.[122] A study published by the *Columbia Journalism Review* found similar changes in broadcast news, with 62 percent of broadcast news invoking a global rather than U.S. perspective, most of it coming from Africa; Africa rose as an affected population in the news from 1 percent of news stories in 1981 to 19 percent in 2002.[123] In other words, though the coverage of AIDS has remained by and large a U.S. story, the focus has aggressively shifted to Africa.

This means that from the 1990s on, AIDS in Africa provided the images of possible death that had circulated of both Americans and Africans with AIDS a decade earlier. Not only did the disease's distant locations facilitate the depiction of unnamed dying and dead, but the images were able to "both disturb and comfort: death in a distant and dangerous elsewhere can become a way of affirming life in the safe here and now."[124]

Consider this 2002 AP image from Haiti (fig. 4.8). Though not from Africa, its depiction of a black body performs many of the functions mentioned above. The photo depicted a patient suffering from AIDS at a hospice in Port-au-Prince. Focusing in close-up on the man's closed eyes and large veined hand, as he clutched the bedsheets, the image's accompanying caption offered no additional detail other than tracking the mortality rates from AIDS. The man was given no name, no identity, no context to his possibly impending death, which was never confirmed. His fragility, aloneness, and vulnerability, temporarily suspended by the camera, were magnified by their journalistic display.

Time devoted a cover story to AIDS in Africa in February 2001, featuring a cover image that uncharacteristically poured over the news magazine's masthead. Picturing two faces—ostensibly a mother and child, though the gender of neither figure was clear—the photo showed the two figures oriented toward each other in a jarring juxtaposition of the older figure's anger and the younger figure's innocence. The child's eyes gazed onto a horizon not captured by the camera: tentative, bewildered, and uncertain, his or her gaze was undone in one fell swoop by the anger and concern of the older individual. The image drew its meaning from the dissonance between the two anonymous individuals it depicted. Collapsed into each other's space in a presentation that erased three of the four letters in the news magazine's masthead, the collision of the two figures' contrary emotions was settled, at least temporarily, by the accompanying text: "This is a story about AIDS in Africa. Look at the pictures. Read the words. And then try not to care." But who were the two people? Were they sick? Left alone by the disease? Dying? Tellingly, there was no title to the issue, underscoring the importance of the picture in signifying the story on its own terms, however unclear they were.

Inside, the cover story, "Death Stalks a Continent," tracked the spread of AIDS across Africa. *Time* also provided a twenty-five-image multimedia slide show to accompany the story. Few of the depicted individuals had names or identifying details; little context was provided about their individual circumstances, and many languished in depleted bodies. The coverage generated over $800,000 in public donations to a designated charity.[125]

All of this suggests that the move toward AIDS in Africa as the core representation for what nonetheless remains a U.S. story has allowed the reemergence

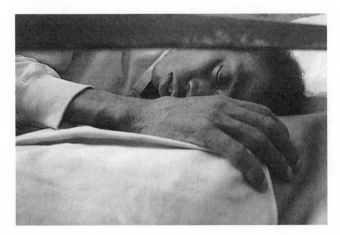

Figure 4.8:
Daniel Morel/AP,
"AIDS in Haiti,"
July 2, 2002.

of old stereotypes that support Africans as bearing the brunt of the illness. Its play to the "as if" of AIDS—by which depleted and unnamed African bodies linger on the cusp of an unconfirmed death—lent the disease an otherworldliness for many Americans. But it also made this motif of the trope of impending death workable in the U.S. news media.

Furthermore, the motif of possible death tends to prevail even when photographers contend that they are interested in other ways of depicting the disease. Photographer Don McCullin, for instance, sought to offset the vulnerability that pictures of people with AIDS depicted alone promote. Photographing his subjects looking directly into the camera, he claimed he "wanted to offer these people some dignity. I didn't want to be taking advantage of wretched people dying on the floor. I wanted to become their voice." Working together with the WHO, HIV/AIDS Alliance, and Christian Aid, he produced an online photo-history of AIDS in the region.[126] And yet, McCullin's photos produced multiple images of frail and decaying bodies, highlighted for their fragility, vulnerability, and disrepair, sometimes unnamed, often dying an unarticulated death. Regardless of his intentions, observed one critic, the photos continued to objectify their targets of depiction, "repeat[ing] recognizable subjects and settings" from early depictions of orientalism.[127]

Similar experimentation with the motif was attempted by Tom Stoddart. An award-winning photographer who had taken pictures of multiple wars, famine, and 9/11, Stoddart's black-and-white photos from a five-year stint in Africa in the 2000s, presented under the title "Scourge" in his book *iWitness* and as an online multimedia slide show, offered stark depictions of the dying and dead in southern Africa.[128] In one photo from 2000, he portrayed a frail man being helped into a bathtub in a Zambia hospice (fig. 4.9). The man's shrunken naked frame, bearing no more girth around his hips than around

Figure 4.9:
Tom Stoddart/Getty Images, "Lest We Forget–Africa's AIDS Crisis," January 01, 2000.

his legs, was supported by the white-gloved hands of unseen hospice workers. Barely able to hold himself aloft, his head teetered precariously parallel to the bathtub's parameter as he was being carefully lowered into it. Describing the hospice as "the frontline in the battle against AIDS," Stoddart claimed that his pictures—"images of dignity"—offered critical documentation of the disease.[129]

Stoddart explained that he decided to document the spread of AIDS in Africa because "wars come to an end, but the AIDS tragedy has been going on for twenty years now and it's getting worse." Setting out to show the face of a disease so widespread that "in sub-Saharan Africa you are either infected or affected, there's no escape from it," Stoddart's stated aim in taking the pictures was to offset the fact that most of those depicted dying of AIDS in the news remained nameless. Deciding he "wanted to give them the respect of using their name, if they wanted that," that aim was not always realized.[130]

Under the title "HIV Victim," this photo was recycled extensively as Stoddart's photos moved across multiple online sites. *US News and World Report* published it online with its full caption:

> AIDS patient Kelvin Kalasa, 30, is helped into a bath at the Mother of Mercy Hospice in Chilanga, Zambia. The hospice is run by Sister Leonia Komas who founded it eight years ago. The nun and her staff provide care to the poorest AIDS victims in the area.[131]

But others displayed the photo while reverting the man in it—Kevin Kalasa—to "an African man dying of AIDS." In many cases Stoddart's preference for displaying the individual's name was not followed, rendering the images more similar to the earlier motif of anonymous decaying bodies without context than he had intended. Even when the photo received the NPPA's best photo award in the POY (Pictures of the Year) Competition, the image's title—"HIV Victim"—was displayed more prominently than the detailed information of its caption in the listing of winners. Instead, the photo was often appended to the fact that nine thousand persons were dying from AIDS across Africa each day. The photo continued to be shown in ways that Stoddart had tried to offset—as the illustration of books on photography, Web sites related to journalism, as the focus of multiple Web sites and gallery exhibits—where one newspaper labeled Stoddart a "witness to horror." Furthermore, sometimes his captions supported an orientation toward suggestibility themselves. In one video show of his still photos, he positioned a picture of the birth of a Malawian baby as the concluding shot. Though this might have been seen as a hopeful gesture, he captioned the image "Baby Mercy has a 35 percent chance of dying from AIDS before she is 15," thus turning an uplifting concluding depiction into a picture of possible death. Even when he tried to do otherwise, the Africans with AIDS in his images continued, in one view, to lack "historicity, community and cause."[132]

For some, the stubborn and familiar persistence of the anonymous decaying bodies on the verge of an unseen death was predictable. In David Campbell's view, "Each of these photojournalists, their stated intentions [of producing different images] notwithstanding, produced photographs that reproduce the icons and stereotypes of the pandemic." That assessment should, at some level, come as no surprise, for it draws from Allan Brandt's early observation that the engagements with disease always draw from preexisting beliefs about it.[133]

But such persistence drives too from a broader need for familiar depictions that can suggest death without showing its graphic detail. Again, form prevails when content is so unsettling. Even when bodily frailty did not depict what was most salient about this disease, it needed to be shown as disease's most workable and familiar signifier. In keeping with the status of AIDS as a global threat, pictures of persons of color dying in distant places thus served multiple functions. Because AIDS needed to be seen in the U.S. news media, it was useful that the bodily frailty it rested on could be shown from elsewhere.

Possible Death from Famine

Journalism's images of famine and its effects have constituted one of the most frequent though uneven repositories for depicting possible death from natural causes. Though images of famine can be found as early as the Great Irish Famine of the 1800s, they have been taken more often than not in a serendipitous fashion, often as a matter of opportunity when representatives from human rights organizations or celebrities visit feeding centers, refugee camps, or other settings established for humanitarian reasons. Though famine has come to be seen as a complex phenomenon associated with war, human rights abuses, opportunistic diseases, poor sanitation and water supplies, inadequate medical facilities, and an ill-fitting relationship between population need and supply,[134] its narratives remain largely simplistic and uncritical, categorizing famine as a natural disaster beyond the control of those it afflicts, and its images tend to reference the most concrete consequence imaginable—the bodily frailty that famine generates in death from starvation.

Because famine tends to evolve over long periods of time, across widespread areas and with initially unseen consequences, its coverage is by no means obvious or simple. Coverage develops in stages, progressing from the provision of terse news briefs, feature stories on regional trends, an enhancement of coverage usually due to celebrity interest, and finally, blanket attention mandating widespread moral concern. Typically, it is only when a known individual—a politician, activist, celebrity, or lobbyist—becomes involved that graphic pictures of dying persons, usually children, tend to proliferate.[135]

The forty years of drought and famine that are ravaging primarily the continent of Africa have captured the news media's attention along such guidelines. But its coverage has been anything but uniform or assured. Images first appeared in 1967, when famine developed following the war in Biafra and caused widespread death. Said to be the last famine that played to the strengths of the black-and-white still photograph, as displayed in newspapers,[136] the war in Biafra created a visual standard for all of the images of famine that followed. Often depicted by images of possible death, where meaning rests on the viewer's recognition of a scope, scale, and magnitude beyond the image, the Biafran famine was depicted by pictures suggesting vulnerability and cued by bodily frailty: these showed generally anonymous individuals—children, women, babies, and the elderly—weak, infirm, and either emaciated and painfully thin with hollowed-out features and threadbare clothes draped across what remained of their bodies or, suffering from chronic protein deficiency, with skin rashes, off-colored hair, and distended stomachs. Their faces showed little affect, their bodies little agency or activity, and their bodies were out of proportion—intense and sorrowful eyes overtaking gaunt faces, heads too large for the frames on which they rested, and bony extremities tacked on like afterthoughts. Often shot in close range, these images offered simplistic and formulaic depictions of the bodily ravages of starvation. Generally pictured in groups, the depicted persons sat, squatted, or lay prostrate on a parched and barren ground, often staring at the camera, and, as recounted in the accompanying captions, revealing little movement other than the usual "awaiting food."[137] Their display, in Susan Sontag's view, encouraged "belief in the inevitability of tragedy in the benighted or backward—that is, poor–parts of the world...inherit[ing] the age-old practice of exhibiting exotic—that is, colonized—human beings...displayed like zoo animals in 'ethnological' conditions."[138]

Such a visual formula prevailed over the ensuing years, as other situations of mass starvation took place across the African continent—Ethiopia in 1974 and 1984, Zimbabwe and Somalia in 1992, Sudan in 2003, to name a few. The news media framed their spread, increasingly over the years on television, as part of a connected series of events, creating a Western image of Africa as "a disaster continent."[139] As Vicki Goldberg commented more broadly on the images of refugees: "The press and television have been glutted with images of starving, emaciated, ragged people in wretched camps, standing in interminable lines for a bit of sustenance, awaiting death with distended stomachs."[140] The *Wall Street Journal* later remarked that the formula had misguided the U.S. news media: "The very power of images of starving children intimidated many print reporters into spending too much of their time at emergency feeding camps. They packaged the famine as a relief issue" and so neglected to focus on the broader structural conditions that made famine an effective governmental strategy of control.[141]

One marked spread of famine took place around the Horn of Africa between 1970 and 1985, killing millions of people across twenty countries. Though Ethiopia was hardest hit, losing more than a million of its residents, by the time its pictures were seen, said an executive with the relief agency World Vision, "most of the people at risk of dying had already died."[142] Coverage was schematic and formulaic, using "stereotyped images, stock phrases and common abstractions" to drive the stories and images that appeared.[143] Though both journalistic and public interest was unremarkable in the early years, the involvement of broadcast news perked public interest. One particular broadcast, shown on NBC and the BBC in October 1984, tracked starving Ethiopians associated with a feeding station near the town of Korem. That footage—filmed by journalists Mohammed Amin and Michael Buerk and later said by one news executive to have used a mesmerizingly slow pacing of camerawork, making each clip "an award-winning still photo"—did not provide new information but showed it in a way that commanded interest. The tape "made the famine a political priority," and drew the attention of multiple celebrities, who then produced a large-scale rock concert—Live Aid—and brought in massive amounts of financial assistance.[144] Images were thus central to the development of interest in the famine across this fifteen-year period, and they moved beyond journalism in patterned ways

The captions and voiceover affixed to images of African famine both recount a fate of impending death and emphasize that many others have already met that fate. Whether or not those depicted in fact meet their deaths has been incidental. In 1983, for instance, a set of three such images decorated the front page of the *Washington Post,* and the story to which the images were appended began as follows:

> By the time you read this article, Bezuayhe Tesema, a 2-year-old wisp of skin and bones, is certainly dead. When I saw her at the Zwi Hamusit "shelter" late last month, Bezuayhe weighed less than 9 ½ pounds and was only 24 inches long. The average healthy American baby usually reaches that weight a month or two after birth and would be three times her weight by age 2. Suffering from pneumonia, often one of the harbingers of death in childhood malnutrition, Bezuayhe had lost more than 10 ounces since her last weighing two months before. Her tiny ribs protruded against her shriveled skin; her arms were like toothpicks.[145]

More often than not, those awaiting death are not identified by name. One such Reuters image, taken by award-winning photographer Corinne Dufka, showed a gaunt, elderly couple staring vacantly at some implied provision of services beyond the camera's frame. In the background, numerous individuals were shown clumped indiscriminately under tents shielding them from the sun. The caption situated the couple against the larger context:

A severely malnourished husband and wife wait outside a feeding center in hopes of being allowed in to receive food aid July 2. Despite a massive aid operation by the United Nations World Food program, aid workers say the numbers of severely malnourished people entering the feeding centers continue to rise. In the Ajiep feeding center run by the medical charity Doctors Without Borders, some 30 people are dying of hunger each week.[146]

It was not made clear whether the husband and wife, whose identities were not mentioned, were among those who died. Rather, it was left to viewers to imagine the couple dead. Similarly, in depicting the famine of Somalia, *Newsweek* featured an image of an unidentified woman lying on the ground, "waiting for help—or death."[147] The function of bodily frailty, then, is to cue a larger story than the possible death of those depicted. Though television has done a fuller job of depicting famine, it followed the same conventions. For instance, when ABC's *Prime Time Live* produced a 1991 program segment on the Somali famine, it flashed an image of an emaciated child and its announcer said, "Look into these eyes. This child is one of two million people who may die if help does not arrive soon in Somalia."[148]

Photographing the victims of famine has raised profound questions among many of the photographers engaged in its documentation. The work of Sebastio Salgado, James Nachtwey, Mary Ellen Mark, and others helped spread the physical horror associated with famine in Ethiopia, Somalia, and the Sudan, but their images raised the possibility of an intervention that was not realized and questions of moral responsibility around images of possible death. Typical was the experience of *Boston Globe* photographer Stan Greenfield, who produced a simple picture in 1985 titled "Ethiopian Famine." The image portrayed a woman and child waiting in line for food in Wad Sharafin Camp. The emaciated child rested on the woman's lap, whose hands maternally cupped the crown of his head. Both stared frontally into Greenfield's lens. Within hours after the shot was taken, the child was dead. Though the image later appeared in numerous retrospectives as one of the top photos of the disaster, it nonetheless remained troubling. As photographer Don McCullin said of photographing dying children in Biafra, "What can I achieve by taking pictures of starving children?... If you photograph a person who's dying, you're not going to save that person's life...Whatever your achievements are, however small or large they may be, you still walk away with a slight crime on your hands."[149] It may be, then, that sometimes cues of bodily frailty do not navigate the inferential tensions necessary for images of possible death to work as assuredly as do those of bodily harm. In particular, the repeated difficulties voiced by photographers about taking these images suggest that unlike other images of impending death, questions about form remain at issue.

Such was the case in one of the most well-known images of African famine—Kevin Carter's picture of a starving, dying girl in the Sudan in March of 1993. Ravaged by civil war, drought, and famine, the region, largely closed to journalists, was rumored to have lost millions of people. Carter, one of a group of South African journalists nicknamed "the Bang-Bang Club" for its photography of black factional violence and apartheid, went to the Sudan in March 1993 to cover the war there. He landed in the village of Ayod, where people were reportedly dying at the rate of twenty per hour.

Although the story of how Carter came to take his acclaimed picture of a starving child differs by the context in which it was told, most versions had him wandering into the open bush where he heard a whimpering sound and saw a small girl collapsed on the ground. Appearing to be no more than five years old, the child had collapsed while crawling toward a United Nations feeding center, a kilometer away. As he crouched to take her picture, a vulture landed a short distance away, awaiting her death. Carter waited for nearly twenty minutes, hoping that the bird would spread its wings so that he might capture a more memorable shot. It did not, and after he took a few images, he shooed the bird away and watched the girl continue to struggle. As he later told it, he sat by a tree, cried, and thought about his own daughter.[150]

The photo he took was striking for both its simplicity and heartfelt human anguish. It depicted the child, lying prostrate in the shot's foreground, being carefully tracked by a plump vulture in the background (fig. 4.10): the child's broken, vulnerable frame, supported by spidery arms that hugged the parched earth as much as they lent on it for physical support, was juxtaposed with the certain, somewhat cocky posturing of the bird. Its head was alertly perched as it waited cannily for its prey to die. No other object appeared in the image, its background clouded by what appeared to be thick dust.

Figure 4.10:
Kevin Carter/Corbis
Sygma, "Vulture
Watching Starving
Child," March 1993.

At the time, the *New York Times* had been searching for an image to illustrate a piece it intended to run on the Sudanese famine; when editors saw Carter's image, they were captivated. Printing the image in its front section on March 26, 1993, the accompanying piece, titled "Sudan Is Described as Trying to Placate the West," addressed the country's widespread starvation and growing acceptance of Western relief efforts. The picture's caption described the Sudanese opening of the famine-stricken region to relief operations and then noted: "A little girl, weakened from hunger, collapsed recently along the trail to a feeding center in Ayod. Nearby, a vulture waited."[151] The girl was mentioned nowhere in the accompanying article.

Public response to the photo was swift. Hundreds of people contacted the *New York Times* with questions about what had happened to the child, and the editors responded publicly in a note four days later: "The photographer reports that she recovered enough to resume her trek after the vulture was chased away. It is not known whether she reached the center."[152] Though it was widely believed, but not confirmed, that the girl died soon after her picture was taken, from the beginning the photo raised questions about the girl's fate.

The photo was picked up by a small number of other news organizations, including *Time* and the South African *Globe and Mail.* Featuring the picture as a three-quarter page image, *Time*'s caption detailed the same frozen juxtaposition of the child's faltering frame with the hovering vulture. As with the *New York Times,* the newsmagazine received scores of public comments, to which Carter responded by reflecting more generally on all famine victims, saying that the photograph depicted "the ghastly image of what is happening to thousands of children."[153] *Time* ran the image again three weeks later alongside letters to the editor, with a plea for donations to relief efforts. Commenting on the numerous letters and phone calls it had generated, the newsmagazine here quoted Carter as being "not sure what happened to the little girl...but he is hopeful that she received food and treatment."[154] *U.S. News and World Report* used the image to illustrate a poll addressing which public issues concerned U.S. citizens (and the word *famine* did not rank highly).[155]

The photo experienced two additional rounds of public display, both of which raised further questions about the viability of its form. Recognizing the subjunctive force created by the girl's vulnerability, anonymity, and the uncertainty of whether she had died, relief organizations saw in it a useful vehicle for increasing aid to the region. The following year, it was used as a poster in a human rights campaign by Amnesty International and other human rights organizations. It was not long before *Time* magazine called the photo "an icon of Africa's anguish," using the opportunity to print it again.[156] That year the image took the Pulitzer Prize, even though Carter was not a recommended finalist. From that point on, the photo appeared widely across the news media, appearing in the *Washington Post, Boston Globe, Salt Lake Tribune,*

St. Petersburg Times, St. Louis Post-Dispatch, and other newspapers.[157] The *New York Times* reprinted it in announcing Carter's win and again the following day in an advertisement heralding the award, noting that the picture of the girl "collapsed from hunger" had become "an icon of starvation."[158] Each time the photo appeared it generated the same discomfort it had raised initially. Many news organizations described the girl's fate in ways that suggested she had survived; she was said to have collapsed, not died. *The Houston Chronicle* went so far as to clarify its earlier reporting of the prize, noting the next day that it had since found out that the girl "was able to reach aid and was treated at a food station."[159] The *New York Times,* covering its own association with the Pulitzer win, repeated its earlier reading of what had happened, echoing the justification articulated a year earlier: "The child recovered enough to resume her trek after the vulture was chased away. It is not known whether she reached the center."[160]

As the photo drew more attention, questions about the girl's fate began to be accompanied by widespread discussions about the aim and shape of news images more generally—questions about appropriateness, decency, vulgarity, and the tasteful function of photojournalism. Specifically, Carter's own behavior in taking the photo raised questions: Why did he not help the girl or make certain the vulture was gone before he moved on? As discussion of the girl's fate gave way to a rapidly building criticism of her photographer—the *St. Petersburg Times,* for instance, in a piece titled "Were His Priorities Out of Focus?" noted of the girl that "no one knows her name, or even whether she lived" and of the photographer that "he moved on"—the photo attracted international attention.[161] In Japan, where in one view the public "had fallen under the spell of the vulture picture like no other society," the photo replayed again and again, rebroadcast on news programs as schoolchildren debated the ethical questions it raised about good journalistic practice.[162] Querying why he had taken the twenty or so minutes to shoot the image but did nothing to help the child, journalists in Carter's native South Africa called the image a fluke and wondered if he had set up the tableau.[163] Viewers continued to express outrage, calling his actions "shameful," "inexcusable," and "inhuman" and complaining that he had "cheapened" both the prizes and the news organizations that printed the image: "Which is the true vulture?" asked one reader.[164]

Provoking questions that had less to do with what was depicted and more with what could be imagined and was not shown, the image rested uneasily in the public imagination. As Susan Moeller later observed, "Where are that child's parents? Siblings? Was the little girl left by her mother to die? Or did the mother die, and now the child is left alone? Did the child manage to crawl to help? Why didn't anyone see the child and help her? Did the child survive?"[165] None of the questions was answerable yet they were asked repeatedly, suggesting that framing the girl's death as possible rested on uneven cues of her bodily frailty.

It was perhaps thus not surprising that the toll of the image's taking grew heavy on Carter. Amidst reports that the "image [had] ignited a global nerve," he grew depressed. Reportedly hounded by phone calls in the middle of the night criticizing him for not rescuing the girl and admitting that "I knew I had a good picture then [but] I had no idea how big it would be," he killed himself in 1994. Before his death he noted that he remained "haunted by the vivid memories of killings and corpses and anger and pain...of starving or wounded children, of trigger-happy madmen." He also expressed his sorrow that "I didn't pick the child up." As is the case with images of impending death more generally, the photo received another round of attention on his death. The *New York Times* reprinted the image atop his obituary, as did numerous other newspapers. NPR ran a piece on Carter's death, in which it added that the girl "is believed to be still alive today."[166]

The persistent attention which the photo generated about Carter's taking of the image, atop questions initially posed about the girl's fate, raised a public discontent not only with the image's content, as is the case with images of impending death more generally, but also with its form. These questions undermined the trope's reliance on a familiar form to sustain the display of distressing content. What had happened undermined what people were able to see from what was shown.

As the image moved into memory, it subsequently followed two contradictory trajectories that drew from the public's discomfort with both the image's content and form. On the one hand, the photo continued to draw acclaim, topping the lists of the most heralded photos and appearing in photojournalistic retrospectives: songwriters composed songs about it, it was imitated in movies, and a 2004 short documentary film tracing the photographer's life and eventual suicide won numerous awards, including an Oscar nomination.[167] The photo's more universal power persevered, remaining what the *New York Times* called "a metaphor for Africa's despair." As one journalist commented, "this photo illustrates in the most significant way the breakdown of humanity, [showing] the hopeless plight of a whole continent." Another said that "if the picture hadn't played, today we still wouldn't know how to spell Sudan."[168] Images following the mold of Carter's picture continue to depict famine to the present day: similar news photos depict starving children in Ethiopia, Guatemala, and Afghanistan, and pictures of famine are used regularly as stand-ins for news stories having little to do with famine. The *Economist*, for instance, used an image of a starving child to illustrate a story about the Ethiopian elections.[169] Moreover, the excessive display of such pictures has not necessarily driven public action, nor has it encouraged the development of more deep-seated structural interventions. As recently as 2006, the head of World Vision, a humanitarian organization for food relief, lamented the lack of continuing aid to Africa amidst predictions of a renewed famine in Africa, and noted that fundraising had remained low because of inadequate media coverage: "The press is not engaged because as yet there are no images of extreme starvation. But if we don't deal with it now, [that] could happen." He then added that "it would be shameful to wait to see images of starving children stalked by vultures before taking action."[170]

On the other hand, the photo's taking has remained an exemplar of problematic photojournalistic practice. Debates over why Carter did not get rid of the vulture or pick the girl up frequent photojournalistic textbooks, while the trade literature, in discussing the quandaries of practicing ethical journalism, has used the incident to launch analyses of the difficulties that arise when shooting disaster. The *Columbia Journalism Review* used it to illustrate a story titled "Covering the New World Disorder," where it displayed the image twice, once in the article and once atop the journal's table of contents. In the latter case, the editors spliced the girl from the image and showed only the vulture, forcing readers to imagine what they by then knew was beyond the image's frame. The image was mentioned nowhere in the article.[171] Years later, Carter's friends from the Bang-Bang Club recounted how variably he had remembered his reaction to photographing the Sudanese child, raising the question of appropriate photojournalistic response from anew. In their recollection, at first he said "he had chased the vulture away, and that he had then gone and sat under a tree to cry. He did not know what happened to the child. But the questions kept coming, and he began to elaborate that he had seen the child get up and walk towards the clinic."[172] Today, nearly twenty years after Carter took the picture, the circumstances surrounding this photo and its form remain a focal point in discussions of journalistic ethics.[173]

In grounding the images of naturally occurring possible death, then, the human body constitutes a valuable vehicle for pushing the public to infer what it does not see. In the case of Kevin Carter's image, however, discussion of the girl's bodily frailty generated such dissonance that the image did not rest comfortably as a news depiction. Questions of content—of whether the girl in fact had died—were accompanied and exacerbated by questions of form—of what Carter did or did not do. Overwhelming the motif of possible death, they made its depiction problematic, not only at the time the picture was taken but across memory as well.

When Possibility Fuels the "As If"

What does it mean to engage with the "as if" through possibility? In much the same way that inanimate structures offer the form through which the presumption of death can take place, here the endangered or weakened human body provides the form through which inference unfolds. Concrete, familiar, and real, the human body must be emotive enough to engage its viewers while carrying cues of either impending harm or its own fragility. Like other images of impending death, these cues blend death by design with death by neglect or accident, but at the same time they must remain sufficiently open— connotatively rich, generalizable, implicative, imaginative, symbolic, and contingent—to facilitate the public's multiple responses to what is being depicted and ensure that its capacity to understand is larger than what they see in the photo. Discussed here across the depiction of illness, political confrontation, mass extermination, and famine, these images are driven by an informational load that remains suggestive but relies on the human body for its meaning. As the Kevin Carter image of the little girl and the vulture showed, at times that load is problematic, paralyzing subsequent acts of inference. Key here is the inherent instability between content and form, by which the trope's reliance on form to make difficult content meaningful cannot always be dependably activated.

This is a tricky path to follow. For if form is to sustain difficult and unsettled content and promote a desired interpretation—that is, the inference of a death not shown that is wider than the image can indicate—then the image needs to carefully tread between the two potential pitfalls of offering not enough or too much information. For this reason, images of possibility and the work of inference they require are most effective when they involve the depiction of information already known. Because, however, the image's content is always about death, it remains easy to refute, deny, or challenge the suggestion of death that these pictures offer.

This invocation of the subjunctive voice and its play to imagined, contingent, and emotional ends was shown here to have multiple shapes. Reinforcing information already in hand, its delayed and retrospective positioning made it possible to recycle the familiar motif of possible death across time regardless of whether or not that recycling made for a more or less effective depiction. In depicting AIDS, for instance, it facilitated a return to decaying bodies that no longer reflected the main trajectory of the disease. In depicting famine, it forced attention to starving bodies at a point in which most had already turned to corpses. Most importantly, it enabled contradictory interpretations of the deaths it was supposed to suggest. Coverage of death in Tiananmen Square, the Warsaw Ghetto, and Pol Pot's Cambodia all became—for some—stories about hope, compassion, persistence, restraint, and of course, life.

Indeed, it is in stories of death by design that contradictory interpretations tend to arise most frequently. This is curious, for their display of purposive action—the approaching tanks, the menacing gun of a Nazi soldier—suggests an unseen death with more resoluteness than do images of human frailty— where the threat is amorphous and already contained within the body. Paradoxically, this may suggest that the clearer the image is about what it shows, the more it invites contrary interpretation and multiple modes of engagement. Though such a notion rests uneasily alongside the longstanding insistence on the sheer force of photographic verisimilitude, it raises important questions about which aspects of visual form facilitate engagement.

At the same time, these images of possible death enjoyed multiple lives as they offered a second stage replay of already digested events in nonjournalistic venues of display. Pushing the possibility of engagement, responsiveness, and strategic action beyond journalistic circles, the depictions of those dying from the Khmer Rouge became more forceful once they were transported into online data banks and prosecutorial tribunals. Because nonjournalists—NGOs, human rights organizations, Holocaust memorial foundations, health advocates—can use the journalistic relay of possible death as a means to an end, the instrumentality of using these images on a public expected to intervene remains salient, and today's digitally mediated environment makes it even more so.

The act of inferring death, then, encapsulates a useful range of responses to the difficult and unsettled events that images of possible death depict. Their play to the emotions, the imagination, and contingency, concretized through the human body, underscores how the response to even the most certain and familiar objects of depiction cannot be guaranteed or taken for granted. Though the informational load of these images offered markedly more information than the inanimate pictures of presumed death, here too that information does not secure or stabilize interpretations as much as it facilitates multiple forms of their engagement.

Chapter 5

Certain Death

The most prevalent use of about-to-die images in the news verbally and explicitly marks individuals as having died after their picture was taken. In much the same way that images of presumption rely on inanimate landscapes and images of possibility on human bodies, these pictures—images of certainty—rely on words to make the image meaningful.

Utilizing an elaborate set of verbal practices, these images provide the greatest degree of informational detail. Titles, captions, adjoining texts, and the verbal information associated with sequenced pictures are all used to confirm that the person about to die is now dead. As with images of presumed and possible death, impending death is established here by activating viewer engagement with what is not shown through a set of interpretive cues, and, like other images of impending death, these depictions blend death by design, neglect, or accident. Though they resemble images of possible death in relying on cues of bodily harm and bodily frailty, they are unlike other kinds of about-to-die images because they add extensive verbal information that tells the public how to interpret the image, so much so that all it needs to do is endorse or reject the verbal cues confirming that the person died. Whereas in other about-to-die images the eventuality of death is left open—presumed or inferred—here the patterned, explicit, and elaborated textual leads establish death's inevitability rather than its likelihood.

The more extensive informational load associated with these images might lead to expectations of the public's straightforward acceptance of death, a greater alignment with journalistic norms, and given the anchoring function that says that words fasten in place what a picture is supposed to mean,[1] less imagination, contingency, and emotions on the part of the journalists, news executives, officials, politicians, and viewers who see them. But that is not the case. Paradoxically, these images often draw more attention, debate, discussion, and ultimately a multiplicity of responses than other images of impending death. Words are used here in ways that paradoxically allow for the most active interpretive play around a depiction, shedding doubt on the fundamental relationship between words and images and raising questions about what the image accomplishes in lieu of informational clarity. Such play facilitates multiple engagements with these images, making them useful as agents of agendas that have little to do with the informational relay of news. Like images of possible death, they often draw extensive involvement from those outside journalism—governmental officials, lobbyists, bereaved individuals, members of militias—who expend considerable effort in their shaping, display, and interpretation. Given that images of certainty underlie all kinds of breaking and continuing news involving death—illness, assassination, crimes, natural disaster, war—they become useful candidates for fostering engagement, particularly when the events depicted remain unsettled and contested themselves.

What Does Certain Death Look Like?

Images of certain death center on the problematic co-presence of a contingent and incomplete image and accompanying verbal features that render it more complete than it looks. Co-presence takes shape on the back of the broader tensions between words and images as complementary or contradictory vehicles of news relay, where supplementary verbal information can be used alternatively to contextualize, expand, and explain an image or challenge and refute what the image shows. Such information appears both at the time of an image's display and in the days, weeks, and months that follow.

Images of certain death can be found among the earliest news pictures. Borrowing from a long tradition of spectacles of suffering, many early images of certain death depicted public executions. In 1861, *Harper's Weekly* depicted a man's execution for military desertion, identifying the man facing the firing squad in the drawing only as "Johnson." In 1865, the *Illustrated London News* published an image of an execution of a samurai involved in an attack on the British Legion; the picture showed the blindfolded man, head bowed, as the executioner raised the blade above him. That same year, Alexander Gardner's image, "The Drop," depicted the individuals convicted of Abraham Lincoln's assassination about to be hanged. Gardner's shots comprised a series of three images, the first of which was an about-to-die photo. In it, the condemned stood atop the scaffold with white hoods placed over their heads; the second and third shots depicted their bodies hanging in the air. Seen as the last act of the war, the trial and execution of the four individuals—and their visualization—helped establish a postwar consensus.[2]

Other images of certain death draw from a lingering fascination with the depiction of war. One early image was the 1916 shot "The Siege of Verdun." Taken during the German attack on the French defenses of Verdun, a World War I battle that left huge casualties on both sides, the image showed a French officer facing the camera as he was being machine-gunned to death. Taken from film footage, it is one of the first known images of front line action and has remained part of the iconic literature of photojournalism. The photo carried with it broad notions about war, sacrifice, and the nation-state, capturing "the moment not just of the man's death but the death of a way of thinking about war, courage and human agency."[3]

Often, the photo of a person about-to-die is presented in place of available documentation that shows the person already dead. For instance, in September 2003, when Korean farmer Lee Kyung-hae stabbed himself to death during the Cancun World Trade Organization summit to protest the organization's lack of responsiveness to small farmers, a Reuters sequence of images portrayed him dying while its caption told readers not only that he died shortly afterward but that his suicide was "an act of sacrifice to show his disgust at the WTO and its policies."[4] No pictures appeared of him dead, though many were available. Viewers almost always know that the person being depicted in an image of certain death is dead before seeing the photo. In 1945, for instance, a widely circulated photo of an Australian POW about to be beheaded by the Japanese appeared both at the time of his beheading—when the picture showed a tall, gaunt blindfolded man under the raised machete of his Japanese captor—and months later when the soldier was identified as one of Australia's outstanding war heroes.[5] Images of certain death thus visually support contingency while undoing it in words. This means that viewers see these images by agreeing to their "as if" depiction—agreeing to be visually suspended in the moment before death while being told that death occurs.

But how much verbal information is necessary to establish certainty? Three photos suggest the range of informational detail that words can offer the depictions of individuals facing a certain death. Chosen because they depict three degrees of verbal identification—anonymity, posthumous personhood, and the renown/notoriety that comes with recognizable persons about to die— these pictures of anonymous victims of war, of a previously unknown girl perishing in a mudslide, and of a well-known politician dying in an assassination all situate certain death across unsettled events (fig. 5.1).

1985 © Frank FOURNIER (CONTACT PRESS IMAGES)

Figure 5.1: Robert Capa/Magnum, "Death of a Loyalist Militiaman," September 5, 1936; Frank Fournier, "Omayra Sanchez–Colombia Mudslide," Contact Press Images, November 16, 1985; Yasushi Nagao/AP, Assassination of Asanuma, October 12, 1960.

The first picture was taken during the Spanish Civil War, when Robert Capa photographed a Spanish militiaman at the moment of his death. Called alternately "Death of a Loyalist Militiaman" and "Death of a Republican Soldier," the image, taken near the Cordoba front in the province of Andalusia in 1936, became the primary iconic representation of the Spanish Civil War: it symbolized Republican sacrifice, a tribute to the Loyalist soldiers who died in the war and to Republican Spain itself. First appearing in the French magazine *Vu*, on September 23, the following year it reappeared in *Life*, where it drew its U.S. audience.[6] Considered by many professionals to be "the best war photograph ever taken"—with Capa called by *Picture Post* "the greatest war photographer in the world"—the photo was fairly elemental—open sky, a natural landscape, an anonymous man falling backward onto the soil he was trying to defend.[7] Though the picture showed the man in the last moments of life, as he fell away from the camera to his death, the accompanying captions and titles pronounced him dead. In a sense, the photo's simplicity made it an apt representation of impending death in wartime, and it has since persisted along those lines, offering a subjunctive valorization of a heroic wartime death and of photography's capacity to depict it.

How did it move from depicting a particular battle to a generalized aspiration of death in wartime and a celebration of photography? The photo had denotative problems from the beginning. Though the caption said the man had just suffered a bullet to the head, no blood or gore was seen anywhere nearby. Instead, the death was clean, almost antiseptic. The photo was also significantly blurred, due to a combination of both camera angle and shutter-speed. And because, in a then-common presentation, the photo's caption provided no information about either the location or date on which it had been taken, those who viewed it could not be certain, at least initially, what precisely it showed. As historian Philip Knightley noted, "The emotive 'moment of death' photograph . . . turns out to be not the clear and simple statement of fact that it at first sight appears." Caroline Brothers concurred: "On the strength of the documentary evidence, it appears that [the photo] provides no documentary evidence of any moment of death; indeed its relationship with the truth in its most orthodox sense is at best heavily undermined."[8]

Debate persisted over the photo's authenticity, rendering further suspect its denotative dimensions. The most generous account argued that Capa had taken the photo by raising his camera blindly above his head in the midst of a ferocious battle, sent it undeveloped to Paris, and only later found out that he had not only caught the soldier in the middle of his camera frame but at the very moment he was hit. Other accounts gave Capa less credit, maintaining that the shot was one of a series of action shots staged for the camera during a quiet period on the front by insurgent soldiers impersonating militiamen. The lack of focus was said to be due to Capa's hand shaking. "If you want to get good action shots," he was quoted as saying, "they mustn't be in good focus. If your hand trembles a little, then you get a fine action shot." Still others claimed that Capa was not present in the zone being photographed, that the man shown was not dead, and that Capa's lover, Gerda Taro, had taken the photo but was unable to claim credit for it because she died in battle. As time went on, none of Capa's associates were able to establish the photo's authenticity. Even his biographer, Richard Whelan, examined Capa's film and found another shot of a second soldier "dying" on the same spot, further suggesting the initial image's staging, though Whelan himself did not support that interpretation.[9]

The image's connotative dimensions were also challenged. What did the image mean if its informational detail was suspect? The picture raised the question of what an image of certain death was supposed to establish and how much information it needed to do so: How was it possible to transform the denotative weaknesses of the image—problematic as real-life documentation—into a meaningful connotative representation about a particular death in the Spanish Civil War? The widespread support for the Loyalists by many Americans at the time, who saw it as a just war fought for the "right" causes, made the image's relevance to the record all the more important.

It was here that the image's subjunctive voice—and its play to the "as if"—helped transform the picture's weaknesses into strengths. The photo's denotative failings—the soldier's anonymity, its absence of blood, blurred focus, lack of documentation—and its connotative uncertainty were bypassed so as to orient to the image's subjunctive value—not as a document of one particular war but as an entry point to multiple broader conversations about wartime death and photography. Absorbing the photo's denotative features and connotative questions within broader interpretive schemes where they were less problematic, subjunctivity shrunk the importance of the photo's failings by transporting it to larger conversations about the meaning of what it portrayed.

This meant that a broader context needed to be established to lend the image meaning. Setting new terms by which the public could engage with the image, extensive recycling moved it away from its moorings in Andalusia and into galleries, books, posters, media retrospectives, postcards, and nearly every available mode of visual representation, where it became emblematic of what a generalized heroic death in war might look like and how its picture had been skillfully taken. Capa himself reprinted the photo in 1938 as a cover image to a collection of his and Gerda Taro's photographs titled *Death in the Making*. The image was included in nearly every collection of memorable photographs, where it was called one of the "most famous, influential and controversial photographs of the twentieth century," its depiction of the militiaman "Christlike," his arms spread in an act of sacrifice that created a lasting "image of martyrdom."[10]

The "as if" of Capa's image had many dimensions. First, the Loyalist soldier embodied a heroic death in wartime. Bloodlessly captured in a near-perfect angling against the grey sky behind him, he prevailed not as a depiction of a concrete instance of death, but as a screen on which viewers were able to project the beliefs and passions of a particular historical era onward in time. His anonymity and the lack of details about who he was were in this regard instrumental. By playing into the "as if" of his dying, the photo became a vehicle to tell people what they wanted to believe about death in wartime— that death mattered, that it was both tragic and heroic, that the single anonymous individual was important. It told them that the soldier's death was not in vain but was enacted for a cause, the support of democracy. The photo supported what many Americans wanted to believe about the Spanish Civil War—that it was a just war, fought honorably and courageously in the service of a higher ideal.

Second, the photo celebrated photographic form—a "new kind of war photograph, a close-up action image," constituting one of the first depictions of death as action. Capa was seen as having "practically invented the photojournalistic idea known as the decisive moment."[11] Celebrating this form said much about what viewers were willing to look at in a just war, creating an aesthetic ground for viewing death and facilitating a willingness to regard violent death as a morally justifiable target of spectatorship. It also suggested that death might look best when it was unrealistic—bloodless, fuzzy, suggestive. As Jay Ruby has argued, "Since death is the last act of a person's life, it is supposed to be meaningful and dramatic, particularly on a battlefield. To die in a war for no apparent reason and without drama is unthinkable for it implies that the deceased's life was wasted."[12] This fictionalized death, then, established a template against which images of certain death could be measured. In this view, it did not matter that the man was anonymous, the photo out of focus, its details unrealistic, or its relationship to the immediate battlefield unclear. The photo prevailed instead via its subjunctive voice, where less attention could be paid to what was shown and more to what it suggested about heroic wartime death and its photographic capture. As one observer noted, "The stop-action quality of the photo [lent] it great realism and [bolstered] the notion that modern camera equipment can supply records of world events as they occur." It made a difference that the photo was taken under danger and in haste, and that Capa took great risk to capture the very moment at which the bullet pierced the soldier's skull. "Even if it were a fake," one critic said, "Capa's photo changed history; it defined the war for everyone who saw it. Spain was the last great romantic war [and] this picture depicts a noble, necessary death.... Even with his last breath, the militiaman seems to embody freedom."[13]

This meant that the photo was forgiven its failings because it told viewers how to read the Spanish Civil War, how to establish a broad notion of a noble wartime death, and how to celebrate its photographic taking. *Life* noted as much in its presentation of the picture:

> Once again *Life* prints grim pictures of war, knowing that once again they will dismay and outrage thousands and thousands of readers...America's noble and sensible dislike of war is largely based on ignorance of what modern war really is. The love of peace has no meaning or no stamina unless it is based on knowledge of war's terrors. Dead men have indeed died in vain if live men refuse to look at them.[14]

The magazine reprinted this last sentence four years later, when it published the first picture of U.S. fatalities during World War II.[15]

Subjunctively, then, the photo reigned triumphant in memory, invoking contingent, imagined, and emotional engagements with those who saw it. Regardless of questions about its content, it had much to celebrate: the photographic form, the photographer and the greater good of the war all supported this preferred mode of engagement. It was for this reason that even questioning the photo's authenticity was seen as treasonous. As Capa's biographer himself said, after discovering a second image that cast doubt on the authenticity of the first: "To insist upon knowing whether the photograph actually shows a man at the moment he has been hit by a bullet is both morbid and trivializing, for the picture's greatness ultimately lies in its symbolic implications, not in its literal accuracy as a report on the death of a particular man."[16] Capa's image was thus central as a moment of certain anonymous death that was celebrated despite the fact that it displayed a marked dissonance between the image and its words, between what people saw and what they were told. Other photographs of certain death from later wars would carry that dissonance forward.

It is telling, then, that even with its verbal detail and extensive recycling over time, people still insist that Capa's soldier did not die. Fifty years after the photo was shot, the unnamed man was rumored to be alive and living in Venezuela.[17] This raises fundamental questions about how much and what kind of information is necessary for an image to establish certainty, which is not guaranteed. It also suggests the enduring power of the "as if," which prevails even in circumstances that logically might be expected to undermine it.

Other photos of death ride on different degrees of identification in establishing its certainty. The second photo of this set (fig. 5.3) followed the eruption of the Nevado del Ruiz volcano in November 1985, when a massive mudslide in Colombia buried more than twenty thousand people. The catastrophic eruption hit the nearby town of Armero particularly hard, wiping out many of its residents. One young teenage girl, Omayra Sanchez, died in the mudslide's aftermath. Caught in mud that engulfed her up to her neck and pulled down by the body of her dead aunt and the timbers of their collapsed house, the girl struggled for nearly three days as rescuers tried to free her before she died, still trapped, in front of them. During her struggle, the girl won the hearts of those trying to help her, singing cheerfully, chatting with journalists and doctors and worrying aloud with her mother, safely on land, about whether she would be able to keep up with her class after missing two days of school.[18] Rescue efforts came to naught, as the on-site personnel did not have the necessary tools to remove her from the mud and the arrival of additional rescue equipment was delayed. She died sixty hours after her entrapment, from a heart attack brought on by prolonged exposure.

Journalists covering the disaster were pulled toward two stories: On the one hand, Armero residents, the dazed relatives of the missing, searched the mud-caked rubble for survivors. On the other, rescue workers' repeated requests for shovels, stretchers, manpower, and helicopters met delays and unresponsiveness. In the *New York Times*' view, as Colombian officials "insisted they had done the best they could with the resources available in their underdeveloped Latin American country, about 23,000 people died."[19] Journalists in the area saw only a handful of Red Cross or civil defense workers, and no army or police force joining the search on the ground. As situations like Sanchez's progressively got worse, the local survivors had no recourse; many turned to prayer. Once her daughter died, the girl's mother, a nurse, "asked for prayers for the dead."[20]

Coverage of the tragedy twinned visual images of the girl still alive with verbal texts that reported her death. Because the girl's struggle was so protracted and photographers and TV personnel were on site for its duration, multiple images of the girl facing death were taken. One AP image captured the anguished girl in the lower quadrant of a picture that was taken up primarily by the bird's-eye views of support personnel trying to help her, and its accompanying caption noted how "rescuers work to save a 13-year-old girl caught in a pit of mud and water in Armero."[21] The visual choice reflected the still-resonant hopes that the rescuers, portrayed more centrally, would prevail in helping her.

Within days, however, the girl died. *The New York Times* printed a picture of her corpse being pulled from the mud.[22] Other news organizations opted to portray her suffering as she faced death, where her prolonged anguish filled the images. Pictures showed side views of her desperately clinging to life.[23] This frontal picture, taken by photographer Frank Fournier for Contact Press Images, depicted a close-up of Sanchez in the midst of her entrapment. The picture centered on the girl's face and upper torso, capturing her struggle from a more proximate distance than any of the other images. Her eyes—doleful, arresting, and accusing—gazed in a fixated fashion on the photographer and by extension the viewer, struggling to stay open though burdened by heavy, dark bags that revealed her growing suffering and fatigue. As she hung onto a log railing crisscrossing the bottom of the frame, one hand grasped it from beneath. Her hands—one holding the log, one engulfed in mud—introduced aesthetic depth to the photo, drawing the viewer into the downward motion of the spreading mud. Mud filled the rest of the frame, spilling over all four of its sides and reinforcing the death that was impending.

Fournier's image first appeared in the non-U.S. news media, surfacing first in *Paris Match* shortly after the girl's death. Appearing both on its cover and an inside page, it spread across Europe within days.[24] The difficulty in viewing his photo did not go unremarked. Fournier himself later remarked how he had "felt totally powerless in front of this little girl, who was facing death with courage and dignity. She could sense that her life was going. I felt that the only thing I could do was to report...what [she] had to go through." How was it possible to lend meaning to such an agonizing moment of personal suffering? As one photo editor commented, "The suffering in this scene is appalling. That it should be photographed and we be able to witness it so intimately is also appalling....The subject stars back at us...Her eyes, like blank sockets, reproach us for staring at her in the moments before her death." Those trying to rescue her and covering the scene were overcome with emotion. As one journalist saw it, her death was "the saddest sight...leaving behind her a circle of full grown men in floods of tears."[25]

The moral questions about using the girl's pain were, as with the denotative problems associated with the picture of the Loyalist soldier, turned into the image's strengths. When U.S. news organizations saw its appearance abroad, they printed it in their own papers and newsmagazines. But here the meanings attached to it exceeded those characteristic of the coverage of a naturally occurring mudslide. *Time* labeled the previously unknown girl a "symbol of Colombia's anguish," while the *New York Times* noted that the girl's death "symbolized a bungled rescue operation in which countless other trapped victims died." With each repeated display the image became an embodiment of a broader message—"the hope so many wanted to feel"—and the girl's posthumous identity and visible suffering became a visual marker of discussions about responses to natural disaster in less-developed regions of the world. Multiple news organizations addressed the primitive nature of the rescue operations, their critical lag time, and the outdated equipment they used.[26]

With each discussion, the photo reappeared. *Time,* for instance, printed Fournier's image twice one month later in its yearly wrap-up—both on the magazine's cover and inside. At year's end the overviews of the mudslide all reshowed the photo, and in 1986 it won the World Press Photo's Picture of the Year.[27] Chosen by various journalistic retrospectives as one of the century's memorable photos, it was hailed in volumes on photography, reproduced in exhibits and discussed in fiction.[28] Though some observers still pondered the camera's intrusive nature—when the wife of then-French president Francois Mitterand challenged Fournier for not saving the girl, the photographer retorted that France should send more rescue machinery than blankets to such disasters—the image's status as a high point of photojournalism was set.[29]

Giving posthumous personhood to one not previously known by the public, this image drew attention to the girl's impending death by appealing to empathy, compassion, and pity, forcefully drawing the involvement of those who saw its unfolding. Moral concerns about the image's taking subsided, as the familiar form of impending death's depiction mitigated its difficult content. Equally important, the relevance of that content for a larger conversation about the relationship between the developed and developing regions of the world in times of natural disaster made Sanchez's posthumous personhood an effective and emotive vehicle for facilitating engagement with those concerns too.

The certainty of impending death evolves differently when the identity of those about to die is known. A third image captured the 1960 assassination of Inejiro Asanuma, chairman of Japan's Socialist Party, on live television cameras (fig. 5.3). A scheduled debate between Asanuma and the Liberal-Democratic prime minister on the U.S.-Japan mutual defense treaty had drawn upward of three thousand onlookers and multiple journalists in attendance, using the photo opportunity to secure coverage. It was a period of unrest in Japan, for students on both sides of the political spectrum had been protesting the direction of Japan's post–World War II international relations. As Asanuma took the podium and began critiquing the party in power for its military agreements with the United States, right-wing students threw wads of paper at him. When a demonstration broke out at the back of the hall, many photographers ran to cover it. The Tokyo daily *Mainichi*'s Yasushi Nagoa stayed where he was. As he sat there, a part-time student charged the stage and fatally pierced Asanuma with a foot-long sword. Nagoa captured the event on his last unexposed negative. Though filmed clips aired on television within ten minutes of the stabbing, his still photo powerfully froze the stabbing in place.[30]

Compelling for its capture of the precise moment Asanuma had been attacked, the photo showed Asanuma and his attacker positioned in forced juxtaposition to each other, their bodies filling up the shot's foreground. The attacker had already struck once, and Asanuma was hunched over from the impact of the sword. His assassin readied it before plunging it into the politician a second time. One man writhed in agony, hands raised in self-defense, eyeglasses askew across his chin; the other hunched forward, his face contorted with determination, holding would-be rescuers at bay as he aimed his sword into Asanuma's midsection.

The photograph was rushed back to *Mainichi* in minutes, where UPI, holding exclusive rights to all *Mainichi* news pictures, released it worldwide. Appearing on the front pages of numerous papers around the world the next day, the picture showed Asanuma wincing as his assailant prepared to stab him a second time; photos on internal pages showed additional pictures of the eighteen-year-old student rushing the politician, the politician hunched in pain and the assailant being led away.[31]

The assassination sent the Japanese public into profound grief. Asanuma had been respected as a pragmatist who both supported ties with the United States and sought further cooperation with the Communist world. Leaders from across Japan's political spectrum joined in publicly grieving his death. A murder that "brought genuine grief and shame" to Japan, the event also raised questions about the country's postwar identity. In one Japanese newspaper's view, Japan was "still in an infant stage so far as democracy was concerned."[32]

Grief for the slain leader accompanied an energetic celebration of the photos of his death. News executives excitedly applauded the "spectacular photographs" obtained of Asanuma's assassination, captured because "many still photographers and television cameras were on hand when the slaying took place." Though *Life*'s larger story was on the assassination itself, it ran a special side bar alongside its table of contents, where, together with a small version of Nagoa's photo, it hailed "the camera's selective eye." Inside, the magazine showed the image again as part of a ten-photo sequence of what had happened. Significantly, what the magazine—and many newspapers—also showed were pictures of people—the prime minister, his widow—grieving the slain leader.[33] Unlike other images of certain death, which do not generally depict mourners, these images provided a visual context in which to come to terms with the death being depicted.

Within the year the photo took on its own life. It received the photography award from the George Polk Memorial Awards in Journalism, where Nagoa was cited for "a picture that is a ballet of horror." Named one of the "great news photos" by the historian of the National Press Photographers Association, it was discussed widely in retrospectives on photojournalism and secured Nagoa the 1961 Pulitzer Prize for photography, making him the first foreign photographer to win. Each time Nagoa won another award, the image appeared again.[34]

Unlike the photos of less renown that involved the Loyalist soldier and Colombian girl, this photo of certain death did not need an extensive linkage with other discourses to be seen and remembered. Playing to the newsworthiness implicit in the death of a famous person, Asanuma's renown, itself the reason for Nagoa's presence at the event, encouraged the image's automatic display. Because Asanuma's death followed a life in the public eye, its photographic capture provided a visible way of marking, remembering, and grieving his passing, its capture of that decisive moment hailed. Nagoya's celebration as its photographer was similar to that evidenced following the *Hindenburg, Challenger,* and *Columbia* air disasters, suggesting that when certain death occurs around photo opportunities, where journalists are already present, the act of hailing photographic technology can become critically coupled with the coverage itself. Though the discomfort of looking repeatedly at the politician being stabbed remained, particularly for many in the grief-stricken Japanese nation, the formulaic turn to its coverage and celebration of its photographic capture mitigated the unsettled content of what it showed.

Over time, the image's reflection of then-resonant tensions between the left and right over Japan's ties with the U.S. propelled it into various discussions about Japanese politics and the budding collaboration between Japan and the West. Years later, when the picture drew parallels with the killing of Lee Harvey Oswald on U.S. television, it was remembered as an important display of a critical incident that had tested the waters of Japan's post–World War II position.[35] The renown of Asanuma thus generated usable and familiar cues for the image's interpretation, facilitating coverage of his certain death, celebration of its capture as breaking news, and the establishment of an emblem for postwar Japan-U.S. relations.

Taken together, the Loyalist soldier, the Colombian girl, and the Japanese politician reveal the central premise by which words drive images of certain death: they establish death's role as the great equalizer. Whether or not a depicted individual is known before or because of his or her impending death allows these images to travel onward in time in different ways. Though here too the familiarity of the form makes content more manageable, even in a version of the trope that depends on elaborate verbal details, these images show that such detail does not come in equal doses. The Loyalist soldier's death was crafted through his anonymity, facilitating its useful symbolic importation into multiple discourses about photography, death in wartime, and heroism. The previously unknown Colombian girl, who became well-known because of her death, was given a posthumous personhood that encouraged a strong emotional identification with human suffering and raised the inequities associated with responses to natural disaster in different regions of the world. The death of the Japanese politician, killed because of his public renown, drew from that same renown in pulling those who saw its image into grief and mourning. Though not all who saw it grieved, his public identity enabled an automatic emotional response to his death that was more readily accessed than that associated with depictions of either anonymous or previously unknown people. On the back of this emotional engagement, the photo became an emblem of post–World War II politics, made visible by a news medium celebrated for its ability to visibly mark his passing. Thus these three levels of explicitness in verbally identifying individuals facing certain death—anonymity, personhood, and renown/notoriety—all facilitate an engagement with uncomfortable content. Because their workability rests on whether their interpretive cues are accepted or rejected, it is worth considering a number of cases in which that outcome has been variously negotiated.

Certain Death and Anonymity

When the people about to die in images of certain death are given no names or identities, death becomes easily symbolically representative of a larger malaise or problem—suicide, euthanasia, terrorism. Reflecting a broader trend that favors the infamous over the famous in news photos, "ever more drawn to telling the major dramas of our day through bit players,"[36] these images suggest that a dying person's anonymity can be fruitfully used to mark a larger cause. Death thus functions here as an enabler of repute, not for the individuals who die as much as for the issues and events on which they cause viewers to reflect.

The certain death of anonymous individuals surfaces repeatedly across the breaking and continuing news of events involving naturally occurring, accidental, and intentional death. Individuals who die in disreputable circumstances— drug dealers in Iran, robbery suspects in Brazil, or drug users in Spain—are often depicted anonymously. But so are victims of random violence. For instance, in May 1992, Serbian photographer Bojan Stojanovic captured an unidentified policeman in a small town in Northern Bosnia shooting an anonymous Moslem man in the back of the head, among the first images to show evidence of Serbian ethnic cleansing. The incident almost cost the photographer his life: when he received the 1993 World Press Photo Award and went to claim it in Holland, he was abducted by two armed Serbo-Croats but narrowly escaped. A 2004 *U.S. News and World Report* article about the civil war in Darfur, Sudan, ran a picture of a doctor from Doctors without Borders treating an anonymous, malnourished baby. Under a title proclaiming "Too Late," the caption told readers that the doctor "tries to help a baby, who later died of malnutrition." That same year, the violence in Iraq was captured by a front-page *New York Times* photo, which showed an unidentified election official in Baghdad kneeling over a colleague on the ground. The caption remarked that "Two other officials were also killed, including, moments later, the man kneeling."[37] Like the anonymous people in images of possible death, these individuals stand in for the collectives that they represent. Anonymity here is critical, because though words help viewers recognize the death as certain, the absence of naming facilitates engagement and the symbolic incorporation of these images into broader discourses.

Consider the case of photographer Martha Rial of the *Pittsburgh Post-Gazette*, who took a three-month journey to Central Africa intending to photograph the vulnerability of Rwandan refugees who had been ordered to leave the refuge of Tanzania in December 1996. One of her photos of the refugees, taken from a group of forty-three images collectively titled "Trek of Tears," depicted a young unidentified boy lying on a bed in a hospital ward filled with other empty beds (fig. 5.2). The picture focused on the boy as he lay huddled under a thin blanket, his head resting immobile on his forearms and

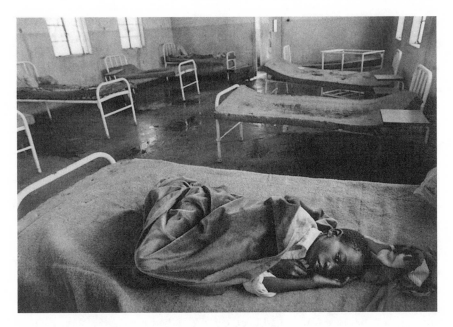

Figure 5.2: Martha Rial/Reuters, "Trek of Tears," 1996–1997.

hands. His eyes were vacant and did not make contact with Rial, conveying a sense of resignation and hopelessness. Titled as a depiction of certain impending death—"A Rwandan boy lies dying of anemia in a nearby empty ward at the Kibondo District Hospital in Tanzania"—the image's appending text gave no additional information about the boy—no name, no identity, no personal storyline or context. Published the year after it was taken (in June 1997), the photo portrayed the boy as still dying, despite the fact that he had died a year earlier. In this regard, the photo functioned like other images of certain death—it was emblematic of the event, not the individual, making the boy's death important to Rial's proclaimed aim of demonstrating the fragility of Rwandan refugees but almost inconsequential as the loss of a particular life. As Rial herself noted, "I wanted people to know that these children paid a high price for the genocide."[38]

Invoking the subjunctive voice over the picture's denotative and connotative dimensions, the *Pittsburgh Post-Gazette* did what it needed to do to keep the photo in the public eye. It ran it several times and made Rial's full visual documentation available online to its readers.[39] Rial's work drew public praise in letters to the editor and editorials—one of which called it "powerful journalism that truly did peer into the soul of the refugees"—and garnered a Scripps Howard Foundation National Journalism Award and a Pulitzer Prize for spot photography. The photos continued to be exhibited for over a decade, where in 2007 their display was used to draw fundraising for the International Rescue Committee responsible for Rwandan refugees.[40] The anonymity of Rial's depicted persons helped establish the universal plight of children and genocide. Functioning in a similar way to the anonymous images of possible death, which are used too for fundraising, their anonymity helped draw attention to the larger issues the images raised.

But anonymous images of certain death do not always work in intended ways. In 1994, the first major confrontation between the emerging new South African order and its racist past drew journalists to the region eager to document the passing of the apartheid regime. The unsuccessful invasion of Bophuthatswana by white right-wing vigilantes intent on propping up the autocratic apartheid government caused scores of deaths over two days of chaos. One incident, involving a summary execution of the right-wingers as they were trapped in a stranded Mercedes by a black "Bop" policeman, produced pictures that were splashed across the news media on March 12 and 13, 1994. One image appeared under the masthead of the *New York Times'* front page. Claimed to have been taken by Kevin Carter, it depicted three vigilantes, two already dead and one—burly, bearded, and terrified—pleading for his life as the policeman trained his gun on him. Because Carter had been certain he had missed the shot, having loaded his film while the first two men were shot, he was surprised to see that he had actually captured the moment that best conveyed the event's sheer brutality and he readily claimed credit. A mix-up in labeling, by which another photographer—Nike Zachmanoglou—had actually caught the image, was never revealed by Carter, despite the fact that the other photographers present claimed Carter knew he had not taken the shot. When reports circulated among journalists that Carter had falsely claimed credit for the photograph, it became widely referenced as a low point in professional practice.[41]

Thus, while anonymity remains a prevalent aspect of images of certain death, it does not always work in pushing an image toward its subjunctive voice. In fact, anonymity—considered here as the lowest load of information an image of certain death provides—can hijack the image's own visibility, stifling its capacity to be seen.

Anonymity: Certain Death in Liberia

Images of certain death often depict anonymous individuals who die at the behest of intentional violent actions. The slaughter of scores of student members of the Krahn ethnic group in Liberia during the early 1990s constituted one such case, when rival militias engaged in gun battles through the streets of Monrovia and other towns. Anonymity in the depiction of these killings was instrumental, for the shootings happened so erratically and quickly that it was difficult to attach names to bodies while they were still alive.

Though Liberia had a history of public executions that dated to the ascendance of the Samuel K. Doe government in 1980, there had been few images of those executions in the international news media, which by and large had been denied access to what was happening. But an outburst of violence that began in December 1989 in protest over the Doe government led to massive and undiscriminating government reprisals amidst reports of a "shoot to kill" policy against anyone associated with "suspicious activity." The rebels, said to be under the leadership of exiled ex-Doe minister Charles Taylor, went on rampages in the southern Krahn territory, slaughtering unarmed civilians and leading to a civil war that lasted seven years and reportedly killed as many as 10 percent of Liberia's 2.5 million people.[42] The war became the prototype for many of the African conflicts that followed during the 1990s: it was among the first to conduct warfare on the basis of ethnicity, among the first to use child soldiers to conduct executions, and among the first to wage war on unarmed civilians.

Two images of this violence experienced different trajectories of display (fig. 5.3). The first was taken in 1990 before much public attention had focused on the Liberian atrocities, the second six years later at the cusp of such attention. Considered here together, they show how the same cues of interpretation at two different times can produce multiple responses from journalists, news executives, officials, politicians and viewers, who either accept or refute what the photos are said to depict.

The first image, taken by photographer Joel Robine and distributed by the Agence France Presse, showed two men—one with his back to the camera, the other facing it—confronting each other in a patch of roadside brush in Bentol, Liberia. The man with his back to the camera, a member of Charles Taylor's National Patriotic Front, wielded a gun, the one facing it, in his mid-twenties, stared open-mouthed at his killer, his hands raised in a gesture of surrender. His knees were bent, suggesting a move of supplication toward his aggressor.

The title to the image told readers that the man, whom it named as student William Weah, was gunned to death because he was suspected of being a member of the Krahn ethnic group. The image, haunting for its frontal view of the student about to die, received first prize at the Festival International Scoop du Angers in 1990, but it was hardly published at the time.[43] Appearing at a point when people were only minimally interested in what was occurring in Liberia, it petered out almost as soon as it appeared.

By 1996, however, the public had had seven years of coverage about the Liberian atrocities. A short period of access for a group of journalists in May of that year made available a series of images that displayed with brutal detail how truly horrific the events in Liberia had become. A number of Western photographers, particularly from France, made their way to the streets of Monrovia during a series of gun battles there. Their pictures set new standards

Figure 5.3: Joel Robine/AFP/Getty Images, Liberian Gun-Running. August 3, 1990; Corrine Dufka/
Reuters, "Prisoner Execution," Monrovia, Liberia, May 9, 1996.

of gruesomeness: they displayed bodiless heads and headless corpses strewn dispassionately across the streets, being visually inspected by wild-looking, sometimes nude young men brandishing guns, swords and other tools of violence.

The images primarily appeared in France. The French magazine *Jeune Afrique* showed a cover photo of a man standing atop a headless corpse, his machine gun thrown over his shoulders as two other men gazed at the body; an internal photo in the same magazine showed a decapitated head lying atop a table. *L'Express* followed with its own series of images, showing not only decapitated heads but naked soldiers waving their swords, soldiers standing atop corpses, and a soldier dragging a Krahn member through the streets. The latter was captioned "a soldier dragging an injured Krahn," but it provided no specification of his fate.[44]

In the United States, the images of what was transpiring in Liberia were both less graphic and less centrally shown. It was against that timid and uneven display that depictions of the about-to-die moment emerged as a relevant picture of what was transpiring. These images showed young men in their late teens and early twenties being run down and beaten; captions said they were killed in full daylight. Many of the pictures displayed frontal views of the young men about to die, as they faced their executors in sheer terror. In other words, these images provided an almost exact replication of the Robine photo of six years earlier, now made potentially more workable by the story's ongoing coverage and the circulation of more graphic pictures elsewhere. They were also now made anonymous.

Images of these later street executions by Reuters' Corrine Dufka received the most widespread media display. A two-shot sequence—collectively titled "Prisoner Execution"—was displayed in varying configurations on May 9, 1996. It first depicted a young naked man running alongside a ditch at the side of the road, a group of soldiers roughly of the same age training their machine-guns on him; the second image showed one of the soldiers standing at right angles to the camera as he loomed over the unnamed man lying face up in a ditch below him, either about to die or already fatally shot (fig. 5.4). His legs were bent in mid-air, heightening his vulnerability and making it unclear whether he was about to be shot or was already dead.

In retrospect, Dufka recounted that she did not know what was going to happen; neither did the man: "He stood up and said to the wrong side that he was part of the Krahn ethnic group." His killers "stripped him down to his underwear...walked him across the street [and] pushed him. By that point we realized that they were going to execute him." The images evolved in record time, with a mere 20 seconds or so stretching from the point at which the young man was being interrogated to the point at which he was killed. As she later told it:

As I developed these pictures I thought I hope these pictures come out because they're going to be very dynamic images. On the other hand, I felt physically sick because someone had just been murdered in front of me. Someone who was unarmed. I wanted for my own sense of ego to please my boss and my organization, but on the other hand it was at the expense of a man's life.[45]

The display of the photos was telling. In some places, they appeared as a sequence; on an internal page of *El País*, they were displayed one atop the other alongside this caption:

> Liberia experienced yesterday a new episode of the orgy of blood and death that has lashed the African country since the beginning of last April... with the execution of a guerilla of the Krahn ethnic group. Half a dozen combatants loyal to Charles Taylor disarmed, stripped and beat the prisoner and in the end shot him in the back. Minutes later, another member of the militia gave him the coup de grace in the head.[46]

But the more common choice was to publish only the second of the two about-to-die photos. It appeared in the *New York Times*, as an illustration to an article about a prospective Liberian peace plan, whose caption offered details of precisely what had happened and was about to happen: "A Liberian fighter from Charles Taylor's faction, shown executing an unknown Krahn militiaman in the capital, Monrovia, yesterday, after the unarmed man was shot in the back, then captured, stripped and beaten."[47] Other than implying that the violence depicted was representative of the actions that West African leaders were seeking to stop, the appending story was in no way related to the image. Significantly, the image appeared only on an inside page and, despite or perhaps because of the horrific scene it depicted, only once.

The photo appeared similarly in a handful of other newspapers, in each case on internal pages accompanying verbal reportage which linked it with a larger story about the ongoing battles in Liberia. The *Boston Globe* used it to illustrate an Associated Press story titled "Battle Rages in Liberian Capital." One paragraph in the accompanying story detailed how fighters from one faction "grabbed an unarmed man from a rival group, beat him, stripped him naked and ordered him to run—then shot him in the back and killed him." The *Chicago Tribune* used the same text and picture, titling it "When Warlords Don't Show, Liberian Talks Are Called Off."[48]

One of the few places where the image received front-page display and directed attention to what it depicted, rather than what it represented about the broader Liberian circumstances, was the *Philadelphia Inquirer*. Displayed centrally on the newspaper's front page as a stand-alone image, it received an unambiguous headline "A Liberian Prisoner Faces Death."[49] Complaints from the public were immediate: More than 150 letters to the editor critiqued the central attention that the paper had given the image and 30 paper subscriptions were cancelled in protest. Lamenting that the image was "too violent," "disgusting," revolting," and "irresponsible," readers' letters prompted the paper two days later to issue an ombudsman's column criticizing its decision to publish the image on its front page.[50] Apologizing for having "missed the carnage in the hazy lower right of the picture," the paper noted that because it had assumed the man was still alive, the photo's publication would have been appropriate. Though it likened the image's display to that accorded pictures of starvation in Somalia or executions in Vietnam, the Liberian execution picture was now said to be "gratuitous" because "it seems unlikely that anything will come of it." In response, the newspaper initiated a new section, titled "Reader Reaction," to address issues that evoked "unusually intense reaction." Though the paper's backtracking prompted another round of readers' letters, this time also remarking on the newspaper's responsibility to publish even gruesome pictures, the modified stance nonetheless stood.[51] Within days, the photo was being discussed by a federal judge in a case testing the constitutionality of the Communications Decency Act.[52]

It is telling that the photos of the Liberian executions did not appear in the majority of U.S. newspapers and newsmagazines, reflecting what some observers considered a general lack of interest in issues, problems, and events related to Africa.[53] Though a handful of other images appeared showing the Liberian violence, they were few and far between.[54] The fact that few graphic photos of Liberia appeared; that the one image that did suggest brutal violence was generally shifted to internal pages with captions that did not fully detail what was happening; and that the one frontal display of an image depicting brutality was critiqued, backtracked, and used in legal proceedings about decency underscore the problematic parameters that the photo raised.

And yet, paradoxically, the image received professional awards once the actual newsgathering gave way to professional evaluation. Hailed among her peers for her visual capture of the execution, Dufka and her photos placed for two separate prizes in the global news category of the "54th Annual Pictures of the Year" Contest and received first prize in the World Press Photo competition, the Robert Capa Gold Medal from the Overseas Press Club in 1996, the International Women's Media Foundation's "Courage in Journalism Award," and a Pulitzer Prize Honorable Mention in 1997, which recalled her "chilling photo of the execution of a Liberian prisoner in the streets of Monrovia."[55] The acclaim prompted one photographic trade magazine later to call her photos depictions of Africa that were "winning awards but not publication."[56]

The irony of granting awards to news pictures that had been generally rebuffed by the news media underscored the deep-seated ambivalence that these images raised. For Dufka's part, the toll of photographing Africa and other crisis-ridden regions proved too much: too many executions made her uncomfortable pushing a story at the expense of its humanity, and she left journalism shortly afterward, becoming a human rights activist and winning a MacArthur Fellowship for her human rights work.

What this suggests is a divided and ambivalent response to the images as news relay and as markers of journalistic professionalism. Though Dufka's pictures showed a largely unknown atrocity, it remained a largely unseen one. It also remained a highly celebrated one among journalists. Unlike the acclaim that built around the anonymous Loyalist soldier, it may be that the anonymity of the young Liberians in these images stifled their deaths' display. Though the images paved the way for the photos' professional recognition, this case of certain death seemed better suited to the deployment of awards than to news relay.

The paradox of awarding the highest possible journalistic honors to a photo that the U.S. news media either minimized or bypassed altogether raises questions about the power of anonymous images of certain death. Was it their Africanness that undermined their visibility? The brutality of what they showed? Distance from the United States? Was it the unavailability of a workable discourse onto which they could piggyback in facilitating interpretation and engagement? Given that the acts depicted here gave rise to a Truth and Reconciliation Commission in Liberia only seven years later, which laid out the horrendous scope of the crimes committed, the implications of failing to engage around the unsettled and difficult events of intentional death brings pause. As the *Washington Post* wrote at the time, "This is news we can't use, these foreigners killing each other for incomprehensible reasons."[57] Not only does this suggest that anonymous images of certain death can work in multiple ways, but it points to how journalists, news executives, politicians, officials, and viewers can be marshaled into illogical and internally contradictory engagements with them as well.

Certain Death and Personhood

When about-to-die images depict the certain death of individuals who become known through their death's capture on camera, words offer more explicit informational detail. As with the picture of the Colombian girl dying under a mudslide, words here help make the death public, offering posthumous personhood to otherwise unknown people who die. The emotion-driven demeanor of these photos is marked: details of the individual's death support subjunctive linkages to larger discourses, facilitating public engagement not only with the event but with the broader issues into which it has been imported, but those details target the common and thereby human parameters of the settings in which previously unknown people die. Attention is paid here to grieving relatives, anguished friends, networks of caretakers, many of whom are depicted and all of whom weigh in on the death that is shown. For this reason, images involving posthumous personhood tend to tug powerfully at the heartstrings of those who view them.

Examples abound: after the 1995 Oklahoma City bombing, an amateur photographer took a Pulitzer Prize–winning photograph of a fireman holding a dying one-year-old Baylee Almon in his arms: "The photograph," said the *New York Times*, "pierced the heart: a limp, bloodied baby cradled in a police officer's arms. But what might have been a picture of hope brought only disappointment. The child did not survive the bombing." A top U.S. college rower pushed for his last stroke in a nationwide 2005 regatta in Philadelphia and died within the hour from dehydration. Though the picture showed Boston College rower Scott Laio crossing the finish line before he collapsed, the scene on the dock turned chaotic as emergency medics attempted to revive him before hundreds of horrified spectators. Suspicions of insufficient hydration, often practiced among lightweight rowers to keep within their weight class, made the incident a lightning rod for changing weigh-in procedures in rowing competitions. In 2007, a Pulitzer Prize–winning Reuters photo from Myanmar showed Japanese video journalist Kenji Nagai being shot fatally by police as he recorded protests against the government's crackdown on Buddhist monasteries. Dying in full view of the police but beyond any offer of assistance, the death horrified journalists and signified what could happen when "a ruthless regime fights the spirit of freedom."[58] In each case, images of the individuals facing death, newly identified by name, were catapulted into discourses—about acts of terror and innocence, the drive to win and the excesses of sports, photojournalism and police brutality—larger than their own death, a transport that was facilitated by the emotional impact of the photos.

These images of certain death tend to appear repeatedly when their initial linkage to a news story has proved fruitful. In early 2004 a security camera captured eleven-year-old Carlie Brucia as she was led away from a Florida car wash by a tattooed stranger who shortly thereafter killed her; the image of her being taken was played and replayed across the print, broadcast, and online media so repetitively that the *Washington Post* labeled it "logo-tization—"when a journalistic image ceases to tell a story but becomes a symbol for a story, denuding it both of its actual news significance and of its inherent drama." Its emblematization—across the print, broadcast, and online media on which it played—of the risks of child abduction was unambiguous. The recycling of images of suicide bombers in the Middle East or of individuals on death row has tendered a similar effect, lending a macabre before/after tension to the repeated depiction of impending death.[59]

Sometimes these images are more posed than accidental. When terminally ill Karen Janoch drank a Seconal solution to kill herself under Oregon's Death with Dignity Act, the *New York Times* recorded the collective scene at her deathbed with a series of impending death photos. The recycling of the images of Terri Schiavo, as she hovered in a comatose state while the courts debated whether or not to remove her life support, displayed "the power of an image to raise an issue, foment debate and inform personal convictions." Not only did the image, which showed Schiavo physically oriented toward her mother, find its way into right-to-life posters, but it appeared continually as the case was being legally debated, despite the fact that news executives admitted their discomfort with its repeated display. In CBS News president Andrew Hayward's view, "Every time we used [the image], we discussed that this was not new." And yet, the image persevered, even after Schiavo was legally dead.[60]

Affording personhood to people who die tends to occur when the events by which they die can be generalized in the service of broader concerns. Certain death here thus becomes subordinated to the subjunctive message—about brutality, poor working conditions, terrorism, illness—that it services. Yet underlying these photos are questions about which kinds of deaths propel their victims into posthumous personhood. Given that they tend to be emotion-driven and can be seen as relevant or central to a pressing issue or problem, the question remains as to whether they need to be also particularly tragic, unusual, or dramatic.

Personhood: Certain Death and the Intifada

In the autumn of 2000, the renewal of the latest turn in a longstanding dispute between Israelis and Palestinians, the Intifada, generated a number of heart-stopping photographs that showed how complex events in the region had become. Many of these images involved children whose impending death was laid out clearly in many of the accompanying titles and headlines that accompanied the evolving story of bloodshed and heartache in much of the region. "Eight year old Palestinian Hassan Majde Lies Dying in Hospital after Being Shot by Israeli Troops," read one such title.[61]

A September 30 event hiked the intensity levels of emotion on both sides of the conflict. A twelve-year-old Palestinian boy, Mohammed Aldura, was killed while trapped in an open square in the Gaza Strip with his father. Caught in a volley of gunfire between Israeli soldiers and local Palestinian residents, the boy and his father crouched for nearly forty minutes between a cement barrel and concrete wall. As camera personnel for French 2 television looked on with cameras rolling, both the boy and his father were shot. The sequence of events was captured on video, and it ended when the boy died of his wounds and his father lost consciousness. The video sequence was later reduced to individual frame grabs that were available free of charge as still images to anyone who asked.

The fifty-seven-second sequence of filmic shots made available by cameraman Talal Abu Rahma seemed to be sequentially sound: TV viewers saw the shots ring back and forth, the father seeming to plead to hold fire, the boy screaming hysterically and clinging to his father. Additional frames documented increasing fire, as additional holes appeared in the wall to the boy's left. Three or four seconds passed, until the boy loosened his grip on his father and then slumped over, dead. Within 48 hours, video footage of the event was screened by most news organizations. While some newspapers printed a two-shot sequence—of the boy and his father screaming as they were under fire or of the boy slumped dead onto his wounded father—nearly every news organization around the world displayed in print, broadcast, and online form one still shot of the terrified twelve-year-old facing his death.

The shot was engulfed by the helplessness of its two depicted figures (fig. 5.4). Both father and son exuded sheer terror as they crouched futilely alongside a hard concrete block wall that served as the backdrop for their inability to escape. The protective gestures of the father as he attempted to shield his son were framed by the two faces in full frontal view, pulled with the conflicting emotions of incomprehension, fear, and dread. The image refracted the complexity of a political conflict through the body of an individual about to die and provided a memorable and heart-rending loading of a complicated foreign battle onto the terrified face and body of a young child and his father.

The photo's display was incessant and repeated. Appearing across the front sections of nearly every major U.S. newspaper, some papers printed the image more than once; very few printed a second shot of an "already dead" boy, and when they did so it was on an internal page.[62] Newscasts showed both the film and still shots, and every news organization with online capabilities posted the pictures there too. Most displayed the photo of the child about to die in their most visible spaces—front pages or tops of broadcast lineups—and the sequence of him dying on inside pages or later in broadcasts.[63] In each case of the photo's appearance, its accompanying words noted clearly and explicitly the fact of Aldura's death. For instance, the *Cleveland Plain Dealer* appended a headline to the article which noted his death as did the text itself: "PHOTO BY FRANCE 2 / ASSOCIATED PRESS Jama Aldura shouts toward the television camera as he tries to protect his son, Rami [*sic*], 12, yesterday at Netzarim in the Gaza Strip. Moments later Rami was killed and his father seriously wounded."[64] No ambiguity was left for interpreting the image as anything but a certain death.

The photo continued to appear in the weeks and months that followed, with the boy suspended at the brink of death, reliving time and again his last

Figure 5.4: AFP/Getty Images, Combo of TV grabs from France 2 footage of Israeli Palestinian clashes, Gaza Strip, Israel, September 30, 2000.

moments in heart-stopping visibility. For instance, already the next day, the photo and what it depicted began to take on symbolic overtones, put up on posters as "a symbol of Mideast violence" and the boy called a martyr, giving the U.S. news media additional reason to rerun it. It was used to document timelines of the Mideast violence and became the target of cartoonists, as when the *Chicago Tribune* offered a caricature of the boy and his father paired with the caption "Ariel Sharon's Wailing Wall."[65] As the news media continued to run the story, Aldura's death—emotionally chronicled through his grieving family members—became about something larger than one person's loss of life. As the *San Francisco Examiner* noted, "Mention The Picture to people who care about Israeli-Palestinian relations and they don't ask "which one"? Instead they tell of tears that flowed across their faces when they saw the image of a Palestinian man and his 12 year old son.... It is the image of a boy about to die."[66]

Viewers were simultaneously enthralled and overwhelmed. One reader called the photo a symbol of "the chaotic nature of Palestinian-Israeli relations," while others saw "the terror in Mohammed's eyes and imagine[d] the eyes of [their] own children in a reflexive act of empathy." As the boy was suspended in a point between what had gone before and what was to follow, many entertained the impossible notion that perhaps his death did not occur. Disbelief was rampant. One *Chicago Tribune* reader observed that the images "made me wish I could shout "stop" so loud it would be heard halfway round the world. Looking at those photos, I wanted God himself to put out his hand and stop the bullets, but he didn't." Even James Fallows, who later wrote a scathing article on the veracity of the Abu Rahma tape for the *Atlantic Monthly,* wanted to disbelieve: "The footage of the shooting is unforgettable, and it illustrates the way in which television transforms reality. I have seen it replayed at least a hundred times now, and on each repetition I can't help hoping that this time the boy will get himself down low enough, this time the shots will miss."[67]

Such disbelief was prescient, for from the beginning the photo stimulated contradictory interpretations. On the one hand, its widespread visualization and extensive accompanying detail made it a clear candidate in far-reaching discussions about the brutality of the event. Editorials addressing the image appeared across the news media. "What's at stake?" the *New York Times* asked. "It's right there on tape, the body of a 12 year old caught in a crossfire in Gaza." The photo generated discussions on the futility of parental authority, on children and political violence, and on the tensions in the Middle East. The *Detroit News* justified its display in a note to readers, where it said that showing the photo of the dead boy was both "gruesome and inappropriate" but that showing him still alive was necessary. Both NPR's Talk of the Nation and ABC News ran shows on the photograph, interviewing Abu Rahma, who said that the event "was the most terrible thing that's happened to me as a journalist."[68]

As pages of readers' letters were published—a reader in the *Dallas Morning News* said of the initial Israeli denials of responsibility, "Does one believe that Israeli soldiers couldn't detect a child, as the TV photo depicted?"—and discussions of ethical journalistic practice centered increasingly on the image, the Israeli authorities provided an aerial picture of the gun battle in which Aldura had been killed, with arrows positioning the boy and his father, the cameraman, and both of the battling sides.[69] This made Abu Rahma part of the story surrounding the photo, and his statement as its cameraman was widely distributed as evidence of what happened. Like the incident involving Kevin Carter, unanswered questions of form undermined the already unsettled questions of content. The photos reignited old debates—about who bore responsibility when innocents were killed and about the relevance of the photographer to the action.

The public and journalistic acclaim continued over time. With journalists noting that the image had become a "rallying cry for peace," it was included on nearly every list of the year's top photos, in what one journal called "a year of unforgiving images." Up for grabs as "the defining image of the decades-old

Arab-Israel conflict," the photo fit into what one newspaper called "the long history of powerful images that sear themselves into global consciousness and divert the course of history." Numerous papers likened the photo to other prize-winning images of about-to-die moments—the 1968 Vietnamese execution by General Loan, the 1972 picture of a Vietnamese girl running naked from her napalmed village, the slaying of Robert Kennedy, the image of a protestor in Tiananmen Square—that in like fashion had reduced a complicated political conflict to an agonizing moment of impending death. The photo became the focus of an audience-driven contest by MSNBC that awarded it photo of the year; other awards followed. Reviews at year's end centered on the event and its visual depiction.[70]

The image also had a populist revival. Copied into murals and plastered on nearly every street corner in Palestinian enclaves around the world and superimposed on a picture of the Dome of the Rock, the photo of the terrified twelve-year-old facing his death was used to adorn the Web site of the Islamic group Hamas and carried in protestors' signs in anti-Israel demonstrations. Called the "pieta of the Arab world," a symbol of the "chaotic nature of Palestinian-Israeli relations," and a poster image in the "battle for Jerusalem," the image was recycled and recontextualized extensively. At the same time as it was being readily labeled "a symbol of Israeli indifference to Arab lives," the Arab League declared October 1 (the day he was killed) as Arab Child Day, Egypt and Iraq named streets, parks and monuments in his honor, Hezbollah guerrillas dedicated their operations to him, Morocco named a park al-Dura Park, and sculptor Adam Pincus made a sculpture based on the photo.[71] The scene of his killing, copied from the still photo, became its own postage stamp in multiple countries (fig. 5.5). The image also appeared in various news organizations' photographic "decades in review" in 2009, and in the decapitation video of *Wall Street Journal* reporter Daniel Pearl, superimposed atop his head as his killers brandished their knives.[72]

Central to this discourse was a celebration of the photographer. In May of 2001, Abu Rahma received the Arab Media Award in Dubai for best coverage of breaking news, where much was made of the risks the cameraman had taken to get his footage. AP photographer Nick Ut, who had taken the prize-winning photo of the napalmed Vietnamese girl during the Vietnam War, likened Abu Rahma's camera work to his own. When he saw the footage, he said, "I'm sure people reacted to it exactly like they did to my picture many years ago." Unlike Ut, however, Abu Rahma welcomed the media attention, giving numerous media interviews, speaking about the event, and repeatedly noting how terrifying it had been to experience it.

On the other hand, a second population emerged over time with a different interpretation of the image. It challenged the photo's evidentiary quality, criticizing its visual shots for being of poor resolution, grainy and out of focus,

Figure 5.5: Egyptian postage stamp of Mohammad Aldura, Public Domain.

due less to the trembling hand of the photographer, as had been the case with Robert Capa, and more to the technological limitations of transforming a video clip onto a still shot. The cameraman's placement and involvement were also discussed, both vis-à-vis the focus of his footage and the barrage of bullets exchanged between Israelis and Palestinians. Video of the volley of shots was analyzed in books, films, magazine articles and scholarly publications. Already by 2002, two separate documentaries—one French, one German—raised questions about the video's authenticity, and one of them—"Three Bullets and a Child: Who Killed the Young Muhammad al-Dura?"—forced open the cause of the boy's death.[73]

Primary among these efforts was a 2003 front page story in the *Atlantic Monthly* which criticized the claims that French 2 TV had made about the incident; as was the case with other about-to-die images, the picture of Aldura was again plastered on the cover and on internal pages in the journal's tracking of the events leading up to the boy's death. Other overviews of the debates regarding the shot's authenticity continued to appear; one, published nearly five years after the incident in February 2005, again reprinted the original photo of the boy being shielded by his father before he died. These later investigations introduced numerous inconsistencies and misinformation in the visuals: they pointed to selective editing of the available materials, revealed unexplained gaps in the depicted sequence of action, challenged the unvisualized death of the boy, and raised fundamental questions as to the truthfulness of the France 2 TV video sequence. In 2007, demonstrations were held outside the television headquarters in Paris, and the Jerusalem correspondent of France 2 TV, which took the footage, began to receive death threats; there were calls for the resignation of its top news executives. By September 2007, France 2 Television was ordered to hand over its videos for French court perusal. The station won its round in court but in May 2008 lost on a counterattempt to keep media watch organizations from evaluating the truthfulness of the video sequence. As one observer wrote in 2008 (alongside an image of the boy facing death) after seeing the full version of the French 2 video, it was unsupportable because "the boy is seen walking away after he's been declared dead and there is no blood on the father, who was (reportedly) seriously wounded. Nowhere is the killing shown."[74] Again, for these viewers, unsettled questions of form undermined the ability to sustain the difficult content of the image. At the heart of their skepticism was who was culpable for the boy's death and what role the cameraperson played in it.

It is worth noting that both for those who felt the documentation was accurate and those who found it erroneous, the still photo in effect accommodated both interpretations. As one observer commented in 2008, "The image's impact is difficult to exaggerate. The look of terror in the boy's eyes as he and his father take cover behind a barrel amid a shootout at the Netzarim Junction in Gaza has become indelibly etched in the collective mind of the Middle East."[75] While the full video provoked censure, the still photo eclipsed it, sidestepping the contrary appraisals of what had happened in the fuller visual sequence.

This suggests that while the dissonance about the larger video sequence lingered, the still picture had already achieved a status in public memory. It continued to reappear, not only illustrating the ongoing battles for interpretation about what had happened but also readily imported into other topics—media spin in 2003, voting in the Middle East in 2005, Mideast violence in 2006.[76] In each case, a possibly long-dead, twelve-year old boy relived in still photography his greatest moment of personal terror.

Although the controversy over the image continues to play out, making a clear assessment difficult, the intensity and prolonged nature of the debate deserves mention. The elaborate and contradictory interpretive play surrounding the Aldura image underscores how complicated and unpredictable is the relationship between an image of certain death, its informational load, the geopolitical context, and the degree to which journalists, news executives, officials, politicians, and viewers are prone to accept or reject its interpretive cues. Clearly, the Aldura image did not produce a unified response, but rather ignited a complicated battle of meaning over what was seen and its relationship with what was known. Its emotional overload enabled contradictory interpretations to prevail about the photo: one side saw it as proof of the boy's death and hence of Israeli military brutality, the other as a tampered image that underscored both a lack of professional integrity and image management by the Palestinians. Both interpretations had "as if" qualities that underplayed the other side's perspective. Significantly, the still photo accommodated the entertainment of both, in a way not possible with the video. As seen with other images of impending death, when questions of form prevail, the content of what is depicted remains that much more contested. Not only does this underscore the degree to which all images of impending death depend on the right mix of circumstances to become meaningful, but it highlights how tenuous that mix can be.

Certain Death, Renown, and Notoriety

In some images of certain death, death's depiction is relevant because the individuals about to die are already familiar to the public. As seen in the image of the Japanese politician's stabbing on television, these images extend an individual's renown or notoriety into death, depending on how they were regarded while alive, and that predisposes journalists, news executives, officials, politicians, and viewer to engage emotionally with what they see; hence, feelings of grief, loss, vengeance, relief, or celebration often surface here. Receiving immediate and automatic coverage because the people who die are recognized figures, these images serve as markers for remembering the individual who died. But they also enable the image's transport to larger contexts than the circumstances for which they are depicted, positioning the person's death as part of a larger subjunctive message about values—integrity, justice, immorality, revenge, virtue, heroism, patriotism—at issue for the collective with whom they had a public relationship before they died.

Images of executions, assassinations, and suicides—which abruptly end the lives of known individuals, often in public space—tend to surface here. For instance, images of Martin Luther King as he lay dying on the balcony where he had been shot surfaced widely within days of his assassination on April 8, 1968. The resulting photo—showing multiple people pointing above King's fallen body in the direction of where they thought the shots had come from later proved instrumental in a civil jury's finding that the civil rights leader had been killed in a government plot and not as originally claimed.[77] One well-known image of certain death captured Robert Kennedy dying on the kitchen floor of Los Angeles' Ambassador Hotel, moments after he was shot on June 5, 1968. Taken by a number of photographers, the depictions showed Kennedy lying prostrate and bleeding on a concrete floor. His head was pitched slightly forward as if he were about to take his last breath. The image not only appeared widely at the time but in numerous retrospectives over time, where it was often nostalgically connected to a diminished Kennedy family legacy.[78] As recently as 2008, forty years after his death, the photo marked the killing's anniversary: the *Baltimore Sun* ran an interview with one of its original photographers, printing the image yet again. In many recycled displays online, the image has been used to forward assumptions about conspiracy in Kennedy's death and surfaced extensively in that regard.[79] At the time of their original display, both the images of King and Kennedy were accompanied by multiple pictures of a grieving public, offering a usable visual context for the photos of a death not seen.

Figure 5.6: John
Moore/Getty Images,
"Benazir Bhutto Killed
in Suicide Attack,"
December 27, 2007.

The assassination of Pakistani political leader Benazir Bhutto on December 27, 2007, killed while campaigning for a return to the premiership, was among the more recent deaths depicted by this motif of certain death. Because the news media were gathered to attend a rally at which she was to speak, they were in full attendance at the moment of her assassination. On the day of her killing, numerous pictures were taken of her as she was driven around Rawalpindi, standing in the roof-top opening of her armored car. They showed her smiling and waving, unaware that her death was near. John Moore, a photographer for Getty Images, said two shots rang out and she fell back into the vehicle as a bomb blast rocked the scene. Dying out of sight, her death sent Pakistanis spiraling into public grief and mourning over a leader many had hoped would reestablish the country's political and social stability. Hordes of mourners crowded the square where she had been shot, and their depiction gave visual form to the public grief spawned by the killing.[80]

This Getty image of Bhutto, taken shortly before her death by Moore, showed her vibrantly gazing across the crowds who had come to celebrate her candidacy (fig. 5.6): used by multiple news organizations, it was emblematic of a set of photos showing the former prime minister on her last day. Though they did not all depict the same moment, the capture of one temporal piece of that day was enough to ensure their recognition as about-to-die photos.

The pictures were titled as such across the print, broadcast, and online news media. For instance, the *St. Louis Post-Dispatch* featured a front-page picture of her smiling, alongside the caption "A Peaceful Force: Former Prime Minister Benazir Bhutto at a campaign rally minutes before she was assassinated in a suicide attack Thursday in Rawalpindi, Pakistan." The *Sun-Sentinel* featured a picture of Bhutto gazing across the crowd under a banner headline,

"Assassinated." Its caption read: "Final Appearance: Shortly before she was killed leaving a rally in Rawalpindi, Pakistani opposition leader and former premier Benazir Bhutto, 54, looks out at a throng of supporters." The *New York Daily News* devoted its front cover to a full size image of Bhutto waving to the crowd, proclaiming to its readers that the image was "Seconds from Death: Chilling Image Captures Last Moments of Benazir Bhutto." Broadcast news organizations featured still photos of Bhutto waving through the sun-roof of her car, with before and after videos of the day's events, paying particular attention to the chaos that swept the crowd after the explosion. Multiple private videos surfaced online that had been taken at the rally, but they generally showed ill-focused sequences of the crowd before Bhutto was shot. Though they made available new information about the assassin, none clearly showed the assassination itself.[81]

That made the same still pictures—showing Bhutto alive and well on the day of her death—the most visible signifier of her shooting. They continued to appear after she was dead, weeks, months, and even the following year. Included in retrospectives that appeared, on posters at rallies commemorating her death, and in online memorial tributes, in each case they were used as vehicles for the expression of loss and grief and as markers of nostalgia for the political doctrines she had embodied and concern over the turpitude of Pakistani politics.[82]

Images of certain death are also used to underscore public approbation or dislike for the person about to die. Though pictures of the corpses of deposed Romanian Premier Nicolai Ceausescu and his wife Elena on December 25, 1989 were made available immediately after their executions—where headlines proclaimed "people were incredulous at the pictures" and public crowds were reported to have energetically booed the slain leader and his wife—images of their impending death came at a strategic delay. A graphic ninety-minute videotape was aired exclusively by the French television network TF1 on April 22 of the following year, playing the about-to-die moment in extensive detail and showing the former leader crying and begging for his life and his wife cursing at their executioners. Paradoxically but in a manner that often surfaces around images of certain death, the images and their verbal texts convinced viewers that death was anything but certain. Numerous reports recounted how most Romanians, on seeing the images of the dead couple, still had not convinced themselves "that the TV images are incontrovertible proof" that they were dead. Though forensic experts conceded that the execution video was faked and that the Romanian dictator and his wife had died much earlier than the video suggested, the footage, today easily accessed on YouTube, has, in one reporter's view, "lost none of its power to shock."[83]

Similarly, the suicide of Pennsylvania State Treasurer Budd Dwyer in front of media cameras in 1987 produced a troublesome image that continues to be the focus of journalism ethics discussions. Facing sentencing in a trial in which he had been convicted, wrongly in his view, of bribery, Dwyer called a news conference and then killed himself in front of a large group of journalists with a handgun to his mouth. Though the events unfolded so quickly that few journalists felt that they could have stopped him, questions nonetheless turned to the media's display of the suicide. Numerous pictures showed the moments before Dwyer's death, and most of the major newspapers carried them either on their front pages or inside. WPXI, the Pittsburgh NBC affiliate, showed footage of Dwyer as he pulled the trigger, and it was followed by WPVI in Philadelphia; the news station's switchboard was immediately overloaded with viewer complaints. Even today, the case remains a textbook example in discussions of media ethics, where the moral and ethical implications of showing a violent impending death remain front and center.[84]

In both the deaths of the Ceausescus and Budd Dwyer, the notoriety of those who died helped establish the initial coverage of their deaths and its repeated— and strategic—reshowing over time. In much the same way that people may be more predisposed to engage with the deaths of renowned individuals than with those they do not know out of a sense of grief or loss, these images often draw viewers who seek justice, revenge, or clarity from the deaths themselves. This is particularly the case when those who die have committed heinous acts, like dictators, murderers, or terrorists. Often, because of a viewer's excessive need to see justice done, these images provoke too a skepticism about the fact of death, requiring the images' reshowing as an act of bearing witness to their demise and what it represents.

What happens, however, when an image of certain death is not clear enough to generate either renown or notoriety? What happens when the geopolitical circumstances are too varied to encourage journalists, news executives, officials, politicians, and viewers to accept or reject an image's interpretive cues? The death of Princess Diana of Wales on August 31, 1997, was such a case. Though images were taken of her dying on the back seat of a car, the British news media did not use them. Shaken by the incident and the involvement of paparazzi, British journalists instead used the incident to address the establishment of new restraining measures as part of the codes governing photojournalism. But the images traveled in less-restrained circles elsewhere, and nine years after her death the Italian magazine *Chi* and the paper *Corriere della Sera* showed Diana in the back seat of a car, her head turned to one side as a paramedic attempted to fit an oxygen mask over her face. In Britain, the response was widespread disgust; both news executive and viewers denigrated the editorial judgment involved. Pictures of Diana facing death became available again years later, when in 2004 CBS News' *48 Hours Investigates* broadcast a special report on Diana's death. In the report, CBS showed close-ups from the 1997

Parish crash scene, two grainy black and white photocopies that had been taken from a French investigation report of her death and which had been available immediately after the crash but not displayed in the media. The photos showed Diana being treated by a doctor while slumped unconscious on the back seat of her smashed car; her eyes were closed but her face clearly visible. CBS published its own rejoinder about the images, where it pronounced them neither graphic nor exploitative.[85]

News organizations critiqued the CBS decision to show the images; the *Denver Post* noted wryly "Even British Tabs Knock CBS." The British media offered what one U.S. newspaper called a "fit of resentment." Mohammed Al-Fayed, father of her boyfriend Dodi Fayed, sued the network, and British prime minister Tony Blair called the display "distasteful." In one view, "the shots of Diana dying repulsed even the bare-knuckled British media," while *The Guardian* declared that CBS's action had "reawakened demand for a privacy law." British viewers decried what they saw as "the sickest intrusion yet. Photos of anyone's life slipping away should never be used as entertainment."[86] That said, throughout the debate, multiple images of Diana's last moments could be readily found online, raising the question of whose propriety was being protected. In this case, images of Diana reflected a larger ambivalence about British royalty and its role in public life; left unmentioned were the multiple other instances in which images of other people about to die had been widely displayed.

Freezing the person about to die in an immortal or notorious space, where facing death time and again becomes a final depiction of a life lived already in the public spotlight, these images show that even when people are known, an image's display needs the right circumstances to engage those who see it. Though these images merit attention because they are newsworthy—events involving a critical change of state of famous people—aspects of their depiction can mute or even suspend their display. In part this has to do with the fact that these images act too as ways to remember the dead person and often to grieve over their death. Because grieving is not always about clear informational detail but is rather an emotional response to loss, the certain deaths of known individuals often generate extensive debate about what people are willing to see.

Significantly, this can differ between renowned and notorious figures. Images of the certain death of renowned people tend not to be shown or tend to generate debate if they are too graphic, particularly showing blood or gore; if they are too intimate, showing too close a view of a known person's face; if they depict a person who is too culturally proximate or powerful, showing a person whose impending death provokes widespread grieving and unmitigated emotional response; if they are too detailed, prompting accusations of a violation of privacy. Sometimes the same impulses characterize notorious figures but they are characterized by one additional impulse as well: even when images of the certain death of notorious people are shown they tend to raise repeated questions about their veracity. Though such questions arise at times with the depiction of renowned individuals dying, their predictable appearance around notorious individuals suggests a linkage with longstanding spectacles of suffering, by which seeing death—of a brutal ruler, abuser, or other wrongdoer— repeatedly is the only way to confirm its unfolding, and the need to do so is paramount.

Because these photos are structured to provide confirmation of death, this is telling. It suggests that death's certainty may be more than journalists, news executives, officials, politicians, and viewers are willing to show and see. How certain does certain need to be remains at the heart of the death images of people who are publicly known.

Renown/Notoriety: Certain Death and the JFK Assassination

The assassination of U.S. president John F. Kennedy in November 1963 was an event that stretched across a long, four-day weekend, taking the American public from shock and grief over the death of a popular president toward a resigned orientation toward the future. Though it remained a story told mainly through television, the photographic recounting of what happened played a central part in creating a visual memory of that fateful event.[87] As Vicki Goldberg noted, the still photos of that weekend "show the killing much more clearly than anything that flashed across the TV screen.... The photographs provide the details, and they give the mind images to hang on to."[88] Two visual depictions of impending death structured the coverage of the weekend's events—the killing of Kennedy on November 22 as he progressed in an open motorcade through Dallas' Dealey Plaza and two days later the shooting of his alleged assassin, Lee Harvey Oswald, as he was being moved from one Dallas jail to another (fig. 5.7).

Though both shootings occurred in close proximity to journalists, who had converged on Dallas to cover Kennedy's visit there, and still photos and videos of each have lingered over time, the two killings show that renown and notoriety can be differently etched into certainty's depiction, particularly when the two deaths are differently recorded by journalists to begin with. As the trade press then commented,

> The actual shooting down of the President was caught mainly through out-of-focus pictures taken by non-professional photographers. But the actual shooting of his accused assailant was recorded in full view of press photographers with their cameras trained right on him and this produced pictures which may rank with the great news shots of all time.[89]

Figure 5.7:
James "Ike" Altgens/
AP, "JFK Assassination–
Rear View of Car,"
Dallas, Texas,
November 22, 1963;
Robert Jackson/AP,
"Lee Harvey Oswald
Shooting," Dallas,
Texas, November 24,
1963.

The two about-to-die moments thus became from the beginning complementary depictions of a story whose complications refused to die—one reflected journalism's inadequacies, the other its zenith. One produced a general refutation of the interpretive cues people were given about what had happened, the other a blanket acceptance. One image worked poorly as an image of certain death, the other flourished powerfully.

Kennedy's shooting generated images of a certain death that did not fare well as part of its coverage, not at the time of recording nor over time. From the beginning, journalists fell short in covering an event of great significance. Although many news organizations had representatives on hand for Kennedy's visit to Dallas, Texas, they were corralled in a press bus that was part of the presidential motorcade taking Kennedy around the city. When the shots rang out from Dealey Plaza, many journalists did not see or hear what had happened. Robert MacNeil for NBC Television recounted it thus:

At about 12.32, the motorcade turns a corner into a parkway. The crowds are thinner...three shots are heard, like toy explosions. [NBC Cameraman Dave] Weigman jumps from his car, running toward the President with his camera running. People scream, lie down grabbing their children. I leave the motorcade and run after police, who appear to be chasing somebody. The motorcade moves on fast.[90]

Though the motorcade took Kennedy to Parkland Hospital, he was soon pronounced dead.

Journalists tried to piece together the story, but their record of events remained riddled with hearsay, rumor, and faulty information. There was no live televised coverage of what had happened, only a handful of wire service pictures—none of which showed what had unfolded—and a number of amateur snapshots and films of the motorcade. This meant that the news media by and large missed covering Kennedy's actual shooting. As one photographer later told it, when he realized he had no pictures, "I thought, 'Man, have I screwed up.'"[91]

The one professional photographer on the scene who did photograph the motorcade was the Associated Press' staff photographer, James Altgens. It was his eyewitness account that went out over the wires: "I saw it," he told his editor. "There was blood on his face. Mrs. Kennedy jumped up and grabbed him and cried 'oh no!' The motorcade raced onto the freeway." Altgens took the only professional shot as the shooting unfolded—an unfocused rear-end shot of the car's trunk, as Security Service agents jumped on top of it (fig. 5.7). Transmitted over the wires within twenty-five minutes, the photo earned him the title of "the only professional cameraman who caught spot pictures of the assassination." Though it was limited in what it showed, the photo was celebrated, appeared widely, and won him a World Press Photo Award the following year.[92]

Undepicted was the moment of Kennedy himself being shot. A number of amateur photographers, standing on the motorcade route, did better than Altgens, and though there were reports of professional photographers taking shots from amateurs by force, the news media incorporated them the next day—unaccredited—into their coverage. One shot, taken by amateur photographer Mary Moorman and accredited to UPI, produced a blurred side view of the president's car as his wife leaned over him; another shot, accredited to the Associated Press, showed a different side view of the car, with thepresident's foot hanging out the back.[93] This meant that most of the images of Kennedy's death were taken primarily by amateurs after he had already been shot. It also meant that from the beginning the moment of his death was visually crafted across numerous photos taken from a variety of temporal and spatial vantage points scattered across the motorcade route.

Alongside these amateur photos were three separate amateur films, all of which caught a fuller sequence of what had happened. Abraham Zapruder, Orville Nix, and Mary Muchmore each recorded side views of the president being shot. Though not accredited as such, they appeared sparingly in the media: WNEW TV New York used Muchmore's film, and later *Life* printed stills from Zapruder's. *Editor and Publisher* pronounced the quality of Zapruder's film "slightly dark" and "out of focus," but the amateur visuals still constituted the fullest visual documentation available, and stills from the film were shown to the public in small increments: six black and white frames first, another nine color frames in *Life* the following week, and more images in a special memorial issue of *Life* that December. By the following year, the Warren Commission's twenty-six volumes of supporting identification included black-and-white enlargements of nearly all of the sequence's thirty-one still frames, and that October *Life* ran another issue showing more of the still images. The actual filmed sequence did not appear on television until 1975.[94]

The visual unraveling of Kennedy's death was thus delayed, unpredictable, and uneven. By the time it appeared in full, documenting in graphic detail the impact of the bullets striking Kennedy, the assassination had become severely tainted in the public imagination. Conspiracy theories—blaming the right, the left, the Soviets, the Mafia—generated deep-seated suspicion over what had happened. That suspicion extended too to the images of Kennedy's death, as extensive discussions over missed frames, misplaced frames, and gaps in the visual sequences shed doubt on the ability to claim an authentic visual representation of what had happened.[95] All of this made it difficult for a single depiction to assume a lead position in giving visual shape to what had happened.

It made sense, then, for the news media to use multiple images to signify the shooting. Broadcast news showed early footage from the motorcade or journalists huddling in groups outside Parkland Hospital waiting for news. The print media circulated pictures of Kennedy and his wife Jacqueline driving through the city streets earlier in the day, waving and smiling at throngs of onlookers. Photos of this moment appeared widely, telling readers that the image showed "the President and Mrs. Kennedy moving through downtown Dallas moments before he was shot." When the *New York Times* published such a picture, it did so alongside four paintings of other U.S. presidents about to be shot, underscoring the parallel in the moment of impending death but showing too how coverage of Kennedy's assassination had misfired.[96] Over the weekend, as more of the amateur photos were collected, both the print and broadcast media were able to provide more detail. Three days later on November 25, Charles Collingwood of CBS gave the following brushed-up scenario of the shooting, now armed with a still photo of the motorcade displayed on the TV screen behind him:

> This was the scene in the big open Lincoln a split second after that shot. The President is slumping to his left. Mrs. Kennedy, half rising, seems to stretch out an encircling arm. Governor Connally, in the seat ahead of the President, is half-turned toward the President. He's either been hit himself or is about to be. At this moment, no one knew how seriously the President had been wounded.[97]

All of this meant that the early visualization of Kennedy about to die had multiple shapes. The photos that surfaced in the news media were not always the same and did not always depict the same about-to-die moment.[98]

Alongside these photos was a patterned focus on the grief that Kennedy's death generated. As Kennedy's body was moved to the Capitol rotunda where it would lay in state until his funeral, television cameras focused nonstop on individuals viewing the presidential coffin. NBC broadcast continuously for nearly forty-two hours. Newspapers and journals showed multiple pictures of people paying their respects.[99] As with other images of certain death involving renowned people, these images offered a visual context for emotionally engaging with a death not seen.

As the story moved on in time, the pattern of using multiple about-to-die images prevailed. Even as more detailed and graphic footage and still photos became available, the images that continued to appear reflected variety rather than uniformity. Various about-to-die images were used to illustrate ongoing coverage of the assassination, appended to debates over evolving interpretations of what happened, anniversaries of the assassination, and retrospectives on Kennedy. Some of the images moved into popular culture, such as one frame from the Zapruder film that appeared on the cover of *Esquire* in 1991 to illustrate its story about the Oliver Stone movie, *JFK*.[100]

The images of JFK's certain death that were seen by journalists, news executives, officials, politicians, and viewers were thereby anything but certain. Offering variable moments of a larger temporal sequence that implied death, they fit an interpretive environment in which all available documentation was contested, debated, analyzed, and often rejected. These images thus reflected the death of a beloved figure, which failed to rise above the multiple contradictory interpretations of what had happened and therefore could not generate agreement about what its images showed. Driven by grief, confusion, fear, and anger, in most quarters this disbelief did not extend to the fact that Kennedy had died, only over the manner and fashion in which he was killed.

By contrast, the shooting of Kennedy's accused assassin, Lee Harvey Oswald, was marked by a clear and memorable image of impending death. When Oswald was killed, the American public was thrown into uncertainty about who had shot Kennedy. Though evidence pointed in Oswald's direction, it was far from certain and became even less so over time. At the point of Oswald's death, many were angry, bewildered, and uncertain over what he had reportedly caused. At the same time, the coverage of his killing was as much a triumph for the news media as covering Kennedy's had been a failure, and that triumph was critical in setting up its image of certain death.

Oswald's killing came on the third day of the weekend, where its capture on camera in front of a large group of journalists, photographers, and camera personnel inscribed the shooting visually in memory. Though his killing threw the nation riddled with doubt and grief into limbo regarding the possibility of finding the cause of Kennedy's death, covering Oswald's killing, which followed the largely amateur visual coverage of Kennedy's death, constituted a triumph for journalism that helped the news media offset their failings in capturing Kennedy's death. As one trade journal noted, if the assassination "was left for the amateur photographers to record, the situation reversed itself on Sunday, November 24," when Oswald was to be transferred to the county jail from the city jail.[101]

Armed with details of the transfer, journalists crowded the jail for a photo opportunity, with an estimated fifty reporters, photographers, and TV camerapersons in attendance in the basement by 10:00 A.M. As the transfer began, reporters jostled to get a word with Oswald. As one participant recalled, "All the newsmen were poking their sound mikes across to him and asking questions, and they were everyone sticking their flashbulbs up and around and over [Oswald] and in his face."[102] The scene was mayhem. Out of the crowd of reporters stepped Jack Ruby, who drew a gun, pulled the trigger, and watched Oswald slump to the floor.

The images that circulated of Oswald's death were far more schematic and limited than were those that had appeared after Kennedy's. Written accounts dwelled on the incredibility of Oswald having been shot in view of the photographic and television cameras. Still photographs, which "fixed an image on the mind more lastingly and precisely than television had been able to do," pushed newspapers into second editions.[103]

Two still pictures emerged. *Dallas Morning-News* photographer Jack Beers captured Ruby stepping from the crowd and aiming his pistol at Lee Harvey Oswald. Robert Jackson, working for the *Dallas Times-Herald,* caught the sequence of events a fraction of a second later, as Oswald hunched over from the impact of being shot.[104] Though Beers's photo went out immediately over the wires, the Jackson photo caught the decisive moment of Oswald being shot. As Vicki Goldberg observed, "A tiny fragment of time made the different between imminence and occurrence, between danger and death." Both photographers were uncertain whether or not they had even gotten the picture, and Jackson tried to shoot a second photo but his equipment failed. As Oswald grimaced, the detective cuffed to his right hand recoiled. Viewed in "stopped time," said Goldberg, the photo remained simultaneously "horribly fascinating" and "painful."[105]

The photo showed the burly back of a man entering the frame from the lower right hand corner, his hand training a gun on Oswald, who was positioned in the center of the shot (fig. 5.7). Oswald was depicted crumpling from the blast, his face contorted with pain. Afterward, Jackson remembered having focused his camera on Oswald:

> I was looking at Oswald's face, because he's the subject, and I was aware of somebody stepping in my line of view. Just maybe two steps and then bang. The hand and gun went up so fast, I leaned to the left and snapped my shot. It was just too quick. Maybe if it had taken Ruby five seconds to step out there, I'd have known what he was doing."[106]

Television caught the event masterfully. As the *New York Times* noted in its recounting of what had happened, "Out of the lower right hand corner [of the screen] came the back of a man. A shot rang out, and Oswald could be heard gasping as he started to fall." NBC's Tom Pettit remarked that "those of us who were literally here and watching are not sure of what we saw." NBC ran the story live nationwide, underscoring the triumph of capturing a real homicide nationally in front of live cameras.[107]

Both footage and still photos were widely shared. Displayed in papers ranging from the *New York Times* to the *Saturday Evening Post,* the *Los Angeles Times* showed a four-shot sequence of images, titled "Struggle," "As the Bullet Hit," "Gasping in Pain," and "Shot" (as Oswald was being transported out on a stretcher). CBS recorded the event on a local camera, replaying immediate coverage from a video monitor, and ABC, whose cameraman had already moved on to the county jail, had to make do without visuals.[108]

The acclaim for both television and photography prevailed over time. *Broad-casting* magazine—hailing the manner in which "out of the lower right hand corner of the TV screen came the back of a man"—called the shooting "a first in television history...television came of age." Broadcast journalism garnered multiple awards. Jackson won the 1964 Pulitzer Prize. Both Jackson's and Beer's images were heralded as being among the nation's great photos, restoring to photojournalism "some of its tragic power." In 1989, *Time* named Jackson's image one of history's ten most important images.[109]

Though mention of television permeated all of the retellings of Kennedy's death, it was its still photos that were used to signify the event across the print media. The pictures illustrated retrospectives on Kennedy's death, discussions of conspiracy theories, overviews on journalism, exhibits, and articles about photojournalism as well as numerous anniversary retellings of the Kennedy assassination and developments in the story, such as the discovery of hidden files and recovery of the Oswald gun.[110] They surfaced too to depict post 9/11 security measures or a 2003 article about the new Dallas police headquarters, replete with a picture of a policeman holding the photo of Oswald being shot; they helped signify an exhibit of the 2002 Pulitzer Prize photos and an opening of the Sixth Floor Museum's new exhibit space; and they traveled into car exhibits, Broadway musicals, and fictional novels. Jackson continued to speak publicly about his taking of the photo for more than forty years, later called "one of the most frequently reproduced photographs of the twentieth century.[111] Oswald's certain death thus made sense for journalists, news executives, politicians, and viewers needing to assign accountability for the killing of the president. It was an image that legitimated journalism as well.

In sum, the certain deaths associated with John F. Kennedy's assassination were not displayed or received in an equivalent fashion. Though significantly both moments of impending death were visualized and recycled in many retrospectives, they differed from each other in marked ways. Kennedy's death invoked his immortality to a grieving public but his death continued to be challenged and debated vociferously by many who saw its images. At issue was its timing, its sequencing, its veracity, its cause, and its agent. It was as if an excess of interpretive play kept Kennedy's certain death from being accepted. Its visualization by a wide range of about-to-die photographs—including his earlier display in the motorcade, various unfocused shots of the motorcade, and graphic images showing his body being blown apart—thus suited the multiple prevailing sentiments. No one still image of his impending death could have emerged over time.

By contrast, Oswald's death invoked notoriety, and it was a notoriety that many people—still angry and bewildered by his reported act—were all too eager to recognize. Contextualized against larger conversations that assigned culpability to a variety of individuals, governments, and political forces, the mention of Oswald's death—and at times of Kennedy's assassination—gravitated in almost every case to one of the two photos provided by Jackson or Beers, which documented with precise detail his certain impending demise. In a sense, this echoed the display of the images from the beginning, when the week after the assassination *Life* published multiple frames from the Zapruder film of Kennedy's death but only one image of Oswald's.[112] The lack of debate over the latter cemented the image as the depiction for a relatively consensual story over time, while the continuing debate over the former made it difficult to settle on one image as the preferred depiction of certain death.

What this suggests is that certainty works most fully when the degree and nature of its accompanying verbal information match larger impulses in the environment in which an image of certain death appears. While such an assumption belabors the obvious, it also highlights how central contingency, the emotions, and the imagination are to visual representation in all of its forms. Most important, it suggests that the larger informational load that certainty offers about death does not necessarily generate a problem-free acceptance of the picture's interpretive cues. More information about what is shown does not necessarily lead to more understanding or to more agreement about what is seen.

When Certainty Fuels the "As If"

The notion that certainty itself can fuel the "as if" suggests how paradoxical is the relationship between what viewers see and what they understand from news images. Undercutting a longstanding linkage between news images and photographic verisimilitude, the images of certain death suggest that more informational detail does not necessarily engender a fuller understanding of what is depicted. Though the words associated with the images of certain death are the conduits for interpreting what is shown, these images show that the impact of words on journalists, news executives, officials, politicians, and viewers is neither reliable nor predictable. Often, rather than anchoring meaning, as words have been thought to do for images, they create openings for an image's uneven interpretation, its vigorous debate, and its strategic employment. In other words, more information does not guarantee certainty.

This chapter has shown that images of certain death service multiple aims. The motif of the certainty of death is helped along by appending varying degrees of identification to the people they depict, each differently invoking the "as if." While anonymous figures drive death's certainty by connecting symbolically to larger issues and problems, individuals given posthumous personhood drive it with little pragmatic or proximate effect on the lives of those who see their depiction but by invoking compassion, empathy, and pity for their plight. Famous or notorious people drive death's certainty by activating a collective and public expression of grief, vengeance, relief, betrayal, loss, celebration, and other emotions that belie the shared impact of the death that has occurred: when a ruler or abuser dies, the lives of those they affected before death can be affected too by death itself. Though none of these emotions involve all those who see the pictures, they exist here as potentialities. What more information does, then, is provide more capacity to engage emotionally, imaginatively, and contingently with the unsettled events of the news.

This chapter has shown that images can powerfully force attention, exposure, and involvement, but where they go from there depends on people who want to see them, a journalistic context that supports them, and a link with a surrounding environment that needs certain sustainable messages about its collective life. Often, as seen in the images of certain death involving the Liberian shootings, insufficient information stifles the image's display. Other times, as seen in the killing of Mohammed Aldura and the Kennedy assassination, images carry too much information, which in turn facilitates the sustained entertainment of contrary interpretations.

What this demonstrates is that images work by their own logic, even in a milieu like journalism, which strives to make them more like words than not. The more information an image receives, the more it can become less about the "as is" and more about the "as if." And yet, without the reliability of a familiar form, the unsettled content of these images stays suspect. Remaining unsettled not only characterizes the event, but the long-term understanding of the wars, terrorism, illnesses, and natural disasters that the images depict.

Chapter 6

Journalism's Mix of Presumption, Possibility, and Certainty

Most news does not involve a single event recorded at one time in one place but tends instead to be positioned across time and space. This makes a news story's meaning dependent on multiple images used to depict an ongoing sequence of events. Perhaps nowhere is this as critical as in the coverage of those unsettled events where too much of a temporal span—a story that goes on for long—or too much of a spatial spread—a story affecting a large number of places—can reduce the possibility of engagement. In drawing on the imagination, the emotions, and contingency to facilitate an engagement with the image, the different motifs of about-to-die images become useful because their mix of presumption, possibility, and certainty can offset news that is either too temporally prolonged or too spatially diffuse. Yet their invocation in such events raises questions about whose deaths invite intrusion and about the circumstances under which a migration across levels of informational detail takes place. What does it mean when the public is asked to presume, infer, or accept that which it is not shown, and what do such choices say about its engagement with the events they depict?

Though theorists of time and space have long argued for an inability to consider one without the other—what Derrida famously called the "becoming-space of time [and] the becoming-time of space"—a consideration of many of journalism's most memorable difficult events suggests that one or the other tends to take precedence as news stories unfold.[1] This chapter considers U.S. journalism's coverage of the Vietnam War and the 2004 tsunami as two cases in point. Though at first glance they might suggest starkly different events, in fact a patterned spatial-temporal reliance on the trope of impending death—Vietnam toward temporality, the tsunami toward spatiality—drove the surfacing of images of presumed death, possible death, and certain death. Though the U.S. news media gave close, sustained coverage to the multiple deaths of distant lands, in each case they differed because space or time facilitated a different coexistence of its images. Coverage of the Vietnam War was driven by its prolonged temporal unfolding. The war, which began by most accounts in 1959, did not end until 1975, making each of its images reflective of a series of events that transpired over sixteen years. By contrast, the 2004 tsunami involved a natural disaster whose spatial spread caused deaths in fourteen countries, making its images necessarily generalizable from a series of localized tragedies. In each case, the temporal or spatial parameters of the larger story made its images responsible for depicting more than could possibly be captured by even multiple cameras at one point in time and space. The suggestive nature of the about-to-die image was useful in this regard, for it accommodated the prolonged and diffuse spatial/temporal parameters of both events. While the about-to-die images of Vietnam changed over time, those associated with the tsunami changed over space, underscoring how different kinds of about-to-die images can emerge at different points in both the temporal evolution and spatial diffusion of a news story. The patterning that they reveal suggests that the utility of images of impending death is reflected not only within a given image but across the relationships it strikes with other images depicting the same news story.

About to Die in Vietnam: Variance across Time

The about-to-die photos of the Vietnam War reflected a shift in U.S. public sentiments about the war that gradually took place over the sixteen years of its prosecution. As journalists, news executives, officials, politicians, and viewers moved from a general if not staunch support for the war and its strategic aims toward a pronounced and sometimes vehement disavowal of the U.S. presence in Southeast Asia, news images reflected their shift. Although the images that moved public sentiment were largely televisual, still pictures were nonetheless powerful carriers at the time of their display and even more so as time moved on. Furthermore, as Susan Moeller has demonstrated, a change in the aesthetic display of war, exemplified by a preference during Vietnam's photographic coverage for shots of individual soldiers and civilians over large-scale battle scenes,[2] rendered about-to-die images central.

Among Americans, the change in climate from support to disavowal of the war was gradual. In the early years of the war, most Americans remained solidly on board with the war's prosecution but as the war escalated in the early 1960s,

much of that support diminished. At the same time, the Johnson administration's "policy of minimum candor," which pushed stories of progress over
stories of setback to the news media, planted seeds of skepticism among U.S.
journalists. Following the 1968 Tet Offensive, presumptions of U.S. strategic control began to rapidly diminish and questions regarding the war's purpose, efficacy, legitimacy, and morality came to the forefront of its discussion.
Images of the war in particular foregrounded attention to a series of indignities
and wrongdoings transpiring in Southeast Asia, as the depiction of bombings,
shootings, and self-immolations offered an uneven but morally troublesome
visual inventory through which to engage with what was happening. When
seen against the lack of a plausible or consistent military or political strategy
on the part of the U.S. government, images thus rose to fill the spaces emptied
by the official platforms regarding the war's continued justified prosecution.
Whether or not these images actually affected policy has been debated,[3] but
the point remains that by the early 1970s images were helping to push a more
critical public response to the war.

The Vietnam War hinged in visual memory on four separate news images
that appeared over the course of the war, none depicting battle scenes per se
but each delivering a heart-wrenching visualization of death caused by the war.
Capturing individuals poised at the moment of death but not yet dead, the
images depicted human agony, picturing "almost without exception...rupture
and displacement rather than reconciliation."[4] Taken and circulated at different
points in the conflict, each image was retrospectively responsible for depicting key changes of status in the war and thus had staying power beyond the
particular event it depicted. The four images not only generated attention,
debate, and discussion at the time they were taken and published, but they
were recycled extensively over time, reappearing on demonstration placards; in
newspaper, magazine, and broadcast retrospectives; in books on the Vietnam
War; in overviews of the sixties and seventies; in reviews of photography and in
memorial volumes on Southeast Asia. This meant that each image worked on
two planes—as an initial news relay and as a memory tool—where it continued
to show people about to die long after they were already dead and long after
people knew of their deaths. Each image thus had more than one opportunity
to move the public through the "as if" of the war's depiction, a useful stance
because communicating the certainty of death when opposition to the war was
nascent was often more than those viewing the images wanted.

Significantly, the about-to-die images of Vietnam displayed different motifs
of impending death over nearly a decade of their taking because they appeared
at different points in the development of sentiments critical of the war. Early in
the war, when its public support was still intact, images of certain death called
on the public to accept an explicit set of interpretive cues about a death not
shown. As is often the case with images of certainty, however, these pictures

fostered more attention, debate, interpretive play, discussion, and multiplicity of response than journalists, news executives, officials, politicians, or viewers were able to engage, revealing that images of certain death could not be relied on to encourage the public to accept the verbal cues it was offered. Later in the war, when the U.S. news media gravitated backward in informational detail, offering an image of possible death that was more suggestive than definitive, the public was better situated to infer death through the depiction of endangered human bodies than accept its confirmation through words. But in only hinting at death's possibility and in calling on viewers to engage with a suggestive and symbolic death as the war's primary depiction, this image facilitated an engagement with the war that gravitated away from what was happening and toward the emotional, imagined, and contingent dimensions of what was hoped instead.

Certain Death in Vietnam

Three of the four photos often touted as being among the iconic depictions of the Vietnam War established the ground for depicting the war in its early years through the trope of certain death. Taken over a six-year period during which the war's public support disintegrated, the images—of the immolation of a Buddhist monk in 1963, the shooting of a suspected Vietcong collaborator in 1968, and the 1968 massacre of a group of Vietnamese villagers whose photo did not appear till the following year—constituted a collective visual message that forced the attention of journalists, news executives, politicians, officials, and viewers to the war's underside. In each case, the deaths of the depicted— pictured still alive—were confirmed by adjoining verbal texts, which called on the public to engage with the picture by accepting or refuting the human loss suggested by a sequencing of action not detailed by the camera.

Burning Monk

In 1963, tensions over a lack of religious freedom in South Vietnam were high, as the longstanding Buddhist community was being discriminated against by the Diem administration. A series of killings involving Buddhist monks the month before, following a riot in Hue, had thrown the community into turmoil, and one Buddhist monk, Quang Duc, planned his own sacrificial immolation to protest. The immolation took place on June 11, 1963, in a public plaza populated by thousands of Saigon residents. Shocking in its stark simplicity, the event unfolded like a series of carefully choreographed and oft-rehearsed movements. The monk entered the plaza, followed by hundreds of devotees as he proceeded into its center. As they formed a circle around him, he seated himself cross-legged under a multicolored Buddhist flag and, cordoned off from the police by his followers, allowed his body to be doused with gasoline before he set himself on fire. As his body lit up, the blazing inferno engulfed his slight frame amidst the piercing wails of the attending monks and nuns. Throughout the ordeal, Quang Duc remained silent, upright, and stoic, barely flinching as he was burned alive.

A number of journalists had been forewarned that an important event was about to unfold, and Associated Press journalist Malcolm Browne, one of the few to heed the call to witness the ceremonies outside the Saigon pagoda, was among the throng of Buddhist devotees. Later, he said as he watched the monk walk to the center of the plaza, "I realized at that moment exactly what was happening, and began to take pictures a few seconds apart."[5] Browne took four rolls of film of the monk setting himself on fire and burning and afterward of his charred corpse lying on the pavement.

A number of Browne's images went over the AP wire. Though the photos showed the entire sequence of action, the picture that was singled out showed the monk about to die, a clear outline of a still-upright and identifiable human figure being engulfed by fire. All of the photo's accompanying texts confirmed that he died in the fire (fig. 6.1). In the picture, Quang Duc's stoic demeanor contrasted starkly with the flames that blazed wildly around him. His posture was stiff and formal—head held erect, mouth slightly ajar, arms clasped behind his back—all juxtaposed with the fire's erratic movement, its flames dancing in a free for all above the monk's head and offering the only aesthetic freedom associated with the shot. In the picture's background were an unexplained automobile and a group of monks and other individuals. Blurred

Figure 6.1: Malcolm W. Browne/AP, Burning Monk, June 11, 1963.

and out of focus, they embodied varied practices of witnessing: some watched Quang Duc, some averted their gaze, and some seemed to focus on unidentified objects on the distance. The image had an ethereal quality, its force reified in the monk's upright bodily posture. His stoic response to death, no apparent bodily reaction to the onset of pain, and refusal to cry out were all details that became part of the photo's clearly moral message: as the editor of one Syracuse paper said on seeing it, "If you can publish a picture of the crucifixion, you can publish this picture."[6]

And yet, the idea of publishing the image met widespread initial resistance. The *New York Times* refused, in Browne's words, "on the grounds that this was not fit fare for the breakfast table."[7] Recounting the story of the immolation in text, the paper printed a different image of another event—monks taking part in a Buddhist protest by blocking the movement of a fire truck—while noting in the caption that "some distance away, another monk committed suicide by fire on a street." Broadcast news gave the immolation no visualization. Other newspapers were similarly reticent: the *Chicago Tribune* reported the story on an inside page without a picture, while the *Los Angeles Times* ran the image a week late. Though the reluctance to publish had precedent—earlier photos taken by Nick Ut of a different monk's immolation had been deemed too horrific and rejected by AP photo editor Horst Faas, who had observed, "These pictures are ugly. Newspapers won't publish these. A better picture would be somebody covering the body, people in the background looking, crying"—the reticence this time around had other implications.[8]

For Quang Duc's immolation was central to the emergent Buddhist response to the Diem government and the protestors needed an image to capture public attention. Within days, mass protests began across the city and Quang Duc became a symbol of Buddhist resistance, forcing the U.S. news media to reexamine their reluctance to give his immolation visual form. As the government established virtual martial law over Saigon, sealed off its main pagodas, blocked streets, and clamped down on foreign journalists, arresting photographers and confiscating or exposing their film, it rapidly became clear that the immolation meant more than the suicide of one individual Buddhist monk. As Malcolm Browne wrote later, the "Buddhists desperately needed the eyes of the world in support of their cause, and sought an appropriate eye-catcher."[9] Quang Duc became one.

It was then that the U.S. news media rethought their initial reticence about depicting the suicide. When the newsmagazines and picture magazines reached their deadlines at week's end, they lead the way in offering the event fuller visual treatment. A two-page spread in *Life* under the title "An Angry Buddhist Burns Himself Alive" ran three pictures—one before the immolation, one after, and in the middle a full page version of Browne's photograph; *Newsweek* ran the same pictures alongside a column about a protest in Southeast Asia; *Time* ran Browne's picture as a stand-alone, under the titled article "Trial by Fire."[10] This meant that within ten days of the immolation, the news media provided viewers with coverage, even if it was missing from the event's initial relay. As the pictures appeared, letters to the editor streamed in, critical of Browne for not helping the monk, a criticism he roundly rejected.[11] Nonetheless, in providing a retrospective depiction of information already known, the image of the monk's impending death became front and center to the larger story of religious repression in Vietnam.

In the meantime, the immolation continued to play a central role in marking Buddhist protest. When Quang Duc's ashes were cleared from the crematorium, his heart was reported undestroyed, a fact that encouraged his fellow monks to proclaim him a saint. Buddhist leaders had Browne's picture blown-up, hand-colored, and carried in demonstrations, making it the protest's insignia. U.S. clergymen reproduced a picture of the monk's immolation as a full-page advertisement in the *New York Times* and *Washington Post* with the caption "We, too, protest." The Communist Chinese reprinted the image for distribution in Southeast Asian countries. Weeks later, when esteemed Vietnamese writer Nguyen Tuong Tam committed suicide, banners on his funeral car likened his death to the martyrdom of Quang Duc; reports streamed in from across the region of imitation immolations in India, France, Japan, and Korea.[12]

Thus, though the photo's initial display came from only a small sector of U.S. journalism—the news magazines and picture magazines—the news media were able to redress journalism's failure to understand the importance of the image on the first round. Suggesting that squeamishness about graphic content could be overlooked when it reflected issues of public import or signified a broader moral message, the reversal of the rejection to depict graphic pictures would have significant impact as the war moved on. For it underscored how even an image of content clearly known could generate its own engagement with the event at a later time. It presaged the importance of still photos in reflecting the meaning of the Vietnam War.

This was supported by the photo's recognition as a tool of memory, when, by the end of the month, it resurfaced in other news coverage and advertisements, such as one sponsored by a community church protesting the death of a "Vietnamese Buddhist martyr."[13] Henry Cabot Lodge went on record saying that "no news picture in recent history had generated so much emotion around the world," the historian of the National Press Photographers Association proclaimed the photo one of the "great news photos" of all time, and the photo was held responsible for prompting President Kennedy, who kept a copy of it on his White House desk, to rethink U.S. support for Vietnam. Over time, the photo joined photojournalism retrospectives, special issues, and volumes about photojournalism's high points. Called by the World Press Photo Organization "an early marker of the power of photos to play a significant role in the

Vietnamese conflict," it won the World Press Photo Award in 1963 and was featured forty years later in a well-regarded collection of the "world's greatest photographs." Remarking that the photo "helped to bring down a government, changed the course of a war and found a place in the history books," Browne himself used the photo to illustrate both retrospective pieces and his memoirs some thirty years later. And it reappeared decades later as the focus of song lyrics and popular music videos.[14]

All of this shows that the photo was in some ways more important over time than at the time of the immolation's unfolding. Though the delay and resistance associated with its initial display raised questions about the viability of certain death as the visual motif for making sense of public sentiments that were only then emerging, the image nonetheless sketched the parameters by which graphic pictures of death and impending death might be displayed in association with the Vietnam War. Capturing viewers' attention not as a vehicle of primary information but as a secondary circulation of known information, the image functioned in ways associated with images of possible death, where the intervention of nonjournalists after its initial display heightened the image's instrumentality. Publishing the photo raised the possibility that about-to-die images in the war might have more than one chance to grab the attention of the journalists, news executives, politicians, officials, and viewers who saw them. This made the strategic importance of the photo—the uses to which it could be put—as important as what it conveyed.

Shooting by General Loan

Five years later, during a fierce outbreak of fighting in Saigon associated with the Tet Offensive, when both the war and protest against it intensified, a summary wartime execution drew signal attention. A street battle broke out near Saigon's An Quang pagoda on February 2, 1968, and South Vietnamese police broke through the pagoda's main gates to capture its instigators. The South Vietnamese chief of national police—General Nguyen Ngoc Loan—captured a suspected Vietcong collaborator and was in the process of marching him down the street, when AP photographer Eddie Adams, in search of a street battle together with an NBC news crew, made his way toward the pagoda. Adams recounted what happened:

> Half a block away I noticed a policeman and an airborne trooper bring a suspect out of a building. He was a small barefooted man in civilian clothes with his hands tied behind his back. As they walked toward me, I ran up just to be close by in case something happened. I felt it was just another ordinary street arrest since they were heading for a nearby jeep. My friend Vo Su kept filming as we saw another policeman on my left start walking toward the prisoner. He was drawing his pistol from

its holster. I thought he was going to threaten the V.C. so I framed my 35 mm rangefinder camera, making the picture as I heard a gunshot.[15]

Adams let his camera roll as Loan turned on the detainee, shot him in the head, and the man fell over backwards, stopping only when, in one view, "the blood gushing from the dying man's head made the scene unbearable." Though he later said that the officer "gave no indication that he was to shoot the prisoner until he did it"—noting that "as his hand came up with the revolver, so did my camera, but I still didn't expect him to shoot. When he fired, I fired"—Adams nonetheless captured a sequence of shots that tracked the man as he was being pushed around by the Vietnamese officer until he was lying on the ground, dead.[16] One photo showed the man in his last moment before death (fig. 6.2).

Labeled alternatively "Execution in the Streets of Saigon" or "Vietnam Execution," the photo juxtaposed two figures: Loan, with his back to the camera, face turned sideways and outstretched gun-bearing arm toward his detainee, versus his soon-to-be victim, grimacing as he faced the photographer in an anticipatory gesture that showed he recognized what was to come.[17] Methodically and almost offhandedly pointing the gun at close range toward his detainee's head, Loan's stiff posture suggested an almost contemptuous disregard for what he was about to do, making the proximity and certainty of death all the more outrageous. By contrast, the man about to die was a study in agony: his arms were tied behind his back, his shoulders tersely pulled back, his face riddled either with terror or pain—eyes half closed, mouth tightly pursed, ruffled hair. One soldier stood at Loan's side, his face clenched too. The background of the shot was empty of people, showing seemingly vacant buildings,

Figure 6.2:
Eddie Adams/AP,
Shooting by General
Loan, February 1,
1968.

deserted streets, and little to draw attention from the impending action in the foreground. The frame was built around the tension it displayed, forcing the viewer to wait for the impact of the shot. All of the accompanying texts confirmed the man's death.

From the time of its taking, Adams was uncomfortable with the photo. When he turned in his exposed film to the AP office, he left before the photos could be developed, later contending that he had had his fill of the brutal killing. In fact, six years earlier photographer Dickey Chapelle had photographed a similar shot that was, in editor Harold Evans's view, "universally rejected" and appeared only in an obscure periodical, suggesting that then the time for such a photo had not yet been ripe.[18]

But Adams's discomfort did not resonate more widely among his peers. Editors at the Associated Press were thrilled with the image and sent it over the wires within hours of the shooting.[19] When the AP's subscriber organizations received the photo, the reaction was uniform and immediate. The photo made it onto the front pages of nearly every newspaper across the United States, mostly under the masthead. It appeared twice in one edition of the *New York Times,* stretching across four columns of newsprint on the front page and an inside page—bracketed by photos that Adams had taken before and after the execution and bearing the different but notably unambiguous captions of "Guerrilla Dies" and "Execution." Both the *Los Angeles Times* and the *Washington Post* displayed it on their front pages, where it took up multiple columns of newsprint. The *New York Daily News* gave it the bottom half of its front page, and the *Chicago Tribune* showed it on an internal page as part of a three-shot sequence. In each case, captions appended to the photo left no doubt as to the victim's fate: "A Viet Cong officer is shot and killed," noted the *Los Angeles Times.*[20] The display extended to the broadcast media. That evening the image was shown as a still photograph on NBC, ABC, and the BBC. When NBC showed the photo, the network blacked out its screen for three seconds, thereby increasing its impact, a significant move because the network would receive its own footage 46 hours later, which it then showed to an estimated 20 million people.[21]

The photo continued to surface during the following week: the *New York Daily News* reran it alongside the rejoinder that "the grim and ghastly picture" showed "how perilously idiotic are the demands of our doves for a one-sided allied pause in bombing." It appeared in *Time, Newsweek,* and *Life* the following week, and in *Time* again two weeks later in a twelve-page wrap-up of the war. *Life* reprinted it the following month.[22]

News executives' eagerness to publish the image was not matched by viewer support for the display, however, and many viewers echoed Eddie Adams's discomfort. As one columnist noted (alongside the photo's display), "Every publication which ran [the photo] received outraged letters deploring the display of horror for its own sake." Letters to the editor blasted the decision to show the image. "Do we have to endure the picture of a gruesome execution on the front pages?" asked one reader. "Realistic as the picture is, many of us find such starkness extremely upsetting." "Why did you publish that picture of death?" asked another. Of the letters received by NBC after it aired film of the shooting, two thirds accused the network of "bad taste." A minority of readers, though shocked by the photo, recognized its use-value in bringing to light the horrors of the war. One *New York Times* reader called it a depiction of a "summary lynching."[23]

Unlike news organizations' delayed response to the images of the burning monk, then, news executives, with journalists behind them, spoke at every opportunity to the persuasive appeal that this picture could wield. Within days, commentators began noting that the image was already mobilizing public opinion against the war. On February 5, a mere three days after it appeared, Anthony Lewis of the *New York Times* commented on its role in fueling growing sentiments against U.S. involvement in the region: "The startling pictures that came out of Vietnam last week—on television and in the press—evidently had an enormous impact. They brought home to the public the effects of the surprise Vietcong raids and of South Vietnamese and American measures in response."[24] That same day, the *Sunday London Times* used Adams's photo as a silhouette to mark its three-page roundup on Vietnam, and within the week *Time* reprinted the photo—asking "Will [it] go into the history books?"—and again two weeks later when it noted that the photo raised the question of "how should prisoners in a guerrilla war be treated?" When the International Committee of the Red Cross went on record against the executions taking place in Vietnam, the *New York Times* noted that the image of Loan was responsible for facilitating discussions between the Red Cross and South Vietnamese officials.[25]

Despite the attention, Adams continued to protest the image's reception. Within a short period of time, the photo's widespread visibility negatively impacted Loan, who was removed from all police responsibilities.[26] Adams argued to anyone who would listen that the photo had unfairly maligned the South Vietnamese officer; he also protested what seemed to him to be the image's instant and wide-ranging acclaim. "The general killed the Viet Cong," he said. But "I killed the general with my camera....What the photograph didn't say was, 'What would you do if you were the general at that time and place on that hot day, and you caught the so-called bad guy after he blew away one, two or three American soldiers?' "[27] However, because so much of journalism was already wrapped up in the photo's celebration, not much attention was paid his discomfort.

When the picture went on to be evaluated by professional circles, it captured nearly every first place honor in news photo contests around the world, winning the 1968 World Press Photo and 1969 Pulitzer Prize. Called a "classic example of the decisive moment in photography," the photo was praised for its "composition, lens choice and timing" and the fact that it captured "the literal reality of a man being shot in all the horror and finality of that moment of death." The photo, said one observer, shows "an individual's fear written on his face a fraction of a second before the loss of his life." Photojournalist David Hume Kennerly later called it "one of about five great photographs of the 20th century that really changed history," and *Newsweek's* former director of photography argued that the photo revealed "in graphic detail the injustice and madness that war breeds."[28] The photo was part of nearly every photographic retrospective on photojournalism, which over time drew note of the image's eventual tie-in with antiwar sentiments.[29]

It thus made sense that the news organizations that initially displayed the photo continued to reprint it over time. In 1972, *Time* used it in its "Gallery of Photos that Brought the War Home," again in a 1985 cover story on "Vietnam: Ten Years Later," where the photo illustrated both the news-magazine's table of contents and the story itself, and yet again in 1989 in a special issue on photojournalism. It reappeared in *Newsweek* in a 2004 column on the damage caused by images of the Iraq War. It ran in both the *New York Times* and the *Washington Post* five times each over the following years, used to illustrate events as wide-ranging as the invasion of Nicaragua, the campaign into Afghanistan, the violations at Abu Ghraib, and other problematic linkages between militaristic and moral impulses in U.S. society.[30]

Significantly, one person not part of the celebration was Adams himself. Said to be haunted by the photo, he refused to display it in his studio and repeatedly told people he wished he had never taken it. Complaining that he was "identified with that picture, nothing else," he admitted to pressure "to find another picture I'd rather be remembered for." He claimed he could not look at it for years, maintaining that "sometimes a picture can be misleading because it does not tell the whole story" and admitting that the "picture hurt [him] in a lot of ways" and "it destroyed [Loan's] life."[31] Adams later apologized to Loan, who by that time had experienced additional humiliation, leaving Vietnam for the United States but then becoming the target of denunciations in Congress, attempts at deportation, death threats, and general harassment. When Loan died, Adams published his own eulogy in *Time* and praised him as a hero.[32]

The effect of the photo on Loan's life was played out across the media, but in ways that fit journalism's earlier celebration of the photo. *Newsweek* in particular linked Loan's personal difficulties with the picture: the Adams shot accompanied a 1976 article on Loan's difficulties in attracting customers to his Virginia pizza parlor, a 1978 article tracing the beginning of INS proceedings against him, and, more appropriately, a 1985 cover story about the legacy of Vietnam. Similar linkages showed up elsewhere, as when the *Washington Post* used the picture to illustrate an article about Loan's problems with immigration.[33] Ironically, given both Adams's and Loan's reluctance at being associated with the photo, it was nonetheless used on their deaths to illustrate their obituaries—Loan's in 1998 and Adams's in 2004.[34]

The image also made its way out of journalism. The antiwar movement used the image extensively, in posters, promotional material, magazines, and books. It gained repeated exposure on television, illustrated book reviews on Vietnam, and was featured in retrospectives on the era; today it remains on contemporary display as the largest picture in the war museum in Ho Chi Minh City (formerly known as Saigon).[35] Over time, however, the image's strident role as an antiwar icon softened as it traveled into unpredictable terrain, becoming the backdrop for a socialist road show in Bonn, Germany; the foundation for a French art installation in 2004; and a conservative icon via its recycling through popular films and comics.[36]

That recycling produced responses echoing some of Adams's earlier misgivings. After he wrote a laudatory column about Loan in *Time* in 1998, letters to the editor nearly unanimously decried the photo's display thirty-odd years earlier, and conservative news media used the incident to argue against the contextless display of images. Following Adams's lead, news organs like the *Weekly Standard* and the *National Review* argued that the photo had scapegoated Loan. The picture, wrote the *National Review,* failed "to expand on 'our right to know.' It didn't answer questions or give us the story. It deceived. It gave no context. It confirmed the biases of the antiwar journalists, and they used it."[37] As media scholar Peter Braestrup commented already in 1977, "What information did the photograph actually convey? That a brave but overwrought South Vietnamese police director...inexcusably shot an enemy?"[38] It was a sentiment shared by many viewers and by Adams but not widely addressed in the rush by news executives and journalism more broadly to celebrate the photo.

In dealing with the image, then, the U.S. news media corrected the reluctance with which they had depicted the burning monk image years earlier and forged ahead with a full-out display of the Adams photo, despite its problems. As Robert Hamilton remarked, the image showed not how the photograph "could change the course of history" but how "the course of history changes photographs."[39] Sidestepping Adams's repeated articulations of dissonance over the photo's display and viewers' discomfort with what it showed, the response of news executives and journalists to the Adams photo—repeated, formulaic, self-congratulatory, and tied to broader agendas associated with the antiwar movement—showed how the consistent and frequent verbal framing of an image of certain death could drive engagement around an unsettled public event. It also, somewhat unwittingly, displayed the degree of efforts that needed to be invested in a photo that was not supported by either the photographer himself or many of the viewers whom it targeted. Such efforts also signaled that at least in some quarters there was a growing though unstable willingness to show and see the graphic violence of the Vietnam War, even if its depiction rested on verbal texts confirming death rather than images of death itself.

My Lai

One month later, a signal massacre of Vietnamese civilians demonstrated a dark and brutal underside to the U.S. military presence in Vietnam. On March 16, 1968, an American military group called Charlie Company, led by Lt. William L. Calley Jr., killed a group of civilians when the expected Vietcong opposition did not materialize. Although the company had anticipated strong resistance from a Vietcong battalion, it instead found civilian men, women, and children, many of whom were still cooking their breakfast rice. The soldiers herded the barefoot villagers into groups, shooting those who resisted, or, as one partici- pant remembered, engaging in a repertoire of brutal acts—"shooting them to cutting their throats to scalping them to cutting off their hands and cutting out their tongues."[40] Estimates of casualties in the event—later called the My Lai massacre—ranged between 150 and 500 persons.

It is telling that the event's photographic capture relied on a military pho- tographer acting in dual roles as soldier and citizen. Ronald Haeberle was in the area to cover operations for a division's military newspaper. With two cam- eras in hand—a black-and-white army issue camera and his own color film camera—he accompanied the military unit as it encountered the villagers. Hae- berle's account of what happened changed over time, but he consistently main- tained that he unknowingly stumbled onto the massacre as it unfolded. At first he admitted understanding that the villagers were going to be killed, as relayed in the caption he supplied alongside one of his photo's earliest displays: "Guys were about to shoot these people. I yelled 'hold it,' and shot my picture. As I walked away, I heard M-16s open up. From the corner of my eye, I saw bod- ies falling, but I didn't turn to look." Later accounts of his actions somewhat softened when he contended that "I thought they were just going to question the people, but just as soon as I turned and walked away, I heard firing."[41] The pictures Haeberle took documented a full sequence of events—soldiers jump- ing from helicopters and setting fire to the village, wounded and dying Viet- namese villagers, and corpses lying amidst rubble. Taking pictures with both cameras, he kept the color film for himself. Among the shots he held onto were images of people about to die and of mangled corpses on the road.[42]

The slaughter at first received no coverage. Haeberle's military tour ended two weeks after the massacre and he returned from active duty to Cleveland, Ohio. Later, he maintained that he found it difficult to remove the scenes of the killings from his mind: "You think back, could I have prevented this? How could I have prevented this? And it's a question I still kind of ask myself today." He began to give lectures on Vietnam, showing slides of what he had seen to

Rotary Club luncheons, the Kiwanis, and Lions Club circuit and other informal local meetings. But the response was muted. As one observer later commented, "Apparently nobody in Haeberle's audiences contacted journalists who might be interested in writing about an alarming event. The rationales for silence are many."[43]

It was not until a year later—March 1969—that the massacre was disclosed. Former soldier Ronald Ridenhour wrote letters to Congress describing what he had seen and prompting an investigation of the incident, on which journalists, among them Seymour M. Hersh, began tracing the story. Hersh's account, first refused publication by both *Life* and *Look,* appeared in thirty-five newspapers on November 13, 1969.[44] Seeing Hersh's story, Haeberle called the *Cleveland Plain Dealer* and offered the paper his photos. At first news executives were hesitant about printing them. Only after they received a phone call from military officials warning that the pictures, if shown publicly, would "inflame public opinion" and drive sentiments against Calley did the paper proceed with publication. Pushing aside visual coverage of a moon walk that same day, eight of Haeberle's images appeared on November 20, 1969—a year and a half after the massacre.[45]

The photos were positioned under the masthead on the *Plain Dealer*'s front page and on a double page inside spread. Two of the eight images drew specific attention. One, appearing on the front page under the headline "A clump of bodies on a road in South Vietnam," documented a blood-soaked heap of twenty-five corpses or so, amidst scattered clothing. Disfigured and missing body parts, the torsos, which included children and babies, looked like a scene from Dante's *Inferno.* In the accompanying graph of introductory text, the newspaper told readers that the image "will shock Americans as it shocked the editors and the staff of the *Plain Dealer.* . . . Why they were killed raises one of the most momentous questions of the war in Vietnam." On a second page, the newspaper printed both the army's request that the paper not publish the images and the *Plain Dealer*'s reply, that it would do so because readers were entitled to see them for themselves.[46]

Inside, the *Plain Dealer* displayed additional images, one of them showing a group of women and children about to die, a depiction of the same group of slaughtered people that the newspaper had portrayed on its front page. This photo depicted a handful of women and small children, huddling together in abject terror (fig. 6.3). Almost everyone in the frame looked to its left corner, suggesting that some undepicted tool of their impending death rested there. Though collectively huddled in fear, the people were engaged in various secondary activities—one teenage girl buttoned her blouse while clutching a toddler on her hip; a young crying child clung to a partly depicted older woman; a taller woman clasped her hands around the waist of an elderly one, whose

Figure 6.3:
Ronald S. Haeberle/Getty Images, My
Lai Massacre, March 16, 1968.

face seemed to have captured the majority of light in the frame. Its centrality emphasized her vulnerability—her weeping, raised eyebrows, crouched frame. The photo drew its cogency from human agony; it so filled the shot that it overran its corners, where another child huddling with those depicted was partly shut out of the frame. None of the individuals was identified. Nowhere were the U.S. soldiers depicted, separating agency from consequence. At the same time, the caption left nothing to the imagination: "A group of South Vietnamese women and children, cowering. Minutes later, they were all dead."[47]

The photos received some attention from the U.S. news media but it was not uniform. Screened on CBS that night, they played to total silence as the camera offered 22 seconds of no voice-over or music, only the pictures—without captions or commentary. The next day they appeared in the *New York Times* and the *New York Post*, and the *Los Angeles Times* ran them under the headline "Point Blank Murder." Within the month they appeared twice in both *Time* and *Newsweek*. After paying Haeberle twenty thousand dollars, *Life* ran

234 • About to Die

a ten-page pictorial spread in December 1969 that included the about-to-die picture as a full-page color image.[48]

Viewers did not wholeheartedly accept what the images tried to show. Commentary in the U.S. news media remained cautious, offering justifications for the company's behavior, refraining from commenting editorially and reminding viewers that the Vietcong had long engaged in the killing of civilians. The *Plain Dealer* was criticized for displaying the images, with 85 percent of the paper's switchboard calls registering protest. People refused to believe that the images were true, and some protested the nudity of the corpses. Readers' letters to *Life* reacted, in the magazine's view, "with horror, shame and shock, but also with disbelief, uncaring acceptance and even benumbed lack of interest." On seeing *Life*'s display, a stunned President Richard Nixon convened a meeting of his advisers in which he told them to "get out the other side of the story." In many cases, as the pictures' distribution spread, so did public disbelief. In Minnesota, where over 49 percent of the public were said to disbelieve the story, one U.S. congressman contended that "you know our boys would never do anything like that." As Vicki Goldberg later noted, the photos underscored that when "the moral import was unbearable," then "denial was widespread."[49]

Critics also decried Haeberle's actions. Accused of not stopping the killings, not showing the images to his superiors, and taking money for their distribution, Haeberle generated little empathy, an impression intensified when he was cross-examined at Calley's court-martial and said he had decided not to report the incident but "to keep quiet until someone came to us." Only when the investigation continued and former company members began to publicly confess their actions did resistance to the story dissipate. From that point on, the pictures received fuller coverage. The *Washington Post* devoted a full three pages to the story, while the *Philadelphia Inquirer* called the event "the kind of atrocity generally associated with the worst days of Hitler and Stalin." The investigation culminated in the court martial of the company leader, William L. Calley Jr.[50]

In the years after the war, the images were given an afterlife by proponents of a variety of causes. The women and children facing their death appeared repeatedly, but, unlike other about-to-die photos, the image's matching photo—which showed the same individuals lying dead in the road—was actively recycled as well.[51] In 1985, for instance, when *Time* ran a special issue on "Vietnam: Ten Years Later," it included the picture of the massacred rather than the shot of people about to die alongside other iconic Vietnam images. The photo of the corpses became a touchstone for many antiwar proponents, when it was used by the New York Art Workers Coalition, which appended a caption—"And babies?"—to its display. Transported into a poster that became "an easily recognized symbol of what was wrong with America," over time the photo graced record covers, promotional literature for art exhibitions, and public events protesting war atrocities. The twinning of the pictures, however, only increased their interpretive flux: in Kendrick Oliver's view, the pictures "offered the option of shame, a chance to map out any continuities that existed between what they had done (at home, in work, in politics) and what they now saw (Vietnamese bodies on a trail)." In that vein, all of Haeberle's pictures were redisplayed as a slide show by the *Plain Dealer,* forty years after the massacre, and remain displayed in the My Lai Museum; they are also rumored to reemerge in association with Oliver Stone's film "Pinkville."[52] In some views, their potency dissipated more markedly than that of other images of the war: "What was once an image of incandescent horror has become at most a vague recollection of something unpleasant that happened during the Vietnam War." Or, as Kendrick Oliver noted in his discussion of the "mutedness of its memory," Americans "have not made use enough of the massacre ... [failing] to fashion a purpose from its memory. It was an aberration; it was Vietnam; it was the wages of war.... The controversy could not be resolved, but it could slowly be eased towards the dimmer recesses of the past."[53]

This image of certain death, then, shows what happens when the suggestion of death does not promote either acknowledgement or engagement, even when its verbal texts confirm that death occurred. Accompanied by delay, resistance, unevenness, and an uncertainty about whether the depiction was true, the image gave way to an image of death itself, suggesting that at some level the photo did not quite work in the more formulaic manner displayed by other about-to-die images. Offering a more direct depiction of U.S. brutality than any of the other about-to-die images, the photo at some level had more to prove and raised the ante of what an image of the Vietnam War needed to show, but its match of image to word still made it a poor fit for those struggling to come to grips with the war.

All of this suggests that the acceptance of three images of certain death was far less automatic than the act of display might have implied. Each image was poised to encourage public engagement, but the responses were varied. Each was produced via wide interpretive play among those who made them— the initial delay and reluctance among news executives to publish Malcolm Browne's image of the burning monk; the discomfort of photographer Eddie Adams and viewers about the image of General Loan; and the delay, public disbelief and consequent parallel display of the same individuals dead in Ron Haeberle's images of My Lai. With the photo of General Loan, news executives pushed the display too much, while in both the cases of the burning monk and Mei Lai, they pushed not enough. The interpretive play accompanying these images of certain death thus undercut their value. Because the certainty of death seemed not to be a workable message in the unsettled events of the Vietnam War, a different load of information would be better equipped to engage the journalists, news executives, politicians, officials, and viewers who saw its images.

Possible Death in Vietnam

Four years later, the public climate had changed. By 1972, the opposition to the war and knowledge of its brutality were more intact. Earlier suggestions of a lack of clear military objectives were now stridently displayed in a panoply of images reflecting a war without clear aims, targets, or battle lines. Military units forging across muddy rivers, frantic helicopter evacuations, and the steady unraveling of threadbare villages all provided a visual pastiche without clear direction that reflected the war's growing lack of order: "What was a sorry truth about the war became a dominant feature of its coverage."[54]

On June 8, 1972, an altercation occurred near the village of Trang Bang off of the major highway between Saigon and Hanoi. Air support from the South Vietnamese Air Force was called in and the village's ensuing bombing involved phosphorus and napalm. Rather than initiate antiaircraft fire, as had been expected, the villagers displayed no resistance. Instead a group of children fled from its blazing environs, maimed from the fire.

At the site were a number of journalists, among them AP photographer Nick Ut, *Time* correspondent David Burnett, and NBC cameraman Le Phuc Dinh. As Ut later recalled:

> When we (the reporters) moved closer to the village we saw the first people running. I thought "Oh my God" when I suddenly saw a woman with her left leg badly burned by napalm. Then came a woman carrying a baby, who died, then another woman carrying a small child with its skin coming off. When I took a picture of them I heard a child screaming and saw a young girl who had pulled off all her burning clothes. She yelled to her brother on the left.[55]

Ut took eight rolls of black and white film of the villagers running from their blazing homes. One of his pictures showed five children running frantically down a dirt road, indifferent soldiers at its edges, black clouds of smoke muddying the sky behind them. The children raced headfirst into the camera's field, mouths agape and arms outstretched in terror. A young girl had stripped off her clothes and was fully naked. Later, it would become clear that they were running from a cloud of napalm smoke.

In Ut's photo, the children embodied brutal human suffering thrown full-thrust at the photographer (fig. 6.4). Each of the children ran directly toward Ut, photographed at varying distances that did not diminish the visible signs

Figure 6.4:
Nick Ut/AP, Napalmed
Children Flee Attack,
June 8, 1972.

of their pain or abject vulnerability: the boy on the left side of the frame ran with clenched fists, crying in terror as his open mouth turned downward like a human mask of tragedy; the children at the right clasped hands as they sprinted in the photographer's direction. In the center of the image was the young girl, racing ahead in full frontal nudity, her arms outstretched from her body. She had ripped off her clothes, set ablaze by the napalm.

Ut took the film back to his bureau, where he and another photographer selected eight prints to be sent over the wires, among them the shot of the napalmed children. The photo at first met internal resistance at the AP, where one editor rejected it because of the girl's frontal nudity. A subsequent argument erupted in the bureau, at which point photo department head Horst Faas argued by telex with the New York office that an exception needed to be made; the two offices agreed to a compromise display by which there would be no close-up of the girl alone.[56] Titled "Accidental Napalm Attack," the image went out over the wires.

It was picked up immediately. Already that evening, the three U.S. TV networks all made the same decision: Alongside Le Phuc Dinh's TV footage, Ut's still photo filled the TV studios' backdrop. NBC cropped the photo so it only showed two children. Though the broadcasters spoke in initially innocuous terms about an accidental bombing in South Vietnam, the photo was anything but innocuous. The next morning, the photo was splashed across the U.S. print media, stretching over four and five columns of the front pages of nearly every major newspaper—including the *New York Times, Washington Post, Los Angeles Times,* and *Philadelphia Inquirer.* The Associated Press, which handled the image, estimated that nearly every U.S. paper printed it. In each case, the adjoining caption remarked on the "fleeing children," noting that one girl had ripped off her clothing. No mention was made of the children's death in the captions, but the adjoining texts addressed the dead civilians and the more general undepicted loss of life that had been caused by the attack. In other words, as with other images of possible death, the children in Ut's image signified those who had died from the blast but were not seen.[57]

Displayed with little or no dissonance, widely and repeatedly, and worked into the retrospective literature in ways that paralleled and built on, rather than were differentiated from, its initial work as a news relay, the photo remained "the most famous and the most frequently reproduced image of the war." Or, as Susan Sontag famously offered, it remained "the signature Vietnam War horror-photograph."[58] Significantly, however, it played to the "as if" in a different way than the others had done, offering an image of possibility that called on the public to infer deaths it did not see rather than accept deaths that were verbally confirmed.

The image continued to surface the next day, often in association with verbal texts recounting unseen victims. CBS broadcast it a second time the next night, this time reporting that the young girl was still alive. Over the following two days, on June 10 and 11, updates were offered on the girl's condition as part of the news media's coverage of the bombings, and each time the image was used to illustrate the reports. The *Philadelphia Inquirer*, for instance, ran a cropped version of the image alongside a second image of a small child being cradled by an adult under the title "One Dies, One Lives"; the headline to the adjoining article read "Little Viet Boy Dies of Napalm Burns," while the text remarked that the girl was taken to a Saigon hospital. By June 11—three days after the bombing—the *New York Times* named the girl as nine-year-old Phan Thi Kim-Phuc; it also claimed that the dead boy in the other picture was Kim-Phuc's brother. With each new piece of information, the photo appeared again.[59]

The possibility of the girl recovering positioned the image differently than had been the case with any of the earlier Vietnam images. Recovery moved the image's display further into the realm of the emotions, the imagination, and contingency, for as people were treated to the same repeated image over the following week, they were able to ask themselves if the girl survived, if her health improved, if the children went home, if others met the same or worse fate. By that point, *Time, Newsweek,* and *Life* were repeatedly using the picture to address the girl's unfolding story. *Newsweek* ran the photo—now titled "Inferno"—alongside a picture of a Vietnamese air battle in a three-page wrap-up on the war. *Life* featured a two-page article, titled "Threat of Life," that highlighted the image alongside one of Kim-Phuc's dead brothers.[60]

This is not to say that there was no debate over the image's publication. Editors debated the appropriateness of displaying nudity, and numerous factual discrepancies—concerning whether the bombing was accidental, which troops were responsible for dropping the bomb, and the care provided to Kim-Phuc following the incident—emerged following the photograph's display. Readers' letters labeled the display "nauseating," "obscene," and "poor taste," on the one hand, and urged the photo's widespread display so as to end the war, on the other. One reader went so far as to collect extra copies of her paper and sent them to her congressional representatives. Nonetheless, the debate had less rigor and intensity than that exhibited around previous images. This was not only because people were more agreed about the war's censure but also because the image confirmed less and suggested more. Facilitating the viewers' engagement, it thus suggested various outcomes to what was depicted, for, as Robert Hariman and John Lucaites observed, the photo overflowed with a surplus of interpretive cues, touching on "moral life, including pain, fragmentation, modal relationships among strangers, betrayal and trauma...political innocence, human rights, third world vulnerability and victimhood, mechanized destructiveness, criminal state action, and moral callousness."[61]

It thus made sense that, other than Kim-Phuc, the children were not immediately identified. Their death, signaled here as possible, was not verified, confirmed, or made clear. In fact it made little difference, for the children's fate stood in for the civilian bombings more generally. This meant that viewers could infer numerous things about what they were seeing, responding to the "as if" of the image's display. Thus when *Life* magazine asked of its readers—"These are South Vietnamese children. Would you feel any easier had the children been *North* Vietnamese?"—readers responded energetically, one woman answering that all readers should ask themselves, "If these were my children, would I have put an end to this war sooner?" Six months later, when *Life* reprinted the picture, it shifted its emphasis from children to civilians in general, with the photo "speak[ing] for every one of the millions of civilians who have fled down Vietnam's highways in search of haven from the hounds of war."[62]

As public interest in the girl's recovery continued, the photo continued to reappear in the U.S. news media as an illustration of that recovery. The *New York Times* printed it again two months later, in an article titled "Napalmed Girl Recovering in Saigon," where it was used to raise funds for the plastic surgery unit where the girl was housed; other newspapers followed suit. Over time, the five children in the photo—Kim-Phuc, two of her brothers and two of her cousins—were all identified as having survived the ordeal, while two additional cousins, pictured in other photographs, were said to have died.[63]

As the story of Kim-Phuc's recovery became fuller, the public learned of an ongoing relationship between the girl and her photographer. It became clear that Ut had snapped her picture, doused her burns with the water from his canteen and rushed her to the nearest hospital, even before he turned in his film. Kim-Phuc was quoted as saying of Ut, "he saved my life. He's wonderful. I am so grateful that he didn't only do his job." Newspapers recounted how Ut visited her during her fourteen month hospital stay and continued to visit until he was evacuated with the fall of Saigon three years later. As late as 2007, he remarked on how he and Kim-Phuc remained in touch. Many years later, working with the photo's impact and establishing the Kim Foundation to help children of war, Kim-Phuc also did not miss an opportunity to credit her relationship with the photographer. "That picture," she was quoted as saying, "has given me a powerful gift."[64]

Not surprisingly, the picture received numerous awards. Honored by Sigma Delta Chi, the George Polk Memorial Award, the Overseas Press Club and the Associated Press Managing Editors Association, it won the World Press Photo of the Year in 1972 and in 1973 the Pulitzer Prize. In the words of one Associated Press editor, the continual requests for its reprinting made it the picture "that doesn't rest." Used widely in retrospectives on Vietnam, books on the 1970s and retrospectives on photojournalism, *Life* displayed it under the title "The Year in Pictures: South Vietnam," while *Time* included it as part of a gallery of images from 1972.[65] In *Life's* 1979 review of the decade, the photo was said "more than any other single image—[to have] made America conscious of the full horror of the Vietnam War." Called "one of the most powerful antiwar images of all time," it became a mainstay of professional and scholarly literature on photojournalism, where it was widely referenced as the singly most memorable photo associated with the Vietnam War.[66] In a 1985 anniversary piece, the *New York Times* called it the "most enduring antiwar image of Vietnam," and over the years, it ran as part of the news media's repository of memorable images.[67]

Alongside the unfolding trajectory of the girl's recovery, the image also rapidly travelled into other parts of the news media, reappearing alongside readers' letters, editorial columns, yearly retrospectives, and overviews of the war. Immediately after the photo first appeared, the *Philadelphia Inquirer* reprinted the image alongside a theologian's extended letter in which he urged people to conscientiously object to the war, and with each new sequel of Kim-Phuc's life, it reappeared.[68] In 1996, her visit to the Vietnam Veterans' Memorial in Washington, D.C., drew widespread media attention, giving news organizations another opportunity to display the photo.[69] That visit in turn spawned additional photo opportunities, such as her reconciliation with a U.S. commander, anniversaries of the attack, the release of documentary films about her life, her appointment as a goodwill ambassador for UNESCO, and reviews of books on her life.[70] Sometimes the photo was referenced but did not appear, as when the *Los Angeles Times* noted that the "photo was [a] symbol of [the] Vietnam War" in a story of Kim-Phuc becoming a medical student in 1984, or when the news media reported her naming by UNESCO as a goodwill ambassador in 1997.[71] Two documentary movies chronicled her tragedy and recovery, and it illustrated topics once removed from the event, including the introduction of French legislation regarding graphic news images and promotional literature for the Kim Foundation for healing children of war.[72] It illustrated the coverage of awards ceremonies—when Ut won the Pulitzer Prize and when both were honored by the London Science Museum—and was discussed, though not shown, in stories about Ut's collected photographs, visual coverage of the U.S. fatalities in Iraq, and Ut's career.[73]

As one later overview noted, before the photo Kim-Phuc "had been a private citizen. Afterward, she became a political instrument." Already the same year of the napalm attack, the *New York Times* printed a cartoon that used the girl's figure to represent the war and the U.S. burden of guilt. The North Vietnamese government sent her to Ho Chi Minh City to appear in propaganda films in 1984. In 1989, the photo ran as evidence of war horror at a United Nations exhibit on world disarmament. When the *Toronto Star* ran a story about her in 1997, scores of donations poured in, offering her everything from money to free tuition.[74] In each case, Kim-Phuc became generalized as meaning much more than the victim of one attack, the resistance to the Vietnam War or the universal suffering associated with war. As the *Boston Globe* told it in 1997, her story became "a story about wounding and healing, cruelty and charity, the miraculous persistence of individual love and generosity."[75]

Her photo also traveled into popular culture. Made into an antiwar poster that adorned walls across the United States and Europe, the photo forced "all eyes" to fix "on one powerless child, and it was enough to change world affairs."[76] Her image in the Ut photo was made into the subject of cartoons, paintings, and art installments, and in 2003 Belgian composer Eric Geurts dedicated a song to "The Girl in the Picture."[77]

Unlike the other about-to-die images from Vietnam, then, Ut's image of the napalmed children was given a context against which it could grow. The photo's repeated display—more extensive than that accorded any of the earlier Vietnam photos—made sense not only to mark the horror of what had happened but the hope and possibility that Kim-Phuc's recovery could make that horror less terrible. The photo's employment as an image of possible death, rather than a certain death, played to the "as if" by facilitating public engagement in a continually evolving story that promised a better ending. Like other images of possible death, then, the Ut image took on a secondary function that drew from its earlier display as news by transporting it into new contexts. This image of possible death succeeded at a time when Vietnam's images of certain death were mired by an overload of interpretive play. Instead, through its recycling, the napalm girl photo was loosened from its denotative moorings and established as a subjunctive marker of numerous interrelated messages—about war atrocity, hope, forgiveness, rehabilitation, recovery. Appearing at a point when, unlike in earlier years, opposition to the war was more uniform and people were more willing to engage with its visualization, the photo captured its spectators in numerous "as if" elaborations of the trajectory of Kim-Phuc's recovery and life. Those elaborations inferred the possibility of death while highlighting an individual's triumph over it.

What this suggests about the suggestibility of news images is telling. For it raises the possibility that a lessened degree of informational detail may help engage people in the unsettled events of the public sphere more effectively than those images with a more detailed informational load. As with images of possible death, Ut's photo coaxed journalists, news executives, politicians, officials, and viewers to do the work necessary to complete the image's contingent features, even if doing so took them toward multiple interpretations. The fact that Kim-Phuc did not die mattered less than her ability to stand for those who did, and in doing so she emblematized her own recovery and that of many Americans vis-à-vis the war. Against these parameters, the photo persevered as the most widely circulated and centrally remembered of all Vietnam's about-to-die images.

Immolation, Execution, Massacre, and Bombing

It is significant that despite the availability of film footage of each of these four events, still photos motivate their collective memory. Appearing in documentaries, books, posters, and other popular cultural venues, when taken together, the photos reveal a broad range of possibilities by which the about-to-die moment was used to depict the Vietnam War. As images of certain death, the first three displayed a degree of certitude about death in Vietnam that did not match a more general willingness to engage with the deaths caused by the war. Rather, the levels of certainty implied by the photos ruffled still developing sentiments about the war's meaning and significance; as one White House adviser noted at the time, "The images have been savage—they almost choke the viewer with horror."[78] In this regard, the U.S. news media did not display the photos in a sustainable fashion: they either pushed the images too forcefully or not enough for its corresponding public engagement.

By contrast, the one image of possible death—that of children maimed by a napalm bombing—succeeded as an image of impending death because it was suggestive of death, not definitive. Migrating back to the stance of possibility rather than certainty, it invoked a different kind of engagement from journalists, news executives, politicians, officials, and viewers, who accommodated its impulses in grappling with the war. As Robert Hariman and John Lucaites observed, this photo

> became a template for remaking the public world through its continued circulation in the public media. Or worlds: The audience can choose one world where resilient individuals get on with their lives, where history has the inert presence of a scar, and moral response to others culminates

in personal reconciliation. Or the audience can choose another world in which the past haunts the present as a traumatic memory, one that continues to demand public accountability.[79]

In other words, using inference to activate the imagination, the emotions, and contingency was a more suited act of engagement than the ready acceptance of more definitive verbal cues. The image of possible death emerged as more useful than those of a certain death because it could accommodate a repertoire of interpretive positions vis-à-vis the war. No less graphic than the other about-to-die photos in what it depicted, but made less reprehensible due to a girl's story of recovery, the widespread and sustained embrace of the photo underscored that in the right circumstances images could work effectively even when they stopped short of providing full documentation of what they depicted.

This migration to a reduced informational load fits broader mnemonic patterns about the Vietnam War. Fred Turner showed that public responses to the war, themselves a replication of that of the traumatized veteran, alternated between spasms of amnesia and recollection, never really reconciling the war with Americans' sense of their national identity.[80] Against that zigzagging, the images of Vietnam were powerful because they underscored the Americans as aggressors: as Susan Moeller argued, "More than any other compilation of images from Vietnam, the photos.... challenged the conduct of the war."[81] But in focusing on impending death, they also opened a space in which it was easier to navigate and play with the various quandaries—political, social, religious, economic, and moral—raised by the war and the fact of its aggression. While pictures of corpses might have had the same effect, the fact that the Vietnam War was often depicted by pictures of impending death enhanced public engagement for good and bad without graphic imagery, playing to evolving public sentiments over what the war meant.

In both Caroline Brothers's and David Perlmutter's separate views, the impact of the pictures from Vietnam depended on a multitude of factors and was less certain than assumed. As Brothers observed, "These pictures... articulated and retrospectively pinpointed shifts in the groundswell of attitudes to the war but were unable to bring about these changes of themselves.... Images such as these could only surface when the mood of the country was ripe."[82] In moving away from images that provided more informational detail about a certain death to accommodating an image that allowed the public to at most infer a possible death, the U.S. news media's coverage of Vietnam thus involved news executives, journalists, officials, politicians, and viewers in what images do best—provide less information when the stakes are highest. In so doing, they relied heavily on the "as if" as a route for lending meaning to the war, a route that took shape incrementally over the sixteen years of its prosecution.

About To Die in the Tsunami: Variance across Space

The 2004 tsunami, in which some 230,000 people died and thousands of coastline communities in Sri Lanka, India, Thailand, Indonesia, and eastern Africa were destroyed, unfolded across a vast spatial territory bordering on the Indian Ocean on December 26, 2004. Acute and spatially diffuse, the reverberations of the earthquake that caused the tidal wave cycled for over seven hours and impacted communities, like South Africa, nearly five thousand miles away.

Though the coverage of distant natural disasters had long followed a reliance on affect-driven stories and hackneyed images that facilitated labeling the disaster easily at the time of its initial reportage and visualization,[83] the coverage of this tsunami was different. Due to the proliferation of mobile technologies and a large group of Western holidaymakers on-site with mobile devices, its reportage was not delayed but immediate and needed to accommodate various populations. Though disasters in distant lands had always suffered from a lack of on-site personnel to provide coverage, international news organizations broke records in shuttling journalists to the region but they were late in coming. Instead, local residents and tourists acting as citizen journalists used blogs, camera phones, and digital cameras to send information and transmitted instant and relatively wide-ranging coverage of the tidal wave as it unfolded, establishing a new normal for covering natural disaster. As a Reuters poll the following year observed, the tsunami "attracted more media attention in the first six weeks after it struck than the world's top 10 'forgotten' emergencies did over a whole year."[84]

This was critical because covering the story was logistically complicated. Broadcast news executives remarked that they had never been "so tested" by a story, which constituted the "most complicated logistical crisis [they had] ever covered." One Fox News correspondent likened it to "a war zone with an invisible enemy." A vast landscape, inaccessible territory and widespread extensive destruction all presented difficulties for traditional newsgathering. Even reaching the areas hit by the tsunami was difficult; it took the three main U.S. news anchors nine days to get to its least remote regions.[85]

In some views the U.S. media's response was laudable given the circumstances. CNN led the pack by cancelling preemptive programming, calling correspondents back from vacation, employing substitute hosts and sending an additional fifty people to the region. As Ted Koppel said in his opening remarks on ABC's "Nightline," reporters did the best they could on a story requiring massive and immediate coverage:

> What is it that allows us to turn away from any number of tragedies while opening our hearts and checkbooks to the victims of the tsunami in Indonesia, Thailand, Sri Lanka and India?...We are, it seems, put-off

by tragedies that involve both the heroics and the villanies of war and politics. A giant tsunami, on the other hand, is nonjudgmental.[86]

But judgment was more evident than Koppel implied: the *Financial Times* criticized the influx of reporters covering the high-profile visitors in the region rather than the disaster itself, one reporter in Sri Lanka complained that "the story stopped where the road ended," and Sky TV news was critiqued for sending fifty journalists to Asia to cover the tsunami and only one to cover Africa.[87]

The tsunami coverage was characterized by the complementary strengths of its two newsgathering populations—old media and its traditional journalists and new media and its on-site local residents and tourists. Though online sites at the time still tended to produce largely material from old media, the tsunami offered a different opportunity to display information. These citizen journalists, able to document what they saw through eyewitness accounts, blogs, photos, and video footage, bolstered and personalized the coverage of traditional news organizations. Fostered by video compression technology, fed by digital cameras and traditional video cameras, and supported by mobile phones, satellite phones, videophones, and laptops with uplink capabilities, they made available accounts, photos, and footage within hours of the disaster. So many blogs were posted to yahoo.com that it organized a directory of them, and technorati.com estimated more than fifty-five thousand tsunami-related blogs surfaced during the first three days. Said to create a "tipping point in citizen journalism," the rush of tsunami documentation helped nonjournalistic involvement in newsgathering "grow up a little faster."[88]

Images, in particular, were an important part of nonjournalists' record. Carried by quickly established nonnews Web sites formed to accommodate the unfolding story, they offered a gathering point for a wide-ranging global public seeking to make sense of what had happened and helped create a vital link for the thousands of Europeans and North Americans who had journeyed there for a winter beach vacation. The Australian-based Waveofdestruction.org, for instance, drew close to 700,000 visitors attempting to access its twenty-five "tsunami videos" during the first four days.[89] New blogs—such as The South-East Asia Earthquake and Tsunami Blog, also called Tsunamihelp (http://tsunamihelp.blogspot.com/), which logged in more than 100,000 site visits in its first seventy-two hours, or Tsunami Disaster in Malaysia and Thailand (http://tsunamipenang.blogspot.com/)—were set up immediately as resources for organizing information, assistance, and financial donations. This meant that the usual distinctions between journalist and nonjournalist, local and foreign, or proximate and distant, categories that had tended to occupy generally unmovable positions in the foreground and background of the Western media attention of other disasters, in this case simply turned unstable.

The event's visual coverage began with singular and unusual amateur videos of onrushing water. By the morning of December 27, CNN, Fox News, and MSNBC all aired real-time footage of the tidal wave, filmed from the roof of a building by an Australian tourist in Thailand. As Reuters and Associated Press Television News found themselves awash in video feeds from the region, news organizations began broadcasting a building list of survivors' stories, photographs, and videos that they also posted to home pages, seeking out more amateur documentation at the same time: "There will be, I think, the definitive shot, the wall of water," said the director of news for APTN, but not all were so particular, and representatives of news organizations went "to airports seeking video from returning vacationers."[90] By the time more professional TV crews and photographers arrived, the first videos of moving water gave way to depictions of devastated landscapes, crumpled manmade structures, forlorn survivors, and corpses. Though the about-to-die image appeared across the disaster's rolling imagery, its surfacing shed light on how differently relevant the disaster—itself spatially diffuse—was to populations in different places around the globe. The spatial character of both the tsunami and its coverage, then, relayed a visual story of distant deaths that could engage the "as if" in varying ways.

As imagery rolled across news and nonnews sites, news organizations debated its appropriate use, oscillating between showing too much of the ravaged scenes or not enough. "What you want to do is show the horrific nature of what happened but do it in a way that you don't cause disgust among the viewers," said one ABC news executive. As with other natural disasters, relevant here were the images of dead bodies that were certain to come. While the choice of subdued or graphic coverage varied, depending on who had died, which medium was reporting, and where those deaths were positioned geographically and culturally in relation to the home front, a fundamental rule of coverage seemed to apply across the board: the further geographically and culturally one was from the disaster, the more graphic its coverage would be.[91] Though the actual sites of destruction were more far reaching than either traditional or citizen journalists could cover, the thrust was to work toward usable visuals that could signify the disaster at large. A search for synecdochically relevant pictures drove newsgathering efforts—images particular enough to be aligned with the disaster area but not so particular that they could not stand in for the region writ large. As with other about-to-die images, then, the tsunami's images were slated to work through their generalizability. And yet, TV news executives conducted lengthy discussions about which images to show. Concerned that even their generalizability would not mitigate offense, anchors like CNN's Anderson Cooper or ABC's Elizabeth Vargas warned viewers that the upcoming video would be disturbing. Managing editors published, broadcast, and posted public interest columns and essays detailing the judgment calls they were making about specific images, home pages of news organizations collected scores of reader responses so as to better gauge public reaction to what was appearing, and journalistic think-tanks offered central lists of relevant resources for reporting the story.[92]

At the same time, new media's involvement in the story reduced the relevance of such interventions. Because the story and its images were posted to multiple nonnews sites on the Internet within hours of its breaking, images and stories of all kinds rolled over the Web, leading the news organizations of old media to realize that coverage was only partly in their control. MSNBC's Web site msnbc.com resolved this by setting up a "Citizen Journalists Report" page, where it posed comments from users on stories. As a head editor for Reuters later recounted, "For the first 24 hours the best and the only photos and video came from tourists armed with portable telephones, digital cameras and camcorders. And if you didn't have those pictures, you weren't on the story."[93]

At first U.S. television was circumspect about what it showed, more so than the print media. Some of its treatments raised eyebrows: ABC called its programming "Waves of Destruction," Fox "Killer Wave," and CNN "Turning the Tide." "Good Morning, America" posted a graphic of "Diane's Route," in reference to Diane Sawyer's trek across the disaster zone, prompting one TV critic to comment that "viewers could be forgiven for thinking Hurricane Diane was as powerful as the tsunami damage she was there to inspect." The early TV coverage was described as "subdued," as CNN, which led the U.S. networks in mobilizing available resources to cover the tragedy, "took several days...to move beyond the devastated resorts to photos of the missing dead." As one commentator noted, "When bodies were seen, they were mostly from a distance and usually covered up. From television's perspective, they didn't have a face."[94]

The print media accommodated graphic images more readily. Recognizing the difficult choices they faced in selecting images—*American Editor* ran an overview titled "Editors Face Tough Choices with Tsunami Victim Photos"—already in the first days certain U.S. newspapers showed pictures of piles of bloated and half-clothed corpses that had come aground from the roaring sea and anonymous dead bodies being pulled from the water. The *Philadelphia Inquirer* showed survivors dragging a corpse from the water on its front page already on December 27, and one day later the *New York Times* showed a front-page image of a mother stooped in grief over a row of children's bodies.[95] The *Seattle Post-Intelligencer* published a front-page, six-column photo of unidentified tsunami victims who were about to be cremated and positioned it under the simple banner headline "60,000." Even Asian newspapers beyond the region directly hit by the tidal wave published images of rescue workers piling body bags or residents holding lifeless bodies. Viewer response was varied: the Seattle paper's display drew readers' letters complaining that it was "unnecessary, "inhumane," and "inappropriate," prompting the editor to run a response editorial, and in Europe a weekly news magazine was pulled from the shelves when retailers refused to sell it due to a front page image of corpses, while pictures of corpses prompted complaints to national press councils.[96]

Regardless of what news organizations decided to show, it did not always quell public discomfort. *Newsweek*'s cover the week of the tsunami offered an extreme close-up of the face of a two-year-old survivor in India, while a picture of grieving parents holding the seaweed-covered corpse of their son stretched across two inside pages under the simple caption "Cuddalore, India: A shattered mother wept for her drowned son after the tide returned him to shore." That same week, a photo by Reuter's Arko Datto, later the winner of the 2004 World Press Photo Award, depicted on the front cover of *Time* a woman sprawled across the sand next to a largely unseen corpse, her palms outstretched toward the sky. All that was seen of her dead relative was a hand, for the corpse lay beyond the camera's frame. When a similar Datta photo appeared in the *New York Times,* showing a man holding the hand of his unseen dead son, readers complained about its graphic nature, calling it "exploitative," "disrespectful," and "unduly graphic," and prompting the paper's Public Editor to respond that it was "an indescribably painful photograph, but one that was in all ways commensurate to the event." Some news organizations tried cropping the pictures differently so as to minimize offense. A different Agence France Presse photo also showed an unidentified man holding the visible hand of an unseen child: U.S. readers were told in the caption that the child, his own, was dead; cropped from a larger image that showed both the dead child and its parent weeping over the corpse, its fuller depiction appeared elsewhere in Europe. But not even this quieted the public. When the Associated Press Managing Editors Association polled a group of editors and readers, it found distinct differences between them: only 26 percent of readers agreed that displaying graphic photos of bereaved parents was appropriate, while the decision was upheld by 41 percent of editors. Repeatedly the photos were justified not because they offered useful referential documentation but because they were effective symbolic markers of a tragedy broader than what was depicted. As the *Times'* editor remarked, the photos were "a portrait of generic tragedy.... [The father's] pain was universal."[97]

Efforts in the broadcast and print media to sidestep the offense caused by graphic display were neutralized on the Internet, where a steady stream of eyewitness accounts, amateur videos, and snapshots pushed the coverage from the hands of the old media into new media sites. How TV news responded to that challenge, *Variety* later reported, constituted "the first litmus test" for a medium that had been under scrutiny since the Internet had come on the scene. Taken by private citizens at numerous spots struck by the tsunami, the personal images of the disaster facilitated the event's visual recording in ways that pushed beyond the formulaic template for such disasters. One of a dozen sites hosting tsunami video footage and photos racked up 640,000 hits within the first few days of the disaster, and the images were graphic. As one TV critic with the *Dallas Morning News* framed it, the hand-held videos from "terrified people who were perched on tabletops, balconies and any other higher-ground spot" were compellingly authentic: they facilitated long-range eyewitnessing and made the public into viewers of a new kind of reality television. Columnists pronounced that "a new medium [had come] of age."[98] Its visualization of the disaster was close up, grounded in real time, personal, genuine, explicit, and terrifying.

This spread of the two modes of news gathering meant that the tsunami's coverage would have multiple nodal points. As citizen journalists grew to include medical care providers, volunteers, relief workers, officials, and survivors, the coverage followed their experiences. For instance, a volunteer doctor's blog provided gruesome photos and grisly details about the job of disposing of rotting bodies, coverage which in one view would not have survived the "typical newspaper editorial process—too much potential for squeamish readers to cancel their subscriptions."[99] In some cases, as the images and texts arrived through different channels, it meant that the public knew of a rapidly mounting death toll that was not necessarily reflected in the old media, but that circumstance would change as the images of the dead became more available and the scope and scale of the tragedy more apparent.

Relevant here was the difference between seeing the tsunami in action across a moving video sequence and seeing its crushing arrival frozen in time by still photos. Though the former elicited engagement with the terrifying rapidity, scope, and scale of the onrushing water, the latter availed a more circumspect exposure to frozen aspects of its sequencing, impact, and residue. The sheer multitude of images—both still and moving—intensified the engagement with the scope and scale of the disaster.

Central to the tensions between old and new media was a creeping recognition that not all deaths were equal. Though it was generally impossible to discern which bodies were of which nationality, many observers reacted as though all the bodies belonged to local residents. As the *Denver Post*'s TV critic commented,

> Footage of distended bodies being plowed into mass graves testified to the undeniable inequity: Dead foreigners are somehow deemed fit spectacles for the camera, whereas dead Americans are generally off-limits. No such intrusion on the dead was permitted after the Sept. 11 attacks. The U.S. government won't even allow glimpses of soldiers' flag-draped coffins. American network myopia when it comes to Third World reporting is nothing new.

Jeremy Seabrook of the *Guardian* made a similar point when, writing of British coverage, he noted, "In death, there should be no hierarchy. But even as Sri Lankans wandered in numb disbelief through the corpses, British TV viewers were being warned that scenes they were about to witness might distress them." Comparisons with a more restrained visual coverage of Iraq surfaced repeatedly, as the more lenient treatment of the dead of Thailand, Indonesia, and India was seen as dissonant from that accorded the dead of Iraq.[100] All of this meant that though images had a particular role to play in documenting the tsunami, that role would be differently negotiated, depending on who was depicted.

Against such a context, depictions of the moment of impending death had particular value. Unfolding across so many locations and for so global an audience, the tsunami could not be captured by any one image. Differences—between Indonesia and Africa, brown and white victims, village and tourist resort, high ground and low ground—seemed to be all swept aside as certain visuals made themselves more available than others and thus came to stand in for the coverage writ broadly. But the relation between what one saw and what one needed to imagine was shaped differently depending on where one was, for the capacity to show and see what had happened was not evenly distributed. This meant that an inequity concerning which motifs of impending death would prevail and which faces of death would be amenable for display emerged, making the photographic coverage salient but patterned. Though coverage ranged across photos suggesting presumed death, possible death, and certain death, their intertwining was telling for its strategic value. When death became certain rather than possible, when death stayed presumed, when death was left as possible conveyed much about which populations were central to the story and how the media accommodated an unspoken hierarchy of value in globally covering this particular disaster.

The about-to-die image appeared in varied ways: news organizations in some locations interwove images of presumed, possible, and certain death from the first days of the disaster. Elsewhere, they made it possible for viewers initially to presume death, and only later broadened their disaster coverage to suggest either the symbolic valence of a possible death or delineate the fuller detail of a certain one. Doing so, however, depended on the identity of the victims facing impending death and the location of the news medium reporting the disaster. Cultural and geographic proximity thus played a large part in determining which impending deaths would be shaped through which impulses.

Presumed Death in the Tsunami

The tsunami coverage unfolded first as a set of eyewitness stories accompanied by images of presumed death. Useful to those news organizations which either could not show graphic imagery because they did not have it or would not show it because they did not want to offend viewers, signaling the tsunami through presumption—largely inanimate landscapes, crashing waves, battered structures, and beach devastation—depended on gathering the eyewitness documentation from whomever was there to provide it. Unlike most of the earlier disasters, which had transmitted a visual record after the fact, the multiple on-site residents and tourists with cameras, camcorders, and mobile phones made certain that "we saw the water coming."[101] Their recording of about-to-die images, signaled by an approaching wall of water, became the first trademark visual of most U.S. news organizations.

The footage showed angry waves swirling perilously close to the camera-person, swallowing everything in their path and filling streets, entranceways, and buildings. As one U.S. reporter observed from the comfort of his living room,

> We stared over and over at the same wave plowing through the same beachfront resort; at the same bodies bobbing in a torrent of brown water and debris, then swept away; the same sedan filling with water under a palm tree; the same aerial shots of villages we had never heard of now reduced to carefully scrutinized rubble in Indonesia's Aceh province.[102]

Though the footage of the tsunami waters was among the first images to appear on U.S. TV screens, it continued to replay in newscasts over the following weeks.

In the print media and on the online home pages of news organizations, still images at first showed pictures of crumpled buildings, beach residue, and angry waves pummeling the shore. Filling not only the front pages of U.S. newspapers and magazines but also those of regions directly hit by the tidal wave, these images froze the waves in place before they could wreak more damage.[103] Many news organizations centered on the experiences of Associated Press photographer Gemunu Amarasinghe, on the scene in Sri Lanka:

> The first waves were not huge, not too destructive. They brought fish to the shore, and people rushed to collect them. Smiling young boys ran with fish dangling in their hands. But then another set of waves crashed ashore, much more powerful. I parked my SUV and climbed on its roof, thinking I was safe there.... But the water kept rising. And rising. In a few minutes my SUV was submerged and I suddenly slipped into the water...joining the crowds running for higher ground, some of them carrying their dead and injured....Rows and rows of women and men stood on the road, asking if anyone had seen their loved ones. I was still in a daze, and the enormity of the tragedy still hadn't dawned on me.[104]

Alongside his harrowing account, accompanying images signaled a presumption of widespread, collective death by depicting the ravaged landscape. That landscape included flooded hotel courtyards, smashed fishing boats, beach mattresses crumpled around uprooted trees, and aerial views of whole villages wiped away. Beaten and crushed landscapes prevailed, relaying the forlorn aftermath of a region savaged and then abandoned by retreating water.[105]

The frenetic influx of such images facilitated a display of pictures that could not always be verified. One such photo—which showed an enormous swell of water engulfing the beachside—was printed widely. Called later by *Editor and Publisher* "the most dramatic photo of the many to emerge from the Indian Ocean tsunami," it was in fact a hoax, for the undated and unattributed image showed instead a tidal bore in China from 2002.[106]

One frequently displayed image from Madras, India, powerful more for what it forced the public to imagine than for what it showed, displayed a beach that bore no visible resemblance to recognizable ground. Taken by an Agence France Presse photographer, the image showed water cresting around engulfed tree-tops (fig. 6.5). Murky and ominous, the water was cluttered with the debris of cars, wagons, furniture and pieces of buildings. What was significant was what was not shown—people struggling to survive or corpses which had failed to do so. Viewers thus needed to imagine what rested underneath the muddy water swirls, particularly the dead bodies that they knew to be there. The caption to the photo guided its interpretation: in the *Miami Herald's* words, "Wiped Out: Tidal waters swallow the beach at Madras, India. About 2,300 were reported dead along the southern coasts of India. The toll was

Figure 6.5:
STR/AFP/Getty
Images, "A General
View of the Scene at
Marina," Madras, India,
December 26, 2004.

expected to rise." Filling an initial need to show and see the damage but not the human loss, the image appeared the first day after the tidal wave in multiple U.S. newspapers and was posted to their home pages online. It was also published widely by newspapers in areas touched by the disaster, where it stretched across columns of news text under the mastheads of Indian, Indonesian, Thai, and Sri Lankan papers. When the *Jakarta Post* showed it on its front page, two adjacent pictures depicted ravaged landscapes.[107]

One AP picture displayed widely on December 27 showed an anguished unidentified elderly Sri Lankan woman, portrayed in mid-distance, holding her head as she stood before the rubble of crushed buildings. Her hands, visibly veined and marked by age and hard labor, were aesthetically juxtaposed to heaps of rubble in the image's background, which spilled over the sides of the frame. The caption explained that the woman stood in front of what had once been her house and her survival was unusual given the massive death tolls that were to come: "With thousands missing, the death toll was sure to rise." Displayed on the front pages of U.S. newspapers, the image signaled contradictory impulses of vulnerability and survival, devastation and hope.[108]

Broadcast coverage followed a similar script. Much of its footage of presumed death used oncoming waters to anchor the landscape of devastation. As the broadcast media sought ways of making their coverage relevant—for instance, the Comcast Corporation offered free access to two Asian-based cable channels, TV Asia and International Channel, in New England so that local residents could follow coverage of the tsunami recovery efforts in their native languages—the coverage replayed footage of rushing waters over and over again. One video that was shown repeatedly focused on a street as it was engulfed by water, taken from the vantage point of a hotel rooftop. Underscoring the rapidity with which the water filled the empty spaces of the frame, it called to mind other events whose mechanical fast-forwarding for comic effect generated a similar sense of disbelief. The newsmagazines followed suit with similar images. Both *Time* and *Newsweek* began their cover stories with large images of inanimate structural devastation. In its first issue after the tidal wave, *Newsweek* ran a cover story titled "After the Tsunami" that began with a double-page picture of rising swirls of frothed water spilling beyond all four sides of the image. In the middle of the frame stood a few engulfed palm trees. There was no headline or title, only a quote from a survivor who said, "I knew I was dying." Another image in the same issue showed other moments of presumed death—a two-page airborne image of an Indonesian town almost completely under water. The *Time* cover story that same week opened with a two-page photo of a Phuket beach restaurant totally submerged by water.[109]

These images of devastation reappeared time and again, not only at the point of the disaster's unfolding but over the weeks and months that followed, providing a visual backdrop to the ongoing verbal narrative of what was transpiring in the region and continuing for what some felt was an excessive period of time. For instance, ten days after the tsunami CBS' *60 Minutes Wednesday* began its program with extensive footage of the waves, as co-host Steve Hartman observed, "It's been a week and a half now since the tsunami hit, and I still can't get past those very first pictures." By the end of the first week in January, nearly two weeks after the disaster, *Newsday* offered the view that the "videotapes of tidal waves tearing up a shoreline have been running silently behind anchor people on Fox and CNN news reports, as if the tsunami were wallpaper."[110]

Though the images—both still and moving—were thought to activate an empathetic identification with the victims regardless of where they were situated, the trademark visual of the raging waters depended on people able to imagine what they could not see, and at times intent on disbelieving what they knew was beyond the camera's frame. One CBS reporter said of one video he had watched repeatedly, "I've watched it now a dozen times and could probably watch it a dozen more and still not believe my eyes." Or, as a reporter for the *San Francisco Chronicle* put it, "We watch and watch, mining the endlessly repeated images for comprehension and meaning, wondering if seeing really is believing, denying what we see, believing, watching again in appalled fascination. Staggering. Unfathomable." The proximity of a popular tourist site made the disbelief all the stronger, and people repeatedly voiced the sentiment that "I could be one of them."[111] Subjunctive identification was thereby a central part of public response to the images.

The images of presumed death in the tsunami thus provided an initial visualization of the disaster in ways that allowed U.S. news organizations to encourage exposure while providing rapid coverage of the story without graphic images of death. Forcing the public to imagine the dying and dead it could not see, the images of physical devastation created an emotional contact point and prepared ground for the more graphic images to follow.

Possible Death in the Tsunami

The inanimate images of surging water and destruction did not prevail for long as the primary depiction of impending death, for they were soon followed by pictures of sky-high tidal waves about to engulf both unknowing people tanning themselves and panic-stricken beachgoers and local residents. Such images, recorded in both the film and still pictures of primarily tourists and local residents, depicted raging waves bearing toward the camera as people, none of them identified by name, either paid no attention to the water or tried frantically to outrun it, often in the photographer's direction.

Among the images that displayed death as possible—images that showed a hypothetical but not certain death of those displayed—were some of the most searing images from the disaster. Displaying unnamed people facing death but never confirming whether they in fact died, these photos both showed people walking unknowingly alongside the monstrous wave or in various degrees of engagement with the water—racing from the swelling waves behind them or partly submerged and clinging to pieces of wood or trees. Some images suggested that many people did not ascertain what was happening and walked into a second wave as it was gathering strength.[112]

These pictures of possible death—depicting anonymous beachgoers, tourists, fisherman, or villagers wrestling with the water and about to be overcome by it—appeared already on the first day in some locations. One tape widely distributed by Associated Press Television a week after the disaster, taken by an Indonesian wedding photographer in Bande Aceh, showed swirling dark water engulfing streets and people scrambling up the sides of buildings. On another tape six or seven tiny heads bobbed up and down in an enormous sea and a frame grab of the scene surfaced in multiple newspapers, while multiple video recordings of people clutching whatever stronghold they could find—buildings, limbs of trees, downed structures—depicted the moment the sea swallowed the shoreline.[113]

The act of trying to outrun possible death captured the agony of the disaster. One photo that surfaced repeatedly, taken by John Russell from Zuma, showed a chaotic scene in Koh Raya, south of Phuket, Thailand on December 26, with people frantically running from the building wave in the background. Taken from the vantage point of a resort platform, the picture captured people ensnared in varying degrees of terrified disarray (fig. 6.6). Some ran full force from the mounting water; some remained in place, bewildered; some faced the wave head-on. The picture appeared widely and reappeared on the weekend, when *Newsweek* published it as a full page depiction whose caption underscored the relation between those who died and those who did not: "Vacationers tried to run for safety, but the water moved too fast for many." The same week, *Time* used it to mark its table of contents page. It also appeared at decade's end to signify the tsunami.[114]

In a fashion typical of other images of possible death, the unidentified and unnamed individuals in these pictures performed a symbolic function, standing in for those who died while not requiring confirmation as to whether they themselves were among the dead. These images forced viewers to recognize the fact of widespread death even if it was not the fate of those depicted.

Sometimes those thought dead turned up alive. One image, taken on a beach in Thailand, pictured the monstrous wave surging in the background as a handful of people in the foreground either attempted to race to safety or remained oblivious of what was happening (fig. 6.7). The image, which appeared on the front page of the *New York Times* a few days after the disaster, was disconcerting for the knowing stance that it forced on viewers. The

Figure 6.6: John
Russell/Fairfaxphotos,
People Flee Tsunami,
December 26, 2004.
Reprinted by courtesy
of TIME Magazine.

woman in the lower right frame was depicted going back into the wave from
the beach, trying to rescue her children. As one newspaper phrased its printing
of her picture at the time it was taken, "We assume the worst. No doubt, she
is dead, along with her family, some of the 125,000 victims of a catastrophe
that has numbed the world's senses. But consider the courage inherent in her
last, selfless act of motherhood. Consider the flame that burns within, even as
death looms."

Other people deeper in the ocean shrunk in proportion as an enormous
water surge swelled across the back of the frame. Inconsequential in size, their
presence in the shot relayed in stark visual terms the horror of their circumstances to those who needed to imagine the sequence of action yet to come.
Later, it became clear that the woman, Swedish policewoman Karen Svaerd,
did not in fact die. Featured too in a widely circulated videotape, viewers later
learned she had rushed into the surf to warn her three teenage boys, all of
whom were then swept underwater and believed dead. All were found a few
days later swept safely to high ground, giving the *New York Times* the opportunity to print the image again as it detailed her survival.[115]

Across all of this coverage, which individuals were depicted as victims of
possible death versus a certain death was telling, for it offered a prism through
which to evaluate the loading points for the U.S. media's treatment of the loss
of lives in what had become a spatially diffuse but global disaster. As the images
were shown over and over, they raised questions as to whether the tsunami

Figure 6.7: AFP/Getty Images, Woman Seeks Children in Indian Ocean, December 26, 2004.

disaster area had been turned into what one observer called a case of "disaster porn,"[116] depriving the local residents of privacy and the local dead of dignity. Exacerbated by the fact that many depicted individuals were not given identities, names, or lives, the images disturbed many observers, local and foreign.

Leading the criticism was a reporter for the *Indian Express*. "Why has southeast Asia's biggest tragedy become every American network's Disneyland party?" asked Ashok Malik. "Has disaster finally found its paparazzi?" In a column that was immediately picked up by the Western media, he lamented:

> In the aftermath of the worst terrorist attack on American soil, the networks were remarkably correct. 'Sensitive coverage,' 'respectful of victims,' 'no violation of privacy': the buzz-phrases flew thick and fast. Unlike the aftermath of 9–11, when not one dead body was shown on screen, not one ghastly image recorded for posterity, and about the only objectionable visual was of a man jumping to his death, Asia's tsunami is open season.[117]

Malik's comments prompted discussion of what appropriate coverage might look like.

Journalists, news executives, officials, politicians, and viewers responded to the issue energetically. Editors queried whether a different standard was being applied to pictures of Western and Asian victims. The *Poughkeepsie Journal* launched a readers' forum on January 9, 2005, to discuss whether seeing people in distant lands at their most vulnerable moments constituted news. Columns ran in newspapers clarifying policy on image display and inviting reader response. Journalists publicly pondered which standard should be invoked for determining coverage of a disaster of the tsunami's scope, particularly with September 11 looming as a contrast case. Said the Poynter Institute's official ethicist Kelly McBride, "As horrific as the photos are, the danger—particularly with the Western public—is of being able to turn away from poor, brown-skinned people and their suffering. So you have to err on the side of showing more rather than less."[118]

Whether and how to do so, however, remained at issue. While these images of possible death were instrumental in helping the U.S. news media cover the event, the trope was also useful for the aim with which it had long been associated—that of securing appeals for humanitarian aid. "Seeing suffering is a powerful incentive to give," said talk show host Charlie Rose. Or, as one executive for Oxfam noted, "The media [are] a huge factor in getting people to be generous. If they're visually engaged, that brings [the disaster] home and makes it real." One reader noted that "without those images, most of us would never have been moved to swift action." The pictures of possible death thus enabled the securing of assistance for the disaster-ridden area, providing recognition that help could still make a difference. The potential for using the images for messages of rehabilitation was key, positioning the public in a space by which it could imagine its own successful intervention in what was being depicted. And yet the impact of such intervention was often more hypothetical than real. As one aid worker wrote, "The press and public need to learn that rehabilitation requires time and may be invisible to the camera." Or, as one *Toronto Star* columnist opined, "So much attention [was paid] because so many disaster movie-quality images were so readily available.... Trite but true."[119]

All of this suggests that the tsunami's images of possible death served a purpose other than that related to journalism. Building on the unevenness between what journalists, news executives, politicians, officials, and viewers saw and what they understood, these images enabled an inference of death facilitated by pictures of endangered human bodies, even when death did not occur. This was critical, for like other depictions of possible death, these photos acted as retrospective detail, reinforcing information already in hand. Thus, even though they appeared in the news, they functioned as relays for those outside of journalism—politicians, celebrities, humanitarian, and aid organizations—who hoped to use them for nonjournalistic aims. Western journalism, in this regard, offered a display setting crafted on the backs of anonymous non-Westerners to enhance aid.

Certain Death in the Tsunami

Not all images were left in the inanimate spaces of presumed death or the symbolic spaces of possible death. Instead, some were given the kind of definitive detail typical of certain death—verbal texts confirming death in captions, adjoining stories, headlines, and titles. These texts generally offered personalized tales about particular individuals who had perished. Often illustrated by images of people about to die, the coverage provided a concrete link to the disaster through the lives of specific individuals, nearly all of them from the West. It also provided an effective means of capturing public engagement about the disaster, which through these images became a story closer to home.

This creation of two populations of victims—where the death of local residents was depicted as possible, unconfirmed, unidentified, and unnamed, and the death of tourists and Western holidaymakers was made certain—revealed a hierarchy of value in the U.S. news media that had pragmatic consequences. To be sure, identifying Western victims and making their identity available to media outlets on the home front was relevant because so many Western holidaymakers had visited the popular tourist destination. But alongside stories of narrowly missed alternative destinies and long-awaited vacations turned bad, it was not long before the print, broadcast, and online media oriented their coverage toward the accounts of the deaths of Western celebrities, politicians, artists, and everyday tourists who had come from the West to vacation in the region. Offering detailed and personalized stories of drama, tragedy, and pathos and always identifying the individuals involved, these Westerners were given the coverage of certain deaths, an informational load not typically accorded the disaster's local residents. At the same time, however, this motif lent the story relevance that enabled a distant U.S. public to stay involved.

Though images of certain death can afford anonymity to those they cannot name, posthumous personhood to those whose deaths bring them into the public eye, and renown or notoriety to those who are publicly known prior to their deaths, the tsunami coverage displayed very few images of unnamed individuals about to die a certain death. Though this no doubt had to do with the difficulty of attaching the certainty of impending death to images of victims thought to have already perished, it also had to do with the fact that individuals about to die needed an identity so as to be useful for U.S. news organizations. Instead, many individuals about to die were transported into named certainty, where their identities were made public posthumously or played on an individual's public renown. Consonant with what an aid worker called "the-white-Westerner-in-a-bathing-suit-phenomenon," giving names and identities thus underscored the tourists as key players in the story and relegated the locals to its backdrop.[120]

Here, the online environment proved critical. Images of missing individuals proliferated on Web sites as an assist to those looking for loved ones who had disappeared. For instance, a full year after the tidal wave, parents with missing children, who had been vacationing tourists that December, still hoped to find them through tsunami Web sites. One such Web site—www.phuketremembers. com—posted pictures of children taken in administrative offices after the tsunami in hopes of reuniting them with their parents.[121]

Much coverage was given to a Canadian couple, John and Jackie Knill, whose last moments before the wave hit were recorded in a sequence of images on their cell phone camera. Found in a heap of rubble after the waters receded the following month by a missionary who was doing relief work in the region, the Knills' mobile phone held four photographs that recorded the beach and the couple's smiling visages just as the shoreline behind them turned black. As one newspaper told it,

> Then a pair of photographs taken at 8.30 am shows a wall of water, filled with sand and debris, rampaging toward them. Rather than try to run for their lives, the couple, whom their family suspect knew that they were going to die, instead stood and recorded the murderous natural force that was about to kill them.[122]

One photograph showed the couple looking serenely into the mobile phone's camera, failing to notice the monster wave building behind them. The last image in the series showed the approaching water about to engulf the mobile camera and its owners (fig. 6.8). Like other about-to-die images, the pictures put viewers in the curious position of knowing more than the couple about to perish, but here the evidence of their impending death was made visible by the camera's lens.[123]

The couple was identified when the missionary removed the phone's memory card and took it back to the United States, where, using a Web site for missing tsunami victims, he contacted the couple's surviving children. When they reconstructed the sequence of events, the children found it difficult to

Figure 6.8: AP, Canadian Couple in Last Minutes before Tsunami Overtakes Them, December 26, 2004.

reconcile how their parents had chosen to take a photograph, standing in place, rather than run from the surging water. One of the couple's sons pondered, "I don't know why they didn't run. Either they knew they couldn't or they didn't know the power of the wave," while another noted that 'it was weird to see the pictures. But I'm glad we have them. I can sleep better at night. This is more than we could ever have asked for. It's like being there with our parents and seeing what they were seeing in those final moments." The photographs were recycled widely, appearing on television, in newspapers and in retrospectives on the tsunami. Other stories of crumpled holidays and suddenly reclaimed lives similarly filled the media, turning what began as certain death into its refutation. A Swedish toddler, assumed dead, was found on the Web site for missing persons and rescued by his uncle, while a seven-year-old Scandinavian boy, thought to be drowned at sea, was found washed ashore in a Buddhist temple. One year after the tsunami, reports still circulated of parents searching for their lost children.[124]

Images of certain death also played off of the already recognizable identity of those who died. One prevalent story concerned the disappearance of Simon Atlee, the professional photographer boyfriend of model Petra Nemcova. On holiday in Phuket, Thailand, Nemcova watched Atlee get swept away while she hung onto a tree for eight hours with a fractured pelvis. Her experience, dubbed by one media commentator "the supermodel's ordeal," was recounted by nearly every news organization covering the disaster, as photographs of the couple circulated widely and she was repeatedly interviewed. Two weeks after the event, Atlee's mother wrote a letter to *The Independent,* complaining of a close-up image of a tsunami victim being fingerprinted as being "insensitive and distressing." The letter prompted an editorial column about images of the disaster, in which the editor both delineated the paper's parameters for appropriate display but reminded readers that the images "had drawn people to get out their checkbooks." Other famous individuals who died, including the daughter and granddaughter of filmmaker Richard Attenborough, the Thai-American grandson of Thai King Bhumibol Adulyadej, and Australian rugby player Troy Broadbridge, were recorded in detail. Because many of these stories did not have pictures from the site, they were often illustrated instead with stock photos or footage showing the now-dead person still alive.[125]

Though few of these images of certain death generated disbelief among the journalists, news executives, officials, politicians, and viewers who saw them, suggesting that at some level the certain death of famous people convinced a distant public struggling to make sense of what happened, their prolonged treatment as news suggested that the engagement they enabled was useful to those coming to grips with the tsunami. At the same time, however, the difference in the informational load given images of possible and certain death was revealing for the differential way in which it was applied—the possible deaths of local residents, used for symbolic appeal and humanitarian aid, versus the certain death of Westerners, used to anchor the "as is" of what happened. As the *Guardian's* Jeremy Seabrook noted, the more recognized victims embodied "a different order of importance from those [others] who have died, who have no known biography and, apparently, no intelligible tongue in which to express their feelings."[126]

What this suggests is that the certainty of death in the tsunami, which provided the fullest informational load without indulging in graphic imagery, was reserved for those perceived to be both literally and metaphorically "closest to home," where an American public could wrestle with the meaning of the tsunami through the prism of the loss of renowned individuals. The "othering" impulse implicit here raises questions about how much a news organization can provide in its coverage of a spatially diffuse disaster. Even here, with an impressive involvement of citizen journalists and new media helping to document what transpired, the hierarchization of deaths and impending deaths remained clear, suggesting that the formulaic representation of non-Westerners is as much about propensities of engagement as it is about the logistical details involved in coverage.

Who Gets Which Mode of Impending Death?

The tsunami's images of impending death thus reflect larger assumptions about what matters in a disaster's coverage. The about-to-die image reigned central as the disaster's trademark visual, but it revealed a hierarchy of value that became clear as strands of the story were told in different places. Images of presumed death offered a breathing space for U.S. news organizations to capture public engagement while figuring out how graphic their images could be without causing offense. Images of possible death were reserved for local residents, who received no name or identity but were useful in the appeal to humanitarian aid that U.S. news organizations helped launch. Images of certain death were reserved for the famous, the powerful, the white and the Western. When told of the disaster that was unfolding, the director of foreign news for ABC noted in the *New York Times*, "We knew right away that we needed to get to the beaches of Thailand because that's where the tourists were."[127] It is telling that his comment was printed without a hint of reservation. Even in an age of new media involvement, these parameters did not change, suggesting that they offer a well-established set of value judgments for what matters in the deaths caused by an unsettled distant disaster.

These representational impulses persevered over time, as the tsunami images were recycled into anniversary retrospectives, books, and photographic exhibits. News organizations marked the one-year anniversary in 2005 via discussions with an Indonesian wedding photographer whose video had been one of the first to be broadcast worldwide, exhibits of tsunami photos appeared in public settings, and retrospective volumes reprinted the images alongside explanatory texts. The tsunami images garnered awards, including the World Press Photo Award of 2004. The disaster's photographs became so widely disseminated that they prompted one Australian editor to note that "we came to understand [this event] through photography." Its photographs of trauma, snapshots of the missing, and satellite imagery of the affected areas displayed a macabre turn, when within weeks a large number of video compilations went on sale across Asian holiday resorts, offering an endless loop of tsunami footage repackaged into a flow of about-to-die images.[128]

The variation through which the tsunami's images of impending death appeared says much about the agendas implicit in global disaster coverage. Two responses surfaced as the coverage persevered: in the West, its overall evaluation was positive. One *Variety* editorial, illustrated by a frame grab of CNN correspondent Anderson Cooper standing in front of a ravaged landscape, crowed about the U.S. coverage, noting that "the combined efforts of the networks, cable and broadcast media made the world keenly aware of the magnitude of the tragedy and mobilized resources to aid the victims.... It's moments like this when TV news provides the connective tissues of our increasingly interconnected world." ABC *Nightline*'s Chris Bury said the coverage of the disaster had "an epic, almost Biblical quality." Or, as another reporter summed up the accolades, "There is a consensus in the media industry that the tsunami was covered better than any previous disaster. Journalists said they'd been good at avoiding usual pitfalls of journalists parachuted into disaster zones... they tried to persuade people to donate cash instead of inappropriate old clothes." *News Photographer* magazine put out a special issue on the disaster's visual depiction, in which it celebrated how quickly journalism's pictures had become iconic.[129] Relevant too was the role played by new media, which came into its own in its collaborative and personalized take on the disaster.

But for the local populations affected by the disaster, evaluation spun in a different direction. Cognizant of the transient nature of U.S. news media attention, they recognized that their brief capture of the world's eye would end long before the disaster's ramifications did. As one columnist observed, "While there is the whiff of disaster porn on the airwaves, mesmerizing audiences, boosting ratings and choking Internet connections, the voyeurism and exploitation have been trumped by human spirit and connectivity." Wondering if "when the tide of journalists now in Asia inevitably recedes, and the normal news cycle churns again, will media interest dry up," she noted that it was easy to imagine that the deaths

> even multiplied 100-fold, would have passed largely unmarked by the media had they not happened on beaches frequented by blonde tourists.... If the waves had hit remote coasts without wealthy Westerners to record them, to bear witness to them, and to survive or be swept away by them, it is highly likely that, despite the magnitude of this tragedy, most of the media would have moved on by now.

Calling on photographers to stay with the story, one photojournalist soberly opined that "while the Westerners go home, the Asians' home is gone."[130]

Such assessments proved on the mark, for news organizations did move on. As Tom Plate wrote in *AsiaMedia*, "Literally, whole villages and entire coastal segments of countries disappear before the world's very eyes [and] Asia finally surfaces on the American media map for no more than a few fleeting minutes." One Lutheran relief organization condemned what it called "feel good" stories about Americans donating clothes instead of drawing attention to the more immediate need for cash donations. The pattern was repeated elsewhere too. In Scandinavia, where nearly a thousand victims made it among the hardest-hit regions from the West, coverage migrated from global reportage in the first few days to a near-total focus on local losses by the following month. A reporter with the Israeli paper *Ha'aretz* commented that "anyone watching television in the West might think the tsunami struck Sweden or Switzerland. If it were not for the 10 or so missing Israelis, we would have forgotten about it already."[131]

What all of this suggests is that an unspoken hierarchy of value structures the coverage of disasters, particularly those that take on global parameters, and that despite the spatial diffusion of such disasters, they end up looking more like local stories than not. The rush to cover is both brief, intense, and formulaic, while the more detailed informational load—and its more energetic and sustained discussion—is reserved for those most proximate to the home front. This not only complicates journalism's capacity to offer information and effect engagement, but tensions regarding the movable and strategic distinctions between global and local victims, over the need for "feel-good" stories that encourage monetary donations but do little as news relay, and about the degree to which journalists' and nonjournalists' on site presence makes a difference in the stricken regions they cover all lack easy resolution. Though the about-to-die photo comes on the back of useful conventions for portraying death in a nongraphic way, it nonetheless reflects a broader ambivalence about whose death matters, in which way, and for whom, and reestablishes a hierarchy of death as a naturalized part of the coverage that ensues.

When the "As If" Is a Precious Visual Category

What does it mean when the different modes of impending death become part of a negotiable category of visual representation? In the temporally prolonged coverage of Vietnam, the tension between certain death and possible death showed that the former raised problems, given sentiments then prevalent about the war. Relayed over the protests of both journalists and viewers, reserved for select individuals, and retained for strategic moments in the evolution of public sentiments about the war, the certainty of death showed its limitations in depicting what was transpiring in Vietnam. Paradoxically, news organizations moved backward in detail to images of possible death, where a call for inference about an already known event constituted the more workable act of public engagement in coming to grips with the war. This reliance on a symbolic relay played to the "as if" of the war's depiction, turning news of a horrific event into a message of reconciliation, recovery, and postwar existence. As a relay across time, then, the about-to-die images showed the trope's usefulness in navigating across multiple engagements with the war, not all of them forcing a detailed informational relay about what was shown.

At the same time, the repeated articulation of people's passions about the photos—both for and against their display—underscores the importance of images in igniting emotion, imagination, and ultimately engagement about the world. Their systematic appearances here show that images can help chart their own version of news stories, shaped in conjunction with verbal coverage but often proceeding in ways that are different or contrary to what words reveal about the public sphere. This is no mean feat and suggests how powerful images are.

In the spatially diffuse coverage of the tsunami, the relationship between presumed, possible, and certain death played out differently in the coverage of a spatially diffuse disaster. The play to presumption gave the U.S. news media a space in which to negotiate how to deal with a disaster that turned more global than its formula suggested. Its play to the possible encouraged and secured financial assistance for those devastated by the disaster, and its play to certainty allowed news organizations to signal an unspoken hierarchy of value about whose deaths ultimately mattered, despite the global nature of the event, and to sustain engagement with those closest to home. When seen across space, the about-to-die image was useful in simultaneously accommodating the competing agendas and interests that were brought to the foreground of the tsunami's coverage, but it did so in ways that revealed how strategic the choices regarding news images can be.

In both cases, one need only ask how the Vietnam War or the Indian Ocean tsunami might have been shaped as a news story without visualization? Images displayed here their capacity for holding both the scope of tragedy and its incremental details in a way that eluded words, and the generalizability of each of its many images drove to the center of their subjunctive power. Each could have taken place anywhere, anytime, underscoring how much temporally prolonged and spatially diffuse events hinge on the "as if," where images of people about to die create powerful links between what is and what could be.

In neither case did the trope of impending death play out in simplistic ways. Rather, its variations and motifs showed the strategic uses to which it could be easily put. Significantly, those variations paint a clear picture of how journalism's images facilitate a different kind of public engagement with news events than do words. As one observer said of the tsunami, "The images are the part of the story that has the most power to stir action.... They make the story human... and make the audience feel."[132] But which action gets stirred, by whom and for which purpose resides at the core of these images' power.

What happens to images when the unfolding of events supports powerful contradictory strategic aims is thus worth considering. Not only can such situations reveal much about the images of impending death in the larger linkage between words and images but about the placement of such pictures in the larger mediated environment. Journalists often avoid depicting what they think is most problematic, but as recent events involving citizen journalists show, nonjournalists may have no such reticence. When people other than journalists can exploit the porousness of images of impending death and distribute them at will, decisions about what to show can be taken in journalism's name but without journalism's sanction to varying effect.

Chapter 7

When the "As If" Erases Accountability

The porous nature of today's mediated environment makes the question of how much information to append to an image ever more critical. As images move across digital platforms with increasing ease and accessibility, the meaning of an image that begins in one place with clear verbal texts about what it shows can rapidly change when it moves to other contexts that offer no information at all. As the lines between journalism and nonjournalism increasingly blur and the platforms for information collection and delivery are increasingly shared, the relationship between images and information faces additional challenges. But these challenges are well met by the "as if," where the emotions, the imagination, and contingency provide useful impulses for those intending to use images not for information relay but to suit their own strategic aims. The blending of presumption, possibility, and certainty in the depiction of events involving death enhances the capacity of politicians, news executives, bereaved families, pundits, government officials, activists, bloggers, lobbyists, militants, and others to involve themselves in decisions about what to show in the news, where to show it, and to whom.

At the time of this book's writing, the so-called war on terror still rages. Begun in the aftermath of the events of 9/11, an initiative started by the U.S. government under the Bush administration and an allied partnership with the UK government of Tony Blair moved first into Afghanistan and then jumped to Iraq, all in the name of eradicating world terror. The two wars' prosecution was accompanied by a lack of independent reporting in the U.S. press that

Lance Bennett, Regina Lawrence, and Steve Livingston have characterized as a moment of "blinking" by news organizations that could not figure out how to run with the story.[1] It was also accompanied by a strategic use of images in an attempt to shape the public climate around the war. The about-to-die image, useful because it could accommodate multiple simultaneous interpretations of the deaths caused by the war, can be traced through four central events that occurred during its unfolding—the killing of Taliban soldiers in 2001, the beheadings of Daniel Pearl and Nick Berg in 2002 and 2004, and the hanging of Saddam Hussein in 2006. Their coverage in the U.S. news media offers a valuable prism for understanding what happens to news images when the "as if" is strategically shaped by journalists and nonjournalists alike.

About to Die in the "War on Terror"

The United States' self-proclaimed "war on terror" offers an illustrative set of examples about how the incomplete and suggestive nature of about-to-die images has been used to modify or hide the fact that people died. Which deaths were rendered possible versus certain, which deaths were left presumed, which deaths went unnoticed and which deaths were framed as about-to-die images despite clear evidence of death pushes beyond the question of seeing dead bodies that tends to emerge during war. Instead, it reveals a sophisticated set of visualizing practices across the choices for depicting impending death, revealing much about the strategies for presenting the war and about how involved nonjournalists have been in shaping its depiction.

Starting with the war in Afghanistan of 2001 and continuing into the war in Iraq nearly two years later, the "war on terror" began as what was initially framed as a series of quick actions designed to eradicate Al-Qaeda cells and their Taliban sympathizers but over time ballooned into wide-ranging military activity on both the Afghan and Iraqi fronts. On October 7, 2001, U.S. and coalition forces, backed by local anti-Taliban militias, stormed the Afghan countryside, providing verbal accounts of freshly conquered landscapes depicted by varied and uneven images. From the beginning the Bush administration called for media restraint, and most news executives fell in line. CNN chief Walter Issacson was said to have instructed his international correspondents to avoid displaying an excess of gruesome images of the war, because "it seems perverse to focus too much on the casualties or hardship in Afghanistan." Much of the U.S. public at first supported the war's prosecution, generating one of the few moments in contemporary times with virtually no recognizable dissent. In PBS ombudsman Michael Getler's view, "The public wants the enemy defeated, and [it is] really not concerned about press concerns, access concerns, or security concerns."[2]

By the time a second war started in Iraq, the situation had changed. The justification for going to war against Iraq as part of the "war on terror" was seen from the beginning by many as a flimsy rationale that generated intense scrutiny, and the Bush government's twinning of Iraq and Afghanistan as dual battlefields drew criticism. Coverage of Iraq as a war story was uneven, shaped by an overemphasis on embedded reporters, a failure to discern action on the ground, and tacit support for erroneous and misleading aspects of the Bush administration's rationale for going to war. As the war's prosecution continued over the years, public support diminished.

The "war on terror," then, was prosecuted within a public climate that wavered from largely supportive to highly critical. The switch in sentiment was both enacted on and reflected by the involvement of new media, where an increasing variety of nonjournalists performing journalistic functions could be found. As one newspaper remarked in 2004, "Very few of the most memorable photos of this 'war on terror' are being taken by journalists."[3] Instead, a steady stream of videos, still images, and digital shots from individuals in a wide range of nonjournalistic roles—bystanders, family members, guards, soldiers—made the struggle for the war's meaning reliant on images produced and circulated beyond journalism. Because the digital environment made it possible for them to remain beyond the U.S. government's sphere of influence, many images that surfaced did not reflect what those prosecuting the war would have liked. But those prosecuting the war took part too in pushing the images that they felt best suited their purposes. It was within these circumstances that an increasingly unpopular war was depicted through about-to-die images. Blending impulses of presumption, possibility, and certainty with a reliance on emotions, the imagination, and contingency, the "as if" offered politicians, members of militias, bereaved parents, news executives, military guards, and government officials innovative but strategic ways to etch the war in visual memory.

The Taliban: Death by Beating

Though Afghanistan had been a country suffering from media oblivion before September 11, it became a mere two months later "the most reported–from country on earth." Photographs began to appear of whole families in flight from barren mountain homes, of women joyously removing their burkas, of smiling children and hopeful villagers engaging in previously prohibited activities, and of breathtaking mountainous, sometimes pulverized landscapes. One prewar image from Afghanistan—a 1984 photo of a forlorn orphaned twelve-year-old Afghan girl that became an iconic image of war refugees after gracing the cover of *National Geographic*—reappeared once the girl was located, now grown, in an Afghan village.[4] Images were used in a way that showed less about the war and more about the assumptions held by the forces responsible for its prosecution. United States journalism was thus complicit, if not consciously so, in using images to uphold the larger strategic aims of the administration.

The about-to-die image made sense as a way to depict the deaths incurred during the war.[5] The display of dead individuals in the region dated to the mid-1990s, when members of a then relatively unknown Islamic fundamentalist group, the Taliban, had aggressively executed citizens in public places throughout Afghanistan. Elaborate verbal reports of the public executions appeared primarily in the U.S. print media, which showed pictures of packed public squares holding public beatings and of Afghan citizens hanging from cranes or traffic posts for committing robbery, adultery, and murder.[6] The images were clear-cut, unambivalent depictions of individuals killed by the Taliban, and they continued to appear up until the U.S. invasion in October 2001.

With the invasion, the balance of power shifted. The Taliban, who had received clear and graphic coverage in the U.S. news media as aggressors, now became victims. Once the United States forged ahead with its coalition with the Northern Alliance, one of their shared aims was capturing the Taliban soldiers on the country's northern front. A set of brutal executions that ensued, among the earliest in the war's unfolding, generated relentlessly detailed verbal narratives about the battles between the anti- and pro-Taliban forces and about the executions of the Taliban supporters. Left unpublished, however, was a full visual record of the atrocities committed against the Taliban forces. Though photos were taken of the beating of live Taliban soldiers and desecration of dead ones—local residents kicking the heads of Taliban supporters or anti-Taliban fighters looting their bodies—by and large such images were not published in the U.S. news media. Even *Newsweek,* which featured a photographic essay on the fall of the Taliban, did not include a graphic photograph of how the Taliban sympathizers had died.[7]

One limited set of photos, however, did depict an early set of atrocities, and it did so through the prism of impending death. In November 2001, when scores of Taliban soldiers were beaten to death publicly in the streets of Kunduz, Mazar e-Sharif, Taloqan, Qala-I-Nasro, and elsewhere, eyewitness reports documented the brutal killing by Northern Alliance forces of surrendering and wounded Taliban soldiers. Said to be bent on avenging the deaths of families and friends who had perished under Taliban rule, the Northern Alliance forces engaged in tortuous acts—tying up Taliban soldiers before killing them, gouging out their eyes, castrating them, tying up their shoes so as to prevent escape before shooting, and kicking, looting and desecrating their bodies after their deaths. The Northern Alliance forces were also reported to have targeted foreigners, including Arabs, Pakistanis, and Chechens who had fought alongside the Taliban.[8]

The reports were problematic for the United States, because its on-ground objectives in the "war on terror" were facilitated by its association with the Northern Alliance. As the actions of the Northern Alliance soldiers drew complaints from the International Committee of the Red Cross, other governments, and the non-U.S. media, the lack of response in U.S. governmental circles drew additional criticism. One human rights lawyer was quoted within days of the killings as saying that "the United States has turned a blind eye to what is going on. (There has) been a signal to the Northern Alliance that they can do what they want (with the prisoners)."[9] Linked with earlier statements by President George W. Bush that he wanted Osama Bin Laden "dead or alive" and with Defense Secretary Donald Rumsfeld's admission that American forces attacking the Taliban were "under order to take no prisoners," the U.S. reluctance to harness the Northern Alliance's actions generated complaints about the Alliance's nature, particularly from non-U.S. and nonmainstream media. The *Progressive* noted that the "foreign press has done a better job of reporting all varieties of gruesome deaths and human rights violations," while the *Toronto Star* lamented that "the war establishment, including its media boosters and editorial cheerleaders, has remained gamely supportive of the unpleasant and untidy events." The *London Times* wrote that "the implication that a dead enemy is better than a live one will not have been lost on the murderous warlords of the Alliance. If they think they can get away with killing their Taliban prisoners, they will do so." Once the U.S. signaled that the fate of prisoners depended on the Northern Alliance, it became clear that even if the fighters surrendered, they might still be massacred: "Our common humanity should not be put to death on the bloody streets of Kabul," wrote one journalist. "There can be no comfort in averting our eyes from the scene. As a people and as a society we still have to look in the mirror at ourselves."[10] And yet, no punitive or responsive action was taken by the United States. Nor did the incidents receive more than a flurry of media attention during the two-week-long rampage of killings across the northern sector of Afghanistan. Though the beatings immediately gave way to even larger atrocities—summary executions near the Sheberghan Prison where some two thousand Taliban prisoners were suffocated and shot to death, an incident that also stayed under the radar of the U.S. news media—the implications of the failure to confidently expose this earlier incident, which was documented by photographers, loomed large.

Images of the executions of Taliban fighters appeared over a two-week period during late November 2001 primarily in the print media, portraying numerous instances of the same phenomenon in different localities, captured by different photographers. Though these photos constituted a small sample of the photos from Afghanistan that appeared, they nonetheless occupied a central place in the larger corpus of still images by which journalists, news executives, politicians, officials, and viewers all saw the war unfolding. They also revealed some of the ways in which about-to-die pictures could be put to larger strategic aims. This photo, which later won Tyler Hicks the World Press Photo Award, was emblematic of a set of images that surfaced (fig. 7.1):

Figure 7.1: Tyler Hicks/Getty Images, "Injured Taliban Soldier Pleads for His Life," November 12, 2001.

What did the image show? While the verbal accounts of the executions provided horrific detail—Taliban soldiers pleading for their life throughout the beatings, banknotes or cigarette butts stuffed into their mouths, noses and what remained of their skulls, limbs hacked away, castrations—the visual trope was simple and formulaic: a single man, surrounded by five or so more robust younger men, was depicted in the center of the shot. Various activities unfolded with him at their center: he was portrayed as being stripped, taunted, and kicked and in some images beaten by hands, sticks, and rocks. In some images the victim's hands were tied behind his back, and he was inevitably portrayed as fearful, couched in a supine or otherwise inferior bodily position, and often bloodied. The men crowding around him laughed, jeered, and looked angry. From many of the verbal accounts that accompanied these pictures, it was clear that the men in the middle of the shot were in fact tortured, castrated, shot, and beaten to death. Yet they were depicted as still alive—following the established trope of the about-to-die image.

Numerous images like this one documented the killings. Photos by a range of photographers and photographic agencies—Dusan Vranic for the AP, Tyler Hicks for Getty Images, Lois Raimondo for the *Washington Post*—were displayed primarily in the print media, in the front sections of the *New York Times, Philadelphia Inquirer, Washington Post, Los Angeles Times,* and the *Chicago Tribune;* the *Boston Globe* featured a front-page picture, while *Time* and *Newsweek* showed an image of the beatings inside.[11]

Telling, however, was the amount of missing or ambivalent information that characterized these photos' display. Absent from their accompanying captions was any information that could have identified the deaths as certain: neither the victim nor perpetrators were named, few texts explained what was shown, and the actions depicted were not labeled as killings. Both the *Philadelphia Inquirer* and the *Chicago Tribune* said, "The fighter was later taken away by truck and his fate is unknown." The *Boston Globe* and the *Los Angeles Times* maintained that the victims in their stories were "beaten." The *Washington Post* caption said that the victim was "roughed up"; in its story, it recounted an incident in which the captors relented and allowed the victim to live, but it left unclear the fate of the Taliban fighter in the photo.[12] Most captions did not address the fact that those depicted had been killed, and there was no mention that any of the victims were castrated, as evidenced by the bloodied trousers evident in many photos. The images did not feature prominently across the broadcast media or across the home pages of those news organizations with active online sites, making this primarily a print media story. Yet all of the print media, except the *New York Times* and *Time,* separated the depictions of the "finished murders" from their sequenced images, depicting the executions instead with single images of individuals about to die. In other words, despite clear evidence underscoring the certainty of the Taliban deaths, the U.S. news media by and large portrayed what was definite as only possible.

The *New York Times* and *Time* provided two exceptions by offering a more extended treatment of the about-to-die moment. A three-photo sequence by Tyler Hicks appearing inside the *New York Times* showed members of the Northern Alliance forces executing a Taliban soldier on the way to Kabul. One picture showed the Northern Alliance soldiers dragging the man; a second, similar to images that appeared elsewhere in the media, portrayed him begging for his life; and a third showed him lying prostrate on the ground. Their shared caption read as follows:

> Northern Alliance Troops dragged a wounded Taliban soldier out of a ditch yesterday on the front lines on the way to Kabul. After he had begged for his life, they pulled him to his feet, shot him in the chest and beat him with a rifle butt and a rocket-propelled grenade launcher. Other casualties from the fleeing Taliban forces in the area were also looted.

Though the caption did not explicitly mention that the man died, the *Times* recounted a man's death in detail in the accompanying story—"They chose to celebrate with executions"—though never connecting the two. While this was more extensive informational detail than that offered by other news organizations, the *Times* did not address fully the questions raised by the killings and left its coverage in word and image unmatched. Its words remained so much more graphic than its pictures that readers only considering the image and its caption did not know that the man being depicted was dead—significantly at the hands of the United States' partner in prosecuting the war. As one atypical reader's letter remarked, "If your article had noted that Northern Alliance troops were committing war crimes as they executed wounded Taliban soldiers and looted nearby villages, it would have helped readers understand the real implications of the war in Afghanistan."[13]

A similarly ambiguous display was found in *Time*, which used the photos as part of a larger photographic essay on Afghanistan. Called "Blood and Joy," the photo essay displayed eighteen separate images, five of which depicted a Taliban soldier's public execution under the title "Vengeance." Labeling the Northern Alliance's actions "summary executions" in the larger story, the newsmagazine gave concrete verbal information about what was depicted in each photo but said nowhere in the captions that the man depicted was killed.[14] Devoting such extensive space—ten pages total—to a photo essay but not explicating in the captions the death that viewers were shown underscored the ambivalence showing the photos raised. In both cases—the *New York Times* and *Time*—the news organizations stopped short of using the available means to document fully the brutality.

Not surprisingly, the photos received a largely uncritical response from those viewing them. The *Chicago Tribune* ran an editorial that labeled the photos "troubling," but conversation stopped short, as no viewers' comments, reader's letters, or pundit conversations followed up the assessment. Few editorials pondered the question of how to reconcile the killings with the Alliance. *Time* ran one reader's letter complaining that "the photos of the Taliban soldier being murdered were the saddest things I have seen in a long time. . . . I urge everyone to look closely at the man who is being brutalized in these photos and remember that when violence is institutionalized, this kind of madness will erupt sooner or later." But far more prevalent was the sentiment that the war coverage was too graphic. The same letter in *Time* was positioned alongside a second letter praising images of the smiling faces of Afghan women and children and the "stunning" beauty of the Afghan landscape.[15] In other words, the photos of the soon-to-be-executed Taliban soldiers went largely without comment.

Significantly, the same photos that were treated as depictions of possible death in the United States were treated and received differently beyond the U.S. news media. In the United Kingdom, for instance, the photos were displayed with fuller evidentiary force (fig. 7.2). Photos from the same sequence were printed on the front pages of two tabloids—the *Daily Mirror* and the *Daily Mail*—where they were destined within days, in the *Guardian*'s view, to become "one of the defining images of the Afghan conflict." In the *Daily Mirror*, the four-photo sequence not only included the Hicks image of the Taliban soldier begging for his life but also other images that led up to the chronological end of the sequence of action—the Taliban soldier lying dead. That photo appeared on the front cover of both the *Daily Mirror* and *the Daily Mail*. Bearing the title "Our 'Friends' Take Over..." in the *Daily Mirror,* its caption left no aspect of the depiction unstated: "Vengeful: Alliance troops kill a Taliban supporter outside Kabul." Not only was the man depicted and identified as having died from the beatings and the photo itself made the center of the story, but an accompanying page showed the same photo a second time, together with three other shots of the beating leading up to his death. Titled "The Executioners," the display also bore a small inset picture of U.S. President George Bush. The accompanying text recounted both what happened to the person depicted in the pictures and to other Taliban soldiers too: "In full view of press cameras Taliban prisoners were bound with electric cable, searched and taken to makeshift POW camps. There, away from prying eyes, a single gunshot proclaimed instant justice from the vengeful victors." Lest the point be missed by its readers, the newspaper's staff articulated the photo's role in explaining the war. The photo, said the *Daily Mirror* editor, "shows the people we have stood shoulder to shoulder with. They are particularly unsavory and savage people. The image represents the whole story." The picture was displayed again at year's end, as part of the paper's special issue on the year's unforgettable images.[16]

Figure 7.2: Tyler Hicks/Getty Images, Taliban Soldier Lies Dead, *Daily Mirror*, November 14, 2001, reprinted courtesy of Mirrorpix; *Daily Mail*, November 14, 2001, reprinted Courtesy of *Daily Mail*.

The *Daily Mail* gave the photos similar treatment. Its bold-type headline proclaimed "No Mercy," while the accompanying caption explicitly labeled the sequence of images as an execution shot: "Savage Retribution: A Taliban fighter who stayed too long is summarily executed by Northern Alliance troops." A question posed atop the front cover amplified the image's status as evidence: "On a historic day, Kabul falls without a fight, and Kandahar could be next. But this horrific picture begs the question: Is the Alliance any better than the Taliban?" The accompanying story continued to force the issue, querying "have Taliban's terrors been replaced by callous killers of the Alliance?" Its graphic verbal description of what happened to the man in the sequence of pictures went substantially beyond that accorded the incident in the U.S. news media:

> It was a scene chilling in its brutality. A wounded Taliban soldier lay helpless in the dirt on the road to Kabul. He had lost his weapon. He had been stripped of his trousers and mutilated and then kicked to the ground where he lay—terrified, arms outstretched, pleading for his life.... Ignoring the begging screams of his captors, one of the Alliance soldiers raised his AK-47 to his shoulder and fired two burst of bullets into the man's chest.... A second Alliance man stepped forward and beat the lifeless body with his rifle butt. A third then started smashing his rocket-propelled grenade into the dead man's head. And all the while their comrades, already laden with loot and booty, cheered and laughed.

Calling the action "medieval savagery," the newspaper remarked that the actions constituted "raw vengeance Afghan style—brutal, unforgiving, and deadly."[17]

Viewers in the UK followed the tabloids' lead, reacting far more attentively than had their U.S. counterpart. Letters to the editor literally flooded the papers, as British viewers called the photos "horrifying," "sickening," and proof that "the Northern Alliance is no better than the Taliban." One *Guardian* reader went further: despite the fact that "occasionally, we've glimpsed that people are getting killed (such as) the images of the castrated Taliban fighter pleading for his life before he was shot," she cautioned, the depictions nonetheless remained insufficient. "Our sympathy for these near-feral wildmen is limited.... There has been no sense of outrage at these atrocities." Outrage was expressed elsewhere too, as one Canadian reader lamented their display as "some kind of circus event." How was it possible, he wrote, "that a man's execution was displayed as a justified and natural part of victory in war? It is sad to think about North American journalists standing by, taking not one but many photos as people are dragged in the street, tortured and then shot with rifles."[18]

The photographic treatment in the UK tabloids thus used multiple supportive texts to depict these about-to-die images as certain. Their appearance in the tabloid news media rather than their elite counterpart, however, is worth considering. Unlike the latter, the tabloids did not self-censor images on the grounds of propriety, decency, or tastefulness, but played instead to the image's role as evidence. In other words, the more straightforward reliance on images in the UK tabloids made them more amenable to organizing a story around an image's display, regardless of the degree of dissonance it generated with those who saw it and regardless of the fact that it undermined the official UK role in prosecuting the war.

The beatings' uneven depiction was critical, for as the fighting in Afghanistan intensified, a more widespread violation of the Taliban's human rights, shown here in one of its nascent moments, continued. Within the month, reports began documenting the summary execution and suffocation of two thousand Taliban soldiers who shortly after these beatings had been stuffed into containers and shipped to Sheberghan Prison. By January 2002, Physicians for Human Rights pointed to mass graves with unaccounted numbers of bodies. That documentation built over the next few years, climaxing in both moves to accuse the United States of war crimes in the region and subsequent tampering with the grave site by the local Afghan warlord. Though attention was slow in coming, by July 2009, U.S. president Barack Obama promised to probe the events of 2001. Over that time period, the pictures were uploaded onto the Internet, where they circulated freely as visual evidence of atrocities against the Taliban, in both Afghan nationalist Web sites and less partisan Web sites about current events, and as professional curios connected to photojournalism, such as a book tour by photographer Tyler Hicks.[19]

This suggests that while the U.S. news media's presentation of these early images as a possible death rather than a certain one supported prevalent notions about how much information should be made explicit about the war, it also muted the truth value of what was depicted. When certain death masquerades as possibility, its capacity to engage by drawing on the suggestive ramifications of what it shows turns attention away from the "as is" of depiction. Framing the Taliban deaths by beating as uncertain and, at best, only possible, instead played to its "as if"—to the photos' role as subjunctive markers of a story more supportive of the U.S. aims. Attention was thus deflected from the fact of the Taliban deaths while heeding the larger message of the war's continued prosecution.

Daniel Pearl and Nick Berg: Death by Beheading

As the "war on terror" moved across Afghanistan, a particularly gruesome mode of killing emerged that took much of the U.S. news media by surprise— beheading. Though as a practice, beheading had long been a recognized punishment in Asia and the Middle East, its particular strategic unfolding on video during the "war on terror," carefully choreographed and set in front of cameras readied for global Internet distribution, pushed the impending deaths of the war to new heights of graphicness, till then largely unseen in the U.S. news media.

Two videos associated first with the war in Afghanistan and then Iraq were central to an evolving awareness of how the "war on terror" looked on both fronts. Both depicted beheadings. Taken at two different times—first when public support for the war was still largely intact, then when it had begun to erode—they showed how the uses and interpretations of the trope of impending death could differ in accordance with the public climate at the time.

Images of the abduction and murder of *Wall Street Journal* reporter Daniel Pearl were the first about-to-die images of beheading to surface. Kidnapped from Karachi, Pakistan, during a supposed meeting with a source for a story on the so-called shoe bomber on January 23, 2002, Pearl's whereabouts were unknown until January 27, when select newspapers, including two Pakistani news outlets, the *New York Times,* the *Washington Post* and the *Los Angeles Times,* received e-mail notification of his kidnapping.[20] In the e-mail his abductors, members of the National Movement for the Restoration of Pakistani Sovereignty, stipulated that Pearl would be killed if their demand—the release of Taliban fighters from Afghanistan—were not met. A third e-mail sent on January 31 delayed Pearl's execution by one day. On February 1, CNN and Fox News announced that Pearl had been executed, though that relay, soon retracted, introduced further uncertainty, mostly provided by broadcast news organizations. That same day reports of a phone call demanding a ransom surfaced, and on February 3, ABC, Fox News, and MSNBC erroneously reported that his body had been found. Pearl's death was finally established on February 21, when a videotape of his beheading was received by the U.S. embassy in Islamabad. The following month the video surfaced on theInternet, and in May CBS aired thirty seconds of it. The video received further attention in June, when the *Boston Phoenix* posted a link to it from its home page and then published one of its explicit frame grabs showing the reporter's severed head. The visual unfolding of the story, then, from beginning to end stretched across six months, much of which teetered on uncertainty: death was not confirmed for a month, and the video of his beheading surfaced four and five months after that.

The original e-mail to news organizations, sent by a Hotmail subscriber named "kidnapperguy," contained four photographs of Pearl, one with a gun to his head, another of him holding a copy of the Pakistani *Dawn.* A follow-up e-mail with an additional photo showed his hands shackled (fig. 7.3). In the photo, Pearl looked grim, his eyes subdued and mouth pursed as he stared straight into the camera. His hands, bound together in large link-chains, were out of proportion to his face because they were slightly closer to the camera.

Appearing unnaturally large, the picture's focus on them pushed the message of captivity that the chains signified. Described as "bone-chilling,"[21] the photo left no doubt as to the situation's gravity.

In its first week, Pearl's abduction and murder were structured as a story of a man about to die. In the first days of his disappearance, news organizations fronted the uneasiness that overwhelmed those awaiting news of his destiny: "The family, friends, and colleagues of U.S. journalist Daniel Pearl are anxiously awaiting word of his fate today as a deadline for his execution set by his captors in Pakistan expires," wrote one newspaper.[22] As numerous people scrambled to locate the kidnappers before they could carry out their threat, images of the reporter facing death surfaced. For the six days of his captivity, they were published and broadcast repeatedly, in tandem, in sequence, and across news organizations. Sometimes they appeared more than once in a newspaper or newscast, and when they reappeared on different days it was without indication of the time that had elapsed between their first appearance and the more recent stories they were brought to illustrate. Web sites were filled with the reporter's grim visage. Though attributed variously to the AP, Reuters, and the *Washington Post*, the images all referenced the same photos that had come by e-mail to the news organizations, taken by his captors.

At least one, if not two, of the four original photos were broadcast on television and appeared on the front pages or front sections of most U.S. newspapers and newsmagazines, including the *New York Times, Washington Post,*

Figure 7.3:
Reuters, Daniel Pearl
Execution, January 27,
2002.

Philadelphia Inquirer, Los Angeles Times, Boston Globe, and *Time.* One photo appeared as a *Newsweek* cover photo and was displayed a second time in the same issue alongside two other sequenced photos and a full-page photo of a gun being held to the reporter's head.[23] When a second shot of Pearl shackled in captivity arrived in a later e-mail, that picture too appeared widely, used to illustrate the continuing story in the *New York Times,* the *Chicago Tribune,* and the *Boston Globe,* and appearing twice on two consecutive days in the *Washington Post.* Those news organizations with online portals continued to show the pictures, and they made their way too into Islamic fundamentalist sites, sites concerned with the safety of working journalists, and other discussion groups.[24]

When on February 1, news organizations received two contradictory messages—a ransom for Pearl's release and word that Pearl had been executed—photos that had appeared the first day of Pearl's captivity were again reprinted and rebroadcast. As news organizations tried to make sense of which story was true over the following two weeks,[25] they lamented the increasing role that the digital environment was playing. As the *New York Times* told it in a story about the reportorial errors committed by the broadcast networks, coverage has "been prone to inaccuracies, in part because so much information has come via e-mail—a medium in which people can shift identifies and addresses and disguise their electronic whereabouts with a few keystrokes."[26] By February 21, when Pearl was confirmed dead, pictures of him facing death again appeared across the digital environment; in the broadcast and print media their captions now recounted that the reporter had died.[27]

Thus, against a background of unclear and ambivalent documentation, a continuing story whose threads did not easily come together, the reappearing photos of Pearl about to die constituted one of its few familiar markers. Even when these pictures bore little relevance to what was actually transpiring, that did not matter because Pearl's last moments continued to circulate, long after he was dead, as a reminder of the horrific actions perpetrated by the "other side." Centrally displayed, the images drew from an unspoken rationale that their repeated viewing would remind all those who saw them of the barbarism associated with the region and justify the U.S. military presence. In this regard, Pearl's kidnapping and murder constituted a useful contrast case of about-to-die coverage to that given the photos of the Taliban soldiers. Unlike the Taliban, images of Pearl supported the U.S. prosecution of the war in a way that the photos of the Taliban soldiers had not. Their absence of graphic content allowed the news media to carry that message without overwhelming viewers with discomfort.

Even though Pearl had been confirmed dead, the need to keep the abduction story oriented to its "as if" moment continued to drive the story, made evident when the video of Pearl's execution started circulating on the Web. A Saudi journalist made it available to CBS, which aired a portion on May 15, showing the moments leading up to Pearl's death during which he admitted his Jewish lineage. The airing stopped before he was beheaded. Though CBS received calls from the Justice Department and Secretary of State Colin Powell's office asking the network not to air the clip, the executive producer of "CBS Evening News" declined; when told that airing the program was "helping to spread the terrorists' word," he replied "I don't think that's the case. The word is already being spread. I don't think it's wrong to inform the American people about it." Dan Rather justified the video's display because "Americans can see and understand the full impact and danger of the propaganda war being waged."[28]

The short video forced people to recognize what many had suspected for some time but had left undeveloped. As *Time* told it, "Daniel Pearl's beard had not grown much since our last glimpse of him in the emailed photos.... So the videotape of his execution left investigators to conclude... he had really been murdered weeks ago and we had been living on faint hope and false promise since then." Reaction was negative but for mixed reasons: some argued no portion of the video should have been aired out of respect for the family, others because it constituted Islamic fundamentalist propaganda; only a minority characterized CBS's decision as ethical. Both the White House and Pearl's family blasted the display, saying it served the abductors' purposes.[29]

The digital environment, however, had already proved a ready host for the video's display. Surfacing first in the Middle East and thought to have originated in Saudi Arabia, where it reportedly became "a great hit," the video soon was circulating on multiple continents. In the United States, the Web-hosting company ProHosters.com secured the full unedited footage, making it available to clients within days, among them ogrish.com, which posted it. Though the FBI threatened ogrish.com with legal action, saying it violated laws against publishing obscene content, it backed off the threat once the American Civil Liberties Union was brought in. The video appeared in the UK, where it remained on a British-registered Web site and was sent to multiple radical Islamic organizations for posting. "People," said one person who was sent a copy, "are sending it out like junk mail."[30]

The following month, the *Boston Phoenix* linked the video to its home page and one week later published a frame grab showing the reporter's severed head. Justifying the display as no different than the pictures of people jumping from the World Trade Center, footage of the Challenger explosion, or photos of the Nazi concentration camps, its editor lamented that "The silence on this issue has been deafening. Where's the outrage? Where are our civil libertarians? Our First Amendment absolutists?"[31] Another reporter for the paper explained that the FBI's attempt to keep the story from the Web, as chronicled in a *Wired.com* report, had convinced the *Phoenix* to post the link to the video. In effect, then, the paper had simply "recontextualized" what was already available online.[32]

Nonetheless, the desire to draw the beheading's visualization back to its "as if" moment was so strong that the newspaper was roundly accused by officials, politicians, and other journalists of sensationalism, unethical practice, poor judgment, and insensitivity to the family. Response to the *Phoenix*'s decision to publish remained overwhelmingly negative, as the paper was criticized for "a callous disregard for human decency." When msnbc.com columnist Jan Herman, who supported the *Phoenix,* tried to provide a link to the video too, it was taken down by the network. The Poynter Institute conducted an online chat about the ethics of making the video available. Claiming that the story had been known for months, it pronounced that the harm of showing the video far outweighed the benefits.[33]

Less convinced that the video should not be shown were viewers. Some viewers agreed with the *Phoenix*'s censure: "If a paper can't convey the story of a terrorist kidnapping and murder without relying on photos of and links to a severed head, it may just be time to hire better writers," remarked one. Readers' letters to the *Phoenix* were divided over the video's display, though one report noted that as time went on and the official and journalistic censure grew, so too did viewer disapproval. But many saw the video's availability differently; the majority of posters to the Poynter chat, for instance, stressed that the images had far more staying power than the verbal accounts of what had happened. "Who does the media serve?" posted one viewer, "Showing this tape is not sensitive. But it is truth.... The beheading is the story here." Another observed that

> I've seen Kennedy's head explode in slow motion now about ten thousand times. I've seen Oswald being shot a hundred times or so. I've seen a U.S. [*sic*] soldier shoot a Vietnamese guy right in the head a few dozen times. And now I've seen Daniel Pearl killed. Out of the four, I think the Pearl video is the most important to be seen by the public because it shows an impending threat to all of us... It's a slippery slope when journalists try to shield the public from fact.

One poster accused the media of protesting the video's display because it showed a journalist, and the journalist who had been responsible for the *Phoenix* posting a link to the video on its home page concurred: "Fellow journalists," he wrote, "are sadly showing more consideration for one of their own than they ever would for, say, a dead American serviceman being dragged through the streets of Mogadshu."[34] Implied but not articulated was a consensus among news organizations not to show the videotape and the government not to release it to the public. As the *New York Times* said in its reporting of the *Phoenix* display, it "broke ranks with the rest of the print media." Yet once the *Phoenix* made the video available, numerous online sites linked to it, its discussion proliferating not only across the Internet but back into traditional media as well. At the same time, as the debate ensued about the execution tape, news organizations displayed pictures of Pearl in captivity, recycled yet an additional time.[35]

The response to the images of Pearl dying on tape as opposed to pictures of him about to die is consonant with the fact that a certain but impending death was as close to showing and seeing Pearl's murder as the U.S. news media, politicians, and the family were willing to go. In communicating the certainty of his death without showing his dead body, they kept viewers drawn to the story and invested in the war's prosecution without causing offense by showing more graphic images.

Thus the photos of Daniel Pearl continued to be shown in the U.S. media as an about-to-die-moment of certain death long after he had died. Shown repeatedly across print, broadcast, and online media and with full informational detail confirming he had died, images of Pearl held by his captors, rather than the graphic pictures of his actual execution, became one of the central images of the war in Afghanistan. They appeared on the one year anniversary of his abduction and murder, on the capture of his abductors, and on the date of their trial. That these early pictures of Pearl about to die continued to illustrate the story long after he was dead underscored their play to the "as if" of the story's unfolding. As a *Boston Globe* columnist remarked, seeing "Daniel Pearl's beheading is searing and nightmarish, but the key to its power is not that it shows him dead. It is that it shows him alive."[36]

Images of Daniel Pearl facing death thus made sense because visualizing a reporter's death by "the other side" in wartime was consonant with the U.S. prosecution of its war. Signifying that death through its impending status offered an optimum way to promote exposure, attention, and engagement, while its illogical and contingent suspension of action allowed for interpretive leakages and elaborations as people sought to make sense of the war. Though new media involvement suggested a fuller way to show and see the behead-ing, it was not yet fully realized. Instead, focusing on Daniel Pearl's death—but without its graphic depiction—remained a more certain way to catch the engagement of the U.S. public, keeping it potentially involved, attentive, and empathetic to the prosecution of the "war on terror." That the about-to-die pictures of the Taliban executions were less suited to those same strategic aims made their depiction less viable.

Significantly, underplayed by the repeated display of Pearl's photos was their original choreographing by his assailants. The involvement of his captors in tak-ing the images lent a paradoxical dimension to journalism's embrace of them. Though it underscored how the digitally media environment had blended the distinction between journalists and nonjournalists, facilitating his abductors' drive of the story in the absence of journalism's documentation of it, it also raised questions about how such photos—taken for aims to the contrary—could then be used to promote and sustain support for the war. While doing so altered the original reasons for their taking, it showed how the digital environment magnified the range of uses to which an about-to-die image could be put. Underscoring how suggestive the image remained, how porous the exchange of information had become within and beyond journalism, and—though not the only event during the "war on terror" to illustrate the central role of new media—how easy it had become to drive a story not from its journalistic center, the reliance on the image of Pearl about to die showed too how powerful the play to the "as if" could be. When the imagination, the emotions, and contingency can be so effectively marshaled, even when they are at odds with what transpires on the ground, this suggests yet again how the familiarity of form helps mitigate difficult and disturbing content and, in doing so, transforms the engagement with an unsettled event like the "war on terror."

A similar nonjournalistic push for the news story, relayed through its images, emerged two years later, when a new set of beheading photos surfaced in the war on Iraq. As the "war on terror" continued its expansion into Iraq, from 2004 onward a rolodex of beheading images, taken by the victims' captors shortly before they were decapitated, appeared in the U.S. news media. Imitating the visual trope set in place with Pearl's beheading, these images visually connected the "war on terror" across the two places in which it was being prosecuted. Within twelve months more than two hundred individuals were shown in the news media about to die by beheading.[37]

The first such beheading shot from Iraq—or, as one news organization framed it, "the second American [after Pearl] to die in a show 'execution' by Islamic militants since the start of the War on Terror"—was that of independent businessman Nick Berg in May 2004. Berg had travelled from Philadelphia to the region as a communication tower engineer, and—following a two-week detention by either the FBI or the Iraqi military, depending on whose report one believed—he disappeared on April 9, 2004. His headless body turned up one month later on a Baghdad roadside. That discovery was followed shortly afterward by a video, circulated online, of his death-in-process.[38]

The timing of Berg's decapitation video was critical. Released when a majority of U.S. citizens had gone on record opposing the war for the first time,[39] the beheading occurred not long after images of a terrorist attack in Madrid and the lynching of four Blackwater contractors in Fallujah, Iraq, had dominated the media. It also occurred just as the images of the U.S. abuses in Abu Ghraib prison came to light. This meant that Berg's beheading photos surfaced in a context already filled with contradictory images offering alternative interpretive cues about the war's direction, legitimacy, and salience. Unlike the pictures two years earlier of Pearl's beheading, which dominated journalism's visual landscaping of the war, here how one responded depended on which images fit which larger sentiments about the war. While the Abu Ghraib photos, grue-some shots of the U.S. military denigrating and humiliating Iraqi detainees, underscored the U.S. military's depravity, the pictures of Berg pointed to the Iraqi militia's barbarism. Which set of images prevailed, then, had much to do with which interpretive cues one sided.

At the same time, the video's initial surfacing on the Internet made it dif-ferently available to the users of different media. Though Reuters made the unedited tape available to all of its clients—saying "it was not its place to make editorial choices on behalf of its clients"—different choices ensued.[40] While those reliant on the traditional print and broadcast media were provided with images that reflected journalists' discomfort with graphic imagery, those turn-ing more to online sites—particularly those stretching beyond the home pages of news organizations—found a wide-ranging embrace of imagery, no matter how explicit or uncomfortable. This means that journalists, news executives, officials, politicians, and viewers would not necessarily see the same about-to-die images in Berg's beheading, raising the question of which images would be shown, which would be seen, and how the two would fit together.

The video of Berg's beheading surfaced on a Web site linked to al-Qaeda and was first picked up by Reuters and distributed for broadcast on May 11.[41] Taken by his captors, it showed Berg facing the camera head on, as a group of masked men stood behind him, also facing the camera. The formulaic video used fade-ins and full motion graphics referencing Palestinian refugee camps, 9/11 and other images central to Islamic fundamentalism. Berg sat on a white plastic chair, dressed in an orange jumpsuit, in front of a dinghy-colored room with cement walls and floors. Behind him a group of hooded men stood stiffly to attention. As the video progressed, Berg was made to kneel on the floor. One of the men raised a knife, and he was pushed onto the ground. The video ended with the men grabbing Berg by the hair and sawing off his head.

The horror of the video pulled those who saw it in multiple directions. One forensic pathologist wrote in *New York Magazine:*

> There was no way for me to step back from the images, to gain distance or perspective. Two years after 9/11, the Berg video unearthed emotions I had no desire to feel: fury, despair, the desire for revenge... I wanted every man in that little death club captured, torn from their families, and dragged into the darkest basement interrogation room.

For one viewer, it was evidence of "the sheer personal, hands-on primitive sadism and blood soaked lunacy of Islamic terror."[42]

Journalists and news executives, in particular, did not know what to make of the video. CBS News remarked that its "emotional effect was nearly as strong as watching planes flying into buildings." The images shattered the "veneer of distance and unreality for Americans about the war in Iraq. Somehow these vivid, cruel images pushed emotional buttons that months of combat footage, magnificently reported newspaper stories and grieving mothers hadn't yet. The pictures were the tipping point."[43] When broadcast news outlets reviewed the tape, consternation was so widespread that the Radio-Television News Directors Association issued guidelines for "airing graphic materials." Highlighting nine points for broadcasters to ensure that their subjects would be treated with "respect and dignity" regardless of whether they were dead or alive, the directive underscored a degree of ill-preparedness among the news media, especially given the Pearl beheading two years earlier.[44] It also constituted a somewhat limited response given the wide circulation of such materials—without journalism's intervention—on the Internet.

As news organizations scrambled to figure out how they would respond, the video had already begun to circulate online. From Reuters' first posting onward, the story began to accumulate increasing numbers of hits online. By the next day, online search engines like google.com, lycos.com and yahoo.com all saw Berg's beheading become the top search term online. As the video migrated to multiple Web sites, managers posting it took care to delineate what people were about to see. On www.annoy.com, for instance, editors appended the following Editor's Note:

> The execution of Nick Berg has been made available on Annoy.com to allow those who choose the option to witness the horror for themselves. It is not here for gratuitous reasons, to gloat or make baseless comparisons with other grotesque acts. The horrific beheading speaks for itself.
>
> The wave of media irresponsibility, their nauseating, agenda-driven claim to exclusivity when it comes to this sort of horror, their censoring of body parts and the government's grip on what we should or shouldn't see, compelled us to present this video in its entirety. We simply feel that you are in a better position to make necessary choices as to what you want to witness.[45]

Underscoring how much the digital environment had eclipsed journalism's control of the story already in its inception, interest in the video remained high. It produced the most frequented Internet search in the United States during the week it became available and remained throughout the month of May the second most popular search term on Google. At the same time, teachers in Texas, California, and Washington were placed on administrative leave for showing it in class.[46] This raised the important question of what role journalism would play in a story that was already moving full-force ahead without it.

The broadcast and print media inched toward more explicit imagery. Unlike the Pearl video, the broadcast media agreed to display the Berg footage: NBC news executive Neal Shapiro justified his decision by remarking that "if people can't watch, we've lost our ability to convey information." Unlike two years earlier, CBS, NBC, ABC, MSNBC, and Fox all showed edited clips from the video."[47] But they wavered over which sequence to show. At issue, said *USA Today*, was "how much video to show to illustrate the story accurately, without offending readers, viewers and Berg's family."[48] While NBC and ABC halted their cameras when the killer drew his knife, CBS showed him grab Berg by the hair and put the knife to his neck. MSNBC, CNN and Fox did not show the knife at all. All verbally described what happened after the camera was stopped. Consciously framing the display as one of impending death, despite the availability of footage showing Berg's death, the traditional U.S. news media thus played to the video's suggestibility.

The easy access to the full video online generated particular problems for editors in both the print and broadcast media. Though each had home pages online, the video's circulation beyond news sites presented what *USA Today* called "an ethical dilemma in today's age of interactive information." Some decided against providing links to the video clips, claiming that "the footage would not necessarily add to the reader's understanding of news," while others provided the link "because it illustrated the harsh reality of the Iraq war."[49]

The print media responded to this circumstance by gravitating backward in the amount of informational detail it would provide. As with other about-to-die images, the still pictures of Berg's beheading offered a way to sidestep the video's gruesomeness, their frozen sequencing rendering them more approachable. Frame-grabbed from the video, the still shots side-stepped the display of Berg's corpse and showed him alternately seated atop the chair or kneeling on the floor (fig. 7.4). In each of the pictures, Berg faced the camera frontally. He sat stiffly

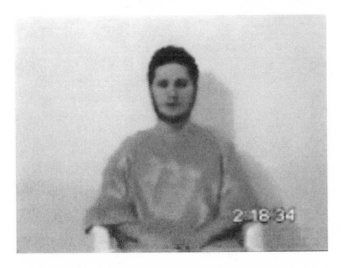

Figure 7.4:
Reuters, Nick Berg
Execution, May 11,
2004.

upright, his facial features almost bland in their lack of expression. He showed no affect, no apparent fear, no clear sense that he knew what was to come. His expression remained the same, even as one of the pictures showed his killer raising the knife behind him. Fuzzily out-of-focus, the images remained otherworldly, profoundly incongruent with what viewers knew was about to happen.

United States news organizations oscillated in terms of which still photo they would show and how. Audio clips from the beheading—referencing an image unseen—were aired on radio shows. The *Dallas Morning News* printed one about-to-die image on its editorial page alongside a photo, frame-grabbed from the video, of Berg's assailant holding his severed head, under the headline "This is the Enemy. Vile Image Shows Why We Should Fight." Though the paper blocked out the face itself "out of respect for the dead man's family," the editorial told readers that the photo "is meant to bring perspective to events in Iraq, to refocus the nation's eyes on the larger picture of the war against radical Islam, and its stakes." In explaining the decision in the *National Review's* online blog, the paper's Rod Dreher noted that he had gotten the idea to print the second image from the blogosphere—where he sensed people wanted it displayed—and that decision was held up the following day, when the paper's letters page was "filled with nothing but Berg related letters, most of them demanding that the DMN show more photos of the Berg execution. Not one of the 87 letters we received yesterday called for these images not to be printed."[50]

Most other news organizations, however, were less visually straightforward. Many showed still shots of the killer with the knife, because, in *Seattle Times* executive editor Michael Fancher's words, "that image shows the calculation behind their act without going farther than we need to tell the reader what happened." Some newspapers showed more than one image of the beheading within one issue of the paper. In all cases, the pictures were accompanied by clear texts that established Berg's death as certain. Though some were quick to strike the parallel with Pearl's death—the *San Francisco Chronicle* called it "chillingly reminiscent of the 2002 slaying in Pakistan of American journalist Daniel Pearl"—missing this time was a hospitable environment for showing the images of impending death.[51] Two circumstances complicated the images' reception: First, the concurrent display of the images from Abu Ghraib had tilted the visual context to such an extent that showing Berg about to die a certain death constituted a countermessage for some viewers rather than a relay to be considered independent of its neighboring news stories. Second, those looking for depictions of the beheading in the print and broadcast media versus those looking for them online found a significantly different visualization of what had happened.

In this context, the pictures of Berg's beheading followed four possible trajectories, depending on one's broader sentiments about the war and on which news medium one depended for its relay. First, they either hardened a resolve against the war or played into a sense that the photos were being used to subvert attention from the concurrent events at Abu Ghraib. Second, they were shaped by either a growing reluctance on the part of the news media to show what they considered images of gratuitous violence or an eager push to visually document online as much graphic imagery as was necessary to ensure that the event be seen. Third and fourth, these camps divided across support for the war and criticism of it, between old media users and new media users, resulting in multiple contexts for showing, seeing, and interpreting the images.

Among those who supported the photos' display was Fox News. "Where is the outrage?" asked the network's John Gibson. "The same people screaming about American abuses at Abu Ghraib are now conspicuously silent about this outrage directed against an American." Readers' letters poured in, demanding to hear more condemnation of Berg's assailants. The *Washington Times* called Berg's death "a painful and expensive reminder of the nature of the war we fight. We're at war against cowards."[52]

But at the same time many remained opposed to the images' display. Berg's family—on record for its opposition to the U.S. military action in the "war on terror"—felt the images diminished the importance of events like Abu Ghraib. News organizations relegated the Berg story to "a second tier story behind repetitive accounts of Iraqi prisoner abuse." As one researcher with the Independent Media Research Center said, "What's shocking is that the beheading of an American is a one-day story. It was gone by Wednesday night." The *Washington Times* recounted the image's circulation thus:

> The *Washington Post* ran a single story on Berg, relegated to an inside page, running two prison abuse stories on its front page and three other related stories in its front section, while the *New York Times* ran three front page abuse stories and three additional stories in its front section, with a single story on Berg, all of which prompted the *Boston Herald* to complain that "the *New York Times,* which has hawked story after story on the prison abuse scandal, saw fit [Tuesday] to run a single column on the upper-right front page about Berg's murder, while prominently featuring accusations of abuse by a former Afghan prisoner."

The uneven display of the Berg images did not escape notice from abroad. In the *Independent*'s view, "Like the murder of Daniel Pearl, Nick Berg's death was designed as blatant propaganda—and we, from television producers to journalists, took up the challenge and ran with it—all in the name of information." Arguing against the image's display, the paper lamented that "publishing these pictures only plays into the hands of the people who made them.... When terrorists within the Arab world see our reaction to this imagery, and the prominence we have given it, they must be delighted."[53]

At the same time, the differences in coverage for those accessing the story through new or old media were critical. In Jay Rosen's view, the difference between old and new news judgment—new judgment referencing the "Web user's hunger to know, see, publicize and discuss," old judgment signifying "the gatekeepers and their ideas about news, the public interest and 'taste'"—meant that a different kind of engagement with Berg's beheading was adrift. Rosen contended that new news judgment could be found in the metanews about popular search terms, and the day after Berg's beheading video turned up, phrases like "nick berg video," "nick berg beheading," and "beheading video" topped the Google charts, indicating where the interest was. Complicated by the concurrent focus on Abu Ghraib, many Internet users complained that the main story was being sidestepped: "They aren't showing us everything: the knife, the throat, the screams, the struggle, and the head held up for the camera. But the sickening photos from Abu Ghraib keep showing up." Conservative pundit Andrew Sullivan observed that "people who have tuned the war out suddenly tuned the war in. They get it. Will the mainstream media?" Or, as one blogger put it,

> One day the media was telling us we had to see the pictures from Abu Ghraib so we could understand the horrors of war. But with Berg's beheading, we're told we can't handle the truth...The media that had—rightfully, in my opinion—showed us the ugly reality of Abu Ghraib prison refused to do the same with Berg's murder.[54]

The mixed responses generated by these differences—support for the war versus its criticism, old media audiences versus new media users—were telling of how diversified and vocal the public had become. They also deprived the coverage of Berg's beheading of its center. As one observer remarked in the *New York Daily News,* Berg had become a symbol but it was unclear whose symbol he was:

> At first, Arab governments greeted the Berg affair with an approving silence....But soon enough it dawned on the region's leaders that Berg's decapitation was diverting attention from the propaganda bonanza at Abu Ghraib prison....The Bush administration saw this distraction as a bonanza...and fully intended for Berg to become its symbol, the personification of the war's underlying rationale. Then Berg's father, Michael, stepped in and snatched his son back.[55]

Though multiple nonjournalists pushed the images, which nonjournalists—members of the Iraqi militias, officials in the Bush administration, bloggers, Berg's bereaved parents—remained indeterminate.

Like many other about-to-die images of a certain death, the interpretive play around the display of Berg's beheading demonstrated how suggestible the images remained. Individuals queried whether he had in fact died. Within days an open letter was posted on islamonline.net, tackling the uproar over Berg's "alleged beheading" and claiming that the video did not provide adequate evidence of his death. Other sites—offering detailed analysis of the video—concluded it was faked. Even in Iraq, there was no clear response to how much graphic imagery should be displayed; in August of 2004 the Iraqi vice premier banned Al-Jazeera from the country for one month, citing its active role in showing the beheading photos.[56]

As the beheadings continued—by mid-August over two dozen people had been kidnapped—the story began to lose its resonance. "This is becoming somewhat monotonous," said one reporter. "It's not like before." A diminishment of interest was suggested soon after Berg's death, when additional beheadings—Paul Johnstone, Eugene Armstrong, Jack Hensley, Margaret Hassan, among others—took on the visual form made familiar by Berg's beheading but did not generate the same degree of attention, however conflicted it might have been. Though the bright orange color of their jumpsuits signaled a genre of beheading photographs that would depict the impending deaths of other U.S., Italian, Japanese, Turkish, Korean and Iraqi individuals, the ongoing—and unsettled—conversations among journalists, news executives, bloggers, politicians, officials, and viewers about "how much" to accommodate of the images, about the strategic aims of the abductors and about the images' value for the prosecuting forces of an increasingly unpopular war all overwhelmed the beheading photos' capacity to visualize the war's brutality. Though images of Berg did resurface in the coverage of other beheadings and in stories about the questioning of his supposed abductors, about the wisdom of Jews traveling to hostile Arab nations, and about the beheadings of other individuals, the beheading photos by then had lost their capacity to engage sentiments on the war, weakly and somewhat vacantly signifying what the Associated Press said had turned an "ancient punishment" into "a 24 hour news cycle's shocking message of defiance." At the same time, the multiple online sites that had forefronted the display of Berg's beheading were now filled with absent links and postings that had since been erased. The waning relevance of the imagery was further underscored three years later, when, in February 2007, the trial of a group accused of planning the 2005 London underground bombing revealed that videos of both Pearl's and Berg's beheadings had been found at the homes of the accused.[57] By then, however, the linkage between the beheadings went almost unnoticed. This was because the decision to obscure death by showing its impending status had changed as the "war on terror" had moved on. It transformed from a depiction contained within journalism to one pushed by nonjournalists on all sides of the political spectrum—both those supporting the U.S. aims in prosecuting the war and those supporting the Iraqi militias' opposition to it. These images thus foreshadowed the conflicted role of visuals in depicting a war whose visual landscaping could not reflect the complicated and contested nature of its prosecution or its evolving platforms for display.

These two instances of death by beheading show how the strategic uses of the about-to-die image in the "war on terror" complemented each other in critical ways: Pearl's beheading—a one of a kind event in the largely supported war in Afghanistan—was widely shown and seen because it encapsulated a key message about the war, embodying the tensions between "us" and "them" and emblematizing why going to war mattered; Berg's beheading—one of hundreds in an increasingly unpopular war in Iraq—was shown unevenly and seen at first but then hardly at all because it competed with visuals that relayed the opposite message of American brutality. Due to their new media involvement, the depictions of both beheadings were managed not only by journalists but by the victims' captors, officials, bloggers, politicians, and bereaved family members. But in Pearl's beheading, journalists, collectively outraged by the death of one of their own, kept the coverage oriented to its less graphic "as if" moment, while a less uniform degree of journalistic outrage in Berg's beheading was offset by the energetic efforts of online bloggers and posters to make sure that the images were seen. Those efforts, however, were shaped by the transient nature of the Internet, which gave the images a short shelf life.

Against these contradictory uses, then, the trope of people about to die, as associated with the "war on terror," showed its holes. Though the trope's familiarity could have been expected to facilitate an engagement with the disturbing content it showed, as was evident with Daniel Pearl's beheading, the questions of whose emotions and imagination were to be drawn, how, where, by whom, and for which contingent or implicative purposes were so prevalent in Berg's beheading that the display seemed to have no clear place in the war's visual documentation. Again, questions of form undermined the pictures' content, for as with other about-to-die pictures whose taking had inspired a lack of confidence—Kevin Carter's photo of the Sudanese child and the vulture, Abu Rahma's picture of a teenage Palestinian boy facing his death—such a marked degree of strategizing was assumed about the images' display, or lack thereof, that it rendered them suspect.

But the uncertainty here exceeded that of form. Bolstered by further variance in the multiple domains in which different images could be seen, the simultaneous images with an opposing message being displayed in the same visual landscape and the intense involvement of multiple nonjournalists trying to secure or prevent display, the video and its frame-grabbed shots caused a flurry of interest among some of the public, which then petered out over time. Typical of the digital environment more broadly, it nonetheless underscored how transient and ephemeral much of its material was.

Though the images' online circulation did not sustain their display over time, however, its initial surge would lay out the parameters of what engaging with the war's visualization could mean in a digital age. Within months of Berg's beheading, by October 2004, a Pew Foundation Survey remarked that 30 million people—or 24 percent of all adult Internet users—reported having sought images online from Iraq that the news media had not published, with 28 percent of them having logged on specifically to find those images.[58] Though the viral display of Berg's beheading played off of journalism's initial news relay to begin with,[59] online relays were able to provide an increasingly compelling rolodex of events that grabbed public attention, even if it petered out over time.

By contrast, the more permanent, material, and multimodal archival repositories of the old media allowed them to function as agents of memory when they wanted to, even when their original news relays had been uneven. The longer staying power and materiality of retrospectives, temporal overviews, special editions, special broadcasts, and books offered traditional journalists additional opportunities to address the unsettled events of the news. Though the Pearl beheading reflected such interest and the Berg beheading did not, as the "war on terror" moved on, about-to-die images would become particularly central as tools of memory, where their frozen slice of time and space would saliently contrast the rapid spin of the digital environment.

Saddam Hussein: Death by Hanging

Though the hanging of Saddam Hussein was expected to bring to final closure many of the issues left open to interpretation during the early stages of the "war on terror," the already divided sentiments about the war made closure a tenuous prospect. Thus how it was staged and interpreted, shown and seen, played to the "as if" of its unfolding, where the emotions, contingency, and the imagination could all be invoked.

Hussein's hanging on December 30, 2006, came at a point of heightened dissatisfaction with the "war on terror," which had reached a turning point with the images from Abu Ghraib. Two weeks before the hanging, the American public was exhibiting manifold signs of discontent. National Public Radio commented on "plummeting public support for the war," after multiple public opinion polls—separately conducted by CNN/Gallup, CBS, *Washington Post*/ABC, and the Pew Research Center—all pointed to marked public dissatisfaction with the war's prosecution. A majority of people had begun to feel the war was going badly, likened Iraq to the war in Vietnam, and characterized the war as a mistake. Dissatisfaction was so high that President Bush delayed a public address on the topic. Even the military had become critical.[60]

A scheduled event whose precise time of unfolding was not made public ahead of time, Hussein's hanging was an event-in-the-making for days before it occurred. Proclaimed by Iraqi officials on December 26 to occur "within the next 30 days" and promised to be filmed on video, the hanging unfolded as the Iraqi and U.S. military forces negotiated over the date, details, and transfer of the former leader from U.S. to Iraqi custody and news executives monitored the signs. Recognizing that the hanging would be seen differently by those feeling differently about the war—those supporting the war's prosecution would look to the execution's coverage to assuage public qualms, while those against the war hoped that it would generate greater opposition—news executives knew that they needed to skirt contradictory public sentiments by finding a middle ground between the two. As had been the case with the beheading pictures of Daniel Pearl and Nick Berg, this meant that portraying Hussein facing death rather than dead would be the less graphic choice of depiction. The about-to-die moment and its suggestibility were thus well-suited to addressing both those who supported and opposed the war, though they were diametrically opposed to each other.[61]

Hussein's execution was approached by those who would show and see it with a mix of reluctance and confidence, stemming from both the event's graphic nature and the opportunities for information sharing offered by the digital environment. Because the execution was anticipated, U.S. news organizations had time to set in place provisional guidelines for how to cover the goriness that would come, and announcing what they hoped would be "tasteful" coverage, they held marathon meetings to debate the shape of the ensuing coverage. At first, ABC and CBS said that they would not air the full execution, noting that "we have very, very strict guidelines with how to deal with that." And yet such guidelines were not clear across the board. The days before the hanging were filled with what the Poynter Institute called "tough decisions about how best to present the news," as professional forums set up helper feeds as ways to think about the impending story. Online seminars under catchy titles like "Displaying Death with Dignity" and "Saddam Hussein Death: Resources for Journalists" advised journalists and news executives ahead of time to maintain "taste and compassion." As the execution's most graphic dimension, images were at the core of these discussions, and a repertoire of tools was suggested— cropping, sequencing, changing placement and size, selective toning, blurring, adding black bars and text, and offering disclosure—to mitigate the event's graphic nature. While on the face of things, news organizations appeared to have many choices—whether to publish the images or link to them online through home pages, whether to show Hussein being prepared for hanging, whether to show the execution, whether to include graphic images on home pages, in front broadcast spaces or on front page, on inside pages or not at all, whether to include verbal warning about the images, and whether to respond if other news organizations and nonjournalistic Web sites decided to do things differently—most news organizations decided ahead of time to set the full execution off-limits, leaving the moment of death off camera. As CNN's Anderson Cooper noted, "We are not going to just get these images and slap them on TV." As late as the day before the hanging, news executives for ABC, CBS, and NBC insisted that even if an execution video were distributed on the Internet, they would not soften their resistance to airing graphic images. Journalists were somberly advised that "images leading up to the moment of death [could] be shown, but not the actual death."[62]

At the same time, as speculative reports surfaced about the precise date and time of the hanging, fueled by the Iraqi government's statement on December 28 that Hussein would be "executed before Saturday," the Internet surfaced as a fertile landscape primed for activation. Reflecting a sustained interest at the time in the Internet, many people flocked to online sites to track the speculation about when the hanging would occur. In particular, evidence of a growth in the online display of digital photography and a growing recognition that online news could provide richer data than that made available by old media generated interest as people actively searched online and engaged in novel practices like tagging and sharing videos.[63] All of this meant that in the period leading up to Hussein's death, many viewers looked to the Internet, where multiple blogs, postings, and Web sites provided a ghoulish countdown to the hanging.

When the hanging occurred the night of December 30, it was as if the public jumped into the online environment and journalists sat on the sidelines, stunned. Access to new media simultaneously enhanced people's capacity to search for the depictions they wanted and pulled the story from journalism's grasp. The lengthy preparation among news executives about which images they would show and in which fashion was quickly nullified because two visual records of Hussein's death—contradictory in what they showed—emerged. The official video of Hussein's hanging, made available to news organizations shortly after the event to "head off skeptics who might not believe Hussein was dead," showed a soundless sequence of him being guided onto the steps of the gallows, a scarf being put around his neck and a noose placed over his head and tightened. One minute long, the video stopped short of his actual death. It played repeatedly on the state-run Iraqi channel, Iraqia, and quickly appeared in the broadcast media and home pages of U.S. news organizations. Later that evening an independent camera phone video—with audio—surfaced on al-Jazeera and al-Arabiya that showed Hussein being taunted as he mounted the gallows. Shot from below, the video showed Hussein being led onto the trapdoor by a group of masked men. As the noose was placed around his neck, the crowd below became audibly abusive. Just after Hussein responded, the trapdoor opened and he plunged to his death. The camera swung erratically and then rested on a close-up of his wide-eyed lifeless corpse. No image was provided of the actual execution. The contrast between the videos was marked. As one news organization noted, "unlike the silent, official film showing a subdued Saddam Hussein, the execution [in the mobile phone version was] a charged, angry scene." From the independent video, taken apparently by a guard, it became clear "that the seemingly quiet, dignified send-off portrayed on the official video [did] not tell the whole story."[64]

Though news organizations faced a quandary about what to do with the independent video, viewers experienced no such hesitation in securing it for their own viewing. The clip went viral almost immediately, traveling aggressively across the Web, where viewers repeatedly downloaded it. When the clip appeared on streaming video Web sites such as Google Image, YouTube and Revver, fed by sites like anwarweb.net, blogsofwar.com, shokk.com, and liveleak.com, and forwarded by e-mail links, blogs, and other postings, many viewers regarded the user-friendly relays as an effortless engagement with the story, requiring no log-in, no wait-time for a Web page to load, and no software compatibility. Within hours, searches for the video began to turn up multiple clips of the same content, often rated or its views tracked, and within forty-eight hours of the hanging, more than 1 million views of the Iraqi official video had been logged on YouTube alone, along with 350,000 views of the cell-phone video."[65] All of this made journalists' earlier decision making—regarding assessments about duty, propriety, and decency—pale in relevance as people bypassed the old media and sought out the video online. What had been codified as an exercise in taste became a clear challenge to traditional print and broadcast media, made acute by the fact that the independent video, as typical of many online relays, had an unverifiable form: journalists did not know who had made it, who had released it, and whether or not the Iraqi government could confirm what it showed. In other words, it was suspect as a journalistic relay but had stunning relevance for what it showed.

Recognizing that they had been eclipsed, news organizations scrambled to vary the story's visual treatment. CNN showed part of the video with subtitles revealing the insults leading up to the hanging, after Larry King had devoted a full hour to the clock ticking on Hussein—at which point he asked, "Is there something ghoulish about this?" ABC offered a few brief clips from the independent video. MSNBC posted an editor's note to its home page, where it explained "Some [of the images] are graphic and we've put that content behind a warning that will allow you to make a choice as to whether you'd like to view them. There is footage that we are not publishing: We believe you count on us to maintain standards and consistency in our coverage."

By contrast, Fox News provided full disclosure of the independent footage: it linked to the video from its home page and provided links to three additional videos that traced the moments before, during, and after the hanging. It also ran side-by-side still images of Hussein, one a file photo titled "Alive" and the other a still taken after the execution labeled "Dead."[66] As the news organization most aligned with those prosecuting the war, Fox's decision to show the fullest visualization of Hussein's death, even if the video raised an interpretation of the hanging at odds with the Iraqi government's gloss on what had happened, was consonant with the scramble two years earlier among viewers to see more graphic footage of Berg's beheading than had been provided by the networks.

For everyone who saw the videos, the meaning of Hussein's hanging changed dramatically depending on which video one believed. Linking to different notions about whether the hanging was justified, necessary, or appropriate, in one Hussein was thought to be submissive and fearful, his handlers silent and reverent, the hanging a considered meting out of justice; in the other Hussein was thought to be defiant and scornful, his handlers derisive, the hanging a hastily organized event motivated by revenge. There were those who saw both videos as too graphic, complaining about snuff photography, bad judgment, and the image's continual replay.[67]

There were also those who saw the videos as not graphic enough, in that they left open the possibility that Hussein was still alive. Remembering the various body doubles who had stood in for Hussein in the past, many people pondered whether the videos left open the possibility that Hussein was still alive. As the Canadian Broadcasting Corporation's Beirut correspondent noted after seeing the independent video:

> It is startling, disturbing, but also informative. It would seem to prove beyond a doubt that the former president is indeed now on the other side. That's important in a part of the world where conspiracy theories abound. There are many who would not believe Saddam was dead unless they saw it with their very own eyes.

Some viewers thus wanted to see more than they were given. As one noted, "The more witnesses the better. If you don't show it someone else will and I will watch. I prefer to set my own filter."[68]

Significantly, that was infinitely more possible in the digitally media environment than it had ever been before. New media involvement—called by Jeff Jarvis "news served raw" and producing what the *Los Angeles Times* labeled a "perfect new media event"—offered extensive latitude for the public to seek and find what it wanted to see. That challenge was not lost on the news media. Lamenting that "one man's citizen journalist is another's spy" in an "era of wrenching journalistic transition" between old and new media, the *Washington Post* warned that journalism's "efforts at gatekeeping are now almost entirely irrelevant. The public will find exactly as much of the death of Hussein as it wants and people will watch for as long as it holds any novelty or fascination."

One editor-in-chief wrote in an open letter on his news organization's Web site that the cell phone video forced journalism to consider its own future: it has "provoked an important debate about how we now get our news. With these images immediately available ... is this a signal that news editors are losing control of the journalistic agenda?"[69]

For many searching for the full independent video of Hussein's execution online, that control had already been lost. Because the online version of the story—with its "inadequate, green-hued light, erratic audio and jerky camerawork" enhancing its authenticity and prompting viewers to ask for more "individual people with mobile phones to show us the truth"—differed so markedly from that of the broadcast and print media, viewers approached Hussein's execution online with independent searching strategies confidently intact.[70]

In much the same way as Nick Berg's beheading, then, the disparate interpretation of the war—and by extension the Iraqi leader's death—and the different settings for seeing its visual relay created multiple different opportunities for engaging the event. There again seemed to be no common nodal point for grounding the execution's coverage at one point in time and space.

And yet, the still photos of Hussein hanging lingered in the background. Because the display of either video was responsive to only part of the public— drawing either support or opposition to the war and relying either on a graphic online display or a more subdued relay by broadcast and print media—news organizations needed to find a visual that could accommodate the various impulses at play. As in other events, the about-to-die image—the still photo of Hussein facing his death—became relevant. Like other about-to-die pictures, it functioned in ways that the moving image could not: static, frozen, and memorable, it accommodated the multiple interpretations that had been generated by the contradictory videos in both their new and old media settings, leaving journalists, news executives, politicians, officials, and viewers to imagine, not see, Hussein's death and by implication the end of his regime.

The still image of Hussein facing death was starkly compelling (fig. 7.5). Frame grabbed from the official video and circulated primarily by the Associated Press, the shot showed Hussein, his face stoic and hard, facing sideways as the hangman placed a noose around his neck. Coarse ropes crossed the forefront of the frame, heralding the bodily drop that they would facilitate. There was no context, environment, or additional actions to complicate the frame. All that viewers saw was a moment frozen on Hussein's impassive visage as he was about to die, "conform[ing] to one of the oldest of dramatic conventions: the act of violence remains off-stage ... the moment of death is not captured."[71]

While people scrambled to decide whether the official or independent video told the story more fully, this image of Hussein facing death—unlike that of Nick Berg—appeared widely across the U.S. print and broadcast media—at the top of broadcast lineups, as logos for broadcast coverage, on front pages,

Figure 7.5: AFP/Getty, Saddam Hussein Execution, December 30, 2006. Reprinted courtesy of the *Chicago Tribune*.

magazine covers, internal pages, as the illustration for cover stories.[72] The image appeared online, both on the home pages of news organizations and across nonnews Web sites, often alongside a fuller relay of Hussein's execution video. Broadcast organizations showed it as part of their coverage logo, and it appeared widely at the top of newscasts. Sometimes it appeared multiple times in one place or site, as when the *Denver Post* ran four front-page images of Hussein facing death alongside one of his corpse or the *Birmingham News* featured three about-to-die images side by side, their titles proclaiming Hussein's "final moments" or "last minutes." The *New York Times* front-paged four shots, three of which showed Hussein about to die and a fourth which showed his corpse wrapped in a shroud. *USA Today,* the *Washington Post,* the *Philadelphia Inquirer,* and the *Los Angeles Times* included a frame grabbed image from the independent cell phone video on an inside page, which showed Hussein dead, but the primary image of Hussein facing death was seen first on the front page. Tabloids, pointedly articulate about what they saw and its relationship to the text, showed the image of Hussein's bruised corpse alongside images of his impending death, and their titles ranged in formulaic ways across "Saddam Swings," "Good Knot," and "Saddam's Last Gasp."[73] Each time the image surfaced, it was presented as an image of certain death, its texts confirming that Hussein was dead, and it remained the signal image of the execution even when news organizations also showed pictures of Hussein dead.

Still adhering to the guidelines they had set up before the hanging occurred, news organizations anticipated negative viewer responses to the image's graphic content, and they established various forums for making the decisions they had taken transparent. Statements of disclosure appeared across the news media: the *Philadelphia Inquirer* offered a boxed-in statement under the bold title "Graphic Pictures Inside," that read: "To Our Readers: A sequence of photos of Saddam Hussein at the gallows appears on A11. *The Inquirer* has chosen to publish these photos because of their news value. Readers should be aware that the photos are of a graphic nature."[74] The *Atlanta Journal-Constitution* directed readers to an inside page where it displayed, in the newspaper's words, "photos of him on the gallows but not of the actual hanging." One editor's blog, titled "The Editors: Saddam's Execution," featured an explanation of how different decisions had been taken about which images to show. Similar forums which ran in *Editor and Publisher* were widely circulated by the AP and Reuters.[75] Significantly, none of these discussions addressed the fact that in the move from video to still photo, most favored the more sanitized depiction of Hussein facing death rather than already dead. Nor did they discuss the obvious fact that regardless of what the news media did or did not display, the more graphic imagery spiraled virally with abandon.

Playing to the about-to-die photo thus enabled news organizations to converge on one image as the core of their depiction. Doing so played to the common denominator of their coverage and facilitated the entertainment of the often contradictory accounts of what had transpired in ways that the videos did not make possible. Though many variations of the hanging were available both in form—still image versus video, with or without sound—and in content—prehanging or hanging, hanging without the drop or the full unedited cut—the news organization's visualization of the hanging pivoted on the one image that allowed both stances—celebration of hanging versus opposition to the hanging—to be simultaneously entertained rather than clarified. For that reason, this still picture of Hussein facing his death was titled and captioned in ways that aligned with both interpretations. Titled as both "Saddam Video Outrage" or "The Tyrant Has Fallen," captions to the same image alternately described Hussein's final moments as dignified, calm, compliant, and muted, on the one hand, and unrepentant, defiant, contemptuous, and feisty, on the other. When Hussein's response to what was happening was noted, captions to the same image said Hussein "was subdued and unresisting," "was scornful of his captors and exchanged angry words with the onlookers," "smiled at taunting onlookers," or "waited with dignity."[76]

Equally important, however, focusing on the about-to-die shot of Hussein allowed news organizations to sidestep the critical questions that new media and the involvement of bloggers and posters raised about their own coverage. Though journalists worried about how the digital environment had affected their capacity to cover breaking news—one columnist cautioned that "we better get used to living without visual boundaries and with the curiosity and flexible morality of the viewer as the only limit on what we can see from now on"—by relying on a simple and familiar formulaic trope that could be repeatedly and easily shown across the print, broadcast, and online media, they held back the online challenge by asserting their singular mode of visually engaging with the event.[77] The about-to-die image signaled the certainty of repeated exposure, so essential for invoking impulses associated with the emotions, the imagination, and contingency among those who saw it. But its suggestive nature meant too that Hussein's execution was documented more fully elsewhere.

Significantly, as the new media involvement in the story began to fade, journalism's reliance on the image of impending death persevered over time. The video clip of Hussein hanging remained available on the Web but increasingly disappeared from the online nonnews sites where it had been given context and nuanced interpretation. By the end of the decade, multiple searches for earlier glints of online wisdom about Hussein's death came up matchless. As has been argued about YouTube but applies more generally to the Internet, it provided "accelerated and exaggerated expectations for availability. Content, once in [the viewer's] grasp, can still be temporary." Conversely, the still image of Hussein about to die continued to appear as frequently as the story moved onward in time as it had at the time of his execution. Illustrating stories as wide-ranging as the arrest of the guard who took the independent video, the execution of Hussein's aides some days later, recountings offered at week and month's end, and anniversary retrospectives, though Hussein was by then long dead, the depiction of him about to die served as a workable and sustainable mnemonic visualization.[78] The pictures of him already dead simply disappeared from view. In memory, then, Hussein about to die was sustained with a vengeance. Topping the retrospectives of the decade in review, his stark visage as the noose was tied around his neck appeared repeatedly in 2009. The same scene also traveled elsewhere—depending on online recycling—where it showed up on refrigerator magnets, as dolls and as the focus of cartoons, book covers, and DVDS.[79]

Thus the gravitation toward the about-to-die image in the U.S. news media was instrumental for finding a common sustainable visual for embodying Hussein's execution not only at the time of the event but across time too. This treatment helped traditional news organizations reinstate control of a story that had slipped their grasp. Portraying Hussein about to die and targeting the moment of contingency allowed for divergent interpretations to persevere about the hanging itself. The powerful effect of seeing Hussein face his own death suspended journalists, news executives, politicians, and viewers at a moment in which they were forced to continue to respond to an event that they did not see. At the same time, its display allowed journalists to sidestep their own professional questions about a video that had challenged their authority. Familiar in form, the about-to-die photo not only settled the disturbing content of what was shown but settled the multiple sources of discontent that surrounded its showing.

The about-to-die image of Hussein hanging thus drew the involvement of journalists and nonjournalists but ultimately enabled a reinstatement of journalism's authority for the coverage of Hussein's execution. By acting as a lowest common denominator—it did not violate the initial journalistic reluctance about showing graphic images, did little to advance either revenge or justice as the motivating impulse for the hanging, sidestepped public concerns over graphicness, and diminished the role played by new media, reducing its threat to traditional news organizations—it allowed the news media to accommodate contradictory stances about the necessity, justification, and appropriateness of the hanging and its coverage, even though the vehicle through which these accommodations were made remained suggestive and contingent. This meant that viewers, news executives, journalists, officials, and politicians could all engage with it emotionally, imaginatively, and without necessary recourse to the fuller and more explicit documentation that prevailed elsewhere.

As shown with other images of impending death, this porousness is a critical aspect of the image's display. In playing to the "as if," death is pushed aside and its anticipation becomes the primary impulse through which people engage. Doing so in the case of Hussein's hanging stopped short of telling the full story that the hanging suggested about the "war on terror"—its incomplete prosecution, unrealized aims, and misjudged rationale. But as tentative and uneven as was journalism's coverage at the time of Hussein's execution, its mnemonic strength reestablished the authority of the news media for the story. Drawn through larger impulses toward propriety, conservatism, and formulaic treatments of the unsettled events of the news, a draw to the common denominators of what had already been set forth put journalism back on top of the coverage over time.

How the "As If" Erases Accountability

The display of about-to-die images in the "war on terror" highlights the degree to which journalism's images remain up for grabs, following the impulses, aims, and strategies of those who use them most effectively to their own ends. Each of the images discussed here reflects the U.S. news media's decision to avoid showing death itself, despite the fact that death was at the center of the coverage, leaving to others to more fully document the events of the war. Four events—the beatings of the Taliban, the beheadings of Daniel Pearl and Nick Berger, and the hanging of Saddam Hussein—chart a trajectory by which journalism's predictable gravitation to a familiar trope whose nongraphic nature enabled an engagement with disturbing content persisted even as some of the public, newly attuned to the energetic relays of the Internet, clamored for more.

The role of new media and of nonjournalists, not always the same, intensified across the four events. In the short span of five years, journalism's multiple shortcomings surfaced in the U.S. news media, by which it stopped short of documenting the deaths of the Taliban and left them as possibilities, piggybacked off assailants' beheading photos to various strategic effect, and sidestepped the larger story, told alternatively by new media, of the enactment of Saddam Hussein's hanging. The role of nonjournalists was central in each event, due partly but not only to the rise of new media, where a depiction of the story offered was contrary to that provided by traditional journalism. New media and nonjournalists went from being almost not present in 2001 to providing the drive for the story in the absence of other documentation in 2004, and onto providing the drive for the story that competed with and emerged as preferable to journalism's own version of what happened in 2006. This enhancement of nonjournalists' role fit the porous digitally media environment in which news images came increasingly to be shown. In each event, the sentiments and actions of government officials, militias, guards with oppositional political views, bloggers, and bereaved families were brought to bear on journalism's images of impending death, shown often in journalism's name but not necessarily with its full sanctioning.

However, though "more" prevailed in the new media environment—more in number, more in graphicness, more in rapidity, more in variety—it also disappeared more quickly, making way for the Internet's similarly energetic engagements with other unfolding news events. By contrast, the steady recycling in broadcast and print media of one still photo, chosen because it accommodated multiple interpretations and modes of engagement at the time of the event, emerged in memory as that which prevailed.

In that an about-to-die image's display has less to do with what people see than with what they are coaxed to imagine it to mean, these images come to resemble each other because they invoke a similar visual trope that hides much of the negotiations that go into its making. Form reigns to the almost complete erasure of content. As one reader wrote in a letter to the *Los Angeles Times,* "I found it difficult to make a qualitative distinction between the photos of Hussein with a rope around his neck and those of terrorist Abu Musab Zarqawi and American hostage Nick Berg prior to Berg's beheading." And yet this is what makes these images so amenable for strategic uses. The *Washington Post* wrote in the days following Hussein's execution that the administration had attempted to construct a "classic media argument in support of the war at a time when 'the media' are dissolving and forming into something new, something in which the images we wish to see are more important than the images we are forced to see."[80] This suggests that the draw to volition—to the emotions, the imagination, and contingency—makes the push for a more graphic depiction of the "as is" driven by a desire for the "as if." But when both desires blend into each other, it is for journalism to sustain what remains as the shards of a journalistic record pulled ahead into memory.

Depictions of impending death work by hinging engagement about the loss of human life on the emotions, the imagination, and contingency. Variations on this abound: images can hide responsibility, as evidenced in the incomplete detail of the about-to-die photos of the Taliban killings. They can marshal broader support, as seen in the images of Daniel Pearl. They can be diminished and invalidated, as seen in the images of Nick Berg. And they can generate legitimacy on a second round of engagement, allowing for the reinstatement of authority lost, as seen in the images of Saddam Hussein. In each case, however, what gets lost is a clear tracking between who took the image, who showed the image and who saw the image, and which purposes were pushing that engagement in each case. Lost is a clear sense of purpose, target, demeanor, community, and objective, leaving the visual depiction of unsettled events void of accountability. When images become such strenuous targets of so many multiple agendas, it becomes near impossible to contemplate them as documents of the "as is." Rather, their strategic uses and lack of accountability highlight the multiple journeys into the "as if" of depiction on which about-to-die images inevitably embark.

Contrary to the popular adage, then, a picture is not worth a thousand words. The words around the picture tell the public what the image means, but the negotiations around a given moment—social, cultural, economic, legal, ethical, technological, moral, and political in nature—determine what the image is worth, and the public exposure and engagement with the image help determine its afterlife. How to display a victim of impending death and how much information is needed to recognize it as such is crafted in conjunction not only with agendas unfolding within journalism's corridors but beyond them too, in the hearts and minds of all those who take about-to-die images to task as depictions of the unsettled events of the public sphere.

Chapter 8

How News Images
Move the Public

Unfolding trajectories of action are pictured everywhere in the news. Athletes crossing the finish line or just-elected politicians about to enter new offices are but some of the anticipatory illustrations that the news media provide. These depictions, frozen as unfinished actions that brim with anticipatory potential, depend on the public to complete their sequencing by imagining what comes when the camera turns off. In so doing, they drive the response to a wide swath of public events through impulses associated with the emotions, the imagination, and contingency. This book has shown how variant these responses have been among journalists, news executives, officials, politicians, and viewers and how broadly these spectators scope an engagement with events of an unsettled nature. Showing that the informational relay of news is often not central to what journalism provides, these depictions underscore the importance of thinking about tools of journalistic relay that complicate the existing picture of what news images are for, and by extension, what news itself is all about. Equally important, they suggest a different kind of public response to the news, a subjunctive engagement accomplished on the back of its visual representation. The energetic patterning of this public response points to the existence of public involvement in the news, regardless of its accompanying degree of rational understanding. Feeling for the unsettled events of the news, then, may take place regardless of what or how much one understands about them.

This book has shown how a certain kind of impending action—that associated with about-to-die pictures—has been valuable on many orders of practice.

Useful in sidestepping the discomfort of showing and seeing graphic images of death; in accommodating evolving, contradictory, and strategic responses to difficult events; and in facilitating imagined and often illogical engagements with what is shown, these images surface with comforting predictability in unsettled times. Though not the only available mode of journalistic depiction, their draw from a mixture of presumption, possibility, and certainty demonstrates that the relationship between what is shown and what is seen travels many roads, and not all of them point toward the enhanced understanding that rational informational relay is supposed to promote.

The "As If" of News Images

The primacy of an alternative voice in the news—one that pushes an engagement fueled by the imagination, the emotions, and contingency as a way of coming to grips with the larger world—raises the "as if" of unsettled events to the status of a default display in much of U.S. journalism. Facilitating a play to multiple emotions, imagined sequences, and incomplete and contingent suggestions of what people see, the "as if" can be utilized by people and institutional settings, which develop it for reasons of their own. This makes an image's strategic use value, instrumental in unsettled times, into a lightning rod for those hoping to coax public sentiment in one way or another. This book has addressed how the "as if" of news pictures helps shape the response to disturbing events, often critical for a public's sense of self: how much and what kind of information is necessary to set the interpretation of news pictures in motion, how and why it travels in so many directions, and how and why people other than journalists have been able to profit by it were key concerns in addressing the more central question of how news images move the public.

As this book goes to press, the ramifications of a massive earthquake in Haiti are still unfolding. Tentatively reported to have killed more than 150,000 people, the quake, which struck on January 12, 2010, was shown through the patterned forms discussed here. Social networking sites and Twitter feeds made stories and pictures available within seconds, and soon after the repetitive display of widespread videos and still photo galleries filled the U.S. print, broadcast, and online news media. Numbering up to sixty new images per day on news sites like msnbc.com and cnn.com, pictures like this one (fig. 8.1) brought the first visual news of the tragedy home, making the widespread devastation wrought by the quake familiar through a sequencing of scenes that unrolled in recognizable ways. As the first pictures of structural damage and crushed buildings gave way to images of anonymous suffering, dying and dead Haitians, and the detailed accounts of the Haitian families of U.S. celebrities and white Westerners caught in the disaster-struck region, the U.S. news media were able to hinge their coverage on the iteration of a familiar form to depict disturbing content. Used to share information, raise funds, and enlist humanitarian assistance, coverage thus took on a predictable shape. The much-repeated invocation of Haiti as the poorest nation of the Western hemisphere, which could nary afford a disaster of this ilk—"tragedy has a way of visiting those who can bear it least," wrote *Time*—relied on pictures of suffering to push public engagement.[1] Not all of the public was convinced, for as one *New York Times* reader complained:

> The people who have suffered the most are being spectacularized by your blood-and-gore photographs, which do not at all inform me of the relief efforts, the political stability of the region or the extent of damage to families and infrastructure. If this had happened in California, I cannot imagine a similar depiction of half-clothed bodies splayed out for the camera. What are you thinking?[2]

Nonetheless, the pictures compelled public attention. For instance, the Red Cross announced it received $800,000 in aid from text messages alone in the first twenty-four hours after the quake: not only did this support the instrumental nature of the disaster's pictures, but it showed yet again that in unsettled times familiar visual depictions mitigate uncomfortable content while simultaneously accomplishing other aims, not all of them related to information relay.

Figure 8.1: UN Photo/Logan Abassi, Port-au-Prince Neighbourhood Destroyed by Quake, January 12, 2010.

It is worth recounting what this book has established about how the "as if" drives news images. The "as if" suggests rather than establishes evidence, invokes generalizability over particularity, plays to the category over the nuance, pushes the familiar over the unfamiliar and the formulaic over the content driven. It suspends temporality and fastens people in the illogical position of knowing more than they see. This means that an about-to-die image's avoidance of what is particular, novel, topical, structural, and logical about the unsettled events it depicts—all long seen as central to news relay—is what coaxes the public to engage. Engagement, then, does not occur through the transference of reasoned information as assumed in traditional analyses of journalism.

Moreover, playing to the "as if" can motivate decisions that range across an image's selection, distribution, and viewing. This book has addressed a number of situations in which journalists capitalize on the about-to-die's nongraphic nature, nonjournalists for their own ends utilize the public's willingness to imagine what is not shown, and viewers respond by agreeing to presume, infer, accept, or reject interpretive cues about the unseen. In this regard, all people associated with these images—journalists, news executives, politicians, officials, and viewers—at times play an irrational game with what they see, projecting altered, conditional, hypothetical and sometimes impossible ends onto the images they see. In entertaining so many emotional, imagined, and contingent impulses, these images thus can soften, mute, simplify, and render contingent the untenable features of the geopolitical realities they portray.

Additionally, they often do so across time. Because images of impending death tend to be familiar from other events, they enter journalism already as memory tools and resurface in parts of the journalistic record in ways that have as much to do with memory, and its rewrites, retrospectives and anniversary journalism, as with the unfolding immediacy of news relay.[3] Primed as memory agents even as they land on the journalistic landscape, these images correspond with the long-standing parameters of the subjunctive voice, which uses the present to look at past action. Thus the same attributes that make them standouts as news relays—simplicity, familiarity, conventionality, universality—outfit them to be strong conduits of remembering. Their prevalence in news blurs journalism's so-called "first draft of history," by which mnemonic work proceeds from the initial relays of news. This nod toward memory relies on unstable and ever-changing interpretations of what matters and makes engagement as important as information relay and the variability and adaptability of its tools critical.

All of this underscores what theorists of modernity have long contended: its representational forms fuse rationality and contingency, determination and chance, evidence and supposal, a paradoxical privileging of progress and linearity alongside an attention to emergent forms, surprises, fugitive events, and undersides. Scholars as wide-ranging as Deleuze, Bauman, Giddens, and

Lyotard have argued that as modernity has become ever more associated with multiple stimuli forcing people to make sense of an intense and rapidly evolving mediated environment, the need grows for representational forms that can navigate the tensions between seemingly oppositional views of what matters.[4] In this regard, the about-to-die image fares well: though their repeated surfacing underscores the fact that time can never be certain or absolute, these images seem discrete and particular even as their audiences receive them as generalizable and universal; they surface as ephemeral but emerge as sustained through their recycling; they are thought to provide reasoned information but engage their audiences primarily through the emotions; and their claims to be evidentiary offer no more testimonial power than that associated with suggestion, imagination, and contingency. On multiple counts, then, the "as if" piggybacks on journalism's devotion to the "as is" and reorients the news toward impulses of the emotions, the imagination, and contingency.

When Form Embraces Flux

The formalistic power of the about-to-die image makes it well-suited to embrace and accommodate the interpretive flux these images raise. Acting as the vehicle for disturbing content, the image's form can assuage the discomfort of its content. As Lauren Berlant noted, "The continuity of the form...provides something of the continuity of the subject's sense of self and of what it means to keep on living on and to look forward to being in the world."[5] This book has shown how journalists and news executives relied on form to sidestep graphic death pictures; politicians and officials used form to carry contradictory messages of compassion and revenge, pity and repulsion; and viewers focused on attributes of form—its appropriateness, sensitivity, degree of vulgarity—as they sought to make meaning of what they saw. Repetitive, patterned, familiar, and predictable, form here was shown to lend a routine and domesticating frame that either offset and neutralized or foregrounded and highlighted the disturbing content relayed. When questions persisted about the picture's form—the circumstances of its taking, the photographer's motive, evidence of manipulation or tampering—the trope faltered, a further indication of how necessary form is to accommodate flux but stabilize it within usable parameters.

Significantly, the about-to-die image, appearing time and again as a still picture of impending action, prevails across imaging technologies rather than withers because of them. Though much of the activity today around about-to-die images stems from the digital environment, images of impending death appear repeatedly across that environment in still shot form. The trope's frozen sequencing of action, play to form over content, and the "as if" character of its depictions, all apparent from the earliest drawings of the illustrated press, are as evident today as they were then. In fact, these still photos of an imagined, incomplete, and contingent moment may offer one way of slowing down the rapid intensity of journalism's trajectories of display. Given the possibility that news, increasingly covered in real time, unfolds too quickly for people to come to grips with what it depicts, these images introduce a different mode of temporality into the news—a pause associated with the emotions, imagination, and contingency. It may be that their delay of unfolding action renders the "as if" into a temporal coping mechanism.

The form of the about-to-die image has been central to its staying power. Offering an opportunity for continued and sustained perusal and relying on its material form to do so, the about-to-die image counteracts the notion that whatever is depicted is over and done. Underscoring the act of viewing as an opportunity for crafting meaningful engagement with unfinished action, its incomplete sequence of action, suspended time, and anticipation of impending death force people to complete what is not shown, regardless of the tragedy being depicted. Like other still photos, it positions the public in a mode of active involvement, which Ariella Azoulay characterized as an attempt to "reconstruct the situation of the act of photography from the surface of the photograph. This motion does not belong to what is seen, as in a movie, but to the spectator. . . . It is the spectator who transforms what is photographed, what happens, into an event."[6] Remaining open to spectatorship, debate, conversation, interpretation, contestation, challenge, exchange, and ownership, the still photo offers a "point of departure for the reading carried out by whomever stands before it, for who decides to look and to watch."[7] Stabilizing what is shown and seen, the about-to-die image thus may prevail as a still picture because it can so easily be contrasted with the video footage of the digital environment. And as the image's frozen sequencing of action is made even more salient by slowing down the rapid spin of digital distribution, it may be particularly useful for journalists needing to sustain their authority in a rapidly evolving technological landscape and for people wanting to continue their engagement with the unsettled events of the news.

This book has shown how the attention to form over content diminishes the salience of an image's distinguishing features and by extension much of the detail characterizing impending death. Though pictures do not usually surface without larger news stories at their side, the readily available posting, easy recycling and exchange activities associated with images of impending death means that the prevalence of a familiar form has made it easier for images of impending death to exclude information that would otherwise be important to news relay. Thus, by leaving out cues of causality, impact, complication, effect, and their distinction between death by neglect, accident, or design, images of the "as if" offer a blended visual category of catastrophes, wars, acts of terror, diseases, and natural disasters. That category invites public engagement with human suffering and death without insisting that people pay heed to each tragedy on its own terms. Not only can people attend to floods and wars as if they unfolded similarly, but any unsettled event can be easily separated from both its planning and its effect. In obscuring death itself and leaving its sequencing up for grabs by the public, these images also make it possible to imagine variable action beyond the camera's eye and to deny, obscure, or challenge death because it is not shown.

And yet, despite the fact that these formalistic aspects of the trope—and its related preference for the category over the nuance, the universal over the particular, the generalizable over the discrete, and the suggestive over the evidentiary—undermine reasoned information relay, about-to-die images powerfully and repeatedly call to attention journalists, news executives, politicians, officials, and viewers, capturing the involvement of many of those who see them. Would people have debated Hiroshima as intensely as they did without an accompanying picture of its mushroomlike clouds? Would people remember the images of Vietnam as clearly as they do today if none had seen the moment of impending death? Though such questions require empirical confirmation, the persistence of about-to-die images suggests that they play a central role in facilitating public engagement, regardless of whether or not they drive public action. Pushing aside reasoned information for engagement, then, these images tend not to be seen and then forgotten but surface instead as strong, memorable depictions not only at the time of their unfolding but across memory as well.

All of this suggests that in taking on a recognizable shape in an evolving digital landscape, where the depiction of stopped time and a frozen sequencing of action summon multiple interpretations, these still photos offer paused invitations to engagement. They remain pregnant though contradictory glimpses of the unsettled moments of public life. In her discussion of the conveyance of temporal continuity and the footage of the Oklahoma City bombing, Mary Ann Doane observed that the footage compelled attention because "part of its attraction is its very resistance to meaning," a meaning she maintained involved domesticating experience and bringing it "back within the domain of the knowable."[8] Such is the paradox of the engagement with about-to-die images: How ultimately does one confer meaning on death? Even for those who look repeatedly at these images, making death meaningful remains an uphill battle. Perhaps for that reason so many people continue to look, hoping to emerge victors in their ongoing struggle to lend meaning to deaths imagined beyond the camera's frame.

Engaging the "As If"

The persistence of about-to-die images also depends on a fundamental link between the public and some agent of a picture's selection, display, and circulation. Journalists—less exclusive than in the past, less authoritative than they want to be, responding to an environment that is as much driven by imagination, the emotions, and contingency as by rational information, and responsible for providing increments of detail more than its final packaging—have become one arbiter among many in a digitally mediated environment that is varied, intense, dynamic, and internally contradictory. As a growing variety of nonjournalists make decisions about which images to show, journalists are no longer necessarily the key agents of an image's taking or its evaluation. Instead, they function alongside bereaved families, politicians, pundits, bloggers, officials, agents of truth and reconciliation commissions, human rights activists, and members of militias and insurgencies, all of whom gravitate at times toward about-to-die pictures. This means that though the agent of these images is no longer necessarily a journalist, the trope of impending death prevails.

But the trope persists over time too, where journalists are central to decision making about which images to show. With the help of institutionally backed mnemonic practices like retrospectives, revisits to unsettled events and anniversary journalism, the U.S. news media continue their display of about-to-die images in memory, where they invoke that same play to form over content that privileges the subjunctive voice. This extended use of earlier about-to-die images as mnemonic tools thus yields extended power to the "as if." The paradox of reshowing a depiction of suspended action long after the original longer sequence of action is over, of invoking instantaneity when it is no longer conceivable, suggests that a need for the subjunctive voice surfaces even when what happened on the ground is widely known and over. In other words, the "as if" continues to displace the "as is" as a presentational choice and a stimulus for interpretation even when the pragmatic task of coming to terms with the event seems to be long settled.

Given such backing for the trope's sustenance, it is thus no surprise that images of impending death continue to surface most pointedly around unsettled events. These images service those who use and view them. The "as if" prevails when journalists and news executives are hard-pressed or unable to provide a clear or graphic account of what has happened, when officials and politicians scramble to register formal responses to upsets in their purview, and when viewers remain entrenched in figuring out what an unsettled event actually means. It does so by pausing time long enough to accommodate the uncertainty, incompleteness, tentativeness, and instability of engagement. Facilitating a connection between an image, its corresponding news event, and distant circumstances that might be tangentially connected or broader than what is depicted, about-to-die images are invitational: they coax those who see them to use emotions, the imagination, and contingency to complete what may not be available as rational information at the time of the event's unfolding or what might be available but rejected as unsavory. Open, suggestive, porous, generalizable, and ambiguous, they thus accommodate the contradictions, qualifications, complexity, and ambivalence that characterize most events of the public sphere and offset expectations for clarity in the reportage of unsettled events. For this reason, the "as if" often leads journalism in periods thought to produce the public's greatest need for information relay, suggesting that informational relay is not all that people want or need, and offsetting the clear information that those supporting news as rational relay have maintained tends to become more important in times of crisis. Rather than offer more information, then, about-to-die images offer less information, and in its place they secure more affective and extrarational engagement.

This book has shown that such has been the case since the earliest evidence of about-to-die images in news. Driven by inanimate structures, endangered and fragile human bodies, and elaborating texts and their corresponding interpretive impulses of presumption, possibility, and certainty, these images encourage public involvement. They coax viewers to criticize and complain or celebrate and admire what is depicted and facilitate the pragmatic steps of politicians and officials to correct or obscure the upsets shown. Important to both the breaking and continuing news of journalistic relay, they provide a reliable way for journalists and news executives to sidestep the graphic depiction of death. Though journalists' response to these images has become over time less uniformly celebratory and territorial and more reflective of contradictory tensions generated by the display of graphic detail, the images still secure awards and resurface in memory work, where images originally provided by nonjournalists are treated as journalistic triumphs, credits for amateur images revert to news organizations, and retrospective work references the airing of such images in the print media, newscasts, and online news sites where they appeared, often alongside now unmentioned nonnews sites. This suggests that the "as if" does not only extend to what is shown initially but, paradoxically, to journalists' authority over time, where their reliance on the subjunctive voice to credential themselves challenges the traditional regard for journalists as arbiters of the "as is."

The "as if" also changes the stakes of what is relevant in news: because these images primarily drive emotional engagement, their ability to blend what elsewhere in the news would seem problematic—about causality, human intervention, malicious intent, degree of purposive action—here can be seen to fuel involvement. It may be that the stronger the association with other unsettled events, the more formulaic and familiar the pictures and the more driven the impulse toward generalizability, the greater the chance that the images will move the journalists, news executives, politicians, officials, and viewers who see them. Raising the possibility that the categorical presentation offers more obvious and accessible cues for interpretation and engagement than would be the case in a discrete tragedy, the about-to-die picture's association with similar pictures and events may be a way of rising above the din caused by the overload of stimuli in the digital environment. In other words, though the blended category of unsettled and disturbing events undercuts journalism's information relay, it may constitute a more effective choice for capturing public attention and securing involvement.

Though much study on public response to the news has addressed exposure, involvement, and engagement as a pathway to critical action—for instance, work on public deliberation has long maintained that engagement facilitates more inclusive dialogue, a propensity toward deliberation, and an increased capacity to barrel through and take part in collaborative action—such an emphasis seems to beg the question.[9] For this book suggests that engagement might have no pragmatic effect on action yet still be meaningful for people. Similarly, it might lead nowhere obvious in the short term yet play a part in moving people over time. Generating variant interpretations, vigorous debates, and contingent and imaginary conversations, engagement appears to have proceeded here on different terms, even when the accompanying informational detail might have been expected to shut down its corresponding interpretive flux. Even when images had explicit supporting information—titles, headlines, captions, and adjoining texts that confirmed an undepicted death took place—they at times generated a more unsettled though energized response than did those images offering less detail.[10] In other words, the more informational detail—either verbal or visual—that is provided, the greater may be the potential for provoking debate, conversation, interpretation, and contestation. This suggests the opposite of what has long been assumed, that more information leads to more agreement and possibly to a clearer understanding of what is depicted. Instead, in slowing down the process of information relay about an unsettled event, the provision of more information is seen here as an opportunity for more sustained engagement. Engagement, in this sense, becomes an end in itself.

On Moving the Public

This analysis suggests that about-to-die images act in ways that are not always in keeping with the aspired parameters of journalistic and public action. Instead, they point toward the healthy growth of an alternative truth value underlying journalism's coverage of unsettled public events and people's responses to them, a truth-value etched on the back of formalistic visual impulses associated with the emotions, the imagination, and contingency and the public engagement they generate.

It is worth returning to the deaths that reside at the core of about-to-die images. Though the referent of their display—death—is definitive, finished, and graphic, death's visual relay in these pictures remains suggestive, in process, and unclear. This makes people's crafting of meaning—the lending of a workable sense or significance to what they see—a critical part of their engagement because they must make an unseen death meaningful. While meaning is hard to measure and appears more fleetingly than not, it arises, said anthropologist Victor Turner, when "we try to put what culture and language have crystallized from the past together with what we feel, wish and think about our present point in life."[11] Though meaning making about death involves "maintaining an attachment to a problematic object *in advance* of its loss,"[12] in this case its visual loss, the continuous and repeated crafting of affective and extrarational interpretations of what people see and imagine seems to fuel engagement with the images. Because the image's incomplete, unstable, and permeable nature provides an ongoing opportunity to air and try out different meanings for unsettled events—as Jerome Bruner observed, "to be in the subjunctive mode is to be trafficking in human possibilities rather than in settled certainties"— journalists, news executives, officials, politicians, and viewers are thus able to use these pictures.[13] They are used to articulate emotional responses to what is shown, experiment with imagined sequences of action, consider the possibility of chance and surprise, and play with suggestion and implication, all as an attempt to lend significance to death. Drawing from the oft-quoted Greek Stoic philosopher Epictetus who said nearly two thousand years ago that "men are not moved by things but by the views which they take of them,"[14] these pictures thus encourage the sidestepping of one true and absolute explanation, unsatisfying in the best of cases when addressing death, for the entertainment of multiple interpretations about it. Because death resists authoritative statements about what its images depict, the "as if" makes the flux of manifold meanings about death a viable alternative for engagement. And because meaning making is primarily an imaginative, affective, suggestive, and extrarational process, it leans on those tools of relay most helpful in drawing on those impulses.

All of this becomes even more central as time moves on, where the emotions, imagination, and contingency have always been central to memory work. This means that what emerges as relevant at an event's unfolding persists and prevails in heightened form over time. The generation of multiple interpretations and affective and extrarational meanings continues into memory, where people continue to engage with the same images, transporting them into diverse scenarios about social life.

It is worth considering the central impulses that come to the fore in this focus on engagement and meaning: relying on viewers for closure, about-to-die images invite people to use the emotions, the imagination, and contingency to complete what is not seen in different ways. In each case, the "as if" displaces the "as is."

Moving the Public through Emotions

The "as if" was shown here to build on the complexity of emotional response, underscoring the specious character of the distinction between emotion and reason and the trope's reliance on emotions for its sustenance. It is telling that the word *emotion* comes from the Latin for *emovere*, which means "to move" or "to move out," for though emotional cues do not have to be dramatic and may signal little more than a piecemeal attachment or fleeting sign of pity, they are nonetheless central in moving the public. Because the involvement of the emotions in images of impending death draws not from an interior notion of emotional response but from an understanding of emotions that resides in social and cultural practice, this sociality of emotions, Durkheimian in origin, is what holds people together in some ways and keeps them separate in others. As Nancy Chodorow observed, emotions give shape to the irrational, but the irrational has its place in meaning making.[15]

About-to-die images play firstly to the human anguish and suffering that is central to the depiction of impending death. This means that their reliance on emotional response is not suggestive or latent, but shouts for attention from the public. They play secondly to the fear of death that underlies many engagements with its depiction, underscoring a profound but often unarticulated investment that death activates. In the space between suggestibility and certainty, these images drive a panoply of emotional cues, none of which are easily predictable but all of which position journalists, news executives, officials, politicians, and viewers in some emotional stance vis-à-vis what they see. In her discussion of photographs of Palestinian resistance to the Intifada, Ariella Azoulay noted that pictures of violence draw public involvement because the lack of resolution in the action that they depict offers the still-redeemable hope of responsive action. Because the people undergoing violence "are still present there at the time I'm watching them, my viewing of these photographs is less susceptible to becoming immoral."[16] The persistent and repeated watching that tends to accompany these photos likewise suggests that the formalistic aspects of the trope help mitigate the guilt of looking at what they depict, establishing the opportunity for a public engagement in which at least some people can temporarily assume more moral, compassionate, and responsible parameters of looking. In this regard, the about-to-die image can arouse compassion, grief, mourning, loss, sadness, anger, speculation, hope for resolution, pity, betrayal, indignation, relief, pleasure, responsibility, celebration, empathy, and sympathy. Conversely, however, that same place for engagement can prolong a public desire for revenge, an overload of horror, or a shutdown through indifference. As Lauren Berlant remarked more generally about the display of suffering:

> Scenes of vulnerability produce a desire to withhold compassionate attachment, to be irritated by the scene of suffering in some way. Repeatedly, we witness someone's desire to not connect, sympathize or recognize an obligation to the sufferer; to refuse engagement with the scene or to minimize its effects; to misread it conveniently; to snuff or drown it out with pedantically shaped phrases or carefully designed apartheids; not to

rescue or help; to go on blithely without conscience; to feel bad for the sufferers, but only so that they will go away quickly.[17]

The same image thus can make possible guilt, hopelessness, resentment, horror, traumatic reenactment, fear of what might be, acting out, distraction, indifference, voyeurism, sadism, disaffection, disgust, rejection of the inevitable, and shock. This simultaneous invocation of what might seem like mirror sides of the emotional landscape—evoking indignation, compassion, pleasure, and relief, on one side, and terror, vengeance, disgust, and disconnection, on the other—underscores the broad reach of the trope's suggestibility.

The fact that the emotional cues activated by the about-to-die image can spread in contradictory directions, signaling both hope and terror simultaneously, suggests that much-repeated fears about compassion fatigue may be off mark. As Stanley Cohen noted, "Baths fill up and overflow; cultures and minds don't."[18] Rather, the about-to-die image channels ready emotional cues in different directions: mobilizing an emotional landscape whose vessels are certain in their ability to front emotional response but unpredictable in terms of which response they raise, about-to-die images thus can be relied on to move the public but in seemingly random ways. And yet, such capricious activity may be more systematic than it seems. For as Lauren Berlant continued, "What if it turns out that compassion and coldness are not opposites at all but are two sides of a bargain that the subjects of modernity have struck with structural inequality?"[19]

This suggests that these images act as a trigger for emotional release, regardless of which emotions they set loose. Involvement and engagement, then, are as important for the fact of their mobilization as for the content of what they stimulate.

Moving the Public through the Imagination

This book has demonstrated how imagined sequences of action drive the public's engagement with images of impending death. This attachment to imagination and fantasy—lauded by a range of scholars like Benedict Anderson, Ernesto Laclau, Chantal Mouffe, and Arjun Appadurai—is seen as functional to the extrarational processes of meaning making, echoing Hannah Arendt's view that "imagination alone enables us to see things in their proper perspective. ... It is the only inner compass we have."[20]

Facilitating a way to engage with emotion-laden depictions that often overwhelm their viewers and offering a subjunctive space in which to temporarily suspend belief in what is known, imagination allows journalists, news executives, officials, politicians, and viewers to construct imaginary, illogical, and fantastical ends to impending death. This is critical because the engagement with about-to-die images suggests that people are not necessarily interested in a clear linkage between what they see and understand. Though at issue here are existential questions about the escape to fantasy—as one observer noted, "the present becomes so uncertain that it devours the future and prohibits thinking about it except as fantasy"—the unseen and ambiguous deaths of the individuals in these pictures facilitate a widespread willingness to proffer illogical and fantastical interpretations of what is seen: people reverse time, construct imaginary sequences of action, disbelieve what is said to be depicted, and imagine that death does not occur.[21] This suggests that at times journalists, news executives, officials, politicians, and viewers all want the engagement that about-to-die images provide because it allows them *not* to connect understanding with depiction. Used equally to generate compassion or indifference, to accuse, distance, critique, empathize, ridicule, manipulate, obscure, deny, neutralize, and dissociate, fantasy and the imagination thus capture public involvement but inextrarational, sometimes illogical, and often contradictory ways. And yet, as C. S. Lewis said long ago, "Reason is the natural order of truth, but imagination is the organ of meaning."[22] The public's capacity to make meaning out of these images hinges on a nurturing of the imagination.

It might be assumed that much of the draw to the imagination has to do with the lack of definitive detail attached to many of these images. Jacques Rancierre noted as much in his discussion of images of suffering on television:

> We do not see too many suffering bodies on the screen. But we do see too many nameless bodies, too many bodies incapable of returning the gaze that we direct at them, too many bodies that are an object of speech without themselves having a chance to speak....The visual [becomes] the lot of multitudes and the verbal the privilege of the few.[23]

As this book has shown, however, imagination flourishes even when such detail is in hand. Often, it flourishes the most when the accompanying informational detail is extensive and explicit.

Imagination is particularly relevant in moving the public because the about-to-die image underscores a paradoxical relationship with death's visibility. While images of violence and death frequent nearly every other visual domain—including cinema, television, and the Internet—in journalism their appearance remains problematic. Instead, by reflecting a repeated choice to gravitate away from death's graphic depiction, contemporary news remains one of the tamer existing visual landscapes. On the face of things, this tameness offsets the notions of newsworthiness that are thought to drive news coverage, where instead of portraying what is most central about news events involving death—consider how the news value of a disaster decreases when people do *not* die—images of impending death stop short of full documentation and visually treat death less explicitly than in words.

But on closer consideration, the persistent gravitation to the imaginary sequence of nondeath suggests a coping mechanism among viewers toward death's inevitability and the fears it raises. Not only do people often not want to see but they refuse the interpretive cues that might direct them to a more rational confirmation of death. This suggests a mode of engagement with the news that is not only emotional but that neutralizes, contests, challenges, and refutes what is shown in either suggestive or elaborated fashion. The impact of this on meaning making involving the unsettled events of the news suggests an active kick-back from people who will absorb what they want about public events, regardless of what journalism provides them.

Moving the Public through Contingency

It has long been argued that people find possibility in moments of suspended action, so that the surfacing of contingency around images of impending death suggests a resistance to accepting the closure of death that they signify. While contingency resists a more widespread gravitation in the news toward the progressively narrowed interpretations of its public events, it also suggests a high degree of unpredictability, interpretive flux, and idiosyncrasy as a way of lending meaning to journalism's unsettled events. Surfacing at the time of an image's initial display, the flux characteristic of contingency perseveres as the image moves across time, where it continues to complicate, modify, and qualify what is shown. The link between what people see and what they understand thus remains unstable, unpredictable, and further amenable to changing agendas. Seen as "beyond or resistant to meaning,"[24] contingency—and its association with chance, play, experimentation, suggestion, possibility, implication, and the ephemeral—thereby upsets the rational and progressive sequencing of events which journalism is thought to provide and which has long underscored journalism's own identification as a project of modernity.

And yet utility can be found in recognizing the play to contingency in journalism. As Richard Rorty noted more than twenty years ago, the recognition of contingency "leads to a picture of intellectual and moral progress as a history of increasingly useful metaphors rather than of increasing understanding of how things really are."[25] The persistence of this suggestive and playful impulse delays a shutting down of interpretation that is central to the settling in of reasoned information, inviting journalists, news executives, officials, politicians, and viewers to cycle instead at their own pace through an interpretive landscape brimming with hope, implication, impossibility, hypothesis, chance, and liminality. In Walter Benjamin's words, "No matter how artful the photographer, no matter how carefully posed his subject, the beholder feels an irresistible urge to search such a picture for the tiny spark of contingency, of the Here and Now, with which reality has so to speak seared the subject."[26]

Relevant here is the relation between contingency and death. Mary Ann Doane has been among those charting such a relationship, which she contended is characteristically "unassimilable to meaning": "The embarrassment of contingency is that it is everywhere and that it everywhere poses the threat of an evacuation of meaning. The concept of the event provides a limit—not everything is filmable—and reinvests the contingent with significance. The contingent is, in effect, harnessed."[27] The difficulty, though, in making death meaningful reinvests the process of meaning making as well. Because even the event cannot sustain a defense against the inevitability of death, people continue to engage with these images, invoking contingency in their attempts to generate meaning both about the deaths they see and those they imagine. Such a prolonged engagement is supported elsewhere too, where keeping death unfinished and incomplete has been regarded a more effective therapeutic intervention than encouraging those who grieve to move past its contingent state.[28]

The engagement with these images at times thereby suspends the provision of closure. It also forces viewers away from an image's specifics—the politics of its taking, the particulars of its context, the gravity of its impact. As people sustain open endedness in their interpretations of what they see, the "as if" thus becomes preferable, even when it leads the public in interminable directions.

On the Value of the "As If"

The American pragmatist philosopher William James stipulated the need to address the value-added status of the "as is," when he asked at the turn of the nineteenth century "under what circumstances do we think things are real?" The flip side of his question, however, focused equally on the implications of the "as if," where, in his corresponding life as a psychologist, he introduced the concept of "acting as if" as a therapeutic intervention for individuals wanting to move beyond their own psychic limitations.[29] This book has elaborated multiple circumstances in which the former fails to make its mark and the latter emerges as robust and healthy. While it is important to remember that the "as if" piggybacks off of the "as is" and cannot thrive without it, the emphasis here on the subjunctive voice, considered out of the shadow of its more recognizable indicative cousin, is worth considering in terms of what it suggests more broadly about news images, journalism, the public, and unsettled events.

The "As If" and News Images

This book has offered parameters by which a certain subset of images surfaces in the news. It has demonstrated that these images work in partial relationship to the events they depict rather than, as words do, attempt to provide a full and complete accounting of them. These images are driven by contingency rather than, as words claim, by certainty, and their fuel is imagination and the emotions, not rational reasoning. Significantly, the more these images are seen, the more opportunities they offer for people to work through them in lending meaning to unsettled events.

How representative is this of news images more broadly? Though a strategically selected universe of pictures of impending death formed this book's core, my analysis of these photos—and the questions, patterns, problems, and inconsistencies associated with their use—reflects much about the workings of the full range of news images. How much one needs to know in order to make sense of what one sees underlies the engagement with news images of all kinds, suggesting that as they are used by people to make sense of events in the world, there is need to better chart the climate and the processes through which certain depictions emerge as critical landmarks of news coverage.

For every news image, not only those of impending death, can at best offer only a slice of what has happened, that "decisive moment" of depiction that calls on viewers to interpret what is left unseen. While about-to-die images ask viewers to fill in an unseen death, other images require other acts of completion: images of families reunited after long absences invite a consideration of the joy that ensues once the camera turns off. Athletic teams shown vying in competition compel attention to unseen victories, regardless of whether or not the image shows them. The multiple partners to this equation—journalists, news executives, politicians, officials, and viewers—thus conspire to make it work. How journalism deals with the problematic copresence of a contingent and incomplete image and accompanying features that attempt to render it more complete than it seems thus goes far beyond the about-to-die image to the broad trappings of news pictures. And how people respond to that copresence is a project fundamental to the workings of the public sphere, more broadly.

This book thus calls for a closer examination of the subjunctive dimensions of news images of multiple kinds. Journalism and its visuals have existed for too long in an uneven relationship that has kept images fastened as second-class citizens. The "as if" offers an opportunity to clarify what is singular about journalism's visual relays and to position those attributes squarely on the table as a choice equal to but different from words.

The "As If" and Journalism

Every time images appear, they have been thought to offer a "new structure of relations between the visible and invisible and between the visible and sayable."[30] If this is so, then what do images of impending death reveal about the workings of the news, writ broadly? Many attributes of about-to-die images surface to a lesser degree in other kinds of nonvisual news relays, and though this analysis focused on U.S. journalism many of the patterns seen here surface globally as well.

Consider how many tools of news delivery run as if they are evidentiary when they are only suggestive, appear as discrete and particular records but stake out universal and generalizable claims, offer human entry points that fail to clarify the structural circumstances at large, emphasize the categorical at the expense of clarifying the nuance, or position themselves as suppositions rather than description. The existence of verbal, visual, audio, and multimodal news relays that operate in much the same way as the about-to-die image suggests that a play to the powerful over the mundane, the memorable over the forgettable, the formalistic over the content driven, the categorical over the discrete, the generalizable over the specific, and the familiar over the novel reflects a wide-ranging set of preferences in journalism. Though U.S. journalism has long been critiqued for its emphasis on such parameters, and particularly their emergence in the coverage of unsettled events,[31] the repetitive nature of their surfacing suggests a more engrained and widespread presence than might originally be assumed. For instance, hypothetical columns, cartoons depicting imaginary situations, investigative stories speculating on potential scenarios, op-eds pondering underdeveloped angles to existing coverage, even editorials anticipating action yet to unfold, all suggest that the "as if" regularly permeates the journalistic record. Moreover, the suggestive, porous, and unstable news relay, typical of the about-to-die image, surfaces regularly as a memory tool, where journalism's memory work across all of its relays is accomplished by the more open and permeable journalistic tools.

It thus may be that the news incorporates more of the "as if" than recognized and that people respond in kind to its display and repeated circulation. Crafting a counterenvironment to the landscape of cool appraisals by which the information environment is presumed to work and understanding thought to be achieved, a parallel world of news work thus may be thriving at the same time, one that makes engagement and the crafting of multiple meanings as primary as information relay and definitive understanding.

To that end, this book calls for a fuller account of journalism's incomplete, ambiguous, suggestive, and unstable relays of the world as much as its finished, clear, and definitive ones. Though theorists of late modernity have long charted a world equally drawn by reality and imagination, by reason and emotion, by evidence and implication, and by certainty and contingency, journalism still remains primarily a modernist project. Moving journalism beyond its modernist moorings, where it can better navigate a digitally mediated environment that left modernity behind some time ago, may stead it well moving forward.

The "As If" and the Public

Central here has been the tenet that people who see images of impending death seem to show involvement and engagement regardless of the information they receive—in quality, quantity, scope, demeanor, pacing or timing. Though engagement works more stridently on a categorical than discrete level—offering cues for emotional, imagined, and contingent involvement in the news—the dictum here seems to be that more information can generate more emotional engagement, more variable interpretation and more sustained extrarational efforts at meaning making. Such a paradoxical situation, which undercuts the longstanding insistence on full information as necessary to the existence of a healthy body politic that coalesces around a reasoned understanding of public events, raises the need to recognize uninformed or less-informed engagement as a thriving public response to the news. Moreover, though notions of a public driven not necessarily by rational reasoning has always lurked at the boundaries of journalism's world—the tabloids, the feature sections of newspapers, and the TV magazines come to mind—this analysis suggests that the "as if" resides firmly within the center of mainstream journalism, asserting itself around events thought to be in most need of full information relay and reasoned public response.

What does this suggest about understandings of the public moving forward? First, it raises the possibility that the news could be envisioned as a multiply tiered journalistic relay, where engagement might precede information. Critical because notions of a healthy public sphere still remain wedded to the relay of reasoned information, such a scenario might accommodate the "as if" as a prevailing voice that powerfully draws in public engagement, often just when information and the "as is" are thought to be most critical to the maintenance of a healthy body politic. In fact, a two-tiered relay may already be in existence, by which the nonnews sites of the digital environment first capture people's involvement in breaking news and traditional journalists follow up with a fuller informational context. But journalism itself can do better in understanding the mechanics of that initial relay and anticipating its resonance for the public.

Second, although this analysis, primarily conducted through texts, can at best project public response moving forward, the centrality here of the "as if" minimizes the centrality of information in news relay. Despite journalism's identification as a project associated with modernity and related notions of the public sphere, which insist on information as conducive to democracy's effective functioning, this analysis raises the possibility that the information that people are interested in securing to understand public events is not automatic or assured. While information sometimes matters and other times does not, the ongoing readiness for involvement in journalism's unsettled events in some way, regardless of what is understood about them, points to a different field of expectations surrounding the intersection between journalism and the public. This suggests that maintaining a healthy body politic depends not only on the words that bring people together in rational ways but on the pictures that make them feel that being together is an endeavor worth pursuing, or not.

This book thus calls for a fuller contemplation of what public engagement without full information might mean for existing understandings of the body politic. What are the implications of meaning making without full understanding, of an information relay that rests happily on the "as if" of public investment in the news? Although any assumption of public response needs further empirical analysis, the suggestion here that the longstanding focus on informed publics may have left behind multiple kinds of viewers who are involved but not necessarily informed, engaged but not necessarily understanding what they see, is worth further consideration. Just as reason is not purely cognitive and engagement not purely emotional, the broader and more variegated landscape on which responses of all kinds take place deserves closer attention.

The "As If" and Unsettled Events

This book has argued that the unsettled nature of multiple kinds of public events does not necessarily get settled despite its reliance on one of journalism's most powerful and memorable visual depictions. Though the images considered here pushed for closure and offered journalists, news executives, officials, politicians, and viewers manifold ways to interpret and complete what was not depicted, many of the events discussed in these pages remain unsettled even today.

This raises the important question of how many public events ever get settled to the satisfaction of those who track their unfolding. Though journalism has long presented itself as an institution dedicated to providing clarity and watertight explanations of what happens in the world, there is evidence to suggest that some events never move past their unsettled status either because the nature of journalistic intervention is not nuanced enough to accommodate it or because journalists are too strategic to let closure occur and public engagement wane. As Keren Tenenboim-Weinblatt showed, the narrative strategies for news making are themselves used to delay closure as journalists strategically transform self-contained news stories into episodes of larger serial stories.[32]

Though the "as if" may seem to fit the unsettled events of the news better than its relay of the everyday, a closer look at journalism reveals that a repeated reliance on speculation, imagination, emotional engagement, and contingency regularly reopens events that seem to have reached clarity at an earlier point in time. From reconsiderations of the Martin Luther King assassination to the debacle over weapons of mass destruction in the war with Iraq, events at one point considered closed were later examined anew. In fact, the capacity to reopen events long thought settled is considered among the high points of journalistic practice: for instance, when the U.S. Justice Department in 2004 reopened its investigation of the murder of Emmett Till, an African American youth killed in a lynch mob in 1955, journalistic professional forums celebrated the case's reopening and many news organizations responded by publishing pictures of his mutilated body that had only before appeared in the African American press. Other cases of wrongful court trials, involving the investigative efforts of students at Northwestern University and the University of Missouri, brought student journalists to the forefront of efforts to unsettle formerly settled events.[33]

This suggests that the unsettled nature of the journalistic record may be more widespread than assumed, that it regularly supports revisits by journalists over time, and that it remains a highly valued and sought after challenge for journalists reconsidering their own accounts of past events. Offering additional evidence about the uneasy combination of a seemingly settled event with unsettled parameters, the push for closure and certainty about news events may remain rhetorically important, but it is not the only route for engaging the events of the public sphere.

The territory of the "as if" is an invitational one: it summons possibility, chance, experimentation, hypothesis, play, elaboration, involvement, supposal, denial, liminality, impossibility, and speculation. Though it cannot exist without the "as is," the presence of the subjunctive voice in the U.S. news media crafts a landscape of far more internally contradictory impulses than might have originally been assumed.

Through the "as if," news images regularly do both more and less than expected. They do more because they allow journalists, news executives, officials, politicians, and viewers to engage with public events as much with their hearts and guts as with their brains. But they do less because the subjunctive voice still awaits widespread appreciation, its capacity to create a richer investment in the world still remaining largely untold. As scholars of the evolving landscapes on which meaning is crafted, we can do better than we have done till now. For investing in the "as if" promises to make the "as is" a bit more bearable, and given the volatility and uncertainty of much of today's world, that might not be such a bad thing.

Notes

Chapter 1

1. Roger Brown and James Kulik, "Flashbulb Memories," *Cognition* 5, 1977, 73–99.

2. Gotthold Ephraim Lessing, *Laocoon* (1776; reprint Noonday Press, 1961), 92. Although much debate has been generated by Lessing's distinction between arts that exist in time versus those that exist in space, I do not engage with it here because the about-to-die image draws from both.

3. Admittedly, these arguments bear differences though all target the moment replete with meaning. See Victor Burgin, "Diderot, Barthes, *Vertigo*," in Victor Burgin, J. Donald, and C. Kaplan (eds.), *Formations of Fantasy* (London: Methuen, 1986), 99; Terence Wright, *The Photography Handbook* (London: Routledge, 1999), 89; Harold Evans, *Pictures on a Page* (London: Heinemann, 1978), 20; Peter Burke, *Eyewitnessing: The Uses of Images as Historical Evidence* (Ithaca: Cornell University Press, 2001), 51, 143. Freezing has, of course, taken varying paces over time, in that early photography was much slower and unable to freeze the action at hand in ways recognizable today.

4. Susan Moeller, *Compassion Fatigue* (New York: Routledge, 1999), 39.

5. Roland Barthes centrally distinguished between denotation and connotation in *Image/Music/Text* (New York: Hill and Wang, 1977), 17–19. Graham Clarke, *The Photograph* (New York: Oxford University Press, 1997); Oliver Wendell Holmes, "The Stereoscope and the Stereograph," *Atlantic Monthly* 3 (June 1859), 739. William Henry Fox Talbot, *The Pencil of Nature* (1844–46; reprint New York: DeCapo Press, 1969); John Berger, "Understanding a Photograph," in John Berger and Jean Mohr, *Another Way of Looking* (London: Writer and Readers Publishing Cooperative, 1984). Admittedly, these terms are not fully coterminous, but I use them here as they reference a similar capacity

of the image to represent things "as they are." Stuart Hall, "The Determinations of News Photographs," in Stanley Cohen and Jock Young (eds.), *The Manufacture of News* (London: Sage, 1974), 176–190; Alan Sekula, "On the Invention of Photographic Meaning," in *Photography against the Grain* (1974; reprint Halifax: Press of the Nova Scotia College of Arts and Design, 1984); John Tagg, *The Burden of Representation: Essays on Photography and History* (Macmillan, 1988).

6. See, for instance, Glasgow University Media Group (GUMG), *Bad News* (London: Routledge and Kegan Paul, 1980) and *Really Bad News* (London: Routledge and Kegan Paul, 1982); Michael Schudson, *The Sociology of News* (New York: W. W. Norton, 2003) and *Why Democracies Need an Unlovable Press* (Cambridge: Polity, 2008); Peter Dahlgren, *Television and the Public Sphere: Citizenship, Democracy, and the Media* (London: Sage, 1995).

7. Hanno Hardt, "The Site of Reality: Constructing Photojournalism in Weimar Germany, 1928–1933," *Communication Review* 1(3), 1986, 373–402; Julianne Newton, *The Burden of Visual Truth* (Hillsdale, NJ: Lawrence Erlbaum, 2000); Caroline Brothers, *War and Photography* (London: Routledge, 1997); Michael Schudson, *Discovering the News* (New York: Basic Books, 1978).

8. Richard V. Ericson, Patricia M. Baranek and Janet B.L. Chang, *Representing Order* (Toronto: University of Toronto Press, 1991), 22.

9. Mike Smith, quoted in Loup Langton, *Photojournalism and Today's News* (Malden, MA: Wiley Blackwell, 2009), 96.

10. Arthur Max, AP Bureau Chief, Amsterdam, personal conversation, January 8, 2010.

11. John Hartley, *Popular Reality* (New York: St. Martin's Press, 1996), 196. Also see John Hartley, *Understanding News* (London: Methuen, 1982). See John Fiske, *Reading the Popular* (Boston: Unwin Hyman, 1989); S. Elizabeth Bird, *For Enquiring Minds* (Knoxville: University of Tennessee Press, 1992); James Carey, "The Dark Continent of American Journalism," in Robert Manoff and Michael Schudson (eds.), *Reading the News* (New York: Pantheon, 1986), 146–196; Kevin Barnhurst and John Nerone, *The Form of News* (New York: Guilford, 2001). John Taylor, *Body Horror: Photojournalism, Catastrophe, and War* (Manchester: Manchester University Press, 1998); Moeller, *Compassion Fatigue;* Jean Seaton, *Carnage and the Media* (London: Allen Lane, 2005); Eleanor Singer and Phyllis Endreny, *Reporting on Risk* (New York: Russell Sage Foundation, 1993); Carolyn Kitch and Janice Hume, *Journalism in a Culture of Grief* (New York: Routledge, 2007).

12. Bonnie Brennen, "Photojournalism: Historical Dimensions to Contemporary Debates," in Stuart Allan (ed.), *The Routledge Companion to News and Journalism* (London: Routledge, 2010), 71–81. Also see Stuart Allan, *Online News* (Maidenhead: Open University Press, 2006); and Mark Deuze, *Media Work: Digital Media and Society* (Cambridge, UK: Polity, 2007).

13. Hall, "Determinations of News Photographs"; Annette Kuhn, *Family Secrets: Acts of Memory and Imagination* (London: Verso, 1995), 11–12.

14. Michael Griffin, "The Great War Photographs," in Bonnie Brennen and Hanno Hardt (eds.), *Picturing the Past* (Urbana: University of Illinois Press, 199), 147. David Perlmutter, *Photojournalism and Public Policy: Icons of Outrage in International Crises* (New York: Prager, 1998). James Fentress and Chris Wickham, *Social Memory* (Cambridge:

Basil Blackwell, 1992), 58–59. Also see Barbie Zelizer, "Reading the Past against the Grain: The Shape of Memory Studies," *Critical Studies in Mass Communication,* 12(2), June 1995, 214–39. Relevant here is Frederic Bartlett's notion of the schema—"an active organization of past reactions or past experiences" which structures recall [*Remembering* (Cambridge: Cambridge University Press, 1932)].

15. Much of this work, called ekphrasis, has established a register of traits that translate the qualities of images—they are simple, memorable, dramatic—into academic terms. See, for instance, W.J.T. Mitchell, *Picture Theory* (Chicago: University of Chicago Press, 1993) and *What Do Pictures Want?* (Chicago: University of Chicago Press, 2005); Jonathan Crary, *Techniques of the Observer: On Vision and Modernity in the Nineteenth Century* (Cambridge, MA: MIT Press, 1991); Paul Messaris, *Visual Literacy: Images, Mind, and Reality* (Boulder, CO: Westview Press, 1994) and *Visual Persuasion: The Role of Images in Advertising* (Thousand Oaks, CA: Sage, 1997). A rich scholarly repository also tracks the various impulses associated with vision, including clarity of thought, agreement, belief, and a metaphor for both position and perspective. See, for instance, Richard Rorty, *Philosophy and the Mirror of Nature* (Princeton, NJ: Princeton University Press, 1981); Barthes, *Image/Music/Text* and *Camera Lucida* (London: Hill and Wang, 1981); Martin Jay, *Downcast Eyes: The Denigration of Vision in Twentieth-Century French Thought* (Berkeley: University of California Press, 1993).

16. Mary Warren Marien, *Photography and Its Critics: A Cultural History, 1839–1900* (Cambridge: Cambridge University Press, 1997), 90. Also see Clement Greenberg, *Collected Essays and Criticism,* vol. 2 (Chicago: University of Chicago Press, 1986).

17. Richard Rorty, *Contingency, Irony, and Solidarity* (Cambridge: Cambridge University Press, 1989); Judith Butler, Ernesto Laclau, and Slavoj Zizek, *Contingency, Hegemony, Universality* (London: Verso Press, 2000).

18. Michele Barrett, *Imagination in Theory: Culture, Writing, Words and Things* (New York: New York University Press, 1999), 76. Nancy Armstrong strikingly documents a similar development in 19th-century British fiction, where in domains of Victorian writing not usually aligned with realism, the image supplanted the word as the grounding of fiction and photography authorized fiction as a truth-telling medium (*Fiction in the Age of Photography* [Cambridge, MA: Harvard University Press, 1999]). Thanks to Ruth Anolik for drawing my attention to this book.

19. John Stuart Mill, *On Liberty* (1859; reprint Cambridge: Cambridge University Press, 1998); Jurgen Habermas, *The Structural Transformation of the Public Sphere* (Cambridge, MA: MIT Press, 1989); Karl Popper, *The Logic of Scientific Discovery* (London: Hutchinson, 1959).

20. Raymond Williams, "Structures of Feeling," *Marxism and Literature* (New York: Oxford University Press, 1978), 128–135.

21. Rorty, *Contingency, Irony, and Solidarity,* 189; Roger Silverstone, *Media and Morality* (Cambridge: Polity Press, 2007), 46; George E. Marcus, *The Sentimental Citizen: Emotion in Democratic Politics* (University Park, PA: Pennsylvania State University Press, 2002), 4; Lauren Berlant, *The Female Complaint: The Unfinished Business of Sentimentality in American Culture* (Durham, NC: Duke University Press, 2008), and "The Subject of True Feeling," in Sara Ahmed et al. (eds.), *Transformations: Thinking Through Feminism* (London: Routledge, 2000), 33–47. These concerns have also been discussed even earlier:

for instance, the 18th-century French mathematician and philosopher Jean d'Alembert argued for a "system of knowledge" drawn equally from reason, imagination, and memory (see Jean d'Alembert, "Discours preliminaire des editeurs," in *Encyclopedie, ou Dictionnaire raisonne des scences, des arts et des métiers* (Paris: Durand), tr. Richard Schwab, *Preliminary Discourse to the Encyclopedia of Diderot* (Chicago: University of Chicago Press, 1995).

22. Catherine A. Lutz and Lila Abu-Lughod (eds.), *Language and the Politics of Emotion* (Cambridge: Cambridge University Press, 1990), 1. Barbara Koziak, *Retrieving Political Emotion* (University Park, PA: Pennsylvania State University Press, 2000), 12.

23. George E. Marcus, W. Russell Neuman, and Michael MacKuen, *Affective Intelligence and Political Judgment* (Chicago: University of Chicago Press, 2000), 1, 9, 124–125. Also see Sianne Ngai, *Ugly Feelings* (Cambridge, MA: Harvard University Press, 2005); Antonio Damasio, *Descartes' Error: Emotion, Reason, and the Human Brain* (New York: Avon Books, 1994); Sara Ahmed, *The Cultural Politics of Emotion* (New York: Routledge, 2004). See also the University of Chicago's feel tank http://www.feeltankchicago.net/. Thanks to Heather Love for bringing this to my attention.

24. Barry Richards, "News and the Emotional Sphere," in Stuart Allan (ed.), *The Routledge Companion to News and Journalism* (London: Routledge, 2010), 304.

25. See, for instance, Nazila Fathi, "In a Death Seen Around the World, A Symbol of Iranian Protests," *New York Times,* June 22, 2009, 1.

26. The quote is from World News Tonight executive producer John Banner, cited in *New York Observer,* June 22, 2009, and discussed on "The Neda Video Becomes a Symbol of Iran's Unrest," *Greater Boston's Beat the Press,* WGBH, June 26, 2009. "Neda: Turning Point for Conflict Reporting?" *Photo District News,* June 22, 2009.

27. "Neda: Turning Point…"

28. Howard Chua-Eoan, "The Moment," *Time,* July 6, 2009, 11; stand-alone picture, *Wall Street Journal,* June 22, 2009, 1.

29. Fathi, "In a Death Seen Around the World," 1; Mams Taylor, *United for Neda Video,* 2009; *A Death in Tehran,* Frontline, November 2009.

30. Daniel Farber, CBS News, June 23, 2009. Fathi, "In a Death Seen Around the World," 1. "Neda Becomes Rallying Cry for Iranian Protests," CNN, June 22, 2009; "Neda: Turning Point…"; "Voices of Iranian Women," *USA Today,* June 23, 2009, 10A; Jessica Ravitz, "Neda: Latest Iconic Image to Inspire," CNN, June 24, 2009; Bill Mitchell, "Iconic Video from Tehran Protests Demands New Skills of Journalists," poynteronline, posted June 22, 2009, 10.36 am. In many of these attempts at building context, pictures of the earlier images were reshown alongside the image of Agha-Soltan. "Time Magazine Names Iran's Neda as One of 2009's Top Heroes," *Time,* December 10, 2009. Agha-Soltan received the number two place in its list, despite a massive online campaign to generate sufficient votes so as to move her into person-of-the-year status. "Our Laureat: Neda of Iran," *Washington Post,* October 10, 2009, 2. Among the 700 postings to the paper following its editorial were multiple observations about the inability to receive a Noble award posthumously.

31. "Neda Agha Soltan's Family Accuse Iran of her Killing," BBC News, December 4, 2009; Bill Mitchell, "Story of Neda's Death Reveals Seven Elements of Next-Step Journalism," poynteronline, posted June 24, 2009, 4.48 pm; Kara Miller (Metrowest Daily

News), quoted on "The Neda Video Becomes a Symbol of Iran's Unrest," *Greater Boston's Beat the Press,* WGBH, June 26, 2009; "Neda: Turning Point...": Megan Garber, "Citizen Journalism vs. 'Tragi-Porn,'" *Columbia Journalism Review,* November 9, 2009; Chua-Eoan, "The Moment," 11.

32. "There Will be Blood: Neda Agha Soltan's Post-Mortem Image in the Media," *Muslimah Media Watch,* posted by Fatemah Fakhraie, June 25, 2009. "She was young, slender and pretty, and so Western media are obsessed with watching her die over and over." "Must Brown People Be Martyred for Americans to be Motivated?" whattamisaid. blogspot.com, posted by Tami, June 22, 2009, 10.30 am.

33. Cited in "Neda Becomes Rallying Cry"; Robert F. Worth and Nazila Fathi, "Iranians Gather in Grief, Then Face Police Batons," *New York Times,* July 31, 2009, 4; cited in Fathi, "In a Death Seen Around the World," 1; pictures appended to "Perspectives," *Newsweek,* July 13, 2009; "An Iranian Martyr," People, July 6, 2009, 64; "What Citizens Saw: The Year in Pictures," *Time,* December 21, 2009, 58; Mams Taylor, *United for Neda Video,* 2009.

34. Mark Johnson, "The Imaginative Basis of Meaning and Cognition," in Susanne Kuchler and Walter Melion (eds.), *Images of Memory: On Remembering and Representation* (Washington, DC: Smithsonian Institution Press, 1991), 85; John Dewey, *Art as Experience* (New York: Capricorn Books, 1958), 348.

35. Walter Benjamin, "Art in the Age of Mechanical Reproduction," in *Illuminations* (New York: Schocken Books, 1988), 83–110, and "Little History of Photography," [1931] in Marcus Bullock and Michael Jennings (eds.), *Selected Writings,* vol. 2 (Cambridge, MA: Belknap Press, 1996), 512; Roland Barthes, "The Third Meaning," *Image/Music/Text,* 52–68, and *Camera Lucida;* Susan Sontag, *On Photography* (New York: Dell, 1977), 23; Wright, *Photography Handbook,* 87.

36. Barbie Zelizer, "The Voice of the Visual in Memory," in Kendall Phillips, *Framing Public Memory* (Tuscaloosa: University of Alabama Press, 2004), 157–186.

37. Clifford Geertz, *The Interpretation of Culture* (New York: Basic Books, 1977).

38. This definition is paraphrased from *Webster's New Universal Unabridged Dictionary.* Also see Emile Benveniste, *Problems in General Linguistics* (Miami: University of Miami Press, 1973) and L. M. Berk, *English Syntax: From Word to Discourse* (New York: Oxford University Press, 1999).

39. Slavoj Zizek, "I Hear You with My Eyes," in Renata Salaci and Slavoj Zizek (eds.), *Gaze and Voice as Love Objects* (Durham, NC: Duke University Press, 1996), 93.

40. Prominent here was the German philosopher Hans Vaihinger [*The Philosophy of "As If"* (1924; reprinted London: Routledge, 1952)], who argued that people willingly accepted imagined action so as to live more peacefully in an irrational world. But also see Cora Lenore Williams, *As If: A Philosophical Phantasy* (San Francisco: Paul Elder, 1914). The phrase was also used to signify the "as if personality" in psychiatry in the 1930s and 1940s, one who conveyed a lack of authenticity in dealings with others (Helene Deutsch, "Some Forms of Emotional Disturbance and Their Relationship to Schizophrenia," *Psychoanalytic Quarterly* 11, 1942, 301–321, while Vaihinger's work was adopted in the mid-1960s as a basis for personal construct psychology [George Kelly, "The Language of Hypothesis," in B. Maher (ed.), *Clinical Psychology and Personality: The Collected Papers of George Kelly* (1964; reprinted New York: Wiley, 1969), 147–162]. See too Lorraine

332 • Notes to pages 15–16

Hedtke and John Winslade, "The Use of the Subjunctive in Re-Membering Conversations with Those Who Are Grieving," *Omega* 50 (3), 2004–2005, 197–215.

41. Victor Turner, "Dewey, Dilthey, and Drama: An Essay in the Anthropology of Experience," in Victor Turner and Edward M. Bruner (eds.), *The Anthropology of Experience* (Urbana: University of Illinois Press, 1986), also *The Ritual Process* (Routledge and Kegan Paul, 1969); Roger D. Abrahams, "Ordinary and Extraordinary Experience," in Victor Turner and Edward M. Bruner (eds.), *The Anthropology of Experience* (Urbana: University of Illinois Press, 1986), 45–72; Jerome Bruner, *Actual Minds, Possible Worlds* (Cambridge, MA: Harvard University Press, 1986); Roger Silverstone, *Why Study the Media?* (Sage, 1999). Michael Schudson, "Deadlines, Datelines, and History," in Robert Manoff and Michael Schudson (eds.), *Reading the News* (Pantheon, 1986), 79–108; Barbie Zelizer, *"Flow" as Ideological Facilitator: The "As If" of Journalistic Performance* (M.A. Thesis, Hebrew University of Jerusalem, 1982). Robin Wagner-Pacifici, *Theorizing the Standoff: Contingency in Action* (Cambridge, MA: Cambridge University Press, 2000), 3. As Charles E. Scott [*The Time of Memory* (State University of New York, 1999), 279] wrote. "The subjunctive mood belongs to states of affairs in which incompletion and contingency, something not stately or directly statable, are joined with statement and fact."

42. Popular songs titled "as if" have been composed and performed by American country singer Sara Evans, the R&B/pop vocal trio Blaque, and the British synthetic pop band La Roux, which called its song "As If by Magic." Movies included a 2009 documentary *Act As If* (dir. Melissa Johnson) which detailed the rise to fame of a Harvard basketball coach; books included an account of the James Bulger killing in the UK (Blake Morrison, *As If: A Crime, A Trial, A Question of Childhood* (London: St. Martin's Press, 1997); and television shows included a cult British comedy-drama series for Channel 4 (dir. John Cuthie and Barnaby Southcombe), broadcast from 2001 to 2004, and a short-lived two-episode U.S. series on UPN-TV, based on the British production, that ran in 2002 before being cancelled. The "As If" webcomic, which ran from 2001 to 2004, can be found at http://www.mimisgrotto.com/asif/index.html, while a blogging collective for intellectual freedom under the same name can be found at http://asifnews.blogspot.com/. The only two of these efforts which were pre 9/11 was Blaque's song, which came out in 2000, and Morrison's book, which came out in 1997. Additionally, the phrase received a popular tilt in the popular 1995 movie "Clueless" (dir. Amy Heckerling), when actress Alicia Silverstone used it to signify her unwillingness to reciprocate a suitor's attention. The association with the movie was so strong that one online slang dictionary traced the word's etymology to "Southern California 'Valley Girl' term."

43. Don McCullin, "Notes By a Photographer," in Emile Meijer and Joop Swart (eds.), *The Photographic Memory: Press Photography—Twelve Insights* (London: Quiller Press and World Press Photo, 1987), 11; Christian Caujolle, "The World Press Photo, the Press and Stereotypes," in Sebastio Salgado and Stephan Mayes, *This Critical Mirror* (New York: Thames and Hudson, 1995), 56; Barbie Zelizer, "On 'Having Been There': 'Eyewitnessing' as a Journalistic Key Word," *Critical Studies in Media Communication* 24(5), December 2007, 408–42.

44. Eric Meskauskas, quoted in Felicity Barringer, "Images of Death," *New York Times,* October 25, 1998, WK1; cited in Annie Lawson, "Editors Show Restraint with War Images," *The Guardian* (online), www.media.guardian.co.uk, posted March 31, 2003.

45. Time Editors, *Four Hours a Year* (New York: Time, Inc., 1936), 20, with similar comments made at the American Society of Newspaper Editors, the American Association of Teachers of Journalism, the British Institute of Journalists, and the National Union of Journalists; Roscoe Drummond, "Keeping Pace with the Picture Parade," *Quill,* June 1937, 11; see Barbie Zelizer, *Remembering to Forget: Holocaust Memory Through the Camera's Eye* (Chicago: University of Chicago Press, 1998), and "Journalism's Last Stand: Wirephoto and the Discourse of Resistance," *Journal of Communication* 45(2), spring 1995, 78–92. Some would maintain this has not changed much: consider how television reporting frontlines reporters while hiding photographers, even when both are in dangerous battle zones.

46. Byron Calame, "Pictures, Labels, Perception, and Reality" (The Public Editor), *New York Times,* July 3, 2005, 10.

47. See, for instance, A. Swofford, "Will You Flinch: Confronting the Images of War," *Columbia Journalism Review,* May/June 2003, 58–60; Bill Marinow, quoted in P. Nesbitt, "Designing for a Tragedy," *Crisis Journalism: A Handbook for Media Response* (New York: American Press Institute, October 2001), 23; Barbie Zelizer, "When War Is Reduced to a Photograph," in Stuart Allan and Barbie Zelizer (eds.), *Reporting War: Journalism and Wartime* (London: Routledge, 2004), 115–135.

48. Zelizer, "When War is Reduced to a Photograph."

49. Caujolle, "The World Press Photo," 56.

50. Philip Gefter, in Marianne Hirsch, "The Day Time Stopped," *Chronicle of Higher Education,* January 25, 2002, B11; Barbie Zelizer, "Journalism, Photography, and Trauma," in Barbie Zelizer and Stuart Allan (eds.), *Journalism After September 11* (London: Routledge, 2002), 48–68; quoted in David Hilbrand and Gail Shister, "A Flood of Images into Homes," *Philadelphia Inquirer,* March 27, 2003, A1, A20; Zelizer, "When War Is Reduced to a Photograph."

51. CNN, Fox News, and MSNBC initially declined to show the charred bodies being strung up and beaten by Iraqi crowds, while CBS and ABC showed them with cautionary notes. In a survey of the 20 highest circulating newspapers, *Editor and Publisher* found that only seven—including the *New York Times, Chicago Tribune, Philadelphia Inquirer, San Francisco Chronicle,* and *New York Post*—showed graphic front-page photos of the bodies (Charles Geraci, "Seven of Top 20 Papers Published Front-Page Fallujah Body Photos," *Editor and Publisher,* April 1, 2004). Moreover, the buzz among journalists, as reflected in editorial statements and ombudsmen columns, over what to do was noteworthy, offering readers an inside look at the decision making that went into the display or lack thereof of the photos. Justification often rested on comparisons likening the photos to those of Somalia, Vietnam, or Tiananmen Square, or even to the removal of Saddam Hussein's statue from Firdus Square.

52. Steve Capus, in Bill Carter and Jacques Steinberg, "Issues of Taste: To Portray the Horror, News Media Agonize," *New York Times,* April 1, 2004, A12; Roy Peter Clark, "You Be the Editor," poynteronline, posted April 1, 2004; Antonia Zerbisias, "Humanity Is First Casualty of War," *Toronto Star,* April 4, 2004, D10; Taylor, *Body Horror,* 7, 9, 14; Adam B. Kushner, "See No Evil," *The New Republic* (online), posted April 2, 2004.

53. Michael Walzer, "On the Role of Symbolism in Political Thought," *Political Science Quarterly* LXXXII (1967), 191–204; Murray Edelman, *Politics as Symbolic Action* (New York: Academic Press, 1971); Zelizer, *Remembering to Forget.*

54. In December of 2003, a NYT/CBS Poll found that 62% of Americans were in favor of seeing pictures of military caskets. Discussion of the Bush administration's ban was sparked by a Tami Silicio photo appended to "The Somber Task of Honoring the Fallen," *Seattle Times,* April 18, 2004, A1, and by photos taken by Defense Department photographers and displayed under a Freedom of Information Act request filed by Russ Kirk (see www.thememoryhole.com). "In Reversal, Obama Seeks to Block Abuse Photos," Associated Press, May 13, 2009, posted 9.30 pm.

55. Doris Graber, "Seeing Is Remembering: How Visuals Contribute to Learning from Television News," *Journal of Communication,* 40(2), 1990, 134–155; Messaris, *Visual Literacy;* David Freedberg and Vittorio Gallese, "Motion, Emotion, and Empathy in Esthetic Experience," *Trends in Cognitive Science* 11(5), March 2007, 197–203.

56. Barbara Norfleet, *Looking at Death* (Boston: David R. Godine, 1993); Jay Ruby, *Secure the Shadow: Death and Photography in America* (Cambridge, MA: MIT Press, 1999).

57. For instance, a 2008 study of photographs of death in the German and Australian press found only 4.5% of stories included photographs of a dead person (Folker Hanusch, "Valuing Those Close to Us," *Journalism Studies* 9(3), June 1, 2008, 341–356). See also Taylor, *Body Horror;* Jessica Fishman, *Documenting Death* (unpublished Ph.D Diss., University of Pennsylvania, 2001); Seaton, *Carnage and the Media;* Jessica Fishman and Carolyn Marvin, "Portrayals of Violence and Group Difference in Newspaper Photographs," *Journal of Communication* 53(1), February 2006, 32–44.

58. While a *Times Daily Mirror* poll, conducted by the Center for the People and the Press on March 24, 1993, asked respondents whether they agreed or disagreed with the idea that "TV news should just tell us about violent news but not show pictures of murder and war," and 50% of respondents disagreed, a decade later the public was less interested in graphic display: see Readers' Letters in the *Boston Globe* (October 6, 2001, A14), *Newsweek* (October 15, 2001, 15–16, and December 10, 2001, 16), and *Time* (October 22, 2001, 14, and November 5, 2001, 5). In December 2003, a NYT/CBS Poll found that 62% of Americans were in favor of seeing pictures of military caskets rather than bodies.

59. *Time*/CNN Poll, 2003; Pew Research Center for the People and the Press, April 5, 2004. Fifty percent of respondents said that the press did a good job of covering the events in Fallujah, while 21% felt that the images were too graphic.

60. "AP Explains Picture of Dying Marine," Associated Press, September 4, 2009, posted 10.30 am. In its statement, the AP noted that it was distributing the picture, taken a month earlier following an ambush in Afghanistan, because it was a document of war. Said the AP's director of photography, Santiago Lyon: "We feel it is our journalistic duty to show the reality of the war there, however unpleasant and brutal that sometimes is."

61. Sydney H. Schanberg, "Not a Pretty Picture: Why Don't U.S. Papers Show Graphic War Photos?" *News Photographer,* June 2005, 52–54; John Rowland, "Letters and Postcards," *News Photographer,* September 2005, 56; J. Max Robinson, "This Time, It's War," *Broadcasting and Cable Magazine,* July 9, 2007; "Talkback on Broadcasting and Cable," http://www.broadcastingcable.com/index.asp?layout=talkbackCommentsFull&talk_back_header_id=6450846&articleid=CA6458171#67785.

62. Randy Cohen, "Neda, Obama and the Power of Pictures," *New York Times,* June 29, 2009.

63. James Pinkerton, "The More the Public Knows the Better," *Newsday,* April 27, 2004, A41.

64. Ashok Malik, "Can CNN, BBC Get Away with This Corpse Show?" *The Indian Express,* December 30, 2004.

65. Antonia Zerbisias, "Humanity Is First Casualty of War," *Toronto Star,* 4 April 2004, D10.

66. I have discussed this in numerous places. See my "When War Is Reduced to a Photograph"; "Journalism, Photography, and Trauma"; and "Journalism through the Camera's Eye," in Stuart Allan (ed). *Journalism: Critical Issues* (Maidenhead, UK: Open University Press, 2005), 167–177.

67. Susan Sontag, in Neal Ascherson, "How Images Fail to Convey War's Horror," *Los Angeles Times Book Review,* March 16, 2003, R8.

68. Aristotle, *Poetics,* 1453; Barthes, *Camera Lucida* and *A Lover's Discourse* (New York: Hill and Wang, 1978).

69. See, for instance W. D. Lutz, "Language, Appearance, and Reality Doublespeak in 1984," in P.C. Boardman (ed.), *The Legacy of Language—A Tribute to Charlton Laird* (Reno: University of Nevada Press, 1987), 103–119; and Albert Bandura, "Selective Moral Disengagement in the Exercise of Moral Agency," *Journal of Moral Education* 31(2), 2002, 101–119.

70. Though the notion of news as spectacle has taken on renewed interest with the contemporary work of Jean Baudrillard, Guy de Bord, Frederic Jameson, and others, in fact spectacles of suffering were used as vehicles of social control over potentially aberrant populations since the earliest known crucifixions and other public executions. Presented as a morality play, such spectacles were used to keep the body politic in place through the usually compulsory viewing of human agony in real time and space, with the spectacle expected to "survive until a certain degree of stability had been reached" (Pieter Spierenburg, *The Spectacle of Suffering* [Cambridge: Cambridge University Press, 1984], 202). Though the copresence of spectators and sufferers persists as the most powerful circumstance for witnessing, made evident in the theatrical origins of public executions, as the media developed the ability to address audiences who were not copresent, scenes of suffering began to be visually represented for those who could not be present in real time and space. Using the specter of punishment to deter and control, spectacles of suffering became a popular visual trope, offering a lesson to be turned with didactic appeal onto the viewing public. Members of the public were turned into voyeurs, who were thought to be collectively stimulated, ordered, and stabilized in some kind of emotionally charged experience brought on by witnessing the suffering of others. Key to the effective functioning of these spectacles was the assumption that the public could and would be deterred from aberrant behavior due to the spectacle's cautionary message. In other words, the spectacle was effected by someone for a reason and was invoked to drive home an effect. See also Samuel Y. Edgerton, Jr., *Pictures and Punishment* (Ithaca: Cornell University Press, 1985); and Dwight Conquergood, "Lethal Theatre: Performance, Punishment, and the Death Penalty," *Theatre Journal* 54 (2002), 339–367.

71. Michael Baxandall, *Painting and Experience in Fifteenth-Century Italy* (Oxford: Oxford University Press, 1972). Philippe Aries established that propriety about dying went hand in hand with its different kinds of mediated representations. From the *artes moriendi*

of the fifteenth and sixteenth centuries, which verbally and visually articulated the proper mode of dying to the masses through the new medium of print, to the contemporary use of photographs to mitigate the finality of the deaths of loved ones, the experience of death was communicated by its visual representation. See Philippe Aries, *Western Attitudes Toward Death* (Baltimore, MD: Johns Hopkins University Press, 1974) and *The Hour of Our Death* (New York: Alfred A Knopf, 1981).

72. Barbara Norfleet in *Looking at Death* addressed the change from an early eagerness to visually document death, embodied in extensive practices for taking postmortem photographs of loved ones, especially babies and children, to a taboo about depicting death that arose in the 1940s and 1950s and then to a more permissive verbal debate about death in the 1980s and 1990s. Also see Taylor, *Body Horror*, and Seaton, *Carnage*.

73. Variously called "shock photos" by Roland Barthes (*The Eiffel Tower and Other Mythologies* [New York: Hill and Wang, 1979]); "photographs of agony" by John Berger (*About Looking* [New York: Libri Books, 1980]); and "shock-pictures" by Susan Sontag (*Regarding the Pain of Others* [New York: Farrar, Straus and Giroux, 2003], 33), images of death can cause their viewers to oscillate, often without prior cue, between compassion, shame, voyeurism, empathy, sadness, disgust, and indifference. That oscillation has puzzled observers, who have found no clear consensus about which images of death affect the public, how they do so, and under which circumstances: photographs of brutal repression in Guatemala, Barthes (*The Eiffel Tower and Other Mythologies,* 71–73) observed, left spectators no room to react, offering little more than "synthetic nourishment" and generating what he later called the predictability of the *studium*, while Sontag argued—at various points in time—that photography of the dead either killed compassion or nurtured it (*Regarding the Pain,* 7). For an historical treatment of the evolution of responses toward Holocaust atrocity photos, see Barbie Zelizer, *Remembering to Forget: Holocaust Memory through the Camera's Eye* (Chicago: University of Chicago Press, 1998); and Lilie Chouliaraki, *The Spectatorship of Suffering* (London: Sage, 2006), for a discussion of contemporary images of suffering.

74. Sigmund Freud was among the first to imply that engagement with memory objects associated with mourning could help ease the trauma and grief involved in loss. Following Freud, trauma theorists have established that the persistent engagement with a traumatic event in need of resolution can either fix an individual or group in a stage of acting out—by which the event's repetition prevents the trauma from being integrated into the existing psychic or symbolic order and forces certain interpretations that are necessary to carry on—or facilitate the process of working through, by which the individual or group carries on in a posttraumatic stage of development. Offering a therapeutic intervention to the experience of loss, encountering objects associated with mourning has value in shaping an individual or collective's response to grief, for, Sigmund Freud, "Remembering, Repeating and Working Through," in J. Strachey (ed.), *Standard Edition of the Complete Psychological Works,* vol. 12 (1914; reprint London: Hogarth Press, 1958), and "Mourning and Melancholia," in Philip Rieff (ed.), *General Psychological Theory* (1917; reprint New York: Collier Books, 1963); Cathy Caruth, *Unclaimed Experience: Trauma, Narrative and History* (Baltimore, MD: Johns Hopkins University Press, 1996); Judith Herman, *Trauma and Recovery* (New York: Basic Books, 1992).

75. Alberto Tenenti, *La vie et la mort a travers le XV siecle* (Paris: A. Colin, 1952); Mary Warren Marien, *Photography and Its Critics: A Cultural History, 1839–1900* (Cambridge: Cambridge University Press, 1997), 82; John Durham Peters, *Speaking Into the Air* (Chicago: University of Chicago, 1999), 59; Roland Barthes, *Camera Lucida* (New York: Hill and Wang, 1981), 92, and *Image/Music/Text* (London, Fontana, 1977), 44; Susan Sontag, *On Photography* (New York: Dell, 1977), 1979, 15. In like fashion, Walter Benjamin pointed to "that which will never entirely perish" in a photograph [Walter Benjamin, "Short History of Photography," *Artforum* 15(6), 1977, 47], and Tom Gunning remarked on photography's creation of the uncanny to exist alongside the concrete world (Tom Gunning, "Phantom Images and Modern Manifestations," in Patrice Petro [ed.], *Fugitive Images* [Bloomington: Indiana University Press, 1995], 42–71). Even the experience of communication from a distance became indistinguishable from communication with the dead as exemplified by photos of the deceased (Peters, *Speaking Into the Air*, 149).

76. Marianne Hirsch, *Family Frames* (Cambridge, MA: Harvard University Press, 1997), 256; Ruby, *Secure the Shadow*.

77. Barthes, *Camera Lucida*; Nancy Armstrong, *Fiction in the Age of Photography* (Cambridge, MA: Harvard University Press, 1999), 37. As Luc Boltansky wrote in *Distant Suffering* (Cambridge: Cambridge University Press, 1999), necessary here is some attention to both what is seen and how it affects the spectator. Often this has to do with disavowing mortality, as Kevin Robins remarked about the visual suspension of death, which "can resurrect the dead…Death-defying simulation is linked to powerful fantasies of rational transcendence" (*Into the Image* [London: Routledge, 1996], 161). Also see Jean Michel Rabate (ed), *Writing the Image After Roland Barthes* (Philadelphia: University of Pennsylvania Press, 1997).

78. The notion of a strategically chosen example comes from Barney Glaser and Anselm Strauss, *The Discovery of Grounded Theory* (Chicago: Aldine, 1977). I chose this subset of about-to-die images because it is useful for addressing both a larger universe of news images (where both share a reliance on impending action and a frozen sequencing of time; a play to the emotions, imagination, and contingency; and a usefulness as both news and mnemonic relays) and a larger universe of journalistic relays, writ broadly (where both exhibit an involvement with death, reliance on unsettled events, and ambivalence about the relationship between word and image). Though there would be value in speaking directly with viewers for a project targeting how news images move the public, the thematic, rather than chronological, organization of the materials I gathered meant that in order to keep the database stable across historical and contemporary circumstances—comprising 170 years of events and pictures—I decided to rely across cases on the same source material. The materials analyzed for this project thus cover a wide swath of primarily textual sources: published, broadcast, or posted images in newspapers, newsmagazines, television, and the Internet; transcripts of broadcast and cable news shows; trade literature, books on photography and journalism, books on specific news events, public opinion surveys, and interviews with journalists and photographers. The project also draws from a close analysis of the Associated Press Multimedia Archive, Reuters Image Database, and Getty News Images, which included both images only circulated over the wires and those that played in the news media. I conducted numerous keyword searches—on "death," "dying,"

338 • Notes to pages 28–32

killing," "illness," "disaster," and "execution" in various electronic databases, including Proquest, Factiva, Lexis/Nexis, and specific newspaper archives, as well as a second tier search of the coverage of specific news events. Once certain pictures were chosen for inclusion, largely on the basis of the debate and attention they had garnered among journalists, news executives, officials, politicians, and viewers, the life history of each photo was tracked across multiple sources and a close thematic analysis was conducted of its shaping and use. Although the primary focus remained with the U.S. news media, when available and relevant I tracked the news media from other countries as well.

Chapter 2

1. Well-known examples from art include Jacques-Louis David's *The Death of Socrates* (1787), Francesco Goya's *The Third of May, 1808* (1814), and Edouard Manet's *The Execution of Maxmilian* (1867). Even as 19th-century realism, imbued with aspirations of verisimilitude, infiltrated artistic representation, the imagined death remained one way of depicting death. In part, this was because a concern with "cause and process rather than the deed itself" (Ron M. Brown, *The Art of Suicide* [London: Reaktion Books, 2001], 150) kept visualization open to multiple interpretive modes. This would have significance for the importation of about-to-die images in journalism, where the informative function of the news and the role of verisimilitude in proving facts were thought to reign.

2. Patricia Anderson, *The Printed Image and the Transformation of Popular Culture, 1760–1860* (Oxford: Clarendon Press, 1991), 60. She also noted that the sculpture of the dying Gaul was originally misnamed the *Dying Gladiator*.

3. Brown, *Art of Suicide*, 159.

4. Illustration titled "Assassination of President Lincoln," *National Police Gazette,* April 22, 1869, np; illustration from *Frank Leslie's Illustrated News,* April 29, 1865, 1; illustrations from *Harper's Weekly,* April 29, 1865, 260.

5. See, for instance, "The Lynching of Frank Embree, July 22, 1899, Fayette, Missouri," in James Allen et al., *Without Sanctuary* (New York: Twin Palms, 2000), photos 42–44. Given that these images were circulated enthusiastically among those who supported lynching, it is telling that most depicted the already dead rather than individuals about to die, for the former sealed off empathetic engagement with the victims in a way that about-to-die images did not. Lynching reemerged in 2000 with a presentist tilt in U.S. public consciousness after lynching postcards were displayed at numerous New York City art galleries (see Roberta Smith, "An Ugly Legacy Lives on, Its Glare Unsoftened by Age," *New York Times,* January 13, 2000, E1).

6. Kevin Barnhurst and John Nerone, *The Form of News: A History* (New York: Guilford Press, 2001), 126.

7. Jack C. Fisher, *Stolen Glory: The McKinley Assassination* (La Jolla, CA: Alamar Books, 2001), 6. Titled "The Shooting of the President," the drawing depicted a hand holding a concealed gun as it discharged into the President's torso (Drawing titled "The Shooting of the President," *Philadelphia Inquirer,* September 7, 1901), 5; Barnhurst and Nerone, *Form of News,* 126.

8. Though the drawing reportedly appeared on the cover by no less than fifteen sources, tracking the issues of the period revealed no picture of the shooting during the

dates mentioned. There are suggestions that the drawing was only created in 1905, which would imply that over time numerous news organizations—including the *Buffalo Courier, Frank Leslie's Illustrated,* and others—erroneously claimed that it had appeared earlier. See, for instance, the *Buffalo Courier*'s tracking of the event in its archives [see "Our President Shot Down," *Buffalo Courier,* September 7, 1901, 1 in buffalonian.com, 2001]. Thanks to Keren Tenenboim-Weinblatt for assiduous research on the appearance of the original drawing.

9. "Story of Shooting Told by Witnesses; Mayor's Official Family Relate What They Did to Aid Their Stricken Chief," *New York Times,* August 10, 1910, 1.

10. Charles E. Chapin, quoted in Ralph Blumenthal, *Miracle at Sing Sing: How One Man Changed the Lives of America's Most Dangerous Prisoners* (New York: St. Martin's Press, 2004), 6.

11. Photo titled "Photograph: Taken Immediately After the Shooting," *New York World,* August 10, 1910, 1; photo titled "Mayor Gaynor Just After Being Shot," *Philadelphia Inquirer,* August 10, 1910, 1; "Snapshot of Mayor Gaynor, Taken a Few Moments After He Was Shot," *New York Times,* August 10, 1910, 2; "Mayor Gaynor After Shots Were Fired," *Washington Post,* August 10, 1910, 1; "Shooting of Mayor Gaynor on Ship at Hoboken, NJ," *Chicago Tribune,* August 11, 1910, 3. Other than the *New York World* photo, which was attributed to Press Publishing Co., the images were accredited to the American Press Association. Warnecke's name appeared in none of the photo's original displays.

12. "Prize Winning Photos in the Annual Exhibition of the New York Press Photographers," *New York Times,* December 5, 1936, 21; "William Warnecke, News Photographer," *New York Times,* May 27, 1939, 20; William E. Berchtold, "More Fodder for Photomaniacs," *The North American Review,* January 1935, 19–30; John Faber, *Great News Photos and the Stories Behind Them* (1960; reprint New York: Dover, 1978), 24–25.

13. "Ruth Snyder Execution," *New York Daily News* (extra edition), January 13, 1928, 1.

14. The execution, which took place on August 6, became fodder in the fight over electrical power between Thomas Edison and Westinghouse, and though it took two full jolts of current to kill Kemmler, who began to smoke under his blindfold, the drawing captured the moment before the failed electrocution got underway. See Mark Essig, *Edison and the Electric Chair* (New York: Walker, 2003). Thanks to Fred Shauer for alerting me to this story.

15. The *Daily News* ran two extra editions that featured the photo (*New York Daily News,* January 13, 1928 and January 14, 1928, 1), but other newspapers did not follow suit. See Faber, *Great News Photos,* 44–45; Cited in Wendy Kozol, *Life's America* (Philadelphia: Temple University Press, 1994), 27.

16. Pronouncing the *Daily News* unworthy of public trust, officials with the Department of Corrections initially contemplated prosecuting the photographer and the paper, but they did not pursue that course of action ("Calls Death Picture Fake," *New York Times,* January 14, 1928, 8; "Tells of Last Plan for Mrs Snyder," *New York Times,* January 15, 1928, 20). Faber, *Great News Photos,* 44; "150 Years of Photojournalism," *Time,* fall 1989, n.p; Ana Mendieta, "Exhibit Captures NY Life, Death," *Chicago Sun-Times,* June 3, 2001, 8; Tim Kirby, "Photojournalism: Diana Is Not Its Greatest Victim," *The Independent,* September 29, 1997, M1.

17. Editors of *New York Daily News, Fifty Years of the New York Daily News in Pictures* (New York: Doubleday, 1979), 42–43; picture appended to William Grimes, "Murder, Madness and Mayhem," *New York Times,* January 26, 1996, C1; Richard Willing, "Florida's 'Ghastly' Electric Chair Revives Debate," *USA Today,* October 28, 1999, 6A; Adam C. Smith, "Journalist Argues for Executions on TV," *St. Petersburg Times,* April 9, 1998, 1A; Alice Reid, "Ad for News Media Museum Dismays Death Penalty Opponents," *Washington Post,* May 29, 1997, D1. Also see Madeline Rogers, "The Picture Snatchers," *American Heritage Magazine,* October 1994, 66–73 and Steven R. Knowlton, "Images of Violence: Ratchet Up? Or Rachet Down?" *Visual Communication Quarterly,* summer 1999, 3.

18. Vicki Goldberg, *The Power of Photography* (New York: Abbeville Press, 1991), 194.

19. Faber, *Great News Photos.*

20. I. R. Sorgi, "Graphic Story of Leap Told by Cameraman," *Buffalo Courier Express,* May 7, 1942. The picture was labeled, alternately, "Genesee Hotel Suicide" and "The Despondent Divorcee."

21. *Life* called the image "breathtaking" (see "Cameraman Catches Final Second of Suicide's Dive," *Life,* May 18, 1942, 36); http://whitewingeddove.blogspot.com/2006/11/fave-foto-friday.html, posted November 10, 2006. For instance, the photo appeared in *Life: The First Fifty Years, 1936–1986* (New York: Little, Brown, 1986); and in Richard Lacayo and George Russell, *Eyewitness: 150 Years of Photojournalism* (New York: Oxmoor House, 1990). An eyetracker experiment used the photo as a stimulus, where only 4% of students viewing the image noticed the woman falling to the ground; see S. Adam Brasel, Philip Zimbardo, and George Slavich, "A Blind Mind's Eye: Perceptual Defense Mechanisms and Aschematic Visual Information," *Advances in Consumer Research* 33, 2006, 305. In *The Photography Handbook* (London: Routledge, 2004), Terence Wright likened the photo to Breughel's "Landscape with the Fall of Icarus": Both shared "an everyday setting, a lack of awareness on the part of passers-by and a moment of death through falling" (86).

22. "Death Is Captivating," http://gustavsgroupieblogspot.com, posted October 17, 2007; posters in response likened the image and the thoughts it provoked to watching people jump from the World Trade Center on 9/11. Also see "Sound and Fury" in Neil Gaiman, *The Sandman,* vol. 1, *Preludes and Nocturnes* (New York: Vertigo, 1993), 192. The photo also inspired a poem titled "Suicide" and a painting called "The Final Plunge" http://katedeannn.deviantart.com/.

23. Faber, *Great News Photos,* 96.

24. Ibid., 96–97.

25. Also see Hal Buell, *Moments* (New York: Black Dog and Leventhal, 2007), 24–25; Cyma Rubin and Eric Newton, *Capture the Moment: The Pulitzer Prize Photographs* (New York: Norton, 2001), 18; Dennis Dunleavy, "A Year in Passing: Remembering Some Photographers Who Died in 2007," http://ddunleavy.typepad.com/the_big_picture/2007/12/a-year-in-passi.html; Faber, *Great News Photos,* 96.

26. "Photo Improved Fire Safety; Amateur Photographer Arnold Hardy Won a Pulitzer for His '46 Shot," Associated Press, December 9, 2007; "The Photo Feed," *Photo District News,* December 7, 2007.

27. Stanley Forman, in "Picture Power: Fire-escape Drama," in "World Press Photo: 50 Years," BBC News, September 30, 2005, http://news.bbc.co.uk/1/hi/world/americas/4245138.stm.

28. See Norfleet, *Looking at Death,* for more on this point.

29. Said Forman: "At the time, I didn't know that the picture was going to be so big or have such an impact. When I started looking at the negatives I was looking at the picture where they were holding onto each other. I didn't even look at the next frame…I didn't realize how dramatic it was until I had developed the film" (quoted in "Picture Power: Fire-escape Drama" in "World Press Photo: 50 Years," BBC News, September 30, 2005, http://news.bbc.co.uk/1/hi/world/americas/4245138.stm).

30. Picture appended to "Heroic Hub Firefighter Dies; Featured in Famous Photo Series," *Boston Herald,* January 27, 2005, 21; Faber, *Great News Photos,* 146–147; Rubin and Newton, *Capture the Moment,* 94–95; Buell, *Moments,* 114–115.

31. When interviewed, a Fox News Channel cameramen became teary when he described filming people jumping from the towers. "I stopped," he said, "but I saw 25 more jumping, holding hands, in groups" (Rob Ginnane, in "Behind the Camera," *TV Guide,* September 29–October 5, 2001, 15).

32. David Westin and Bill Wheatley, in Jim Rutenberg and Felicity Barringer, "The Ethics: News Media Try to Sort Out Policy on Graphic Images," *New York Times,* September 13, 2001," A24.

33. Tom Junod, "The Falling Man," *Esquire,* September 2003.

34. Cited in Junod, "Falling Man." The Drew photo appeared in the *New York Times* (September 12, 2001, p. A12), *Philadelphia Inquirer* (September 12, 2001, A14), *Chicago Tribune* (September 12, 2001, A12), and *Washington Post* (September 13, 2001, C1). Pictures of the burning towers appeared on both pages A1 and A8 of the *Washington Post* on September 12, 2001. A different photo of people jumping, taken by Getty Images, appeared in the *Los Angeles Times* (September 12, 2001, A13) and *Time* (special September 11 edition, n.p). Interestingly, this was not the first time Richard Drew shot a moment of impending death: years earlier he had taken the famous image of Robert Kennedy dying on the floor of a Los Angeles restaurant kitchen.

35. Reuters was alerted to the people in the shot by a European subscriber who noticed small incongruous blobs on the original larger print. See Valerie Basheda, "An Unforgettable Picture," *American Journalism Review,* October 2001, 27. The photo appeared in the *Boston Globe* (September 12, 2001, A8), *Chicago Tribune* (September 12, 2001, A12), *Washington Post* (September 12, 2001, A16 and September 13, C3), and *Newsweek* (September 24, 2001, Special Report, n.p.).

36. Rutenberg and Barringer, "Ethics," A24; Alice Tugend, "The Simple Act of Getting to Work was An Ordeal," *American Journalism Review,* October 2001, 25. By contrast, the *Philadelphia Inquirer* ran a column entitled "The Most Horrific Images," where it did not mention the bodies at all. Tugend, "Simple Act," 24–25. The newspapers which ran the photograph included *The New York Times, Detroit News, Newsday, Denver Post,* and *Philadelphia Inquirer.* The *Washington Post* included a front-page discussion of the bodies jumping (Barton Gellman, "I Saw Bodies Falling Out—Oh God, Jumping, Falling," *Washington Post,* September 12, 2001, A1), but the accompanying picture depicted two grieving women holding each other. The Reuters photo of people hanging out of the

towers appeared on A16. In one collection of the front pages of newspapers the day after the attacks, not one of 122 national papers showed an image of people about to die on their front pages; see Poynter Institute, *September 11, 2001: A Collection of Newspaper Front Pages Selected by the Poynter Institute* (Andrews McMeel, 2001). Quoted in Rutenberg and Barringer, "Ethics," A24; Junod, "Falling Man," 180.

37. French television and the BBC were among those news organizations that continued to show the footage. Mexico City's *El Universal* front-paged the Reuters photo of people hanging out of buildings (September 12, 2001, p. A1) as did Rio de Janeiro's *O Dia* and *O Globo* with the AP photo of a man falling headfirst to his death, under the caption "desperado" (September 12, 2001, p. A1). Both images were reminiscent of depictions of an earlier event—the Triangle Shirtwaist factory fire in 1911, where approximately fifty people gestured hysterically at bystanders from inside a fiery warehouse and then jumped from the building rather than burn to death inside.

38. The image did appear in *Newsweek,* September 24, 2001, as a double-page spread (n.p.), while a similar Getty photo appeared in *Time*'s special issue on September 11. But the image of people jumping did not appear in the regular issues of *Time, Business Week, People,* or *In These Times.*

39. Junod, "Falling Man." See picture appended to Kevin Flynn and Jim Dwyer, "Falling Bodies: A 9/11 Image Etched in Pain," *New York Times,* September 10, 2004, A1, B8.

40. Comment made at a public viewing of TV coverage, University of Pennsylvania, Philadelphia, Pennsylvania, September 11, 2001; Don Dahler, in "Ground Zero," *TV Guide,* September 29-October 5, 39.

41. Magnum Photographers, *New York;* and Reuters, *September 11: A Testimony,* which included the Jeff Christiensen shot of people hanging out of the windows; World Wide Photography and Associated Press, *Day of Terror* (Beaverton: Or.: America Products Publishing, 2001); Joseph P. Fried, "Etched in 9/11 Pain, Statue Finds Its Place," *New York Times,* October 10, 2004, 43; "Artist Stages 'Falls' to Recall 9/11 Horror," Associated Press, June 16, 2005; Junod, "Falling Man," 180.

42. *9/11: The Falling Man* (Henry Singer dir), aired 2006. Also see Michiko Kakutani, "A Man, A Woman and a Day of Terror," *New York Times,* May 9, 2007, E1. See too Marita Sturken, *Tourists of History: Memory, Kitsch, and Consumerism from Oklahoma City to Ground Zero* (Durham, NC: Duke University Press, 2007).

43. "Death Plunge No. 4: NYU's Grief," *New York Post,* March 10, 2004, 1. The paper also depicted a smaller earlier close-up shot of the woman as a high-school track star that created some ambivalence as to whether or not it depicted her face as she leapt.

44. See, for instance, "NYU Student Photo Published, Her Frat Boyfriend Revealed, and NYU's Grief," nyuview.com, March 10, 2004.

45. The letters appeared in the *Post* on March 11, 2004. Also see "Outrage over Plunge Picture," newyorkpostonline.com, March 11, 2004; "NYU Falls."

46. John Beckman, in Amy Westfeldt, "Fourth Building Plunge Death of an NYU Student," Associated Press, March 10, 2004; Stevenson Swanson, "Student Suicides Spur Action on Campuses," *Chicago Tribune,* October 12, 2004, A8; Maki Becker and Alison Gendar, "A New Low For Post," *New York Daily News,* March 11, 2004, 6; "Paper's Coverage of Suicide Draws Fire," *Psychiatric Times,* May 1, 2004.

47. Timothy McDarrah, "Jumper Photo is OK," in Jim Romanesko, poynteronline, posted March 11, 2004.

48. Barry Gross, "Sorry, Folks, We Are a Tabloid," in Jim Romanesko, poynteronline, posted March 12, 2004.

49. James McGowan, "Did NYDN Lose Jumper Pic Auction?' in Jim Romanesko, poynteronline, posted March 11, 2004; Becker and Gendar, "A New Low For Post," 6.

50. Geneva Overholser, "NY Post Readers Upset Over Suicide Photo," poynteronline, posted March 11, 2004; "NYU Falls Lead to Appalling Journalism" (Editorial), *Massachusetts Daily Collegian,* March 11, 2004; Katha Pollitt, "So Grotesque, So Cruel, So Voyeuristic," in Jim Romanesko, poynteronline, posted March 11, 2004.

51. Alan Cowell, "BBC to Use Time Delay Device to Weed Out Upsetting Images," *New York Times,* June 24, 2005, A4.

52. Gisele Freund, *Photography and Society* (London: Godine, 1979), 149.

53. Quoted in Peter Howe, *Shooting under Fire* (New York: Artisan Books, 2002), 52.

54. Quoted in Piers Moore Ede, "Horst Faas: After Two Pulitzers and Five Decades of Pictures, He Looks Back at History," *News Photographer,* July 2004, 30.

55. The photo was appended to "An Exodus to Uncertainty, *Philadelphia Inquirer,* September 2, 2005, A19; "Life on the Brink," *Newsweek,* September 12, 2005, 37; "An Exodus to Uncertainty," *New York Times,* September 2, 2005, A19. It was also used to depict a commemorative editorial on the hurricane four years later ("Third-World Week," *Philadelphia Inquirer,* September 5, 2009, A10).

56. Gunther Kress and Theo van Leeuwen, *Reading Images: The Grammar of Visual Design* (London: Routledge, 1996), 186–192. Close-up shots show the subject's head and shoulders, medium-close shots cut the subject around the waist, medium shots cut the subject around the knees, medium-long shots show the full figure, and long shots position the figure about half the frame's height (130). According to Edward Hall, *The Hidden Dimension* (New York: Doubleday, 1966), 71–72, these distances correspond with fields of vision, so that at distances of more than 13 feet, people seem to have little connection with each other. Conversely, public distance can show a figure with four or five surrounding people. Hall also distinguished between close and far personal distance, close and far social distance, and public distance.

57. Horst Faas, in Rubin and Newton, *Capture the Moment,* 55. Also Buell, *Moments,* 62–67. In 1965, Faas received a Pulitzer Prize for his combat photos from Vietnam.

58. Wright, *Photography Handbook,* 105.

59. Susan Meiselas, "Central America and Human Rights," in Ken Light (ed), *Witness in Our Time: Working Lives of Documentary Photographers* (Washington: Smithsonian Institution Press, 2000), 103. One blogger on photojournalism recently observed that "being a good caption writer can actually elevate your standing with your word side colleagues. Sometimes I think they still believe we can't read and just sort of grunt to communicate with one another....So be a good caption writer and elevate yourself from Neanderthal to Cromagnon" (Gary Cosby, Jr., "Writing Captions," http://alittlenewsphoto.com, posted July 12, 2009, at 6.40 pm).

60. W. Eugene Smith was rumored to have fought with his editors over the role of the photographer, claiming his need to have veto power in decisions involving his images over

that of either the writer or editor; see A. E. Woolley, "The Photographer and Writer," in *Camera Journalism: Reporting With Photographs* (New York: A. S. Barnes, 1966).

61. Her name, Daisy McCumber, was made public in Sam Heys and Allan B. Goodwin, *The Winecoff Fire* (Longstreet, 1993).

62. Wright, *Photography Handbook,* 98–99.

63. Jenni Goldman, "Where Do Picture Editors Come From?" *Newsphotographer,* September 2005, 35.

64. Harold Evans, *Pictures on a Page* (London: Heinemann, 1978), 207.

65. Wilson Hicks, *Words and Pictures* (New York: Arno Press, 1952), 34. The effect occurs when "two pictures are brought together, their individual effects are combined and enhanced by the reader's interpretive and evaluative reaction."

66. Griselda Pollock, "Feminism/Foucalt—Surveillance/Sexuality," in Norman Bryson, Michael Holly, and Keith Moxey (eds.), *Visual Culture, Images and Interpretation* (Hanover, NH: Wesleyan University Press, 1994), 15.

67. Quoted in Howe, *Shooting Under Fire,* 90.

68. Tom Shales, "Horror of the Fire in the Sky," *Washington Post,* January 29, 1986, B1. Similar comments were voiced after other powerful events of impending death, including 9/11, the shooting of 12-year-old Mohammad Aldura during the Intifada, and the assassinations of John F. Kennedy, Robert F Kennedy, and Benazir Bhutto. Much of the replay of the *Challenger* explosion had an additional macabre effect. As former astronaut Michael Collins wrote in the *Washington Post,* "We watch the rockets explode, over and over again, in slow motion, backward and forward, in vivid color. Christa's parents watch their daughter's spacecraft being blown to bits. We watch them watching it. Not once but as often as we can stomach it. This 'you are there' lens, coupled with instant replay, magnifies that which needs no magnification" (Michael Collins, "Riding the Beast," *Washington Post,* January 30, 1986, A25). This is what Adrian Piper called "modal imagination"—the capacity to imagine what is impossible ("Impartiality, Compassion and Modal Imagination," *Ethics,* July 1991, 726–757).

69. Picture appended to *Life,* November 1990. Kirby had died the preceding May.

70. Paul Lester, *Visual Communication: Images with Messages,* 4th ed. (Belmont, CA: Thompson Wadsworth, 2006), 70. See, for instance, Joan Gibbons, *Art and Advertising* (London: I. B.Taurus, 2005); Paul Jobling and David Crowley, *Graphic Design: Reproduction and Representation Since 1800* (Manchester, UK: Manchester University Press, 1997).

71. "After Complaints, Rockefeller Center Drapes September 11 Statue," *New York Times,* September 19, 2002, B3; Eric Fischl, "A Memorial That's True to 9/11," *New York Times,* December 19, 2003, A39. Thanks to Jonathan Glick for pointing this out to me.

72. Don DeLillo, *Falling Man* (New York: Scribner, 2007).

73. Paul Grice, *Studies in the Way of Words* (Cambridge, MA: Harvard University Press, 1989). Thanks to Joseph Cappella for pointing me to this literature.

74. Sol Worth and Larry Gross, "Symbolic Strategies," *Journal of Communication* 24(4), 1974, 27–29. Also see Larry Gross, "Life Versus Art: The Interpretation of Visual Narratives," *Studies in Visual Communication* 11(4), fall 1985, 2–12.

75. Taken for the Venezuelan paper, *La Republica,* later photographer Hector Rondon said "I don't know how I made the pictures. I was prone on the street with my camera" (Buell, *Moments,* 58).

76. The photo by Eamon McCabe, showing soccer fans crunched against a fence, appeared in the *Guardian,* May 29, 1985, 1, and ten years later in John Duncan, "Ten Years On From Heysel: The Day Football Nearly Died," *Guardian,* May 29, 1995, 3. McCabe was quoted widely for having said he arrived at the stadium a sports photographer and left a war photographer ("Night That Shamed Soccer," *Express,* May 24, 2005, 39). Other photos showing the swelling crowds appeared in Richard Bernstein, "Riot in Brussels at Soccer Game Leaves 41 Dead," *New York Times,* May 29, 1985, 1; and "41 Killed as British, Italian Soccer Fans Riot," *Los Angeles Times,* May 29, 1985, 1, as well as more graphic images of the fans being crushed (Milt Freudenheim and Henry Giniger, "The Score is 1 to 0; the Toll is 38," *New York Times,* June 2, 1985, E4). The event resulted in a 5-year European ban on British soccer teams and a 10-year ban on the Liverpool team (see pictures appended to Steve Lohrs, "After 93 Die, British Again Anguish Over Soccer," *New York Times,* April 17, 1989, A12).

77. In Harold Evans's view, "some photographers and a television crew departed without taking a picture in hopes that in their absence the acts might not be committed....Others felt that the mob was beyond the appeal to mercy. They stayed and won Pulitzer Prizes." See *Pictures on a Page* (London: Pimlico, 1978), vi–vii.

78. The series of images was called "Death in Dacca" (Buell, *Moments,* 99).

79. "India Bars 5 News Photos on Executions," *Los Angeles Times,* December 21, 1971, A9.

80. Buell, *Moments,* 99.

81. See, for instance, commentary in Rubin and Newton, *Capture the Moment,* 97.

Chapter 3

1. Jean Baudrillard, *Simulacra and Simulation* (Ann Arbor: University of Michigan Press, 1992); Guy de Bord, *Society of the Spectacle* (New York: Zone Books, 1994); Douglas Kellner, *Media Spectacle* (London: Routledge, 2003). In de Bord's view, the spectacle, which he defined as a social relationship mediated by images, offered an inverted image of society, where relations between commodities supplanted relations between people and identification with the spectacle supplanted authentic engagement.

2. John Taylor, *Body Horror: Photojournalism, Catastrophe, and War* (Manchester, UK: Manchester University Press, 1998), Jessica M. Fishman, *Documenting Death: Photojournalism and Spectacles of the Morbid in the Tabloid and Elite Newspaper* (Ph.D. diss., University of Pennsylvania, 2001), and Jean Seaton, *Carnage and the Media* (London: Allen Lane, 2005) have all addressed this tendency.

3. For instance, "An unidentified Chicago police officer tries to drag people to safety from a stack of people jammed into the bottom of a crowded staircase in this security camera image of the E2 nightclub stampede that killed 21 people" (AP Photo/Courtesy Chicago Police Dept., February 28, 2003, Chicago, Illinois, #6657829 [3YP7P]) or "Rescue workers pause while searching for missing people in the rubble of the National Guard Armory in downtown Pierce City, Mo., after it was destroyed by a tornado

Sunday night" (AP Photo/Charlie Riedel, May 5, 2003, Pierce City, Mo., #6755497 [40SKP]).

4. "Tay Disaster," HultonArchives/Illustrated London News/Getty Images, 1880.

5. "Media Event" and "The Eyewitnesses," *The Web of Memory* (Chicago: Chicago Historical Society and Northwestern University, 1996), http://www.chicagohs.org/fire/. This was due to technological developments in printing, transportation, and communication.

6. Eric H. Monkkonen, *America Becomes Urban: The Development of U.S. Cities and Towns, 1780–1980* (Berkeley: University of California Press, 1980), 70; Carl W. Smith, *Urban Disorder and the Shape of Belief: Great Chicago Fire, the Haymarket Bomb and the Model Town* (Chicago: University of Chicago Press, 1995), 5, who noted that the fire's earliest coverage "expressed a longing for a finer world now beyond recapture" (89).

7. Smith, *Urban Disorder*, 1, 91.

8. James O. Brayman, in "Eyewitnesses."

9. "Chicago in Ruins," *Philadelphia Inquirer*, October 10, 1871, 1.

10. Smith, *Urban Disorder*, 23–24, 30.

11. Quoted in "Eyewitnesses"; quoted in "Chicago in Ashes," *Harper's Weekly*, October 28, 1871, 1010; quoted in John McGovern, *Daniel Trenthworthy: A Tale of the Great Fire of Chicago*, 1889.

12. Quoted in "Eyewitnesses."

13. Quoted in Peter Charles Hoffer, *Seven Fires: The Urban Infernos that Reshaped America* (New York: Public Affairs, 2006), 135.

14. John J. Pauly, "The Great Chicago Fire as a National Event," *American Quarterly* 36, 1984, 673. In fact, a much larger rural fire the same day in Peshtigo, Wisconsin, that took 1,500 lives received only a fraction of the coverage.

15. "Chicago," *Scribner's Magazine*, December 1871, 235; "The Chicago Fire," *Religious Magazine and Monthly Review*, November 1871, 463.

16. Ross Miller, *The Great Chicago Fire* (Champaign: University of Illinois Press, 2000), 64. The local news media's advocacy stance in times of disaster is typical of contemporary calamities too. See, for instance, Nikki Usher, "Recovery from Disaster: How Journalists at the New Orleans *Times Picayune* Understand the Role of a Post-Katrina Newspaper," *Journalism Practice* 3(2), April 2009, 216–232.

17. *New York Tribune*, October 13, 1871, 2; quoted in Smith, *Urban Disorder*, 91.

18. "Reader's Letter," *Harper's Weekly*, November 11, 1871, 1059.

19. "The Chicago Fire! 8,000 Lives Lost," *Idaho Statesman*, October 14, 1871, 2.

20. Horace White, in "The Eyewitnesses."

21. *Harper's Weekly* showed images of burnt buildings or safe survivors (October 28, 1871, 1012–1013). Its cover photo showed a group huddled together in front of a brightly lit landscape. By contrast, when a fire broke out twenty years later on the grounds of the Chicago Exposition, *Harper's Weekly* featured a drawing that showed a building and people falling from it on the way to their deaths (Charles Graham, "The Chicago Fire," *Harper's Weekly*, July 22, 1893, 702).

22. *Harper's Weekly*, for instance, depicted multiple images of specific buildings on fire—the Chamber of Commerce, the Opera House, the central grain elevators (October 28, 1871, cover, 1012–1013).

23. Theodore R. Davis, "A Bird's Eye View of Chicago as It Was before the Fire," *Harper's Weekly*, October 21, 1871, 984–985.

24. Drawings collectively titled "Chicago in Flames," *Harper's Weekly*, October 28, 1871, 1004–1013; quoted in John R. Chapin, "Chicago in Ashes," *Harper's Weekly*, October 28, 1871, 1010.

25. Chapin, "Chicago in Ashes," 1010.

26. Ibid., 1010–1011.

27. It was thought to have provided the impetus for other about-to-die photos of a city ablaze, including a photo in *Illustrated London News*, November 11, 1871, and lithographs both by Kellogg and Bulkeley and by Currier and Ives; "Human Brotherhood" (editorial), *Every Saturday*, November 4, 1871, 3, a remark made not only about the Chicago Fire but also about the less covered but more horrific Peshtigo disaster in Wisconsin and Michigan.

28. Quoted in Chapin, "Chicago in Ashes," 1010.

29. "As They Are" (editorial), *Christian Union*, December 20, 1871, 4.

30. *Report of the Chicago Relief and Aid Society of Disbursement of Contributions for the Sufferers by the Chicago Fire* (Cambridge, MA: Riverside Press, 1874), 8.

31. Frank Luzerne, *The Lost City! Drama of the Fire-Fiend* (New York: Wells, 1872); Hunter and Company engraving, whose advertisement appeared in *Harper's Weekly*, February 3, 1872, 111; a widely reprinted lithograph by Currier and Ives, which depicted the large-scale scene of the moment from the other side of the lake, flames blowing in the wrong direction.

32. "Commemorating Catastrophe" and "Fire Diorama," *The Web of Memory* (Chicago: Chicago Historical Society and Northwestern University, 1996), http://www.chicagohs.org/fire/.

33. Reenactment image depicted in Smith, *Urban Disorder;* Hoffer, *Seven Fires*, 133. Also see Fire Prevention Week informational pamphlet, Carson City, Nevada (October 2006) (http://www.carson-city.nv.us/Index.aspx?page=336), which noted that the fire "started people thinking about fire prevention rather than only firefighting" and image appended to "Best Laid Plans," Scottish-American History Club Newsletter, April 2005, 2 (on Scottish immigration to Chicago). (http://www.chicago-scots.org/clubs/History/Newsletters/2005/apr05-2.htm).

34. "War Photography: Past and Present," *Camera*, March 1943, 39. Also see Susan Moeller, *Shooting War* (New York: Basic Books, 1989); Caroline Brothers, *War and Photography* (London: Routledge, 1997); Barbie Zelizer, *Remembering to Forget: Holocaust Memory through the Camera's Eye* (Chicago: University of Chicago Press, 1998).

35. William L. Laurence, "Heat in the Heart of an Atom," *New York Times*, May 1, 1937, 36.

36. Gregg Herken, *The Winning Weapon: The Atomic Bomb in the Cold War, 1945–1950* (New York: Knopf, 1980), 11.

37. Hanson W. Baldwin, "The Atomic Weapon," *New York Times*, August 7, 1945, 10.

38. Vicki Goldberg, *The Power of Photography* (New York: Abbeville Press, 1991), 147.

39. William L. Lawrence, "War Department Called Times' Reporter to Explain Bomb's Intricacies to Public," *New York Times*, August 7, 1945, 5, and "Eyewitness Tells First

Story of A-Bomb Blast," *New York Times,* September 9, 1945, 1, coverage that earned him a Pulitzer Prize. For criticism of the prize, see Amy Goodman, "Hiroshima Cover-Up: Stripping the War Department's Timesman of His Pulitzer," *Democracy Now!,* http://www.democracynow.org/2005/8/5/hiroshima_cover_up_stripping_the_war.

40. Brigadier General Thomas Farrell, in Lewis Wood, "Steel Tower Vaporized in Test of Mighty Bomb," *New York Times,* August 7, 1945, A5, where the only displayed images portrayed the enrichment plant at Oak Ridge, Tennessee, aerial pictures of Hiroshima before the attack, and members of the Manhattan Project (Jay Walz, "Atom Bombs Made in Three Hidden 'Cities,'" *New York Times,* August 7, 1945, 1). Other news organizations followed suit, using their front pages and editorial columns to assess the bomb on August 7, while broadcast news organizations extended their relay time to report the story.

41. "Bomb Pictures Delayed," *New York Times,* August 10, 1945, 4; Goldberg, *Power of Photography,* 147.

42. Vincent Leo, "The Mushroom Cloud Photograph: From Fact to Symbol," *Afterimage,* summer 1985, 8.

43. Photo titled "First Photo of Atomic Bombing of Japan," *Los Angeles Times,* August 12, 1945, 1; "Hiroshima—Site of a City That Used To Be," *Los Angeles Times,* August 12, 1945, 3; "Smoke and Fire Reach toward the Sky as Atomic Bombs Are Dropped on Japanese Cities," *New York Times,* August 12, 1945, sec. 1, 28; "Targets of Fate," *Newsweek,* August 20, 1945, 22, where only the picture of Nagasaki appeared under the caption "The atoms of Nagasaki rise 50,000 feet high." As Vincent Leo has argued, the delayed timing turned the photos into images of victory rather than destruction ("Mushroom Cloud").

44. "The War Ends," *Life,* August 20, 1945, 26–27, where images included the fire-bombing of Tokyo and before and after aerial views of the ground around Hiroshima. Additionally, the *Los Angeles Times* printed a five-shot series showing what it would look like to photograph an atomic bomb from six miles ("Atomic Bomb Explosion Photographed at Distance of Six Miles," *Los Angeles Times,* August 18, 1945, 8).

45. Susan D. Moeller, *Shooting War* (New York: Basic Books, 1989), 237.

46. They were taken by a Japanese photographer, with extensive visual documentation taken by Yosuke Yamahata for the Japanese military of Nagasaki. See photo entitled "First Ground Photo of Atomic Bomb Devastation," *Los Angeles Times,* September 2, 1945, 3, showing Japanese workers clearing away debris, and "Atomic Bombing of Nagasaki Told by Flight Member," *New York Times,* September 9, 1945, 35.

47. Wilfred Burchett, *Shadows of Hiroshima* (London: Methuen, 1984), 9. A more critical round of coverage later that month, provided by Burchett and John Hersey for the *New Yorker,* prompted Burchett to write, "in Hiroshima, thirty days after the first atom bomb destroyed the city and shook the world, people are still dying, mysteriously and horribly…Hiroshima does not look like a bombed city. It looks as if a monster steamroller has passed over it and squashed it out of existence. The damage is far greater than photographs can show"; Stuart Allan, "When Worlds Collide: Reporting the Realities of Hiroshima," in Hillel Nossek, Annabelle Sreberny, and Prasun Sonwalkar (eds.), *Media and Political Violence* (Creskill, NJ: Hampton Press, 2007), 88.

48. "Letters to the Times" (from Walter Niebuhr, Francis R. Walton, and Wm. Church Osborn), *New York Times,* August 11, 1945, 12.

49. "Atomic Bomb Film Is Made in Color," *New York Times,* October 23, 1946, 48; Leo, "Mushroom Cloud," 6.

50. "Release Photos of First A-Bomb," *Chicago Daily Defender,* December 8, 1960, 15; picture appended to "The Man in the White House, *Newsweek,* November 12, 1956, 74. The image also appeared in a 1963 advertisement for the U.S. Committee for the United Nations in a discussion about containing communism.

51. See, for instance, "Atomic Bomb in Japan Is Focus of Photo Show," *New York Times,* May 13, 1970, 48, and the "Daisy" political TV advertisement for Lyndon Baines Johnson's 1964 political campaign. After the Committee for the Compilation of Material on Damage Caused by the Atomic Bomb in Hiroshima and Nagasaki published *Hiroshima and Nagasaki: The Physical, Medical, and Social Effects of the Atomic Bombings* (New York: Basic Books, 1981), sentiments became more strident, exemplified in novels like Betty Jean Lifton's *A Place Called Hiroshima* (1985) and the reprinting of John Hersey's *Hiroshima* (1985).

52. "Exhibit Plans on Hiroshima Stir a Debate," *New York Times,* August 24, 1994, 26.

53. Robert Jay Lifton, *Indefensible Weapons* (New York: Basic Books, 1982), 61; Goldberg, *Power of Photography;* Peter Stepan, *Photos That Changed the World* (Munich: Prestel, 2000), 68–69; Kevin G. Barnhurst and John Nerone, *The Form of News: A History* (New York: Guilford, 2002).

54. Leo, "Mushroom Cloud," 6.

55. The gamble, they wrote, is "the wager that the long-term dangers of a technologically-intensive society will be avoided by continued progress" (Robert Hariman and John Louis Lucaites, *No Caption Needed* (Chicago: University of Chicago Press, 2007, 244). Thanks to Jonathan Glick for his thoughts on natural, accidental, and intentional death.

56. "Dateline San Francisco," *New York Times,* April 18, 2006, A26. Typical here have been the spectacular representations of tiny human figures scrambling to find unseen dying individuals across vast, barren landscapes: captions recount how residents of Burma struggled to find survivors after the 2008 cyclone or villagers searched in vain for those still alive in the mountains of Afghanistan or villages of China, Algeria, and Iran after they were buried by earthquakes [AP Photo/Nabil, Reghaia, Algeria, May 28, 2003, # 6785712 (41FW0) or AP Photo/Zaheeruddin Abdullah, Dashtak, Afghanistan, June 5, 1998, #2793932 (1NVT8)].

57. Christine Gibson, "Our Ten Greatest Natural Disasters," *American Heritage Magazine* 57(4), August/September 2006, 26–37.

58. Kevin Starr, *Americans and the California Dream, 1850–1915* (New York: Oxford University Press, 1973); Edward A. Wicher, "Training Presbyterian Ministers," *New York Observer,* August 8, 1907, 178. "The San Francisco Horror," *Christian Observer,* April 25, 1906, 17; "The Ruin at San Francisco" (editorial), *New York Observer and Chronicle,* April 26, 1906, 523. Alvin E. Magary, Readers' Letter, *New York Observer and Chronicle,* October 25, 1906, 84. Comments about sinfulness tend to repeatedly surface following natural disaster: Voltaire's observations on the Great Lisbon Earthquake of 1755 or linkages by conservative pundits Pat Robertson and Charles Colson between Hurricane Katrina and gay pride, legalized abortion and other so-called "sins" of the American people. Thanks to Gideon Glick for pointing out the relevance of the Gold Rush and to Larry Gross for these examples.

59. Editorial, *San Francisco Call,* October 22, 1868.

60. J. S. Holliday, *Rush for Riches: Gold Fever and the Making of California* (Berkeley: University of California Press, 1999), 126; Douglas Frith Anderson, "'We Have Here A Different Civilization': Protestant Identity in the San Francisco Bay Area, 1906–1909," *Western Historical Quarterly* 23(2), May 1992, 204.

61. Cited in Philip L. Fradkin, *The Great Earthquake and Firestorms of 1906: How San Francisco Nearly Destroyed Itself* (Berkeley: University of California Press, 2005), 5. Magary, Reader's Letter, 84.

62. "Plucky News Gatherer Sticks to His Work in Grave Peril," *San Francisco Chronicle*, May 7, 1906, np; "Earthquake and Fire, San Francisco in Ruins," *Call-Chronicle-Examiner*, April 19, 1906, 1; "HUNDREDS DEAD! City Seems Doomed For Lack of Water," *San Francisco Daily News*, April 19, 1906, 1.

63. See, for instance, the accounts reprinted in Gladys Hansen and Emmet Condon, *Denial of Disaster* (San Francisco: Cameron, 1989). Miriam Michaelson, "The Destruction of San Francisco," *Harper's Weekly*, May 5, 1906, 624. Almost without exception, headlines in every daily U.S. newspaper focused on the number of fatalities, as in "Heart is Torn From a Great City: San Francisco Nearly Destroyed by Earthquakes and Fire—Hundreds of Killed and Injured," *Los Angeles Times*, April 19, 1906, 1; or "Over 500 Dead, $200,000 Lost in San Francisco Earthquake," *New York Times*, April 19, 1906, 1.

64. H. Morse Stephens, "How the History of the Disaster Is Being Made," *San Francisco Examiner*, April 18, 1908, np.

65. James Hopper, "Our San Francisco," *Everybody's Magazine*, June 1906, np; Commentary, Virtual Museum of City of San Francisco, http://www.sfmuseum.net/1906.2/daynews.html.

66. Gertrude W. Page, "Sins of Exaggeration," *The Independent*, December 25, 1926, 117; M. Roeel, Letter to the Editor, *Forest and Stream*, June 16, 1906, n.p.

67. Fradkin, *Great Earthquake;* Hansen and Condon, *Denial of Disaster;* Gladys Hansen quoted in Tom Graham, "90 Years Later, Quake Victims Get Names," *San Francisco Chronicle*, April 14, 1996, SC-3.

68. Arnold Meltsner, "The Communication of Scientific Information to the Wider Public," *Minerva* 17(3), 331–354, autumn 1979, 333; Fradkin, *Great Earthquake*, 263.

69. George Kennan, Letters, *Outlook*, May 11, 1912, 101.

70. Fradkin, *Great Earthquake*, 264.

71. Edgar A. Cohen, "With a Camera in San Francisco," *Camera Craft*, June 1906, 183.

72. "Dateline San Francisco," *New York Times*, April 18, 2006, A26.

73. Cohen, "With a Camera," 284.

74. Jack London, "The Story of an Eyewitness," *Collier's*, May 5, 1906; "Cities that Have Suffered," *Los Angeles Times*, April 21, 1906, 114.

75. The motif also extended to drawings; the cover photo of *Harper's Weekly* showed a burning city, rescue workers, and police personnel in the foreground. No corpses were shown (Drawing by Arthur Lewis, "The Heart of the Ruins," *Harper's Weekly*, May 5, 1906, cover image). In some cases, the badly wounded and corpses lying amidst the rubble were depicted by artists. See, for instance, illustrations in Hansen and Condon, *Denial of Disaster*.

76. Quoted in Fradkin, *Great Earthquake*, 60.

77. Photo appended to Harry G. Carr, "The Epic of the Dynamited Metropolis," *Los Angeles Times,* April 21, 1906, 1.

78. See Virtual Museum of City of San Francisco, http://www.sfmuseum.net/1906.2/daynews.html.

79. James D. Phelan, "Personal Notes at the Time of the San Francisco Earthquake" (unpublished ms), quoted in Hansen and Condon, *Denial of Disaster,* 24–25; Fradkin, *Great Earthquake,* 59.

80. Photo titled "Wreck of the Southern Pacific Company Hospital," Virtual Museum of the City of San Francisco, http://www.sfmuseum.org/.

81. Photos appended to "Views of San Francisco—Some of the Districts Destroyed," *New York Times,* April 19, 1906, 6–7; "San Francisco's New Peril: Gale Drives Fire Ferryward; Hundreds of Bodies Found in the Ruins of Buildings," *New York Times,* April 21, 1906, 1.

82. In *Leslie's,* a photo of a still intact city appeared the first week, a burning city center the second week and a barren city center the third week (Cover photos, *Leslie's Weekly,* April 26, 1906, May 3, 1906, May 11, 1906. The May cover of *Sunset* magazine superimposed a female figure, signifying hope and the future, arising from a still burning city from which tiny human figurines were escaping ("The Spirit of the City," *Sunset,* May 1906, cover). Other monthlies—such as *Overland Monthly*—also depicted the still-burning city, the death of its citizens implied but not shown (photo appended to Pierre N. Beringer, "The Destruction of San Francisco," *Overland Monthly,* April 1906, 4).

83. For instance, of the images included in his book on the quake, nearly a fifth depicted still burning buildings, one of them the Valencia Street Hotel (Fradkin, *Great Earthquake*). Another volume with hundreds of photographs showed more than thirty images of buildings in the process of crumbling or burning, while only two (paintings) showed corpses (Hansen and Condon, *Denial of Disaster*). Also see Stepan, *Photos That Changed,* 14–15. The Valencia Street Hotel image also illustrated a report about Lawrence Livermore seismic experts' attempt to simulate the 1906 earthquake a hundred years after the fact ("Recreating the 1906 San Francisco Earthquake," *Science and Technology Review,* September 2006, https://str.llnl.gov/).

84. Some observers maintained that the images were touched up to support official versions of what happened (Gladys Hansen, in Tom Graham, "90 Years Later, Quake Victims Get Names," *San Francisco Chronicle,* April 14, 1996, SC-3). Hansen pointed to a deliberate effort to spread disinformation that involved images and noted that insurance companies were willing to pay up to $15,000 for amateur photos of heavy earthquake damage before the fires came. Also see Tim Walton, "Quake Spurred Birth of Citizen Photojournalism," msnbc.com, April 18, 2006, http://www.msnbc.msn.com/id/12358766.

85. Justin Ewers, "Nightmare in San Francisco," *U.S. News and World Report,* April 17, 2006, 42–46.

86. Fradkin, *Great Earthquake,* xi, 195. Other setbacks caused by the earthquake—increased U.S. vulnerability to Japan, stalled commerce in much of the United States, a negative effect on the nation's monetary stability that set the stage for the Panic of 1907 were all seen as part of this larger context. See Kerry A. Odell and Marc D. Weidenmier,

"Real Shock, Monetary Aftershock: The 1906 San Francisco Earthquake and the Panic of 1907," *The Journal of Economic History* 64, 2004, 1002–1027.

87. H. W. Brands, *The Age of Gold: the California Gold Rush and the New American Dream* (New York: Anchor, 2003), 442.

88. See, for instance, *Life*'s special commemorative online 2006 gallery of images on the earthquake's 100th anniversary, "California Observes the 100th Anniversary of the 1906 San Francisco Earthquake, *Life*, http://www.life.com/search/?q0=%221906%20san%20francisco%20earthquake%22 or the cover drawings of Lawrence Yep, *The Earth Dragon Awakes* (New York: Harper Collins, 2008) and Dan Kurzman, *Disaster!* (New York: Harper Perennial, 2002).

89. "The Loss of the 'Titanic'" (editorial), *The Independent*, April 18, 1912, 856. See picture appended to "Titanic Sinks Four Hours after Hitting Iceberg," *New York Times*, April 16, 1912, 1.

90. Picture appended to "Lusitania Sunk by a Submarine," *New York Times*, May 8, 1915, 1.

91. Pictures appended to "Andrea Doria and Stockholm Collide," *New York Times*, July 26, 1956, 1; "1,117 Andrea Doria Survivors Arrive Here," *New York Times*, July 27, 1956, 1; "Liners Collide," *Los Angeles Times*, July 26, 1956, 1; "Death Plunge of Proud Ship," appended to "Story of Terror on Doomed Liner," *Los Angeles Times*, July 27, 1956, 1. Harry Trask's version of the ships sinking, taken for the *Boston Traveler*, earned a Pulitzer Prize in 1957.

92. Allan Grist, "Zeppelin was 130th of Her Famed Line," *Philadelphia Inquirer*, May 7, 1937, 12.

93. George M. MaWhinney, "Explosion Blamed on Back-Fire," *Philadelphia Inquirer*, May 7, 1937, 1; Joseph Nelson, "Like 'End of World' When Zep Exploded," *Philadelphia Inquirer*, May 7, 1937, 1.

94. Robert J. Brown, *Manipulating the Ether: The Power of Broadcast Radio in Thirties America* (Jefferson, NC: McFarland, 1998), 142.

95. Herbert Morrison, *The Hindenburg Broadcast*, May 6, 1937 http://www.eyewitnesstohistory.com/vohind.htm. Also see *Broadcasting*, May 15, 1937, 14–15. Interestingly, the relay has been repeatedly codified as having been delivered live. Even *Broadcasting and Cable*'s 75th anniversary issue, which pointed to Morrison's broadcast as a high point of U.S. broadcasting, called it a "live account of the explosion" *Broadcasting and Cable*, May 22, 2006, np.

96. See the Hindenburg overview on radio at http://www.otr.com/hindenburg.shtml.

97. Cited in Brown, *Manipulating the Ether*, 142.

98. The former included Paramount, Fox, Universal, and News of the Day ("Films of Disaster Viewed By Millions," *New York Times*, May 8, 1937, 3).

99. "Hindenburg Burns in Lakehurst Crash; 21 Known Dead, 12 Missing, 64 Escape," *New York Times*, May 7, 1937, 1; "Hindenburg Explodes with 97 Aboard," *Washington Post*, May 7, 1937, 1; "Forty Die as Hindenburg Explodes," *Los Angeles Times*, May 7, 1937, 1; "The Hindenburg Makes Her Last Landing at Lakehurst," *Life*, May 17, 1937, 27–7. This was not the first report of a failed dirigible: seven years earlier, 46 passengers died in Britain's R101, but it was only visualized by a file photo ("British

Airship R101 Is Destroyed in Crash and Explosion in France," *New York Times*, October 5, 1930, 1).

100. Photos appended to "Torch from Sky Sears New Horror in Airship Annals," *Philadelphia Inquirer*, May 8, 1937, 12; "Hindenburg Blast Kills 35," *Philadelphia Inquirer*, May 7, 1937; "U.S. Maps Zep Probe," *Philadelphia Inquirer*, May 8, 1937, 1, 12; "Forty Die as Hindenburg Explodes," *Los Angeles Times*, May 7, 1937, 1, 2, 3, 8, 9, 16. Sketches appended to "Times' Artist's Sketch of Disaster," *Los Angeles Times*, May 8, 1937, 2 and "Artists' View of Hindenburg," *Los Angeles Times*, May 9, 1937, 3.

101. Hariman and Louis Lucaites, *No Caption Needed*, 249; Stepan, *Photos That Changed*, 8–9. Shere's picture—or other photos taken from the same vantage point—appeared in "Hindenburg Explodes With 97 Aboard, "*Washington Post*, May 7, 1937, 1; "The Hindenburg Makes Her Last Landing at Lakehurst," *Life*, May 17, 1937, 26–27; "Hindenburg Blast Kills 35," *Philadelphia Inquirer*, May 7, 1937, 1. A similar photo from the AP was appended to "The Hindenburg on Fire in the Air and Views After Crash at Lakehurst," *New York Times*, May 8, 1937, 3, and the *Inquirer* photographer's image appeared on an inside page ("Passengers Blown Alive From Zeppelin By Force of Blast," *Philadelphia Inquirer*, May 7, 1937, 11). Left somewhat unattended was the fact that amateur photographs were also produced by the group of bystanders in Lakehurst. See, for example, "Amateur Photographs at the Hindenburg's Last Loading," *Life*, May 17, 1937, 26–30, which included images from Arthur Cofod Jr. alongside those of Shere.

102. Comdr. C. E. Rosendahl, "New Zeppelin Is Described By American Airship Expert," *Science News Letter*, April 30, 1938, 281; Stepan, *Photos That Changed*, 53.

103. "The Hindenburg Disaster" (editorial), *Los Angeles Times*, May 8, 1937, A4; and Russell Owen, "Hindenburg Disaster Hard Blow to Airships," *New York Times*, May 9, 1937, E12. Cartoon titled "Indestructible," *Philadelphia Inquirer*, May 8, 1937, 10. Martin Kelley, "The Hindenburg Disaster," http://americanhistory.about.com/od/hindenburg/a/hindenburg.htm.

104. See, for instance, "Photos of the 20th Century," *The Columbia (S.C.) State*, December 19, 1999, S1; R. B. Stolley, ed., *Life: Our Century in Pictures* (Boston: Little, Brown, 1999), 138; Stepan, *Photos That Changed*, 52–53; Richard Lacayo and George Russell (eds.), *Eyewitness: 150 Years of Photojournalism* (New York: Time 1990), 81; Goldberg, *Power of Photography*, 194; "150 Years of Photojournalism," *Time*, fall 1989, n.p.; Beaumont Newhall, *The History of Photography* (New York: Little, Brown, 1988), 257.

105. See, for example, Onion Editors and Scott Dikkers, *Our Dumb Century: The Onion Presents 100 Years of Headlines from America's Finest News Sources* (New York: Three Rivers Press, 2007), 53; R. Conrad Stein, *The Hindenburg Disaster* (Chicago: Children's Press, 1993); and episodes of "The Simpsons." See Gregory Solman, "New History Channel Ads Remember Things Past," *Adweek*, June 14, 2004, where the picture appeared again in the article. Hariman and Lucaites maintain the Shere photograph was recycled more than others because it did not show the Nazi swastika on its tail (*No Caption Needed*, 247).

106. Goldberg, *Power of Photography*, 195.

107. Joe Garner, *We Interrupt This Broadcast* (New York: Sourcebooks, 2002), 4.

108. Kathy Sawyer, "The Horror Dawned Slowly," *Washington Post*, January 29, 1986, A1.

109. Jack Thomas, "TV Serves as Hearth for Country," *Boston Globe*, January 29, 1986, 8.

110. Boyce Rensberger, "Fire Engulfs Ship with 7 Aboard," *Washington Post*, January 29, 1986, A1.

111. Ibid., A1. Children's responses to the coverage wavered between impersonal regret and personal involvement, largely divided by gender (John C. Wright et al, "How Children Reacted to Televised Coverage of the Challenger Shuttle Disaster," *Journal of Communication* 39(2), 1989, 27–45).

112. Tom Shales, "Horror of the Fire in the Sky," *Washington Post*, January 29, 1986, B1.

113. Lance Morrow, "A Nation Mourns," *Time*, February 10, 1986, 23.

114. J. Miller, "The Impact of the *Challenger* Accident on Public Attitudes Toward the Space Program," *Report to the National Science Foundation* (Public Opinion Lab, Northern Illinois University, 1987).

115. Martin Merzer, "Space's Age of Innocence Ends," *Miami Herald*, January 29, 1986, 1S.

116. Pictures appended to "The Last Moments," *New York Times*, January 29, 1986, A5; "Space Shuttle Explodes in Midair, Killing Crew," *Philadelphia Inquirer*, January 19, 1986, 1; "Space Shuttle Mission 51-L: The Disaster," *Washington Post*, January 19, 1986, A6-A8; "The Shuttle Explodes," *New York Times*, January 29, 1986, 1; "Shuttle Explodes, Crew Killed," *Los Angeles Times*, January 29, 1986, 1, 5.

117. Quoted in Karlyn Barker and John Ward Anderson, "Vivid TV Images Spread Disaster's Shock Wave," *Washington Post*, January 29, 1986, A9. The comparison underscores the greater acceptance of violent graphic images in fictional formats than in news.

118. Subheading to Shales, "Horror of the Fire," B1.

119. Richard Cohen, "In Space, Still," *Washington Post*, January 29, 1986, A23.

120. Shales, "Horror of the Fire," B1. The replay had a macabre effect. As former astronaut Michael Collins wrote in the *Washington Post*, "We watch the rockets explode, over and over again, in slow motion, backward and forward, in vivid color. Christa's parents watch their daughter's spacecraft being blown to bits. We watch them watching it. Not once but as often as we can stomach it. This 'you are there' lens, coupled with instant replay, magnifies that which needs no magnification" ("Riding the Beast," *Washington Post*, January 30, 1986, A25).

121. See, in particular, Diane Vaughan, *The Challenger Launch Decision: Risky Technology, Culture, and Deviance at NASA* (Chicago: University of Chicago Press, 1997). Because the launching has come to be seen as "an archetypal example of bad decision-making arising from poor decision-making processes and institutional culture," a focus on the faulty mechanics of the launching—specifically, the so-called O-rings which failed to seal due to the cold weather—has faded; see Jill Edy and Miglena Dardanova," Reporting Through the Lens of the Past: From Challenger to Columbia," *Journalism* 7(2), 2006, 135.

122. C. P. Jeevan, "The Rise and Fall of the Space Shuttle," *Social Scientist*, May 1986, 48; Martin Merzer, "Space's Age of Innocence Ends," *Miami Herald*, January 29, 1986, 1S; Thomas H. Maugh, "Why Shuttle Exploded Still a Major Mystery," *Los Angeles Times*, January 29, 1986, 1; Murray Dubin, "Some Question Value of Manned Missions," *Philadelphia Inquirer*, January 29, 1986, 7A; Collins, "Riding," A25.

123. William J. Cook, "Shifting Cautiously Ahead, 10 Years Later," *U.S. News and World Report,* January 29, 1996, 10, illustrated by the *Challenger* exploding yet again.

124. See, for instance, Jeffrey Smith, "Shuttle Inquiry Focuses on Weather, Rubber Seals and Unheeded Advice," *Science,* February 28, 1986, 909–911. Suspicions of negligence grew when the Presidential commission charted to investigate the disaster, The Rogers Commission, returned with an indictment not only of mechanical failure but of institutional culture gone amok.

125. Ellen Livingston, "The Last Thing I Wanted Was to Be a Reporter Now," *Miami Herald,* January 29, 1986, 4S; "Oh, the Humanity" (editorial), *Washington Post,* January 29, 1986, A22; Cohen, "In Space, Still,"A23; Shales, "Horror of the Fire." B1; Cynthia Gorney and Stephanie Mansfield, "A New Tragedy Calls Back the Sorrows of the Past," *Washington Post,* January 30, 1986, B1; Dick Polman, "In Calamity, A New Lesson in Courage," *Philadelphia Inquirer,* February 2, 2003, A9.

126. "Oh, the Humanity," A22. Some observers noted the irony in the comparisons: for instance, *The New Republic* decried the fact that "the explosion in the sky bore little resemblance to those tragedies" and the commonality between earlier assassinations and the explosion was "the presence of the camera and the swarm of anchormen," a comparison that "exalt[ed] television as the legitimate creator of a common national emotion" ("When *Challenger* Fell From the Sky," *The New Republic,* February 17, 1986, 7. "Hindenburg Announcer's Reaction," *San Francisco Chronicle,* January 29, 1986, 14. Jack Thomas, "TV Serves as Hearth for Country," *Boston Globe,* January 29, 1986, 8.

127. "Photos of the 20th Century," *The Columbia [S.C.] State,* December 19, 1999, S1; Jerry Adler, "Putting Names in the Sky," *Newsweek,* May 13, 1991, 69), where it was called "a brilliant solution to the problem of reconciling the sober function of a memorial—which in some way must acknowledge that its subject is dead and in the ground—with a celebration of spaceflight, in a literal sense the highest achievement of humankind." The picture arises online when inputting "*Challenger* explosion" as a search term into the websites for MSNBC, the BBC, Wikipedia and YouTube.

128. Dan Steinberg, "As Tragedy Unfolds, Networks Stay Tuned," *Philadelphia Inquirer,* February 2, 2003, A9.

129. Tom Shales, "Networks Struggle to Convey Another Day of National Anguish," *Washington Post,* February 2, 2003, A3. Even in coverage there were similarities, as when Shales's column recycled ideas from the column he wrote following the *Challenger* disaster in 1986.

130. "Television News at Its Best and Worst," *Electronic Media,* February 10, 2003, 10.

131. Seth Borenstein, quoted in Edy and Dardanova, "Reporting Through the Lens," 144.

132. Chris Suellentrop, "The *Columbia* Disaster on the Web," slate.com, posted February 3, 2003, 6.57 pm.

133. Staci D. Kramer, "Shuttle Coverage Mixed But Strong Overall," *Online Journalism Review,* February 2, 2003.

134. Mike Braun, "*Vindicator*'s Coverage Followed 9/11 Blueprint," poynter.org, posted February 5, 2003, 4.51 pm; James Kauffman, "Lost in Space: A Critique of NASA's Crisis Communications in the *Columbia* Dis aster," *Public Relations Review* 31, 2005, 263–275. space.com was established in response to a reduced interest among mainstream

journalists in topics related to space exploration (Rosen, "Taking a Walk on Space"); http://www.slate.com/id/2078072/.

135. Steve Saffran, "Convergence at NECN," poynter.org, posted February 6, 2003, 9.51; Kramer, "Shuttle Coverage Mixed."

136. Mark Jurkowitz, "Again on TV, Riveting Scenes and Gathering of Grief," *Boston Globe,* February 2, 2003, A26.

137. Robert Daugherty, in Kenneth Irby, "A Digital Icon in Time," poynter.org, February 5, 2003, 2.00 am; Paul Richard, "*Columbia,* Gone in a Frustrating, Imprecise Blur," *Washington Post,* February 4, 2003, C1. Both photographs appeared across the covers, front pages, and news sites of the *New York Times, Los Angeles Times, Washington Post,* the *Philadelphia Inquirer, Time, Newsweek,* and ABC News, among others. See, for instance, picture appended to "Shuttle Breaks Up, 7 Dead," *New York Times,* February 2, 2003, 1; "'*Columbia* is Lost,'" *Los Angeles Times,* February 2, 2003, 1; "'*Columbia* is Lost,'" *Washington Post,* February 2, 2003, 1; "*Columbia* Lost," *Philadelphia Inquirer,* February 2, 2003, 1; "Not Again," *Newsweek,* February 10, 2003, cover; "'The *Columbia* Is Lost,'" *Time,* February 10, 2003, cover.

138. Lisa Granatstein, "Shuttle Scramble," *MediaWeek,* February 10, 2003; Pictures appended to "Shuttle Breaks Up, 7 Dead," *New York Times,* February 2, 2003, 1; "Drifting Particles," *New York Times,* February 2, 2003, 26; James Glanz, "Space Flight's Dangers Are Raised by Speed," *New York Times,* February 2, 2003, 28; "2003 Sigma Delta Chi Awards," *Quill,* June/July 2004, 10.

139. See, for instance, accounts regarding charred human remains that surfaced outside Nacogdoches (http://www.io.com/~o_m/clfaq/s3.htm) and Hemphill, Texas, where pictures of "debris" were displayed alongside a story about the surfacing of body parts, "Body Parts Reportedly Found," *Cincinnati Enquirer,* February 2, 2003.

140. See, for example, picture titled "Silent Vigil," *Los Angeles Times,* February 2, 2003, A6.

141. "Turning Point for US Space Effort," BBC News, February 2, 2003; http://news.bbc.co.uk/1/hi/world/americas/2718353.stm.

142. Jill Rosen, "Taking a Walk on Space," *American Journalism Review,* March 2003, 10–11; Joan Ryan, "A Measure of What We've Lost," *San Francisco Chronicle,* February 2, 2003, A34; Buzz Aldrin, "'Just Doing Their Duty,'" *Los Angeles Times,* February 3, 2003, B11; Polman, "In Calamity," A1, A9.

143. Aldrin, "'Just Doing Their Duty,'" B11; "Letters to the Times," *Los Angeles Times,* February 4, 2003, B12; "Space in Our Hearts" (Editorial), *Philadelphia Inquirer,* February 2, 2003, C4. NASA, trying to counteract memory of how it had poorly handled public queries about the *Challenger* disaster, nonetheless could not counter the stiff public, journalistic, and official opposition to its reasoning about the *Columbia* explosion. See Kauffman, "Lost in Space."

144. Crispin Sartwell, "A Place Like…The Sky," *Los Angeles Times,* February 3, 2003, B11; Gregg Easterbrook, "What Went Wrong? *Time,* February 2, 2003; "American Mourns, Again" (editorial), *New York Times,* February 2, 2003, 24; Polman, "In Calamity," A9.

145. Pictures appended to Rob Stein, "With the Loss of *Columbia,* Echoes of the Challenger," *Washington Post,* February 2, 2003, A11; "A Look At the Fleet," *Washington*

Post, February 2, 2003, A29; Paul Richard, "*Columbia,* Gone in a Frustrating, Imprecise Blur," *Washington Post,* February 4, 2003, C1; "Space Travel Won't End," *Philadelphia Inquirer,* February 2, 2003, A8; "Seventeen Years Ago in Time," *Time,* February 10, 2003, 24; "The Shuttle's Glory and Tragedy," *Time,* February 10, 2003, 40. Edy and Dardanova ("Reporting Through the Lens," 2006) track how journalists' interpretive strategies drew from the earlier explosion; Howard Rosenberg, "Television Once Again Plays Its Role as Conduit of Nation's Grief," *Los Angeles Times,* February 2, 2003, A19. Said one editor, "You go with what impacts your readers most" (quoted in Rosen, "Taking a Walk on Space," 11).

146. Mark Cantrell and Donald Vaughan, *Sixteen Minutes from Home* (Boca Raton: AMI Books, 2003), back cover and unnumbered inside pages; Jonathan Curiel, "2003: The Year in Pictures," *San Francisco Chronicle,* December 28, 2003, D1. Also see *Newsweek*'s "One Dazzling Decade," http://2010.newsweek.com/essay/one-dazing-decade.html; MSNBC's "The Decade in Pictures: Events," http://news.uk.msn.com/photos/photos.aspx?cp-documentid=151078358&page=13; http://2010.newsweek.com/photo/visions-of-the-decade/2003.slide1.html; WFAA-TV's "Photos: Decade in Review," http://www.wfaa.com/news/slideshows/Photos-Of-The-Decade-78346827.html?gallery=y&c=y&img=1; Robert Sullivan, *2000–2009, The Decade That Changed the World* (New York, Life Books, 2009), n.p.

147. Barbie Zelizer, "CNN, the Gulf War, and Journalistic Practice," *Journal of Communication* 42, winter 1992, 66–81.

148. For more on this, see Barbie Zelizer, "The Voice of the Visual," in Kendall Phillips, *Framing Public Memory* (Tuscaloosa: University of Alabama Press, 2004), 157–186.

149. Rutenberg and Barringer, "Ethics, A24.

150. D. Murray, "Behaving in the Face of Tragedy," *Crisis Journalism: A Handbook for Media Response* (http://www.americanpressinstitute.org/articles/publications/crisis-journalism: American Press Institute, 2001), ii.

151. Though 11% of people in the United States used radio as their primary source of information in the first days after the attacks, television remained the most widely used source of information (Pew Research Center for the People and the Press, *Terror Coverage Boosts News Media's Influence,* November 2001).

152. See Barbie Zelizer and Stuart Allan (eds.), *Journalism after September 11* (London: Routledge, 2002) for extensive discussion of the 9/11 coverage.

153. Mike Phillips in *Crisis Journalism: A Handbook for Media Response* (http://www.americanpressinstitute.org/articles/publications/crisisjournalism/: American Press Institute, 2001), 13; Stuart Allan, "Reweaving the Internet," in Zelizer and Allan (eds.), *Journalism After September 11,* 123; Steve Outing, "Attack's Lessons for News Web Sites," *Editor and Publisher,* September 19, 2001; Pew Internet and American Life, "How Americans Used the Internet After the Terror Attack," September 15, 2001, http://www.pewinternet.org/.

154. Barbie Zelizer, "Photography, Journalism and Trauma," in Zelizer and Allan (eds.), *Journalism After September 11,* 48–68; "September 11," *Newsweek,* December 31, 2001–January 7, 2002; Joe Russin in W. Robins, "Newspaper Web Sites Bring Tragedy Home," *Editor and Publisher,* October 15, 2001; Philip Gefter, in Marianne Hirsch, "The Day Time Stopped," *Chronicle of Higher Education,* January 25, 2002. This turn to the

visual had precedent, however, as it was displayed following the liberation of the Nazi concentration camps in 1945, when, unlike the coverage of 9/11, bodies were also shown; see Barbie Zelizer, *Remembering to Forget: Holocaust Memory through the Camera's Eye* (Chicago: University of Chicago Press, 1998).

155. New York *Daily News*, September 12, 2001. Editor in chief Ed Kosner later said that "I felt that it would be dishonest, almost, not to use images like that. It was the situation that was horrible, [not] the 'graphicness' of the pictures," in David Friend, *Watching the World Change* (New York: Farrar, Straus and Giroux, 2006), 128.

156. "September 11, 2001." *People*, September 24, 2001; "Special Report: God Bless America," *Newsweek*, September 24, 2001; Steve Outing, "Attack's Lessons"; J. Scott, "Closing a Scrapbook Full of Life and Sorrow," *New York Times*, December 31, 2001.

157. Caryn James, "British Take Blunter Approach to War Reporting," *New York Times*, November 9, 2001; Alessandra Stanley, "Opponents of War are Scarce on Television," *New York Times*, November 9, 2001; Silvio Waisbord, "Journalism, Risk and Patriotism," in Zelizer and Allan (eds.), *Journalism after September 11*, 201–219.

158. *Crisis Journalism*, 2001, iii; "Before and After—Special 40th Anniversary Issue," *Columbia Journalism Review*, 2001; J. Geisler, "Covering Terror and Tragedy," Radio-Television News Directors Association and Foundation, www.rtnda.org, October, 2001; Andrew Heyward, in J. Gay, "Network Lions and Cable Jackals Find Essence of TV News is News," *The New York Observer*, September 24, 2001; Patricia Cohen, "When Repetition is Helpful Rather Than Annoying, *The New York Times*, September 17, 2001; Caryn James, "Live Images Make Viewers Witnesses to Horror," *New York Times*, September 12, 2001, A25.

159. Deborah Potter, "It Isn't Over," *American Journalism Review*, November 2001, 76; Poynter Institute, *September 11, 2001: A Collection of Front Page Newspapers Selected by the Poynter Institute* (Kansas City, Mo: Andrews McMeel, 2001). The sequences of the tower's destruction appeared on the front pages of the *Los Angeles Times*, the *Lexington Herald-Leader*, the *Sacramento Bee*, the *Arizona Republic*, *The Tennessean*, the *Denver Post*, and the *Dallas Morning News*, among others.

160. Personal communication with author; James, "Live Images," A25.

161. Erik Sorensen, in Rutenberg and Barringer, "Ethics," A24.

162. Quoted in "Terror Hits Home," *TV Guide*, September 29–October 5, 2001, p. 10; "Terror in America," *Business Week*, September 24, 2001, 35.

163. One exhibit, entitled "Here Is New York: A Democracy of Photographs," displayed over 4,000 images by hundreds of professional and amateur photographers, stringing them on wires across the ceilings and walls. In one organizer's words, "the photographs are the memorial to September 11" (Charles Traub, interview with author, November 13, 2001.) See Barbie Zelizer, "Finding Aids to the Past: Bearing Personal Witness to Traumatic Public Events." *Media, Culture, and Society* 24 (5), September 2002. It is also worth noting that many pictures also showed people looking at the towers without showing the towers themselves, a telling kind of photo that forced viewers to fill in what was known but not pictured.

164. Andy Grundberg, "Photography," *New York Times Book Review*, December 2, 2001, 35.

165. The burning towers appeared repeatedly across the media, including *TV Guide* (September 29–October 5, 2001, cover, 8–9, 10 and 18); *Business Week*

(September 24, 2001, cover, 34); and *People* (September 24, 2001, cover, 6–7). Book covers included those of Magnum Photos, *New York: September 11, 2001* (New York: Powerhouse Books, 2001); World Wide Photos and Associated Press, *Day of Terror;* Editors of *New York* Magazine, *September 11, 2001: A Record of Tragedy, Heroism, and Hope* (New York: Henry N. Abrams, 2001); Ethan Casey (ed.), *9:11 8.48 A.M.: Documenting America's Greatest Tragedy* (New York: Booksurge.com, 2001). At year's end, they appeared in *Newsweek* (December 31, 2001- January 7, 2002, cover) and "The Year in Pictures," *New York Times* (December 31, 2001, section G); *New York: September 11, 2001* [New York: Magnum Photographers]; *In the Line of Duty* (New York: Regan Books, 2001). Other examples included World Trade Center 2002 Memorial Wall Calendar, Heroes 2002 Wall Calendar, *American 911: We Will Never Forget* (VHS Tape Set).

166. Pictures appended to "Decades in Review," *Philadelphia Inquirer,* December 31, 2009, A8; Robert Sullivan, *2000–2009, The Decade That Changed the World* (New York, Life Books, 2009), n.p. "Minute By Minute: Real Terror in Real Time," *New York Times,* September 11, 2008, E2. See, for example, *Newsweek*—http://2010.newsweek.com/essay/one-dazing-decade.html; MSNBC—http://www.msnbc.msn.com/id/34261690/ns/news-picture_stories/displaymode/1247/?beginSlide=1; Dallas TV WFAA—http://www.wfaa.com/news/slideshows/Photos-Of-The-Decade-78346827.html.

167. Colson Whitehead, "The Image," *New York Times Magazine,* September 23, 2001, p. 21.

168. See, for instance, Rebecca Solnit, "The Ruins of Memory," in Mark Klett and Michael Lundgren, *After the Ruins: 1906 and 2006* (Berkeley: University of California Press, 2006), 18–31; Fradkin, *Great Earthquake.*

169. Richard Edward Larsen, "Did Palestinian Boy Die in Vain?" *Ventura County Star,* October 5, 2000, B9.

170. Leo, "Mushroom Cloud," 8; Paul Richard, "*Columbia,* Gone in a Frustrating, Imprecise Blur," *Washington Post,* February 4, 2003, C3.

Chapter 4

1. Interview with Jean-Marc Boujou, January 2005, Los Angeles, California.

2. For instance, a Reuters photo of a Guatemalan drought-stricken child lying in a hospital bed in 2002 was described by the following statement: "Some 6,000 Guatemalan children under five are in danger of dying from hunger in the coming months, with 126 dead already" (Reuters Pictures/Photo by Jorge Silva, May 2, 2002, Jocotan, Guatemala, #x011370020020503dy53000b5). It was not clear whether the child depicted actually died.

3. "Plague Spot," (1840), accredited to Hulton Archive/*Illustrated London News*/Getty Images), # 3325442; "The Black Death in the 14th Century," Mary Evans Collection, www.bbc.co.uk/.../photos/2007/5/31/20878_2.jpg; Michael L. Carlebach, *The Origins of Photojournalism in America* (Washington, DC: Smithsonian Press, 1992), 93.

4. With the pictures called "not portraits painted from fancy, but photographs taken from life, taken of men in the agonies of death," Congress debated retaliating over what they depicted for months [Vicki Goldberg, *The Power of Photography* (New York: Abbeville Press, 1991), 24]. The same engravings were also appended to "Further Proofs of Rebel

Inhumanity," *Harper's Weekly*, June 18, 1864, 387. John Peffer, "Snap of the Whip/Crossroads of Shame," *Visual Anthropology Review* 24(1), spring 2008, 55–77.

5. Robert Hariman and John Lucaites, *No Caption Needed* (Chicago: University of Chicago Press, 2008).

6. Elaine Scarry, *The Body in Pain* (New York: Oxford University Press, 1985).

7. Mahmood Mamdani, "Karamoja: Colonial Roots of Famine in North-East Uganda," *Review of African Political Economy*, September—December 1982, 66.

8. Richard Longhurst, "Famines, Food, and Nutrition: Issues and Opportunities for Policy and Research," *Food and Bulletin* 9(1), March 1987, np.

9. Will Ross, "Guns and Drought in Karamoja," BBC News, February 18, 2003, http://news.bbc.co.uk/2/hi/africa/2777059.stm; Susan Robinson et al., "Famine Relief in Karamoja, Uganda," *The Lancet,* October 18, 1980, 850–851; Mahmood Mamdani, "Karamoja: Colonial Roots of Famine in North-East Uganda," *Review of African Political Economy,* September—December, 1982, 66–73.

10. Marcel Marceau, in Sebastio Salgado and Stephan Mayes, *This Critical Mirror* (London: Thames and Hudson, 1995), 129.

11. See, for instance, http://www.vinodlive.com/2007/02/15/some-of-the-most-powerful-images-from-around-the-world/. See too Salgado and Mayes, *This Critical Mirror,* 129.

12. See, for instance, http://iconicphotos.wordpress.com/2009/11/19/famine-in-uganda/; Filip Spagnoli, "Iconic Images of Human Rights Violations: Starving Boy in Uganda," May 14, 2009, http:/filipspagnoli.wordpress.com/2009/05/14/iconic-images-of-human-rights-violations-6-starving-boy-in-uganda/; Vinod Ponmanadiyil, "Some of the Most Powerful Images From Around the World," http://vinpon.wordpress.com/2007/04/03/some-of-the-most-powerful-images-from-around-the-world/; http://tokasid.blogspot.com/2007/03/wars-of-world.html; Norbert Mao, "Famine in Northern Uganda is a Wake-Up Call For Everybody," July 27, 2009, www.friendsforpeaceinafrica.org.

13. Stuart Franklin, in Patrick Wright, "Icon of the Revolution," *Guardian,* June 4, 1992, 23. There were in fact three images: one by Stuart Franklin for Magnum Photos, one by Jeff Widener for AP, and one by Charles Cole for UPI, which won the World Press Award.

14. Peter Stepan, *Photos that Changed the World* (Munich: Prestel, 2000), 162. One photographer later recalled that "there was no doubt in my mind he was going to be killed. They'd shot so many others, and I was certain he'd die" (quoted in Wright, "Icon," 23).

15. The photo appeared on both June 5 and 6 in the *New York Times, Los Angeles Times,* and *Chicago Tribune,* and as a picture appended to "China on the Brink of Civil War," *St. Louis Post-Dispatch,* June 6, 1989, 1; Russell Watson, "Reign of Terror," *Newsweek,* June 19, 1989, 19; Strobe Talbot, "Defiance," *Time,* June 19, 1989, 10–11, and cover, "Revolt Against Communism," *Time,* June 19, 1989; "History Through a Cloudy Lens," *U.S. News and World Report,* June 19, 1989, 18–19. The photo's impact was discussed in "Bush Halts Military Sales to China," *Los Angeles Times,* June 5, 1989, 1 and "China Teeters on Edge of Civil War as Rival Forces Mobilize," *Los Angeles Times,* June 6, 1989, A1.

16. James Barron, "One Man Can Make a Difference," *New York Times,* June 6, 1989, A16, which called the picture "powerful in its simplicity." Also see James P. Sterba, "For A Moment, This Man's Lonely Act of Defiance Held Chinese Army at Bay," *Wall Street*

Journal, June 6, 1989, A25; and David R. Schweisberg, "One Man's Defiant Gesture," *New Pittsburgh Courier,* June 17, 1989, 1. The picture's most cited precedent was "Prague Summer," where photographer Ladislav Bielik depicted a man standing down a Soviet tank in Bratislava, August 21, 1968.

17. Quoted in David D. Perlmutter, *Photojournalism and Foreign Policy: Icons of Outrage in International Crises* (Westport, CT: Praeger, 1998), 69.

18. The photo appeared in *Time* twice on June 19, 1989, once on July 10, 1989 and once on December 12, 1989. It appeared in *Newsweek* in its June 19, 1989, and December 12, 1989 issues. It appeared on *Life*'s cover for its "Year in Pictures" section.

19. Though numerous claims were made about the man's identity, they were never sufficiently resolved. Even when the *Guardian* did its ten-year anniversary round-up on the event, it named the man but admitted "he has disappeared from sight, though not from history. China's president Jiang Zemin said the police had checked morgues, prisons and computer registers but were unable to find any trace of him" ("The Price of Dissent," in "Tiananmen: 10 Years On," *Guardian.co.uk,* May 31, 1999, posted at http://www.guardian.co.uk/world/1999/may/31/china); Wright, "Icon," 23; "Barbara Walters, "A Smile and Eyes That Go Cold," *New York Times,* May 18, 1990, A31. For more on the man's various identities and sightings, see Perlmutter, *Photojournalism;* and Hariman and Lucaites, *No Caption Needed.*

20. Richard Gordon, "One Act, Many Meanings," *Media Studies Journal,* winter 1999, 82. See Wu Hung, *Remaking Beijing* (Chicago: University of Chicago Press, 2005); and Hariman and Lucaites, *No Caption Needed* for a discussion of these artifacts.

21. Perlmutter, *Photojournalism,* 67.

22. Pico Iyer, "The Unknown Rebel," *Time,* April 13, 1998, 192–195; "Photos of the 20th Century," *Columbia (S.C.) State,* December 19, 1999, S1; Susan D. Moeller, *Compassion Fatigue* (London: Routledge, 1999), 50; Gordon, "One Act," 82; Trudy Rubin, "An Image of Defiance, An Image of Possibility," *Philadelphia Inquirer,* June 4, 2008. A15, where the picture again illustrated the article.

23. Jeffrey Wasserstrom, "History, Myth and the Tales of Tiananmen," in J. Wasserstrom and E. J. Perry, *Popular Protest and Political Culture in Modern China* (Boulder, CO: Westview Press, 1994), 297.

24. The picture appears repeatedly in retrospectives. See, for instance, Stepan, *Photos That Changed,* 162; "150 Years of Photojournalism," *Time,* fall 1989, 71; and Goldberg, *The Power of Photography,* 251; Richard Lacayo and George Russell, *Eyewitness: 150 Years of Photojournalism* (New York: Time, 1995), 164; Richard B. Stolley, *Our Century in Pictures* (Boston: Little, Brown, 1999), 375.

25. Longhurst, "Famines, Food and Nutrition," np.

26. Mamdani, "Karamoja: Colonial Roots of Famine," 66.

27. Perlmutter, *Photojournalism,* 63.

28. Taylor, *Body Horror,* 49.

29. "Further Proofs of Rebel Inhumanity," *Harper's Weekly,* June 18, 1864, 387; Reuters Pictures, August 5, 1998, Baghdad, Iraq, #x007000020010920du8502i3; Associated Press photo, Jinga, Uganda, June 26, 2001. #589961 (31G6B).

30. For more on this, see Barbie Zelizer, *Remembering to Forget: Holocaust Memory through the Camera's Eye* (Chicago: University of Chicago Press, 1998).

31. Janina Struck, "The Death Pit," *Guardian*, January 27, 2004, 9.

32. Michael Berenbaum, *The World Must Know* (Boston: Little, Brown, 1993), 112.

33. Ibid.

34. Ibid., 110.

35. Ibid., 109. The picture appeared over time with varying degrees of informational detail. Typical captions read "Roundup of Jews during the Warsaw Ghetto uprising. More than 56,000 Jews surrendered as in one caption that read "Warsaw Ghetto: A group of Jewish fighters before their extinction" (Yitzhak Arad, *The Pictorial History of the Holocaust*, New York: Macmillan, 1990), 334.

36. Jurgen Stroop, *The Stroop Report: The Jewish Quarter of Warsaw Is No More!* (1943; reprint New York: Pantheon Books, 1979), n.p.

37. Robert H. Jackson, *The Case against the Nazi War Criminals* (New York: Knopf), 1946; Charles Alexander and Anne Keshan, *Justice at Nuremberg: A Pictorial Record of the Trial* (New York, 1946); Robert H. Jackson, *Nurnberg Case As Presented by Robert H. Jackson Chief of Counsel for the United States Together With Other Documents* (New York: Cooper Square, 1947).

38. Alexander and Keshan, *Justice at Nuremberg*, 181.

39. Gerhard Schoenberner, *Der gelbe Stern* [*The Yellow Star*] (Germany,1960). The photograph appeared inside each edition of the book but also on the cover of the British, French, Canadian, and Dutch editions. The exhibit using the photo, held in April and May 1960 in Berlin's new Congress Hall, initially drew objection from Berlin's minister of culture, who protested the image's use because he did not believe it was authentic; see Richard Raskin, *A Child at Gunpoint: A Case Study in the Life of a Photo* (Denmark: Aarhus University Press, 2004), 156.

40. Gideon Hausner, *Justice in Jerusalem* (New York: Harper and Row, 1966).

41. Picture appended to David Ben-Gurion, "The Eichmann Case as Seen by Ben-Gurion," *New York Times Magazine*, December 18, 1960, 7, 62. Using specific images to illustrate broad texts in regards to the Holocaust is discussed in Zelizer, *Remembering to Forget*.

42. The photo was captioned: "Grim roundup of young Jews takes place in Warsaw after conquest of Poland. Germans sent some to ghettoes but the killings had already begun." See "Eichmann's Own Story (Part I and II)," *Life*, November 28, 1960, 106, and December 5, 1960, 22–23; picture appended to David Ben-Gurion, "Eichmann and His Trial," *Saturday Evening Post*, November 3/10/17, 1962, 39–41; picture appended to David Binder, "Nazi Photograph Helps Convict Nazi Murderers," *New York Times*, May 24, 1969, 2, whose caption read, "A Nazi soldier with a rifle, at rear, guarding Jewish prisoners during the ill-fated 1943 Warsaw Ghetto uprising." The picture was cropped so that the boy was in front of only three or four other individuals, and the photograph was described as having been taken in April 1943, not May.

43. Books using the image on their front cover included Emanuel Ringelblum, *Notes from the Warsaw Ghetto* (New York: Schocken, 1974), Stewart Justman, *The Jewish Holocaust for Beginners* (New York: Writers and Readers, 1995); Peter Neville, *The Holocaust* (Cambridge: Cambridge University Press, 1999); French L. MacLean, *Ghetto Men* (Atglen, PA: Schiffer Military History, 2001). Also see Chena Byers Abells, *The Children We Remember: Photographs from the Archives of Yad Vashem* (London: Kar-Ben Publishers,

1983). Beyond course syllabi and primary pedagogic materials, the image appeared too on the cover of the Anti-Defamation League's *Holocaust Denial: A Pocket Guide* (New York: ADL, 1997).

44. Artwork included that of Italian painter Renato Gutusso, who painted the boy with raised hands, U.S. artist Judy Chicago, who used the photo in her piece "Im/balance of Power," in *Holocaust Project: From Darkness into Light* (New York: Penguin, 1993), and Holocaust survivor Samuel Bak, who produced a series of 25 paintings between 1995 and 1998 incorporating the image. Swedish filmmaker Ingmar Bergman used the image in his film *Persona* in 1966, Israeli filmmaker Haim Gouri in *The 81st Blow* in 1974, and in 1985 Yugoslavian Mitko Panov's short film *With Raised Hands* crafted a fictional story around the photograph, winning an award for him and the Polish National School for Film, Television and Theatre, which produced it at the Cannes Film Festival in 1991. Poems included Peter L. Fischl's "To The Little Polish Boy Standing with His Arms Up" (1965), which was a featured part of the Simon Wiesenthal Center archives in Los Angeles, and Yala Korwin's "The Little Boy With His Hands Up" (1987). All of this underscores the image's remarkable durability across locations and decades of representation.

45. Holocaust survivor and artist Samuel Bak gave him the name of one of his lost childhood friends; see Samuel Bak, *Between Worlds* (Boston, Pucker Art Publications, 2002).

46. Erwin Kroll, "The Uses of the Holocaust," *The Progressive,* July 1993, 15. The article reproduced not the photo of the boy but a drawing instead.

47. Stepan, *Photos that Changed,* 58; Sue Fishkoff, "The Holocaust in One Photograph," *Jerusalem Post,* April 18, 1993.

48. "Clay Harris, Warsaw Ghetto Boy: Symbol of the Holocaust," *Washington Post,* September 17, 1978, L1, L9; Edward Kossoy, "The Boy From the Ghetto," *Jerusalem Post,* September 1, 1978, 5; Heidi Gleit, "When History is Forgotten," *Jerusalem Post,* September 20, 2000; Helen Schary Motro, "Worth More Than a Thousand Words," *Jerusalem Post,* February 22, 2001; Stepan, *Photos that Changed,* 59.

49. David Margolick, "Rockland Physician Thinks He is the Boy in Holocaust Photo Taken in Warsaw," *New York Times,* May 28, 1982, B1. Nussbaum recalled, "I remember there was a soldier in front of me," he told the newspaper, recalling the picture, "and he ordered me to raise my hands." After his uncle intervened, he was allowed to rejoin his family.

50. Margolick, "Rockland Physician," B1. In response to the controversy his identity caused, Nussbaum maintained, "I never realized that everyone puts the entire weight of 6 million Jews on this photograph. To me it looked like an incident in which I was involved, and that was it." A video on the story was also made: "Tsvi Nussbaum: A Boy from Warsaw (A Video About a Photograph)," Helsinki: MTV and Ergo Media, Inc., 1990.

51. Dr. Lucjan Dobroszycki, in Margolick, "Rockland Physician," B1. Dobroszycki maintained that several elements in the picture made Nussbaum's claim dubious: the scene was on a street rather than the courtyard he remembered, the Jews were wearing armbands while he said he had been in hiding, the heavy clothing suggested May rather than the July he remembered, and every other photograph in the Stroop report was taken in the Warsaw Ghetto, where he said he never lived.

52. See http://images.google.com/imgres?imgurl=http://www1.yadvashem.org/exhibitions/nuremberg/img/4414425.jpg&imgrefurl=http://www1.yadvashem.org/exhibitions/nuremberg/nuremberg_16.html&h=280&w=400&sz=43&hl=en&start=67&tbnid=pO2i_cWIkpFSCM:&tbnh=87&tbnw=124&prev=/images%3Fq%3Dwarsaw%2Bghetto%26start%3D54%26gbv%3D2%26ndsp%3D18%26svnum%3D10%26hl%3Den%26client%3Dfirefox-a%26channel%3Ds%26rls%3Dorg.mozilla:en-US:official%26sa%3DN.

53. John Darnton, "Does the World Still Recognize a Holocaust?" *New York Times,* April 25, 1993, section 4, 1; "What He Saw," *New York Times,* January 7, 2001, 14; Judith Judson, Reader's Letter, *New York Times,* January 28, 2001, SM6.

54. Mark Weber, "The Warsaw Ghetto Boy," *Journal of Historical Review* 14(2), March/April 1994, 6–7; Robert Faurisson, "Warsaw Ghetto 'Uprising,'" *Journal of Historical Review* 14(2), March/April 1994, 8–9.

55. Raskin, *Child at Gunpoint,* 162–163.

56. Ibid., 166–168.

57. The cartoon was published by Indymedia—Switzerland, while the Greek cover photo appeared on *Eleutherotypia,* April 1, 2002; quoted in Dorothy P. Abram, *The Suffering of a Single Child: Uses of an Image from the Holocaust* (Ph.D. diss., Harvard University, 2003), 249.

58. See http://images.google.com/imgres?imgurl=http://www.thepeoplescube.com/images/NYT_Warsaw_uprising_editors.gif&imgrefurl=http://www.thepeoplescube.com/red/viewtopic.php%3Ft%3D797&h=645&w=554&sz=52&hl=en&start=126&tbnid=dY9czfrFZWS14M:&tbnh=137&tbnw=118&prev=/images%3Fq%3Dwarsaw%2Bghetto%26start%3D108%26gbv%3D2%26ndsp%3D18%26svnum%3D10%26hl%3Den%26client%3Dfirefox-a%26channel%3Ds%26rls%3Dorg.mozilla:en-US:official%26sa%3DN.

59. The musical, "David," was part of Staffordshire's "2004 program dedicated to teaching the impact of World War II in the United Kingdom" and was organized with the Imperial War Museum. The genealogy site, which called over the Internet to Polish citizens looking for their descendants or relations, was http://www.soulwork.net/polish_roots.htm.

60. Abram, *Suffering.*

61. David Roskies, *Against the Apocalypse* (Cambridge, MA: Harvard University Press, 1984), 295.

62. Samuel Bak, in Raskin, *Child at Gunpoint,* 152.

63. Sydney H. Schanberg, "The 'Enemy' Is Red, Cruel and, After 5 Years, Little Known," *New York Times,* March 2, 1975, sec. 4, 1; Jacques Leslie, "Bloodbath Not a Certain Fate," *Los Angeles Times,* March 16, 1975, 9; "Massive Cambodia Bloodbath Reported," *Los Angeles Times,* May 4, 1975, 4; Samuel A. Adams, "Signing 100,000 Death Warrants," *Wall Street Journal,* March 26, 1975, 16; William Safire, "Get Out of Town," *New York Times,* May 12, 1975, 25.

64. John J. O'Connor, "TV: 'What's Happened to Cambodia' on CBS," *New York Times,* June 7, 1978, C24.

65. John J. O'Connor, "TV: The Great Tragedy of Cambodia," *New York Times,* November 6, 1979, C19.

66. Zelizer, *Remembering To Forget.*

67. On discovery, the photos underwent a double process of conservation, first by East German photographers in 1981 and later in 1993 by U.S. photojournalists Douglas Niven and Chris Riley of the Photo Archive Group. Riley and Niven published 100 of the images in *The Killing Fields* (Twin Palms, 1996).

68. Stepan, *Photos that Changed,* 140–141.

69. Seth Mydans, "Faces From Beyond the Grave," *New York Times,* May 25, 1997, BR21.

70. See, for instance, a picture appended to "Museum Tells Tale of Death in Cambodia," *Los Angeles Times,* November 30, 1979, 1, whose title read: "Faced Camera, Then Death." Also see pictures appended to Robert J. Caldwell, "Cries from the Grave," *San Diego Union,* May 3, 1987, C1; Sharon Noguchi, "Killing Fields, the Sequel," *San Jose Mercury News,* January 8, 1989, 7C; Denis D. Grey, "Evidence of Asian Holocaust," *Houston Chronicle,* December 10, 1994, 28.

71. Key here were the efforts of David Hawk, who mounted the exhibitions after doing relief work for the United Nations. Around this time the cinematic release of *The Killing Fields* in 1984 gave the story additional form, when it visually recounted the experiences of Cambodian Dith Pran, an assistant to *New York Times* reporter Sydney Schanberg, during his reportage of the event. See Herman Wong, "Cambodia Genocide Pictures," *Los Angeles Times,* November 1, 1984, E1; and Samuel G. Freedman, "In 'The Killing Fields,' Cambodian Actor Relives His Nation's Ordeal," *New York Times,* October 28, 1984, H1.

72. Steven Erlanger, "Museum for the Things Too Painful to Forget," *New York Times,* December 30, 1988, A4.

73. Picture appended to Seth Mydans, "Flawed Khmer Rouge Trial Better than None," *New York Times,* April 16, 2003. Also see Seth Mydans, "Side by Side Now in Cambodia: Skulls, Victims, and Victimizers," *New York Times,* May 27, 1996, 1, and "Cambodia's Bureaucracy of Death: Reams of Evidence in Search of a Trial," *New York Times,* July 20, 1997, E7. Because much of the United States was indifferent to the prosecution of the Khmer Rouge, the images were important for larger efforts to get an international tribunal underway.

74. Seth Mydans, "Cambodian Killers' Careful Records Used Against Them," *New York Times,* June 7, 1996, A1. The article was illustrated with a picture of a wall in Tuol Sleng bearing images of the about to die, with schoolchildren around them. The group was headed by Ben Kiernan from Yale University.

75. Tina Rosenberg, "Cambodia's Blinding Genocide," *New York Times,* April 21, 1997, A14. Also see Pico Iyer, "Into the Shadows," *Time,* August 16, 1999,

76. Michael Kimmelman, "Hypnotized By Mug Shots That Stare Back: Are They Windows or Mirrors?" *New York Times,* August 27, 1997, C9.

77. Mydans, "Faces," BR21. In the end, the attempts to try Pol Pot's henchmen came to fruition after substantial delay. In July 1997 he was given what was widely seen as a "show trial," which condemned him to life under house arrest. As reports of his possible capture and trial came to light in the U.S. news media, he died the following spring, though his cause of death remained unclear. (Seth Mydans, "Cause Unclear in Death of Creator of Killing Fields," *New York Times,* April 17, 1998, A1. The article was illustrated by a series of photos titled "Faces of the Countless Victims of Pol Pot," A15.) Even after the Khmer

Rouge collapsed and piles of skulls were discovered across more than 400 killing fields, the efforts by the Cambodian Genocide Center to prosecute those who remained did not have impact. But in 2002, the privately owned Documentation Center of Cambodia began to collect its own Khmer Rouge records, slightly raising the probability of a future trial, and the following spring, after six years of negotiations between Cambodia, the United Nations, and individual countries, a trial began (Seth Mydans, "Researchers Put Together Story of the Khmer Rouge," *New York Times,* September 15, 2002, 18, and "Flawed Khmer Rouge Trial Better Than None," *New York Times,* April 16, 2003, A4). Though reporting that tribunal no longer made the front page, pictures of Cambodians facing their death again topped the coverage (Rosenberg, "Cambodia's Blinding Genocide," A14).

78. Michael Kimmelman, "Poignant Faces of the Soon-to-Be Dead," *New York Times,* June 20. 1997, C1.

79. Mydans, "Faces," BR21; Kimmelman, "Poignant Faces," C1, and "Hypnotized," C9.

80. The pictures also received generally front-page coverage from other newspapers: See Robin McDowell, "Photography Mystery Unshrouded," *Seattle Post Intelligencer,* February 4, 1997, A1; "The Grim Reminder," *Sun Herald,* February 23, 1997, C24; Guy Trebay, "Killing Fields of Vision, *Village Voice,* June 3, 1997, 34; "The Terror of Pol Pot Lives on in Cambodia," *St. Petersburg Times,* June 24, 1997, A2; Ben Barber, "A Return to Cambodia's Vicious Past?" *Washington Times,* July 21, 1997, A1.

81. Thomas Roma, "Looking into the Face of Our Own Worst Fears through Photographs," *Chronicle of Higher Education,* October 31, 1997.

82. Roma, "Looking." Also see Rachel Hughes, "The Abject Artefacts of Memory: Photographs from Cambodia's Genocide," *Media, Culture and Society* 25(1), January 2003, 23–44.

83. The Cambodian Genocide Program, run by Yale University under Ben Kiernan's efforts with U.S. congressional funding, involved gathering evidence for the possible trials of the Khmer Rouge leaders. See www.yale.edu/cgp.

84. Mydans, "Faces," BR21; Kimmelman, "Poignant Faces," C1, where Kimmelman asked "Can genocide be art?"; "Cambodia's Bureaucracy of Death: Reams of Evidence in Search of a Trial," *New York Times,* July 20, 1997, E7; Kimmelman, "Hypnotized," C9; Seth Mydans, "Cause Unclear in Death of Creator of Killing Fields," *New York Times,* April 17, 1998, A15; Brook Larner, "Facing a Grisly Past," *Newsweek,* August 13, 2001, 12.

85. See *Bophana: A Cambodian Tragedy* (1996) and *S21: The Khmer Rouge Killing Machine* (2003), both directed by Rithy Panh.

86. Steve Silva, "Genocide Tourism: Tragedy Becomes a Destination," *Chicago Tribune,* August 5, 2007, 1; J. John Lennon and Malcolm Foley, *Dark Tourism: The Attraction of Death and Disaster* (London: Continuum, 2000).

87. Siem Reap, "Touring the Tragic Kingdom," *Boston Globe,* October 28, 2007;

88. Doug Bandow, "The Man Who Shot Death," *The Straits Times* (Singapore), November 28, 2007; Paul Williams, "Witnessing Genocide: Vigilance and Remembrance at Tuol Sleng and Choeung Ek," *Holocaust and Genocide Studies* 18(2), fall 2004, 244.

89. See, for instance, http://www.offbeattravel.com/cambodian-genocide-museum.html or http://www.virtualtourist.com/travel/Asia/Cambodia/Phnom_Penh-1194372/

Things_To_Do-Phnom_Penh-Tuol_Sleng_Museum-BR-1.html. For more, see Paul Williams, "Witnessing Genocide," 234–54.

90. David Simmons, "Atrocity Tourism's Overkill?" (Commentary), *Asia Times,* October 10, 2002.

91. See, for instance, Jerry Adler and Ron Moreau, "Pol Pot's Last Days," *Newsweek,* April 27, 1998, 38–42; Guy de Launey, "Khmer Rouge Trial Raises Hope of Justice," BBC News, November 20, 2007.

92. Bandow, "The Man."

93. See, for instance, "Cambodian Tribunal Summons Former Khmer Rouge Prison Photographer," Associated Press, October 23, 2007; Anthony Faiola, "The Surviving Lieutenants of Pol Pot: After Many Delays, A Tribunal Appears Close," *Washington Post,* November 18, 2007, A18; Anne Hyland, "A Grim Picture," *South China Morning Post,* February 1, 2007, 16.

94. Stepan, *Photos that Changed,* 140–141.

95. Reuters Pictures, March 28, 1997, Ubilo, Zaire, # x000910020011003dt3s000my.

96. Photo by Jean Marc Boujou, appended to Joseph Contreras and Marcus Mabry, "On Scene in the Hot Zone," *Newsweek,* May 29, 1995, 49; Knight Ridder Tribune Photo Service/Photo by Cheryl Diaz Meyer, 16 April 2003, Baghdad, Iraq, #krtps00020030416dz4g00340.

97. Hariman and Lucaites, *No Caption Needed;* Pictures appended to Sheri Hall, "The Cost of Dying: End-of-Life Choices Wrench Michigan Families," *The Detroit News,* August 29, 2004, http://www.detnews.com/2004/specialreport/0408/29/a01–256783.htm.

98. See, for instance, "A Court for King Cholera," *Punch,* July-December, 1852; "Emergency Hospital During 1918 Influenza Epidemic, Camp Funston, Kansas," or "U.S. Army Camp Hospital No. 45, Aix-Les-Bains, France, Influenza Ward No. 1, 1918," www.vaccineinformation.org/photos/flu; "Starving Irish Children," *Illustrated London News,* http://z.about.com/d/history1800s/1/G/1/-/-/-/London-ill-cahera.jpg.

99. See, for instance, Brian Williams, "Bono Leverages Celebrity to Impact Africa," MSNBC, May 23, 2006, in which the rock star said he was a "traveling salesman for the continent"; Gordon Crovitz, "Can Rock Stars Stem Ethiopian Hunger?" *Wall Street Journal,* April 24, 1985, 28.

100. Sander Gilman, *Disease and Representation* (Ithaca: Cornell University Press, 1988), 1.

101. Moeller, *Compassion Fatigue,* 57, 67–68, 77, see in general 55–96. Alongside images of possible death from illness has been a gravitation toward photo essays around the impending death of named persons, made particularly prevalent in the contemporary digitally mediated environment. One early instance involved *Life* photographer Gordon Parks, who in 1961 documented a twelve-year-old Brazilian boy, then thought dying from malnutrition and bronchial asthma ["Freedom's Fearful Foe: Poverty," *Life,* June 16, 1961, 86–93; Gordon Parks, *Flavio* (New York: Norton, 1978)]. While the boy recovered, the form of the photojournalistic engagement with a dying individual moved on to chronicle persons dying from cancer, AIDS, and other terminal diseases in photo-essays.

102. Mary Tillotson, *CNN & Company,* CNN, June 10, 1994; quoted in Moeller, *Compassion Fatigue,* 60; Roland Bleiker and Amy Kay, "Representing HIV/AIDS in

Africa: Pluralist Photography and Local Empowerment," *International Studies Quarterly* 51, 2007, 159.

103. For instance, see "Nachtwey's Wish: Awareness of XDR-TB," *Boston Globe,* October 3, 2008; Steve Sternberg, "Photojournalist Documents Toll of Tuberculosis," *USA Today,* October 3, 2008; Meghan Keane, "Photographer Awarded TED Prize for Work on War, Disease," *Wired,* October 3, 2008.

104. James Nachtwey, "Raising Awareness about TB," www.huffingtonpost.com/james-nachtwey/raising-awareness-about-t_b133060.html; "Technology Elite Use Internet to Fight TB," Agence France Presse dispatch, October 3, 2008.

105. Laurie Garrett, *HIV and National Security: Where Are the Links?* (New York: Council on Foreign Relations, 2005), 20; Kristen Alley Swain, "Approaching the Quarter Century Mark: AIDS Coverage and Research Decline as Infection Spreads," *Critical Studies in Media Communication* 22(3), 2005, 258–262; Nilanjana Bardhan, "Transnational AIDS-HIV News Narratives: A Critical Exploration of Overarching Frames," *Mass Communication and Society* 4(3), 2001, 283–309.

106. See James Kinsella, *Covering the Plague* (New Brunswick, NJ: Rutgers University Press, 1992); Randy Shilts, *And the Band Played On* (New York: Macmillan, 1994); Larry Gross, *Up From Invisibility* (New York: Columbia University Press, 2001).

107. Douglas Crimp, "Portraits of People with AIDS," in Lawrence Grossberg, Cary Nelson, and Paula Treichler, *Cultural Studies* (New York: Routledge, 1991), 129; Jenny Kitzinger, "The Face of AIDS," in Ivana Markova and Robert Farr (eds.), *Representations of Health, Illness and Handicap* (Harwood Academic Publishers, 1995), 49–67; Paula Treichler, "AIDS, Africa and Cultural Theory," *Transition* 51, 1991, 86–103; Mollyann Brodie et al., "AIDS at 21: Media Coverage of the HIV Epidemic 1981–2002," supplement to the *Columbia Journalism Review,* March/April 2004.

108. Garrett, *HIV and National Security,* 20.

109. Bianca Brijnath, "It's About TIME: Engendering AIDS in Africa," *Culture, Health, and Sexuality* 9(4), 2007, 372; Jorge Luis Andrade Fernandes, *Challenging Euro-America's Politics of Identity* (London: Routledge, 2008), 67; David Campbell, "The Visual Economy of HIV/AIDS," 2008, www.visual-hivaids.org.

110. Gideon Mendel, in Campbell, *Visual Economy,* part 5, 49; Don McCullin, in Campbell, *Visual Economy,* part 5, 57; "Don McCullin—From Images of War to Portraits of AIDS," Reuters Alert Net, www.alertnet.org/thefacts/imagerepository/237661; Kitzinger, "Face of AIDS," 49.

111. Kitzinger, "Face of AIDS," 49; Crimp, "Portraits," 120.

112. Bleiker and Kay, "Representing HIV/AIDS in Africa," 144, 149.

113. Ibid., 141, 144, 149.

114. Personal correspondence with Edward Hooper, February 9–15, 2010; Edward Hooper, *Slim: A Reporter's Own Story of HIV/AIDS in East Africa* (London: Bodley Head, 1990), 47–49, photo 170; Edward Hooper, *The River: Journey to the Source of HIV and AIDS* (New York: Little, Brown, 1999).

115. See Rod Nordland, Ray Wilkinson, and Ruth Marshall, "Africa in the Plague Years," *Newsweek,* November 24, 1986, 44; picture appended to *Washington Post's* affiliated journal *Health,* May 24, 1988, cover; picture appended to "Dispelling Myths about AIDS in Africa," in "AIDS and Africa," *Africa Report,* 1988, 16–31; picture appended

Notes to pages 157–163 • 369

to Catharine Watson, "Africa's AIDS Tim Bomb," *Guardian*, June 17, 1987, 10–11; *Weekly Review*, (Nairobi), June 24, 1988, 18. These appearances of the photo were tracked in Paula Treichler, *How to Have Theory in an Epidemic: Cultural Chronicles of AIDS* (Durham, NC: Duke University Press, 1999), 107–110.

116. Treichler, *How To Have Theory*, 108.

117. Crimp, "Portraits."

118. Robert Atkins, "Nicholas Nixon," *7 Days*, October 5, 1988. Nixon later published the photos in book form in *People with Aids* (1991).

119. Crimp, "Portraits," 117–118.

120. Campbell, *Visual Economy*, part 2, 4; part 4, 6.

121. Ibid., part 4, 7–8; part 2, 4.

122. Brodie, "AIDS At 21."

123. Ibid.

124. Bleiker and Kay, "Representing HIV/AIDS in Africa," 151.

125. Shown as a multimedia presentation titled "The Plague," the images also portrayed a picture of a Zimbabwean—Fortunate Chitofu—first lying ill in bed and then masked by his coffin. See James Nachtwey, "The Plague," photo-essay appended to Joanna McGreary, "Death Stalks a Continent," *Time*, February 12, 2001; Brijnath, "It's About TIME," 373.

126. "Don McCullin—From Images of War."

127. Jane Elliott, "Recording the African HIV Tragedy," BBC News, November 24, 2004, cited in Campbell, *Visual Economy*, part 5, 69.

128. Tom Stoddart, *iWitness* (London: Trolley, 2004); Tom Stoddart, "AIDS in Africa," *Getty Images News Blog*, http://blogs.gettyimages.com/news/2007/11/27/aids-in-africa/.

129. Stoddart, "AIDS in Africa."

130. Quoted in Chris Bond, "Capturing the Human Faces of Africa's AIDS Nightmare," *Yorkshire Post*, September 14, 2007.

131. The photo appeared in an online gallery on "AIDS in Africa" in *U.S. News and World Report*, http://www.usnews.com/usnews/photography/aids/aids1.htm.

132. See, for instance, David Elliott Cohen, *What Matters* (New York: Sterling Publishing, 2008); The Digital Journalist (September, 2004), http://www.digitaljournalist.org/issue0409/stoddart40.html; "Lest We Forget—Africa's AIDS Crisis," photographic exhibit in the UK (September 2007); www.inmycommunity.com.au/funstuff/galleries/Tom-Stoddart/; Stoddart, "AIDS in Africa"; Annwen Bates, "Wearing the Tee-Shirt: An Exploration of the Ideological Underpinnings of Visual Representations of the African Body With HIV or AIDS," *African Journal of AIDS Research* 6(1), 2007, 71–72.

133. Campbell, *Visual Economy*, part 5, p. 64; Allan M. Brandt, *No Magic Bullet* (New York: Oxford University Press, 1985).

134. See, for instance, Amartya Sen, *Poverty and Famines: An Essay on Entitlement and Deprivation* (New York: Clarendon Press, 1981).

135. Michael Marren, "Feeding a Famine," *Forbes MediaCritic* 2(1), 1994, 32–34.

136. Jonathan Benthall, *Disasters, Relief, and the Media* (London: I. B. Taurus, 1993).

137. For instance, a typical caption might read: "An Ethiopian woman waits for food," AP Photo/Eyal Warshavsky Staff, April 13, 2000, Didhara, Ethiopia, #4494313(2OBU1).

138. Susan Sontag, in Neal Ascherson, "How Images Fail to Convey War's Horror," *Los Angeles Times Book Review,* March 16, 2003, R9.

139. Stepan, *Photos that Changed,* 119. At the same time, a more general lack of interest in the West about Africa made images from the continent less compelling for publication (see Jay Mallin, "Images From Africa: Why Don't We Care?" *PhotoDistrict News,* January 1998, 58–64).

140. Vicki Goldberg, "Beyond Clichéd Interpretations of Exile, Suffering, and Death," *New York Times,* 1 January 1999, E38.

141. Robert D. Kaplan, "False Images of Ethiopian Famine," *Wall Street Journal,* January 6, 1988. 15.

142. Andrew Natsios, "Illusions of Influence: The CNN Effect in Complex Emergencies," in Robert Rotberg and Thomas Weiss (eds.), *From Massacres to Genocide* (Washington, DC: Brookings Institute, 1996), 164.

143. Moeller, *Compassion Fatigue,* 104; Michael Maren, *The Road to Hell* (New York: Simon and Schuster, 1997).

144. Mohammad Amin and Michael Buerk, "The Faces of Death in Africa," NBC and BBC, October 23, 1984. William Lord, in Moeller, *Compassion Fatigue,* 117, also 112.

145. Jay Ross, "Ethiopian Famine Claims Children First," *Washington Post,* June 27, 1983, sec. 1, A1.

146. Reuters Pictures/Photo by Corinne Dufka, AIJEP Feeding Center, Sudan, July 3, 1998, # x000910020010920du730012y.

147. Photo appended to Russell Watson, "It's Our Fight Now," *Newsweek,* December 14, 1992, 26–27. Its title read: "The bodies of dead children are as light as bundled sticks. Here, one waits for its grave."

148. *PrimeTimeLive,* ABC News, May 9, 1991 (quoted in Moeller, *Compassion Fatigue,* 132).

149. Quoted in Peter Howe, *Shooting under Fire* (New York: Artisan Books, 2002), 134; "Trials with Editors" (Interview), Nieman Reports, June 22 1998. Also see, for example, Cyma Rubin and Eric Newton (eds.), *The Pulitzer Prize Photographs: Capture the Moment* (New York: Norton, 2001), n.p.; Buell, *Moments,* 168–169.

150. Accounts of Carter taking the picture have appeared in a wide range of source material, including videotaped interviews with the photographers, memoirs written by his friends and colleagues, and documentary films. The account offered here provides a composite version generated from Greg Marinovitch and Joao Silver, *The Bang-Bang Club* (London: William Heinemann, 2000).

151. Picture appended to Donatella Lorch, "Sudan Is Described as Trying to Placate the West," *New York Times,* March 26, 1993, A3.

152. "Editors' Note," *New York Times,* March 30, 1993, A2.

153. "Concerned Response," *Time,* April 26, 1993, 6.

154. Picture titled "In Extremis," *Time,* April 5, 1993, 16; picture appended to "Concerned Response," *Time,* April 26, 1993, 6.

155. Picture appended to "Outlook: Snapshots," *U.S. News and World Report,* April 25, 1994, 22.

156. Scott MacLeod, "The Life and Death of Kevin Carter," *Time,* September 12, 1994, 70.

157. Picture appended to Howard Kurtz, "Post Columnist Raspberry Wins Pulitzer; "Disaster, Radiation Reports Also Cited," *Washington Post,* April 13, 1994, A13; David Mehegan, "Schuller, Schwartz, Proulx Win Pulitzers," *Boston Globe,* April 13, 1994, 15; "*New York Times* and *Chicago Tribune* Top Awards List," *St Louis Post-Dispatch,* April 13, 1994, 8A. It also appeared as a stand-alone image in "A Picture Worth a Pulitzer Prize," *Salt Lake Tribune,* April 13, 1994, A1; and "Pulitzer Prize Series," *St. Petersburg Times,* April 13, 1994, 1A; The photo was described, but not printed, in *The Wall Street Journal, USA Today,* and the *Philadelphia Inquirer.*

158. Picture appended to "Feature Photography," *New York Times,* April 13, 1994, B7; advertisement, *New York Times,* April 14, 1994, D19.

159. Picture appended to "Gut-Wrenching Photos Win Pulitzer Prizes This Year," *Houston Chronicle,* April 13, 1994, 8. The correction appeared the following day.

160. James Barrons, "Radioactivity Experiment and the Human Aftermath Wins a Pulitzer," *New York Times,* April 13, 1994, B7.

161. Reena Shah Stamets, "Were His Priorities Out of Focus?" *St. Petersburg Times,* April 14, 1994, 1A.

162. Greg Marinovich, "The Killing Eye," *Sunday Star-Times,* September 3, 2000, 1.

163. Quoted in MacLeod, "Life and Death," 73.

164. Lois Kabelitz, in "Readers React to Pulitzer Photo," *St. Petersburg Times,* April 21, 1994, 21A.

165. Moeller, *Compassion Fatigue,* 139.

166. Transcript of "Tribute to Kevin Carter, Prize-Winning Photographer," NPR (segment number: 14; show number: 1082), July 30, 1994, n.p.

167. See Buell, *Moments,* 224–225; Rubin and Newton, *Capture the Moment* (New York: Norton, 2001), n.p.; Top photography lists included http://www.worlds-famousphotos.com/stricken-child-crawling-towards-a-food-camp-1993.html. Its association with popular music involved singers Richey Edwards from the Manic Street Preachers, Martin Simpson and Jessica Ruby Simpson's Band of Angels, and a cover photo on the Dead Kennedys album *Plastic Surgery Disasters.* In film, a scene involving Angelina Jolie luring a vulture away from a dying baby was depicted in the 2003 film *Beyond Borders; The Death of Kevin Carter,* directed by Dan Krauss and produced by El Cerritto in 2004, won an Oscar nomination (2006), Emmy nomination, and numerous other awards; and the image and Carter's story appeared in 2006 in Alfredo Jaar's documentary *The Sound of Silence.*

168. Bill Keller, "Kevin Carter, the Pulitzer Winner for Sudan Photo, is Dead at 33," *New York Times,* July 29, 1994, B8; Dieter Steiner, in Salgado and Mayes, *This Critical Mirror,* 188; Paul Velasco, in "The Death of Kevin Carter," 2004.

169. Pictures of impending death from famine continue. See, for instance, Reuters Pictures/ Photo by Peter Andrews, April 6, 2000, Gode, Ethiopia, #x0001000200010820dw46000b5.

170. David Scheiman, in http://www.worldvision.org/donate.nsf/child/ africa_erdm_index?Open&cmp=ILC-africafoodcrisis#more.

171. April Peterson and Meg Spratt, "Choosing Graphic Visuals: How Picture Editors Incorporate Emotion and Personal Experience Into Decision Making," *Visual*

Communication Quarterly 12 (1/2), September 2005, 4–19; Leon Hadar, "Covering the New World Disorder," *Columbia Journalism Review,* July/August 1994, 3, 26–27.

172. Marinovich and Silver, *Bang-Bang Club,* 151.

173. Gina Lubrano, "Journalists' Struggles with Their Bias," *San Diego Union-Tribune,* June 10, 1996, B7; Sherry Ricchiardi, "Confronting the Horror," *American Journalism Review,* January 1, 1999, 35–39; Charles Paul Freund, "The Atrocity Exhibition," *Reason,* June 1, 1999, 44; Sumiko Tan, "Journalists Do Have Feelings Too," *The Straits Times,* August 14, 1994, n.p.; Lynne Duke, "The Shooters: They Aimed Their Cameras in War's Face," *Washington Post,* October 18, 2001, C1; George Eppley, "While the Vulture Sat and Watched," *Plain Dealer,* April 15, 1995, 11B.

Chapter 5

1. Stuart Hall, "The Determinations of News Photographs," in Jock Young and Stanley Cohen, *The Manufacture of News* (London: Sage, 1973).

2. "Execution of a Samurai," *Illustrated London News,* February 25, 1865; Alexander Gardner, "The Drop," Stereo Card, July 7, 1865, Daniel R. Weinberg Lincoln Conspirators Collection, 1865–1997, William Henry Smith Memorial Library, Indiana Historical Society (Photographs: Box 1, Folder 2).

3. Peter Stepan, *Photos that Changed the World* (Munich: Prestel, 2000), 30–31; Alistair Horne, *The Price of Glory: Verdun 1916* (London: Penguin, 1994), cover.

4. The sequence of pictures, titled "Korean Protestor Is Treated Before Dying After Stabbing Himself Near Cancun WTO Summit" (Reuters/Daniel Aguilar, September 10, 2003, Cancun, Mexico, # 90024), appeared widely the day after the farmer died, appended to "Rich, Poor Countries Face Off in Cancun," *Boston Globe,* September 11, 2003, E4; S. Lynne Walker and Diane Lindquist, "S. Korea Farmer Fatally Stabs Self at Trade Talks," *San Diego Union-Tribune,* September 11, 2003, C1; and "Desperate Protestor Dies From Injuries," *Seattle Times,* September 11, 2003, A2. Said one observer a week later, two images lingered from the Cancun summit: "One is Mr. Lee and the other is jubilant protestors…Mr. Lee's suicide dramatizes the desperate plight of farmers around the world" (John Cavanaugh, in S. Lynne Walker, "Suicide Underscored Power Shift in WTO," *San Diego Union-Tribune,* September 16, 2003, C1).

5. The victim was Lt. William Newton, winner of the Victoria Cross. His picture appeared on the front page of the *Philadelphia Record,* under the caption "Lest We Forget: A Picture Editorial," September 4, 1945, 1. Thanks to Monroe Price for locating this.

6. The photo appeared in *Vu* on September 23, 1936, as part of a seven-photo spread titled "La guerre civile en espagne" and as a half-page photo in Robert Capa, "Death of a Republican Soldier," *Life,* July 12, 1937, 19, alongside an article titled "Death in Spain: The Civil War Has Taken 510,000 Live in One Year."

7. Philip Knightley, *The First Casualty* (New York: Harcourt, Brace Jovanovich, 1975), 227. Knightley offered the quote but countered it to protest the unearned fame that the photo garnered—in his words, "an essentially ambiguous image" that "does not tell us anything as a picture."

8. Knightley, *First Casualty,* 230; Caroline Brothers, *War and Photography: A Cultural History* (London: Routledge, 1997), 183.

9. See, for instance, Richard Whelan, "Robert Capa's Falling Solider: A Detective Story," *Aperture*, 2002, 48–55; and Haim Breesheeth, "Projecting Trauma: War Photography and the Public Sphere," *Third Text* 20(1), January 2006, 57–71.

10. Robert Capa and Gerda Taro, *Death in the Making* (New York: Covici-Friede, 1938); Stepan, *Photos that Changed,* 51; Kenneth Kobre, *Photojournalism* (Focal Press, 2008, 442).

11. Raymond Demoulin, "Photojournalism and Tomorrow's Technology," in Emile Meijer and Joop Swart (eds.), *The Photographic Memory: Press Photography—Twelve Insights* (London: World Press Photo Foundation, 1987), 187. Also see "150 Years of Photojournalism," *Time,* fall 1989, n.p.

12. Jay Ruby, *Secure the Shadow: Death and Photography in America* (Cambridge, MA: MIT Press, 1995), 16.

13. Michael Griffin, "The Great War Photographs: Constructing Myths of History and Photojournalism," in Bonnie Brennen and Hanno Hardt (eds.), *Picturing the Past* (Minneapolis: University of Minnesota Press, 1999), 138; Stepan, *Photos that Changed,* 51. Along these lines, the *New York Times* continued the investigation of the photo's veracity. See Larry Rohter, "New Doubts Raised Over Famous War Photo," *New York Times,* August 18, 2009, C1.

14. Text accompanying Capa, "Death of a Republican Soldier."

15. Text accompanying photo accredited to George Strock, "Dead GI's on Buna Beach," *Life,* September 20, 1943.

16. Richard Whelan, *Robert Capa: A Biography* (New York: Knopf, 1985), 99–100.

17. Whelan, "Robert Capa's Falling Soldier," 51.

18. Marjorie Miller, "Armero: 'White City' Turned into 'Land of Dead.'" *Los Angeles Times,* November 17, 1985, A14; Donna Eberwine, "Colombian Volcano Death Toll Now Put At More Than 25,000," *San Diego Union-Tribune,* November 17, 1985, A1.

19. Joseph B. Treaster, "Colombia's Rescue Operation Draws Divided Assessments," *New York Times,* November 24, 1985, A1;

20. "Trapped Girl, 13, Dies," *New York Times,* November 17, 1985, 18;

21. The longer view of the girl struggling, surrounded by support personnel, appeared widely, appended to "Rumblings of Volcano Continuing," *Philadelphia Inquirer,* November 16, 1985, 10A; Marjorie Miller, "Armero," A14; "Rumblings of Volcano Continuing," *Philadelphia Inquirer,* November 16, 1985, 10A.

22. "Trapped Girl, 13, Dies," 18.

23. Carol Guzy, picture captioned "In the Path of Destruction," *Newsweek,* November 25, 1985, 53.

24. The picture first appeared in *Paris Match,* November 29, 1985, then was printed in *Observer Magazine,* December 1, 1985, cover and internal page; *Bunte,* December 23, 1985, 14; *Panorama* (Holland), December 26-January 3, 1985/6, 1–29. Thanks to Frank Fournier for graciously compiling parts of this list.

25. Quoted in "Picture Power: Tragedy of Omayra Sanchez," BBC News, September 30, 2005; Kathy Ryan, "Newsmakers," in Sebastio Salgado and Stephen Mayes, *World Press Photo: This Critical Mirror* (London: Thames and Hudson, 1996), 34; Tony Jenkins, "Armero Becomes Tomb After Last Survivor Saved," *Guardian,* November 18, 1985.

26. "Symbol of Colombia's Anguish," *Time*, November 25, 1985, 49; Treaster, "Colombia's Rescue," A1; Donna Eberwine, "Colombian Volcano Death Toll Now Put At More Than 25,000," *San Diego Union-Tribune*, November 17, 1985, A1. Showing a two-page image, *Newsweek* called her "the face of calamity" ("Under the Volcano," *Newsweek*, January 6, 1986, 40–41).

27. "Symbol of Colombia's Anguish," 49; "Images '85," *Time*, December 30, 1985, cover and 43; "Messages Are Varied," *Atlanta Journal-Constitution*, July 16, 1995; "Eyewitness: Picture of the Century," *Life*, October 1, 1999, 38; "50 Years of Shock and Awe," *London Sunday Times*, September 18, 2005, 36–43; "Colombia Volcano Disaster Picture Gets World Press Photo Award," Associated Press, February 6, 1986.

28. This included Andy Grundberg, "Photojournalism Lays Claim to the Realm of Aesthetics," *New York Times*, April 12, 1987, 29–30; *Tele Loisirs*, November 1989, 20; *Life* (The World's Best Photographs, 1980–90), December 1990, 64; *Time* (150 years of Photojournalism), 1989, 70; *Photo Selection* (Canada), March-April 1991, 10–11; *VSD*, December 11–17, 1997, 90–92; *Le Figaro*, September 12, 1998; "Eyewitness: Pictures of the Century," *Life*, October 1, 1999, 38; Salgado and Mayes, *This Critical Mirror*; Isabel Allende addressed the lingering resonance of Sanchez's death image in her fiction (Sylvie Drake, "Latin Lady of Letters," *Variety*, March 28, 1994–April 3, 1994, 40). Thanks to Frank Fournier for compiling and sharing this record and to Michael Serazio for helping him do so.

29. Quoted in "Picture Power."

30. "Many Cameras Record Assassination in Japan," *New York Times*, October 13, 1960, 3; Hal Buell, *Moments* (New York: Black Dog and Leventhal, 2007), 52.

31. See, for instance, photo appended to Richard Johnston, "Assassination of Leftist May Change Japanese Election Campaign," *New York Times*, October 13, 1960, 1.

32. Quoted in "Murder in Public By a Berserk Boy," *Life*, October 24, 1960, 30.

33. "The Camera's Selective Eye," *Life*, October 24, 1960, 1; "Murder in Public," 24–30.

34. Philip Benjamin, "All Way Home Pulitzer Play," *New York Times*, May 2, 1961, 40. The photo appeared, for instance, on May 2, after Nagoa won the Pulitzer (*New York Times*, 2 May 1961, 40). Vicki Goldberg, *The Power of Photography* (New York: Abbeville, 1991), 223–224; John Faber, *Great News Photos and the Stories Behind Them* (1960; reprint New York: Dover, 1978), 126–127; Buell, *Moments*, 51–52.

35. Jack Gould, "Millions of Viewers See Oswald Killing on Two TV Networks," *New York Times*, November 25, 1963, 1. Asanuma's widow was quoted consoling Jackie Kennedy.

36. Kathy Ryan, in Salgado and Mayes, *This Critical Mirror*, 43.

37. Reuters picture titled "A Man Lies Dying on the Main Street of Rio De Janeiro," November 13, 1996, reutpix0020011106dsbd00i1e; Reuters picture titled "Filer of Vagabond Dying of Drug Overdose in Downtown Madrid," September 17, 1996, #x00037; Hans Moleman, "Killers Focus on a Photographer," *Guardian*, April 26, 1993; picture appended to Kathy Evans, "I Feel Numb, I Have Seen Islamic Justice Firsthand," *Guardian*, April 27, 1995; picture appended to Benjamin Joffe-Walt, "A Grim Cyclone of Grief," *U.S. News and World Report*, June 28–July 5, 2004, 26; Associated Press picture appended to Monica Davey, "The New Military Life: Heading Back to the War," *New York Times*, December 20, 2004, A1.

38. Quoted in Marylynne Pitz, "History Center Exhibit of Pulitzer Winning Photographers Honors Their Sacrifices," *Pittsburgh Post-Gazette,* April 10, 2007.

39. It ran on January 26, 1997, and again on April 15, 1998, after Rial won the Pulitzer Prize for spot photography. Also see "Post-Gazette Photographer Wins Award," *Pittsburgh Post-Gazette,* February 22, 1998, B3.

40. Mark Macedonia, "Newspapers Do Make an Impact with Detail of World Events," *Pittsburgh Post-Gazette,* April 22, 1998, A22; Pitz, "History Center Exhibit."

41. Picture captioned "A Call to Battle Ends in Execution," *New York Times,* March 12, 1994, A1. Three weeks later, the man was given a name—Alwyn Wolfaardt–when the *Independent* printed a story titled "Alwyn's Last Trek," about his history of support for the AWB—Afrikaner Resistance Movement; see David Cohen, "Alwyn's Last Trek," *The Independent,* March 30, 1994. Quoted in John Marchese, "Final Exposure," *Village Voice,* May 9, 1995.

42. Howard W. French, "Liberian Slayings Began Brutal Trend in Africa," *New York Times,* February 4, 1998, A3.

43. See Joel Robine's discussion of his photo, in www.grandreporters.com. It did appear, however, in Agence France-Presse's retrospective volume, *Facing the World: Great Moments in Photojournalism* (New York: Harry N. Abrams, 2001), 98.

44. Pictures accredited to Nanzer/SIPA Press, appended to "Liberia: Chaos et Barbarie," *Jeune Afrique,* May 28, 1996, cover and 6; pictures accredited to P. Robert/Sygma, appended to "Les ados tueurs du Liberia, *L'Express,* June 12, 1996, 104–105. The caption to the about-to-die photo stated no more than that the student was being dragged through the streets: "En haut, capture d'un Krahn blesse."

45. Personal conversation with Corinne Dufka, Cambridge, MA, May 5, 2004. Also see Interview with Corinne Dufka, "Beyond Words," CBC Television, November 4, 2005, http://www.cbc.ca/beyondwords/dufka.html.

46. Photos titled "Ejecucion sumaria en las calles de Monrovia," *El Pais,* May 9, 1996, 6.

47. Agence France-Presse picture appended to Howard W. French, "Peace Plan for Liberia Seeks to Demilitarize the Capital," *New York Times,* May 9, 1996, A3.

48. It appeared in the *Chicago Tribune, Boston Globe,* and *Pittsburgh Post-Gazette,* among others. "Battle Rages in Liberian Capital," *Boston Globe,* May 9, 1996, 34, whose picture was captioned "A prisoner is shot yesterday in Monrovia, Liberia, by a member of Charles Taylor's forces." Reuters Photo appended to "When Warlords Don't Show, Liberian Talks are Called Off," *Chicago Tribune,* May 9, 1996, 4. Also see "Monrovia a Battle Ground Again as Peace Talks Fail; Unarmed Prisoner Executed; Threat of Cholera Mounts," *Pittsburgh Post-Gazette,* May 9, 1996, A10.

49. Reuters/Corrine Dufka picture, titled "A Liberian Prisoner Faces Death," *Philadelphia Inquirer,* May 9, 1996, 1. The caption read as follows: "A man from a rival Liberian group was executed yesterday in Monrovia after pleading for his life as he was held at gunpoint by a fighter with Charles Taylor's National Patriotic Front."

50. "Reader Reaction," *Philadelphia Inquirer,* May 10, 1996, A4; John V.R. Bull, "Execution Photo Should Not Have Been on Page One" (Ombudsman's Report), *Philadelphia Inquirer,* May 12, 1996, E4.

51. "A Sampling of Mail on the Liberian Photo," *Philadelphia Inquirer,* May 16, 1996, A26.

52. Reid Kanaley, "Is Internet Different from Print?" *Philadelphia Inquirer*, May 11, 1996, A04.

53. See Jay Mallin, "Images of Africa: Why Don't We Care?" *Photo District News*, January 1998, 58–64. For instance, the image did not appear in the *Washington Post*, *U.S. News and World Report, Time, Newsweek, Life, Paris Match, Le Pointe*, the *Guardian, Le Monde, London Times*, or the *Economist*.

54. See, for instance, Reuters picture appended to "Talks Collapse as Rivals Battle in Liberia," *Los Angeles Times*, May 9, 1996, A4. The caption said, "Prisoner taken on front line of factional fighting in Monrovia is beaten. The man was executed minutes later."

55. The various photos were titled "Prisoner Execution," "Prisoner Execution (2)," "Stabbing," and "From a Dead Man's Wallet." Dufka herself received numerous awards, including a MacArthur Fellowship and a 1997 International Women's Media Foundation "Courage in Journalism Award." In 2002, she co-wrote a book on war crimes. See Corinne Dufka, "Liberia: Do Not Forget the Crimes," *International Herald Tribune*, February 6, 2004. Dufka's photos also appeared in *The Art of Seeing: The Best of Reuters Photography* (London: Pearson Education, 2000), 123.

56. Mallin, "Images of Africa," 60. With a touch of irony, the author noted that "looking at recent winners of major photojournalism awards, you may wonder whether the competitions list a passport stamped with an African visa among the entry requirements" (59).

57. Blaine Harden, "Who Killed Liberia? We Did; The Ugly American Policy: Create the Mess, Then Stand Back and Watch the Slaughter," *Washington Post*, May 26, 1996.

58. Charles Porter/Sygma photo, April 20, 1995; "Tiny Victim Shown in Dramatic Photo," *New York Times*, April 21, 1995, A23; picture appended to "Witness Describes Effort to Save Rower," *Philadelphia Inquirer*, May 17 2005, E1; "Rowers Reflect on Worries About Making Weight," *Philadelphia Inquirer*, May 22, 2005; "Race-Day Weigh In Eliminated," *Philadelphia Inquirer*, May 11, 2006; Picture appended to "Today's Photo: Japanese Journalist Shot to Death Covering Protests in Burma," *USA Today*, September 28, 2007; Martin Fletcher, "Two Pictures that Show How the Protest Was Crushed," *London Times*, September 28, 2007, 2.

59. Bob Garfield, "Images That Flicker and Fade," *Washington Post*, February 8, 2004, B1. See, for example, photo of Palestinian suicide bomber Reem al-Reyashi, (Reuters/HO, January 14, 2004, Gaza Strip, #x80001). Also see photos of executed serial killer Aileen Wuornos (AP Photo/Florida Department of Corrections, October 9, 2002, # 6449905).

60. Photos appended to James Estrin, "A Woman Ends Her Life Among Her Friends," *New York Times*, June 1, 2004, F5; Gina Bellafante, "The Power of Images to Create a Cause," *New York Times*, March 27, 2005, 3; Quoted in Jonathan Storm and Alfred Lubrano, "Cable Got a Boost But TV Saturation Had Its Low Points," *Philadelphia Inquirer*, April 1, 2005, A18.

61. Reuters/Osama Qashoo, February 12, 2003, Qalqilya, X80004.

62. See, for instance, picture appended to "Mideast Violence Continues to Rage," *New York Times*, October 1, 2000, A1 and A10; "Jerusalem Riots Escalate," *Chicago Tribune*, October 1, 2000, 1 and 6; "Clashes Kill 12, Hurt 500 Palestinians," *Dallas Morning News*, October 1, 2000, 1A; "Middle East Bloodshed Mounts," *Washington Post*, October 1, 2000, A30; Tracy Wilkinson, "TV Image of Boy's Death Captures Terrible Conflict," *Seattle Times*, October 2, 2000, A8; Hugh Dellios, "Palestinians Call Boy, 12, A Martyr," *Chicago Tribune*,

October 2, 2000, 6; "Caught in the Crossfire," *Dayton Daily News,* October 1, 2000, 9A; William A. Orme Jr., "Images of Boy's Death Televised," *Ventura County Star,* October 1, 2000, A16; "Riots Escalate in West Bank," *Sacramento Bee,* October 1, 2000, A1.

63. Pictures appended to "Mideast Violence Continues to Rage," *New York Times,* October 1, 2000, A1 and A10; picture appended to "Jerusalem Riots Escalate," *Chicago Tribune,* October 1, 2000, 1 and 6.

64. "Boy, 12, Dies in His Father's Arms in Gaza Strip Violence," *Cleveland Plain Dealer,* October 2, 2000, 6A.

65. For instance, the picture appeared in the *Detroit News* on October 1, 2000, 11A and on October 2, 2000, 5A, the *Chicago Tribune* twice on October 1, 2000, 1 and 6 and again on October 2, 2000, 6, and the *New York Times* twice on October 1, 2000, A1 and A10. Picture appended to "Sticks and Stones: A Deadly Brand of Child's Play," *New York Times,* October 8, 2000, WK16. Picture appended to "Two Weeks of Violence in the Middle East," *Chicago Tribune,* October 15, 2000, 14; cartoon captioned "A Step Back from Mideast Chaos," *Chicago Tribune,* October 5, 2000.

66. Michael Dougan, "Haunting Image Becomes Rallying Cry for Peace," *San Francisco Examiner,* October 5, 2000, A1.

67. Atyah Akbar, Letter to the Editor, *Toronto Star,* October 9, 2000, LTO1; Julian Borger, "A Picture Can Change the World, Or Maybe Not," *Houston Chronicle,* October 5, 2000, A39; Michel Agriopoulos, "Stop the Guns" (Commentary), *Chicago Tribune,* October 5, 2000, 22; James Fallows, "Who Shot Mohammed al-Dura?" *Atlantic Monthly,* June 2003, 49–56.

68. Editorial, *New York Times,* October 3, 2000; "Should We Use the Picture?" *Detroit News,* October 4, 2000, O2A; "Impact of Photographs on Public and Political Opinion," *Nightline,* ABC News, October 13, 2000; Quoted on NPR, October 1, 2000.

69. Paul Waverly, Reader's letter, *Dallas Morning News,* October 8, 2000, 4J; picture appended to Readers' Letters, *USA Today,* October 6, 2000, 24A; Borger, "A Picture Can," A39.

70. See, for example, "2000 Year in Photos," *Florida Times-Union,* December 24, 2000, G1; Dougan, "Haunting Image," A1; Borger, "A Picture Can," A39; Richard Edward Larsen, "Did Palestinian Boy Die In Vain?" *Ventura County Star,* October 5, 2000, B09; Dougan, "Haunting Image," A1; Results of the MSNBC contest were pulled because of suspected ballot stuffing ("Internet Photo Competition Pulled Due to Ballot Stuffing," Associated Press, March 22, 2001); Robert Fisk, "Review of the Year," *Independent,* December 29, 2000, 9; "2000 Year in Review," *San Francisco Chronicle,* December 29, 2000, A16.

71. "Arab World on March to Mark the Anniversary," *The Glasgow Herald,* September 29, 2001, 6 ; Akbar, Letter to the Editor, LT01; Charles M. Sennott, "Fighting Rekindled in Mideast," *Boston Globe,* October 4, 2000, A1; William M. Stewart, "The Struggle Goes On," *Santa Fe New Mexican,* December 31, 2000, F1; "The Boy Martyr" (editorial), *Cleveland Plain Dealer,* October 3, 2000, 8B; Doreen Carjaval, "Photo of Palestinian Boy Kindles Debate in France," *New York Times,* February 7, 2005, C6.

72. http://www.msnbc.msn.com/id/34261690/ns/news-picture_stories/ displaymode/1247/?beginSlide=1; Frida Ghitis, "When Bad Journalism Kills: The Mohammed Al-Dura Story," *World Politics Review,* May 30, 2008.

73. Fallows, "Who Shot," 49–56; Carjaval, "Photo of Palestinian," C6; Richard Landes, "How French TV Fudged the Death of Mohammad Al-Durra," *New Republic,* October 17, 2006.

74. Fallows, "Who Shot," 49–56; Carjaval, "Photo of Palestinian," C6; Ghitis, "When Bad Journalism"; Brett Kline, "Was Arab Boy's Death Staged?" *Canadian Jewish News,* September 26, 2007, 1.

75. Ghitis, "When Bad Journalism."

76. Picture appended to Tara Weiss, "Making Sense of Media Spin," *Hartford Courant,* February 25, 2003, D1; "Remembering, Voting," *St. Paul Pioneer Press,* October 1, 2005, A4; Craig Nelson, "Israelis and Palestinians: Two Sides to Every Image," *Atlanta Journal Constitution,* June 18, 2006, C1; "French TV Loses Gaza Footage case," *BBC News,* May 22, 2008; Ghitis, "When Bad Journalism."

77. See, for instance, picture titled "It Came from That Way," *Chicago Daily Defender,* April 9, 1968, 1. Ruben Castenada, "A Conspiracy of Silence?" *American Journalism Review,* March 2000, 60–63.

78. Pictures appended to "Kennedy Clings to Life," *Chicago Daily Defender,* June 6, 1968, 3. Photographers capturing virtually the same picture included Richard Drew for the AP (who also took the shot of the "falling man" after the 9/11 attacks), Bill Eppridge for *Life,* and Boris Yaro for the *Los Angeles Times* and *Washington Post.*

79. Picture appended to Christopher T. Assaf, "Epic Vision: Forty Years Ago Today, Photographer Bill Eppridge Captured the Image That Many Can't Forget: The Assassination of Robert F. Kennedy," *Baltimore Sun,* June 4, 2008, A33; "The Sound of History," *The Gazette* (Canada), June 5, 2008, A3; " 'We All Just Plain Loved Him,' " *Gulf News* (UAE), June 7, 2008, 12; "Democrats Must Heal Rift—Unlike after RFK," *Irish Times,* June 6, 2008, 13. See too pictures appended to "Cover-Ups and Conspiracies: A Unique Investigation into the Dark Side of the Kennedy Legend," *Revelations,* summer 1988, 22, 26.

80. John Moore, quoted in "Benazir Bhutto Assassinated," CNN, December 28, 2007.

81. For instance, see pictures appended to "Assault on Democracy," *St. Louis Post Dispatch,* December 28, 2007, A1; "Assassinated," *Sun-Sentinel,* December 28, 2007, 1A; "Seconds from Death: Chilling Image Captures Last Moments of Benazir Bhutto," *New York Daily News,* December 28, 2007, front cover; "Bhutto's Last Picture Before Attack," *London Sun,* December 28, 2007, 1; "Benazir Bhutto Assassinated," CNN, December 28, 2007; Zain Verjee, "Bhutto Assassination," CNN, December 28, 2007; "Benazir Bhutto: The Dying Seconds," YouTube, posted by fcukpg, December 29, 2007; "Last Seven Seconds of Benazir Bhutto," YouTube, posted by rimkhan1, December 30, 2007.

82. Pictures reappeared in the *New York Times'* yearly retrospective of memorable images, where its caption informed readers that they were looking at "the opposition leader...seconds before she was assassinated in a suicide attack" ("The Year in Pictures," *New York Times,* December 31, 2007, 4).

83. Romanian television did broadcast images of the couple in captivity but none of them facing their execution (Mort Rosenblum, "Ceausescu Troops Surrender After TV Shows Body of Dictator," Associated Press, December 26, 1989); "Romania: People Incredulous at Pictures of a Dead Dictator," IPS-Inter Press Service, December 26, 1989);

"Ceausescus Beg For Mercy, Weep in New Execution Footage," Associated Press, April 22, 1990. "Ceausescu Execution Video Faked, Experts Say," Associated Press, April 30, 1990; Patrick McDowell, "French and Romanian TV Networks Argue over Ceausescu Execution Tape," Associated Press, April 24, 1990; Alan Elsner, "Trial and Execution: The Dramatic Deaths of Nicolae and Elena Ceausescu," Huffington Post, December 23, 2009, www.huffingtonpost.com/alan-elsner/trial-and-execution-the-d_b_401497.html

84. See, for instance, William K. Stevens, "Official Calls in Press and Kills Himself," *New York Times,* January 23, 1987, A1. Pictures of Dwyer in varying degrees of holding the handgun to his mouth appeared on the front pages of the *New York Times* and the *Washington Post* and on the inside pages of multiple newspapers. See pictures appended to "Witnesses to Death," *Washington Post,* January 23, 1987, A1, A4; "White-Collar Shame," *Newsweek,* November 28, 1988, 58; "Treasurer Dwyer Kills Self," *Philadelphia Inquirer,* January 23, 1987, 1; Robert Bianco and Ken Guggenheim. "Use of Suicide Film Debated News, Television Desks," *Pittsburgh Press,* January 23, 1987, A6; Also see Patrick R. Parsons and William E. Smith, "R. Budd Dwyer: A Case Study in Newsroom Decision Making," *Journal of Mass Media Ethics* 3(1), 84–94; Elizabeth B. Ziesenis, "Exploring Questions of Media Morality," *Journal of Mass Media Ethics* 6(4), 1991, 234–244; Jeffrey Lord, "A Plea for Mercy: Budd Dwyer Merits a Pardon," *Philadelphia Inquirer,* Jaunary 11, 2009, C1.

85. See Taylor, *Body Horror,* 73; "Fury as Di Pic Shown," *The Sun,* April 4, 2007, 1; Episode titled "Diana's Secrets," CBS News, *48 Hours Investigates,* April 21, 2004.

86. Joanne Ostrow, "Even British Tabs Knock CBS," *Denver Post,* April 25, 2004, F16; James Pinkerton, "The More the Public Knows the Better," *Newsday,* April 27, 2004, A41; cited in "Anger at CBS Use of Diana Photos," CBS News, 23 April 2004; Martin Soames, "Whose Life Is It Anyway?" *Guardian,* April 26, 2004, 10; "Diana's Fans' Fury at Crash Images on TV," *Citizen,* May 1, 2004, 7.

87. See Barbie Zelizer, *Covering the Body: The Kennedy Assassination, the Media, and the Shaping of Collective Memory* (Chicago: University of Chicago Press, 1992).

88. Goldberg, *Power of Photography,* 225.

89. Rick Friedman, "Pictures of Assassination Fall to Amateurs on Street," *Editor and Publisher,* November 30, 1963, 16.

90. Robert MacNeil, NBC News, November 22, 1963.

91. Zelizer, *Covering the Body,* 51–55; Bob Jackson, in Rich Toschies, "History Shot in Black and White," *Colorado Springs Gazette,* November 22, 2003, A1. Significantly, this is the same photographer who then received a Pulitzer for his shot of Lee Harvey Oswald being killed.

92. Quoted in Saul Pett, AP Log, rpt. "The Reporter's Story, *Columbia Journalism Review,* winter 1964, 8; "Lone 'Pro' on Scene Where JFK Was Shot," *Editor and Publisher,* December 7, 1963, 11. Picture appended to "When the Bullets Struck," *New York Times,* November 23, 1963, 1; "The Day Kennedy Died," *Newsweek,* December 2, 1963, 43; "President Is Killed," *Chicago Daily News,* November 23, 1963, 1. Altgens, however, was better known for other pictures he took that day: a few moments earlier he had taken what is believed to be the last professional picture made of the president while still alive, a frontal view of the car with a fairly visible Kennedy inside it. And during the shooting, he snapped an image of what is believed to be Lee Harvey Oswald, standing on the front steps of the

Texas School Book Depository at the moment he was supposed to be shooting Kennedy from its sixth floor; see David R. Wrone, *The Zapruder Film: Reframing JFK's Assassination* (Lawrence: University Press of Kansas, 2003).

93. For instance, Moorman's image was appended to "The Day Kennedy Died," *Newsweek,* December 2, 1963, 42; picture titled "Moments After Assassination," *New York Times,* November 24, 1963, 5.

94. "The Assassination of President Kennedy," *Life,* November 29, 1963, 23–24; *Life* (special memorial issue), December 1963; *Warren Report: Report of the President's Commission on the Assassination of President John F. Kennedy,* vol. 18 (Washington, DC: US Government Printing Office, 1964); "The Warren Report," *Life,* October 2, 1964. Also see David M. Lubin, *Shooting Kennedy* (Berkeley: University of California Press, 2003).

95. The film was widely discussed (and its still images published) in Ben H. Bagdikian, "The Assassin," *Saturday Evening Post,* December 14, 1963, 25–26; Richard B. Stolley. "The Greatest Home Movie Ever Made," *Esquire,* November 1973, 133–135. "JFK's Assassination: Who Was the Real Target?" *Time,* November 28, 1988, cover photo and p. 32; Robert Hennelly and Jerry Policoff, "How *Time-Life,* the *New York Times,* and CBS Killed the Conspiracy Theory," *Village Voice,* March 31, 1992, cover photos.

96. For instance, see picture appended to "The Day Kennedy Died," 42; "Kennedy Fourth President Killed by an Assassin," *New York Times,* November 23, 1963, 10, alongside drawings of U.S. presidents Abraham Lincoln, William McKinley, James A. Garfield and the would-be assassin of Franklin Roosevelt.

97. Quoted in "The Four Dark Days: From Dallas to Arlington," CBS, November 25, 1963.

98. "Assassination—Behind Moves to Reopen JFK Case," *U.S. News and World Report,* June 2, 1975, 30–31; "John Kennedy's Death: The Debate Still Rages," *U.S. News and World Report,* November 21, 1983, 49; Bill Marvel and Delia M. Rios, "Flashback," *Dallas Morning News,* April 21, 1991, F1; Leonard Boasberg, "A Market for Conspiracy," *Philadelphia Inquirer,* November 22, 1993, E1.

99. Zelizer, *Covering the Body,* 61–63.

100. See, for instance, pictures appended to Michael Beschloss, "The Day that Changed America," *Newsweek,* November 22, 1993, 58–65; "November 22, 1963: Where We Were," *People,* November 28, 1988, 69; Tanya Barrientos, " 'JFK' Film Has Students Talking About History, *Philadelphia Inquirer,* January 24, 1992, D1; Robert Sam Anson, " 'JFK' The Movie: Oliver Stone Reshoots History, *Esquire,* November 1991, cover; Lisa Grunwald, "Why We Still Care," *Life,* December 1991, 35.

101. Friedman, "Pictures of Assassination," 17.

102. *Warren Report: Report of the President's Commission on the Assassination of President John F. Kennedy* (Washington, DC: U.S. Government Printing Office, 1964), 216.

103. For example, "The Day Kennedy Died," 21; Goldberg, *Power of Photography,* 223.

104. The photo, copyrighted by the *Times-Herald* and serviced by UPI and AP, November 24, 1963, came after Beers's photo by a fraction of a second. Both AP and UPI gave Jackson a bonus and the *Times-Herald* raised his pay (Friedman, "Pictures of Assassination," 67).

105. Goldberg, *Power of Photography,* 224.

106. Bob Jackson, in Michael A. Lednovich, "Immortal Image Lost," *Los Angeles Daily News*, November 21, 1993, U1.

107. Jack Gould, "Millions of Viewers See Oswald Killing on 2 TV Networks," *New York Times*, November 2, 1963, 10; Quoted in Lubin, *Shooting Kennedy*, 237; Zelizer, *Covering the Body*.

108. Cecil Smith, "Camera Watches as Oswald Is Shot," *Los Angeles Times*, November 25, 1963. Jackson's photo was also appended to "An Assassin Assassinated," *Chicago Daily Defender*, November 25, 1963, 4; Jack Gould, "Millions of Viewers See Oswald Killing on Two TV Networks," *New York Times*, November 25, 1963, 1; Ben H. Bagdikian, "The Assassin," *Saturday Evening Post*, December 14, 1963, 27. Beers's was appended to Thomas Thompson, "Assassin: The Man Held—and Killed—for Murder," *Life*, November 29, 1963, 37; Herbert Brucker, "When the Press Shapes the News," *Saturday Review*, January 11, 1964, 77; Zelizer, *Covering the Body*, 58–61.

109. "Oswald Shooting a First in Television History," *Broadcasting*, December 2, 1963, 460; "Icons: The Ten Greatest Images of Photojournalism," *Time*, special collector's edition, fall 1989, 8; "New Challenges: 1950–1980," *Time*, special collector's edition, fall 1989, 56. Also see Faber, *Great News Photographs*, 134; Rubin and Newton, *Capture the Moment*, 52–53; Paul Lester, *Photojournalism: An Ethical Approach* (Hillsdale, NJ: Lawrence Erlbaum, 1991), 52.

110. See pictures appended to Priscilla McMillan, "That Time We Huddled Together," *New York Times*, November 22, 1973, 37; "A City is Tried and Convicted," *The Quill*, November 1987, 55; "JFK's Assassination: Who Was the Real Target?" *Time*, November 28, 1988, 40; Melinda Beck and Anne Underwood, "'I Wanted To Be a Hero,'" *Newsweek*, November 22, 1993, 95; Pictures appended to Keith McKnight, "Veteran Reporter Recalls Moment Camelot Ended," *Akron Beacon Journal*, November 22, 2003, A1; Michele Cohen, "JFK: For Those Who Were There, That November in Dallas Was A Day That Never Ended," *Sun-Sentinel*, November 20, 1988, 1A; "John F. Kennedy Memorial Edition," *Life* (Anniversary Special), winter 1988, n.p.

111. Picture appended to Robert Tharp, "Police Close Door on History," *Dallas Morning News*, October 12, 2001, 33A; Jason Trahan, "Police Move Stirs Sentiment," *Dallas Morning News*, March 17, 2003, 15A; Selwyn Crawford, "For Museum, A Photo Opportunity," *Dallas Morning News*, February 19, 2002, 15A, which was captioned as follows: "1. The obscure, the horrifying, the historic: The exhibit that launches the seventh-floor gallery of the Sixth Floor Museum takes in the many emotional images that have won Pulitzer Prizes for news photographers for 60 years. 2. "It's just an honor to be a part of this exhibit," says Robert Jackson, who captured Jack Ruby shooting Lee Harvey Oswald"; Nancy Moore, "Photographer Retraces His Steps," *Dallas Morning News*, February 23, 2007, 16.

112. Pictures appended to "The Assassination of President Kennedy," 22–32.

Chapter 6

1. Jacques Derrida, *Margins of Philosophy* (New York: Harvester Wheatsheaf, 1982), 13; Anthony Giddens, *The Consequences of Modernity* (Stanford, CA: Stanford University Press, 1991). Also see Andrew Quick, "Time and the Event," *Cultural Values* 2 (April 1998), 223–242.

2. See, for instance, Daniel Hallin, *The "Uncensored War": The Media and Vietnam* (New York: Oxford University Press, 1986); and Marita Sturken, *Tangled Memories: The Vietnam War, the AIDs Epidemic, and the Politics of Remembering* (Berkeley: University of California Press, 1997), 89; Susan Moeller, *Shooting War: Photography and the American Experience of Combat* (New York: Basic Books, 1989).

3. David Perlmutter, *Photojournalism and Foreign Policy: Icons of Outrage in International Crises* (New York: Praeger, 1998).

4. These included the Malcolm Browne photo of a Buddhist monk self-immolating, the Eddie Adams shot of the shooting of General Loan, the Ron Haeberle image of a group of women and children about to be shot in Mei Lai, and the Nick Ut shot of a young Kim-Phuc running naked from a napalmed village (who did not die but others in the bombing did); Judy Lee Kinney, "Gardens of Stone, Platoon and Hamburger Hill: Ritual and Remembrance," in Michael Anderegg (ed.), *Inventing Vietnam: The War in Film and Television* (Philadelphia: Temple University Press, 1991), 156.

5. Malcolm Browne, "Viet Nam Reporting: Three Years of Crisis," *Columbia Journalism Review,* fall 1964, 6.

6. Quoted in Vicki Goldberg, *The Power of Photography* (New York: Abbeville, 1991), 212.

7. Malcolm Browne, in Moeller, *Shooting War,* 405.

8. Picture titled "Monks Take Part in Buddhist Protest," appended to David Halberstam, "Diem Asks Peace in Religion Crisis," *New York Times,* June 12, 1963, 3. In fact, the newspaper continued to refer to Quang Duc's suicide numerous times over the following weeks—nearly every day between June 13 and June 21 and intermittently between June 22 and July 1—but did not include a photograph until thirty years later (picture appended to Malcolm W. Browne, "Death Benefits: Life and Times," *New York Times,* October 3, 1993, 273). Curiously, on September 12, 1993, Dan Rather's *New York Times* review of Browne's book called on readers to "remember the shocking photographs of the Buddhist monk Thich Quang Duc, who immolated himself in 1963 to protest the Vietnam War," but the image had not yet appeared in the newspaper. "Burns Self to Death in Viet Protest," *Chicago Tribune,* June 11, 1963, 3; "The World: South Vietnam: Death in a Saigon Intersection," *Los Angeles Times,* June 16, 1963, K4. Quoted in Denise Chong, *The Girl in the Picture: The Story of Kim-Phuc, the Photograph and the Vietnam War* (New York: Viking, 1999), 50. And yet, one such picture, taken by Faas, did appear in a retrospective years later (Piers Moore Ede, "Horst Faas," *News Photographer,* July 2004, 28–29). Even later, Faas (together with Michel Laurent) took similar pictures in what was to become Bangladesh in 1971, when Bengali soldiers bayoneted Bihari prisoners in front of the press. The pictures won them the Pulitzer Prize.

9. "Saigon Riot by Buddhist Women Barely Averted," *Los Angeles Times,* June 14, 1963, 26; "Saigon Police Out in Force as Buddhist is Cremated," *New York Times,* June 19, 1963, 3; Browne, "Viet Nam Reporting," 6. The journal reprinted Browne's picture alongside the piece.

10. Pictures appended to "An Angry Buddhist Burns Himself Alive," *Life,* June 21, 1963, 24–25; "Fiery Protest," *Newsweek,* June 24, 1963, 63; "Trial by Fire," *Time,* June 21, 1963, 32.

11. Admitting that he felt no compunction about not saving the monk, he offered that "I probably could have done nothing in any case, since the monks and nuns had clearly rehearsed their role for the ceremony many times....But frankly it never occurred to me to interfere. I have always felt that a newsman's duty is to observe and report the news, not to change it" (Browne, "Viet Nam Reporting," 7). Part of the reason for the initial unevenness of the photo's display may have derived from the frames competing for its meaning: it simultaneously signaled a protest against religious oppression and a war for freedom from the Communists (Lisa M. Skow and George N. Dionisopoulos, "A Struggle to Contextualize Photographic Images: American Print Media and the "Burning Monk," *Communication Quarterly*, fall 1997, 393–409).

12. "The Heart of Quang Duc," *Time*, July 5, 1963, 33; Browne, "Viet Nam Reporting," 7; David Halberstam, "Rites for Leading Writer," *New York Times*, July 14, 1963, 16; "Vietnamese Girl Tries Suicide to Aid Buddhists," *Los Angeles Times*, August 13, 1963, 5. The immolations multiplied in number, and by 1965 Buddhist followers in Saigon were being urged to stage suicides by burning (Jack Foisie, "Viet Mob Wrecks 2nd U.S. Library," *Los Angeles Times*, January 24, 1965, D1).

13. "Two Modern Martyrs" (advertisement), *New York Times*, June 22, 1963, 11. In September, *Life* repeated its photographic treatment of the Quang Duc immolation in a second event of the same order "Another Monk Gives Himself to Flames," *Life*, September 6, 1963, 30–31. The coverage assumed a later place in memory too, when ten years later a black Vietnam veteran set himself on fire in the middle of an Atlanta parade, and leaders compared it to the self-immolations of Buddhist monks in Vietnam ("Black Leaders Compare Fire Death, Monks," *Chicago Daily Defender*, October 9, 1972, 4).

14. Quoted in Moeller, *Shooting War*, 404; John Faber, *Great News Photos and the Stories Behind Them* (1960; reprint New York: Dover, 1978), 132–133; Browne, "Viet Nam Reporting," 7; for instance, Faber, *Great News Photos*, 132–133, and "The 60s: Decade of Change," *Life*, December 26, 1969, 65; texts accompanying the photo's display as the World Press Photo of the Year, 1963; "The World's Greatest Photographs," *London Sunday Times*, October 22, 2006, 12; Malcolm W. Browne, *Muddy Boots and Red Socks* (New York: Time-Life Books, 1993), 3. When Browne wrote a column about his life, the photo was used as illustration (Malcolm W. Browne, "Life and Times," *New York Times*, October 3, 1993, 273). Music included a Billy Joel video and the sleeve photo for a record by Rage against the Machine.

15. Quoted in Faber, *Great News Photos*, 136.

16. Faber, *Great News Photos*, 136; quoted in Peter Howe, *Shooting under Fire* (New York: Artisan Books, 2002), 26. The prisoner was later identified as either Nguyen Van Lem or Le Cong Na, both said to be operatives of the Vietcong.

17. Analysts differ as to how proximate death was in this photo: some argue it depicted the final moment before death; others maintain it was taken after the bullet discharged into the prisoner's head.

18. Harold Evans, *Pictures on a Page* (London: Heinemann, 1978), n.p.

19. George A. Bailey and Lawrence W. Lichty, "Rough Justice on a Saigon Street: A Gatekeeper Study of NBC's Tet Execution Film," *Journalism Quarterly*, summer 1972, 223.

20. Picture captioned "Guerrilla Dies," *New York Times*, February 2, 1968, 1, and "Execution," *New York Times*, February 2, 1968, 12; "Death Strikes in Saigon," *Los Angeles Times*, February 2, 1968, 1; and "Execution," *Washington Post*, February 2, 1968, A1. The *Washington Post* again displayed the entire page years later in a feature titled "The Century in the Post," where the recycled front page illustrated a short blurb about the Tet offensive that was positioned in the comics section ("Tet Offensive," *Washington Post*, February 2, 1999, C13); untitled photo in both the *New York Daily News* (February 2, 1968, 1) and *Chicago Tribune* (February 2, 1968, 3).

21. At the time that NBC News showed the still shot, it did not yet know that its own Saigon crew would have available color film of the execution the following day. The film aired twice more, once on the "Frank McGee Report" on March 10 and again nineteen months later, on October 7, 1969, on a special NBC broadcast, "From Here to the 70s." See Bailey and Lichty, "Rough Justice," 221–229, 238, for a detailed discussion of the NBC crew's experience of shooting the event. Also see Goldberg, *Power of Photography*, 226.

22. Pictures appended to "Grim and Ghastly Picture," *New York Daily News*, February 3, 1968; "The War," *Time*, February 9, 1968, 24–25; "Hanoi Attacks," *Newsweek*, February 12, 1968, 29; *Time*, February 29, 1968, 24–25; Shana Alexander, "The Feminine Eye: What Is the Truth of the Picture?" *Life*, March 1, 1968, 19.

23. Alexander, "Feminine Eye," 19; Lynette Moss, Letter to the Editor, *London Times*, February 5, 1968, 9; G. M. Buxton, Letter to the Editor, *London Times*, February 6, 1968, 9; Bailey and Lichty, "Rough Justice," 238; S. Kenneth Nelson, Letter to the Editor, *New York Times*, February 7, 1968, 46.

24. Anthony Lewis, "Outrage and Horror in Europe Tempered by Some Sympathy for U.S.," *New York Times*, February 5, 1968, 16.

25. Lewis, "Outrage and Horror," 16; photo appended to "The War," *Time*, February 9, 1968, 24–25; and "By Book and Bullet," *Time*, February 23, 1968, 32, where *Time* oddly characterized the person about to die as "stubborn-looking." "Red Cross Assails Executions in War," *New York Times*, February 10, 1968, 14.

26. He was, however, promoted to Brigadier General after the incident (Faber, *Great News Photos*, 136).

27. Eddie Adams, "Eulogy," *Time*, July 27, 1998.

28. Thomas R. Kennedy, in Sebastio Salgado and Stephen Mayes, *This Critical Mirror* (London: Thames and Hudson, 1996), 163; Peter Stepan, *Photos that Changed the World* (London: Prestel, 2000), 114; cited in Andy Grundberg, "Eddie Adams, Journalist, 71; Showed Violence of Vietnam," *New York Times*, September 20, 2004, 10; Thomas R. Kennedy and James K., Colton, in Salgado and Mayes, *This Critical Mirror*, 163.

29. See "150 Years of Photojournalism," *Time*, fall 1989, cover, 9; and "Eyewitness: Pictures of a Century," *Life*, October 1, 1999, cover, 32. It was also selected as one of the top photos by numerous photo editors, where Stepan (*Photos that Changed*, 114–115) called it "one of the most memorable war images in the history of war photography." See too Salgado and Mayes, *This Critical Mirror*, 60–61; Cyma Rubin and Eric Newton, *Capture the Moment: The Pulitzer Prize Photographs* (New York: Norton, 2001), 64–65; Faber, *Great News Photos*, 136–137; and Paul Lester, *Photojournalism: An Ethical Approach* (Hillsdale, NJ: Lawrence Erlbaum, 1991), 52. The photo also appeared in a 2004 article

about an exhibit of prize winning photographs (Mary Voelz Chandler, "Through the Lens of History: Museum Displays Pulitzer Prize Winning Photographs Since 1942," *Rocky Mountain News,* August 26, 2004, 1D).

30. Picture appended to "A Gallery of Photos that Brought the War Home," *Time,* November 6, 1972, 20; "Vietnam: Ten Years Later," *Time,* April 15, 1985, 1, 22; and "150 Years of Photojournalism," n.p; picture appended to Jonathan Alter, "The Picture the World Sees," *Newsweek,* May 17, 2004, 31. It appeared in the *New York Times* in 1963, twice in 1998, in 2004, and 2007, and in the *Washington Post* in 1968, 1978, 1982, 1999, and 2004; Alter, "Picture the World Sees," 31. Its importance continues to be debated, as in the 2007 film *Looking for an Icon* (dir. Hans Pool and Maaik Krijgsman and released by First Run/Icarus Films), which considered the photo's function as an icon of war.

31. Quoted in Liz Nakahara, "Pulitzers: The Power and the Pressure," *Washington Post,* September 12, 1982, G12; Richard Pyle, "Eddie Adams, 71, Photographer," *Philadelphia Inquirer,* September 20, 2004, B10. Also see Seymour Topping, "Introduction," in Rubin and Newton, *Capture the Moment,* 5–6; and "War Stories," Newseum, http://www.newseum.org/media/ws/mp3/bio_adams_1.mp3.

32. Robert McG. Thomas Jr., "Nguyen Ngoc Loan, 67, Dies: Executed Viet Cong Prisoner," *New York Times,* July 16, 1998, A27; Eddie Adams, "Killing With a Camera," *Time,* August 1, 1998.

33. Picture appended to Betsy Carter, "The Haunted General," *Newsweek,* May 3, 1976, 11; "The Vietnam War: The Executioner," *Newsweek,* November 13, 1978, 70; "The Legacy of Vietnam" (Special Report), *Newsweek,* April 15, 1985, 64. Picture appended to "Ten Years Later: A Photo Haunts Men and Nation," *Washington Post,* December 17, 1978, 5.

34. On the former, see McG. Thomas, "Nguyen Ngoc Loan," A27; "Ex S. Vietnam General Who Executed Prisoner," *Chicago Tribune,* July 16, 1998, 10; "Vietnamese Executioner Who Shocked the World Dies at Home in the US," *Guardian,* July 16, 1998, 18. On the latter, see Pyle, "Eddie Adams," B10; and Adam Bernstein, "Photojournalist Eddie Adams, Pulitzer Prize-Winner, Dies," *Washington Post,* September 20, 2004, B6.

35. See, for instance, Richard Bernstein, "In Vietnam the Pen Was as Mighty as the Sword," *New York Times,* December 1, 1998, E2. The image illustrated Bernstein's review of *Reporting Vietnam,* appearing with the simple caption: "This execution is credited with turning public opinion against the war." Also see Robert Goldsborough and Mike Ryan, "The Year of Indelible Memories," *Advertising Age,* May 16, 1988, 54; and Matt Zoller Seitz, "When Images Take on Lives of Their Own," *New York Times,* May 9, 2007, 5. The picture was even used to illustrate a more pointed story about the connection between the Zapruder film and the history of the JFK assassination, driving home the point that images of violence have regularly populated the historical record (Thomas Doherty, "Forever Linked: Zapruder and…History," *Boston Sunday Globe,* July 26, 1998, D2). For more on this, see H. Bruce Franklin, *MIA, or Mythmaking in America: How and Why Belief in POWs Has Possessed a Nation* (New Brunswick, NJ: Rutgers University Press, 1993), 47.

36. See AP Photo/Stf, "Germany Protest 1968," May 11, 1968 (# 07022008535); "The Remix Saigon," artist Olivier Blanckart, displayed at 'ART COLOGNE,' in Cologne, Germany, October 28, 2004. Also see H. Bruce Franklin, *Vietnam and Other American Fantasies* (Amherst: University of Massachusetts Press, 2000).

37. Jonah Goldberg, "Goldberg File—There are Tears in My Eyes: Eddie Adams and the Most Famous Photo of the Vietnam War," *National Review Online*, August 26, 1999, 7.20 pm, http://article.nationalreview.com/print/?q=M2QxNWY0N2ZkY2IxMW JhZGQ4MTU3ZjhlZjg3NTk0NzE=. Also see "Photographs Do Lie," *Weekly Standard*, http://www.weeklystandard.com/Content/Public/Articles/000/000/004/666noxlw. asp?pg=2.

38. Peter Braestrup, *Big Story: How the American Press Reported and Interpreted the Crisis of Tet 1968 in Vietnam and Washington* (Boulder, CO: Westview, 1977), 461–462.

39. Robert Hamilton, "Image and Context: The Production and Reproduction of the Execution of a VC Suspect by Eddie Adams," in Jeffrey Walsh and James Aulich (eds.), *Vietnam Images, War and Representation* (Basingstoke: Macmillan, 1989), 182.

40. Varnado Simpson, interviewed for "Remember My Lai," May 23, 1989, transcript of TV show, *PBS: Frontline*, http://www.pbs.org/wgbh/pages/frontline/programs/ transcripts/714.html.

41. Ronald Haeberle, in Joseph Eszterhaus, "The Massacre at Mylai," *Life*, December 5, 1969, 40; Ron Haeberle, in "Remember My Lai," *Frontline*, PBS Broadcasts, originally broadcast May 23, 1989. http://www.pbs.org/wgbh/pages/frontline/programs/ transcripts/714.html.

42. Goldberg, *Power of Photography*, 230. Also see "My Lai Massacre: Something Dark and Bloody," Asia Pacific Network: Café Pacific, http://www.asiapac.org.fj/cafepacific/ resources/aspac/biet.html.

43. Ronald Haeberle, in "Remember My Lai"; Steve Weinberg, "War Crimes," *Investigative Reporters and Editors, The IRE Journal*, March/April 2004.

44. David L. Anderson (ed.), "Ron Ridenhour's Letter of March 29, 1969," in *Facing My Lai: Moving Beyond the Massacre*, Appendix A (Lawrence: University of Kansas Press, 1998), 201; "The Press—Miscue on a Massacre," *Time*, December 5, 1969, 75; Seymour M. Hersh, "How I Broke the My Lai Story," *Saturday Review*, July 11, 1970, 47.

45. Seymour M. Hersh, "The Massacre at My Lai," (1970) in John Pilger, *Tell Me No Lies: Investigative Journalism That Changed the World* (Thunder's Mouth Press, 2005), 113.

46. The photo appeared alongside a single word heading—"Exclusive." Lower on the front page the headline to the accompanying news article gave more information: JosephEszterhaus, "Cameraman Saw GIs Slay 100 Villagers," *Cleveland Plain Dealer,* November 20, 1969, 1A. Other pictures appeared in the same issue on a double-page photo spread (4B and 5B); "Don't Use Photos, Army Urges," *Cleveland Plain Dealer,* November 20, 1969, 6-A; "Plain Dealer Reply," *Cleveland Plain Dealer,* November 20, 1969, 6-A.

47. Picture appended to "PD Prints 1st Photos of Viet Mass Slaying," *Cleveland Plain Dealer,* November 20, 1969, 4-B. In fact, the group of photos was curious for its disconnect between the actions of the U.S. soldiers and the results of those actions on the Vietnamese civilians. Although one of the eight photos showed an American soldier firing his rifle at an undepicted village and another showed a U.S. soldier throwing baskets onto a fire, all of the other photos in the set targeted the loss of human life. Five of the eight photos depicted dead civilians and one showed the group of civilians facing death, but nowhere were the soldiers and civilians depicted in one collective shot. Haeberle later said

he kept for himself images that might have identified soldiers; see Evelyn Theiss, "My Lai Photographer Ronald Haeberle Exposed a Vietnam Massacre 40 Years Ago Today in the *Plain Dealer*," *Cleveland Plain Dealer*, November 20, 2009, posted 4.10 am, http://www. cleveland.com/living/index.ssf/2009/11/plain_dealer_published_first_i.html.

48. For instance, see picture appended to "Former GI Took Pictures of Dead," *New York Times*, November 22, 1969, 3; "Point Blank Murder," *Los Angeles Times*, December 1, 1969, 14; "MyLai Massacre," *Time*, November 28, 1969, 17–19; "My Lai: An American Tragedy," *Time*, December 5, 1969, 23; picture appended to "Song My—A U.S. Atrocity?" *Newsweek*, December 1, 1969, 35; "The Killings at Song My," *Newsweek*, December 8, 1969, 33; and Joseph Eszterhaus, "The Massacre at Mylai," *Life*, December 5, 1969, 41.

49. Hersh, in Pilger, *Tell Me No Lies,*114; Goldberg, *Power of Photography*, 234; Letters to the Editor, *Life*, December 19, 1969, 46–47; Kendrick Oliver, *The My Lai Massacre in American History and Memory* (New York: Manchester University Press, 2006), 76; Quoted in Claude Cookman, "An American Atrocity: The My Lai Massacre Concretized in a Victim's Face," *Journal of American History*, June 2007, 160; Goldberg, *Power of Photography*, 234. The congressman was Mendel Rivers, chair of the House Armed Services Committee.

50. Cookman, "American Atrocity," 157–158. The coverage followed the televised confession of Paul Meadlo on November 21 (Hersh, in Pilger, *Tell Me No Lies,* 115–116). The commission of inquiry that later reviewed misconduct in the incident, the Peers Commission, found Haeberle's deficient on five counts, including his failure to try and prevent the massacre, to inform authorities of what had happened, and to make available the evidence he had collected. See Joseph Goldstein et al, *The My Lai Massacre and Its Cover-up: Beyond the Reach of Law* (New York: Free Press, 1976).

51. See, for instance, picture appended to Walter Goodman, "My Lai: Hard to Forget, Hard to Remember," *New York Times*, May 23, 1989, C18.

52. Picture appended to "Vietnam: Ten Years Later," *Time*, April 15, 1985, 23–24. The newsmagazine also printed the Eddie Adams and Nick Ut pictures; Goldberg, *Power of Photography*, 236; Oliver, *My Lai Massacre*, 135; Theiss, "My Lai Photographer."

53. Michael Bilton and Kevin Sim, *Four Hours at My Lai* (New York: Penguin, 1992), 4; Oliver, *My Lai Massacre*, 3, 280.

54. Robert Hariman and John Lucaites, *No Caption Needed* (Chicago: University of Chicago Press, 2007), 177.

55. Quoted in Horst Faas and Marianne Fulton, "The Bigger Picture," http://www. digitaljournalist.org/issue0008/ng2.htm.

56. These details were fully recounted in Faas and Fulton, "Bigger Picture."

57. NBC also included film that showed the burnt backs of the children (Goldberg, *Power of Photography*, 241). Picture titled "Accidental Napalm Attack," *New York Times*, June 9, 1972, 1; " Tragic Error," *Los Angeles Times*, June 9, 1972, 1; "Vietnam: Scents of Success," *Washington Post*, June 9, 1972, 1; "The Horror of War," *Philadelphia Inquirer*, June 9, 1972, 1; "A Misplaced Bomb…and a Breath of Hell," *Stars and Stripes*, June 10, 1972. Also see Goldberg, *Power of Photography*, 242.

58. Patrick Hagopian, "Vietnam War Photography as a Locus of Memory," in Annette Kuhn and Kirsten McAllister, *Locating Memory: Photographic Acts* (New York: Berghahn

Books, 2006), 213; Susan Sontag, *Regarding the Pain of Others* (New York: Farrar, Straus and Giroux, 2003), 57.

59. Picture appended to "Little Viet Boy Dies of Napalm Burns," *Philadelphia Inquirer*, February 10, 1972, A2; "Girl, 9, Survives Napalm Burns," *New York Times*, June 11, 1972, 17. This pattern was repeated by other papers. See "Napalm-Burned Girl Recovering in Hospital," *Los Angeles Times*, June 11, 1972, 1. Another brother, pictured in the original photo, was also said to have died, but that fact was reported only much later. See Peter Cheney, "Vietnam Photo Girl Kim Now 'Smiles All the Time," *Toronto Star*, February 6, 1997, A1. In fact, numerous contradictory claims were made about the other children in the photo and their relation to Kim-Phuc: she was said to have lost one brother, two brothers (both in the photo), one cousin and two cousins. Each report underscored the fact that some of those depicted with Kim-Phuc had died.

60. Picture appended to "Pacification's Deadly Price," *Newsweek*, June 19, 1972, 42–43; "Threat of Life," *Life*, June 23, 1972, 4–5.

61. Howe, *Shooting under Fire*; Jim Renello, "Letters to the Editor," *Philadelphia Inquirer*, June 18, 1972, A10; Donna Westerman, "Letters to the *Times*," *Los Angeles Times*, June 15, 1972, D6; Evelyn Silver, "Letters to the Editor," *Life*, July 14, 1972, 29; S. Leeds, "Letters to the *Times*," *Los Angeles Times*, June 15, 1972, D6. One reader thanked *Newsweek* for publishing it, saying it "will haunt me eternally" (Jane Rubey," Letters," *Newsweek*, July 17, 1972, 6); Mrs. Leo V. Corbett, "Letters to the *Times*," *Los Angeles Times*, June 15, 1972, D6; Hariman and Lucaites, *No Caption Needed*, 175, 199.

62. "Threat of Life," 4–5; "Letters to the Editors," *Life*, July 14, 1972, 29; *Life*, December 29, 1972, 55. The entire citation appeared in Goldberg, *Power of Photography*, 244.

63. "Napalmed Girl Recovering in Saigon," *New York Times*, August 9, 1972, 1; picture titled "Life Looks Up," *Los Angeles Times*, August 9, 1972, C2; "Misfortune Revisits a Vietnamese Girl," *New York Times*, November 12, 1972, 3; and "Napalm-Burned Girl Again Victim of War," *Los Angeles Times*, November 12, 1972, 21. Also see http://digitaljournalist.org/issue0008/ng_intro.htm.

64. Quoted in Howe, *Shooting under Fire*, 27; David Hinckley, "A Far Cry from Vietnam," *New York Daily News*, June 12, 2007, 49. For more on this, see Hariman and Lucaites, *No Caption Needed*, 171–207.

65. Goldberg, *Power of Photography*, 243; picture appended to "The Year and Kim-Phuc: Memories Masked by a Smile," *Life*, December 29, 1972, 54–55; "Images, 72," *Time*, January 1, 1973, 9; "Vietnam: Ten Years Ago," *Philadelphia Inquirer*, April 28, 1985, 4C; and George Judson, "Stepping Out from the Lens of History," *New York Times*, October 11, 1995, B1. Also see "150 Years of Photojournalism," 62.

66. *Life*, December 1979, 185; Howe, *Shooting under Fire*, 28. See also Chong, *Girl in the Picture*; "Accidental Napalm," *New York Times*, 9 June 1972, 1A; Terence Wright, *The Photography Handbook* (London: Routledge, 1999), 78; Goldberg, *Power of Photography*, 241–245; Rubin and Newton, *Capture the Moment*, 80–81; Hal Buell, *Moments: The Pulitzer Prize Photographs, A Visual Chronicle of Our Time* (New York: Black Dog and Leventhal, 1999), 102; Lester, *Photojournalism*, 52; Sturken, *Tangled Memories*, 89–93; Hariman and Lucaites, *No Caption Needed*, 171–207; Horst Faas and Marianne Fulton, "The Bigger Picture," http://www.digitaljournalist.org/issue0008/ng2.htm. Observers

have remained divided over the image's impact on public sentiment. See, for instance, Perlmutter, *Photojournalism and Foreign Policy.*

67. John Corry, "Sorting Out Coverage of Hanoi's Celebration," *New York Times,* May 2, 1985, C26. See picture appended to "150 Years of Photojournalism," n.p., where it was the only one of the four Vietnam images to appear. Also see picture appended to "The 70s," *Newsweek,* January 3, 1994, 44–45; "100 Milestones of the Century," *Time,* April 13, 1998, 87; "Eyewitness: Pictures of a Century," 126–127; and Cynthia Dockrell, "Century's Photo Album," *Boston Globe,* November 3, 1999, E6.

68. Rev. Francis X. Meehan, "Youth Urged to Shun 'Unjust War,'" *Philadelphia Inquirer,* June 17, 1972, A14; picture appended to Peter Eng, "A Symbol of Vietnam War, A Young Woman Still Suffers," *Philadelphia Inquirer,* July 14, 1964, 1.

69. Picture appended to Eliane Sciolino, "A Painful Road from Vietnam to Forgiveness," *New York Times,* November 12, 1996, A1; Bill Miller, "A Vietnamese Victim Makes Call for Peace," *Washington Post,* November 12, 1996, B1; Harry F. Rosenthal, "A Wreath from a Famous War Victim," *Philadelphia Inquirer,* November 12, 1996, A7; "A Long Journey to Reconciliation," *People,* November 25, 1996, 29.

70. Picture appended to Peter Pae, "At Last, A Conflict Ends," *Washington Post,* February 20, 1997, 2; "Girl Who Learned to Live Without Hate," *Evening Standard,* June 6, 1997, 5; John Koch, "Icon of War, Pillar of Peace," *Boston Globe,* November 7, 1997, D1; "Milestones," *Time,* November 17, 1997, 17; Peter Pae and Maria Glod, "Vets Challenge Minister's Account of Napalm Attack," *Washington Post,* December 19, 1997, C5; Jonathan Yardley, "Review of *The Girl in the Picture,*" *Washington Post Book World,* August 6, 2000, 2; Nhat Minh, "Telling a Thousand Stories," *Sydney Morning Herald,* March 17, 2001, 11.

71. Peter Eng, "Napalm Student Now a Medical Student," *Los Angeles Times,* July 22, 1984, 17; Joseph Schuman, "Victim in Famed Vietnam Photo Gets U.N. Job," *Philadelphia Inquirer,* November 11, 1997, A21.

72. "Kim-Phuc," dir. Manus van de Kamp, 1985; "Kim's Story: the Road from Vietnam," dir. Shelley Saywell, also broadcast on A&E as "The Girl in the Photograph," 1997; picture appended to Patricia Strathern, "Tell—But Don't Show," *Time,* June 26, 2000, 25; picture appended to www.kimfoundation.com.

73. See http://digitaljournalist.org/issue0008/ng_intro.htm. In its review of the exhibit, the *London Observer* called the photograph "the most haunting image of the horror of war since Goya" (Deyan Sudjic, "Architecture: The Appliance of Science," *London Observer,* June 25, 2000, reviews sect., 9); "The Bigger Picture," *Guardian,* June 27, 2000, 4; Martha Brant, "Off Beat," *Newsweek,* October 13, 2003. When Ut took a 2007 photo of Paris Hilton 35 years to the day after he took the photo of Kim-Phuc, journalists made much of the coincidence: See Philip Kennicott, "Images: Poles and Decades Apart, Two Silent Screams Issue Discomfiting Reverberations," *Washington Post,* December 30, 2007, M01 and David Hinckley, "A Far Cry From Vietnam," *New York Daily News,* June 12, 2007, 49.

74. Peter Cheney, "Vietnam Photo Girl Kim Now 'Smiles All the Time," *Toronto Star,* February 6, 1997, A1; Goldberg, *Power of Photography,* 244; Peter Cheney, "Vietnamese Woman's Story Stirs Readers," *Toronto Star,* February 17, 1997, A2. The article concluded with an address for contributions. A second story followed the first and detailed the result

of Canadians "open[ing] their hearts and wallets to Phan Thi Kim-Phuc" (Andrea Hopkins, "New Life for Napalm Survivor," *Toronto Star,* March 21, 1997, 34).

75. John Koch, "Icon of War, Pillar of Peace," *Boston Globe,* November 7, 1997, D1. There were also those who argued the flip side of the image's porous and open nature. In 1986, retired General William Westmoreland refuted evidence that Kim-Phuc was burned by napalm. "He said an investigation determined that she had been burned in an accident involving a hibachi, an open grill," but the army found no records of such an investigation ("Viet War Photo Is Challenged," *Washington Post,* January 19, 1986).

76. Goldberg, *Power of Photography,* 243; Salgado and Mayes, *This Critical Mirror,* 25, where three editors in the book independently referenced the image as a key news photo.

77. For instance, in 1999 the photo was transformed into an art installation of pigment and melted wax (Deirdre Kelly, "Portrait of a Woman Reborn," *The Globe and Mail,* June 5, 1999, C12), where artist Tony Scherman was quoted as saying he had "done to the canvas what napalm did to her body." The song was sung by Yanah and released by Flying Snowman Records. Also see Hariman and Lucaites (*No Caption Needed*) for discussion of the photo's incorporation in popular culture.

78. Harry McPherson, in Oliver, *My Lai Massacre,* 27.

79. Hariman and Lucaites, *No Caption Needed,* 207.

80. Fred Turner, *Echoes of Combat: The Vietnam War in American Memory* (New York: Anchor Books, 1997).

81. Moeller, *Shooting War,* 403.

82. Caroline Brothers, *War and Photography: A Cultural History* (New York: Routledge, 1997), 203–4. Also see Perlmutter, *Photojournalism and Foreign Policy.*

83. Susan D. Moeller, *Compassion Fatigue* (London: Routledge, 1999), 42.

84. "Tsunami Fundraising Efforts May Adversely Affect Other Disasters," *Reuters Expert Poll: AlertNet,* January 24, 2005. http://about.reuters.com/pressoffice/pressreleases/index.asp?pressid=2406.

85. Chris Cramer and Greg Palkot, in Michele Greppi, "News Copes With Disaster," *Television Week,* January 10, 2005, 1; Joanne Ostrow, "Tsunami Tests TV Journalism," *Denver Post,* January 10, 2005, F-01. The delay in getting the network anchors to the region generated some discussion (i.e., Gail Shister, "TV's Big Guns Join Coverage of Disaster," *Philadelphia Inquirer,* January 4, 2005, D1).

86. Ted Koppel, *Nightline,* ABC News, January 11, 2005. Many theories were offered, such as the tsunami's timing at the front end of the 2005 budget cycle, the widespread scale of the disaster, and the exotic appeal of the region for Western tourists.

87. Tim Burt, "Media Accused of Too Much Coverage after Slow Beginning," *London Financial Times,* Asia Edition, January 8, 2005, 1–2; V.S. Sambandan, "Global Journalism About a Regional Catastrophe," *Nieman Reports,* spring 2005, 76 (who also noted that once the high-profile visitors left, so did the journalists, though "the devastation remains, and so do its victims," 77); Ruth Gidley, "Debate: Has Tsunami Carved a News Niche for Disasters?" AlertNet, March 11, 2005, http://www.alertnet.org/thefacts/reliefresources/111056581462.htm.

88. Steve Outing, "Taking Tsunami Coverage into Their Own Hands," poynteronline, January 6, 2005; Steve Outing, "Managing the Army of Temporary Journalists," *Nieman Reports,* spring 2005, 80. The BBC was far ahead of the U.S. news media, and it set up an

online web site for tsunami blogs already by the end of the first week, at Shefali Srinivas, "Online Citizen Journalists Respond to South Asian Disaster," *Online Journalism Review,* January 7, 2005. Also see "Online," www.stateofthemedia.org/2004/.

89. Jennifer Harper, "Vacation Videos Make Big News," *Washington Times,* 7 January 2005, A10.

90. "Media Outlets Scramble for Tsunami Footage," zap2it.com, December 29, 2004. Also see "Taking Tsunami Coverage Into Their Own Hands," poynteronline.

91. Chuck Lustig, in David Bauder, "TV News Avoids Graphic Tsunami Images," Associated Press, January 2, 2005. This, of course, depends on the event. Coverage of Hurricane Katrina produced images in the U.S. news media that were in many ways more graphic than those of the tsunami, though it can be argued that their graphicness resulted from psychic distancing from the disaster in New Orleans.

92. David Bauder, "Are Standards Different for Newspapers and Television in Tsunami Coverage?" *Associated Press,* January 3, 2005; In the United States, for instance, the Poynter Institute, Journalism.org, the website of Jim Romanesko, and numerous columnists in individual newspapers debated the issue (i.e., David McCumber, "The Reasoning Behind Our Use of Tsunami Victims' Photos," *Seattle Post-Intelligencer,* January 1, 2005; and Susan Llewelyn Leach, "How To Tell the Story of the Dead Without Offending the Living," *Christian Science Monitor,* January 19, 2005).

93. Tom Glover, in Edward Wasserman, "We Don't Own the News Anymore," *Miami Herald,* August 7, 2006.

94. Ostrow, "Tsunami Tests," F-01; Leach, "How to Tell," 11; Bauder, "Are Standards Different."

95. "Editors Face Tough Choices with Tsunami Victim Photos," *American Editor,* January–February 2005, 28. Corpses appeared on the front pages of the *New York Times* and the *Philadelphia Inquirer.* The *Inquirer's* picture was positioned directly under the main headline, and it portrayed three men, looking frontally into the camera, as they pulled a corpse from the water (M. Lakshman/AP photo appended to "Tsunami Kills 13,340 from Asia to Somalia," *Philadelphia Inquirer,* December 27, 2004, A1). The picture in the *New York Times* was positioned under a banner headline which stretched across nearly an entire page and a caption telling readers that the woman "sat yesterday with the dead, among them her own children" (Guaram Singh/AP photo, *New York Times,* December 28, 2004, A1). The *Times* editor who chose the picture later recounted that it elicited such an emotional reaction from her coeditors that she knew it was a dramatic photo and needed to be included.

96. Front-page photo appended to "60,000," *Seattle Post-Intelligencer,* December 29, 2004, 1. See, for instance, the front page pictures on December 27, 2004, of Malaysia's *New Straits Times,* Hong Kong's *South China Morning Post,* Malaysia's *The Sun,* and Malaysia's *Harian Metro.* The front page of India's *Indian Express* showed a person carrying a corpse but this was anomalous to other news media in areas directly hit by the tidal wave, which tended at first to display inanimate pictures of presumed death. David McCumber, "The Reasoning Behind Our Use of Tsunami Victims' Photos," *Seattle Post-Intelligencer,* January 1, 2005; "Magazine Issue Withdrawn After Complaints Over Tsunami Dead Picture," Danmarks Radio web site, Copenhagen, January 6, 2005; provided by BBC Monitoring Service, January 7, 2005; Ullamaija Kivikuru, "Tsunami Communication in Finland," *European Journal of Communication* 21(4), 2006.

97. Gurinder Osan/AP photo, "India," *Time,* January 10, 2005, 24–25; Arko Datta/Reuters photo, "After the Tsunami," *Newsweek,* January 10, 2005, cover; Gurinder Osan/AP photo, untitled image, *Newsweek,* January 10, 2005, 24–25; Arko Datta/Reuters photo, taken in Tamil Nadu, December 28, 2004; appended to *Time,* January 10, 2005, cover; Daniel Okrent, "The Public Editor: No Picture Tells the Truth, *New York Times* January 9, 2005, sec 4, 2. Prakash Singh/Agence France Presse photo, appended to "Massive Waves Leave 14,000 Dead," *San Jose Mercury News,* December 27, 2004, A1. It appeared cropped on the front page of the Dutch *Rotterdams Dagblad;* APME poll, in Kathleen Norton, "Disturbing Photos Tell the News," *Poughkeepsie Journal,* January 23, 2005, 9A; Okrent, "No Picture Tells," 2.

98. "News That Matters" (editorial), *Variety,* January 5, 2005, 32; Paul O'Grady, "A New Medium Comes of Age," *New Statesman,* January 10, 2005, 14; Tom Maurstad, "I Saw It on Tsunami TV," *Dallas Morning News,* January 16, 2005, 1G; "A New Medium Comes of Age," *New Statesman,* January 10, 2005, 14–15.

99. Outing, "Managing the Army," 80.

100. Ostrow, "Tsunami Tests," F-01; Jeremy Seabrook, "In Death, Imperialism Lives On," *Guardian,* December 31, 2004; See, for instance, Mike Whitney, "Iraq Vs Tsunami: The Duplicity of the Media," *Znet,* December 31, 2004.

101. Stacy Palmer, in Kathleen Megan, "Friends in Need: What Is It about the Tsunami Coverage that Has Made Americans So Generous?" *Hartford Courant,* January 20, 2005, D1.

102. Steven Winn, "Caught Up as Spectators to a Far Away Disaster," *San Francisco Chronicle,* January 4, 2005, E1.

103. See the December 27, 2004, front pages of India's *Hindustan Times,* Thailand's *The Nation,* Indonesia's *Jakarta Post,* Indonesia's *Kompas,* and Indonesia's *Koran Tempo.*

104. This account appeared widely: Gemunu Amarasinghe, "Witness Recounts Deadly Chaos Amidst Waves," *Miami Herald,* December 27, 2004, 1A; Gemunu Amarasinghe, "Photographer Witnesses Lives Swept Away by Sea," *Fresno Bee,* December 27, 2004, A1; Gemunu Amarasinghe, "Eyewitnesses Stunned By Swift Devastation," *San Jose Mercury News,* December 27, 2004, A1.

105. Picture appended to "Sea Surges from Massive Quake Kill Over 13,000 Across South Asia," *Washington Post,* December 27, 2004, A1 or "Quake, Waves Kill Thousands," *Chicago Tribune,* December 27, 2004, 1.

106. Mark Fitzgerald, "Canadian Media Hoaxed By 'Tsunami' Photo," *Editor and Publisher,* January 3, 2005; Samiran Chakrawertti, "After Deadly Tsunami, International Media Suffer Photo Hoax Wave," *The Times of India,* January 8, 2005. The picture appeared in the *Deseret Morning News,* the Canadian *Calgary Herald,* Sky News, Channel 9 of Australia and the New Zealand *Taranaki Daily News.*

107. Picture titled "Wiped Out," *Miami Herald,* December 27, 2004, 1A; picture appended to "Thousands Die as Quake-Spawned Waves Crash Onto Coastlines Across Southern Asia," *New York Times,* December 27, 2004, 1A; "Wiped Out," *Miami Herald,* December 27, 2004, 1A; "Waves of Devastation," *Cleveland Plain Dealer,* December 27, 2004, A1; and "Tidal Waves Kill 13,000," *Chicago Sun-Times,* December 27, 2004, 1. The picture also appeared on the front pages of India's *Hindustan Times,* India's *Indian Express,* Indonesia's *Koran Tempo,* and Malaysia's *New Straits Times.* Pictures appended to "Tsunami Sweeps Sumatra," *Jakarta Post,* December 27, 2004, 1.

108. Eranga Jayawardena/AP photo, appended to "Waves of Death," *Rocky Mountain News,* December 27, 2004, 1. The same picture also appeared on the front pages of the *Los Angeles Times, Newsday, San Francisco Chronicle, Denver Post, The Globe and Mail,* and *International Herald Tribune.* The *New York Times* showed it alongside two other images of physical devastation.

109. Untitled pictures, appended to cover story, *Newsweek,* January 10, 2005, 22–23, 26–27; Joanne Davis/AFP/Getty photo, appended to "Sea of Sorrow," *Time,* January 10, 2005, 22–23.

110. Steve Hartman, "Haunting Tsunami Images," *60 Minutes Wednesday,* CBS, January 5, 200; see, for example, picture appended to Julia Day, "How the Tsunami Hogged the Headlines," *MediaGuardian,* March 11, 2005; Peg Finucane, "We Behold Disaster at Our Own Remove," *Newsday,* 7 January 2005, A45.

111. Steve Hartman, "Haunting Tsunami Images," *60 Minutes Wednesday,* CBS, January 5, 2005; Winn, "Caught Up," E1; Ullamaija Kivikuru, "Tsunami Communication in Finland," *European Journal of Communication* 21(4), 2006, 512.

112. See picture appended to Andrew C. Revkin, "How Scientists and Victims Watched Helplessly," *New York Times,* December 31, 2004, A1.

113. http://video.google.com/videoplay?docid=-4276800493180740813& ei=ibFkS_usEKf6qgKf94nRCA&q=tsunami+video+%22wedding+photographer%22& hl=en&view=3#; see Beth Gardiner, "Video Shows Tsunami Roar Through Indonesia," Associated Press, January 10, 2005; newspapers in Brazil, Finland and Sweden—*Diario do comercio, A Gazeta,* and *Iltalehti*—were among those that published the same grainy image of possible death on their front pages on December 22, 2004.

114. Picture appended to *Newsweek,* January 10, 2005, 28; picture appended to *Time,* January 10, 2005, 5; Robert Sullivan, *2000–2009, The Decade That Changed the World* (New York, Life Books, 2009), n.p.

115. Picture appended to Revkin, "How Scientists," A1; "A Mother's Courage," *Sunday Herald Sun,* January 2, 2005, 74. The original image was taken on Rai Lay Beach, in Krabi, Thailand, on December 26, 2004. It appeared on the front page of the *New York Times* on December 31, 2004, and again on January 3, 2005, in an article about the family's survival (Alan Cowell, "From Image of Disaster to a Safe Homecoming," *New York Times,* January 3, 2005, A10). Also see Peter Zimonjik, "Found Alive and Well, The Family Pictured Fleeing the Tsunami," *Sunday Telegraph,* January 2, 2005, 3.

116. Antonia Zerbisias, "Will We Still Care When Media Leave?" *Toronto Star,* 6 January 2005, A21.

117. Ashok Malik, "Can CNN, BBC Get Away With This Corpse Show?" *The Indian Express,* December 30, 2004.

118. Nick Morrison, "When Every Picture Tells a Horror Story," *Northern Echo,* January 7, 2005; Kathleen Norton, "Readers Invited to Join Debate Over Tsunami Images," *Poughkeepsie Journal,* January 9, 2005, 9A; Ian Mayes, "The Readers' Editor on *Guardian* Coverage of the Tsunami Disaster," *Guardian,* January 8, 2005, 24; Michael Williams, "Readers' Editor: Painful Imagery of Disaster," *Independent,* January 16, 2005, 27; Eugene Kane, "Images, Though Horrific, Help Us Grasp Tsunami Tragedy," *Milwaukee Journal Sentinel,* 2 January 2005, 3; Leach, "How to Tell," 11.

119. Charlie Rose, "One Year Anniversary Show—Charlie Rose," December 2005 in Susan Moeller, "'Regarding the Pain of Others': Media, Bias and the Coverage of

International Disasters," *Journal of International Affairs,* spring/summer 2006, 182; Orla Quinlan, in Julia Day, "How the Tsunami Hogged the Headlines," *Guardian,* March 11, 2005; Eugene Kane, January 3, 2005, 11.29 am, poynteronline, http://www.poynter.org/column.asp?id=45&aid=76346&; Michael Stone, "How Not to Respond to a Disaster," *New Statesman,* January 9, 2006, 14. Zerbisias, "Will We Still," A21. In fact, it was not the more gruesome photos that necessarily pushed public response. As the first images gave way to recovery efforts, the structural issues at heart forced the public to take heed. As the *Ottowa Citizen* remarked, "Judging by public reaction, some of the most disturbing images to come out of the Indian Ocean tsunami disaster contained no corpses. They were photographs of tourists sunning themselves while Thais labored in the background, clearing the debris that had been their homes. Some newspaper readers were disgusted by what they saw as gross selfishness. Others felt the photos a perfect depiction of the West's relationship with the developing world. A few suggested that because tourism is vital to the economies of the devastated countries, the pale man holding a beer, his stomach hanging over a Speedo, was doing exactly what he should to help. Whatever the reaction, the comments rested on the same assumption: that the pictures were a fair and complete representation of the facts" (Dan Gardner, "Pictures That Speak Louder than Words," *Ottowa Citizen,* 22 January 2005, B4).

120. Sue Dwyer, in Mark Bixler, "World's 'Silent Tsunamis' Take Quiet, Deadly Toll," *Atlanta Journal-Constitution,* February 9, 2005, 1F.

121. See, for instance, "Pictures of the Missing," *New York Times Upfront,* January 24, 2005, 1c; Sutin Wannabovorn, "Grainy Picture Sparks Couple's Hope of Finding Missing Daughter," Associated Press, December 9, 2005.

122. Tim Reid, "Holiday Couple Left Record of Their Last Moments as Waves Engulfed the Beach," *The London Times,* February 25, 2005, 41.

123. This stance is common to horror films, where the audience sees the killer but the victim does not. Thanks to Larry Gross for making this parallel.

124. Christian Pilet, "The Couple on the Beach," *Guideposts,* January 2007 61(11), n.p.; Reid, "Holiday Couple," 41; Ted Chernecki, "Images Discovered of Canadian Couple's Last Moments Before Tsunami Hit," *CBS Morning News,* February 25, 2005; Lyod Robertson, "More Images From December's Tsunami," *CTV News,* February 23, 2005; Matthias Karen, "Swedes Are Coming to Grips with Tsunami," *St Louis Post-Dispatch,* June 26, 2005, A14; Wannabovorn, "Grainy Picture."

125. Zerbisias, "Will We Still," A21; Leslie Bennetts, "Petra's Story," *Vanity Fair,* May 2005, 216–17, 220–221, 263; Michael Williams, "Readers' Editor: Painful Imagery of Disaster," *Independent,* January 16, 2005, 27; "Model Recounts Horrifying Experience Being Swept Up in the Waves," *ABC Primetime Live,* March 8, 2005; "Attenborough Mourns Tsunami Dead," BBC News, March 7, 2005; "Names and Faces: The Tsunami's Celebrity Victims," *Washington Post,* December 29, 2004, C-03.

126. Seabrook, "In Death." Who received names and who did not extended across the tsunami coverage. For instance, one caption in the *Cincinnati Post* read as follows: "An Indian woman bursts into tears as others stand in line to collect relief items from a van in Cuddalore, India. Photo by J. T. and Caroline Malatesta via Birmingham News. Caroline and J.T. Malatesta of Mountain Brook, Alabama survived the killer Asian tsunami while on

vacation in Thailand," picture titled "Tsunami's Aftermath," *Cincinnati Post,* December 31, 2004, A14. Practices like this had the effect of positioning the local residents as supporting players to the story of Western tourists.

127. Chuck Lustig, in David Carr, "With Thousands of Images from the Region, Broadcasters Struggle to Make Sense of a Disaster," *New York Times,* December 28, 2004, A12.

128. Dan Harris, "A Second Look," *ABC World News Tonight,* December 24, 2005; "A Wave of Images From Tsunami-Hit Areas," *Hindu,* May 27, 2005; "Pictures That," *Canberra Times,* June 19, 2005; " 'Ocean of Tears' Worth a Thousand Words," *Jakarta Post,* April 10, 2005; "Indian Photographer Wins World Press Photo Award for Tsunami Image," *Agence France Presse,* February 11, 2005; "AP Tsunami Coverage Wins Awards from APME," Associated Press, July 28, 2005; Andrew Meares, in "Images They'll Never Forget," *Canberra Times,* June 19, 2005; "Horrors on VCD," *Hindu,* January 25, 2005; "Thailand's Tsunami-Hit Phuket Island Offers Gory Souvenirs," *Asia News,* January 18, 2005.

129. "News That Matters" (Editorial), *Variety,* January 5, 2005, 32; Chris Bury, *Nightline,* ABC News, January 11, 2005; Gidley, "Debate"; Donald Winslow, "An Unforgettable Story" (Editor's Notebook), *News Photographer,* February 2005, 10.

130. Zerbisias, "Will We Still," A21; John B. Zibluck, "The Dead Are the Context, the Living are the Story," *News Photographer,* February 2005, 15.

131. Tom Plate, "From Oceanic Tsunami to Geopolitical Teutonic Shift," *AsiaMedia,* December 30, 2004; Jennifer Harper, "Vacation Videos Make Big News," *Washington Times,* January 7, 2005, A10; See, for instance, Ullamaija Kivikuru, "Tsunami Communication in Finland," *European Journal of Communication* 21(4), 2006, 499–520; Gideon Levy, in Zerbisias, "Will We Still," A21

132. Zibluck, "Dead Are the Context," 14.

Chapter 7

1. Lance Bennett, Regina G. Lawrence, and Steven Livingston, *When the Press Fails: Political Power and the News Media from Iraq to Katrina* (Chicago: University of Chicago Press, 2007), 28.

2. Sanford J. Unger, in Stephen Hess and Marvin L. Kalb, *The Media and the War on Terrorism* (Cambridge, MA: Brookings Institution Press, 2003), 99; Howard Kurtz, "CNN Chief Orders "Balance" in War News," *Washington Post,* October 31, 2001: C1; Marvin Kalb, "Dissent: Public Opinion, Media Reaction," *Nieman Reports* 57(4), wir ter 2003, 72; Michael Getler, in Hess and Kalb, *Media and the War,* 99.

3. Antonia Zerbisias, "The High-Tech Delivery of Depraved Horror," *Toronto Star,* May 13, 2004, A23.

4. Jeremy Seabrook, "Peep Empathy from Rubble," *Statesman* (India), November 4, 2001. The photo, called the single most recognized image in the magazine's 114-year history, would also be featured on a repeat cover (Michael Kilian, "Haunting Afghan Face Gets a Name," *Chicago Tribune,* March 14, 2002, D10).

5. For more on this, see my "Death in Wartime: Photographs and the 'Other War' in Afghanistan," *Harvard International Journal of Press/Politics,* 10 (3) 2005: 1–30.

6. Anthony Spaeth, "Kabul's New Islamic Rule Young and Fundamentalist," *Time,* October 7, 1996, 48. Also see photo by Alan Chin/NYT, John F. Burns, "Afghan Professionals Fleeing Rule by Clerics," *New York Times,* October 7, 1996. For a thorough discussion, see Roy Gutman, *How We Missed the Story* (Washington, DC: USIP Press, 2008).

7. See, for instance, David Rohde, "Foreigners Who Fought for Taliban Shot in Head," *New York Times,* November 19, 2001, B1; or Carlotta Gal, "Fortress Awash with Bodies of Taliban," *Chicago Tribune,* November 29, 2001, 10. Some pictures of dead individuals did appear, usually Taliban supporters and soldiers. For example, see Tyler Hicks/Getty Images photo appended to David Rohde, "The Volunteers," *New York Times,* November 18, 2001, B1; or Carolyn Cole photo appended to Paul Watson, "A Roadside Graveyard for Taliban Stragglers," *Los Angeles Times,* November 27, 2001, A10. Also see images in online archives (i.e., AP Photo/Darko Bandic, Mazar-E-Sharif, November 27, 2001, #XDRB110, #XDRB114, #XDRB116 and AP Photo/Dusan Vranic, Kunduz, November 26, 2001, #DV103). Photos by Luc Delahaye/Magnum appended to "Fall of the Taliban," *Newsweek,* November 26, 2001, 21–29.

8. First reports appeared from November 17 onward. See, for instance, "A Nation Challenged: The Battle," *New York Times,* November 17, 2001, 1.

9. Peter Rosenthal, in Richard Gwyn and Linda Diebel, "Rage Grows Over War Atrocities," *Toronto Star,* November 28, 2001, A1.

10. Matt Rosenthal, "Just Massacres?" *The Progressive,* December 3, 2001; Dalton Camp, "We Are Silent as Barbarians Are at Gates," *Toronto Star,* November 18, 2001, A13; Ian Cobain, "America Will Take No Prisoners," *London Times,* November 20, 2001, A1.

11. AP/Dusan Vranic photo appended to Drew Brown and Sudarsan Raghavan, "In Kunduz, Residents Cheer Alliance Arrival," *Philadelphia Inquirer,* November 27, 2001, A11; Lois Ramondo/Washington Post photo appended to Sharon LaFraniere, "Revenge Shapes Struggle for Taliban Holdout," *Washington Post,* November 18, 2001, A1; Agence France-Presse photo appended to Maura Reynolds, "Response to Terror, Taliban Under Siege," *Los Angeles Times,* November 27, 2001, A10; and to Bryan Bender, "Land Force Faces a Two-Front Fight with Bin Laden," *Boston Globe,* November 27, 2001, A1.

12. Caption to AP/Dusan Vranic, Kunduz, November 26, 2001 (#APA5620925). The photo appeared in the *Philadelphia Inquirer,* November 27, 2001, A11, and in the *Chicago Tribune,* November 27, 2001, 8; Captions appended to a Lois Raimondo photo for the *Washington Post,* November 18, 2001, A1, and an Agence France-Presse photo that appeared in the *Los Angeles Times,* November 27, 2001, A10 and the *Boston Globe,* November 27, 2001, A1.

13. Tyler Hicks/Getty images appended to David Rohde, "Executions and Looting as Alliance Nears Kabul," *New York Times,* November 13, 2001, B1, B3; Eric Stover, "Reader's Letter," *New York Times,* November 15, 2001, A30.

14. Nancy Gibbs, "Blood and Joy," *Time,* November 26, 2001, 30.

15. "Liberation and Revenge" (Editorial), *Chicago Tribune,* November 14, 2001, 22. The editorial asked the obvious question: "Have we supported a band of liberators or a band of thugs?" Or, as a columnist for the paper commented the next day, "The people on our side in Afghanistan are not necessarily folks you'd want baby-sitting your kids" (Steve Chapman, "In Need of the Northern Alliance," *Chicago Tribune,* November 15, 2001, 31); Jonathan Brown, "Reader's Letter," *Time,* December 17, 2001, 8; Misook Kim, "Reader's Letter," *Time,* December 17, 2001, 8.

16. Dan Milmo, "Morgan Lambasts Sun's Pro-War Editorial," *Guardian,* November 14, 2001; Tyler Hicks photos appended to "Our 'Friends' Take Over...," *Daily Mirror,* November 14, 2001, cover, and *Daily Mail,* November 14, 2001, 1 and 3; Gary Jones and Graham Brough, "Battered, Stripped, Mutilated, and Then Riddled with Bullets...A Revenge on the Taliban at its Most Merciless," *Daily Mirror,* November 14, 2001, 5; Piers Morgan, in Milmo, "Morgan Lambasts"; "2001: The Year in Unforgettable Images," *Daily Mirror,* December 29, 2001, 14.

17. Tyler Hicks photo appended to "No Mercy," *Daily Mail,* November 14, 2001, cover; Ross Benson and Matthew Hickley, "Have Taliban's Terrors Been Replaced by Callous Killers of the Alliance?" *Daily Mail,* November 14, 2001, 2; Gary Jones, "War on Terror: The Executioners," *Daily Mirror,* November 14, 2001, 1, and Gary Jones and Graham Brough, "Battered, Stripped, Mutilated," 5.

18. Carl Morrisroe and Margaret White, Reader's Letters, *Daily Mirror,* November 15, 2001; Madeleine Bunting, "Reader's Letter," *Guardian,* December 17, 2001; Simon Neufeld, "Reader's Letter," *Toronto Star,* November 17, 2001, K7.

19. See, for instance, Celeste Bohlen, "Food for Refugees, Raids on Caves and the Fate of Taliban Prisoner," *New York Times,* December 11, 2001, B1; Babak Dehghanpisheh, John Barry, and Roy Gutman, "The Death Convoy of Afghanistan," *Newsweek,* August 26, 2002; "As Possible Afghan War-Crimes Evidence Removed, U.S. Silent," *McClatchy Newspapers,* December 11, 2008; James Risen, "U.S. Inaction Seen After Taliban POWs Died," *New York Times,* July 10, 2009; "ICC Prosecutor Eyes Possible Afghanistan War Crimes, Reuters, September 9, 2009. Also see James Risen, *State of War* (New York: Free Press, 2006). The 2002 documentary film *Afghan Massacre: The Convoy of Death* (earlier called *Massacre in Mazar*), dir. Jamie Doran, was the first attempt to visually address the development. Though shown widely across Europe that year, it was only screened in the United States in May 2003 by *Democracy Now* http://i4.democracynow.org/2003/5/23/afghan_massacre_the_convoy_of_death. See, for instance, www.alkhilafah.info; www.downwithtyrannyblogspot.com; www.freemasonrywatch.org/executions.html; "Westport to Afghanistan and Iraq," westportnow.com, November 28, 2004 at http://www.westportnow.com/index.php?/v2/comments/7296/.

20. See, for instance, Erick Eckholm and Felicity Barringer, "American Reporter Held Captive in Pakistan, a Message Says," *New York Times,* January 28, 2002, A6; Molly Moore and Kamben Khan, "Pakistan Group Says It Has US Journalist," *Washington Post,* January 28, 2004, A16; Bob Drogin, "US Reporter Is Seized in Pakistan," *Los Angeles Times,* January 28, 2002, A1.

21. Unmesh Kher, "The Odd Ordeal of Daniel Pearl," *Time,* February 11, 2002, 34.

22. Andrew Duffy, "Kidnappers' Deadline Expires for U.S. Reporter," *Ottowa Citizen,* February 1, 2002, A11.

23. Pictures appended to Eckholm and Barringer, "American Reporter," A6; Moore and Khan, "Pakistan Group Says." A16; Drogin, "US Reporter," A1; "Group Claims to Hold US Reporter," *Philadelphia Inquirer,* January 28, 2002, A2; Farrah Stockman, "Sheikh Sought in Missing Reporter Case," *Boston Globe,* January 29, 2002, A9; Kher, "The Odd Ordeal," 34; "Kidnapped: The Ordeal of Daniel Pearl," *Newsweek,* February 11, 2002, cover.

24. Picture appended to Felicity Barringer with Erick Eckholm, "New Message Threatens Execution of US Reporter and Others Who Stay in Pakistan," *New York Times,*

January 31, 2002, A14; Molly Moore and Kamben Khan, "'We Will Give You One More Day,'" *Washington Post,* February 1, 2002, A14; Molly Moore and Kamben Khan, "Kidnapped US Reporter Is Threatened With Death," *Washington Post,* January 31, 2002, A22; Bob Drogin, "Threat on Reporter's Life," *Chicago Tribune,* January 31, 2002, A8; Susan Milligan and Mark Jurkowitz, "Death Threat Issued for US Reporter Held Captive," *Boston Globe,* January 31, 2002, A1.

25. Pictures appended to Molly Moore and Kamben Khan, "Pakistanis Search Cemeteries for Missing Reporter," *Washington Post,* February 2, 2002, A16; Dave Goldiner, "Grim Search as Email Says Reporter's Dead," *New York Daily News,* February 2, 2002, 3; Jack Kelley, "Fate of Kidnapped U.S. Reporter Remains a Mystery," *USA Today,* February 4, 2002, 4A; Martin Kasindorf, "Respect Has Long Followed Pearl," *USA Today,* February 5, 2002, 3A; Evan Thomas, "A Reporter Under the Gun," *Newsweek,* February 11, 2002, 18; "Countdown to Tragedy: Key Dates in the Abduction and Apparent Murder of *Wall Street Journal* Reporter Daniel Pearl," *New York Daily News,* February 22, 2002, 2.

26. Felicity Barringer, "Networks Erroneously Report US Reporter's Death," *New York Times,* February 4, 2002, 11.

27. Pictures appended to Colin Nickerson, and Anthony Shadid, "Fighting Terror, Journalist Slain," *Boston Globe,* February 22, 2002, A1; Timothy J. Burger and Corky Siemaszko, "Kidnappers Cut Pearl's Throat; Videotape Shows Newsman's Brutal Slaying," *New York Daily News,* February 22, 2003, 3; Richard Pyle, "Videotape Shows Kidnappers Killing U.S. Reporter in Pakistan, *National Post,* February 22, 2002, A1.

28. Jim Murphy in David Bauder, "Pearl Family Denounces Broadcast," cbsnews.com, May 15, 2002; Dan Rather, "Terror, Lies, and Videotape," *CBS Evening News,* May 15, 2002; video titled "The Slaughter of the Spy-Journalist, the Jew Daniel Pearl," in "The First Victim," *London Times,* May 12, 2004, 12.

29. Nancy Gibbs, "Death in the Shadow," *Time,* March 4, 2002, 28; "White House: CBS Erred Showing Pearl Video," cnn.com, May 16. 2002; Bauder, "Pearl Family"; "Freedom to Choose," *Boston Phoenix,* June 7–13, 2002, 6.

30. Jeff Jacoby, "Pearl Video Brings the Horror Home," *Boston Globe,* June 13, 2002, A19; "Freedom to Choose," *Boston Phoenix,* June 7–13, 2002, 6; "Video of Reporter's Slaying Posted on Web," *Ottowa Citizen,* June 30, 2002, A11.

31. "Freedom to Choose," *Boston Phoenix,* June 7–13, 2003, 6. The newspaper's editor compared the photo with that of a dead soldier being dragged through Mogadishu, a dying baby being carried out of the Federal Building in Oklahoma City, and pictures of Nazi concentration camps. Those opposing its display said it was not newsworthy because the fact of Pearl's death had been known for months.

32. Declan McCullagh, "FBI Seeks Pearl Video Ban on Net," wired.com, May 23, 2002; "Declan McCullagh, "Besieged ISP Restores Pearl Vod," wired.com, May 28, 2002; Dan Kennedy, "Witness to An Execution," *Boston Phoenix,* June 14–20, 2002, 20.

33. Peter Johnson, "Pearl Murder Photos: To What End?," *USA Today,* June 6, 2002, 50; Mark Jurkowitz, "When Horror Makes News," *Boston Globe,* June 7, 2002, B1; Felicity Barringer, "Traces of Terror," *New York Times,* June 7, 2004, 24; Felicity Barringer, "Paper Publishes Photo of Head of Reporter Who Was Killed," *New York Times,* June 7, 2002, A24; Bruce Shapiro, "Yes, I Have Looked at It," Dart Center for Journalism and Trauma, posted July 16, 2003; Ken Beaumont, "Reader's Letter," *Boston Phoenix,* June 14–21, 2002, 4; Tunku Varadarajan, "Revulsion at the Boston Phoenix," wallstreetjournal.com,

posted June 11, 2002; Bob Steele, "Pearl Photo: Too Harmful," poynteronline, posted June 7, 2002.

34. Response to Steele, "Pearl Photo," Fran Hutchinson, "Need to See?" posted June 8, 2002, 2.47 am; "Letters," *Boston Phoenix,* June 14–20, 2002, 4–6 (The letters were equally divided between those who supported and opposed the video's display); Barringer, "Paper Publishes," A24; Responses to Steele, "Pearl Photo," Larry, "Tough Call," posted June 7, 2002, 10.47 am; David Poland, "Who Do We Serve," posted June 7, 2002, 9.25 am; Thomas Davis, "Pearl Photos," posted June 6, 2002, 5.12 pm. Of 12 posters, nine favored the poster's display. Some journalists also supported the video's availability: "This is no time to be covering our eyes," wrote Jeff Jacoby ("Pearl Video Brings," A19); Dan Kennedy, "Witnesses to an Execution," *Boston Phoenix,* June 14–20, 2002, 20.

35. Barringer, "Paper Publishes," A24; also Kevin Canfield and Tara Weiss, "Boston Paper Creates Controversy with Video," *Hartford Courant,* June 5, 2002; "Face to Face With Terror," on "The Connection," WBUR-Boston Radio, www.theconnection.org/shows/2002/0620020607_6_main.asp; Jacoby, "Pearl Video," A19; "The Daniel Pearl Video," usatoday.com, June 20, 2003.

36. "A Year after Daniel Pearl's Abduction, Questions Remain," *Holland Sentinel,* January 23, 2003, A1; "Under the Gun," *World Press Review* (online), 49 (5), May 2002; Jacoby, "Pearl Video," A19.

37. "The Ever Growing Catalogue of Killings," *Australian,* May 3, 2005.

38. "First Victim," 12; Julie Rawe, "The Sad Tale of Nick Berg," *Time,* May 24, 2004,

39. An opinion poll conducted by Gallup Polls on May 9, 2004, showed that a majority felt that the war was not worth fighting. See "The Final, Cruel Cut," *Middle East Economic Digest,* May 14, 2004.

40. Quoted in Jacques Steinberg, "Kidnapping, Beheading, and Defining What's News," *New York Times,* August 1, 2004, 1.

41. "Abu Musab al-Zarkawi Shown Slaughtering an American" appeared on a website operated by Muntada–Ansar on May 11, 2004. The video was discussed by all of the broadcast news organizations, including Melissa Block and Michele Norris, "Beheading of an American in a Video Posted on an Islamic Web Site," National Public Radio, May 11, 2004; Execution Hostage Decapitated in Iraq," ABC News, May 11, 2004.

42. Jonathan Hayes, "Second Opinion," *New York Magazine,* May 24, 2004; Dick Meyer, "Benumbed by Beheadings?" www.cbsnews.com, September 24, 2004.

43. Meyer, "Benumbed."

44. Jennifer Harper, "American's Beheading Old News for Media Elite," *Washington Times,* May 14, 2004, A14.

45. http://www.annoy.com/sectionless/doc.html?DocumentID=100614.

46. "Behead Video a US Hit," *Geelong Advertiser,* May 21, 2004; Lynne Smith, "Web Amplifies Message of Primitive Executions," *Los Angeles Times,* June 30, 2004; "School Suspends Teachers for Video," *Washington Times,* May 21, 2004; "More Teachers in Trouble for Showing Berg Images to Students," *Dallas Morning News,* May 22, 2004.

47. Quoted in Lynne Smith, "Web Amplifies Message of Primitive Executions," *Los Angeles Times,* June 30, 2004; Susan Moeller, *Packaging Terrorism* (Malden, MA: Wiley Blackwell, 2009), 159.

48. Peter Johnson, "A Death Caught on Tape: Should It Run or Not?" www.usatoday.com, May 11, 2004.

49. Stacy Lee, www.onlinejournalism.com, posted October 20, 2004; Peter Johnson, "A Death Caught on Tape: Should It Run or Not?" www.usatoday.com, May 11, 2004.

50. Picture appended to "This is the Enemy: Vile Image Shows Why We Should Fight," *Dallas Morning News,* May 13, 2004, 22A; Rod Dreher, on instapundit.com, May 24, 2004, http://pajamasmedia.com/instapundit/; Rod Dreher, "DMN Publishes Berg Picture," in "The Corner," *National Review Online* www.nationalreview.com/thecorner/04_05_09_corner-archive.asp.

51. Quoted in Johnson, "A Death Caught"; picture appended to Robert Moran, "Tape Shows West Chester Man Beheaded by Captors in Iraq," *Philadelphia Inquirer,* May 12, 2004, A1; Sandy Bauers, "Victim Called Bright, Caring, Inventive," *Miami Herald,* May 12, 2004, 2A; "Savages: Qaeda Beheads Hostage on TV," *New York Post,* May 12, 2004, 1; "American Civilian Beheaded on Video," *St. Petersburg Times,* May 12, 2004, 1A; "U.S. Civilian Beheaded in Iraq," *Seattle Times,* May 12, 2004, A1; "Degrees of Depravity," *San Francisco Chronicle,* May 12, 2004, B8.

52. John Gibson, "American Beheaded on Camera By Iraqi Militants, Fox News, May 11, 2004; "Reader's Letters" from Joseph J. Barbano, *Washington Post,* May 13, 2004, A28; Harold J. Gross, *Dallas Morning News,* May 13, 2004, 22A; Bob McElree, *Dallas Morning News,* May 13, 2004, 22A, and Robert S. Buick, *Gold Coast Bulletin,* May 14, 2004; Suzanne Fields, "An Echo from an Earlier War," *Washington Times,* May 17, 2004, A19.

53. See, for instance, Jeff Gammage, "Berg Faults 'Cycle of Violence,'" *Philadelphia Inquirer,* June 9, 2006; Tim Graham and others, in Jennifer Harper, "American's Beheading Old News for Media Elite," *Washington Times,* May 14, 2004, A14; quoted in Janet Street-Porter, "Do We Really Need to See All This Horror?" *Independent,* May 13, 2004, 33.

54. Jay Rosen, "News Judgment Old and News Judgment New: American Nicholas Berg Beheaded, Now What?" *BlogCritics.org,* May 17, 2004, www.blogcritics.org/culture/article/news-judgment; Andrew Sullivan, May 14, 2004; Evan Coyne Maloney, in Rosen, "News Judgment."

55. Zev Chafets, "The Berg Dilemma," *New York Daily News,* May 17, 2004.

56. "The "Alleged Beheading" of Nicholas Berg," *The Weekly Standard,* June 21, 2004; Anthony Gregory, "The Unanswered Questions of Nick Berg's Murder," http://www.antiwar.com/orig/gregory.php?articleid=2582 ; "Nick Berg Beheading Video is A Fake," http://www.topplerummy.org/berg/; "15 Anomalies Surrounding Death of Nick Berg," http://www.rense.com/general52/anom.htm; Aabrina Tavernise, "Iraqi Leader Orders Temporary Closing of Al Jazeera's Bureau in Baghdad," *New York Times,* August 8, 2004, 14.

57. Quoted in Susan Moeller, *Packaging Terrorism* (Malden, MA: Wiley-Blackwell, 2009), 160; Harper, "American's Beheading," A14; Meyer, "Benumbed"; Louis Meixler, "Militants Worldwide Copy Iraq Beheadings," AP Dispatch, November 5, 2004; Sinan Salaheddin, "Iraq Beheadings: Medium Becomes Message," AP dispatch, September 23, 2004; "Beheading Videos 'Kept at Homes of 21/7 Bomb Plotter,'" *London Times,* February 13, 2007, 2.

58. Deborah Fallows and Lee Rainie, "The Internet as a Unique News Source," *Pew Internet and American Life Project,* cited in "Waving the Bloody Jpeg," *Atlantic Monthly,* October 2004.

59. See, for instance, Henry Jenkins, *Convergence Culture* (New York: New York University Press, 2006), 13–18; Lucas Hilderbrand, "YouTube: Where Cultural Memory and Copyright Converge," *Film Quarterly,* Dall, 2007, 48–57.

60. Don Gonyea, "Support for War Dives as Bush Seeks New Iraq Plan," NPR, December 12, 2006. See Joel Roberts, "Poll: Iraq Going Badly and Getting Worse," December 11, 2006, www.cbsnews.com/stories/2006/12/11/opinion/polls/main2247797.shtml; "Poll: Pessimism About Iraq War Growing," CNN, March 16, 2006, .www.cnn.com/2006/POLITICS/03/16/Iraq.poll/; Scott Keeter, "Trends in Public Opinion About the War in Iraq, 2003–2007, March 15, 2007, Pew Research Center, www.pewresearch.org/pubs/431/trends-in-public-opinion-about-the-war-in-iraq-2003–2007.

61. For more on this, see my "Journalists as Interpretive Communities, Revisited," in Stuart Allan (ed.), *The Routledge Companion to News and Journalism Studies* (London: Routledge, 2009).

62. Paul J. Gough, "TV Plans Tasteful Coverage of Saddam Execution," Reuters, December 19, 2006; Al Thompkins, "Saddam Hussein Death: Resources for Journalists," poynteronline, December 29, 2006, and Pat Walters, "Weekend Update: Coverage of the Execution and Its Aftermath, poynteronline, December 29, 2006; Kenny Irby, "Displaying Death With Dignity," poynteronline, December 31, 2006; Kenny Irby, "Weekend Update: Coverage of the Execution and Its Aftermath," poynteronline, December 29, 2006. Anderson Cooper, in Walters, "Weekend Update." Gough, "TV Plans"; Kelly McBride, "Weekend Update: Coverage of the Execution and Its Aftermath," poynteronline, December 29, 2006. Journalists were advised to "share the historic background of this predicament and situation, offering cultural and political justification for the hanging."

63. Though there was evidence that public trust in the Internet had declined since 2001, particularly concerning nonnews web sites, for instance, online searching nonetheless prevailed, with 33% of Internet users visiting sites like YouTube. Moreover, online searching tended to increase around unfolding news events. See, for instance, "Online Public Attitudes—2006 Annual Report," *Project for Excellence in Journalism,* www.journalism.org/node/1328; "Online Content, A Day in the Life—Annual Report 2006," Project for Excellence in Journalism, www.journalism.org/node/1242; Lee Rainie, "Online Video Audience Surges," Pew Research Center, January 9, 2008, http://pewresearch.org/pubs/682/online-video-audience-surges. Thanks to Michael Delli-Carpini for help in locating these data. Also see http://www.talkleft.com/story/2006/12/29/17463/653; http://blogcritics.org/politics/article/countdown-to-the-execution-of-saddam/.

64. Quoted in Alexandra Zavis, "The Conflict in Iraq," *Los Angeles Times,* January 1, 2007, A1; "Video Shows Taunts at Execution," BBC News, December 31, 2006.

65. Susan Moeller, "Death's Strange Spell," *Los Angeles Times,* January 3, 2007, A15.

66. "He Couldn't Die Fast Enough for Cable News," *Philadelphia Inquirer,* December 31, 2006, A11. One reporter noted that "Mr. King looked a little let down when he had to sign off before the execution, promising viewers, 'It is really imminent now'" (Alessandra Stanley, "An Overnight Death Watch, and Then Images of the Hangman's Noose," *New York Times,* December 31, 2006, 14); Jennifer Sizemore, "Editor's Note on Saddam Images," http://www.msnbc.msn.com/id/16401180; David Bauder, "TV: Few Tough Decisions on Saddam Pictures," Associated Press, December 31, 2006.

67. "Readers Letters," *New York Times,* January 1, 2007, 18.

68. See, for instance, "Readers Letters," 18. It is telling that beyond the U.S. news media, responses were similarly polarized. Those viewing the event from the Arab world noted a resurgence of admiration and awe. As his Shiite executioners tormented and abused him, Hussein's death turned the spectacle on its head, with Egyptian president

Hosni Mubarak noting that the hanging "turned him into a martyr." Quoted in Olivia Ward, "Saddam's Hanging Deepens Divide," *Toronto Star*, January 6, 2007, A4; Keith Gardner, response to Kevin Bakhurst, "The Editors: Saddam's Execution," BBC News, December 30, 2006, http://www.bbc.co.uk/blogs/theeditors/2006/12/saddams_execution.html. "We didn't see the execution. That is the whole point—we don't even know if he is dead," he wrote (Nahlah Ayed, "Saddam Video: A Spotlight on Iraq's Problems," www.cbc.ca/news/reportsfromabroad/middleeast/2007/01/saddam_video_a_spotlight January 2, 2007); Jim Letourneau, response to Tony Burman, "The Power of Cell Phones, After Saddam," posted January 11, 2005, http://www.cbc.ca/news/about/burman/letters/2007/01/the_power_of_ce.html.

69. Tim Rutten, "Regarding Media," *Los Angeles Times*, January 6, 2007, E1; Phillip Kennicott, "For Saddam's Page in History, A Final Link on YouTube," *Washington Post*, December 31, 2006, D1; Tony Burman, "The Power of Cell Phones, After Saddam," http://www.cbc.ca/news/about/burman/letters/2007/01/the_power_of_ce.html; January 9, 2007.

70. Dan Glaister, "Saddam Execution: Images," *The Guardian*, January 1, 2007, 3; Ali M, response to Bakhurst, http://www.bbc.co.uk/blogs/theeditors/2006/12/saddams_execution.html. In a similar vein, in July 2008, the Israeli activist group B'tselem started a "shoot back" program where it gave Palestinian children video recorders to document abuses by Israeli soldiers.

71. Dan Glaister, "Saddam Execution: Images," *The Guardian*, January 1, 2007, 3.

72. Among the newspapers featuring the about-to-die image without a corresponding image of Hussein dead on its front page were the *Washington Post*, the *Chicago Tribune*, the *Philadelphia Inquirer*, the *Los Angeles Times*, *Newsday*, the *Boston Globe*, the *Atlanta Journal-Constitution*, the *Dallas Morning News*, the *Charlotte Observer*, the *Hartford Courant*, the *San Jose Mercury News*, the *Pittsburgh Post-Gazette*, the *Sacramento Bee*, and the *Detroit Free Press*, all on December 31, 2006. The picture was posted at the top of the websites of the *New York Times*, *Los Angeles Times* and *Washington Post* (see "Newspapers, Online Editors, TV Show Images of Saddam Hanging," editorandpublisher.com, December 30, 2006). It illustrated the cover story of *Newsweek* (see image appended to Christopher Dickey, "Death of a Tyrant," *Newsweek*, January 8, 2007, 19).

73. Pictures appended to "Noose Still and Taut," *Denver Post*, December 31, 2006, 1, and Larry Kaplow, "Execution Brings Little Solace," *Birmingham News*, December 31, 2006, 1A; caption title to a three-image sequence appended to Marc Santora, "As Attacks Go On, Iraqis Are Riveted by Hussein Video," *New York Times*, December 31, 2006, 1. But the *New York Times* was one of the few U.S. newspapers to show a front page image of Hussein's body. Other exceptions included the *St Petersburg Times*, which displayed two front page images—one of Hussein about to die and one of Hussein dead—and *The Press of Atlantic City*, which showed only a picture of Hussein's corpse under the caption "This image from Biladi Television...appears to show Saddam Hussein's body wrapped in a white shroud" ("Saddam Gone, Shiites Rejoice But Violence Still Rules Iraq," *The Press of Atlantic City*, December 31, 2006, A1). It was the only newspaper of 257 front pages to opt solely for the display of Hussein's body. Pictures appended to Santora, "As Attacks Go On," 1; pictures appended to "Good Knot," *New York Post*, December 31, 2006, cover; "Saddam Executed," *New York Post*, December 31, 2006, 3; "Saddam's Last

Gasp," *New York Daily News,* December 31, 2006, cover; "Defiant Saddam's Flicker of Fear," December 31, 2006, 5.

74. "Graphic Photos Inside," *Philadelphia Inquirer,* 31 December 2006, 1; caption to picture appended to Larry Kaplow, "Tyrant Gone, Realities Remain," *Atlanta Journal-Constitution,* December 31, 2006, A1.

75. Bakhurst, http://www.bbc.co.uk/blogs/theeditors/2006/12/saddams_execution.html. In response, the majority of readers complained of impropriety in showing the images, calling them "appalling," "barbaric," "propagandistic," and "an absolute disgrace." One such reader was Anthony S., who likened them to the day on which viewers would see "the next militia beheading in full (right up to the point when the knife touches the neck—we want to keep our moral compass don't we?)"; "Newspapers, Online Editors"; Paul J. Gough, "Networks Air More Saddam Execution Video," Reuters, December 30, 2006; Bauder, "Few Tough Decisions."

76. Picture appended to "Death Taunts—What They Didn't Want You To See: Camera Phone Footage Captures Saddam's Insult-Filled Execution," *Chicago Tribune,* January 3, 2007, 9, and "Execution Not End of Iraq Drama," *San Antonio Express-News,* December 31, 2006, 1A; "Final Minutes: Ex-Dictator Appeared Confident, Calm," *Philadelphia Inquirer,* December 31, 2006, 1; Stephen R. Hurst, "Saddam Defiant to the End," *Buffalo News,* December 31, 2006, A1; caption to picture titled "Saddam Meeting His Fate," *Charlotte Observer,*" December 31, 2006, 1A; "Execution Not End of Iraq Drama," *San Antonio Express-News,* December 21, 2006, 1A; and "Saddam's Last Moments," *Colorado Springs Gazette,* December 31, 2006, A1.

77. Edward Helmore, "Saddam's 'Snuff Video' Signals the End of Editorial Control," *Observer,* January 7, 2007, 10.

78. Hilderbrand, "YouTube," 50; "In Days Before Hanging, A Push for Revenge and a Push Back from the U.S.," *New York Times,* January 7, 2007, 12; Murray Armstrong, "Saddam on the Gallows: Editors' Blog," commentisfree.guardian.co.uk, posted January 2, 2007; Lewis Williamson, "In Pictures: Saddam Hussein Before His Execution and the Reaction of Iraqis To His Death," *Guardian,* posted December 30, 2006; http://blogs.guardian.co.uk/news/archives/2006/12/30/in_pictures_saddam_hussein_before....html. The same gravitation toward the image of Hussein's impending death was displayed in British journalism, a partner in the war coalition. Though the *Guardian* initially showed a front-page image of the dead Iraqi leader, the climate against its display was so strong that the paper issued numerous apologies and by the following week included only a picture of Hussein before his death in its online photographic gallery. In explaining its about-to-die image, *The Observer* noted that every British paper, with one exception, and the majority of U.S. papers had used that image on their front pages. Left unsaid was why the images of Hussein after his death were no longer shown. See, for instance, Armstrong, "Saddam on the Gallows"; Stephen Pritchard, "The Readers' Editor on Images of Saddam's Execution," *The Observer,* January 7. 2007, 26; The London *Observer,* for example, used the image of a dead Hussein to illustrate its front cover and then also as part of a six-photo sequence on inside pages Cover photo titled "Final Judgment," *Observer,* December 31, 2006, cover; and as pictures appended to Ned Temko and Peter Beaumont, "He Ruled For Years," *The Observer,* December 31, 2006, 2–3. Choosing impending death over death was a less prominent strategy in settings not associated with prosecuting the war. The front pages of

newspapers in Peru, Israel, Taiwan, Colombia, Chile, Brazil, and India, among other places, showed not only the picture of Hussein about to die but full photographic sequences that included varied moments of Hussein facing death and images of his bruised corpse.

79. See, for instance, *Newsweek*, "One Dazzling Decade," http://2010.newsweek.com/essay/one-dazing-decade.html. The slide show attached to "Katie Couric: Decade in Review" included two pictures of him facing death. See "Katie Couric: Decade in Review," CBS News, December 29, 2009, http://www.cbsnews.com/video/watch/?id=6035461n&tag=cbsnewsVideoArea;cbsnewsVideoArea.0. The magnet was advertised on amazon.com, where its product details heralded a "beautiful image of the rope being tightened around Saddam Hussein's neck just before he was hung." See http://www.amazon.com/Saddam-Hussein-Hanging-Refrigerator-Magnet/dp/B001LRD8N2/ref=sr_1_17?ie=UTF8&s=miscellaneous&qid=1263057967&sr=8–17; Kevin Robinson, "Beyond the Punchline: Saddam Hussein Execution," January 1, 2007, http://images.google.com/imgres?imgurl=http://4.bp.blogspot.com/_b9IqT2FYq3E/RZiVpC-cFerI/AAAAAAAAAEY/Gzr9ilzPsnY/s400/01_01_07.gif&imgrefurl=http://beyon-dthepunchline.blogspot.com/2007/01/todays-cartoon-saddam-hussein-execution.html&usg=___-L9AHc02zUR9sBngt4moUri-s0=&h=313&w=400&sz=123&hl=en&start=64&tbnid=Zpt9ZTn8o1uAWM:&tbnh=97&tbnw=124&prev=/images%3Fq%3Dexecution%2Bof%2Bsaddam%2Bhussein%26gbv%3D2%26ndsp%3D18%26hl%3Den%26sa%3DN%26start%3D54, and in Faithmouse, where the noose around his neck was connected with eroticasphyxiation. See http://images.google.com/imgres?imgurl=http://www.faithmouse.com/cartoon487.jpg&imgrefurl=http://faithmouse.blogspot.com/2007/01/saddam-hussein-execution-video-porn.html&usg=__MxLyK18K0FGv8iYiDc0RbW7ldOE=&h=350&w=550&sz=59&hl=en&start=81&tbnid=PXHXt2GhxPhOnM:&tbnh=85&tbnw=133&prev=/images%3Fq%3Dexecution%2Bof%2Bsaddam%2Bhussein%26gbv%3D2%26ndsp%3D18%26hl%3Den%26sa%3DN%26start%3D72. Hussein about to be hung was transformed into a doll; called the "Doll of Hussein," he wore a T-shirt proclaiming "dope on a rope," http://images.google.com/imgres?imgurl=http://www.hollyscoop.com/BlogImages/50070624—-sad.jpg&imgrefurl=http://www.hollyscoop.com/breaking-news/saddam-hussein-hang-man_8939.aspx&usg=__L-eE9oeXLaEllhQEfTnDuluSY30=&h=500&w=306&sz=46&hl=en&start=383&tbnid=X7HNsHPqSKKoSM:&tbnh=130&tbnw=80&prev=/images%3Fq%3Dexecution%2Bof%2Bsaddam%2Bhussein%26gbv%3D2%26ndsp%3D18%26hl%3Den%26sa%3DN%26start%3D378. T-shirts and bumper stickers proclaiming the "Saddam Hussein Swing Set" did not reproduce the image but suggested it nonetheless.

80. Peter Bresler, "Letter to the Editor," *Los Angeles Times*, January 3, 2007, A14; Kennicott, "For Saddam's Page," D1.

Chapter 8

1. Michael Elliott, "Haiti's Agony," *Time*, January 25, 2010, 33.

2. Christa Robbins, in Clark Hoyt, "Face to Face with Tragedy" (Public Editor), *New York Times*, January 24, 2010, 10.

3. See, for instance, Barbie Zelizer, "Why Memory's Work on Journalism Does Not Reflect Journalism's Work on Memory, *Memory Studies* 1(1), January 2008, 75–83;

Barbie Zelizer, "News: First or Final Draft of History?" *Mosaic* 2–2/3, Spring/Summer 1993, 2–3. Jill Edy, "Journalistic Uses of Collective Memory," *Journal of Communication,* Spring 1999, 71–85; Carolyn Kitch, "'Useful Memory' in Time Inc Magazines," *Journalism Studies* 7(1), 2006, 94–110; Kurt Lang and Gladys Engel Lang, "Collective Memory and the News," *Communication,* 11, 1989, 123–139.

4. Mary Ann Doane, *The Emergence of Cinematic Time: Modernity, Contingency, the Archive* (Cambridge, MA: Harvard University Press, 2002), 208. Also see Gilles Deleuze, *Cinema 1: The Movement-Image* (Minneapolis: University of Minnesota, 1986); Zygmunt Bauman, *Liquid Modernity* (Cambridge: Polity Press, 2000); Anthony Giddens, *The Consequences of Modernity* (Stanford, CA: Stamford University Press, 1991); Jean-Francois Lyotard, *The Inhuman: Reflections on Time* (Stanford, CA: Stanford University Press, 1991).

5. Lauren Berlant, "Cruel Optimism," *differences* 17 (3), 2006, 21.

6. Ariella Azoulay, *The Civil Contract of Photography* (New York: Zone Books, 2008), 342, 356.

7. Ibid., 356.

8. Doane, *Emergence,* 208, 254.

9. See, for instance, the promotional language associated with CAPE, the Center for Advances in Public Engagement, http://www.publicagenda.org/cape.

10. Such was the case in images from Vietnam, from the Kennedy assassination, and from the Mohammad Aldura shooting, among others.

11. Victor Turner, "Dewey, Dilthey, and Drama: An Essay in the Anthropology of Experience," in Victor Turner and Edward M. Bruner (eds.), *The Anthropology of Experience* (Urbana: University of Illinois Press, 1986), 33.

12. Berlant, "Cruel Optimism," 21.

13. Jerome Bruner, *Actual Minds, Possible Worlds* (Cambridge, MA: Harvard University Press, 1986), 26

14. Epictetus, in Aaron T. Beck, *Cognitive Therapy and the Emotional Disorders* (New York: Penguin, 1979), 47.

15. Nancy J. Chodorow, *The Power of Feelings* (New Haven, CT: Yale University Press, 2001).

16. Azoulay, *Civil Contract,* 16.

17. Lauren Berlant (ed.), *Compassion* (New York: Routledge, 2004), 9.

18. Stanley Cohen, *States of Denial* (Cambridge: Polity Press, 2001), 188.

19. Berlant, *Compassion,* 10. Also see Berlant's argument about national sentimentality, where she demonstrates that nationhood rests on channels of affective identification and empathy. See, for instance, Lauren Berlant, "The Subject of True Feeling: Pain, Privacy, and Politics" in Sara Ahmed et al., *Transformations: Thinking through Feminism* (New York: Routledge, 2000), 33–47.

20. Hannah Arendt, *Essays in Understanding 1930–1954,* ed. Jerome Kern (New York: Harcourt Brace and Company, 1994), 323. Also see Benedict Anderson, *Imagined Communities* (London: Verso, 1983); Ernesto Laclau and Chantal Mouffe, *Hegemony and Socialist Strategy* (London: Verso, 1985); Arjun Appadurai, *Modernity at Large* (Minneapolis: University of Minnesota Press, 1996).

21. Loic J. D. Wacquant, "Inside the Zone: The Social Art of the Hustler in the American Ghetto," in Pierre Bourdieu et al. (eds.), *The Weight of the World: Social Suffering in Contemporary Society* (Stanford, CA: Stanford University Press, 1999), 156.

22. C. S. Lewis, "Bluspels and Flalansferes: A Semantic Nightmare," in *Rehabilitations and Other Essays*, 1939, 265.

23. Jacques Rancierre, *The Emancipated Spectator* (London: verso, 2009), 96–97.

24. Doane, *Emergence*, 10.

25. Richard Rorty, *Contingency, Irony, Solidarity* (Cambridge, MA: Cambridge University Press, 1989), 9.

26. Walter Benjamin, "Little History of Photography," in Marcus Bullock and Michael Jennings (eds.), *Selected Writings*, vol. 2 (1931; reprint Cambridge, MA: Belknap Press, 1996), 512.

27. Doane, *Emergence*, 144–145.

28. See, for instance, Lorraine Hedtke and John Winslade, "The Use of the Subjunctive in Re-Membering Conversations With Those Who Are Grieving," *Omega* 50 (3), 2004–2005, 197–215, where they outline the therapeutic value of maintaining relationships with the dead rather than accepting death's finality. Also see T. Attig, *How We Grieve: Relearning the World* (New York: Oxford University Press, 1996).

29. William James, in Roger D. Abrahams, "Ordinary and Extraordinary Experience," in Victor Turner and Edward M. Bruner (eds.), *The Anthropology of Experience* (Urbana: University of Illinois Press, 1986), 66; taken from William James, "The Will to Believe," 1897.

30. Azoulay, *Civil Contract*, 93.

31. The literature on this is vast. See, for instance, James Carey, "The Dark Continent of American Journalism," in Robert Manoff and Michael Schudson (eds.), *Reading the News* (New York: Pantheon, 1986), 146–196; Lance Bennett, Regina G. Lawrence, and Steven Livingston, *When the Press Fails: Political Power and the News Media from Iraq to Katrina* (Chicago: University of Chicago Press, 2007); Dan Nimmo and James McCombs, *Nightly Horrors: Crisis Coverage by Television Network News* (Nashville: University of Tennessee Press, 1989); Susan Moeller, *Compassion Fatigue* (New York: Routledge, 1999).

32. Keren Tenenboim-Weinblatt, "Fighting for the Story's Life: Non-Closure in Journalistic Narrative," *Journalism* 9 (1), 2008, 31–51.

33. See, for instance, Meg Spratt, "The Till Case: A Picture of Torment," *Dart Center for Journalism and Trauma,* May 11, 2004; Ben Poston, "Missouri Journalism Student Documents Wrongful Conviction," *Missouri School of Journalism*, March 4, 2009; Dan Fletcher, "Medill-McKinney Case: Are Student Journalists Protected?" *Time*, October 22, 1999.

Index